Approaches to Teaching the Works of D. H. Lawrence

Edited by

M. Elizabeth Sargent

and

Garry Watson

The Modern Language Association of America
New York   2001

For information about obtaining permission to reprint material from
MLA book publications, send your request by mail (see address below),
e-mail (permissions@mla.org), or fax (646 458-0030).

Library of Congress Cataloging-in-Publication Data

Approaches to teaching the works of D.H. Lawrence / edited by M. Elizabeth Sargent
and Garry Watson.
  p. cm. — (Approaches to teaching world literature ; 70)
  Includes bibliographical references and indexes.
  ISBN 0-87352-763-1 — ISBN 0-87352-764-X (pbk.)
1. Lawrence, D. H. (David Herbert), 1885–1930—Study and teaching. 2. Lawrence,
D. H. (David Herbert), 1885–1930—Criticism and interpretation.   I. Sargent, M.
Elizabeth, 1948– II. Watson, Garry. III. Series.
PR6023.A93 Z557 2001
823'.912—dc21   2001030124

ISSN 1059-1133

A section of "Major Issues in Teaching Lawrence and Otherness" in the Introduction to the
"Approaches" section of this volume is drawn from M. Elizabeth Sargent and Garry
Watson's "D. H. Lawrence and the Dialogical Principle: 'The Strange Reality of Otherness' "
in *College English* 63.4 (2001): 409–36.□"Some Notes toward a Vindication of the Rites of
D. H. Lawrence," by Sandra M. Gilbert, is a revised version of the preface in the second
edition of her book *Acts of Attention: The Poems of D. H. Lawrence,* © 1990 by Southern
Illinois University Press. Used with permission.□"Teaching 'Woman': A Cultural Criticism
Approach to 'The Woman Who Rode Away,' " by Pamela L. Caughie, is a revised, shorter
version of chapter 4 in her book *Passing and Pedagogy: The Dynamics of Responsibility,*
© 1999 by the Board of Trustees of the University of Illinois. Used with permission of the
University of Illinois Press.□"The Resurrection of Pan: Teaching Biocentric Consciousness
and Deep Ecology in Lawrence's Poetry and Late Nonfiction," by Keith Sagar, is a con-
densed and revised version of "Lawrence and the Resurrection of Pan" in *D. H. Lawrence:
The Centre and the Circles,* edited by Peter Preston, © 1992 by the D. H. Lawrence Centre,
University of Nottingham. Used with permission.□"Lawrence and Rites of Passage," by
Langdon Elsbree, is based on chapters 1–4 in his book *Ritual Passages and Narrative
Structures,* © 1991 by Peter Lang. Used with permission.□"Teaching Lawrence's Tortoise
Poems as a Sequence," by David Ellis, is a revised version of his introduction to D. H.
Lawrence's *Tortoises,* edited by Ellis, © 1982 by Yorick Books. Used with permission.

Cover illustration of the paperback edition: Figure from the Tomb of the
Augurs at Tarquinia worked in wool by D. H. Lawrence and Frieda
Lawrence. With acknowledgments to Laurence Pollinger Limited and
the estate of Frieda Lawrence Ravagli.

Published by The Modern Language Association of America
26 Broadway, New York, New York 10004–1789
www.mla.org

Approaches to
Teaching the Works of
D. H. Lawrence

Approaches to Teaching World Literature

Joseph Gibaldi, series editor

For a complete listing of titles,
see the last pages of this book.

Art-speech is the only truth.
—D. H. Lawrence,
Studies in Classic American Literature

All vital truth contains the memory of all that
for which it is not true.
—D. H. Lawrence
Letter to Gordon Campbell
20 December 1914

CONTENTS

PREFACE TO THE SERIES

In *The Art of Teaching* Gilbert Highet wrote, "Bad teaching wastes a great deal of effort, and spoils many lives which might have been full of energy and happiness." All too many teachers have failed in their work, Highet argued, simply "because they have not thought about it." We hope that the Approaches to Teaching World Literature series, sponsored by the Modern Language Association's Publications Committee, will not only improve the craft—as well as the art—of teaching but also encourage serious and continuing discussion of the aims and methods of teaching literature.

The principal objective of the series is to collect within each volume different points of view on teaching a specific literary work, a literary tradition, or a writer widely taught at the undergraduate level. The preparation of each volume begins with a wide-ranging survey of instructors, thus enabling us to include in the volume the philosophies and approaches, thoughts and methods of scores of experienced teachers. The result is a sourcebook of material, information, and ideas on teaching the subject of the volume to undergraduates.

The series is intended to serve nonspecialists as well as specialists, inexperienced as well as experienced teachers, graduate students who wish to learn effective ways of teaching as well as senior professors who wish to compare their own approaches with the approaches of colleagues in other schools. Of course, no volume in the series can ever substitute for erudition, intelligence, creativity, and sensitivity in teaching. We hope merely that each book will point readers in useful directions; at most each will offer only a first step in the long journey to successful teaching.

Joseph Gibaldi
Series Editor

PREFACE TO THE VOLUME

This book aims to serve not only specialists but also those teaching D. H. Lawrence's work for the first time. In the development of this volume, we've been in dialogue with forty-seven faculty members who have written detailed responses to a questionnaire about their teaching of Lawrence (twenty-five from the United States, eight from Canada, nine from the United Kingdom, and one each from Poland, Germany, Portugal, Italy, and South Africa). In this brief overview of their comments on the challenge of teaching Lawrence (1885–1930), a Q after an author's name signals that the idea or comment comes from one of these questionnaires rather than from one of the essays that follows or from the works-cited list.

The survey responses raise some key concerns for the teaching of Lawrence's work: Lawrence's constant rewriting and revising, which resulted in multiple extant versions of his stories, novels, and poems; the major role of anthologies in determining what does and does not get read (or how certain works are taught: see Ellis, in this volume); Lawrence's role in the development of the novel in English, particularly in his move beyond realism and his experiments with characterization and form but also in his essays on the novel; his focus on relationships, marriage, and the family and on the ineluctable fact of otherness; the dangers and complications of connecting Lawrence's biography and his art and yet the rich interrelations between the two; the historical, political, and class contexts of Lawrence's writing; the need for careful attention to chronology; the violent swings in Lawrence's critical reception; and his current reputation in not only the academy but also the wider culture, established perhaps mainly through film adaptations and Kate Millett's *Sexual Politics*.

But the largest concern is that Lawrence's work is hardly known at all: for instance, Gordon Harvey (Q) finds fewer and fewer entering Harvard students familiar with Lawrence; of the roughly one-third who recognize his name, most have read only "The Rocking-Horse Winner" or a few poems. In fact, Tony Tanner, in a 1996 review of the second volume of Lawrence's three-volume biography (Cambridge UP), sees the neglect of Lawrence as even more widespread and growing:

> When I was an undergraduate reading English in the 1950's, we all read Lawrence passionately (Leavis's book on him came out while I was at college—in 1955). I can still remember the excitement when *Phoenix* was republished in 1961. . . . For my generation, there is no doubt that he was a tremendously emancipating writer. . . . Then—I can't say when—he suddenly came to seem dated. By the time the feminists gave him a going-over in the 1970's, most of us had lost interest; and, asking around,

I have found no one who has re-read one of his novels in years. Nor have recent generations of students shown much interest.

The difficulties of teaching Lawrence are real and troubling, even if first-year university students have read more Lawrence than we might expect—as they seem to in England, at least according to Anne Fernihough, at Girton College, Cambridge (Q). Fernihough finds that the "eighteen-year-old students who come for interviews . . . are often highly enthusiastic about Lawrence"; they appreciate his frank approach to sex and his sensitivity to the natural environment. But, she goes on, "something happens when they get to university and by the second year (having realized he is unfashionable), they disown him . . . as antifeminist, politically incorrect in every way, tiresomely repetitive in his prose-style."

Is Lawrence thus an author one eventually grows out of? Questionnaire respondents don't think so. They repeatedly emphasize that the rewards of working with Lawrence's texts are often identical to the challenges or difficulties of doing so: "The greatest problem in Lawrence can also be his greatest attraction" (Jorgette Mauzerall [Q]). Antony Atkins (Q) writes, "Many students are alienated by the very features that appeal to others . . . the energy, the high-octane set-piece scenes [and] the heady mixture of the expressionistic and dialectical qualities of Lawrence's prose with his deep appreciation of realist modes of writing." Many respondents stress the appeal of Lawrence's writing ("prose of remarkable variety and technical bravado" [Charles Ross (Q)]) for students; Harvey (Q) finds students enjoy in Lawrence's essays "the vivid patter, so full of voice, easily shifting between irony and religious feeling." His Harvard students also like that Lawrence worries over some of the same things that worry them, not least of which are the dangers of self-consciousness and overintellectualizing. Harvey enjoys "seeing these very knowing Harvard students get knocked over by this or that passage, by the power of Lawrence's perception and language—especially since they've mostly heard that they're not really supposed to like Lawrence. . . . They come to realize that a great writer may need sifting, that the intelligence and tiresomeness can't always be easily separated." Isobel Findlay (Q) finds that in Canada few students have read Lawrence "in high school or are prepared for the sorts of demands he makes on readers." Thus, in her classes, Lawrence serves as a site for students to examine and alter past habits of reading.

The question of misogyny in Lawrence will always be a live one, though many of the contributors to this volume suggest the importance of reading Lawrence in the context of women writers contemporary with him (Bonnie Scott's anthology is repeatedly mentioned as a useful resource for such reading). Most survey respondents find feminist issues a good way in to Lawrence, reporting that students' extreme reactions provoke animated discussion. A feminist critique is, in any case, unavoidable, since, as Louis Grieff (Q) puts it, "the fundamental questions he asked—and all of us are still asking—remain unchanged: What has gone wrong between the sexes? How can it be repaired?" Mauzerall (Q) deals with the sexism in Lawrence "by pointing to the honesty with which he presents it. He admits to desires that others, less honest, deny."

Even more important, Mauzerall continues, Lawrence uses the novel to examine those desires, to challenge and complicate his beginning ideas:

> Most authors bury their ideas in the narrative flow and therefore leave their philosophic assumptions unquestioned. Lawrence puts a Lawrence-surrogate in the text and then has other characters call that character's ideas into question—and this is not done to prove those ideas correct. The narrative flow refuses, as I have put it, to grant the author's supposed ideological wishes. . . . Lawrence's honesty, his strong sense of otherness, does not allow him to let, for instance, Birkin's ideas triumph over anyone else's in *Women in Love*.

Mauzerall recommends Sabin for related reflections on Lawrence's narrative technique. The novel itself becomes a larger, richer idea, more fully "his" than any idea challenged within it. Part of Lawrence's enterprise is to extend our everyday notions of what an idea or thought might be (something more physical than we had previously imagined, "a man in his wholeness wholly attending," according to his poem "Thought" [*Complete Poems* 673]). Lawrence was committed to the novel as "thought-adventure" (*Kangaroo* 279), to the heuristic powers of the form itself, the lively relations and opposing tensions it makes possible and even likely; he wrote fiction to push his thinking, to test and unsettle his opinions. However, his best nonfiction equals and even surpasses the "art-speech" of some of his novels and stories, becomes "art-speech" itself (Lawrence, *Studies* 8; see Wallace, "Circling" and " 'Study' "; see also Mills in this volume). Thus questionnaire respondents repeatedly mention certain of Lawrence's essays on the novel as essential for their teaching of him, often requiring students to read a few of them, in full or in part (most are in "*Study of Thomas Hardy*" or *Selected Critical Writings*; see the list of recommended essays on page 10, this volume).

In "Morality and the Novel" Lawrence claims:

> The novel is the highest complex of subtle inter-relatedness that man has discovered. Everything is true in its own time, place, circumstance, and untrue outside of its own place, time, circumstance. . . . Morality in the novel is the trembling instability of the balance. When the novelist puts his thumb in the scale, to pull down the balance to his own predilection, that is immorality. (172)

Studies in Classic American Literature reveals why Lawrence felt he could do his best thinking only in his art, and this famous dictum on the work of the literary critic results (in *Studies* itself) in reversals that prefigure the insights and methods of deconstructive criticism:

> Art-speech is the only truth. An artist is usually a damned liar, but his art, if it be art, will tell you the truth of his day. And that is all that matters. Away with eternal truth. Truth lives from day to day, and the marvellous Plato of yesterday is chiefly bosh today. . . .
>
> Never trust the artist. Trust the tale. The proper function of a critic is to save the tale from the artist who created it.   (8)

Thus the dialectic and oppositions of Lawrence's works are no accident—and they lead to extreme and opposing reactions in readers. Expounding Lawrence's beliefs about anything except his life's work—writing, the "struggle for verbal consciousness" (Foreword to *Women* 486)—is usually misleading and nonproductive; certainly his novels and stories are too complex to support any single position. Joyce Wexler (Q) suggests that we should have students "identify contradictions rather than complain about them," should teach them to "see contradiction, repetition, excess as purposeful rather than as lapses" and to "understand that Lawrence's work is structured by contradictions." And we shouldn't be surprised if it takes our students a while to hear the polyphony in Lawrence's work; after all, it took even Wayne Booth nearly an entire career to do so ("Confessions"). The problem is not just that Lawrence sets voices in opposition to each other but that he enters so fully into each voice in its turn, goes as far as he can with a particular idea or feeling, that readers often assume one particular voice is Lawrence's own and forget he wrote the other voices as well, with their equally trenchant and extreme perspectives.

Certainly, the risks Lawrence took as a writer make him an uncomfortable classroom presence. Nicole Ward Jouve (Q), who is "interested in the crisis of masculinity precipitated by World War I and Lawrence's attempts to deal with it at every level," argues that Lawrence "remains one of the few writers to have gone so deep and unguardedly, to the edge of ridicule . . . into areas of sexual and other *relating*. Also, his 'feminine' side he explores with more daring than most male writers." Charles Ross (Q) also finds that Lawrence's daring, as "one of the first authors to articulate the stress points in male/female relationships," leaves Lawrence open to attack—but simultaneously reveals in his work a "sympathy for women in their effort to shape an identity and find a place in a man's world" that has led undergraduate women in Ross's classes to comment that Lawrence "writes as we feel." Ross closes his questionnaire with the hope that a volume on Lawrence in this series will provide

> strategies for introducing and teaching a provocative author whose work needs to be read with an open mind and an unconstrained heart. That sounds, I realize, quite unfashionable in the age of "interpretive communities." But I would reply that we need to be more self-aware as teachers

of the communities in which we force our students to live, making sure that there are enough such communities to include a protean artist like Lawrence.

We hope that the interpretive communities unavoidably created in and by this volume are spacious enough, allowing enough room for opposing voices, to serve teachers of Lawrence's work and their students well.

ACKNOWLEDGMENTS

Despite all our reminder notes to ourselves, we've had so much help that we will inevitably fail to mention somebody—for which we apologize up front. Our thanks, to begin with, go to those who participated in the Modern Language Association teaching survey. Their responses to the questionnaire were invariably thoughtful and stimulating, and we would have liked to have included even more excerpts from them in our introduction. We are grateful for the generous support given by Joseph Gibaldi, general editor of the series, throughout the project; for the work of the MLA Publications Committee; for the meticulous copyediting of the editorial staff; and for Elizabeth Holland's careful, patient oversight in bringing the manuscript to book form. Every project like this one has its darker moments, and during those it was a constant source of encouragement to be able to consult the perceptive comments and suggestions made by the two readers of the manuscript, Charles Rossman, University of Texas, Austin, and Judith Ruderman, Duke University.

While doing most of her work on this volume, Sargent was at Western Oregon University, and she gratefully acknowledges the course-release and the travel and research funds her institution granted her for this work. Watson similarly acknowledges the fact that he was able to devote part of his last University of Alberta sabbatical to this project. We both fondly remember the huge labor performed by our computer expert in Oregon, Terri Tuma, who not only transferred manuscript files coming in from widely varying word-processing programs (and from all over the world, from Portugal to South Africa) into one standard file-type we could work with but also used her considerable writing expertise to build the first drafts of our long works-cited lists and to eliminate inconsistencies throughout the manuscript—we would have been overwhelmed without her help. Paul Chafe, a graduate student at the University of Alberta, helped us compile the two indexes; and Ann Bliss, of Western Oregon University, in addition to supplying many forms of moral support, performed what amounted to a minor archeological dig to unearth a reproduction that we suspected might work for the cover of this volume—and, happily, the MLA staff members agreed with us once they saw it.

John Worthen has been unflaggingly cheerful and prompt in answering many questions by international e-mail, especially about the new and forthcoming Cambridge and Penguin editions of Lawrence's work. Our work has been enriched in countless ways by the support of the international community of Lawrence scholars and of those who have organized international Lawrence conferences over the years. The Lawrence manuscript collections at both the University of Nottingham and the University of New Mexico, Albuquerque, gave generous assistance. And, of course, without our contributors, this volume would not exist. They did not always agree with us, and we did not always agree with them; the strengths of this volume are primarily due to their good work and to our continuing dialogues with them. We thank all of them for the patience, good-humor, and understanding they have shown. Finally, on a more exclusively personal note, we would like to thank our children and stepchildren—Molly and Hannah, Sophie and Martin—for the patience, good-humor and understanding *they* have shown on numerous occasions while we have worked on this book. All four were exposed to Lawrence at an early age and seem to have survived the experience. If it is true, as Tony Tanner has observed (*TLS* 23 Aug. 1996), that Lawrence is hardly read any more by the young, that he is read only by an "aging band" of Lawrentians (to which we suppose we must belong), we have been happily sustained in our work on this volume by the exceptions—the many young scholars and teachers who have contributed to it and the many students in our own classes who have pushed our teaching and thinking about Lawrence's work. We have also been sustained by the hope of supporting others who are teaching Lawrence's work to the younger generation, a generation represented for us most immediately by the four splendid adults who have trained us as parents.

Part One

MATERIALS

Introduction

In the following discussion of materials, we pull together the most frequently recurring suggestions for teaching from the questionnaires we received; we also highlight a few startling ones that strike us as particularly intriguing. There is certainly no need for us to be either overwhelming or exhaustive in our suggestions, in any case, since many fine bibliographies of Lawrence exist, from those by Warren Roberts and by James Cowan to the specialized bibliographies in the *D. H. Lawrence Review*—a rich resource for Lawrence study since its first issue in 1968—to the recent and extensive bibliographies on individual works in Paul Poplawski's *D. H. Lawrence: A Reference Companion* (1996), a necessity for library collections. We do, however, want to give the lay of the land, a snapshot of what's going on in Lawrence scholarship at the beginning of the twenty-first century, so that beginning teachers of Lawrence can quickly get their bearings—and veteran teachers can glimpse already familiar terrain through an occasional unaccustomed lens or from a previously untried vantage point.

Literary Criticism

Lawrence's literary reputation has swung from one extreme to the other. He was dismissed as either a prophet-preacher given to tirade or a sex-obsessed genius who couldn't think (or both) until F. R. Leavis convincingly insisted in 1955 that Lawrence was a novelist, first and foremost, and one of our greatest novelists at that (*D. H. Lawrence*). New Critics continued to resist that conclusion, however, certain that the poise and detachment of the true artist were revealed by Henry James, James Joyce, and T. S. Eliot, right up to the moment Kate Millett delivered her coup de grâce in 1970. Since then Lawrence has been assumed to be politically incorrect in just about every way imaginable. Simultaneously, however, theorists have been busy redefining what a novelist was and is—and their work, especially that influenced by Mikhail Bakhtin, makes Lawrence's essays on the novel seem remarkably contemporary. His famous contention—"Never trust the artist. Trust the tale"—is now an accepted tenet of twentieth-century literary criticism (see Lodge, "Reading"; Watson, "Real Meaning"), although that this is Lawrence's position tends to be overlooked. If in many other ways Lawrence seems to have anticipated items that are on our current agenda—

> the reassessment of modernism,
> the centrality of sexual and gender theory,
> the changing role of women,

the postcolonial,
the dangers of idealism and its link to fascism,
the critique of positivism (entailing revised theories of knowledge),
the critique of whiteness ("the old white psyche has to be gradually broken down before anything else can come to pass" [*Studies* 70]), and
the recognition and acceptance of difference, otherness (central to all of
   the above)—

Lawrence's prescience is not currently anywhere near as widely known as it ought to be.

Yet recent critical work reveals a revaluation of Lawrence going on. While Jonathan Dollimore could still refer to him in 1991 as "increasingly disregarded and often despised" (268) and Tony Tanner still found no one reading him in 1996, probably more of certain kinds of critical and scholarly work have been done on Lawrence recently than on any other twentieth-century writer. We are referring to the immense collective scholarly project associated with Cambridge University Press and begun under the direction of Michael Black, a project that is giving us not only major new editions of each of Lawrence's works (as well as complete early versions of *Sons and Lovers* and *Women in Love*) but also Lawrence's collected plays, a new biography, and eight volumes of letters, many of them never before published. An international team of scholars has edited these CUP volumes (a total of forty volumes is anticipated). Many are now available in inexpensive Penguin paperbacks (see "Editions" below). The Cambridge and Penguin CUP notes and introductions represent a remarkable outpouring of thoughtful recent criticism of Lawrence's work and meticulous scholarship on the composition history of his novels, stories, poems, essays, plays, and travel books; they should be considered essential reading for the teaching of any individual text, as should the introductions to the recent Oxford World Classics editions of Lawrence.

Thirty years ago, teachers tended to turn to Prentice Hall's *Twentieth Century Interpretations* or Macmillan's Casebook series (published in the United States by Aurora) to steer them through the welter of D. H. Lawrence criticism. In the late 1960s and early 1970s both presses brought out collections on *Sons and Lovers*, *The Rainbow*, and *Women in Love*, still the three most frequently taught Lawrence novels, if responses to our survey are representative. Even earlier (in 1963), Prentice Hall brought out a general collection of essays on Lawrence, edited by Mark Spilka.

Twayne has studies available, in its Masterwork series, on *Sons and Lovers*, *Women in Love*, and *Lady Chatterley*. The centenary of Lawrence's birth, in 1985, resulted in the publication of a spate of essay collections on Lawrence in general (e.g., Balbert and Marcus; Squires and Cushman; Salgado and Das). While innovative work continues to be done on Lawrence in relation to contemporary critical theory (see Widdowson's 1992 collection—which was burned in self-defense, apparently, by Geoff Dyer, according to his *Out of Sheer Rage*

[101]—as well as many of the essays in this volume), teachers of Lawrence still recommend certain groundbreaking early texts in Lawrentian criticism to their students as particularly readable and accessible: Leavis's *D. H. Lawrence: Novelist*, H. M. Daleski's *The Forked Flame*, Spilka's *The Love Ethic*, George Ford's *Double Measure*, Julian Moynahan's *Deed of Life*. However, it should be noted that, as Carol Siegel argues in her *Lawrence among the Women*, these are some of the texts of the 1950s and 1960s that had the effect of briefly canonizing the normative Lawrence that feminists felt the need to rebel against. Several surveys mention L. D. Clark's *The Minoan Distance*, with its evocative photographs by LaVerne Harrell Clark, as the best single-author book currently available on Lawrence. Among feminist studies, Siegel's and Anne Fernihough's are recommended most frequently; Hilary Simpson's volume is cited as an excellent source for setting Lawrence's writings about gender in a historical context.

Lawrence's work—neglected after his death, rediscovered in mid-century, then attacked for its misogynist and fascist tendencies from the late 1960s on—will never be politically correct in any age or under any government. The tensions between the opposing voices Lawrence sets in dialogue with one another are too engaged, too strong. When formalist criticism reigned, there was no place for him; and, oddly, the last twenty-five years of engaged political and cultural criticism have made few places for him either. How do we account for what Fernihough refers to as "the extraordinary history of Lawrence's literary reputation (adulation turned to bitter vilification in a startlingly short space of time)"? Fernihough attributes the dismissal of Lawrence not only to the feminist critique but also to a literary critical climate bent on discrediting notions of "the organic" (5). Her task in *D. H. Lawrence: Aesthetics and Ideology* is to show how "rigid adherence to the notion of the 'constructedness' of all cultural categories can be as ideologically loaded as speaking of the 'natural' or the 'organic'" (8) and how the organic in Lawrence does not betray a certain idealism but rather works to support his consistent warning against the dangers of idealism. Both Fernihough and Barbara Mensch reexamine Lawrence's supposed "authoritarian personality," arguing that his aesthetic is ultimately anti-imperialist and a "celebration, not a suppression, of difference" (Fernihough 186).

Lawrence wrote so much in so many genres, not a great deal can be done in a short space here to suggest the range of criticism available on individual works. We mention only a few directions one might take in preparing classes on some of the most frequently taught novels and stories (often consulted on Lawrence's poems are Gilbert, *Acts*; Laird, *Self*; and Pollnitz; see also Ellis and Cushman in this volume).

For teaching *Sons and Lovers*, Michael Black's little volume receives high praise, focusing as it does on the new Cambridge edition of that novel. The introductions by Helen Baron and Carl Baron to the Cambridge edition and to the Penguin CUP edition are also excellent (the Penguin edition gives a much-needed deft and clear overview of Garnett's restored cuts [xlv], essential information to help a teacher justify the choice of a particular *Sons and Lovers* reading text to students). David Trotter's introduction to the 1995 Oxford edition of *Sons and Lovers* is a forceful argument for reading and teaching the shorter 1913 version of the novel (which was all we knew up until 1992—see the "Editions" section below) and should spark lively classroom discussion (see also Atkins in this volume). Finally, in addition to the old standbys for context and criticism (Moynahan's Viking Critical Edition, Tedlock), Karyn Sproles and Judith Ruderman each get special mention as resources for teaching *Sons and Lovers*.

This volume contains several long essays on teaching *The Rainbow* and several shorter pieces on teaching *Women in Love* in part 2, "Approaches." In addition, the surveys recommend Virginia Hyde's *The Risen Adam*, along with Paul Delany, Samuel Hynes, and Paul Fussell, to help students understand the impact of the First World War and hence the extraordinary differences between the worlds of those two novels. Raymond Williams's *Long Revolution* offers strong cultural and historical background as well.

Those interested in teaching Lawrence's short stories should begin by consulting Janice Harris (*Short Fiction*), Keith Cushman, and Black (*Early Fiction*). The survey results suggest that, of the full-length novels, hardly anyone ever teaches *The Trespasser, The White Peacock, The Boy in the Bush, Mr Noon, Kangaroo* (except in relation to its film version), or—least of all—*Aaron's Rod*. *The Plumed Serpent* seems to be having something of a resurgence (two essays on it are in this volume) as is *The Lost Girl* (Siegel's introduction to the Penguin CUP edition and John Worthen's to the Cambridge edition, along with Hyde's "'Lost' Girls" and M. Elizabeth Sargent's essay on the novel, would give a beginning teacher plenty to go on). And see Louis Martz in this volume for sources on *Lady Chatterley* in its three incarnations.

Finally, we need to acknowledge that the twenty years or so between the publication of R. P. Draper's *Critical Heritage* in 1970 (still a useful resource for students) and the appearance of David Ellis and Ornella De Zordo's four-volume *D. H. Lawrence: Critical Assessments* (again, a necessity for reference in any library attempting to support and encourage scholarship on Lawrence), more literary criticism has been produced on Lawrence than any one faculty member could absorb in several lifetimes and quite a bit more than one would expect on an author no one is reading. Two brief general introductions to the world of Lawrence criticism and scholarship—Richard Beynon's volume on *The Rainbow* and *Women in Love* and Worthen's *D. H. Lawrence* (published by Arnold)—might be a good way to get started.

Editions

For the teacher of Lawrence, it's a textual jungle out there. The copyright on most of Lawrence's works (except the Cambridge edited texts) has recently expired: thus, a bewildering variety of new and inexpensive paperback editions exist (used ones are everywhere), and they are far from interchangeable. The biggest differences are in *Sons and Lovers*. Edward Garnett cut approximately one-tenth of the novel to help Lawrence get it published in 1913, pages that appeared for the first time as an integral part of the novel in the 1992 Cambridge edition. But "corrupt" texts have been a problem for Lawrence from the beginning. The legal battles over *Lady Chatterly* (see Rolph) resulted in many pirated, unauthorized editions of that novel, but other of Lawrence's writings suffered under various forms of overt and covert censorship (see Templeton in this volume) and therefore present curious problems. For instance, *The Rainbow*, banned and seized immediately after publication in England in 1915, was released in the United States in 1916 with many passages cut, some long, some just a few words. The original American plates continued to be used by Viking and then by Penguin right up into the 1990s without any warning or explanation to the reader that the text was incomplete. In fact, for a few years, Penguin had two editions available simultaneously: the incomplete one from the old Viking plates (with an introduction by Richard Aldington) and a full and reliable text (with an introduction by Worthen, published in 1981), very close indeed to the more recent Cambridge one (edited by Mark Kinkead-Weekes)— now also available from Penguin (with an introduction by Fernihough, published in 1995).

Those who feel differences between these editions are insignificant have perhaps not had the experience of one of the coeditors of this volume, who once argued at ridiculous length in a graduate seminar over the interpretation of chapter 12 ("Shame") of *The Rainbow*—whether Ursula and Winifred ever consummated their lesbian affair—until someone pointed out to her that four lines present in everyone else's edition were missing in hers (the top four lines of 316 in the CUP edition).

True, not every printer's or transmission error, not every cut for the sake of decency (to ensure orders of *The Lost Girl* from the lending libraries, for instance) or for concision, not every alteration to standardize Lawrence's punctuation or spelling, is equally significant. Further, scholars disagree over the value of the Cambridge editions and over specific editorial decisions. However, at the very least, faculty members need to know enough to help their students choose among this plethora of editions, especially since nothing clearly signals the differences between the multitude of new and used texts on bookstore shelves.

In fact, even the new Penguin versions of the Cambridge editions look no different from other new Penguin Lawrence texts: one needs to look on the back cover, two-thirds of the way down, for the small words in bold print: "The

Cambridge D. H. Lawrence." Currently, all the major novels from *The White Peacock* (1911) and *The Trespasser* (1912) on are available both in Cambridge editions, which include the full textual apparatus, and in Penguin CUP editions, which do not, although they usually include appendixes and some maps, if any were in the original Cambridge edition. The Penguin CUP editions also have new introductions and notes and a slightly different but still detailed version of Worthen's chronology of Lawrence's life and work. The Penguin CUP list includes *The Boy in the Bush* and *Mr Noon*, but not the two early versions of *Lady Chatterley* (CUP editions, however, do exist for those). *Apocalypse* and most of the short stories and novellas are available in both Cambridge and Penguin CUP editions, with the notable exceptions of *The Escaped Cock* and *The Virgin and the Gipsy* (which are, however, readily available in the Penguin *Complete Short Novels*, edited by Sagar and Partridge; CUP, but not Penguin CUP, editions are planned). All the travel books are out in both, except *Mornings in Mexico*, which has yet to appear in the full Cambridge edition. Three additional volumes (selected essays, selected poems, and selected stories) are projected to appear in Penguin CUP editions. Cambridge still has in the works an edition of the psychology books, *Fantasia* and *Psychoanalysis*; *Studies in Classic American Literature*; two additional volumes of essays, introductions, and reviews; one volume of early stories; and four volumes of poems.

Most of these editions are included in the works-cited list at the end of this volume, with a clear notation—"(CUP)"—if a Penguin includes the Cambridge edition text and a clear indication if a Cambridge edition is currently available in Penguin. The pagination of the Lawrence text itself—excluding notes and front matter, but including any appendixes—is identical in CUP editions and the corresponding Penguin CUP editions.

Clearly, an author so easily misread and misrepresented and, from the beginning of his writing career, so often cut, censored, and expurgated benefits more than most from close scholarly attention to restored, accurate texts. But the choice of which text to teach from is rarely a simple one. For instance, it's not a foregone conclusion that a teacher will assign the 1992 *Sons and Lovers*, the Cambridge text that is most radically altered from previous published versions. Not only do some feel the novel is better *without* the restored eighty pages cut by Garnett (Schorer took it for granted that Garnett did Lawrence a favor—and one can find evidence in the letters to suggest Lawrence thought so too); others feel that a text that's been read and accepted as the only *Sons and Lovers* for eighty-five years has a socially constructed authority that outweighs considerations of original authorial intention. In other words, good reasons exist for using either version—instructors simply need to know what those reasons are so they're not using older editions out of habit or for monetary considerations alone. Otherwise, one is easy prey to the archetypal teacher's nightmare: being grilled without warning by a student who would have preferred to use the new *Sons and Lovers* when one didn't even know a new version existed or couldn't explain one's choice, not knowing the major differences between the two versions and thus not having decided whether they mattered or not.

Garnett's cuts, of course, are not the only concern in deciding which *Sons and Lovers* to teach; the Cambridge editors have also eliminated many other confusing transmission errors. For instance, until 1992 when the Cambridge edition came out, the word *not* appeared in chapter 4 in the sentence "Let my father *not* be killed at pit" (italics ours); but Lawrence originally wrote this sentence with the young Paul Morel praying for his father's death in a mining accident, as Mark Schorer's *Facsimile* of the *Sons and Lovers* manuscript makes clear (102). A printer's error muddled the boy's wish for many years (and continues to do so in many new editions). The erroneous insertion of one word can affect our teaching not only of the novel but also of other works closely related to it. For instance, the wish fulfillment at work in the early versions of "Odour of Chysanthemums"—when the miner's death sets everything right in the family and restores him as "a clean young knight" ("Odour," ed. Atkins 226) to his wife and to his supposedly true self (and provides a pension to his widow in the process)—is much more apt to leap out at students who know the original version of Paul Morel's childhood prayer.

Other errors exist in non-Cambridge editions of the novel. At the very least, make sure your students check that the last word in chapter 3 is *file*; the manuscript makes clear that Lawrence never once considered using the humdrum, unwriterly *life*, which has been printed in editions of the novel since the 1950s. Also, have students change *whimpered* to *whispered* if *whimpered* shows up anywhere in the last ten lines of the novel. Two editions brought out in 1999—Modern Library, with a moving introduction by Dyer, and Wordsworth, with an introduction and helpful notes by Howard Booth—both get *whispered* right and the boy's prayer wrong. Booth's edition gets *file* right; Dyer's gets it wrong but includes commentaries by Anthony Burgess, Jessie Chambers, Frieda Lawrence, V. S. Pritchett, Kate Millett, and Alfred Kazin that would be useful in generating class discussion. (Trotter's 1995 Oxford edition gets Paul's prayer right but uses both *life* to end chapter 3 and *whimpered* in the final chapter!)

There have been important critiques of various Cambridge editions and, at times, of the entire project. John Worthen (one of the Cambridge editors and the advisory editor for the Penguin CUP editions) believes the true test of an authoritative edition is whether or not the reader has all the information needed in order to *undo* what the editors have done, to deconstruct the edition if necessary. The annotations, textual apparatus, and variant readings in the Cambridge editions all seem to support this principle of reversibility. While they do, of course, privilege the Cambridge editors' chosen text, they also offer the possibility of reading other versions of the text within the Cambridge version, something previous editions cannot offer. (See Ross and Buckley in this volume, however, on the advantages of hypertext for working with textual variants.)

Lawrence's Letters and Essays: Essential Tools for Teaching His Fiction and Poetry

Of special interest to teachers of Lawrence will be the forthcoming Penguin CUP volume of selected essays; many of these essays are currently available only in expensive Cambridge editions (see *"Study of Thomas Hardy," "Reflections on the Death of a Porcupine"*) or in the still-useful posthumous collections of Lawrence's essays, reviews, prefaces, and introductions, *Phoenix* and *Phoenix II*. The recent paperback of Lawrence's *Selected Critical Writings*, edited by Michael Herbert, thus fills an important gap in available classroom texts, although it unfortunately prints only excerpts from *"Study of Thomas Hardy."* The following titles are mentioned by almost all survey respondents as essential for teachers of Lawrence (all are included in the works-cited list at the end of this volume; an asterisk indicates that the essay is available in Herbert's collection):

> *A Propos of* Lady Chatterley's Lover
> "Art and Morality"°
> "Books"
> "Foreword to *Women in Love*"
> "The Future of the Novel" (also known as "Surgery for the Novel—or a Bomb")°
> "Morality and the Novel"°
> "The Novel"°
> "The Novel and the Feelings"
> "Study of Thomas Hardy"° (only the sections on Hardy are in Herbert's collection)
> "Why the Novel Matters"°

Several respondents also mention using the following in full or in part: "Autobiographical Sketch," "Chaos in Poetry"° (also known as "Introduction to *Chariot of the Sun* by Harry Crosby"), "Foreword to *Sons and Lovers*" (first printed as a section of a letter in Huxley's *Letters of D. H. Lawrence*), "Foreword to *The Collected Poems of D. H. Lawrence*," "German Books: Thomas Mann,"° "Hymns in a Man's Life," "Introduction to *The Dragon of the Apocalypse*,"° "Introduction to These Paintings,"° "Making Pictures,"° "Nottingham and the Mining Countryside," "On Being Religious," "Pan in America," "Poetry of the Present,"° "Pornography and Obscenity,"° "The Proper Study,"° and a few chapters from the psychology books. Many of these selections were once available in one paperback—*D. H. Lawrence on Education*, edited by Joy Williams and Raymond Williams, now unfortunately out of print.

Almost everyone who responded to the survey mentions the importance of Lawrence's letters; the Cambridge letters have recently been completed with an eighth volume of latecomers and strays (plus a complete index to all eight volumes). While these are essential for any library collection, they are beyond the pocketbooks of most students. There is, however, a one-volume paperback Cambridge *Selected Letters*. No Penguin CUP edition of selected letters is planned (a 1950 Penguin *Selected Letters* is still available, edited by Richard Aldington). Harry T. Moore's edition (*Collected Letters*) and Huxley's introduction to his 1932 collection of letters, which is reprinted in full in the Penguin *Selected Letters*, remain valuable. Questionnaire respondents emphasize the necessity of sharing at least excerpts of certain key letters with students. The *Norton Introduction to Literature* (Beaty and Hunter 354–59) stands out among anthologies in including excerpts from both Lawrence's essays and letters in its expanded section of three Lawrence stories. The following letters are mentioned most often:

> 3 December 1910. To Rachel Annand Taylor. Relationship with his dying mother: "Nobody can have the soul of me. My mother has had it, and nobody can again."
>
> 19 November 1912. To Edward Garnett. Justification of the Paul Morel manuscript he has just sent off: "It's the tragedy of thousands of young men in England."
>
> 14 December 1912. To Else Jaffe. Why he and Frieda should assert rather than renounce their desire and why Frieda shouldn't sacrifice herself for the sake of her children.
>
> 17 January 1913. To Ernest Collings. "My great religion is a belief in the blood."
>
> 1 February 1913. To Edward Garnett. "I think . . . I have inside me a sort of answer to the *want* of today: to the real, deep want of the English people."
>
> 24 February 1913. To Ernest Collings. Making "one's mood deep and sincere": "One has to be so terribly religious, to be an artist."
>
> 26 October 1913. To Cynthia Asquith. Explains that he had to scrub the floor of the adorable four-room cottage he and Frieda found in Italy.
>
> 2 December 1913. To Henry Savage. Though Lawrence does not himself use the word, this is the letter in which (according to Mark Kinkead-Weekes, *D. H. Lawrence*) Lawrence effectively admits to being bisexual.
>
> 22 April 1914. To Edward Garnett. Explains that "The Wedding Ring" is the work of both himself and Frieda; claims he is "common" only when he fails to express his deepest religious feeling "and a sort of jeer comes instead."
>
> 2 June 1914. To Arthur McLeod. Futurism interesting but too "purely male"—need to make art "the joint work of man and woman."
>
> 5 June 1914. To Edward Garnett. "You mustn't look in my novel for the old stable ego of the character."
>
> 20 December 1914. To Gordon Campbell. "All vital truth contains the memory of all that for which it is not true."

8 December 1915. To Bertrand Russell. Reading Frazer's *Golden Bough* and *Totemism and Exogamy* persuades Lawrence of the existence and importance of "blood-consciousness."

16 December 1915. To J. B. Pinker. On Arnold Bennett's idea of "rules of construction."

16 July 1916. To Catherine Carswell. Explains what he admires about Christianity and why he is not a Christian: "God in me is my desire."

9 October 1916. To Mark Gertler. Reaction to first seeing Gertler's *The Merry-Go-Round*: "terrible and dreadful"—"the best *modern* picture I have seen."

27 July 1917. To Eunice Tietjens. "[A]bnormal sex" is when we go against our desire, which is holy.

15 May 1921. To Earl and Achsah Brewster. "Give me *differences*."

25 October 1922. To William Hopkin. On death of Hopkin's wife, Sallie.

10 November 1923. To Baroness Anna von Richthofen, Lawrence's mother-in-law. "[W]omen today always have more courage than men"—men don't need love but strength from their wives, "battle-strength."

9 January 1924. To Mabel Dodge Luhan. Admires her "dauntlessness," advises her to have "the courage *not to care*, and the power to laugh a bit."

22 January 1925. To Carlo Linati. "[W]hoever reads me will be in the thick of the scrimmage."

29 August 1925. To Molly Skinner. On death of her brother—on money, bourgeois people, and life.

3 December 1926. To Rolf Gardiner. Utopian dreaming: hiking, dancing, singing.

13 March 1928. To Witter Bynner. "[T]he leader-cum-follower relationship is a bore."

14 November 1928. To David Chambers. Remembers visiting the Haggs farm as a boy.

20 May 1929. To John Middleton Murry. Tells Murry they belong to different worlds.

Also, Jack Stewart (Q) recommends that his students read all of Lawrence's letters from Cornwall, 30 December 1915 to 12 October 1917, to get a fuller continuous sense of a crucial period in Lawrence's life, the "nightmare" years Delany's book describes that produced *Women in Love*.

In addition to excerpts from the letters and essays listed above, certain paragraphs from Lawrence's other books work well as handouts for teaching or as epigraphs for a course: for example, the passages in *Apocalypse* on rereading (60) and on "the marvel of being alive in the flesh" (149), written during the last year of his life; the passage on the working of the emotional mind (like a circling hawk) in the preface to his translation of Giovanni Verga's *Cavalleria Rusticana* (*Phoenix* 249–50); the poem "Thought" (*Complete Poems* 673); the first page of the piece "John Galsworthy" discussing the necessary qualities of a critic; and the lines on "an act of pure attention" and discovery in *Sketches of Etruscan Places* (62).

Biography

It seems everyone who ever knew Lawrence wrote a memoir or two about him; these range from embarrassing hagiography to equally embarrassing and revealing attacks. Edward Nehls, realizing this fact, put together *D. H. Lawrence: A Composite Biography*; its three volumes have been a standard Lawrence reference work since they appeared (1957–59) and remain an essential research and teaching tool even in the shadow of the monumental three-volume Cambridge University Press biography of Lawrence (which has three authors— on the principle that multiple authors are more likely to do justice to multiple Lawrences). Survey respondents make grateful mention of the solid scholarship and readability of Worthen's 1991 *D. H. Lawrence: The Early Years, 1885– 1912*; Kinkead-Weekes's 1996 *D. H. Lawrence: Triumph to Exile, 1912–22*; and David Ellis's 1997 *D. H. Lawrence: Dying Game, 1922–30*.

However, some earlier biographies deserve mention, primarily Moore's *The Intelligent Heart* (1954), revised and reissued under the title *The Priest of Love* in 1974; Sagar's *D. H. Lawrence: Life into Art*; and Burgess's *Flame into Being*. Both Sagar (*Life of D. H. Lawrence*) and Moore (with Roberts, 1996) wrote briefer illustrated biographies that many teachers recommend to students for a swift verbal and visual overview of Lawrence's background and travels. Memoirs offering irreplaceable insights into Lawrence include those by Jessie Chambers, his boyhood sweetheart; Frieda Lawrence; and Catherine Carswell, a friend from 1914 on and a fellow writer. However, such memoirs should not be taken at face value; they need contextualizing. Nehls is useful for this purpose, as are three short biographies by Worthen—the highly condensed ninety-page "Biography" in Poplawski's *Reference Companion*; his *D. H. Lawrence: A Literary Life*, which focuses on Lawrence as a working writer, earning his living by his pen; and his forthcoming condensation of the three-volume Cambridge biography for Penguin.

Reference Works

Obviously, the Cambridge *Letters* and three-volume biography are crucial reference works, as are Nehls, and Ellis and De Zordo. Other works that remain handy tools for teachers of the peripatetic Lawrence include *Poste Restante: A Lawrence Travel Calendar*, by Moore, and *D. H. Lawrence: A Calendar of his*

Works, by Sagar (with a checklist of manuscripts and their locations, complied by Warren Roberts and Lindeth Vasey). *A D. H. Lawrence Handbook*, edited by Sagar (published in 1982), contains a checklist of Lawrence's reading, information on productions of Lawrence's plays, and a thematic index to *Phoenix* and *Phoenix II*. Poplawski's *D. H. Lawrence: A Reference Companion*, the most recent and exhaustive collection of bibliographies (including bibliographies of bibliographies) now available, has already been mentioned (see also Poplawski, *Works*). And for teaching an author who changes so much (see Kinkead-Weekes's essay, "Which Lawrence, When?" in this volume), the usefully detailed and complete *D. H. Lawrence Chronology*, by Peter Preston, is essential.

Audiovisual and Electronic Resources

Many film and television adaptations of Lawrence's work exist, some more useful or more honorable than others (and there seems to be little consensus about which adaptations fall into which category). Nigel Morris's extensive filmography in Poplawski's *Reference Companion* lists most of the adaptations to date (although some difficult-to-locate ones, like *Second Best*, starring Alan Bates, and *Fanny and Annie*, both shown on British television in the early 1970s, do not appear; nor does the short film of "The Horse-Dealer's Daughter"). Suffice it to say that the best adaptations seem unavailable for rent or purchase anywhere (Stuart Burge's excellent *Sons and Lovers*, done for British television and starring Eileen Atkins, heads the list) while dismal films like Ken Russell's *Rainbow* are all too easy to find in the local video store. One exception is the sensitive Australian production of *Kangaroo* starring Judy Davis, which often shows up in collections of foreign videos. Most survey respondents find class time too tight to show film adaptations of Lawrence and prefer to focus on the works themselves, unless teaching a course specifically about literature and film.

A few, however, do mention showing sections of Christopher Miles's film biography *Priest of Love* or the recent documentary on Lawrence (played by Kenneth Branaugh) and Frieda (played by Helen Mirren) called *Coming Through* to give students a quick sense of Lawrence's life. More useful for the classroom are two recent documentaries on Lawrence listed with Films for the Humanities and Sciences (1-800-257-5126; PO Box 2053, Princeton, NJ 08543; www.films.com) as available for purchase or rental:

> *D. H. Lawrence* (BBC, 1996; 53 min.). A thoughtful production: John Worthen, Glenda Jackson, Dorothy Brett, Helen Corke, and Margaret Needham discuss Lawrence's life and work; scenes from the 1960 ob-

scenity trial of *Lady Chatterley's Lover* are dramatized. This is one of the best documentaries on a writer we've ever seen.

D. H. Lawrence: "Odour of Chrysanthemums" (1991; 20 min.). Straightforward analysis of the style and structure of the story; no mention is made of the multiple drafts.

Also available (for purchase only) from the same source is *D. H. Lawrence as Son and Lover* (1984; 52 min.). This biography uses Lawrence's own letters, essays, and autobiographical sketches as the sound track. The description, however, is better than the film itself, which is self-indulgent and hard to follow and which irritatingly gives no attributions (titles or dates) for the many Lawrence passages read out loud or displayed on screen. The same company also lists *A Portrait of Katherine Mansfield* (1997; 60 min.), a lovely film that briefly touches on her friendship with D. H. Lawrence and gives glimpses of, among other places, Garsington, Cornwall, and Bandol (though the instructor should be warned that the section on living with the Lawrences in Cornwall focuses—with intentional broad humor—on a pair of fighting cocks, not on the landscape!). These videos are all in color and can be previewed for a period of fifteen days.

Finally, two new volumes, Louis Greiff's *D. H. Lawrence: Fifty Years on Film, 1949–1999* and Jane Young's *D. H. Lawrence on Screen* (focusing on *Sons and Lovers, The Rainbow,* and *Women in Love*) complement Nigel Morris's filmography and bibliography for instructors wanting to help students evaluate Lawrence on film.

Sagar's *D. H. Lawrence Handbook* lists Lawrence-related audio recordings available up to 1982. Since then many of Lawrence's works have been recorded on cassette tape, and new recordings seem to appear monthly (Penguin Audiobooks are the most recent, with actors reading abridged versions of *Sons and Lovers, The Rainbow, Women in Love,* and *Lady Chatterley*—tapes may be ordered by calling 1-800-253-6476). The major distinction is between abridged and unabridged recordings (although several abridged recordings, like the *Lady Chatterley* read by Janet Suzman—now unfortunately no longer available—are excellent). The companies below have unabridged Lawrence tapes available for rent or purchase (no information is given about which edition is being read from, but one assumes CUP editions are not used because of copyright issues). Since new readings come out often, call for the most recent additional titles:

Books on Tape, PO Box 7900, Newport Beach, CA 92658; 1-800-626-3333 ("England, My England," *Women in Love, Aaron's Rod, Lady Chatterley's Lover, Twilight in Italy, Sea and Sardinia*)

Recorded Books, Box 409, Charlotte Hall, MD 20622; 1-800-638-1304 (*St. Mawr, "The Prussian Officer"* stories, *Ladybird, The Captain's Doll, The Fox, Lady Chatterley's Lover, The Virgin and the Gipsy*)

Audio Book Contractors, Inc., Box 40115, Washington, DC 20016; 202 363-3429 (*Sons and Lovers, The Rainbow*)

Spoken Arts, Inc., Box 289, New Rochelle, NY 10801; 914 633-4516 (*The Poems of Lawrence*, read by Wendy Hiller, Peter Jeffrey, David King, and Peter Orr)

In addition to the unabridged recording of *Women in Love* listed above, two curious dramatized versions exist, both originally done for the BBC. One, dated 1981 and featuring Penelope Wilton, is available through Audio-Forum in Guilford, CT (call 1-800-243-1234 to order). It has its moments, but in general it seems based on the principle that Lawrence's novel needed extensive rewriting, including some supplementary and composite scenes. The other is more recent (1996), features Nicholas Farrell as Birkin and Geraldine Fitzgerald as Hermione, and suffers from the same problems, but less eccentrically so (order online at www.bdd.com). Any of the abridged (as opposed to dramatized) versions would be preferable: Jennie Linden's (HarperCollins, 1992) is surprisingly good, slightly stronger (and funnier) than the 1994 Juliet Stevenson version; both are produced in the United Kingdom, but Stevenson's is brought out on the elusive Listen for Pleasure label that produced the no-longer-orderable Suzman *Lady Chatterley* tapes in Canada (no phone listings are available on these). Michael Maloney (Penguin, 1995) tends to swallow the ends of words and sentences, which makes him nearly impossible to hear in a moving vehicle, but he does a powerful rendition of a condensed version of "Mino" that is quite audible in a quiet classroom. If teachers use abridged tapes in class, they should do a dry run and mark skipped passages ahead of time in the text; otherwise, students tend to be frustrated and confused by trying to follow along and getting lost in the middle of passages. Unabridged tapes are obviously preferable, for a multitude of reasons; but occasionally an actor can render a particular scene in a way that transforms student reactions to it: Ian McKellen's 1983 reading of *Sons and Lovers* (Newman, Albuquerque, NM) and Judi Dench's 1987 version of *Lady Chatterley* (Multilingua, Inc., NY) are both impressive for that reason, but they are nearly impossible to locate. Book-on-cassette companies seem to appear and disappear with the rapidity of mushrooms.

If audiotapes are well done, they work beautifully in the classroom to give students a sense of the dialect Lawrence uses and of the heat, tension, and balance of his dialogues. As several surveys mention, Lawrence's work needs at times to be read out loud. Theresa Thompson (Q) uses CDs and tapes of Native American songs and chants to give her students a sense of the oral tradition represented in *The Plumed Serpent*: she finds *Music of New Mexico: Native American Traditions* (Smithsonian-Folkways Recordings, distributed by Rounder Records) especially effective. She also speculates on why students "struggle with Lawrence's prose style, its repetitive, chant-like, dense narrative form. . . . Lawrence's prose resists skimming techniques most English majors utilize, and that makes them irate. If you skim, you often miss the point." Audiotapes can help students slow down, can let Lawrence's prose rhythms do their necessary work on the ear. Lawrence's poetry in particular lends itself to audiotape presentation, but the most recent offering—an anthology that includes two Lawrence poems, Jeremy Irons reading "Snake" and William Shatner reading "Whales Weep Not!" (*The Compleat Silver Lining*, 1998, www.bmpmusic.com)—has a distracting musical accompaniment that students would probably find unintentionally funny.

By far the most widely used audiovisual aid in the Lawrence classroom is the slide projector—to show Lawrence's own paintings or the many works of art he wrote about (from Botticelli to Boccioni). Slides of Paul Cézanne's work shown in conjunction with a reading of Lawrence's "Introduction to These Paintings" helps move to a different level students' understanding of Lawrence's commitment to the body and to physical, material reality. Reproductions of Lawrence's paintings are available in several editions (Levy; R. Millett) and work well with Lawrence's short essay "Making Pictures." Nicole Ward Jouve (Q) recommends showing photographs of the First World War; to help students deal with the "Rabbit" and "Moony" chapters in *Women in Love* Atkins (Q) shows reproductions of German expressionist paintings. Gertler's *Merry-Go-Round* appears in full color on the dust jacket of Lawrence's Cambridge biography, volume 2; students have a richer understanding of Loerke in *Women in Love* if they are familiar not just with Gertler's painting but also with Lawrence's letter to Gertler about it (see the list of letters above). Survey respondents mention that student difficulty with Lawrence's prose diminishes when students shift their attention for a moment to visual art by Lawrence's contemporaries—they can see more quickly by comparison the experiments Lawrence was trying out in language.

Instructors who have traveled to Eastwood, where Lawrence grew up, or to other Lawrence locations often show slides to give students a sense of Lawrence's travels and the many different settings that appear in one form or another in his fiction. Paul Hogarth's watercolors, the result of fifteen years of following in the footsteps of Lawrence (from Nottingham to Florence, Taos to Bandol) were exhibited in the Djanogly Art Gallery at the University of Nottingham from 13 July to 11 August 1996; the catalog of this exhibition—*Escape to the Sun*—does not include all the paintings but nevertheless gives a swift and colorful sense of Lawrence's rich visual life as he moved from place to place.

The Internet will soon make it easier for scholars to search through databases on the holdings of Lawrence manuscript collections around the world, the two major collections being the Humanities Research Center at the University of Texas, Austin, and the D. H. Lawrence Research Centre at the University of Nottingham, under the direction of John Worthen and Peter Preston. Dorothy Johnson, of the University of Nottingham Library, has created an online database describing the university's Lawrence manuscript collection, although it will be several years before that database will include the extensive George Lazarus collection Nottingham acquired in 1996 (see the library's Web page [www.mss.library.nottingham.ac.uk/dhl_home.html] for a description of this collection; Trotter's introduction to the Oxford *Sons and Lovers* describes two of the many unpublished Lawrence papers the Lazarus collection contains and gives a sense of how it will affect Lawrence scholarship).

Students may enjoy prowling the various Lawrence offerings on the Web or participating in a Lawrence discussion list but should be given some hints on discussion-list manners and protocol before subscribing: they should be advised to listen in on the conversation quite awhile before contributing themselves. For links to much interesting Lawrence material (biography, censorship issues, and online texts of Lawrence novels, including *Lady Chatterley's Lover*, visit www.home.earthlink.net/~jgertzma/dhl/index.html. A poetry site on Lawrence is located at www.ymaverick.com/vance/lawrence—courtesy of Vance Maverick and Helen Croom. Information on the Web comes and goes even more quickly than do books-on-cassette companies, so the best advice is simply to use a good search engine and check occasionally under Lawrence's name. Obviously, students should always be cautioned about the reliability of anything they read on the Web; the most reliable material they're likely to find on Lawrence is through links from the University of Nottingham Library's Manuscripts and Special Collections Web site given above. For instance, the complete text of Worthen's condensed biography of Lawrence ("Biography") is available, as is information on collections of Lawrence materials and manuscripts from around the world.

Also, Helen Croom in Bristol manages both a Lawrence announcement list (dhlawrence-announce@onelist.com) and a discussion list (rananim@onelist.com); the first serves to disseminate information of interest to those teaching or studying Lawrence (on forthcoming events, seminars, articles, plays, exhibitions) and is only for messages that desire or require no reply. To subscribe directly to one of the lists send e-mail to dhlawrence-announce-subscribe@yahoogroups.com or rananim-subscribe@yahoogroups.com. If you have queries or problems with either list, write to Helen Croom at aitch@pmail.net or rananim@ukonline .co.uk. The address for her well-managed Web pages on Lawrence is web .ukonline.co.uk/rananim/lawrence; her site provides links to many other Lawrence sites.

Organizations and Conferences

A growing number of international D. H. Lawrence societies exist, most with their own publications (either a newsletter or academic journal or both). Korea, Japan, China, France, Australia, and Italy have active organizations for the study of Lawrence's work, as do North America and the United Kingdom. A newsletter for the D. H. Lawrence Society of North America (DHLSNA) appears twice a year and is edited by Eleanor Green, Dean of Arts and Sciences, University of Maine, Presque Isle, ME 04769 (e-mail greene@polaris.umpi .maine.edu). DHLSNA publishes a directory of members every two years (currently produced by Louis Greiff—e-mail greiff@alfred.edu), which also lists addresses of current presidents of the other Lawrence societies. *The D. H. Lawrence Review* is not affiliated with DHLSNA and is currently edited by William Harrison, Department of English, State University of New York, Geneseo, NY 14454 (e-mail harrison@geneseo.edu). Information about the D. H. Lawrence Society in the United Kingdom is available through the editor of its journal, Catherine Greensmith (c.greensmith@selc.hull.ac.uk).

International Lawrence conferences are organized every two or three years by a board made up of representatives from duly constituted Lawrence societies. Eight such conferences for the sharing of current scholarship on Lawrence have been held, the most recent in Boston (at Tufts University in 1985), Montpellier (1990), Ottawa (1993), Nottingham (1996), Taos (1998), and Naples (2001). The *DHLSNA Newsletter* gives information on all upcoming conferences as well as on the activities and publications of other Lawrence societies. Students often seem unaware of this dimension of contemporary literary scholarship—that published literary criticism, history, theory, bibliography, and biography are all part of an ongoing conversation among real people who meet occasionally to share the work they're doing and to test their ideas out on fellow scholars. The level of international interest in Lawrence intrigues students; Takeo Iida's *The Reception of D. H. Lawrence around the World* (a recent collection of essays by scholars in fourteen countries) makes clear that Lawrence is taught in a global context (see also Phelps in this volume).

Part Two

APPROACHES

Introduction

We agree with Jonathan Dollimore's claim that "there is more to be said about Lawrence; much more than was usually said in the days when he was celebrated as a prophet of straight liberation, and more than is often said when he is castigated from the vantage point of contemporary sexual politics" (269). Thus part of the function of this volume is to draw attention to the work—with its new insights and approaches—that has been produced over the last decade or so and to make it more available for our teaching. Stereotypes about Lawrence are alive and well both in academia and in the wider culture: Lawrence was a racist, a fascist, a sexist, and a careless writer to boot. Luckily students often come to our classes free of these stereotypes about Lawrence because they've never read him or even heard of him. It would indeed be a shame if they left with these same stereotypes because of careless or uninformed teaching.

Regardless of the level of students' familiarity with Lawrence, however, teaching Lawrence is problematic because of the strong responses he arouses in readers. More than almost any other modern author, Lawrence creates difficulties for undergraduates on a first reading. His use of oxymoron, his play with opposites and extremes (both in characters and in ideas), mislead many who filter out much of the text as they react quickly and antagonistically to one side of the opposition, never even seeing the other. Lawrence's forceful language, imagery, and rhythms only intensify the feeling of being attacked or challenged that many readers have. An apt example comes from a recent modern-novel course taught by M. Elizabeth Sargent: a young man wrote in his journal, "I think we should be warned at the beginning that *The Rainbow* is such a feminist novel," while an older woman complained, "This novel is so sexist." Getting students to read more accurately, closely, sensitively, to learn how to complicate their own first readings, has become a primary goal in our teaching of Lawrence; opposing voices have become the central metaphor. The strengths of Lawrence's work can be made available to students through teaching that regularly encourages, enables, and discovers such complications; we hope, in this volume, also to suggest the rich intellectual possibilities inherent in teaching material that generates such heat.

A central difficulty, however, presents itself: How do you teach a teacher to your students? This question works in two ways. First, Lawrence was himself a teacher, and, according to evaluations by his peers and superiors, a good one, especially of botany. He also wrote essays (and poems and sections of novels) on education, on teaching and learning. Joy Williams and Raymond Williams's collection of Lawrence's writings on education (*D. H. Lawrence on Education*, now out of print) reveals how Lawrence's experience in the classroom shaped a lifelong interest in theories of knowledge and education. Lawrence's epistemology needs reexamining now in a context where prevailing theories of knowledge have changed and are still changing.

Second, Lawrence clearly sees himself as a teacher in his writings, someone who has a message. He has been dismissed as a preacher whose art too often collapses under the weight of its teaching mission. But the author who put these words into the mouth of the resurrected man in *The Escaped Cock* (also known as *The Man Who Died*)—"What a pity I preached to them! A sermon is so much more likely to cake into mud, and to close the fountains, than is a psalm or a song" (31)—is no simple sermonizer, even if individual works (like *Lady Chatterley's Lover*) fail to transcend their didactic function. Lawrence unsettles the classroom not least because he upsets comfortable assumptions about works of literature as so many commodities or cultural artifacts. He does not have the detachment twentieth-century readers were taught by Eliot, Pound, and the New Critics to expect of our "real" artists. How do we teach a writer who believes he has a message—even if it isn't a simple one and even if the message is primarily to be found in the medium itself, the lively relations and opposing tensions of the novel? How does a teacher avoid sounding either like a proselytizer or, conversely, like someone who is suspiciously dismissive, perhaps frightened and defensive? We hope the following essays will help teachers of Lawrence's work negotiate these challenges creatively.

In an effort to be as useful as possible to as many teachers as possible, we have included both theoretically based essays (in sections entitled "Words of Encouragement and Caution" and "Major Issues in Teaching Lawrence and Otherness") and briefer, more pragmatic essays (in the section entitled "Course-Context Sketches"). If readers are curious to find out where we, as editors, stand in relation to Lawrence, they will find our views set out below, under "Major Issues in Teaching Lawrence and Otherness" in this introduction.

Words of Encouragement and Caution

One common sticking point in teaching Lawrence occurs when we fail to recognize the extent to which Lawrence changes—not once but many times—during the course of his approximately twenty-year writing career. Therefore, as Mark Kinkead-Weekes argues in this volume, we should try to ensure that students qualify generalizations about this writer by paying careful attention to chronology and by identifying which Lawrence they have in mind (a practice we have tried to follow conscientiously throughout this volume). Just as you make a statement about one Lawrence, another Lawrence emerges with a different voice or argument from a different perspective. Just as you think you have one story or novel figured out, like *Lady Chatterley's Lover*, you discover two completely "other" earlier "versions"—which are actually separate novels in their own right (see Martz's essay in this volume—or his recent edition of *Quetzacoatl*, discussed in Hyde's essay, also in this volume).

During the late 1960s, writing PhD dissertations simultaneously at Columbia

University, Sandra M. Gilbert and Kate Millett seem to have been listening to or studying at least two of these completely different Lawrences. Gilbert's essay in this volume is a revised version of the preface to the second edition of the book that grew out of her dissertation on Lawrence's poetry, *Acts of Attention* (first published in 1972). In it Gilbert offers a "vindication" for feminist scholars teaching Lawrence, a faculty category that came to seem an oxymoron after the publication of Millett's dissertation (as *Sexual Politics*).

Finally, A. A. Markley provides strategies to help a teacher keep an investigation moving forward when it threatens to get stuck or bogged down in misunderstanding. Sexual issues are often problematic for students reading Lawrence, so teachers may find it useful to consider Markley's argument that Lawrence's treatment of sexuality is best understood in terms of a general historical definitional crisis over what constitutes homo- and heterosexuality. All three essays in this section promote a fresh look at Lawrence's work by encouraging teachers to help students complicate too-easy or insufficiently supported generalizations and to destabilize unproductive labels and categories.

Major Issues in Teaching Lawrence and Otherness

In "Democracy" (1919), Lawrence wrote that "the fact upon which any great scheme of social life must be based . . . is the fact of otherness" (78). What ought we to make of this claim? We can note first that it is followed, a couple of pages later, by this:

> When I stand with another man, who is himself, and when I am truly myself, then I am only aware of a Presence, and of the strange reality of Otherness. There is me, and there is *another being*. That is the first part of the reality. There is no comparing or estimating. There is only this strange recognition of *present otherness*.   (80)

The significance of this reality to Lawrence is evinced by his claim that it gives us "the first great purpose of Democracy: that each man shall be spontaneously himself—each man himself, each woman herself, without any question of equality or inequality entering in at all; and that no man shall try to determine the being of any other man, or of any other woman" (80).

Second, we can note that "Democracy" is by no means the only work in which Lawrence makes us aware of the vital importance he attaches to "the fact of otherness." As J. C. F. Littlewood argued in 1976, our teaching of Lawrence should be informed by the knowledge that this concern with otherness was central from at least 1914 on. The earliest major evidence of Lawrence's "breakthrough"—when that is understood as his discovery of "his new relation to all that was not himself" (Littlewood, *D. H. Lawrence* 47)—is to be found in the final revisions Lawrence made to the two short stories "Odour of Chrysanthemums" and "Daughters of the Vicar," most dramatically in the passage near the end of "Odour" in which Elizabeth Bates contemplates the naked body of her dead husband and realizes "what a stranger he was to her": "She looked at his face, and she turned her own face to the wall. For his look was other than hers, his way was not her way. She had denied him what he was—she saw it now. She had refused him as himself" (197, 198). In this passage, Littlewood claims, "we have the characteristic Lawrentian intuition, that of the otherness of other life, making its first appearance in his work . . . and doing so before it becomes a *doctrinal* truth in his writings" (*D. H. Lawrence* 18).

The breakthrough Lawrence achieved in 1914 was to a large extent made possible by the relationship he entered into in 1912 with the extraordinary Frieda Weekley—the "woman of the future," as one of her lovers, the psychoanalyst Otto Gross, once described her (qtd. in Worthen, *D. H. Lawrence: The Early Years* 443). Much has been made of Lawrence's third-hand exposure to Freud's theories, specifically of the Oedipus complex (through Freud's disciple Gross, through Frieda), at this time in Lawrence's life, and certainly Frieda's connection to European intellectual culture was part of her fascination for Lawrence: glimpsing how his insights, so hard-won through the writing of *Sons and Lovers*, were corroborated by theories discussed up until that time only by a small group of European psychoanalysts (*The Interpretation of Dreams* was first published in English in 1913; see Worthen, *The Early Years* 442–43) gave Lawrence more distance on the final draft of his novel, helped him see Paul Morel's dilemma as less abnormal than representative. However, much more crucial to his development as a writer was his daily interaction with Frieda, a woman completely different from his mother and from the other women he had known. Frieda was not only sexually liberated, believing in the free expression of her physical desires, but she also had a highly developed theory to support her position; she loved ideas, literature, argument, and sex. In Frieda, Lawrence had chosen a worthy and lifelong opponent, as well as ally, a woman who wanted neither to absorb him nor to be absorbed by him. As she read the manuscript of *Sons and Lovers*, she quarreled with Lawrence about his portrayal of his mother, forcing him to see his mother as "other" than he had previously seen her and to see his father as "other" than he had seen him (on Frieda's impact on that novel see Worthen 441–46; Kinkead-Weekes, *D. H. Lawrence* 42–49).

But it was not until the final revisions he made to "Odour of Chrysanthemums" and to "Daughters of the Vicar" in 1914 that Lawrence's extraordinary insight into otherness comes into full view; and as teachers, we need to stress that, from this point onward, the exploration of otherness becomes a central preoccupation of his work. Let's briefly consider two more examples, the first from a piece of literary criticism, the second from a novel.

In November 1918 "The Spirit of Place," the first version of what was to become the opening chapter of *Studies in Classic American Literature*, appeared in the *English Review*. In this essay Lawrence contests the view that "we" (that is, he and his English readers) "should regard American literature as a small branch or province of English literature." He maintains that "the quality of life-experience, of emotion and passion and desire, . . . has changed . . . in the English-speaking Americans." And not just changed—for in Lawrence's view "the familiar American classics, of Hawthorne, Poe, Whitman, or Fenimore Cooper" have "surpassed and exceeded" the English classics. The English therefore have to realize that their "way of feeling" has been "superseded" (*Symbolic Meaning* 16). Instead of assuming they already know what American literature has to offer them, the English would do better to study it in the hope of learning from it—learning that is more likely to occur, Lawrence implies, if they read it in the defamiliarizing ways he recommends:

> We have thought and spoken till now in terms of likeness and oneness. *Now we must learn to think in terms of difference and otherness* [our emphasis]. There is a stranger on the face of the earth, and it is no use our trying any further to gull ourselves that he is one of us, and just as we are. There is an unthinkable gulf between us and America, and across the space we see, not our own folk signalling to us, but strangers, incomprehensible beings, simulacra perhaps of ourselves, but *other*, creatures of an other-world. . . . The present reality is a reality of untranslatable otherness. . . . The oneness is historic only.   (17)

If the English want to live in the present and not "in a state of confusion," they must accept that these "strangers" have something to teach them: specifically, "the best approach to the knowledge of this othering" (17).

Consider next the central role that the concept of otherness or difference plays in the developing argument of *Women in Love* (1920). At the end of "Moony" the Brangwen sisters are walking along a lane and see "a robin sitting on the top twig of a bush, singing shrilly." Gudrun reacts first by deciding that the bird looks as if "he feel[s] important." Infected by Gudrun's observation, Ursula then proceeds to delight her sister by suggesting that he is "a little Lloyd George of the air!" And we are told that for days afterward "Ursula saw the persistent, obtrusive birds as stout, short politicians lifting up their voices from the platform, little men who must make themselves heard at any cost" (263). But she then experiences a revulsion of feeling and her attitude changes:

> Some yellow-ammers suddenly shot along the road in front of her. And they looked to her so uncanny and inhuman, like flaring yellow barbs shooting through the air on some weird, living errand, that she said to herself: "After all, it is impudence to call them little Lloyd Georges. They are really unknown to us, they are the unknown forces. It is impudence to look at them as if they were the same as human beings. They are of another world. How stupid anthropomorphism is!"   (264)

What is going on here if not an exploration of how "to think in terms of difference and otherness"? (See also the discussion of the daisy [130–31].) But then, it might reasonably be said that a great deal of the novel is devoted to the task of teaching us to think in these terms, the crucial passage being the one in the "Breadalby" chapter in which Rupert Birkin takes issue with Hermione Roddice's contention "that in the spirit we are all one, all equal in the spirit, all brothers there." "It is," Birkin insists, "just the opposite, just the contrary. . . . We are all different and unequal in spirit—it is only the social differences that are based on accidental material conditions. We are all abstractly or mathematically equal, if you like. . . . But spiritually, there is pure difference and neither equality nor inequality counts. It is," he then claims, "upon these two bits of knowledge that you may found a state" (103)—or, we might add, a university or a classroom. And, if this statement reminds us of the passage we have just looked at from "Democracy," the resemblance becomes even stronger as Birken continues:

> But I, myself, who am myself, what have I to do with equality—with any other man or woman? In the spirit, I am as separate as one star is from another, as different in quality and quantity. Establish a state on *that*. One man isn't any better than another, not because they are equal, but because they are intrinsically *other*, [so] that there is no term of comparison.
> (103–04)

Hermione isn't the only one to disagree with Birkin on this point. Like Elizabeth Bates (who had denied her husband "what he was," "had refused him as himself"), Gerald Crich also refuses "to accept the fact of intrinsic difference between human beings" (*Women in Love* 209). This is surely at least part of the reason Gerald conspicuously fails to achieve the fulfillment in difference that is prophesied in the "Man to Man" chapter ("There is now to come the new day, where we are beings each of us, fulfilled in difference" [201]) and that we see Birkin and Ursula experiencing at the end of "Excurse" ("For she was to him what he was to her, the immemorial magnificence of mystic, palpable, real otherness" [320]).

Nevertheless, Gerald's complexity and enormous attractiveness—not only to Birkin but to the other characters and to the reader as well—make it impossible for us to read *Women in Love* as Birkin's tract. Gerald (the man of action, the doer) is in a real sense the other, the essential criticism of Birkin, all that Birkin the talker is not—which must be why Birkin continually hopes for and seeks a committed friendship with him throughout the novel and why Birkin is so devastated by (and feels so much to blame for) Gerald's death at its close.

Such passages, as well as the structure of the novel as a whole, demonstrate that Lawrence often practiced a novelistic mode of thought that was centrally concerned with the ethical and political implications of otherness or difference. Wherever else he belongs, instructors who teach Lawrence should recognize that he occupies an important place alongside other writers who have reflected on the same subject, a recognition we argue for at greater length in "D. H. Lawrence and the Dialogical Principle: 'The Strange Reality of Otherness'" (Sargent and Watson). In that essay, we situate Lawrence in the company of, among others, Martin Buber, Mikhail Bakhtin, Julia Kristeva, Luce Irigaray, Emmanuel Levinas, and Tzvetan Todorov, in a tradition of dialogic thought still in the process of being constructed. And while our essay definitely presents a case *for* this tradition, it does so by tackling head-on some of the problems generated by the attempt to give otherness a wholly positive meaning. Among other things, this means acknowledging (in response to criticism brought by S. P. Mohanty) that when we affirm our differences, we need to preserve a strong sense of what we have in common, as well as take care to see that our respect for otherness, for hetereogeneity, is not bought (as Leo Bersani and Dollimore have argued it easily can be) at the price of a denigration of sameness, of homogeneity. And it also means that we need to keep in mind the question recently formulated by Diana Fuss, "How can the other be brought into the domain of the knowable without annihilating the other *as other*—as precisely that which cannot be known?" (4), and to keep it in mind not as a question that permits a simple answer but rather as a reminder of the problem each new case of otherness presents us with.

Hence our decision to invite contributions to this volume that would focus on teaching Lawrence's various engagements with otherness. And, as a logical extension of this, since it seems to us that we ought to be better able to read, teach, and understand Lawrence, to appreciate his importance, if we are prepared to familiarize ourselves with—at least to the extent of becoming aware of the existence of—other practitioners of the mode of thought he practices, we also invited contributors to draw on those practitioners whenever it appeared appropriate to do so.

We are anxious not to be misunderstood on this point. We are not saying that students have to be familiar with Bakhtin or Irigaray or Kristeva (to mention only three of the names that crop up more than once in the following pages) before they can approach Lawrence. That would be as ridiculous as saying that they have to be familiar with Lawrence before they can approach those other theorists of difference or otherness. It is a matter not of obligation but of potential illuminations working both ways: if some of the currently better-known theorists of difference can sometimes deepen our understanding of his work, Lawrence, in turn, can sometimes manage to illuminate theirs too.

The essays we have assembled in this section reveal a range of classroom approaches to Lawrence so various that they succeed in helping us "to think in terms of difference and otherness" in our own reading and teaching—while nevertheless affirming what we have in common with our colleagues and our students as we encounter Lawrence's work and then struggle to interrogate our responses to that encounter.

We have arranged these essays into groups, starting off with two pieces on

"Odour of Chrysanthemums," the story in which, as mentioned above, Lawrence is thought to first register his discovery of the importance of otherness. Though both of these pieces show us how to make good use of the various draft versions of this short story, their approaches are otherwise very different. Gordon Harvey focuses on using Lawrence to teach students to write meaningfully about literature in its cultural, historical, and literary contexts, while Charles L. Ross and Donald Buckley (who discuss *The Rainbow* as well as "Odour") demonstrate how hypertext can help students participate in Lawrence's process of composing and endlessly revising his fiction.

The second group of essays ("Psychoanalytic Approaches") is primarily devoted to *The Rainbow*, the major work in which, as Maria Ferreira argues, Lawrence makes his own discovery and in-depth exploration of what Kristeva was later to term "the foreigner within" (*Strangers* 191). Although these three pieces may be described as broadly psychoanalytic and feminist in approach, they nevertheless demonstrate that psychoanalysis and feminism can each mean many different things. Luba Slabyj (who also discusses *The Virgin and the Gipsy*) and Ferreira derive their main inspiration from the French (Slabyj from Lacan; Ferreira from Kristeva, Irigaray, and Cixous), while Jorgette Mauzerall draws on the Americans (Nancy Chodorow, Dorothy Dinnerstein, and Jessica Benjamin). All three contributors, however, are concerned to show us how, by helping to illuminate the literary text, the insights of these theorists can be profitably put to work in the classroom.

In grouping the next four essays under the heading "Cultural Criticism," we mean to designate the kind of cultural studies work that could almost be called cultural theory, except that this work uses theory in the service of (primarily feminist) literary criticism. After the preceding psychoanalytic approaches, it seems appropriate to turn next to the essay in which—with *Women and Love* and *Sons and Lovers* in mind, as well as the example provided by certain feminist Foucauldians—Carol Siegel explains why, in the sometimes heated atmosphere of the feminist classroom, she encourages a move away from "the familial paradigms of psychoanalysis." Pamela L. Caughie describes how she teaches "The Woman Who Rode Away"—alongside such cultural texts as *A Room of One's Own* (1929), Fanny Hurst's popular melodrama *Imitation of Life* (1933), and the 1934 film *Tarzan and His Mate*—in a core course in women's studies investigating "the cultural construction of 'woman' in early-twentieth-century Anglo-American society." This essay is followed by Cynthia Lewiecki-Wilson's account of teaching *The Captain's Doll* in a cultural studies class "thematically focused on an inquiry into how representations affect us." Drawing on Brian Massumi's distinction between *affect* and *emotion*, Lewiecki- Wilson argues that we need "a pedagogy of affect, one that challenges the pedagogy now in the ascendancy." That is to say, to teach Lawrence's work more effectively, we need to acknowledge and use our students'—and our own—resistances to his work. And finally, in an essay on teaching *Studies in Classic American Lit-*

erature, Isobel M. Findlay and Garry Watson remind us that this text is itself an early and distinguished example of cultural criticism. In the effect it has had on the teaching—and indeed construction—of American literature, it has also been an enormously influential work. But what, Findlay and Watson ask, should we make—and encourage our students to make—of the work's unacademic and unauthoritative style?

Since North American literature and culture was, from Lawrence's point of view, foreign, Findlay and Watson's essay provides—along with Caughie's discussion of Marianna Torgovnick's *Gone Primitive* in relation to "The Woman Who Rode Away"—a transition to the last section of long essays, "Other Cultures and Religions." Keith Sagar opens this group by arguing that, if students of Sagar's generation turned to Lawrence because of "the refreshing sanity of his attitude toward sex," today's students may be less interested in his treatment of sexuality and more likely to appreciate his work once they realize that what is now called deep ecology is but the latest name for the religious consciousness Lawrence sometimes referred to as Pan, of which he found traces in the religions of Mexico, Native America, Etruria, and Eastwood. But if there is a sense in which Lawrence can be described as a religious writer, it is important to add that he did not adhere to any orthodox system of belief. Langdon Elsbree, introducing his students to the three-stage model of ritual laid out by Arnold Van Gennep (and later developed by Victor Turner), points out that Lawrence clearly favored the middle phase of liminality, in which the possibility of change—of death and rebirth (which is, after all, as Elsbree says, an "essentially religious phenomenon")—is kept perpetually open.

Whereas Sagar and Elsbree both touch briefly on a wide range of Lawrence's writings, the last two essays in this group each focus on one text. Howard Mills maintains that if we can teach only one of Lawrence's works, it ought to be *Sea and Sardinia*. Mills values this work for the way in which, "like the country, [it] offers what Burgess calls an 'unspoilt pocket of strangeness.'" If we can resist the temptation to insist that Lawrence must have a message or a design on us, then we will be able to see in this book just how changeable, self-contradictory, and funny—in a word, just how strange (or different from his usual self)—Lawrence could sometimes allow himself to be. Here, in other words, appropriately enough when he is relaxed and on holiday, we can best encounter Lawrence in his otherness, just as he was encountering that of Sardinia.

The Plumed Serpent is widely perceived as giving us just the opposite—Lawrence as dogmatist, misogynist, masculinist, and even proto-Fascist. Whether or not readers believe the novel succeeds as a novel—or even succeeds at Lawrence's goal of resurrecting a dead religion within the world of the novel—they may have to reconsider their assumptions about *The Plumed Serpent* after taking in Hyde's discussion of this controversial text, especially her argument that perceiving it as monological is a serious mistake. Reading it in the light of Lawrence's urging us to "pick up the life-thread" from Native American peoples ("America" 90), Hyde argues that this novel is actually dialogic through and through and that its critique of colonialism and its obvious respect for multiculturalism ought to make it of special interest to students today.

Course-Context Sketches

Our aim in this section is to give a sense of the wide variety of courses in which Lawrence can be taught and to provide quick sketches of classroom possibilities. Quite simply, if these pieces are to function as useful resources for overburdened teachers, they have to be brief and to the point.

Most of the titles—David Ellis's "Teaching Lawrence's Tortoise Poems as a Sequence," for example—are self-explanatory. We have organized the essays into three subsections, the first relating to the poems and short fiction, the second to the major novels, and the third to the plays and nonfiction. When a piece focuses on a particular work, its title is included in the title of the piece. The essays include ideas for courses—or for contributions to courses—on a variety of topics. For suggestions on how to make use of myth, ritual, and archetype in teaching Lawrence, readers should turn, for example, to Hyde and to Jack Stewart. For a discussion of homosexuality in the context of an analysis of the Bible as literature, they should read Raymond-Jean Frontain. For anyone especially interested in treatments of multiculturalism and postcolonialism, the essays by James Phelps, by Rebecca Carpenter, and by Theresa Thompson can be recommended. For the history of the book see A. R. Atkins and for censorship Wayne Templeton. Phyllis Perrakis and Louis Greiff each write about literature and psychology, and Gordon Harvey discusses teaching writing to first-year undergraduates. Cushman and Martz help students consider multiple versions of a work (the poem "Piano," *Lady Chatterley's Lover*). And finally, Tim Middleton, Carol Peirce and Lawrence Markert, and Hans-W. Schwarze suggest a range of contexts—cultural, historical, and literary—in which to teach Lawrence's fiction.

Certain of the essays also connect in other ways. One example concerns style: Lawrence is a repetitive writer, often deliberately so, and students usually want to know why (especially if they've been taught consciously to avoid repetition in their own prose). This question is addressed briefly by Kinkead-Weekes in an earlier section and, from different perspectives, by Stewart, Hyde, and Harvey in this section. Lawrence was aware of the "pulsing, frictional to-and fro" of his prose style, as he described it in "Foreword to *Women in Love*" (486), and was articulate on how it worked to discover, express, enact, and embody his meanings (see Donna Miller on how Lawrence's characteristic sentence structures revealed his commitment to equal opposing voices and positions).

Our hope is that, closing the volume as it does, Harvey's essay on teaching writing will lead readers' attention back to Lawrence's language—not just his skill as a shaper of sentences but also his extraordinary ear, his receptivity to the rhythms of the English language, to the dialect in which he was raised and to the dialogues (indeed arguments) he overheard as a child and learned to attend to all his life—that is, not only to his way with words but to words' ways with him.

WORDS OF ENCOURAGEMENT
AND CAUTION

Which Lawrence, When?

Mark Kinkead-Weekes

I am ancient enough to have begun teaching Lawrence in the mid-1950s, before the unbanning of *Lady Chatterley's Lover*. Indeed, I had at one point to take my telephone off the hook to avoid being pestered by a Scottish tabloid about having dared to lecture on the banned work—in order, as it happens, to contrast it unfavorably with the imagination at work in *The Rainbow* (see Kinkead-Weekes, "Eros"). Yet my answer to the question of how much has changed over forty years in the response of undergraduates to their reading of Lawrence would have to be "surprisingly little."

In the mid-1960s I moved to the south of England to help set up a new university whose English school made optional courses on single twentieth-century British novelists a regular part of the undergraduate syllabus. Every year since, Lawrence has attracted a full enrollment (two seminars) as consistently as Hardy and more so than Conrad, Joyce, or Woolf. Of course students who had been told by their schoolteachers that Lawrence, according to F. R. Leavis, was the climax of the "great tradition" of the English novel may have swelled the numbers in the early part of my career, and those told latterly that they should not bother to read such an "antifeminist" or "facist" author may have avoided the risk of contamination altogether, but there have always been enough who have wanted to make up their own minds. And whatever the climate of critical fashion, those students have (in my experience) been troubled most by the same question: how to come to terms with their varying responses to an unusually variable writer. A great part of Lawrence's work—now as always—seems to my students extraordinarily vital and valuable, but some emphatically does not, while being (disturbingly) no less Lawrentian. Can there be an overall verdict, whether in praise or blame? or perhaps some definitive discrimination, throwing away the worst part in order to live better with the rest? Or, as students get deeper into Lawrence's writing career as a whole, is not the real challenge the need to relate one apparently contradictory Lawrence to another?

For the prime difficulty in teaching Lawrence is to make students aware of the dangers in generalizing from whatever work they happen to be considering. A sense of chronology seems absolutely crucial in dealing with him. He believed with William Blake that "without contraries is no progression," and his marked shifts of view and vision make it certain that to generalize about him is indeed to be an idiot. I try to persuade students never to write a sentence beginning "D. H. Lawrence . . ." without clarifying which Lawrence they are talking about. The Lawrence of 1918–22 came to subvert and contradict (to a surprisingly great and detailed extent) the vision of the Lawrence of 1912–17, while yet remaining unmistakably the same man with many of the same concerns. The Lawrence of 1922–25 and the Lawrence of the final years reacted and reacted again, showing that what was most consistent in him was his sense that life means change and renewal, definitiveness only death.

Attention to this flux and changeability is enough in itself to discount a great deal of false generalization from all sorts of ideological quarters and to focus such criticisms more accurately only when and where they serve to discriminate and to explain. Students—and critics more interested in politics than in literature—may dislike and resist this approach. Exploration becomes more difficult and criticism more complex when one tries to pay adequate attention to development and change in the man and the writer, year by year. Students want the sort of certainties that help shape essays and exam answers. Even when convinced of the need to trace development, they are reluctant to scrap simplistic notions of linear growth or deterioration—but Lawrence's achievement is constant only in variation. Moreover, this assessment accords with his own deepest beliefs about creative writing and living. His conception of character (subverting "the old stable ego" [*Letters* 2: 182–84]), his opposition to "Flaubertian" ideas of artistry and style (see "German Books"), his practices of open-endedness and of re-vision, all stem from these beliefs and are markedly different from Joyce's, for instance. Lawrence had a Whitmanesque view of self-contradiction and might equally have said that he contained multitudes.

A second major difficulty follows. Lawrence never thought of his works as finished, even when they had been published, and he often made radical changes at a later date. Therefore, care is needed to establish which version of a work one is talking about, and students need to be constantly challenged to define the major differences between earlier versions and the products of reseeing in rewriting and hence to think of works as processes rather than as achieved texts. The two versions of *Studies of Classic American Literature*, written in 1917–18 and in 1922, are different books (the first not published until 1962 as *The Symbolic Meaning*) and must not be confused or conflated— nor should the two stories called "England, My England" (1915 and 1921) or the novels "The Sisters III" (see *Women in Love* [CUP] xxiv–xxix) and *Women in Love* or the novels *Quetzalcoatl* and *The Plumed Serpent*. Examples abound. One must also be careful of inferences from a later text to an earlier Lawrence text, or vice versa. There is no such things as *the* text of a Lawrentian work, unless one means either a particular published edition or the whole process of composition, subject only to the author's not getting his hands on it again. Lawrence began to alter *The Rainbow* yet once more, we now know, in his sister's presentation copy. He changes the title of "Shame," for instance—the chapter that would figure prominently in the trial and banning of the book—to "Schwarm" (German for *crush*) so that the shame at the lesbian relationship of his heroine with her schoolteacher is clearly seen to be not his but Ursula's. He also changed the ending. The Cambridge text of *The Rainbow*, as its editor stated before this discovery, aimed to be inclusive rather than definitive.

Related to the problems mentioned above are the familiar ones of character and style. My students find it difficult to see character as continually fluctuating and changeable, particularly because they seem almost as unwilling as Lawrence's first readers to imagine that they themselves might be subject to unknown, contradictory, and even violent subconscious forces and be similarly unstable as a result. They want to get hold of a character and don't like feeling at sea in the next chapter. They complain of inconsistency or manipulation—the latter particularly because Lawrence's attempts to uncover what the character cannot articulate or be fully conscious of are necessarily authorial narrative. Students (and critics) constantly fall into the trap of confusing the Lawrentian voice lent to a character with D. H. Lawrence himself. My students are regularly surprised at the results of a challenge to plot the shifting points of view in, say, the rosebush scene in *Sons and Lovers* (195–96). To this, one would have to add the constant complaint about Lawrence's repetition. Here one needs to test whether what seems merely repetitious may or may not turn out on closer examination to be a process of varying and orchestrating associations—even in a notorious case ("fecund" in *The Rainbow* [413–14])—rather than a merely monotonous harping on one note.

The most testing problem of all is persuading students not to shy away from Lawrence's difficulties in finding language to articulate what had been imperceptible before and getting them to tackle apparently unintelligible or "weird" passages with sufficient patience and imagination (including historical imagination about what *could* be made articulate then). What may seem the worst sentence Lawrence ever wrote, for example—how looking at the rip in Gudrun's arm "tears" Gerald's "ultimate consciousness, letting through the forever unconscious, unthinkable red ether of the beyond, the obscene beyond" (*Women in Love* 242; see Kinkead-Weekes, Introduction xx–xxi)—not only has meaning but, if one puzzles patiently enough, also turns out to encapsulate exactly how and why the relation of the two characters is becoming an obscenely sadomasochistic mirror image of the one between Birkin and Ursula. The extraodinariness of the language comes from having to suggest the sexual excitement of blood cruelty while relating it (both like and unlike) to what might seem simply and utterly different, the "little death" of self-abandoning sexual love. And as the fictions end, students looking for conclusions tend to be unhappy at how often Lawrence's stories and novels leave one with a question or a challenge or an irony or a pointer to an indeterminate future; they may need to ponder the critical implications of his opposition to the idea of finished artistry or conclusive view.

One also needs to combat the tendency to see the work as autobiographical or the characters as portraits of actual persons—though Lawrence did make imaginative, creative, and sometimes ruthless use of people he knew. We have learned to be careful about reading even *Sons and Lovers* as though it were biography. Walter Morel is not a portrait of Lawrence's father but (as the name privately registers) draws on both Arthur Lawrence and his drunken and violent brother, Walter. Mrs. Morel differs from Lawrence's mother in several important ways. Imaginative justice to the fictive character Miriam and justice to the person Jessie Chambers are questions of different orders, which ought not to be confused. The supposedly confessional *Look! We Have Come Through!* is more accurately regarded as a dramatized sequence composed in 1917 than as an anthology of poems actually written at the earlier places and dates ascribed to them (see Kinkead-Weekes, "Shaping"). We also ruin Lawrence's mock-heroic and comic structure, as well as promote inaccurate biography, if we treat *Mr Noon* as though it were a memoir. The relation of Lawrence's art to his life is an unusually complex question: like many writers, Lawrence so constantly drew on life that the two cannot be regarded as entirely distinct—as modernism tried to pretend they were. Yet they should never be conflated or confused. Biography and literary criticism are different disciplines, with different criteria, and for no author is it more important to guard the boundaries than it is for Lawrence.

I suggest that the best time to read the critics is after students have struggled to discover their own response to each work. I encourage students to pin down the critical questions they think most crucial on a page of notes before the seminar discussion and then to follow these up in such recommended criticism as they have time for afterward, before reading and thinking about the next work. Hence my recommendations, given usually at the end of a seminar, tend to be critiques on particular works; I am reluctant to require the reading of overall critical treatments at the beginning of the course. The best time for these, I think, is in the middle. I try to get students to familiarize themselves with the Cambridge editions, the Cambridge *Letters*, and both the *Composite Biography* of Edward Nehls and the Cambridge biographies, so that they know how to use for particular purposes what they will not have time to read in full. But my emphasis falls on reading Lawrence for themselves, chronologically work by work, and seeking to interrogate their own responses. Most seem to find him as alive as ever and as challenging.

Some Notes toward a Vindication of the Rites of D. H. Lawrence

Sandra M. Gilbert

Many questions are hard to answer if you take them seriously, but some are especially hard. One query that has stopped and often stumped me over the last twenty years has to do with D. H. Lawrence, and it usually goes more or less like this: How do you reconcile your work as a feminist critic with your admiration for the art of D. H. Lawrence; in other words, how can you be a feminist and a Lawrentian? This is a question my students ask all the time, and it's not at all surprising that it should arise whenever in the course of classroom discussion we analyze what seem to be the implications of some of Lawrence's most radical political claims. And indeed, especially in the time since Kate Millett attacked Lawrence's misogyny in *Sexual Politics* (esp. 237–93)—and, worse still, Norman Mailer defended Lawrence in *The Prisoner of Sex* (esp. 134–60)—this query has, of course, been both relevant and recurrent.[1] But it is in any case one that would naturally have occurred to any self-respecting woman confronted, in a range of Lawrence texts, with countless statements of the kind that we would now label sexist.

How, then, do I account for my abiding fascination with his writing? I could, to be sure, repudiate or revise some of my earlier expressions of regard. *Acts of Attention*, I could claim, represents an apprentice self that I want now to disown. Parts 1 through 3 of the book started out, after all, as a doctoral dissertation that was presented to Columbia University in 1968, more than three decades ago, and the rest of the volume was completed in the years right after I got my degree. At that point, I had barely embarked on Millett's *Sexual Politics*—which didn't appear until 1970—and Mailer hadn't yet published *The Prisoner of Sex*. Can't I say I was just a wimp, a good-girl graduate student dutifully churning out a conventional study of an officially certified major male modernist?

Even if I can, I don't want to, don't want to because I still know in my soul (as Lawrence would say) exactly how transformative reading and writing about this apparently sexist artist was for me. To begin with, the Lawrence I wanted to examine—Lawrence the poet—was not really officially certified. In those days, the proper Lawrence was F. R. Leavis's "mature" and politically correct *D. H. Lawrence, Novelist*, while the author of *Look! We Have Come Through!*; *Birds, Beasts and Flowers*; *Pansies*; and *Last Poems* had been contemptuously dismissed by New Critical éminences grises like R. P. Blackmur and Leavis himself as intellectually embarrassing and aesthetically incompetent. Over such judgments, I felt, hovered the long (and, at that time it seemed, inescapable) shadow of T. S. Eliot, who had virulently chastised Lawrence's ethical unorthodoxy in *After Strange Gods*. Indeed, it often appeared that the only defenders of Lawrence's poetry were a handful of disaffected anti-Eliotians who were poets themselves—most notably, William Carlos Williams, Karl Shapiro, and Kenneth Rexroth. (For yet another poet's sympathetic view of Lawrence's verse, see Auden)

Far from being a decorous project, then, my work on Lawrence seemed to me a kind of exercise in rebellion. How could I, I wondered at the time, analyze and discuss poems that didn't meet the rigid criteria of the New Criticism, poems that didn't present themselves as well-wrought urns, poems in which you usually couldn't count *three* types of ambiguity, let alone seven? How could I explain and justify such aesthetic unorthodoxy while linking it with the ethical unorthodoxy of a prophet who did frankly worship what Eliot scathingly called "strange gods"? These were, I suppose, the major theoretical problems that intrigued me, and, interestingly, they forced me at the outset of my professional career into a questioning of critical and canonical assumptions that was not, I now see, incompatible with the feminist enterprises that would later engage me.

Equally or more important, though, I found Lawrence's writing so compelling that, quite simply, I couldn't read enough of it. Of course I struggled against his misogyny. Looking at *Acts of Attention* today, I can tell that in my fairly negative appraisals of, say, "Figs" ("The year of our women is fallen overripe"[*Complete Poems* 284]) and "Purple Anemones" ("Poor Persephone and her rights for women"[*Complete Poems* 309]), I was really arguing political points on aesthetic grounds, as if trying to camouflage my own discomfort with the writer's stridency about gender issues. Yet in these problematic poems, too, I felt the Lawrentian charisma that I was attempting to define and describe in more congenial works.

I sensed that Lawrence, even at his most overtly masculinist, did not quite fit into what I'd now call the "patriarchal modes" in which I had been educated. He didn't pontificate about tradition. He didn't lecture about "law" or "form." Scrupulous artist though he was, he didn't have grandiose and authoritative authorial intentions. Instead, he *attended*—as he himself said and as I tried to stress through the title of my book—nakedly, with a sort of mystical passivity, to the flux of experience and the fluidity of language. Like Birkin in *Women in Love*, therefore, he could be said to have had two aspects. One was a sermonizing "Salvator Mundi and a Sunday-school teacher" who excoriated women (and men, too, for that matter) when they didn't submit, as he thought they should, to the powers he heralded. The other was a being with "wonderful, desirable life-rapidity," who himself submitted, eagerly and joyously, to the forces of otherness in all creatures and things (130).

It was, finally, for this "life-rapidity"—this intuitive acquiescence in and transcription of powers outside the self—that I honored Lawrence. Nor was I the only female reader to do so. Over the years, I've noticed that women students are often especially drawn to this writer's work, as if, oddly enough, they sensed something quasi-feminist in it. And for some time now, Susan Gubar, my collaborator on a number of feminist critical projects, has been threatening to write an essay called "Women in Love," about the many early-twentieth-century women of letters, most of them protofeminists, who revered this artist—including HD, Katherine Mansfield, and Anaïs Nin, along with such other literary figures as Amy Lowell, Catherine Carswell, and Mabel Dodge Luhan.

Certainly these talented artists were all clever enough to realize precisely how problematic some of Lawrence's doctrines might be for them as writers. In her roman à clef *Bid Me to Live*, HD summarized her own abiding disagreement with the more regressive notions propounded by the character she called Rico, and in doing so she spoke for most of her female contemporaries. Julia, the heroine of her novel, resolutely protests Rico's "sex-fixations, his man-is-man, woman-is-woman," and argues, instead, for a sort of creative androgyny, insisting that the imagination is "sexless, or all sex" (62). Yet despite this quarrel with the author of *Women in Love*, HD regarded him as one of her "initiators," and *Bid Me to Live*, like the later *Advent*, can be considered as much a tribute to Lawrence as the more famous *Tribute to Freud* was a ceremonial offering to the Viennese psychoanalyst. Rico/Lawrence's words, she wrote, "flamed alive, blue serpents on the page" (52).

Similarly, even after personal fallings out with Lawrence, Katherine Mansfield declared that he "is the only writer living whom I really profoundly care for" (*Letters* 477–78) and remarked about the strikingly masculinist "leadership" novel *Aaron's Rod* that though "[t]here are certain things in this book I do not like, . . . [they] are trivial, encrusted, they cling to it as snails to the underside of a leaf. . . . [Apart] from these things is the leaf, is the tree, firmly planted, deep thrusting, outspread, growing grandly, alive in every twig. All the time I read this book I felt it was feeding me" (*Novels* 320–21). More specifically—and more surprisingly—Anaïs Nin defined Lawrence's work as "*[a]ndrogynous writing*" (her emphasis), as if responding in advance to some of the objections HD would level against Rico's sexual theories in *Bid Me to Live*. "The intuitional quality in Lawrence resulted in a curious power in his writing which might be described as androgynous," Nin insisted, noting that he "had a complete realization of the feelings of women. In fact, very often he wrote *as a woman* would write" (59). And Mabel Dodge Luhan agreed. In "Plum," a poem that wittily parodies the style of his own *Birds, Beasts and Flowers*, she defined this artist as a "chameleon!" and added, insouciantly,

> Why do women like Lorenzo?
> They do.
> Maybe because no one, so well as he, knows
> How to stick in his thumb and pull out the plum
> of their available, invisible Being.[2]

What explains the striking sympathy of these women with a man who, as sexual Salvator Mundi, frequently elaborated what we would now consider essentialist theories of gender and, in the name of such theories, often celebrated what we would now regard as the most pernicious sort of feminine submissiveness? For one thing, all were aware that, by background and affinity, Lawrence was a radical outsider and rebel, not an authoritative spokesman for a hierarchical status quo. All knew, in other words—and who could not have?—that as a working-class artist, the son of a coal miner, he had grown up pretty near the bottom of late Victorian England's rigidly defined social ladder. Thus, like the few other poets of his class whom Virginia Woolf discussed in *A Room of One's Own*, he was as alienated from the Oxbridge-Bloomsbury circles that shaped much of England's modernist literary culture as any woman was. (For a full discussion of Woolf's reaction to Lawrence, see Siegel, *Lawrence* 90–99.) In fact, he was more of an outsider than, say, Woolf herself, who after all had, among other advantages, her father's library to compensate her for being kept off the grass outside King's College Chapel.

All these women knew, too, that even when Lawrence's literary success, along with his marriage to a bohemian German aristocrat, more or less detached this working-class writer from a predestined position of social obscurity and inferiority, he never forgot his origins, never relinquished his allegiance to his roots. "I cannot make the transfer from my own class . . . cannot, not for anything in the world, forfeit my passional consciousness and my old blood-affinity with my fellow men and the animals and the land," he wrote late in his life in "An Autobiographical Sketch" (596). Raging against middle-class gentility and the "nerve-brain" consciousness—the "thin, spurious mental conceit"— it fostered, he always (as the women who admired him must also have understood) spoke for the "blood" consciousness that bourgeois ideology would repress and for the supposedly satanic Blakean energies that would overturn fixed hierarchies altogether (596).

Many of Lawrence's sophisticated female readers must have realized, moreover, that a number of his major literary models had been *women* writers. The aspiring novelist told Jessie Chambers that his first extended fiction would be a kind of homage to George Eliot: "The usual plan is to take two couples and develop their relationships. . . . Most of George Eliot's are on that plan. . . . I shall try two couples for a start" (Chambers 103). But of course anyone enthralled by such ferociously intense texts as *The Rainbow* and *Women in Love* would recognize their debt to quasi-Gothic products of the female imagination like *Jane Eyre* and *Wuthering Heights*. Naturalistically "regional" as the Brontës' Yorkshire, Lawrence's landscape is also, like theirs, a region of romance in which, say, Birkin Byronically "stalks" apart in "joyless reverie" like a neurasthenic, twentieth-century Heathcliff.

And that Lawrence actually depended not just on the female imagination but also on women's memories and manuscripts for some of his works might have been as apparent to some of his early feminine admirers as it was to me. Did a few know that he had asked Jessie Chambers to supply reminiscences on which he based significant passages of *Sons and Lovers*? that Frieda put in "bits" of the "woman's part" now and then? Surely many were aware that he had "collaborated" with an Australian nurse, Mollie Skinner, on *The Boy in the Bush* (1924), and even if that collaboration was (on Lawrence's part) a kind of usurpation, it also constituted a tribute to the power of the material produced by a woman writer.

Finally, most of Lawrence's female admirers must have sensed that, because the working-class culture in which the artist was reared was in many ways politically radical and egalitarian, women in that world—even the oppressed wives of coal miners—frequently had more privileged roles than did some of their upper-class counterparts. To be sure, Mrs. Morel obediently serves her husband in *Sons and Lovers*, just as she slaves for her children. Yet the central problem of the novel is, notoriously, *her* power, not his. And although such female strength was in many ways painful for the boy who would cast himself in that book as the conflicted Paul, the mother's predominance left her son with a lingering, if sometimes grudging, respect for women, even while it no doubt also fostered the sexual anxieties that underlay his bouts of misogyny. Many of Lawrence's most perceptive women readers must have agreed, then, that given his upbringing, for this writer—as a (male) scholar at a Lawrence conference long ago remarked to me in passing—man is always "the second sex."

One need only review the titles and plots of some of Lawrence's novels to realize how much they emphasize female primacy, male secondariness. *Sons and Lovers, Women in Love, Lady Chatterley's Lover*—all these phrases suggest that, in various ways, men exist chiefly in relation to women. Equally to the point, women are frequently the central consciousnesses in this writer's fiction. *The Rainbow* is both a family chronicle novel and a *female* bildungsroman. *The Plumed Serpent* recounts Kate Leslie's confrontation with male/Mexican otherness. *Lady Chatterley* tells the story of Connie's sexual awakening. Moreover, it is frequently the men in these works who are most blocked in their "blood" consciousness, most (as we would now say) "patriarchal" in their rigidity. Gerald Crich, the captain of industry, is destroyed by his own willfulness. Clifford Chatterley is paralyzed by "nerve-brain" solipsism. And indeed, even when Lawrence's heroes seem to triumph, his heroines point ironically to the Salvator Mundi roles in which they have trapped themselves. Ursula warns Birkin at the very end of *Women in Love* that his theories are "false, impossible" (481), and, in response to the neo-Aztec masculinism Lawrence develops in *The Plumed Serpent*, Kate Leslie muses toward the close of the book that "I've had it put over me" (371). To be sure, precisely the vision of female primacy offered in many of these works sometimes left their author shaken and angry, so that the theology of the phallus which he proposed in the middle and late 1920s was clearly only one strategy in an ongoing sexual battle that (as many critics have pointed out) intensified as he grew older and sicker. "Fight for your life, men. Fight your wife out of her own self-conscious preoccupation with herself. Batter her out of it till she's stunned," raged Lawrence in *Fantasia of the Unconscious* (217). And the melodramatic vision of female sacrifice that, soon after this, he offered in "The Woman Who Rode Away" can certainly be seen as a dramatization of such woman battering, such a fight for male life.[3] In its way, the phallic "hunting out" of Connie Chatterley in *Lady Chatterley's Lover* was a comparably combative tactic, despite the novel's preaching of sexual "tenderness."

How could women as diverse as HD and Nin, Mansfield and Luhan tolerate what seems to have been such violent hostility? Perhaps a few of Nin's remarks best begin to explain their response. For Nin, Lawrence's "truthfulness"—his unfailingly keen attention, that is, to the dynamics of relationship—appears ultimately to have justified even many of his worst excesses. "In all the descriptions of conflict," she commented, "the man and the woman's response is equally stated. He is absolutely conscious of the twofold currents, in even measures. There are no soliloquies. There is always a question and an answer" (56, 59). And indeed, although one can find exceptions to this observation, Lawrence does seem to have had an uncanny ability to transcribe with unusual clarity energies and emotions at the edge of consciousness, psychological phenomena that other writers (e.g., Eliot and Stevens) were inclined to repress or distort. Even Lawrence's agonistic participation in what Susan Gubar and I have elsewhere called a "war of words" with women, then, paradoxically reveals his awareness of gender issues in a society still struggling to marginalize such matters (Gilbert and Gubar 1: 37–40).

More to the point, however, Lawrence's battle against women was often a battle against exactly the same force this artist excoriated in men: the fixed will, the "nerve-brain" consciousness that would subordinate flesh and blood to an idealized authority. The "strange gods" to whom Lawrence would have women submit, in other words, were the same strange gods to whom he himself submitted, in what we would today call a *renversement* of traditional hierarchies. As I tried to say even in my earliest work on his poetry, he wanted to substitute Pluto for Plato, the flux of the material world for the fixity of an abstract spiritual order, so that in a curious sense he was actually trying to undo precisely the binary oppositions—light/dark, culture/nature, mind/body, self/other—that such contemporary theorists as Hélène Cixous (63–69) and Luce Irigaray deplore (see "Plato's *Hystera*," in her *Speculum*).

Lawrence as a proto–French feminist? I know the idea sounds strange, to say the least. And yet it is possible that, as my students and I have sometimes mused, in the presence of those Lawrentian words that "flamed alive" like "blue serpents" a number of early-twentieth-century literary women became "women in love" because, despite his often hectically masculinist rhetoric, they sensed his profound rejection of the cultural metaphysics that would suppress darkness, nature, the body, otherness—and women. Certainly he himself knew, at his clearest, that he and his female acolytes had a community of interests. "As for me and my 'women,'" he once wrote to Cecil Gray, "I know what they are and aren't, and though there is a certain messiness, there is a further reality. Take away the subservience and feet-washing, and the pure understanding between the Magdalen and Jesus went deeper than the understanding between the disciples and Jesus . . . [and] my 'women' . . . represent . . . the threshold of a new world, or underworld, of knowledge and being" (*Letters* 3: 179–80).

NOTES

[1]See also my "D. H. Lawrence's Uncommon Prayers," an "Afterword" to the second edition of *Acts of Attention* that reads *Birds, Beasts and Flowers* as a defiantly demonic verse narrative.

[2]For a recent and consciously feminist analysis of Lawrence's appeal to women from the perspective of reader-response theory, see Schweickart 43–44.

[3]On the ferocity of "The Woman Who Rode Away," see K. Millett 285–93. For a more complex feminist reading than Millett's, a reading informed by a highly developed cultural criticism approach, see Caughie in this volume; other post-Millett feminist readings of the novella are listed in Sargent, "Wives" 230–32.

The Crisis in Homosexual/Heterosexual Definition in the Lawrence Classroom

A. A. Markley

Jonathan Dollimore reflects, in his *Sexual Dissidence*, that Lawrence, "this one-time prophet of heterosexual liberation[,] is now recognized to have been intensely, ambivalently steeped in homosexual curiosity and desire" (29–30). As Dollimore points out, "the homosexual, the homoerotic, or the homosocial" has recently been discovered in the works of many other apparently heterosexual artists too, and "the more homosexuality emerges as culturally central, the less sure become the majority as to what, exactly, it is: a sensibility, an abnormality, a sexual act, a clandestine subculture, an overt subculture, the enemy within, the enemy without?" (29, 30).

. As students ponder Dollimore's question about what exactly homosexuality is (as well as, perhaps, Sedgwick's concept of a homosexual/heterosexual definitional crisis [1]), they might also turn to the essay in which the "discovery" of Lawrence's homosexuality was first announced, Jeffrey Meyers's "D. H. Lawrence and Homosexuality" (1973). Read in this context, what, by contrast, is immediately striking about Meyers's essay is its tone of certainty. Meyers tells us, for example, that "Lawrence's conflicting attitudes about the possibility of male love are expressed . . . most specifically in four overt homosexual scenes: the swimming idyll in *The White Peacock* (1911), the wrestling match in *Women in Love* (1920), the nursing episode in *Aaron's Rod* (1922) and the initiation ceremony in *The Plumed Serpent* (1926)" (135). Students who have read one or more of these novels and who have begun to think about what has been at stake—politically, legally—in the crisis of homosexual/heterosexual definition, might well be struck by the unhesitating way in which Meyers labels the scenes in question. They are also likely to be struck by his reading of "Excurse" in *Women in Love* (145). Leaving aside for the moment the entire debate about whether or not Lawrence is describing anal intercourse between Ursula and Birkin (Meyers clearly believes he is, as does Worthen [Rev. 76], along with many other critics), Dollimore's comment that for Meyers "heterosexual sodomy is surrogate homosexuality and homosexual sodomy is surrogate heterosexuality" seems accurate. "Perhaps," Dollimore adds, "such interpretations are intriguing not so much because of their desperate commitment to the metaphysical primacy of heterosexual genital intercourse—that is merely banal—but because they reveal the tortured cultural and psychic logic which that commitment entails" (274).

It may be, as Dollimore suggests, that the cultural and psychic logic Meyers employs is simply mistaken. What if heterosexual sodomy and homosexual sodomy are not surrogate versions of each other after all? And beyond this,

Dollimore raises the possibility that we might be better off dispensing with such categories altogether:

> Should such passages [as what has been read as a description of anal intercourse in chapter 16 of *Lady Chatterley's Lover*] lead us to say that Lawrence was a heterosexual sodomite or "repressed homosexual"? Neither: let us say rather that what is most significant about such passages is the way so much is fantasized from the position of the woman. . . .
>
> (274–75)

Students should, of course, be asked to decide for themselves—on the basis of their reading of whatever passages are in question—what exactly seems to be going on and what is significant in the passages. They may, in that process, find helpful the pages that Mark Kinkead-Weekes devotes to the subject of Lawrence's sexuality in *Triumph to Exile, 1912–1922*, his massive contribution to the Cambridge Lawrence biography (see the bottom half of the second column of the index on page 905 and the top of the first column on page 906). After explaining, for example, why he thinks it unlikely that Lawrence had a homosexual affair with William Henry in Cornwall, Kinkead-Weekes offers the following reflections:

> In fact our culture is seriously at fault in having no language for the whole spectrum of possibility and satisfaction that lies between the admission of sexual attractiveness between men, and the fulfilment of sexual desire in acts of sodomy and mutual masturbation. The word "homosexual"—especially if opposed to "heterosexual" as though they were categorically exclusive—is of confusing span, and hence intolerable crudity. In many of the world's cultures male friendship is expressed physically, quite naturally. Men touch each other, put their arms around each other, kiss each other, admire and love each other, without either shame or necessary implication that they wish to go to bed; and without any sense that their behaviour is incongruous with their relations with women. Yet our culture apparently finds it necessary to label someone as "a homosexual" as *categorically opposed* to "a heterosexual," and to find in any sexual attraction between men the evidence of categoric "homosexual" preference. Lawrence himself seems far wiser, more honest, and more humane, though he was so much a child of his Englishness as to have been probably rather physically inhibited than otherwise in his relations with other men. It is only after the wrestling match that Birkin can tell Gerald he is beautiful, or that their hands can clasp and stay clasped. One rather hopes that, after some bout of work in the fields, it got as close as that with William Henry. (381)

Students ought to be urged to consider Meyers's essay in the light of these comments.

Whether or not we can realistically hope to get rid of the terms *homosexual* and *heterosexual* any time soon, we can at least try, as Kinkead-Weekes says, to avoid using them "as though they were categorically exclusive." But isn't that, unfortunately, the way Lawrence himself used them (or used whatever equivalent terms were available to him)? Sometimes, yes. Kinkead-Weekes concedes, for example, that Lawrence's "first encounters with sodomites in 1915 had aroused" in Lawrence an "instinctive outburst of shock and homophobia (and some self-recognition)" (377), but he also claims that Lawrence worked hard to understand this outburst and that by November 1919, when he was in Florence with his friends Norman Douglas and Maurice Magnus, there was no longer any hint "of the repulsion from homosexuals that Lawrence had felt earlier" (538; Sedgwick argues that the repulsion is back in full force in 1924 in the form of "male homosexual panic" [182, 195], but her evidence is debatable).

Here too, of course, students should be encouraged to make up their own minds, considering perhaps Kinkead-Weekes's argument that Lawrence was neither homo- nor hetero- but rather bisexual; that he struggled with his bisexuality as early as 2 December 1913, in a letter to Henry Savage (*Letters* 2: 115) and insisted later on that bisexuality "was a universal and creative condition" (377, 162); and that this constituted a challenge to—or, as some might prefer to put it, a deconstruction of—the binary opposition of homosexuality and heterosexuality. Perhaps Lawrence's challenging of this binary is one way in which Lawrence anticipates Kristeva's recommendation that we should recognize and struggle with the stranger within ourselves, rather than try to maintain that stranger on the outside, as our scapegoat (*Strangers*).

Lawrence was often criticized for his extreme and abnormal attitudes to sex, but his own definition of abnormality—in a letter to Eunice Tietjens on 21 July 1917—is worth sharing with students as they consider these aspects of his work:

> There is all the difference in the world between *understanding* the extreme and awful workings of sex, or even fulfilling them, responsibly; and abnormal sex. Abnormal sex comes from the fulfilling of violent or extreme desire, *against the will*. It is not the desires which are wrong, nor the fulfilment . . . but the fixed will in ourselves, which asserts that these things *should not be*, that only a holy love should be.—You see, it is impious for us to assert so flatly what *should be*, in face of what *is*. It is our responsibility to know how to accept and live through that which *is*. It is the labouring under the burden of self-repudiation and shame which makes abnormality. And repudiation and shame come from the false doctrines we hold. Desire is from the unknown which is the Creator and . . . is holy . . . no matter *what* the desire.   (*Letters* 3: 140–41)

While Lawrence's work—from *The White Peacock* to "The Prussian Officer" to *Lady Chatterley's Lover*—is bound to raise questions in the classroom about his attitudes to homosexuality (his own or others'), the reflections above (in addition to a historical awareness of which sexual acts could and could not be described in any detail in Lawrence's day [see Worthen, Rev. 76]) may usefully complicate student discussions of these important issues and encourage more nuanced and attentive readings of Lawrence's work, including those passages Meyers so confidently categorized over twenty-five years ago.

MAJOR ISSUES IN TEACHING
LAWRENCE AND OTHERNESS

"Odour of Chrysanthemums" and the Freshman Essay: Teaching Literature by Contextual Sequence

Gordon Harvey

American college students reading Lawrence are usually reading him for the first time. Of the fifteen students in my freshman seminar The World of D. H. Lawrence last year, five had heard somewhere that he was scandalous, three had actually read him. Of these three, two had discussed an anthology piece in the twelfth grade—"The Rocking-Horse Winner" or "Snake"—and one girl's father had forced *Lady Chatterley* on her in the summer after high school. One of the pleasures of teaching Lawrence to college freshmen, then, is witnessing—and in some measure reliving—that first encounter with his vivid and profound way of seeing.

The temptation, for teachers who care about Lawrence, is to leave it at that—to let him be read and discussed but not written about in assigned papers. The traditional approach to freshman writing about literature not only accommodates but invites superficial treatment of assigned topics. Given the natural limitations on what freshmen can learn about reading literature, a teacher might as well shift some emphasis onto matters students *can* learn, such as how to make certain moves in writing about it. Only after I made my teaching of literature more writing-centered and less reading-centered (by making my reading and discussion topics serve the larger aim of learning to write a literary essay) did I begin to have freshmen write about the works—such as "Odour of Chrysanthemums"—that I care most deeply about.

In a reading-centered course, typically, one surveys a large number of major works, discussing each in class and at selected intervals assigning a paper. This paper invites students to interact with one of these works and arms them with the well-meaning advice to "stick to the text" and "give your personal response." But not only is this advice paralyzing for eighteen-year-olds ("OK now, Bob, *respond* to *Hamlet*"); it's also false to the way that personal interaction with texts—and thoughtful writing of any kind—actually occurs. One doesn't write all of a sudden, on cue, but rather prepares by reading around and doing a good deal of jotting, at some point writing a draft that gets things a bit wrong or blurry and then revising it. And in writing, one isn't involved in a naked confrontation with a text but always perceives the text in a landscape, in relation to other texts and facts and ideas. One isn't ever merely responding or defending a response but is always comparing, placing, applying, connecting. When writing about literature, in other words, not only when writing a research paper, one is always using various sources, though not necessarily mentioning them, to help one think.

A writing-centered course needs to acknowledge and work with this situation by reducing the number of major texts taught in a semester and developing sequenced, contextual units around the remaining few texts—units structured with essay-writing moves in mind. These units, which may take three or more weeks each to work through, consist of short source materials designed to create an intellectual landscape in which students might situate themselves as they plan and write their essays. The essay assignment isn't present in the class sessions merely as a thought in the back of the mind or a notation beside a date on the syllabus; it is the explicit aim and end point of the unit—examined early, brought up often, and modeled in class discussions. And students don't work on the paper only the evening before it's due; they write in their journals—toward if not on the paper—all along.

For this approach to student writing, Lawrence turns out to be a good candidate, since contextual material on him abounds. And in this regard "Odour of Chrysanthemums" in particular is an obvious choice. It is, in itself, a good story for freshman to discuss in their Intro to Lit course, since it takes them with exemplary literary vividness into another world and other lives (a collier's family in Britain around 1900) and has a distinct structure that is readily graspable by readers just coming to literary analysis: a long buildup that establishes an emotional circumstance (Elizabeth Bates and her children waiting bitterly for her husband, Walter, to return from the pub after work); an unexpected and complicating event (the revelation that Walter has been suffocated in the mine); and a concluding reflection by the protagonist (prompted by the physical presence of Walter's corpse, which Elizabeth washes and dresses) in which the significance of the previous events emerges as tragic wisdom. That wisdom—the story's theme—isn't dependent on subtle hints or nuances of tone (as such wisdom often is in pieces by Joyce, Hemingway, or Flannery O'Connor, for example), nor yet is it one of those universal themes about which students think,

Who cares? Rather it has clear and immediate psychological interest. The story dramatizes, namely, how hard it is, especially if you have moral rectitude on your side, to respect the otherness of people close to you—to let them have a real existence in your emotions as other human souls, as more than mere mental images created by your self-absorbing anxieties, needs, thwarted hopes, and feelings of being put upon. Respecting otherness can be so difficult, in fact, that to bring it about may require an event as extreme and as alienating as death: "Life with its smoky burning gone from him had left him apart and utterly alien to her" (197).

Most freshmen haven't seen a corpse to know that particular alienation. Nor, since they have most of life ahead of them, can most freshmen fully participate in the feeling of wasted life that hangs over the end of the story. And for freshmen to empathize with the "fear and shame" (199) that Elizabeth Bates feels, on realizing that she has denied Walter's otherness, is a challenge—freshmen being still in transition from childhood (when one is permitted to see others only in relation to one's own needs) to adulthood (when one isn't permitted to do this but often does anyway and may occasionally realize it). Yet this transition, this difficulty of coming to emotional knowledge, is precisely the life situation that the story takes on—is precisely the moral challenge it puts to the reader's own life. Lawrence himself wasn't fully capable of coming to this knowledge when, in his early twenties, he first wrote down the events of the story—which brings us back to the story's aptness for giving students the experience of contextualized thinking and writing. "Odour" is a particularly situated, interconnected text: it exists in different versions, which gives us a reason for paying attention to the text; the changes in the text are related to significant biographical and intellectual events; and it connects in more and less obvious ways to other stories and essays by Lawrence and others. I want now to outline how, in my experience, a three- or four-week unit on "Odour of Chrysanthemums" can make use of these connections as a way of teaching freshmen to write a critical essay.

Before teaching the unit for the first time, I assembled a packet of sources, which students buy at a copy shop to supplement the texts. My texts were the Viking *Portable D. H. Lawrence* (out of print, but widely available used) and the Penguin CUP *"Prussian Officer"* collection. (I have often used the Dover edition instead, which currently offers the full collection for one dollar, but teachers should be aware that its version of "Odour," like that in the Oxford 1995 edition, still contains eighty-five of the two hundred small alterations made by Louie Burrows in 1911, which remained in the first English edition in 1914 and were not removed until the 1983 CUP edition.) The packet consists of photocopied items, the longer of which require publisher's permissions; alternatively, some of these items can be put on reserve in the library and students can make their own copies. Many of the items, however, are short excerpts and snippets— for where a whole critical essay will cause student eyes to glaze, a pithy and provocative paragraph will spark reactions and ideas. The important thing, for teaching the skills of contextual thinking and writing, is that the materials represent a range of *kinds* of sources: actual drafts of the text in question; texts both on and by Lawrence and by others on similar topics and situations; interpretive opinions (concerning both particular works and Lawrence generally); evidence of the biographical and intellectual circumstances of writing; and general concepts or theories that can be applied to particular texts.

Certain items of the last sort—short, general observations about the nature of literature or fiction or reading or criticism—I use as points of reference, epigraphs for the whole course. These I therefore don't include in the unit packet but rather give out at the start of the semester. These brief reflections—by writers as different as Aristotle, Marx, Flannery O'Connor, and Lawrence himself (e.g., "Never trust the artist. Trust the tale." [*Studies* 8])—become part of every student's intellectual landscape, and they appear—applied to various texts, agreed with, challenged, or extended—in class discussions and in papers throughout the semester. I do include in the Lawrence packet many excerpts of a page or more from critical essays that not only supply ideas for students to position themselves in relation to but also illustrate for them how critics use sources of these various kinds—show how much or little of a source is included, how one leads into a source and follows through on it, how one cites it. The assignment makes clear, from the start, that several sources will be required for the analysis. The work of the reading sequence, of the short writing tasks, and of class discussions is to suggest why one might *want* to use several.

For the first class, students have read "Odour of Chrysanthemums" and responded in their reading journal to two basic, transferable literary questions: (1) Whose story is this and what, in a nutshell, is it the story *of*—what's the essential inner action that happens to that person? And (2) is this a successful story? To get students thinking right off in terms of writing and argument, I ask them to cast their answers as statements (hypotheses) that an essay might defend or demonstrate. In this class, as in all classes, I start discussion by having several students read out their jotted responses to questions I have asked; like the rest of us, students have more stake in what they have written than in what they have merely thought. Moreover, making class discussion explicitly an occasion for inferring, assembling, and testing evidence and counterevidence for proposed general claims helps model the basic task of writing an essay.

Students mostly agree that "Odour" is Elizabeth's story, though some will argue that it's the story of the marriage. But the question of what it's the story *of* is harder for the class to articulate ("A couple that didn't spend enough quality time together?"). The other question, whether the story is successful or not, is always a vexed one for freshmen ("Isn't that just subjective?"), which is why many teachers avoid it. But in a writing-centered course the question of subjectivity is worth introducing right away, since it's at the heart of all academic writing in the humanities, writing that—although always located in subjects and never a matter of mathematical certainty—is always a matter of argumentation, of persuading other subjects to the greater plausibility of one's own way of feeling and perceiving by making more sense of more details of the reading experience than they can. It's also important to discuss early on the sometimes subtle distinction between students' evaluative responses that aren't supportable by a critical essay and therefore aren't critical judgments—for example, that the story is "too depressing" or "too pessimistic" (adjectives that mostly respond to the atmosphere of the tale and to the morally severe ending but also reflect certain existential fears characteristic of early adulthood)—and genuine critical questions and responses that some students will have: Are we to take the story as a comment on marriage or only on *a* marriage, constituted by specific circumstances? Isn't the story just too long—or at least misshapen, since nothing except waiting happens for most of the story and the action happens only at the very end? Isn't the wise self-analysis by Elizabeth at the end of the story out of keeping with the tone of the rest and even a bit implausible? Isn't it weak to have a story resolve in explicit analysis (the didactic moral of the story) rather than in action? Because such questions often become the starting point for essays—and to help make sure they do—I try to draw them out in discussion and recur to them throughout the unit.

Along with the story, students read Lawrence's 1929 "Autobiographical Sketch," which, besides giving a concise account of his life, defines its central problem in terms related to the temperamental difference between his father and his mother ("I cannot make the transfer from my own class to the middle class" [596]). I want students to recognize on their own the parallel to the Bates family; for many students this is their first deep recognition of the relation between literature and life. The "Autobiographical Sketch" also makes Lawrence (the Great Author) human and real to students, since it asks a question that all kinds of students secretly ask about themselves or soon will: Why is it that I don't feel like the success that other people think I am? In this class and throughout the unit, I pass around pictures of Lawrence, his family and friends, and his early places, indoor and outdoor.

For the last fifteen minutes of class, I have students turn to their source book and consider a page on which are assembled a series of two- or three-sentence claims, excerpted from critical essays, about the story's meaning or value. We read out several of these claims and let them sink in; then I ask students to write for five minutes in response to one of them as it bears on "Odour"—for example, to Frank O'Connor's claim that Lawrence's early tales are all "miracle stories" in which "physical contact bears a strong resemblance to what we know as Christian charity" (153)—saying how the statement applies or doesn't or needs qualification (e.g., how exactly is "contact" related to otherness?). We end with a debate about one or two of the critical claims, based on what students have just written. Time runs out too soon, of course, but this debate sends students out with something on their minds—with some active stake in the text besides mere appreciation of its greatness (which they may or may not feel) and with the beginnings of an intellectual landscape in which to situate themselves when they write.

For the second class of the unit, the syllabus instructs students to do three things. One is to read over the instructions for the essay assignment that will be the end result of the unit on "Odour" and to come to class with questions about it. The assignment is included in students' source book, so it's always adjacent to the contextual materials that I want students to use in writing it and so they always have the assignment in class when I mention some aspect of it in the light of a certain discussion, which I do frequently. This essay assignment—one of four in the semester—entails more explicit comparing of texts than do the others, but the wording of the assignment stresses argument and demonstration (without which comparing and contrasting is merely an exercise). Although I spend some time on my assignment sheet amplifying, explaining, and warning of pitfalls or paths of least resistance, the gist of the assignment is to compose an analytical argument of eight to ten pages that demonstrates something about the relation of the versions of "Odour of Chrysanthemums," that involves close analysis of the story's concluding paragraphs, and that refers to at least five sources. Since this assignment requires students to write a paper longer than ones they are used to writing and to use texts they haven't yet read (e.g., the other versions) and kinds of texts they haven't worked with before in papers (e.g., drafts, letters, criticism—all needing to be cited properly), they come to class with many questions. Answering these, at the start of the second class, provides an opportunity to talk about the upcoming essay to an audience that's all ears and that is eager to see an example of the kind of analysis I mean.

The second thing students do to prepare for this class is respond in their journals to the rest of the critical snippets in the packet (ten in all), starting from where we left off at the end of the first class, which will have shown them how such opinions can spark ideas and are therefore useful aids to writing. In fact, we don't take up students' responses to these critics in the second class (students need to see that they can do useful reading and thinking on their own), but the critics' assertions and language ("contact," "tragedy," "sacramental," "symbol") do start to creep into class discussions, along with the language of the intellectual epigraphs that I mentioned earlier.

The main reading for the second class, however, is another kind of source text: famous works by other writer to which "Odour" might usefully be compared to illuminate its distinctive qualities. Students read Joyce's "The Dead" (currently available in the one-dollar Dover *Dubliners*) and Kate Chopin's two-page "Story of an Hour" (in which a woman who hears of her husband's accidental death is inwardly thrilled because finally liberated and then, when her husband appears, dies suddenly of disappointment). Reading these stories alongside "Odour" helps students gather what constitutes notable similarity between literary works and how perceiving similarity can invite subtle perceptions of difference. Like "Odour," these stories are revelations about the nature of a marriage, revelations brought about by an unexpected death that causes an epiphany in a main character. Joyce's story also resembles "Odour" in its basic structure: a long lead-up—during which circumstances are established but little seems to happen—to a fairly short epiphany: the protagonist's realization that he hasn't really known his spouse all those years and the altered sense of life and death that this brings with it.

Students come to class having responded to a writing prompt like this one:

> Comparisons that illuminate a focal text, by showing its striking similarity to or difference from another text, are useful tools of persuasion; but even if you stress difference, you first need to establish sufficient points of similarity to make the comparison apt (i.e., more than arbitrary: you can usefully compare apples and oranges only if you've first established that the common ground is fruit). Make a list of five main similarities and then five main differences—in plot, focus, theme, emotional effect—between the stories by Lawrence, Joyce, and Chopin.

Having the other stories as points of comparison and engagement (to repeat my basic premise) takes students deeply into each work and sets them struggling for language that articulates the differences in meaning and effect. Chopin's short piece, with its heavy irony, its more predictable theme of female imprisonment, and its slightly gimmicky twist ending (in the Maupassant manner that many students know from high school), eventually falls away as serious art, thereby making real for students the idea of greater and lesser works. (The value of teaching lesser works in college courses—even outright bad works— beside great works is widely underestimated.) But articulating the difference between the death-haunted states of Gabriel Conroy ("his soul had approached the region where dwell the vast hosts of the dead" [151]) and Elizabeth Bates ("from death, her ultimate master, she winced with fear and shame" [199]) makes for a thoughtful and sustained discussion of both stories. And, on the writing front, it becomes apparent to students how comparing a work to a similar yet different work that most readers will know can bring out (first for the writer, then for readers) the distinctiveness of the first work. Comparing and contrasting becomes something more than an exercise.

For the last fifteen minutes of the class I distribute two or three short passages from critical essays that make analytic comparisons. Students won't necessarily know the works being compared, but the knowledge that they will themselves have to make such comparisons makes them attend to the rhetorical lessons of the passages: that comparison can't be just decorative but needs to be cast as evidence, as something that helps persuade a reader of a claim; that effective comparisons therefore usually involve a focal text that is the subject of a claim and a lens or foil text that illuminates the focal text; that such comparisons can be made passingly (as allusions) or developed at length, in one of two or three standard structures; that any orienting information needs to be given deftly at the start.

For the third class, students read ahead of time yet another kind of source, the central one for the essay assignment: a draft, or earlier version, of "Odour."

Alongside the final version, they read the 1910 draft, printed in full by James Boulton in 1969 (I give them only the text, none of Boulton's notes or his collations with changes made in proofs and in the *English Review* text of 1911; the CUP edition reprints as an appendix the last few pages of an even earlier version [1909] from a manuscript fragment at the University of Texas.) I ask students to mark in their text all alterations they encounter, list in their journal the five most important differences, and conclude with a sentence that defines the general effect of the changes. This assignment involves close attending and careful rereading of a text they have just read—which in reading-centered literature classes is difficult to get young students to do seriously, even when they are writing a paper on the text. But again, since students are contextualizing and making connections—work that they can see immediately how to get started on (as they can't with a request to respond, analyze, or discuss)—and since students know that this work will be part of the essay they must soon write, they dig right in.

Students are excited to notice the differences between early and late versions of the story. They are also interested and secretly relieved to find that great writing doesn't spring full-formed from the mind of the writer—crucial lesson in a writing-centered class! They see that some of Lawrence's changes simply cut or improve bad writing (e.g., passages that tell what is already shown), and even the subjectivists see that most alterations are obvious improvements. And they see that other changes make for a shift of emphasis: the lessened role of the children, for example, but particularly the new conclusion, which inevitably becomes the focus of most of the class.

At least initially many students prefer the 1910 ending, in which the love of Elizabeth for Walter is finally released in weeping as she holds his beautiful and now harmless body, childlike in its innocence: "She loved him again—ah, so much! . . . She did not want him to speak. She had him again, now, and it was Death which had brought him" ("D. H. Lawrence's 'Odour'" 44). The earlier ending pleases some students since it's apparently happier and "less pessimistic" than the revision; this is another good point at which to have students identify the particular language in the revised ending that feels to them pessimistic and get them to be more exact about the effect of the language. For many students the earlier ending also fits better with the attention the story elsewhere gives to innocence, children, and parents and has a strong logic of character: the bitterness of Elizabeth in the first part of the story is the bitterness of a woman who wants to be happy, who once cherished romantic hopes for a happy marriage and (as the chrysanthemums symbolize) has merely suppressed these feelings in the face of unromantic reality and the need to raise her family—until these feelings are suddenly released in a flood when her husband is returned to her in the state (or so she imagines) that she first fell in love with, before things went bad.

Other students—perhaps the minority at first—counter that this Elizabeth, compared with the tragically self-aware character of the 1914 revision, is deluded and pathetic, someone to whom the reader feels superior. And so the question usually arises, in some form, whether literature should give us acute psychological portraits or characters of dignity and wisdom. It's a false dichotomy, of course, but the question reflects a genuine if simple bit of literary theorizing.

Toward the end of this class, to the wonder of most students, I have them turn to the ending of an intermediate draft of "Odour," the one published in the *English Review* in 1911 (a 1995 Oxford paperback of *"Prussian Officer,"* edited by Antony Atkins, prints the final four pages of this version, in which Lawrence is starting to feel his way toward the final ending). We read aloud a few key passages that show the ending articulating a fuller and more mature understanding of Walter's experience than the original does ("The miner turned miscreant to himself, easing the ache of dissatisfaction by destroying the part of himself which ached" [432]). The understanding is more cerebral and sociological than that of the final "Odour," which will eliminate much of the new analysis—an interesting demonstration for students of how less can be more. And certainly the 1911 draft has not yet achieved the final version's religious awe at otherness and at the wonder of life as seen through death (in particular, students should compare the final sentence of each version). But the analysis, though not clearly given to Elizabeth herself, dignifies her character: "Faithful to her deeper sense of honour, she uttered no word of sorrow in her heart" (432). This intermediate draft can also be effectively introduced as evidence later, when students are wondering whether the 1914 ending was made possible by Lawrence's elopement with Frieda in 1912 or was already latent in pre-Frieda revisions. (I put the whole issue of the *English Review* on reserve at the library, so students can browse through it and see what the story looked like to its first readers and what was written and thought by other contributors.)

As a complement to these versions and as easy reading after the hard work of closely comparing them, I have students read bits of Ford Maddox Ford's reminiscence of receiving the manuscript of "Odour" when Ford was editing the *English Review*. Ford's analysis, sentence by sentence, of details in the story's opening that bespoke Lawrence's genius ("D. H. Lawrence" 72–74; rpt. in Nehls 1: 106–09; excerpts also in Beaty and Hunter 310–12, 314) illustrates the kind of attention I expect students to pay to the story's close. Students also enjoy Ford's account—self-flattering though it is and remembered through the filter of Lawrence's subsequent writings—of an unannounced visit by the unabashed young writer to the magazine's offices ("the fox-colored hair and moustache"; "that fellow was really disturbing" [77–78; Nehls 1: 111–13]). The whole scene gives students a salutary glance at the material and social world of literary production and reputation making.

Around this time I ask students to compose and submit an early, provisional thesis that they might want to demonstrate in their essay, along with a few supporting observations (in list form) and the contrasting or alternative thesis that another reader might hold. Formulating an arguable general idea is difficult for some students, but better they encounter the difficulty now than the night before the essay is due. Other students easily come up with a thesis, but a superficial or obvious one that, in response to a few queries from me or to subsequent reading and class discussion, they end up modifying. The importance of being willing to modify or abandon a thesis, however, and of formulating one provisionally as a way to engage the mind in the process of arriving at a final thesis is the whole purpose of this exercise.

Working through a contextual reading and writing sequence like this one, besides providing students a textual landscape in which to maneuver, prompts a natural curiosity about a work's background. At this point in the unit, students are wondering what Lawrence thought and wrote elsewhere about the subjects of marriage and colliers' lives and what was happening in his own life or thinking that might have caused him to change the ending of "Odour." Therefore, though I will eventually complicate the landscape of story versions yet further, I assign for classes 4 through 6 a large group of research readings that potentially bear on these questions and that also introduce two new kinds of sources that students need to learn to handle: other writings by the author on the same or related topics and personal letters in which the writer touches on similar themes and indicates current ideas and moods. For each of the texts grouped below, I ask students to jot some notes in their journal that answer the question, How does this text relate to or intersect with "Odour" and the story of its development? For each text students must come prepared not only to give their answers about points of intersection but also to support those answers with particular passages or phrases in the texts.

The first group consists of other stories from the "*Prussian Officer*" period or earlier that deal with marriages, colliers, or both. "The Miner at Home" and "Her Turn" are early sketches—it can be discussed whether they are fully stories in the sense that "Odour" is—that show other kinds of mining marriages, similar struggles between husband and wife that, however, involve more emotional contact. From "*The Prussian Officer*" collection itself, if time allows, I sometimes have students read "The White Stocking," "The Shadow in the Rose Garden," "The Prussian Officer," and especially "The Christening," in which the proud, superior girls have chosen (as Elizabeth Bates and Lawrence's own mother might have) to remain unmarried and the collier father is—like Walter Bates—both impressive and embarrassing. But most important is "Daughters of the Vicar," in which love and physical attraction (as in "Odour," of a superior girl to a young collier) seem to triumph over class and money. Students can also be given the pre-1914 version of the back-washing scene in "Daughters" (available as "Two Marriages" in the CUP ed., 231–32), which Lawrence has revised with language that resembled the philosophically heightened revised ending of "Odour" (e.g., "There was this living center" [qtd. in Littlewood, "Tales" 109–10; see also Littlewood, *D. H. Lawrence* 45–49]).

The second cluster of items in the research group comprises the essay "Nottingham and the Mining Countryside," excerpts from the late articles "Enslaved by Civilization" and "Women Are So Cocksure," and snippets from other articles. "Nottingham" gives not only a concise history of the rise of mining communities but also a picture of the married life that these pointlessly ugly communities fostered—a picture that students can compare with that drawn (twenty years earlier) in "Odour." The criticism of colliers' wives, who have been turned morally shrill and materialistic in part by the ugliness of their physical existence and who are increasingly alienated from the instinctual pit and pub lives of their husbands, is continued in "Women Are So Cocksure" and "Enslaved" (where the women are schoolteachers). Students read these lively pieces eagerly, looking for some direct evidence of what Lawrence "really thought" about marriage, but ultimately find that the mode of generalizing sociology in these essays—though like the revision of "Odour," the essays come down "against" his mother's view of his father—is much blunter and harsher than the story's study of an individual case. They find, in fact, that these essays are most useful for illuminating what "Odour" is *not* saying.

Along with these passages students read a page of ten or so snippets from various Lawrence essays on relations between men and women (e.g., "You have to balance love and individuality, and actually sacrifice a portion of each" ["Love Was Once" 332]) and on Lawrence's aims in writing (e.g., "[I]t is this that I want to restore into life: just the natural warm flow of common sympathy between man and man, man and woman" ["State of Funk" 569]). Included here too are brief quotations about the experience of otherness realized or denied: for example, from "Democracy," on the uniqueness of "the actual man present before us" (78); from the poem "She Said As Well to Me," in which Lawrence, "feeling trammeled," rejects Frieda's lovingly imaginative description of him ("don't touch me and appreciate me. / It is an infamy" [255]); from the poem "Fish," with its rejection of Lawrence's own imaginary constructions ("I had made a mistake. I didn't know him" [338]); and from a letter to John Middleton Murry ("I provided the speck of dust on which you formed your crystal of an imaginary man; we don't know one another" [*Letters* 7: 369]). Alongside these items I place the warning from Lawrence's chapter on Poe, seemingly at odds with the conclusion of "Odour," that "to try to *know* any living being is to try to suck the life out of that being [and] to try to know [a woman] mentally is to try to kill her" [*Studies* 76]). Again, the idea is for students to try to say something about each of these passages as they pertain or don't pertain to "Odour."

Finally, students read a series of excerpts from letters and biographies. There is first a summary of Lawrence's life from 1909 to 1914, which makes clear that the immediate source for the events in "Odour" was the marriage of Lawrence's Aunt Polly and Uncle Jim and that the story was first written when Lawrence's mother was alive but was revised after her death and, more important, after Lawrence's elopement with Frieda. In this group there are also excerpts from letters by Lawrence about meeting Frieda and about the seriousness, sacredness, and difficulty of marriage. The sense in these letters that Lawrence is leaving his particular land and his particular job as teacher and perforce taking on certain larger ambitions as a universal writer is relevant to the revised ending of "Odour," as is the wondering sense of marriage as a salvation. Some students will be perplexed that Lawrence composed a tragic story about marriage during the same period that he celebrated and idealized marriage and its effects in his own life. I suggest to them that exploring such a perplexity could initiate an essay on "Odour."

This is a lot of reading for three or four classes. But though the list could easily be shortened, it's remarkable how much even freshmen will read when they have something specific to do with their reading, some specific point of reference for the various plots and ideas and images that pass before their eyes. (And this, after all, is how scholars approach the reading they do for writing; they don't start with a blank slate.) It's also remarkable how much more confidently students speak and write after they have completed this reading marathon and filled in their intellectual landscape a little. Some readings naturally interest some students more than they do others, and it's interesting to see what strikes a chord with whom. I don't discuss every one of these texts in class: I try to touch on all the major groups of texts that students read, but I generally let the discussion follow the interests of the class. In each of the classes, however, I do try to spend some time looking at a passage of writing in which a critic makes use of these kinds of sources—other stories by the author, letters and biography, authorial remarks in essays.

In class 7 I focus back down on a single text and again on "Odour." Students read Lawrence's play *The Widowing of Mrs. Holroyd*, probably written in 1910. I withhold the play until this late stage partly so as not to interfere with students' reading of the early draft of "Odour" but also because, as a telling of the "Odour" story in a different mode and medium, the play comes as more of a bombshell and thus works to refresh students' attention. Here, among other remarkable things, the Walter character (Holroyd) comes through the door (drunk) in the living flesh! And the Elizabeth, instead of seeming only stuck and bitter, is here tempted to run off with another man—who loves her! I have students respond to three questions in their journals: (1) Would you guess that the play was written before or after the original story? the revised story? (2) Do you find the play more or less satisfying than the story? (The play after all, and surprisingly, gives much more character background and motive than does the story—for example, we learn what Elizabeth's thinking was when she married Holroyd.) And (3) can you keep the play and story separate in your head, as separate works? That is, can you read the play without thinking of the story or, having read the play, think of the story without thinking of the play (e.g., the portrait of the living "Walter")—and if not, are you sorry to have read the play? Are they really separate works?

Discussion of these questions is lively and introduces important literary topics, such as the demands and effects of different genres. Some students, remembering from their reading for the previous week that when Lawrence wrote the play he was boarding in Croyden with a married couple and their two children (and flirting with the mother and children) or remembering the "Autobiographical Sketch" and the critical snippet on Lawrence's oedipal conflicts, will see in the genteel yet manly character of Blackmore, the would-be savior of Elizabeth, an idealized portrait of the author. They are thus reminded that there are many reasons for writing imaginative literature, not all selfless.

At the end of the unit, in class 8 (it could also be done earlier), I broaden the focus and link up again with the general topic of social class, which will recur in the course and which was raised at the start of the unit by the "Autobiographical Sketch." I have students read several nonfiction treatments of working-class life that can be compared with Lawrence's treatment in "Odour." They read excerpts from Virginia Woolf's essay "Memories of a Working Woman's Guild," which concerns her difficulty as a member of the middle class in fully sympathizing with the plight of working women. They may also read the first three chapters of George Orwell's *Road to Wigan Pier* (cheaper to have students buy than to get permissions), which describe in detail the mine as a workplace and the home life of mining families (particularly worth noting are the last few pages of chapter 1). And finally students read Philip Larkin's lovely short tribute to miners killed in mine collapses, "The Explosion." The first two of these texts add thickness to the students' historical picture—relay information about mining and also about the interest of literary intellectuals (in both Lawrence's generation and the next) in representing and understanding the working class. The ensuing discussions bring out the fact that in nonfiction, authors express attitudes toward their subjects even when they are merely reporting. Students also discuss whether Larkin's poem owes something to Lawrence's picture of miners in "Nottingham" and to pieces like "Adolf" (there is often lively debate on how and whether one can recognize such debts of one author to another). Students can see that both Woolf and Orwell, in writing about the working class, are alienated, while Lawrence is at home. Is Lawrence, however, equally at home in all the versions of "Odour"?

The essays that students submit near the end of the unit are a mixed lot. Most commonly students argue for the superiority of one version of "Odour"— or of Elizabeth Bates—over another or argue that the versions reflect distinct intentions or visions and can't really be compared as drafts. But, though all pay attention (as required) to the language of the endings and integrate sources in ways that we have discussed, they draw on different sources and in an unpredictable variety of ways. And the very act of drawing on a number of sources gives most of the essays more intellectual movement, more twisting and turning, than they would otherwise have. In my freshman seminar, where I have the luxury of a small class, I ask students to revise their papers after they have read my initial comments and met with me to discuss how they will proceed (with the source book of readings beside us). Revision is obviously a crucial feature of a writing-centered course. But a virtue of the contextual sequence as a method of teaching is that, even in a large class where reading student drafts and revisions is impossible, the gradual accretion and shaping of knowledge still gives a teacher more control over the writing process and produces more confident and informed essays than does the traditional survey course. The kind of introductory course I have in mind is composed of three or four of these intensive units, each one resulting in a different kind of essay. I have assembled and taught similar contextual units on many other texts and themes, from Sophocles to Flannery O'Connor (some of these units, including the one on "Odour," will be published by Bedford). The "Odour" sequence and assignment described here focus on comparison; other essay assignments emphasize other uses of sources: applying a theory to or testing it on a text; locating a text in a historical context; interrelating several primary texts by the same author or by different authors who share a common topic, method, or situation.

Valid objections can be raised to this way of teaching—that is, in addition to the objection that it doesn't allow a class to survey several centuries of great works. Responding to various sources inevitably does take students' time away from the main business of close reading. A bigger problem is that students don't and can't know enough when they refer to the sources: they've been given a few bits and pieces—the larger context of which they don't begin to understand—that invite them to play at literary criticism and to speculate about historical and biographical influences. This method works best with short works and excerpts; students who want fully to understand Lawrence's revisions of "Odour" and the context of those revisions would read *Sons and Lovers* followed by *The Rainbow* followed by Littlewood, James Boulton, Keith Cushman, Mara Kalnins, Brian Crick, John Worthen (Introduction), and other commentators. And my method, though it pretends to let students discover connections on their own, really predetermines the kind of connections to be found—isn't a leap taken into the unknown, Lawrence might say, but only a "jiggling and twisting of already existent ideas" ("Thought," *Complete Poems* 673).

Well, yes: one is always making trade-offs with the possible—with what is possible for a group of first-year undergraduates in a semester. But this method at least gets most students to pay close, interested, and sustained attention to a literary text. And although a preselected body of material does indeed shape and constrain their essays (as does the sequence of classroom discussions, which I encourage students to draw on in their writing), the idea here is for students to practice making certain moves with sources in writing—to learn to sail by tacking around a harbor before they venture alone onto the deep seas of research. Such a process seems to me better preparation for real research writing—since knowing how to use a source in an essay is a prerequisite for knowing what to look for in the library—than is the exercise in book hauling (or Net surfing) that is the usual freshman research paper. The point is to give students the experience, by whatever means, of writing a confident and interested essay—something that doesn't insult Lawrence. Indeed most of the essays I get from this unit, if less neatly organized than the students' high school writing, do engage in close reading more willingly and intelligently for having a larger context that gives close reading a purpose; on the whole the essays reach an intellectual plane that students could not have imagined for themselves at the start of the semester. The knowledge in the essays may be thin and artificially obtained, but so is most knowledge for most people, initially. And if students make large speculations based on too little evidence, that speculative energy can be harnessed later—the challenge is to release it in the first place.

Lawrence in Hypertext:
A Technology of Difference for Reading/Writing
The Rainbow and "Odour of Chrysanthemums"

Charles L. Ross and Donald Buckley

As teachers in the Age of Hypertext, we should seize the opportunity of computer technology to bring the riches of textual scholarship into our classrooms. In doing so, we may overcome the skepticism of many teachers who fear that hypertext will "thin" the reading page or that readers will trade their absorbing engagement with the past in books for a multimedia, CD-ROM future of "grazing" information (Hartman 383; Birkerts 1635).

D. H. Lawrence is a particularly good subject for hypertext presentation. Archival research in the last quarter century has radically altered our image of Lawrence at work. From the ashes of a "daimonic" but sloppy craftsman has risen a writer whose copious revisions before and after publication enriched his art.[1] So extensive was Lawrence's rewriting that editors of the ongoing Cambridge edition (1979–) feel justified in fashioning new works from Lawrence's prepublication papers, both work he left unpublished, like *Mr Noon*, and unpublished versions of well-known works such as *Sons and Lovers* (forthcoming as "Paul Morel") and *Women in Love* (published in 1998 as *The First "Women in Love"*). Each new Cambridge volume provides textual evidence with which to study his revisions and, at least ideally, to reconstruct new versions of his texts.

But has this process reached our literature and writing classes in effective ways? Elsewhere Ross has argued that a print critical edition hinders the reconstructions its textual apparatus should enable and that popular editions, like the Penguin reprints of the Cambridge texts, drop the apparatus altogether, thereby eliminating the possibility of reconstructions ("Electronic Editing"). We shall not rehearse those arguments here because most of them disappear if we change media. By hypertext we mean, to adapt Ted Nelson's definition, nonsequential reading and writing of texts (0/2). Hypertext reconceives each text as, in George Landow's formulation, "a dispersed field of variants and not . . . a falsely unitary entity" (*Hypertext* 56). With this technology students can re-create texts on screen in synchrony with ongoing, collaborative acts of interpretation. This would seem to be the answer to a teacher's prayer of using textual research in the classroom. The pedagogical goal, in short, is a more interactive environment in which to reinterpret and rewrite D. H. Lawrence.

Hypertext foregrounds the variability of texts; it is a technology of difference as opposed to the book's technology of presence. Through electronic collaboration between readers and writers, texts come to life. That cliché revives because readers literally change the reading text, thereby becoming its creators or editors. While manipulating a hypertext archive, readers learn that the apparently fixed text is really a weave of strands or variants given coherence by what Michel Foucault calls an "author-function," an interpretive idea of the author, which is always retrospective and renegotiable.

There has been surprisingly little experimentation in what we call substitutive hypertext, as compared with the well-known linking of fixed texts in George Landow's web of Dickens and Landow and Jon Lanestedt's web of Tennyson or the World Wide Web itself.[2] At the 1996 MLA convention, for example, the Joyce scholar Michael Groden demonstrated a beta version of *A Multimedia Ulysses*. Although Groden's team has woven a wondrous web of annotation, it has tethered all multimedia effects to Hans Walter Gabler's reading text. When asked about the rich history of the text itself, whose versioning has been the cause of heated debate, Groden replied that hypertextualizing that history would be "difficult." Yet a novel's textual history, when displayed interactively, is every bit as interesting to readers as the other histories (e.g., biographical, linguistic, and political) customarily linked in a multimedia display.

For the past three years we—the authors of this essay—have been building "literary machines" (Nelson's phrase) that turn readers into co-creators of the literary texts they study. Using first *Hypercard* and recently *Supercard*, we have devised interfaces that permit reader-controlled versioning or *writing* of digitized textuality. We aim to improve pedagogy in three ways.

First, students may access a content area hitherto unavailable to all but a few scholars who can decipher the textual apparatuses in critical editions or who conduct research in archives. Our substitutive hypertext enables students to make use of scholarship and to explore the process of rewriting. Our interface minimizes the extent to which a student must rely on memory to reconstruct texts. All the relevant data for a decision is available within the span of an eye on screen.

Second, students practice textual scholarship. After doing research the old-fashioned way, students can scan, mark up, and turn texts into hypertexts. Fields for annotation and response encourage dialogue with fellow readers about choices among variants. Third, students become coauthors by restructuring and editing Lawrence's *textuality*, not only replaying Lawrence's choices but also creating new versions.

In hypertext, of course, the proof is in the performance, though in print our descriptions of interactivity must substitute for the real thing. Following are a few examples of writing and interpretation enabled by hypertext.

The first edition of *The Rainbow* was banned and burned despite Lawrence's efforts to modify certain phrases in proofs. Forced by publishers to censor himself, Lawrence characteristically seized the chance to revise. Since those proofs have not survived, editors must speculate about which changes are the result of self-censorship and which were aesthetically motivated. And different choices will lead to quite different versions of scenes that carry Lawrence's revolutionary representations of sexuality. A print edition must present one version and

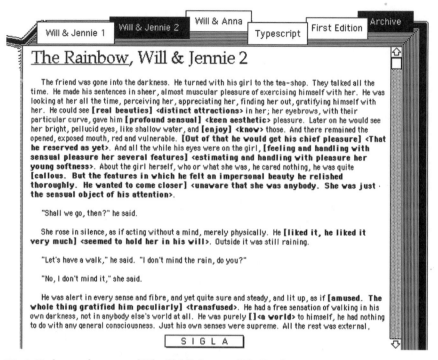

Fig. 1. Exploratory hypertext of "The Child" chapter of *The Rainbow*.

relegate the evidence of variation to the back of the book, where only scholars choose to prospect. With hypertext the variants can be an integral part of a reader's experience.

Our interface preserves the book as metaphor for the sake of familiarity. Students will already have read the novel in either print or digitized format. Sometimes we split the class and assign the typescript to one half and the first edition to the other. The text shown in figure 1 belongs to a scene from "The Child" (cf. 212–13), the chapter in which Will Brangwen nearly seduces Jennie, a warehouse lass, before returning home to Anna and a night of love both "immoral" (220) and liberating. The imaginative logic of the heavily revised scene is a famous interpretive crux of the novel. On opening our digitized book, readers encounter Typescript, First Edition, and Archive buttons that offer choices among, respectively, the typescript Lawrence sent to the printer, the Methuen first edition, and interactive pages in which not texts but textuality can be manipulated.[3] Revised passages in the typescript and first edition appear in bold so that readers can gain a preliminary sense of how much change they will be dealing with and where changes occur. This is particularly effective when the class has read different texts. Then readers select Archive and delve into compositional history. By clicking on bold-faced and bracketed hot spots they toggle between typescript variants (in square brackets) and first edition variants (in pointed brackets). Having these interchangeable variants on screen at once re-creates the writing scene in the lost proofs, allowing readers to peer over the shoulder of the author. Interpretive questions of varying sophistication immediately arise: What are the effects of changing "real beauties" to "distinct attractions" or "profound sensual" to "keen aesthetic" or later "know the touch of" to "discover"? or of deleting "sensual" from "sensual pleasure"? Has Will become an epicure? or confused religion and sensuality? Has self-censorship played a role in Lawrence's revisions? Will's appetite for extreme sensuality was again muted in revision of his revels with Anna. Indeed, the Cambridge editor suspects censorship but doesn't restore the passage. So, what would be the effect of restoring Will's exorbitance in both, interrelated scenes? Finally, readers edit the text, creating their own versions on the basis of interpretations developed in class discussion and their reading in secondary sources.

The pedagogical advantages of this mode of reading are nothing less than revolutionary. Such questions rarely if ever arise in traditional classrooms because reprints lack apparatus and critical editions make revisions hard to see or effect. In hypertext, however, readers see that local changes always have broader implications, like ripples expanding in a pool. As genetic studies have shown, Lawrence kept in mind the rhythm of the whole, submitting entire texts to revision and rarely tinkering at isolated passages. It has been extraordinarily difficult, however, to demonstrate this to students, much less to give them the opportunity to replay Lawrence in the act of seizing creative opportunities, even outright rejection or censorship, and to rewrite his texts. Hypertext brings versions alive under the increasingly sophisticated guidance of readers who can see the effects of minute changes without losing sight of holistic structures.

Our second interface (fig. 2) provides means for readers to write comments, to organize variants under interpretive categories, and finally to reconstruct an entire text according to those interpretive decisions. In this scene from "Anna Victrix" Anna Brangwen, great with child, dances naked in her room as a gesture of freedom from her husband's claims for attention (cf. 169–70). By linking text, comment field, and variant list, our interface coordinates modes of reading, writing, and editing. All this activity amounts to a rationale for the version readers will eventually create on screen.

This is, we believe, a crucial move in hypertext pedagogy: readers now become collaborators and authors within the computer's writing space. In the classroom, for example, readers would weigh the differences made by the excision of the preliminary allusion to David or by the various substitutions for "God." Then, noting that "exception was *particularly* taken" to this scene at the novel's obscenity trial, some readers might suspect that Lawrence censored himself (Ross, *Composition* 46). Having written a rationale in the comments field, the reader would then press the Self-Censorship button to add variants to a growing list. Other buttons—Free Choice, Collaboration, and Corruption—encourage the accumulation of variants in other interpretive categories. Additional categories could be imagined and all have merely interpretive boundaries: Did the author seek or accept collaboration? Or did the change result from

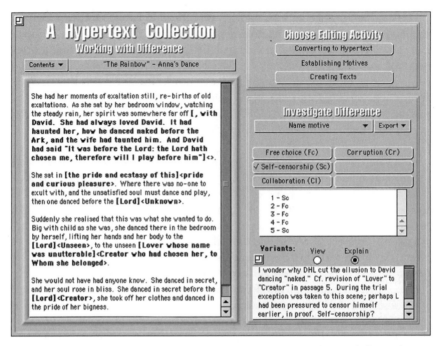

Fig. 2. Constructive hypertext of the dance scene in the "Anna Victrix" chapter of *The Rainbow*.

error? (*Corruption* is the morally loaded word editors use for *error*. One reader's error, however, might be another's happy chance.) Clicking on a variant in any list returns the text to the relevant spot and calls up the saved comment. Readers see variants, comments, and interpretive categories linked in space; they needn't rely on memory to overcome linear presentation. Finally, having visited each interactive spot and decided the author's motivation for change, readers can reconstruct the whole text on interpretive principles. Clicking on the button "Creating Texts" and then selecting motive(s) has the effect of authorizing certain variants or certain sorts of change. In figure 3 Free Choice has been selected, so the reconstructed text retains the opening allusion to David dancing naked before the lord that the reader has judged to be the result of self-censorship. Put another way, the reconstructed text was written by an author who, according to the reader, deleted the David allusion in an act of self-censorship from which he and his text should be saved.

Having learned how to explore and reconstruct already prepared texts, readers will want to create and link their own in a growing web of related texts. So our program turns marked text into hypertext. Readers must prepare marked texts by conducting research in textual apparatuses and first editions, scanning print, and producing digitized texts with sigla (markup signs). Scholarship becomes more of an adventure now that it leads to the actual production of texts. The program recognizes these marked texts, then groups, sets in boldface, and activates the variants as interactive hot spots. In this prototype as many as four

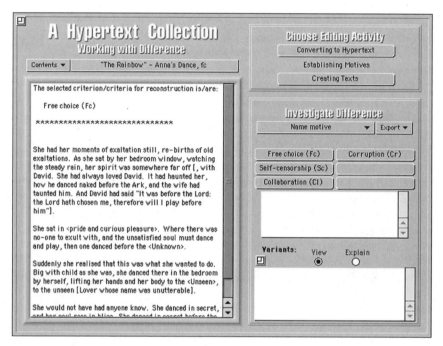

Fig. 3. Text of the dance scene in the "Anna Victrix" chapter of *The Rainbow*, reconstructed on the basis of free choice.

versions of a literary work may be created by choosing different sigla. The interface also offers both a dialogue space for the responses of fellow readers and a link to another interface where the reader may import and annotate related texts. Thus the program enables the construction, annotation, and linking of both texts and hypertext in expandable webs.

And what's happening pedagogically? The reader's experience of textuality has become fully interactive. By toggling between variants and commenting on change, readers reach provisional judgments about meaning. Theory and practice converge seamlessly as readers invent the author or "author-function" that gives coherence to a version. What sort of an author was Lawrence in this particular project? Whose help did he accept? Were there mixed motives for revision? In short, by which portrait of the author at work should we reconstruct his text? Excitement builds in anticipation of producing new versions of the novel. The scene of reading has become a scene of writing; as Stanley Fish asserts, "Interpretation is not the art of construing but the art of constructing. Interpreters do not decode poems: they make them" (327). In our hypertext the verb "make" acquires literal force.

All the activities described so far take place in a branch of our program called "Author's Variants." Here all the variants are Lawrence's, and the structures change only in the sense that any reedited, eclectic text will differ from its historical incarnations. In the "Reader's Variants" branch of the program, however, we offer means to recombine and rewrite texts. We call this mixing and matching. One prototype allows students to affix as many as three endings to any of three bodies; another allows choice among beginnings, middles, and ends. Students combine and rewrite on screen in class, then export their creations to their own disks for work at home. This is a particularly good means of comparing and combining the endings of stories.

The three published versions of "Odour of Chrysanthemums," each with a radically different ending, present a good test case for hypertext pedagogy.[4] Since the tragedy of Elizabeth Bates and her miner husband concerns difference (of class, gender, humanity), it seems appropriate to use a technology of difference for studying and rewriting the story. Its history also illustrates the convergence of aesthetic motive and publishing necessity. Although Ford Madox Ford tells us he accepted an early version after reading only its first paragraph (Nehls 1: 106–10), his successor at the *English Review*, Austin Harrison, advised substantial cuts because, as Lawrence reported, "The story must work quicker to a climax." Lawrence cut 1,550 words from the opening section in which Elizabeth and the two children wait for the miner's return from the pit. His cuts fell most heavily on what he called "the playing part—most of the kiddies share" (*Letters* 1: 252). In a hypertext readers may restore those authentic details of the miner's milieu by attaching the original opening to any one of the three endings. Readers are revising in the sense of reseeing part of the story; from this perspective, realized in hypertext, Lawrence's texts become occasions of original transformation.

Using our literary machine, readers are in control of these transformations, as a student recently commented:

> One thing that I enjoyed was picking and choosing from all parts of the story. Sometimes I did not understand the full meaning of a passage until I saw it paired with its revision in a different version. This type of reading and writing allows for more interaction within the text and, therefore, creates more excitement in the reader.

And that newfound control can increase the reader's involvement and pleasure:

> Overwhelmingly, I enjoyed the first version of *Odour of Chrysanthemums* the most. It was much more real to me. For Lawrence warmed up the story a bit, by adding in more details about the house and home and by giving the children more dialogue and more personality.

Actually, this reader added in, or reintroduced, the details. Having explored the "Author's Variants" interface to gauge the nature and extent of the changes, she substituted the first opening in the third version of the story.[5]

Giving the readers greater control helps solve some of the interpretive problems raised by the very different endings to the story. One preliminary problem is the status of early versions, unpublished or published. In our print culture there is a predisposition to consider all early versions as preliminary drafts, which are therefore inferior to the final product. Even scholars forget that their retrospective assessments differ from the perspectives of the author, for whom the future was uncertain and the text in hand a coherent, perhaps "final" version. Hence our interpretations often dissuade readers from considering a version in its synchronic or holistic integrity. Thus James T. Boulton, who brought to light an early version of "Odour," introduces it with these words: "Initially stimulated, perhaps, by Hueffer's [Ford's] request that *Chrysanthemums* should be shortened, [Lawrence] seems to have recognised the weaknesses of the tale. . . . [H]is revisions reveal a growing alertness to economy, relevance, and significant emotion" (8). Boulton may be persuasive, but his perspective is counterproductive for the classroom teacher who wants to stir interest in the process of writing and revising. Good hypertext presentations, in contrast, encourage students to value each version on its own terms and then to reach interpretations from interactive engagements.

Surely other teachers of Lawrence have shared my surprise when students prefer an early ending to the final. As professional readers we pride ourselves on pinpointing lapses in technique and characterization in, say, the *English Review* version (i.e., the second of three). Who, we ask, makes the trite social and moral comments about "discipleship" and "education"? Elizabeth Bates or Lawrence imitating his censorious mother? Is it plausible, we may continue, that the proud and stoic woman should console herself with thoughts of "knights" and "honor"? or that an artist who had seen the implication of his materials—the tragedy of the man in the miner—would have Elizabeth consider her dead husband to have been a naughty child and feel "joy" that he was not maimed? Having always read the canonical ending, we may have concluded that the *English Review* version lacks the "fear" and "shame" in the face of death—or Elizabeth's recognition of the human soul's ultimate isolation—that we value in the final version. And so on. Yet, as some of us have discovered, many students find reasons for preferring, being more involved in or moved by, the early versions.

Hypertext presentations of textuality can give readers a greater stake in the study, re-creation, and imitation of an author at work than print texts can. Both the process and the products of Lawrence's imagination come alive on screen. Our pedagogies, consequently, can honor differences in interpretations and versions more fully than is possible in print formats and traditional classrooms. And to the degree that hypertext increases collaborations between readers and authors, it helps us also to know both Lawrence and ourselves more fully.

NOTES

[1]Aldous Huxley established one image of Lawrence at work: "It was characteristic of him that he hardly ever corrected or patched what he had written . . .; he re-wrote. In other words, he gave the *daimon* another chance to say what it wanted to say" (xvii). F. R. Leavis followed Huxley. In the 1960s and 1970s, studies of the manuscripts by

Mark Kinkead-Weekes, Charles Ross, Michael Squires, and Keith Sagar showed us a Lawrence who in rewriting copiously was a master of detail.

[2]Landow's webs are published by Eastgate Systems of Watertown, MA, which also publishes the *Eastgate Quarterly* on disk and is the premier source for hypertext fiction.

[3]The typescript is item E331b in Warren Roberts's *Bibliography*. The first edition was published by Methuen in London in 1915.

[4]The first surviving version of the complete story was published by Boulton (1969); the second by the *English Review* (1911); and the third in *"The Prussian Officer" and Other Stories* (Duckworth, 1914). The CUP *"Prussian Officer" and Other Stories* prints the 1914 text with some emendations as well as an early version of the ending (1909) in an appendix (this fragment is the earliest known draft of the story). The Oxford World's Classics edition (1995) includes an appendix that prints the ending of the *English Review* version. For more information on versions and surviving manuscripts, see Worthen, Introduction l-li.

[5]Quotations used with permission.

Fathoming Flood and Father in
The Rainbow and *The Virgin and the Gipsy*

Luba Slabyj

Students usually agree that *The Rainbow*'s most uncannily rendered episode is Ursula's extraordinary confrontation with the band of horses in the novel's concluding chapter. But that scene has a close rival that can hardly fail to arouse students' efforts at interpretation: the catastrophic flood that earlier carries Tom Brangwen to his untimely death. Yet, as with the other scene—indeed, as with so much of Lawrence's writing—the sheer intensity and mysteriousness of presentation that compel speculation about the flood's symbolic significance by the same token defy any simple reading.

Students are quick to associate this flood with its counterpart in the biblical narrative that supplies Lawrence with so much of *The Rainbow*'s structuring allusion and imagery. Lawrence himself, of course, would seem to anticipate if not invite such comparison through Tom's joking references to the story of Noah as Tom prepares to drive home in the rain (227). And yet any attempt to use Genesis 6–9 as a ready-made hermeneutic key that will of itself disclose the fullest meaning of *The Rainbow*'s flood scene risks producing an interpretation no less befuddled—and perhaps no less amusing—than the inebriated and explicitly facetious commentary that Lawrence has Tom offering the stable boy. That is, insisting on any strict or immediate correspondence between mythological model and the artist's use of it will in this case leave students with little choice but to construe the flood as, say, an instance of quasi-divine retribution with the patriarch Tom Brangwen as its sole and deserving, because somehow corrupt, target—a reading not only grossly incompatible with *The Rainbow*'s portrayal of Tom up to this point but also clearly at odds with the Noah story itself. (I argue below how a less immediate interpretation of Tom as a version of Noah can be redeemed, but only with adequate preparation.)

A more elastic construal of the flood motif as here signifying some kind of ineluctable crisis or, perhaps, a precondition for a transition from old order to new, while initially more sensible and serviceable, is—if left undeveloped—less sensitive than it could be to the passage's many subtleties of import. That is, if the interpretation leaves unexplored the more precise possible kind of crisis or transition at issue, it does little to breach that gap of meaning or initial seeming senselessness at the heart of the flood, a gap homologous to the one in the canal embankment, that bids students to interpret the flood in the first place. A more specific approach that (like Miliaras's) links the flood to the disruptive force of industrialization as figured by the burst canal goes some way to lessening this gap, indeed seems to offer symbolic closure of a kind that is both satisfying and readily accessible to many students. However, given that such a reading, when offered on its own, tends to emphasize Tom Brangwen's broadly representative status as historically doomed agrarian to the detriment of his singularity as fully realized fictional being, it seems to me essential that we also encourage students to discern—as they do in Ursula's encounter with the horses—a more intimate relation between symbolic event and the character at its heart and, if possible, a correspondingly richer relation between this episode and the larger text whose dead center it constitutes.

The apparent abruptness with which *The Rainbow* announces the fatal flood might at first seem to preclude such relations by appearing to disconnect a freak accident from its larger context. That is, even the heading of chapter 9, "The Marsh and the Flood," does not adequately prepare us for the shock of the single and deliberately surprising sentence that triggers the episode: "Then suddenly the father died" (226). With respect to exploring connections between this and other passages in *The Rainbow*, then, the laying of some preliminary groundwork for class discussion is almost certainly necessary. One might remind students that, as other of Lawrence's writings show us (most explicitly, *The Rainbow*'s sister novel, *Women in Love*), for Lawrence an accident is never merely an accident, let alone a textually isolated one.

More to the point, though, we would do well to begin our exploration with F. R. Leavis's response to criticisms concerning *The Rainbow*'s supposed lack of narrative cohesion. Using as his example the passage in which Tom covertly observes Will embracing Tom's stepdaughter, Anna, in the fowl loft (111–12) and mournfully recalls the night, described in an earlier passage (75–76), on which Tom himself held the child Anna in the barn while his wife gave birth— an experience that at the time brought its own recollections of his mother, of her attending church in the shawl now blanketing Anna, of Tom himself as a boy at home—Leavis argues that the organizing presence in *The Rainbow* is a "complex rhythm . . . , the movement that, by recurrence along with newness, brings continually a significant recall of what has gone before" (*D. H. Lawrence* 126).

Asked to attend to the flood scene in the light of this observation, students may recognize in the passages Leavis cites certain key elements echoed not only by this episode but also by others both before and well after it. On the most obvious level, in addition to the repeated setting of the farmyard with its buildings and animals, there is the recurrence of the conditions of darkness and rain, conditions that have also featured significantly in Will Brangwen's exploit with the factory girl (210–16) and that will, of course, feature in Ursula's encounter with the horses. Once students have observed that Will's attempted seduction is a notable variation on Will's original embrace of Anna in the fowl loft and that Ursula's confrontation with the horses is arguably a metaphorical reworking of Tom's drowning (see, e.g., Kinkead-Weekes, "Marble" 410), they perceive the beginnings of an associational nexus of scenes that appear somehow to comment on one another. Students might wish to point out those passages that connect Ursula and Will, albeit in differing and even opposing ways, to the mythic Genesis deluge: Ursula's critical musings on the Noah story (301–02) and Will's turmoil of dependence on Anna before he achieves "a new, deeper freedom" (173–76) and particularly the following paragraphs:

> What had he in life, save her? Nothing. The rest was a great heaving flood. The terror of the night of heaving, overwhelming flood, which was his vision of life without her, was too much for him. He clung to her fiercely and abjectly.
>
> And she beat him off, she beat him off. Where could he turn, like a swimmer in a dark sea, beaten off from his hold, whither could he turn? He wanted to leave her. . . . But for what? She was the ark, and the rest of the world was flood. (173)

With the flood motif here betokening masculine anxiety and frustration in marriage, this passage may in turn prompt the students' recollection of the one in which Tom Brangwen's difficulties with Lydia after the birth of their first child are described in similar language:

> He wanted to give her all his love, all his passion, all his essential energy. But it could not be. He must find other things than her, other centres of living. She sat close and impregnable with the child. And he was jealous of the child.
>
> But he loved her, and time came to give some sort of course to his troublesome current of life, so that it did not foam and flood and make misery. He formed another centre of love in her child, Anna. Gradually a part of his stream of life was diverted to the child, relieving the main flood to his wife. Also he sought the company of men, he drank heavily now and again. (79)

This is not the only occasion on which Tom's passion for Lydia is expressed in terms of a flood. Earlier yet, we have this passage on the resolution of an impasse in the marriage:

She lapsed into a sort of sombre exclusion . . . which drove him and the child nearly mad. He walked about for days stiffened with resistance to her, stiff with a will to destroy her as she was. Then suddenly, out of nowhere, there was connexion between them again. . . . The tension, the bond, burst, and the passionate flood broke forward into a tremendous, magnificent rush, so that he felt he could snap off the trees as he passed, and create the world afresh.   (60)

Students, taking their cue from Leavis and the examples he offers, might wish to remark on other instances of "recurrence along with newness" among the finer details of the flood episode. Most striking to my mind are the complex reversals of the aforementioned childbirth scene observable in the particular constellation and circumstances of characters it features. On the memorable night of childbirth, the terrified Anna, unable to go to her mother, refuses to be consoled by the exasperated Tom, who—before he lights on the idea of taking Anna out to the barn—struggles futilely to put her to bed. With Anna's blind crying in our ears, we can now discern echoes (more than strictly figurative) in the flood scene—in Lydia's desperation to locate her missing husband, as well as in the reactions of her younger son, Fred: "'To-om, To-o-om!' rang out the strong, inhuman cry. Fred Brangwen's blood froze, his heart was very angry. . . . Why was she yelling like this? He could not bear the sight of her, perched on her chair in her white nightdress in the doorway, elvish and horrible" (231). Here, not only has the previous familial triangle of father, (absent) mother, and daughter been revised to that of (absent) father, mother, and son, but also the mother, who down to the details of her "elvish" physique, her nightdress, and her perch on a piece of furniture clearly stands in for the frightened child Anna, now repeatedly yells out for a husband/father in the grip of death, just as Anna once called out for a mother in the throes of delivering a new life. In both cases, standing between them is a male figure whose own anxiety renders him painfully, even violently, sensitive to the female's cries. In both cases, too, we might add, a distressed Tilly looks helplessly on.

Having established an abundance—by no means exhausted here—of such textual interweavings of the flood episode with the rest of *The Rainbow*, students perhaps run the risk of being overwhelmed by too much implicit significance and the critical question of where it all tends, particularly with regard to the scene's primary character, Tom. A brief aside about some other famous literary flood scenes—most pertinent, the one in Lawrence's *The Virgin and the Gipsy* and its almost certain prototype, the flood concluding George Eliot's *The Mill on the Floss*—might therefore offer students an opportunity to assimilate the foregoing material from *The Rainbow* while likewise suggesting possible readings of its more precise significance in relation to *The Rainbow*'s flood. Particularly helpful in this respect would be a brief review of critical commentary on *The Virgin and the Gipsy* underscoring the implicit association of this work's flood with the force of desire. Indeed, the mere mention of the titles of two articles, Carol Siegel's "Floods of Female Desire in Lawrence and Eudora Welty" and Garry Watson's "'The Fact, and Crucial Significance, of Desire': Lawrence's *Virgin and the Gipsy*" (incorporating a key phrase from Leavis on the novella [*D. H. Lawrence* 306]), may suffice to boost students' nascent awareness that most of the aforementioned passages in *The Rainbow* also, in one way or another, deal with the issue of desire—its workings, its thwartings, its transmigrations—and thus appear, like the flood episode itself, to represent or comment on the desire of Tom Brangwen.

One can, however, do much more with these two commentaries to lead students into a consideration of desire in *The Rainbow*. For instance, Siegel contends that Yvette's survival of the flood in *The Virgin and the Gipsy* triumphantly realizes desire that is forever tragically repressed in *The Mill on the Floss* by Maggie Tulliver's death ("Floods" 111, 114–16). Students may wonder if a similar relation exists between Yvette's survival and Tom's death—or, more pertinent yet, between Tom's death and Ursula's symbolic rebirth through her own flood-like ordeal.

More effective in helping students determine the nature and constitution of Tom's desire, however, is Watson's closer reading of *The Virgin and the Gipsy*, which points out how intricately Yvette's desire is bound up with two pairings of older women with younger men: Mrs. Fawcett and Major Eastwood and the implicit model couple behind them, Yvette's renegade mother and the man with whom she has run off (141–44). In each instance, Watson notes, Yvette clearly desires to participate in the "potent state of being" ("'Fact'" 142) that the man and woman separately and jointly represent. Taking this much from an argument with a complex aim of its own, I would add yet another such pairing of older woman and younger man to Yvette's mise-en-scène of desire—Yvette's grandmother, or "the Mater," and Yvette's own father—in order to point out that the desire evident in these triangular relationships is not only broadly rivalrous but also, as the figuring of Yvette's mother in them might already hint, specifically incestuous. And this desire is not only on the part of Yvette, who longs for the gipsy (as?) husband-father but also on the part of the rector, who, in the form of the darker reflection of himself that the text plainly constructs the gipsy as, desires the "snowdrop" of Yvette's virginity (54; Watson 142) as he desires that "snow-flower" of "She-who-was-Cynthia" (7; Watson 142), even while worshipping that "faithful wife . . . and mother," the Mater (71; Watson 147).

This positioning of a desiring father figure among a number of familial females whose roles complexly overlap one another and whose absence or presence defines the degree of his potency can serve students as a template for exploring Tom Brangwen's desire. For instance, students should be able to see in certain of the aforementioned passages not only an implicit overlapping of Lydia with Anna in the configuration of Tom's desire but even their conjoint role in channeling the sheer force of this desire, which, when sustained—and, more important, when reciprocated—makes Tom feel powerful enough to "create the world afresh." To these passages, moreover, we can now add others indicating just how critical Anna's presence is to Tom's satisfaction in his relationship with Lydia: "soon" into this relationship, Tom and Anna "were like lovers, father and child" (62), and, of the two parents and "[o]f her own choice," Anna "loved Brangwen most, or most obviously" (79). We might point out that the love between Tom and Anna is not spontaneous, for as Tom's repeated coaxings of Anna into accepting him as her father demonstrate, this relationship is as much a product of Tom's patient courtship as is his marriage to Lydia. Indeed, Anna's centrality to the memorable scene in which Tom gazes at mother and child together through the kitchen window of the vicarage on the night he comes to propose to Lydia underscores our impression that Tom courts the two females as, if one can pardon the term, a package deal.

This is a good moment to observe that, like Yvette's fascination with wife-husband and mother-father pairings, Tom's attraction to this mother and child has its basis in family history. Chapter 1 briefly tells us that through the departure of various siblings and the death of his father, Tom's immediate family has dwindled to the point of leaving Tom in possession of the Marsh farm; here, for a period, he occupies the son-cum-father role in an intimate triad of "mother and son and daughter" (19). If this early connection to a mother and daughter does not in itself seem charged with desire, Tom's attempts to replicate it in his erotic career become evident long before Lydia and Anna appear. First, we are told that "rooted" as Tom is "in his mother and his sister," his first sexual encounter with a prostitute leaves him shaken because "[f]or him there was until that time only one kind of woman—his mother and sister" (20). Again, we might note, the two female figures are equated, even conflated, in Tom's mind. His ensuing endeavor to find a "nice girl" whom he desires as much as those "loose" ones from whom he inevitably recoils once he has possessed them of course follows the familiar pattern of a masculine incest anxiety characterized by dramatic oscillation between the virgin-mother and whore aspects of woman (21).

What proves more interesting and suggestive to students is Tom's progressive resolution of his dilemma. This resolution commences not simply on the death of his mother and the marriage of his sister but on his encounter at an inn with the young woman and the older father figure whose mistress Tom discovers her to be only after he has had sex with her. This experience with "a voluptuous woman and . . . a small withered foreigner of ancient breeding" (26) leaves Tom with a glow that hints at a more involved explanation for his previous trouble in finding a sister-mother figure to desire. That is, the prostitute and other "loose" girls with whom he has slept have been, as "loose" indicates, sufficiently available (unlike his mother, his sister, and "nice girls") and yet (again, unlike them) insufficiently attached to or associated with an older male figure with whom Tom can surreptitiously share them and from whom he can eventually win them. The compromise fantasy scenario created for him by this chance meeting offers Tom a hitherto unknown satisfaction that he can only attempt to sustain through drink until that perfect couple comes along to realize this fantasy: the mother and child who have previously belonged to the foreigner Paul Lensky and who still, in a sense, move in Lensky's shadow (49–50). One might suggest that the strange "vacancy" in Lydia's eyes "inflames" (32) Tom because it signifies that the "small withered foreigner of ancient breeding" has at last, so to speak, checked out of the inn, leaving the mother and daughter to Tom. (We might add that the only female other than Anna to whom Tom, in his difficulties with Lydia, is fleetingly tempted to "divert" his "stream of life" is his older brother's mistress, who reinvokes the earlier fantasy scenario.) Interestingly enough, the broadest effect of Tom's acquaintance with Lydia and her child is to make Tom feel, somewhat à la Noah, "as if a new creation were fulfilled, in which he had real existence" (32).

Just as we might say that Yvette's deepest desire is to be the mother in a multiple, fantasy sense, so might we describe Tom's deepest desire as the need to occupy the lofty position of the father in his idealized capacity of proprietor of his family's women. With some encouragement, students might begin to perceive a similar but even more profound need on the part of Tom's successor in Anna's affections, Will Brangwen, whose initially secure sense of the house in which he honeymoons with Anna as "the Ark in the flood" with "all the rest drowned" (136) soon gives way to pathetic efforts to become "captain of the ship" (161) in his marriage to Anna and, eventually, to the fearful condition in which we have seen him in the aforementioned passage. Those students eager to pursue this issue of the would-be father's desire might observe how Will's passion, like Tom's, extends to his own daughter, Ursula, who is "wakened too soon" (205) by her father's cravings for her love (see also 197) and who hovers as surely as Anna herself behind the childish figure of the factory girl whom Will attempts to seduce. Students particularly attuned to this kind of reading might even discern, in the earliest paragraphs of the flood episode, a masculine preoccupation with attaining a fatherly or potent standing that sets the tone for the event to come. This focus is most obviously embodied by the young Fred Brangwen who, sitting at home that evening, finds himself at an impasse regarding his immediate prospects:

> This wet, black night seemed to cut him off and make him unsettled, . . . aware that he was scarcely living. There seemed to him to be no root to his life, no place for him to get satisfied in. He dreamed of going abroad. But his instinct knew that change of place would not solve his problem. He wanted change, deep, vital change of living. And he did not know how to get it. (226)

Fred's quandary, moreover, has already been prepared for by the plight of his older brother, Tom's namesake, who, we are told just before this passage, has become "undefinably an outsider," belonging "to nowhere, to no society" (226).

If we are to make the most of this pattern that extends outward from Tom to incorporate other males of the Brangwen clan, we must point out to students that its broadest effect is not so much to constitute a series of variations on a common oedipal theme as to indicate with a cumulative force the fatality intrinsic to the position of the father as an idealized, absolute being and, relatedly, the lethal underside of a desire to be this figure. We should not, for example, overlook the fact that Fred's impasse over attaining a footing in life can apparently be resolved only by Tom's losing his own footing as the flood waters literally sweep Tom off his feet—a resolution, we might add, that leaves Fred hardly any less shaken than Yvette is by the flood's drastic disposal of her rival, the Mater. Nor should we fail to note that these other instances of fatherly desire and desire to be the father—desires that are, in a sense, arguably one and the same—play a critical role in prefiguring, as somehow inevitable, Tom's death in his express capacity as "the father" (266).

Even more specifically suggestive in this respect is the occasion, just before Will's exploit with the factory girl, on which Ursula nearly breaks her father's neck as they leap off the canal bridge, causing them to "f[a]ll into the water in a heap, and [fight] for a few moments with death" (209). Clearly, this near breakage has its equivalent—Anna-logue, one is tempted to say—in the symbolic role Tom's own daughter plays in his death—a role neatly evinced in the juxtapositioning of two seemingly separate narrative events:

> Anna Brangwen had left her intimacy with her father undeveloped since the time of her marriage. At her marriage it had been abandoned. He and she had drawn a reserve between them. Anna went more to the mother.
>
> Then suddenly the father died.   (226)

Students may ask why, however, Anna's abandonment of, or absence to, her father by virtue of her marriage should be so singly linked to that "great, raw gap in the canal embankment" (232) that unleashes the fatal flood, when, as we have seen, Anna is apparently only as important as Lydia—and indeed, supplementary to her—in the channeling of Tom's desire.

Without drawing too much on psychoanalytic theory, we can explain the daughter's implicit fatality to her father in terms of culture's prohibition on incest or, alternatively, culture's exogamic dictate that eventually and necessarily deprives the father of his daughter as a bearer of his name, directing her to cancel this name out by assuming another in marriage. We can say that the daughter constitutes the means by which the father is symbolically murdered and replaced by a male successor. We do, however, have to stress the symbolic nature of this murder, inasmuch as Anna does not in fact cancel out Tom's surname any more than she does Tom himself when she marries her cousin Will, who, as circumstances would have it, bears the same last name. That her marriage does, however, constitute a forcible breach—in the paradoxical form of a barrier—in Anna's relationship to Tom is reflected not only in the above passage but also in an earlier one that plays on the fowl loft scene as evidently as the loft scene plays on the one in the barn. The passage in question describes Tom's final gesture to Anna and her new husband on their wedding night, which is to lead a band of reluctant male relatives under Anna's window in order to "carol 'em, for th' last time" (133). Whereas previously Tom has been able to witness the couple embracing above him through "a travelling veil of rain" (111), window blinds now completely obscure from him the bedded Anna and Will, who eventually "[cease] to hear" the hymn in which he leads the men. This passage of course immediately precedes the one in which Will imagines that all others have been "drowned" and swept away, leaving him in sole possession of Anna and their arklike home.

Bearing all this in mind, students are in a good position to grasp the symbolic significance behind the flood's conversion of Tom from "the father" to simply an "unconscious, drowning body" without nomenclature (229). Students are now also able to grasp Ursula's markedly different relation to the flood motif not only in terms of her emergence from her parallel ordeal with the horses but also in terms of her personal revision of the Noah story, an account as wryly aware of the story's underlying masculine urge to proprietorship as it is delightfully amusing:

> After all, how big was the Flood? Perhaps a few dryads and fauns had just run into the hills and the further valleys and woods, frightened, but most had gone on blithely unaware of any flood at all, unless the nymphs should tell them. It pleased Ursula to think of the naiads in Asia Minor meeting the nereids at the mouth of the streams, where the sea washed against the fresh, sweet tide, and calling to their sisters the news of Noah's Flood. They would tell amusing accounts of Noah in his ark. Some nymphs would relate how they had hung on the side of the ark, peeped in, and heard Noah and Shem and Ham and Japheth, sitting in their place under the rain, saying, how they four were the only men on earth now, because the Lord had drowned all the rest, so that they four would have everything to themselves, and be masters of every thing, subtenants under the great Proprietor.
>
> Ursula wished she had been a nymph. She would have laughed through the window of the ark, and flicked drops of the flood at Noah, before she drifted away to people who were less important in their Proprietor and their Flood.   (302)

Far from being the "right" reading of the Genesis myth, this is simply an alternative version that disavows the central problem motivating its complement myth, or, as the latter might better be described, fantasy: namely, the fact that, whether nymph or Noah, one inevitably lacks. Both myths seek to expel lack by projecting it onto another, less righteous party: in the Genesis account onto all those who perish for their iniquities in the flood and in Ursula's account onto Noah and his party, whom Ursula renders absurd and themselves iniquitous in their flagrant greed. More important, both versions disavow lack through a paradoxically utopian vision of a nonlacking culture—a culture that in Genesis is, moreover, conspicuously incestuous.

How, though, should we relate these latter tensions back to the primary occasion for this analysis, Tom's death in the flood episode? Perhaps one of P. T. Whelan's mythic epithets for Tom, "Noah *manqué*," indirectly suggests the best course (25). The phrase, implying as it does not only an inversion of the Noah figure but, when translated literally, a Noah who intrinsically lacks, signals the status of the flood episode as yet another of Lawrence's rewritings of the flood story. Like the two competing versions—the one in Genesis and Ursula's—this one offers a vision that attempts to compensate for lack—here not only the loss of a desired daughter but also the outright loss of life. Students, having considered Ursula's active revision of a story to feature herself as a nymph rather than as only one of the "daughters of men," now have occasion to discern Tom's passive translation, through the mysterious workings of the flood, from a less than complete father into an "inaccessible male . . . beyond change or knowledge, absolute, laid in line with the infinite, . . . a majestic Abstraction, made visible now for a moment, inviolate, absolute" (233). Indeed, from the perspective of Tom's wife and daughter, who pay him "awe-stricken" homage, and arguably from the perspective of the narrative voice itself, Tom is "neither living nor . . . dead" but "both one and the other, inviolable, inaccessibly himself"—and, we might note, inaccessibly now the father he could never be in life. In the spirit of this mythic resolution, then, it would perhaps be most appropriate to view Tom's death neither as a tragic repression of desire a là *The Mill on the Floss* (never mind as retribution for the father's unconscious incestuous desire) nor as desire fulfillment on the order of *The Virgin and the Gipsy* but as both one and the other, in the form of the realization of the death drive, whose powerful current constitutes an undertow in that "troublesome current of life," the libido. In this respect, we could perhaps deem the flood a lethally uncanny "return of the repressed" (see Freud, *Moses* 372–76).

To those interested in developing their students' grasp of contemporary psychoanalytic theory, this approach to *The Rainbow*'s flood episode could be but the beginning of a more complex exploration of the figure of the father in relation to the Lacanian categories of the imaginary, real, and symbolic and—just as fruitfully—in relation to Lacan's notions of the uncanny and of the sublime (on these relations see Žižek, chs. 4–5).

However, in any undergraduate context where teaching a great deal of contemporary theory would be inappropriate, the instructor should at least emphasize how compellingly and realistically *The Rainbow* presents the complex relation between desire and the dictates of culture. Underlying the irresolvable tension between these two forces and intrinsic to both is an ongoing attempt to establish an absolute that is fundamentally impossible, not only inasmuch as desire and the cultural dictates that would legislate desire are inevitably subject to each other but, more important, inasmuch as both desire and culture are equally predicated on the inevitability of lack.

Strange Bedfellows: D. H. Lawrence and Feminist Psychoanalytic Theory in *The Rainbow*

Jorgette Mauzerall

Teaching D. H. Lawrence today means surmounting the hurdle of Lawrence's reputation as one of the arch male chauvinists of modern literature. This reputation, largely defined and established by Kate Millett in *Sexual Politics*, is not totally undeserved, but I would argue that aspects of what we think of as Lawrence's sexism make him worth our attention, especially when they are examined under the new lens of feminist theory, in general, and feminist psychoanalytic theory in particular. Ironically, certain feminist theorists can find an ally in Lawrence. He represents in clear terms problems between the sexes that these theorists believe need addressing, and he emphasizes aspects of human psychology neglected by traditional, male-dominated psychoanalytic theory.

My familiarity with this feminist approach to human psychology helped me understand why I, as a reader, was both drawn to and put off by Lawrence. This ambivalence is often shared by new readers of Lawrence, and I am convinced that they, like me, will find reading him a much richer and less frustrating experience if they begin with an understanding of feminist theory, specifically the branch represented by such writers as Dorothy Dinnerstein, Adrienne Rich, and the psychoanalytic theorist Nancy Chodorow. In the following analysis I outline some important and relevant aspects of this line of thinking and then indicate how these can be used to illuminate one of Lawrence's major novels, *The Rainbow*—although the implications of feminist psychoanalytic theory for any student of Lawrence extend far beyond this work.

Throughout Lawrence's work, the new reader encounters what at times seems an oppressive ideology of gender in which male and female are seen as binaries, complementary and polar opposites: the female principle, Lawrence tells us as early as "Study of Thomas Hardy," represents the body, while the male principle represents spirit (94)—although, as he also makes clear, "the division into male and female is arbitrary, for the purpose of thought," since "every man comprises male and female in his being [and] a woman likewise consists in male, and female" (60, 94). Most of our students have themselves never consciously entertained a theory like the one set forth by Lawrence, but I would argue that he only states forthrightly a belief that saturates the Western cultural tradition: beginning with the Bible's story of Genesis (in which God grants Adam the power of naming but assigns Eve to give birth in pain to new bodies, to perpetuate the cycle of life and death until a male savior redeems humankind from this organic process), through Aristotle's form-matter paradigm (Aristotle believed that in the process of reproduction, "woman's part is . . . entirely passive, the man's active; and she contributes only the matter, while he contributes the soul and the form" [Homans 154]), right up to the recent popularization of this same gender binary by Camille Paglia. All these accounts of the distinction between male and female function to keep women tied to the body while men are associated with spirit and the word, with cultural and intellectual pursuits, with that which transcends the body.

Where does this mutually reinforcing cluster of concepts originate? Is there any truth here? Dinnerstein, Chodorow (*Reproduction*), and Rich, along with many other influential feminist theorists such as Julia Kristeva (*Desire*), Luce Irigaray (*Speculum*), and Sherry Ortner, have explored the gendering of the body as female as well as the way that both the body and the female have been set in opposition to culture. These theorists suggest that we can learn much about gender constructs by seeking their origins in the mother-child bond and the way that bond shapes our conceptions about women, men, and culture. As Dinnerstein points out, "[u]nder the arrangements that now prevail, a woman . . . is the parental person . . . who exists for the infant as the first representative of the flesh." Because she is "the person around whom the . . . ambiguous human attitude toward the flesh begins to be formed," through her we develop "what will be a lifelong internal conflict . . . between our rootedness in the body's acute, narrow joys and vicissitudes and our commitment to larger-scale human concerns," in other words, to culture (29). According to Dinnerstein, this conflict shows up cross-culturally: "People under the most diverse cultural conditions seem to feel an . . . antagonism, between what is humanly noble, durable, strenuous, and the insistent rule of the flesh . . . which is going to die . . ." (126). If one sex can bear the burden of the body—its pleasures and pains—then the other can more easily be thought of as transcending the body.

If we recognize the pervasiveness of this attitude toward culture, of the effort to transcend the (female) body through (male) cultural achievement, then Lawrence's theories about male and female can be seen as a reflection of larger cultural attitudes. Anne Fernihough, in her introduction to the recent Penguin CUP *Rainbow*, observes that many writers of Lawrence's time saw "the educated 'New Woman' [as] a symptom of degeneration" (xvi). Lawrence and his contemporaries were familiar with theories of cultural decay that saw decadence specifically as the blurring of lines between male and female. According to the theory, a woman who took on "'masculine' qualities, . . . by seeking access to higher education and the professions, was taken to be a sign of reversion to degeneracy, just as the male who showed signs of 'effeminacy' was seen to be regressive" (xvii). Lawrence, then, is far from unique in his fascination with and at times anxiety over the move away from life in the body and toward education by "new women" such as Ursula in *The Rainbow* or even the artist Gudrun in *Women in Love*. *The Rainbow*, therefore, can be seen to illuminate anxieties found in the work of other modern authors and in the culture at large.

Also, with respect to *The Rainbow*, Fernihough cites the theories of Irigaray to account for the gendering that goes on as the novel details the emerging modern individual. According to Irigaray, Fernihough explains, "the drive towards individual identity entails a repression of the mother. . . . In order to be a subject, the child must separate from the mother's body and repress all connection with it"; therefore "the search for perfect, detached selfhood as the goal of evolution is based on an implicit erasure of the female body," and this search can be found "implicit" in "the evolutionary theories of the late nineteenth and twentieth centuries" (xxv–xxvi). As Fernihough also observes, the "apparent paradox, whereby women signify both development and decline, is responsible for many of the interpretative difficulties posed by *The Rainbow*" (xvi). Lawrence here set out to write a book based on his lived experience with Frieda Lawrence, her sister Else Jaffe, and other women he knew. The novel was to be about "woman becoming individual, self-responsible, taking her own initiative" (*Letters* 2: 165); and Lawrence's sense of the state of women he knew was so strong and sympathetic, his own talent for observation and depiction so brilliant, that he created female characters, such as Ursula and Gudrun, who compel our identification and sympathy. The narratives in which these characters move, however, show the women at times as threatening—both to the men in their lives and to the culture at large.

Feminist psychoanalytic theory also helps account for another aspect of Lawrence's work that often baffles readers new to Lawrence: the deeply irrational and powerful emotions felt by both female and male characters in the novels. Traditional psychoanalytic theory is based on a concept of evolving subjectivity in which the individual moves from oneness with the maternal toward greater rationality, distinction, and autonomy. The connection with the original caregiver is seen as something to escape and to leave behind, unexamined. As Coppelia Kahn has said of Freud, his "matrophobia takes the form of a nearly lifelong reluctance to confront the child's, especially the male child's, early and close relationship to his mother" (79). For Freud, she argues, "identification with the mother" is "the 'unknown' . . . not because it is unknowable but because he is a man, because manhood as patriarchal culture creates it depends on denying . . . the powerful ambivalence that the mother inspires" (88).

In Lawrence's work, however, we find a deep and penetrating exploration of this ambivalence—one that often confuses or intimidates our students. Feminist psychoanalytic theory again helps here as a way of illuminating Lawrence's vision of the relationship between men and women. Jessica Benjamin says, for instance, that thanks to Freud we now know "that the foundations of erotic life lie in infancy"; that is, "adult sexual love is not only shaped by the events dating from that period of intense intimacy and dependency, it is also an opportunity to reenact and work out the conflicts that began there." We need to recognize that, "[w]here the site of control and abandon is the body, the demands of the infant self are most visible" (51). Moreover, this body and the conflicts it arouses are specifically associated with the female because, as Kahn explains, "a woman is the first significant other through whom both girls and boys realize [their own] subjectivity." At the same time, though, "women in general become charged with the ambivalence of fear and desire" because, in the early stage of development, the infant does not "recognize that the mother exists or has interests apart from it." All that she provides or facilitates is perceived as an extension of its will; all that she denies is seen as incomprehensible betrayal. Therefore, according to this theory, "the mother, and all women perceived in her shadow, are tainted with the grandiose expectations and bitter disappointments of a necessarily alienated subjectivity" (73–74).

Dinnerstein elaborates on the causes of the infant's extreme emotional response to its initial caregiver: "because it is immobile longer and at the same time very much brighter, [the child] has a capacity for feeling powerless unlike that of any other baby animal" (33). Therefore, for this vulnerable infant, especially one raised in the tight nuclear family of Western cultures, the mother represents "the center of everything the infant wants . . . , fears losing and feels threatened by" (93). Or, as Nancy Chodorow puts it, since "mothers have exclusive responsibility for infants who are totally dependent, then to the infant they are the source of all good and evil" (*Feminism* 90).

With this picture of the deepest level of the psyche, we may begin to appreciate why Lawrence's work disturbs readers so much: it deals with what I would suggest is a culturally constructed yet psychologically real fantasy of "Woman." Lawrence reminds us of the body and its power over our emotions and taps precisely those repressed, deeply irrational fears and desires that adult readers have spent a lifetime trying to overcome and to forget. Yet it seems clear that adulthood will remain driven by the irrational as long as we refuse to grasp the nature and persistent power of irrational impulses—those that (because of traditional child-rearing practices) stem from early experiences with the maternal body. It is, then, in his focus on gender, the body, and emotion that Lawrence can offer students, and all his readers, such profound and useful insights.

In *The Rainbow* Lawrence consciously tried to get at the "carbon"—to reach the depths of the psyche (*Letters* 2: 183). The character of Tom Brangwen deserves our special attention because of his unique status in the novel. He is depicted in mythical terms—as larger than life, a being of the past linked to the unconscious, to deep psychic levels. Tom also stands out in *The Rainbow* and in the Lawrence canon as, I would argue, the most positive major male character the author ever created. The others, from Rupert Birkin, of *Women in Love*, to Lady Chatterley's gamekeeper, Mellors, are men of the present, the walking wounded, who reflect the damage that Lawrence believed the twentieth century had inflicted on men. Tom, in contrast, is one of the imagined men of the past, before the sexual fall that Lawrence maintained had occurred in modern life. But the portrait of this most "healthy" and whole of men, Lawrence's prelapsarian Adam, reveals some disturbing cracks. Cursed with a sort of original sin, Tom contains inner psychological fissures that will widen in later generations of men in this novel, in *Women in Love*, and in the works that follow. Since Tom represents the past on which Lawrence quite consciously built the present time of his future novels, we help our students understand all of Lawrence's male characters when we carefully analyze this patriarch's inner emotional stresses. I contend that what I call the labor scene throws most light on these stresses. Here Lawrence demonstrates the awesome power of the *magna mater*—both its threat and its attraction—its hold on both Tom and his stepdaughter, Anna. Focusing on this scene effectively can help students see the profound psychological insights found in much of Lawrence's work.

The labor scene has typically been called the barn scene. Critics have tended to linger in the barn—the place where Tom Brangwen moves toward a secure assumption of fatherly authority—but a focus on the barn ignores the crucial relation between what happens there and the events that both precede and follow, thus stressing the man's success at becoming a father rather than the striking resemblance of his state to the child's. A better understanding can be gained of Lawrence's psychological insights, particularly in *The Rainbow* and in *Women in Love*, by attending to the equivalence of man and girl, rather than to his achievement of a state beyond hers.

During the course of his marriage, Tom is disturbed by the frequent crying of Anna at her mother's absences. He thinks, "There was something heartrending about Anna's crying, her childish anguish seemed so utter and so timeless, as if it were a thing of all the ages" (65–66). The powerful effect on Tom of Anna's weeping seems connected to his own particular torment, his anxious fear that his wife might leave. "Was she here for ever?" he asks himself. "Any moment, she might be gone," he believes; "he could never quite . . . be at peace, because she might go away" (58). There is a childlike simplicity and insecurity in these nagging thoughts. They represent the kinds of fears that plague young children, who are completely dependent on adult support yet without rational understanding of adult life's complexities—precisely the same kinds of obsessive thoughts that overwhelm Anna in the labor scene.

Lawrence presents in this scene the moment at which the woman is simultaneously mother and antimother—in the process of bearing one child while withdrawing support and recognition from another. In becoming a mother, Lydia becomes unavailable as nurturer to both her husband and her older child as they realize that the support and attention of the woman Tom calls "the mother" will not always be there. A panic that has been anticipated by Tom's feelings toward the withdrawn, pregnant Lydia overwhelms Anna, who now goes through what resonates as a primal scene: the child's first cataclysmic experience of loss, of helpless abandonment and subsequent violation, of extreme psychic pain. But in Anna's cries for the absent Lydia, her hysterical repetition of "I want my mother," and her refusal to respond to Tom's voice, Tom recognizes the embodiment of his own fears—as well as a symbol of their cause. Having just returned from Lydia, Tom is "white to the gills" because in her labor pain she can barely recognize him (72). Now Anna, too, denies him recognition—precisely because she shares his state: neither can reach Lydia.

In the image of a tiny girl, then, Tom sees the uncanny reflection of his own deepest anxieties, and, as the ordeal grinds on, the mirror effect persists. Anna cannot stop her nerve-shredding, sobbing chant; and though Tom tries to be rational, to distract her—calmly telling the child to undress for bed—the wailing goes on, and her emotions finally overwhelm his own. "He crossed over the room, aware only of the maddening sobbing." As Anna stands "stiff, overpowered, violated," Tom forces off her clothing; "her body catch[es] in a convulsive sob. But he too was blind, and intent, irritated into mechanical action . . . unaware of anything but the irritation of her" (73). Reflecting Anna's lack of control, Tom's own mindless, mechanical irritation indicates the deep resonance within him of the child's cries. The image of Anna is more than the man can stand, as she becomes, in a sense, an icon of infant despair, the thing itself:

> The child was now incapable of understanding, she had become a little, mechanical thing of fixed will. She wept, her body convulsed, her voice repeating the same cry. . . . She stood, with fixed, blind will, resistant, a small, convulsed, unchangeable thing weeping ever and repeating the same phrase. . . . Unheeding, uncaring . . . alone, her hands shut and half lifted, her face, all tears, raised and blind. And through the sobbing and choking came the broken:
> "I—want—my—mother."   (73–74)

It should be stressed to students that Lawrence does much more here than describe a childish tantrum. The authorial respect accorded this event is striking. Rarely does such a scene receive a novelist's attention, let alone such powerful and emphatic rendering. Earlier Tom called this "childish anguish" "utter" and "timeless"—"a thing of all the ages" (66). Here again Anna is presented as archetypal or iconic—a "living statue of grief." (74). The words used to describe her insist that we read Anna's experience, and likewise Tom's response to it, as deeply symbolic. What begins as a realistic representation of a childhood tantrum transforms into something far more profound. As the focus shifts from Tom to Anna, the narrative emphasizes her solitude, her powerfully blind will, the singleness of her wish and the immutability of her state. In her belief that only one thing can satisfy her, Anna becomes before our eyes a kind of prisoner in a world of absolute lack. But, significantly, her feelings are shared by the adult Tom, produced by the same cause: the woman's indifference.

In Tom's impulse to take Anna outside through darkness and a downpour to the barn, Lawrence continues to demonstrate a kind of intuitive knowledge of ideas now set forth by feminist psychoanalytic theory. After being enclosed within the house, trapped with the mother in labor, after the monomaniacal shrieks of Anna for the one answer, the man and girl break out into another world; but importantly, Anna and Tom do not just undergo separation, a move toward autonomy, but also make a comforting movement toward a new kind of union, both becoming caretakers of the maternal in themselves, as they symbolically feed cows, animals that are themselves sources of nourishment. Held by her father in the rhythm of the feeding pattern, Anna finds an alternative world of comfort, sustenance, and security. "Motherness" can be found in unexpected places. Tom, likewise, recovers the maternal as he discovers it within himself, caring for both child and animals.

It is significant that "motherness" here is connected to sensuous experience, rather than to any words spoken between the two characters. Tom's verbal, authoritarian efforts to reach Anna fail. In the house, Anna uses language in a futile attempt to articulate her lack, but the barn experience—the recovery of the maternal—for man and child is deeply rhythmic and physical, resonating at a level beneath articulation. This sensuously rhythmic experience apparently speaks to some deep need in both of them, replaces what they lacked, what they have left behind in the house. Lawrence's depiction of the barn experience, I would suggest, corresponds to what Kristeva describes as "the irruption within language of the anteriority of language" (*Desire* 32). Because early child rearing is almost always carried out by a female, usually the mother, the prelinguistic state is associated with her. In this scene, although ostensibly the mother has been left behind, Tom and Anna appear to have stumbled into what Kristeva calls the "archaic, instinctual, and maternal territory" (*Desire* 136). Significantly, Lawrence does not present this experience as regressive. If anything, the man and girl seem to circle back in order to move forward.

In teaching this novel, we should point out to students that Lawrence here may be on to something important. Laurence Lerner has specifically noted the honesty, power, and insight of the labor scene, crediting Lawrence's "willingness to say only what he knows, rendering the emotion even if the psychology is guesswork" (78–79). The guesswork in the scene, in fact, again shares much with current feminist psychoanalytic theory. Kristeva, Hélène Cixous (Cixous and Clément), and Irigaray have in various ways pointed to the original bond with the mother—established before the child's entry into the symbolic system of language—as the irrational, repressed, unexplored, and undervalued substructure of consciousness. In the labor scene, as I have noted, Lawrence grants serious attention both to the mother-child relationship and to the preverbal, evoking the power of each as he continues to emphasize the connection between early childhood experience and adult behavior.

The parallels between the adult Tom and the child Anna continue throughout the scene. They both sink into a comforting state of unconscious union and then return to the house—the girl to be settled into the very bed that belonged to Tom as a child. Then, when he hears his wife in labor, she sounds "not human, at least to a man." "A great, scalding peace went over him" when he looks in on her and is forced to recognize her otherness: "He had a dread of her as she lay there. What had she to do with him? She was other than himself" (77). Yet Tom still retains the old insecurities, and they will persist throughout his life. Years later, reverberations of the labor scene continue when Tom looks toward the barn through another driving rain to see Anna embracing her future mate. Tom becomes "blackly and furiously miserable," remembering "the child he had carried out at night into the barn." "She was going away," he thinks, "to leave an unendurable emptiness in him, a void that he could not bear" (111–12).

We recall his former thoughts about Lydia, his "never [being] at peace, because she might go away."

Apparently, though the barn experience powerfully affected Tom, it failed to transform him completely; thus, Lawrence indicates something important about male psychology in particular. In the future, Anna will never again manifest the sort of anxiety she experienced that night; however, in subsequent generations, as women in the novel move toward independence, the men become more and more desperate. Lawrence seemed to understand what feminist theorists maintain: that at the deepest psychological level, men need women more than women need men. In Tom's mirroring of Anna's behavior, there is the suggestion that the fear of female abandonment may be more persistent in adult males. In fact, Dinnerstein and others propose that, although men and women share the wrenching experience of initial dependence on the mother, men are pressured earlier and more completely to separate from her and thus may have more repressed anxiety about female abandonment as well as a less rational image of woman's power. For this reason men seek refuge from women in activity separate from them, thus finding a "sanctuary from the impact of women . . . in which they can recuperate from the temptation to give way to ferocious, voracious dependence, and recover their feelings of competence, autonomy, dignity" (66–67).

If this theory has validity, then we begin to understand why subsequent generations of male characters in the novel become more and more dependent on women toward whom they feel increasing hostility and fear. In Will Brangwen, the man of the second generation with few meaningful outlets beyond his wife, Anna, we see a maddened version of the elder Tom's dependency. The "only tangible, secure thing was the woman. He could leave her only for another woman," but "[a]nother woman would be woman. . . . *Why* was she the all . . ., why must he sink if he were detached from her?" (173). Anton Skrebensky, of the third generation, fares worst, and his horrific breakdown in a public place is an excellent scene to contrast with the labor scene.

When Skrebensky's love, Ursula, says that she will never be his, Anton's reaction uncannily mirrors Anna's in the labor scene. We see the same viscerally physical response, the same blindness and lack of control—all brought on by confrontation with the fact of a woman's unattainability: his "head made a queer motion, the chin jerked back against the throat, the curious, crowing, hiccuping sound came again, his face twisted like insanity, and he was crying, . . . blind and twisted as if something were broken which kept him in control." Like Anna's, Anton's emotions are gut wrenching, welling up apparently from some primal source, beyond his power to stop. And, as in the depiction of Anna, the "living statue of grief," the rendering here goes beyond the merely realistic and personal, approaching the iconic: he weeps "uncontrollably, noiselessly, with his face twisted *like a mask*, contorted and the tears running down the amazing grooves in his cheeks"; he goes on "[b]lindly, his face always this horrible working *mask*" (my emphasis). As Tom attempted to comfort Anna, so Ursula in this scene tells Anton, "It's not necessary." But, again like Anna, Skrebensky "could not gain control of his face . . . weeping violently, as if automatically. His will, his knowledge had nothing to do with it" (433). Echoes of the labor scene, then, resonate from the beginning to the end of *The Rainbow*. The difference here, however, is that this last man finds no comfort—the growing strength and independence of the woman over the course of three generations, Lawrence implies, leave this modern man totally abandoned and helpless.

To teach *The Rainbow* as I have outlined would avoid much of the confused and troubled response to this work, typical even of much Lawrence criticism. A study by David Holbrook, *Where D. H. Lawrence Was Wrong about Woman*, is a case in point. This critic sums up the labor scene as depicting Tom's "tormented concern for his wife, and his urge to distract the child from her anxious need for her mother." Such a view, I would suggest, contributes to this critic's final assessment of the marital portrait of Tom and Lydia as "superb and completely realized" compared with Lawrence's subsequent renderings of relationships that, Holbrook contends, leave the reader "bewildered" (137–38). He suggests, "To most readers . . . the turbulent and seething relationship between Will and Anna comes as a surprise," and admits, "After many readings, I still find it hard to see what goes wrong between Skrebensky and Ursula" (162). Of *The Rainbow* Holbrook says that "some of [its] deepest turbulence . . . feels extraneous and seems not, in some way, inevitable to the novel" (137). And he repeatedly asks such questions as "What are the sources (the etiology) of such turbulence and dread?" (140).

I would suggest that Lawrence's depiction of the source of male psychic development in the novel, as manifested in the patriarch Tom and particularly in the labor scene, goes a long way toward answering Holbrook's question. When Lawrence attempts to get at the psychic core, he does not hesitate to look into the infant's heart of darkness, even though what he discovers there certainly challenges the culturally constructed image of powerful male autonomy. The events of *The Rainbow*, as well as those of Lawrence's subsequent novels, affirm that irrational, early childhood experience profoundly affects the responses of adult men to women—a view in which, as we have seen, Lawrence is supported by much feminist theory. The deep psychic layers revealed in the labor scene can help students understand Lawrence's depiction of brooding, defensive men in subsequent novels, men who manifest irrational emotional extremes or proclaim their omnipotence and their distinction from the women in their lives.

Lawrence was in many ways wrong about women, but, I would argue, he was usually right about "Woman"—the powerful psychological construct shaped by early childhood experiences—and particularly about this construct's impact on men. Rich has said of the female's bearing and parenting of children, "We carry the imprint of this experience for life, even into our dying. Yet there has been a strange lack of material to help us understand and use it" (xiii). She goes further, contending that we must recognize the initial dependency of the male child on woman and the subsequent results of that dependency. In *The Rainbow* and throughout his work, it would seem, Lawrence provides recognition of, as well as profound insight into, this much-neglected and crucial aspect of human life.

The Foreigner Within: Teaching *The Rainbow* with the Help of Cixous, Kristeva, and Irigaray

Maria Aline Seabra Ferreira

> The foreigner is within us. And when we flee from or
> struggle against the foreigner, we are fighting our uncon-
> scious. . . . Delicately, analytically, Freud . . . teaches us
> how to detect foreignness in ourselves. That is perhaps
> the only way not to hound it outside of us.
> —Julia Kristeva, *Strangers to Ourselves*

When teaching *The Rainbow*, I have found it rewarding to examine the beginning of the novel in the light of French feminism—particularly some of the
work produced by Hélène Cixous, Simone de Beauvoir, Julia Kristeva, and
Luce Irigaray. I briefly focus first on Lawrence's account of the predicament of
the Marsh women and then, at greater length, on his account of the relationship
between Lydia Lensky, the Polish widow, and Tom Brangwen. In each case,
what is at stake are different ways of understanding and relating to the beyond.

The Marsh Women: From Nature to Culture

> The women were different.
> —Lawrence, *The Rainbow*

In the opening paragraph of the novel, we learn that "[w]henever one of the
Brangwens in the fields lifted his head from his work, he saw the church-tower
at Ilkeston in the empty sky. So that as he turned again to the horizontal land,
he was aware of something standing above him and beyond him in the distance"
(9). We are then quickly made to feel that the Brangwen men are so richly satisfied by their relation with nature—by their knowledge of "the intercourse between heaven and earth," of how "the earth heaved and opened its furrow to
them"—that they need no more contact with the beyond than that which they
get from the church tower. But the women are different. While the Brangwen
woman also experiences "the drowse of blood-intimacy," for her this is not
"enough" (10):

> Looking out, as she must, from the front of her house towards the activity
> of man in the world at large, whilst her husband looked out to the back at
> sky and harvest and beast and land, she strained her eyes to see what man
> had done in fighting outwards to knowledge. . . . She also wanted to know,
> and to be of the fighting host. (11)

Unlike her husband, the Brangwen woman is not content to merely look at, or in the direction of, the beyond. She wants to actively participate in "another form of life," in "the spoken world beyond" (11, 10).

To help students grasp the significance of this difference between the Brangwen woman and the Brangwen man, I get them to consider the claim Cixous makes that one of the most powerful ways in which women have been subordinated to men has been in terms of traditional associations such as the idea that women are (or ought to be) passive and belong to the realm of nature while men are (or ought to be) active and belong to the realm of culture. According to Cixous, such binary oppositions reveal a solidarity between the "logocentrism" that largely determines "what is thinkable" and the "phallocentrism" that subordinates women to men (64–65). She maintains that "it has become rather urgent to question this solidarity" in order "to threaten the stability of the masculine structure that passed itself off as eternal-natural" (65). But what is Lawrence doing in the opening of *The Rainbow* if not challenging traditional associations? As we have just noticed, it is, after all, the Marsh men who are described as leading a life of profound "blood-intimacy" with the natural and animal world, whereas it is the women who, though also implicated in this life of intimacy with the land and the process of creation, long for culture and knowledge, the possession of which they equate with power.

As we read further into the novel, we gradually realize that the challenge facing the Marsh women is to find a way not just of entering and participating in the predominantly male world of culture but also of doing this on their own terms, of doing this so as to attain their own identity. It is a matter of their wanting to threaten the stability of an essentially masculine system and of their wanting (and of Lawrence's wanting through them) to transform the system—a transformation, the novel implies, that will not be possible so long as women participate as would-be men, one that can only be accomplished on the basis of a full recognition of sexual difference.

In addition, the novel implicitly argues that something else is required to bring about the transformation of a system that has been so long entrenched that it seems to have become part of the nature of things. It is not just sexual difference that needs to be recognized and accepted; it is also the idea of the foreign. In this novel the beyond figures not only as vertical transcendence (the church tower) or as culture (the "spoken world"); it is also embodied in the foreigner, the foreigner within as well as without.

Two Foreigners or Strangers: Tom and Lydia

> They were such strangers, they must forever be such strangers.
> . . . Such intimacy of embrace, and such utter foreignness
> of contact! It was unbearable. He could not bear to be near
> her, and know the utter foreignness between them, know
> how entirely they were strangers to each other.
>
> —Lawrence, *The Rainbow*

The drive to know the beyond is inextricably linked with the idea of the foreign in Lawrence's writings. These notions find privileged expression and dramatization in the figures of foreigners, who embody not only the idea of estrangement from the author's home country but also the idea of travel out of it.

The underlying theme of travel permeates the whole Lawrentian enterprise. Already in *The White Peacock* we can see a growing taste for the distant and exotic and the depiction of traveling as a desirable and enriching experience. From an early stage George Saxton talks of emigration while Cyril dreams of Spain (66), his image of a different, seductive world. Although the characters do not travel abroad (apart from Lettie's brief honeymoon in France), the resonances of change and movement gain in intensity as the novel progresses, such as when George thinks about venturing "into the foreign places of life" (246). At this early stage in Lawrence's writing, the imaginative voyage tends to be emphasized; later, after Lawrence's own experience of other places, the voyages become literal, as they are in *Women in Love*. Yet even in this first novel, in which Lawrence has George cross the border of the valley of his youth "flauntingly" and march "towards the heart of the unknown" (246), essential movements of characters' development are envisaged as spatial displacements.

In *The Rainbow* the travel impulse gains momentum. The language of this novel is crowded with the imagery of travel and of displacement, with the rhetoric of forward movement and going beyond margins. Characters are often depicted in doorways, on thresholds, at windows, "on the brink of the unrevealed" (186), reaching toward "the shore of the unknown" or "the porch of the great Unknown" (188, 191). The concept of the unknown includes travel in space as well as the inner journey toward the unconscious, the unseen, the opening out of the characters' beings. The unknown is perceived as a desirable (although also dangerous and risky) space that holds out the promise of self-realization, hinting at all the possibilities denied the characters in the felt constriction of the home or local space. But it is foreigners who—positioned as they are at the core of Lawrence's centrifugal novel—play a decisive role in *The Rainbow*, contributing to the awakening of the other characters by inspiring in them the sense of the unknown and expectations or dreams of a different life.

Tom Brangwen has his first encounter with a foreigner, Matlock, when he is twenty-four. It makes him reject "the mean enclosure of reality" (26), and after an evening spent in conversation with the smooth-talking foreigner, Brangwen's whole being is "all in a whirl":

> What was it all? There was a life so different from what he knew it. What was there outside his knowledge, how much? What was this that he had touched? What was he in this new influence? What did everything mean? Where was life, in that which he knew or all outside him?   (25)

These pressing questions, so poignantly raised, will go on to inform the whole book.

After this germinal encounter and until Tom meets Lydia Lensky, he finds himself in the grip of "a fever of restless anger" (27). Lydia's foreignness and otherness then provide him with the means of escaping convention. In Lydia are condensed the desirable qualities of those who are perceived to live beyond the prosaic, uninspiring reality of the Marsh farm. She reveals an "extended being . . . as a traveler in his self-contained manner reveals far-off countries present in himself" (13). When Tom first sees her, "he felt as if he were walking again in a far world, not Cossethay, a far world, the fragile reality," a world that, despite its dim contours and distance, seems to him more real than the "unreality" of Cossethay and that encapsulates the wonders inherent in the faraway, mythical beyond (29, 27). In spite of her being a "stranger," of her belonging "to somewhere else," she transforms the unreality of Tom's life into "something real and natural" (32). Before meeting her "he was nothing. But with her, he would be real" (40).

It is tempting to say that, as Tom experiences Lydia ("she was Woman to him" [79]), she is a striking embodiment of the myth of woman as an essentially mysterious creature. Students need to know, therefore, that this myth is not as harmless or as neutral as it might at first appear, that it has been identified and exposed as a position within masculinist discourse by, among others, Beauvoir and Cixous. Of the many myths with which man has chosen to burden woman, none, according to Beauvior, "is more firmly anchored in masculine hearts than that of the feminine 'mystery'" (289). And as Cixous points out (reminding us in passing of Freud's characterization of woman as a "dark continent" ["Question" 212]), the idea of feminine mystery has often been expressed as an equation between women and darkness: "woman is in the shadow. In the shadow he [man] throws on her." Traditionally defined as "night to his [man's] day—that," Cixous maintains, "has forever been the fantasy. Black to his white. Shut out of his system's space, she is the repressed that ensures the system's functioning" (67). Once again, however, on closer inspection, Lawrence's handling of this binary opposition turns out to be no more predictable than his handling of the related passive-active and nature-culture binaries we looked at earlier.

To begin with, while it is, for example, easy to find passages describing Lydia as walking "always in a shadow, silenced" (49), we discover that they refer to the life she led with her first husband, Paul Lensky. We learn that she had been in a position of utter subservience to him, that his work dominated his life to the exclusion of his wife and children. Deprived of a voice, subjugated to her husband's ideas, Lydia "followed him like a shadow, serving, echoing" (49). In short, with Paul Lensky, Lydia was indeed "passive, dark, always in shadow" (50). So it is not surprising that, when she first arrives in England—after not only his death, incidentally, but also the deaths of two of her children—the utter foreignness of the country's customs, language, and people make her recoil into herself, into the darkness, abstraction, and indifference that envelop her:

She was like one walking in the Underworld, where the shades throng intelligibly but have no connection with one. She felt the English people as a potent, cold, slightly hostile host amongst whom she walked isolated. (50)

What we need to remember, however, is the change that occurs when she meets Tom Brangwen.

No longer "always in shadow," in her new relationship with Tom, Lydia emerges into the light: "in herself she [now] walked strong and clear" (91). In this new relationship, furthermore, she is the one who often takes the initiative (see, e.g., 55). Yet it doesn't therefore follow that from this point onward Lydia is always active and in the light, never passive and in the dark. What actually happens is more interesting and more complex, as we can see by briefly glancing at parts of Lawrence's description of the ways in which, in their new relationship with each other, Tom and Lydia are both reborn. This turns out to be a difficult and painful experience and one that requires from both of them something much closer to passivity than to the ability to actively exert oneself. We are told, for example, that Tom "submitted to that which was happening to him, letting go of his will, suffering the loss of himself, dormant always on the brink of ecstasy, like a creature evolving to a new birth" (38). Clearly, then, given "the pain of a new birth" (39), it might be easier to stubbornly hold on to one's will and resist, as we see Lydia tempted to do later on:

Resistant, she knew she was beaten, and from fear of darkness turned to fear of light. . . . She could not bear to come to, to realize. The first pangs of this new parturition were so acute, she knew she could not bear it. She would rather remain out of life, than be torn, mutilated into this birth, which she could not survive. She had not the strength to come to life now, in England, so foreign. . . . (53)

Nevertheless Lydia too manages to muster the necessary strength, the somewhat paradoxical kind (submission to one's fate) that we find Tom displaying earlier on, during the interval between the moments when he first saw Lydia and when he goes to propose to her: "It was coming, he knew, his fate. The world was submitting to its transformation. He made no move: it would come, what would come" (32). So much, then, for what passes in most versions of common sense as weakness!

And so much for the certitudes—especially about what constitutes strength and weakness—that we tend to rely on to help us understand such things as the significance of Tom and Lydia's lovemaking in the second chapter. What are we to make of the fact that in a significant departure from traditional roles attributed to women in late-nineteenth- and early-twentieth-century England, Lydia is the initiator but then subsequently reverts to a passive attitude, enjoying the pleasure Tom takes in her while he assumes a conventionally male, active stance:

> She was sure to come at last, and touch him. . . . They looked at each other, a deep laugh at the bottom of their eyes, and he went to take of her again, wholesale, mad to revel in the inexhaustible wealth of her, to bury himself in the depths of her in an inexhaustible exploration, she all the while reveling in that he revelled in her. . . .   (60)

And what are we to make of the apparent implication that it is the man's responsibility to explore woman's secrets, if not that Lawrence is here subscribing to the idea of woman as the dark continent? Tom and Lydia's lovemaking here is conducted "on the edge of the outer darkness" and is described as a time of exploration principally for the man, "when the secrets within the woman are game for the man, hunted doggedly, when the secrets of the woman are the man's adventure, and they both give themselves to the adventure" (61). The emphasis placed on metaphors of hunting, of the chase, takes us back to the male sphere of activity, while the admission of Lydia's role and participation comes last, in a secondary position, as a patronizing concession. It is emphatically the man's role as explorer and adventurer that predominates here.

However, things are very different in the lovemaking scene between Tom and Lydia in the third chapter. The scene begins with Lydia asking Tom to come to her and then, when he stands before her, putting her arms around him in a gesture that "seemed to reveal to him the mould of his own nakedness, [so that] he was passionately lovely to himself." This gesture makes it difficult for him to look her in the eye, however. It fills him with "fear" and Lydia seems "awful" to him: "[s]he was the awful unknown" (89). We are told that he would have found it easier to kiss her feet than to kiss her on the mouth. But this is not what Lydia wants. She doesn't want him "to bow before her, and serve her"; she wants "his active participation, not his submission." And we learn that, at this particular point, "it was torture to him, that he must give himself to her actively, participate in her, that he must meet and embrace and know her, who was other than himself." Nevertheless, with her help, he manages to do what is necessary, and by now we oughtn't to be too surprised if it looks more like submission than active participation: "he let go his hold on himself, he relinquished himself, and knew the subterranean force of his desire to come to her." Only now, as "[h]is blood beat[s] up in waves of desire," can he hope to approach the "reality of her who was just beyond him" and "be received within the darkness which would swallow him and yield him up to himself." At the same time as Tom is relinquishing one self (having it "destroyed, burnt away") in order to approach Lydia's reality, he is discovering another self, the reality of which is, in a certain sense, every bit as beyond him (or his conscious control at least) as Lydia's otherness (90). And what does this mean if not that this other self—which we assume Lydia discovers too—is Lawrence's way of describing the foreigner within? Perhaps we can say of Lawrence what Kristeva says of Freud, that he "teaches us how to detect foreignness in ourselves" (*Strangers* 191). Here, at any rate, is Lawrence's description of the lovemaking that follows:

Their coming together now, after two years of married life, was much more wonderful to them than it had been before. It was the entry into another circle of existence, it was the baptism to another life, it was the complete confirmation. Their feet trod strange ground of knowledge, their footsteps were lit-up with discovery. Wherever they walked, it was well, the world re-echoed round them in discovery. They went gladly and forgetful. Everything was lost, and everything was found. The new world was discovered, it remained only to be explored.

They had passed through the doorway into the further space, where movement was so big, that it contained bonds and constraints and labours, and still was complete liberty. She was the doorway to him, he to her. At last they had thrown open the doors, each to the other, and had stood in the doorways facing each other, whilst the light flooded out from behind on to each of their faces, it was the transfiguration, the glorification, the admission.   (90–91)

Now, clearly, Tom and Lydia are both explorers. Having achieved a certain balance and equality, they are jointly engaged on an egalitarian quest, a never-ending search for the otherness of the other.

The search is never ending because Lydia and Tom are aware that to know someone else fully is impossible and that the obliteration of otherness would be undesirable and destructive. What the narrator now says of Tom—that "[h]e did not know her any better, any more precisely, now that he knew her altogether"—could equally well be said of Lydia. And the novel surely wants us to feel that remaining foreigners to each other (as well as to themselves) is what makes it possible for Tom and Lydia to experience, from this point onward, the "wonder of the transfiguration," to experience it not just occasionally but "perpetual[ly]" (91).

According to Irigaray, it is "wonder" that maintains the "autonomy" of each of the two sexes and that keeps "a space of freedom and attraction between them, a possibility of separation and alliance" (*Ethics* 13). Irigaray gives us another way of understanding the relationship that Tom and Lydia achieve, a relationship of which it is indeed true to say (with Irigaray) that "[o]ne sex is not entirely consumable by the other," that "[t]here is always a *remainder*" (14). But, of course, the problem (of which Irigaray and Lawrence are obviously fully aware) is that it is always possible to try to destroy, suppress, or deny the existence of this remainder—just as it is always possible to destroy, suppress, or deny the existence of that unknown area inside each of us, a mysterious zone that includes Freud's "uncanny" and what is conventionally called the unconscious.

As this close textual reading has suggested, it is precisely this unknown inside us, this uncanny strangeness, that constitutes one of Lawrence's main thematic concerns, the problematic verbalization and dramatization of the search for, identification with, and recoil from otherness.

Reading *Women in Love* and
Sons and Lovers like Sisters and Brothers:
Lawrence Study in the Feminist Classroom

Carol Siegel

Feminist approaches to D. H. Lawrence's writing abound, as is suggested by the leading role feminist critics have played in Lawrence studies in recent years. However, promoting the study of Lawrence in a classroom devoted to feminist pedagogy—a site where humanity is not universalized as male nor is gender treated as a timeless transcultural absolute but where the social and cultural construction of gender differences and the consequent differences in men's and women's social conditions are open topics of discussion—still presents difficulties. Obviously teaching Lawrence in any classroom involves surmounting the usual obstacles to students' understanding modern British literature: the professor must overcome the students' assumptions that one language means one culture and that every word must have the same meaning it does in local contemporary speech, as everyone knows who has ever struggled to convince an irate student that a textual reference to a man "knocking up" a woman simply means that he is knocking on her door (see, e.g., Lawrence, *Lost Girl*, where we are told that Miss Pinnegar "had to be knocked up, for she was lying down" [216]).

But when some minimal background information and perhaps a short glossary have been given to the students, more severe problems persist. Lawrence's philosophical concerns permeate his work, and because of the political atmosphere of the last few decades, those concerns are likely to be interpreted by students as calls to political action. The way that each student is accustomed to responding to such calls will determine how that student will respond to the Lawrence text—unless the professor intervenes to create a more nuanced and sophisticated response, one that involves engagement with the way Lawrence's ideas are communicated as well as with his ideas themselves. This essay suggests some ways that one may successfully intervene to prevent feminist students from reflexively dismissing Lawrence and antifeminist students from using his work as a mere weapon to bash the others.

The many references in recent political debates to a culture war that is dividing the American people seem sadly accurate. Classrooms, from two-year community colleges to major research universities, are now highly politicized sites where the mood is volatile and students can easily divide into factions that refuse to communicate with one another or with the professor except in slogans. As commentators on popular culture from Gerald Graff to William Bennett have pointed out, this culture war centers in the university because it is above all else a war over changes in our group understanding of what constitutes knowledge and aesthetics; and these changes perforce involve curriculum and canons of artworks and the values pertaining to their construction. Possibly because of the enormous shifts during the last twenty years in gender roles and in the common understanding of gender differences and because of the centrality of these shifts to the disruption of a unified sense of what higher education ideally includes, feminist scholars often find ourselves in the middle of the debate. While this is not always the most comfortable position for a professor who is trying to get students to talk and think about literary form, poetics, and other not overtly political matters, it may be a good position for anyone trying to mediate in undergraduates' first classroom discussion of Lawrence.

Whether or not the professor chooses to mention gender issues, Lawrence's popular reputation as a misogynist, the published opinions of a great many Lawrence critics on this issue, and many of Lawrence's own writings make it likely that teaching any text by Lawrence will polarize the classroom into feminist and antifeminist factions. Professors who want to teach Lawrence are frequently left with three options. The first is to ignore the political situation in the classroom and proceed as if the students were paying attention to the text. While this approach has some appeal—it seems high-minded and will reach the few students whose concern with literature is free of any conscious politicization—I do not advocate it for those who want to teach the whole class. The second approach is popular with professors who see Lawrence as an unmitigated sexist: they simply present him as one. This can be satisfying for many of the feminist students, but it is unlikely to get them involved in analyzing Lawrence's writing. The average undergraduate, preoccupied with determining whether a narrative is "realistic," cannot ordinarily achieve the distance necessary to find literature interesting if it is also deemed morally reprehensible. The third option is to give students a sense of the political situations Lawrence's writings originally addressed.

The problems of the politically polarized classroom can be compounded if students reductively misread Lawrence's many critiques of formal education as advocacy of ignorant reliance on instinct or unquestioning allegiance to a leader. An unpleasant opposition—between support for Lawrence and respect for the analytic approach intrinsic to successful higher education—may develop. Once it has, an especially grave risk of this sort of reductive misreading is that some misogynist and anti-intellectual students will seize on Lawrence's many written tirades against the association of moral art with feminine sensibility and idealized motherhood in late-Victorian society and assume that his political position can best be expressed as a fascistic demand that both female power and high culture be violently swept away. To prevent this counterproductive development and, instead, provide ways for the students to explore the complexities of Lawrence's work, it will generally be necessary for the professor to begin discussion of the text with background information that places Lawrence's thought in relation to the controversies about gender that characterized his personal intellectual world. An important starting point for an in-class examination of Lawrence's gender politics is their contextualization in relation to ideas about gender current in the early part of the twentieth century. Supplemental information or readings can and should be used to some extent. Among the many writings that place Lawrence's thinking in this way, Hilary Simpson's *D. H. Lawrence and Feminism* and Janice H. Harris's "Lawrence and the Edwardian Feminists" most succinctly chart Lawrence's responses to the developing late-nineteenth- and early-twentieth-century feminist ideologies.

Lawrence's own texts also include detailed depiction of the gender norms that Lawrence felt constrained late-Victorian and early-twentieth-century life. A useful initial exercise is to ask the students what the text posits as the sexual and gender mores of its time and then in what ways it articulates resistance to these normative rules. At this point it is not necessary to ask students whether Lawrence takes sides with characters who articulate resistance. In fact, students should probably be asked to defer discussion of this issue until the types of resistance have been identified. One might fruitfully prepare for this exercise in identifying hegemonic and counterhegemonic voices in the text either by asking advanced upper-division students to read Mikhail Bakhtin's essay "Discourse in the Novel" or, when working with less advanced students, by summarizing the concept of dialogism in fiction. Following Bakhtin's dialogic approach to literature, students can identify certain parts of the texts as representing official discourses on gender and sexuality and then examine the mode of presentation of these citations from an ideologically determined foundational narrative of culture. With which speakers are these citations most strongly identified? Are they undermined or called into question by other parts of the text? Are conflicts within and between the characters' ideological positions resolved? Is the voice of the narrator unified and without self-contradiction? Some time should be spent addressing these questions.

Once this discussion is under way, students may exhibit a strong desire to identify Lawrence himself either with the official discourses or with the resistant voices that they have found in the text. Most students will probably refer to Lawrence in a way that conflates the historical figure and author with the narrator and, if they are reading a text with a male protagonist, the main character. Even if they can distinguish between narrator, main masculine character, and "Lawrence," they will generally not see authorship itself as constructed. Instead they will usually insist on the authority of intentionality. In this situation a hard-line poststructuralist approach to the topic of authorship will probably not be successful.

If students are ever to be convinced that the author is not present in the text, one had better not begin with Lawrence. Certain texts seem to call for specific kinds of contextualizations, and, from *Sons and Lovers* on, Lawrence's texts have elicited a biographical approach, as published Lawrence criticism frequently demonstrates. Conceding this to the students will generally create a less contentious atmosphere than will trying to convince the students that an author's intentions are ultimately unknowable or denying that Lawrence's ideas as they are expressed and described elsewhere are relevant to the text at hand. Here, however, is a good place to make a distinction between biographical facts (e.g., Lawrence broke off his engagement to Jessie Chambers in November 1910) and biographical interpretation (e.g., Lawrence broke off his engagement to Jessie Chambers because of his unresolved Oedipus complex).

The introduction of biographical facts into the analysis of Lawrence's writing provides an ideal moment for an outbreak of feminist theory in the classroom. Gerald Graff describes theory as breaking out "when a consensus that was once taken for granted in a community breaks down" and what "has formerly gone without saying now has to be 'argued for'" ("Other Voices" 19). It is known to most American students, even if only through their familiarity with the popular psychology of self-help books, that some feminist theory throws doubt on the central paradigms of psychoanalysis, for instance, penis envy and the Oedipus complex. Feminist criticism of psychoanalytic theory can easily be seen to problematize literary criticism's once almost automatic recourse to the psychoanalytic when decoding biographical information. Students might thus be urged to avoid adopting the reading strategies typical of early readers of psychology, like Jessie Chambers herself, who treat reading fiction as an occasion to search for signs of mental or emotional problems in the author. Instead they may be encouraged to emulate the feminist Foucauldians who see psychoanalytic discourse as determined by political power structures. Consequently the students may be led to read Lawrence's inconsistencies about gender as possible points of resistance to the almost overwhelming pressure to construct himself as a unified being according to socially acceptable gender categories. This is an important interpretive move for study of his work's relation to women's issues because Lawrence's opposition to the developing "science of the mind" creates affinities between his ideas and some central principles of first-wave feminism.

To look at Lawrence this way can help students transcend making direct biographical equations when analyzing his depiction of the maternal, a major component of his work, and instead come to appreciate his anticipation of some ideas associated with postmodernism's critique of the (masculinized) Cartesian individual. For many poststructuralist feminist theorists, belief in this individual is shored up by the twentieth century's preoccupation with what Freud called the family romance ("Question").

A movement in feminist theory away from privileging the familial paradigms of psychoanalysis can be seen in the metacriticism that appeared at the beginning of the 1990s. For example, Jane Gallop asserts that we need to stop "reading everything through the family romance" in order to realize our subjectivity more powerfully (239). And Judith Butler gives a negative answer to the questions, "Is female generativity truly an uncaused case, and does it begin the narrative that takes all of humanity under the force of the incest taboo and into language?" (91). Such theorists are helping effect a rapprochement not only between feminist literary theory and the antiessentialism of philosophers like Michel Foucault, who argues that gender identity is constructed in response to official discourses, but also between academic feminists and the growing number of postmodernists who reject the conventional goal of well-integrated individuality in favor of performative identifications. The latter group might be understood as the inheritors of the 1960s movement away from the talking cure in psychology, with its focus on the individual's family and past as permanently determining the contents of the psyche rather than as providing a staging ground for radical self-revision and political change, a point of view typical of behaviorist approaches to emotional problems and of the spiritual and consciousness-raising practices sometimes dismissively lumped together under the term *new age*. For the postmoderns who share this vision, the forces that have made us what we are seem to be of less interest than the forces that can break us free into a new becoming.

One of postmodernism's major differences from modernism is its refusal to read history as a coherent narrative of causality. Part of the ideology of politically engaged postmodernism is that the discontinuity of history allows for intervention and change. Within this theoretical framework, it becomes possible to think about identity without continually returning to the generalized mother figure that has so obsessed the Western mind since the Victorian period. The struggle to think about something other than maternity, a struggle so easily traceable in Lawrence's work, might be seen consequently not as an indication of oedipal conflict but as a sign of his anticipation of the postmodernist movement beyond the oedipal hermeneutic, a belief system still in its initial stage at the time of Lawrence's death. To look at Lawrence this way also counteracts the apologist tendency to say that his struggle for independence from the dominating figure of the mother marks him as a man of his times, unable to rise above a typical male modernist gynophobia. It can also help students understand that characters in fiction can represent ideas and ways of thinking as well as actual persons.

Before many of Lawrence's contemporaries had even read Freud, Lawrence rejected the Freudian belief that the mother of childhood remains preserved within our unconscious as a latent component of our beings. As Judith Ruderman shows in *D. H. Lawrence and the Devouring Mother*, Lawrence saw any emphasis on connection to the mother as antithetical to self-realization. It is easy to say that in this Lawrence is simply misogynistic, repaying with contempt the debt that we all owe to the mothers who bore us and usually nurtured us through childhood. However, applying Jessica Benjamin's feminist psychology, one might see Lawrence's view as an implicit criticism of Freud's greater interest in the imagined mother (who has been metaphorically killed through reification) than in the real, living woman. This criticism is made explicit in Lawrence's book *Psychoanalysis and the Unconscious*. Although Benjamin argues for greater recognition of human connectedness, she opposes both Freudian and object-relations theories of development because she sees them as reducing the mother to a symbol. Lawrence rails equally against Victorian domestic ideology's treatment of the mother as a sort of introjected soul and against modernist psychoanalytically influenced consideration of her as an imago carried always within us. He also insists on the recognition of her as a being separate from the child, a point he makes beautifully in the poem "Rose of All the World" (*Complete Poems* 218–19).

Lawrence's focus on the autonomy of the woman who is a mother is remarkably free from resentment of her separate existence. He refuses to demonize the mother as the decadents and artists did and instead points the way toward current poststructuralist reassessments of gender that go far beyond mere reversal. Rather than either reflect nostalgia for a mother who must be sacrificed on the altar of art or glory in her removal, Lawrentian texts depicting dead mothers, like *Sons and Lovers, The Rainbow*, and the poem "Spirits Summoned West" (*Complete Poems* 410–12), examine the process through which historically specific gender roles gain new symbolic dimensions.

A brief look at Lawrence's treatment of the mother in his most famous novel reveals how differently this novel can be understood when read through recent feminist theory, which is always attentive to history and cultural change. Critics have generally understood *Sons and Lovers* as an oedipal tale and consequently have emphasized the similarities between Paul Morel's mother, Gertrude, and his girlfriend Miriam. But this reading obscures Lawrence's historicizing of gender roles throughout the novel. Paul repeatedly attributes his failure with Miriam specifically to time-bound differences between her cultural situation and his mother's. Lawrence shows us in scene after scene that Gertrude deliberately embodies the Victorian womanly ideal. While she is religious and proper, she is also pragmatic. Her demands for allegiance divide her son against himself, but she remains smugly sure of her moral superiority to all the men in her life. In contrast, Miriam's more modern gender identity causes her continual uncertainty and self-doubt. Described repeatedly as "hypersensitive," she is unable to reconcile her turn-of-the-century feminist aspirations for equality with her romantic, spiritualized Victorian compulsion to defer to the man she loves. Her perception of her place in the gender hierarchy is confused: "Miriam almost fiercely wished she were a man. And yet she hated men, at the same time" (185). Of her feelings for Paul, we are told that "deep down, she hated him because she loved him and he dominated her" (340). Miriam and Paul both envision their most appropriate and comfortable relation as intellectual and hierarchical, with her acting as student and listener, but they have no way to assimilate this behavior into either an erotic connection that would satisfy sexual and romantic needs or a partnership that would build their sense of themselves as progressive thinkers. An ideal Victorian marriage, presumably what Gertrude wanted, with each partner capably overseeing a separate sphere of physical work, could have little relevance to the younger couple's sense of themselves. Thus Lawrence locates the problematic center of modern love in the movement from the Victorian world's emphasis on gendered productivity to the turn-of-the-century emphasis on shared intellectual life, which fosters competition and resentment. The novel's many scenes in which the women in Paul's life confront Paul with rival accounts of events and even of his own psychology foreground the modern battle between the sexes over representation, analysis, and philosophy that has made it impossible for Paul to hope to find an intelligent woman with the self-confident femaleness of his mother.

In this respect, among others, *Sons and Lovers* is a self-referential text. As a reworking of material from Jessie Chambers's written reminiscence, it competes with a specifically female vision and mode of literary production. The novel's structure itself stresses that the world of the mother, with its safely fixed gender roles, is irretrievably gone. Paul yearns toward her because she gives him meaning but recognizes that having her alongside him would mean death. He must move beyond his mother, not because she is his mother and a woman but because staying with her means staying in a dead mode of dichotomous gender relations. What lies beyond her is marked as new, literally unknowable, because the novel, in taking Paul past her, ends. But by going beyond the mother, Lawrence finishes the novel, bringing it into conversation with the female-authored text it rivals. And it is here that the mixture of facts and interpretations of them in Chambers's famous *D. H. Lawrence: A Personal Record* can be drawn on to provide an approach to *Sons and Lovers* far richer than the one Chambers seems to have intended.

Facts about Lawrence's personal life can be usefully integrated into a presentation of the radical inconsistency of gender roles at the turn of the twentieth century. Texts like Elaine Showalter's *Sexual Anarchy* and Sandra M. Gilbert and Susan Gubar's *Sexchanges* (*No Man's Land*, vol. 2) are good starting places for professors who want some background on this topic. Anne Smith's essay "A New Adam and a New Eve" remains an excellent introduction to some of the problems of gender identification involved in Lawrence's movement from the working class to the intellectual middle class. A brief discussion, perhaps bringing in examples from our own times, of the ways different social classes and cultural groups define masculinity and femininity will help move students beyond the certainty, promoted by unexamined gender ideology, that sex roles are asynchronic and binary.

Depending on the intellectual level of the students, this might also be the time to introduce them to the Foucauldian idea that one can trace the genealogies of discourses by looking at changes over time in symbolic systems and at what power structures those changes served. An example of this that most students find easy to grasp is that, as an increasing number of Americans recognized that racial integration was necessary for social harmony, the word *black* lost more and more of the negative connotation it had once carried in such formerly common terms as *blackhearted.* And likewise the contrastive positing of white as virtuous, as in the phrase *white as snow,* fell out of ordinary speech. Students can then be prompted to give some examples of similar changes in discourses of gender difference. One example that emerges in many of my classes, and which I attribute to the popularization of theories of female-centered epistemology such as those expressed in Carol Gilligan's *In a Different Voice* and collected in *Women's Ways of Knowing* (Belenky et al.), is that the concept of thinking like a woman has come to be roughly synonymous with thinking empathetically and has lost its mid-twentieth-century connotation of solipsistic emotionality.

If students in the class can be brought to an understanding that gender ideologies are unstable and constantly under deconstruction and reconstruction in response to political changes, then they may be able to see that authors do not necessarily merely affirm the gender ideology of their times—no matter what the author's own primary gender identification is. This qualification is tremendously important in getting a fair reading of Lawrence from feminist students. Of course, if no students self-identify as feminists, one should not be quick to conclude that the role of the feminist professor here is to raise the consciousness of students brainwashed by patriarchy. While in most American coeducational classrooms few students will openly claim to be feminists, many are acutely disturbed and deeply angered by the situation feminist reader-response theorists have termed "immasculation."

Judith Fetterley coined this term in *The Resisting Reader* to describe the process through which women immersed in a culture that universalizes masculinity begin to accept the idea that to be female means otherness from the standard of humanity. Immasculated readers identify with male protagonists and in doing so partake of the characters' (and the authors') misogyny. As many feminist critics and theorists have testified, this identification results in intense alienation and corresponding rage. These emotions are often inelegantly articulated in the classroom through a student's dismissal of a book as sick, boring, or stupid. The perpetually irritated and alienated female student may be the one most in need of a feminist reading practice that seeks to grant her agency rather than to dictate to her, once again, how she should understand texts.

In the landmark essay "Reading Ourselves: Toward a Feminist Theory of Reading," Patrocinio Schweickart offers many brilliant suggestions for the development of a feminist praxis within reader-response criticism but finally does not go far enough beyond the usual Kate Millett–style rejection of male-authored texts to enable her to provide a path for the neophyte feminist reader into the dialogic complexity of Lawrence's work. Using *Women in Love* as her test case for developing an approach to masculinist texts, Schweickart describes her "affective response to the novel" as "bifurcated," because as a woman she identifies with Ursula, while she is "also induced to identify with Birkin, and in so doing, [is] drawn into complicity with the reduction of Ursula, and therefore of [herself], to the role of the other" (43). Perhaps the most interesting aspect of the analysis of this painfully fragmenting experience is that Schweickart attributes her identification with Birkin to Lawrence's depiction of him as struggling to attain both "autonomous selfhood" and love (43). A number of questions are begged in this dichotomous vision of the novel. For instance, is Ursula represented as wanting only love and not selfhood? And does Birkin stand for all men or for masculinity in his longing for both selfhood and love? And, finally, although many other problematizing questions could be raised, does it mean anything that Birkin's need for deep connection to others besides Ursula is not satisfied and is apparently unsatisfiable in the world as it is—or that Gerald, not Ursula, fails Birkin?

I cannot endorse Schweickart's recommendation that feminists read male- and female-authored texts differently, in the first case striving to disrupt the immasculation presumed to be the result of uncritical reading and in the second striving to "connect" imaginatively with female authors so as to enter into a feeling of "community" (48). Nor would I ever recommend this practice to my students. But I do agree strongly with Schweickart's claim that "one must identify the nature of the choices proffered by the text and, equally important, what the text precludes—namely, the possibility of reading as a woman *without* putting one's self in the position of the other, of reading to affirm womanhood as another, equally valid, paradigm of human existence" (50). The inclusion of this recommendation in her essay should remind us of how seriously we need to think (and to urge our students to think) about exactly what a text precludes and how it does so, because *Women in Love* itself, even at the core of Schweickart's somewhat schematic reading, challenges her assumption that "[m]en value autonomy [and] individual rights" while women "value relationships" (55). Her guidelines for feminist analysis of texts lead Schweickart, as she says, to concur with Kate Millett about the sexism of *Women in Love*, but they can also confirm the vision of a reader who sees the novel as concerned with men and women who cannot desire only those things culturally deemed appropriate to their assigned gender positions. The deep examination of the identificatory positions a text enables can provide bored and angry students with a means of expressing in great detail what annoys them about a text while at the same time sparing them the further unproductive annoyance of being told to interpret the text in a prescribed manner. It is usually less annoying to see the text as a site of ideological struggle than as a piece of art that must always be understood as coherent.

It is under this imperative to examine deeply the workings of textual dialogism that the class can go from a discussion of the incoherent and shifting nature of cultural discourses of gender into examples of Lawrence's multivocality, looking at a few brief pieces that suggest the wide variety of his speaking positions on gender politics. A few useful pairings to assign are "We Need One Another" (from *Phoenix*) and "On Being a Man" (from *Phoenix II*); "Bavarian Gentians" and "Purple Anemones"; and "Humiliation" and "I Wish I Knew a Woman" (all from *Collected Poems*). If the class is reading one or both of the most frequently taught novels, *Sons and Lovers* and *Women in Love,* it works well to spend some class time reading closely one of the scenes in which characters debate philosophical issues. Students can be asked to identify the social voices that are heard in such scenes, with the reminder that the voices may not have a one-to-one correspondence to characters and that one character may speak from different discursively determined positions at different times. By this point in the class, students will probably feel some of the excitement of placing these debates in relation to unresolved issues of Lawrence's culture and our own. While recognizing that the scenes might sometimes have been meant to instruct and persuade readers, students can now use analytic skills to enter into the communication with Lawrence's intellectual world that his writings make possible.

If there ever was general agreement that a feminist approach to Lawrence meant exposing the inadequacies of his sexual politics and condemning him as a not very complex misogynist, it has this meaning no longer. An approach to Lawrence that is more thoroughly informed by the poststructuralist theories of identity formation and representation that have so deeply influenced feminist and gender studies yields a different set of responses to his work. While students may well conclude that their personal visions of gender and sexuality differ from Lawrence's and may further decide that they dislike his gender and sexual politics, they may still be brought to understand how dynamic and multilayered his engagement was with the cultures he inhabited. A feminist approach to Lawrence can provide an exciting introduction to the literary gendering of modernism, which was under revision even as it took form. And going beyond the project of creating excitement in the classroom about Lawrence's writing and its place in modernist literature, this approach can also help students think productively about two issues central to Lawrence's life and work: the complicated, ever-changing and ever-modifiable relationship between women and men and the problem of addressing that vitally important part of life in literature.

Teaching "Woman": A Cultural Criticism Approach to "The Woman Who Rode Away"

Pamela L. Caughie

"*This was woman herself, with her sudden fears, her irrational whims, her instinctive worries, her impetuous boldness, her fussings, and her delicious sensibility.*" So begins Roland Barthes's influential essay "The Death of the Author." This quotation from Honoré de Balzac's *Sarrasine* gives rise to Barthes's provocative question, one that has changed the very nature of reading: "Who is speaking thus?" Barthes continues:

> Is it the hero of the story bent on remaining ignorant of the castrato hidden beneath the woman? Is it Balzac the individual, furnished by his personal experience with a philosophy of Woman? Is it Balzac the author professing "literary" ideas on femininity? Is it universal wisdom? Romantic psychology? We shall never know, for the good reason that writing is the destruction of every voice, of every point of origin. (142)

Barthes's reading of *Sarrasine*, published in the book-length essay *S/Z*, is often said to mark the turning point from structuralism to poststructuralism in literary studies. I begin with Barthes because his sustained analysis of reading and writing practices raises questions that I explore in teaching D. H. Lawrence in my Women in Literature course. Where do a writer's notions of woman, femininity, and female sexuality come from? How, when, and why do gender ideologies get constituted, produced, and reproduced? Whose voice is speaking in the text? What does the question of voice have to do with "woman herself"? The title of my essay, then, is deliberately ambiguous, referring both to the subject of this essay, Lawrence's story "The Woman Who Rode Away," and to the subject of my course, the cultural construction of "woman" in early-twentieth-century Anglo-American society. In discussing how I teach D. H. Lawrence's "Woman" in the context of my Women in Literature course, I describe a particular form of cultural criticism.

Barthes's poststructuralist critique of the author-as-origin, the intending subject behind the text, and of the classical notion of representation as the representation of a preexisting reality provides the theoretical underpinnings for the emergence of contemporary cultural criticism. In *Marrano as Metaphor: The Jewish Presence in French Writing* Elaine Marks defines cultural studies, the paradigm for much cultural criticism today, by reference to Barthes:

> I understand cultural studies through Roland Barthes's definition of myth as "a chain of concepts widely accepted throughout culture, by which its members conceptualize and understand a particular topic or part of their

social experience." . . . In this sense cultural studies analyzes the noncon-scious presuppositions that organize a text.   (xiv)

For Barthes, writing is no longer conceived in terms of its meaning or content, to be explained by reference to the author, for that humanist model ignores the signifying force of language and cultural discourses that, through disciplines and institutions, provide the terms with which we represent ourselves as sub-jects in relation to others. Instead, writing for Barthes is a "tissue of quotations drawn from the innumerable centres of culture" (146), a "neutral space" where identities and bodies are "lost" (142). To speak of the death of the author is not to deny the reality of identities, bodies, and intending subjects; rather, the coinage refers to the critique of the concepts of author, individual, originality, and intentionality that have long been central to the teaching of literature. A critique does not mean repudiating or negating certain beliefs and values; it means interrogating the historical conditions of their emergence and the "non-conscious presuppositions" they carry with them. If one believes it is "language that speaks, not the author" (143) then one's task as a critic or teacher of litera-ture is to open inquiry into those "innumerable centres of culture" (146) that are the very precondition of the writer's agency and creativity. Or as Mary Poovey has put it, cultural criticism that derives from poststructuralist theory basically takes the form of a "three-tiered enterprise" comprising

> the study of culture as an interdependent set of institutional and informal practices and discourses; the study of the traces this larger social forma-tion produces in individual texts; the study of the role our own practice—in this case, teaching—plays in reproducing or subverting the dominant cultural formation.   (620)

The basic principle of cultural criticism thus defined is that "concepts we treat as if they were things are seen as the effects of representations and institutional practices, not their origins" (621).

The cultural criticism of poststructuralists like Barthes and Poovey provides a useful way of approaching the teaching of Lawrence in a women's studies class-room. I ask my students to take seriously the kinds of questions Barthes asks rather than to assume that Lawrence's representation of woman and his sexual politics are simply expressions of his personal beliefs and values. Instead of seeking origins or culprits, we look at the complex historical, cultural, and psy-chopolitical dynamics in which ideas and representations of woman are pro-duced, naturalized, and contested. The point is not to save Lawrence from criticism but to understand how his characterization of "woman" in particular writings of the 1920s came to produce and reproduce certain meanings and val-ues even as it contested other dominant cultural beliefs about women.

In a core-level course in women's studies, however, I do not begin with

Barthes's and Poovey's theoretical writings (although I teach selections from Barthes's *Mythologies* later in the semester). Instead, I present their notions of representation and culture through two well-known and more accessible works by British writers, which I assign in the first two weeks of the course: Virginia Woolf's *A Room of One's Own* and John Berger's *Ways of Seeing*. Berger and Woolf provide specific examples of visual and narrative representations of women to show how culture—both material conditions and discursive practices—produces gendered, and racialized, identities. In the guise of a lecture to be delivered to students at a woman's college, *Room* explicitly addresses the role teaching practices and educational institutions play in reinforcing and sustaining dominant notions of woman, and it alerts us to key questions about material conditions and their effects on notions of woman and on writings by and about women:

> Here I am asking why women did not write poetry in the Elizabethan age, and I am not sure how they were educated; whether they were taught to write; whether they had sitting-rooms to themselves; how many women had children before they were twenty-one; what, in short, they did from eight in the morning till eight at night.   (46)

Although Woolf takes whiteness for granted when discussing woman, her references to colonialism, psychoanalysis, and patriarchy undermine notions of sex and race as natural attributes and raise questions about their cultural deployment, questions we take to our reading of Lawrence.

When I teach "The Woman Who Rode Away" (the first fictional work we read in the course), I situate its representations of the woman and the Indians within a variety of discourses and media of the late nineteenth and early twentieth centuries: psychoanalysis, anthropology, advertising, cinema, colonialism, and suffrage, to name the most prominent. Freud's and the sexologists' accounts of female sexuality and homosexuality, the highly popular Tarzan stories and films, posters and cartoons depicting women as primitive savages, editorials expressing anxiety over the number of white middle-class women entering the workforce all provide a historical context in which to read Lawrence's story for an understanding of how a literary work comes to be produced and to generate meanings in relation to other cultural productions. This approach enables students to understand literature as Barthes's "tissue of quotations," not as an original and autonomous object to be understood primarily through reference to the author and literary history. More important, this approach encourages students to see culture not just as the creation of social groups, which then has an impact on the experience of individuals, but as the very precondition of what it means to be an individual, a woman or a man (Poovey 617). We look at Lawrence as a *writer* (the term Barthes substitutes for *author*), producing his texts within this complex matrix of cultural discourses, "the matrix from which 'literature' is born" (Haraway 595), not simply as a man expressing certain beliefs—some of which happen to be sexist. The object of study in this course is not Lawrence's story or his life and character or even his British culture but the formal system of relations that makes possible the production of "Woman," both the story and the figure.

I begin our first class on Lawrence by reading the following passage:

> Her kind of womanhood, intensely personal and individual, was to be obliterated again, and the great primeval symbols were to tower once more over the fallen individual independence of woman. The sharpness and the quivering nervous consciousness of the highly-bred white woman was to be destroyed again, womanhood was to be cast once more into the great stream of impersonal sex and impersonal passion. ("Woman" 60)

"Who is speaking here?" I ask my students by way of opening discussion. The authorial voice of these lines, and of the final line of the story, has long been considered problematic (Wallace, "Circling" 114–15). Is it the narrator who speaks, expressing the views of the Indians who will eventually sacrifice the woman? Is it Lawrence the writer offering his hyper-individualist, materialist, and sex-conscious age a philosophy of sexual harmony? Is it Lawrence the man expressing his personal misogyny and what we might call today his inverse racism? Identifying where such notions of (white) womanhood come from is our task in reading this story.

Lawrence wrote "The Woman Who Rode Away" in Taos in the summer of 1924, and the story was first published in the *Dial* in 1925. Set in the Sierra Madre during the recession years following the First World War, the story tells of a woman in her early thirties whose boredom with her isolated surroundings and conventional marriage, coupled with her romantic notions of Mexican Indians, leads her to seek out the Chilchui, "the sacred tribe of all the Indians" (42), living in the mountains beyond her home. When her husband, Lederman, is away on business, the woman (who remains unnamed throughout the story) rides away from her home and children on a spiritual quest to find these "mysterious savages" (42) who still practice the ancient religion of their ancestors. Discovered in the mountains by the Chilchui, the woman is taken hostage and spends several months in the village as the priests prepare to sacrifice her at the winter solstice. The story ends with the sacrificial knife poised above her naked body.

Not surprisingly, most students find the ending disturbing. Through passages such as "She lived on, in a kind of daze, feeling her power ebbing more and more away from her, as if her will were leaving her, . . . as if she were diffusing out deliciously into the harmony of things" (62), students come to see that Lawrence wants to represent the sacrifice of the petty individualism and self-centeredness of Western culture to the cosmic harmony of the ancient religious sensibility. Many students are sympathetic to what they perceive as Lawrence's celebration of Indian culture and values. Lawrence's essay "New Mexico" can help students discern in his representation of the Indians the author's criticism of Western materialism and patriarchy as embodied in that "little dynamo of energy," the husband Lederman (39). "He loved work, work, work, and making things. His marriage, his children, were something he was making, part of his business, but with a sentimental income this time" (40). Through the image of a "red kerchief" knotted around a neck ("New Mexico" 142), Lawrence's essay criticizes Western tourists whose "foolish romanticism" ("Woman" 42) leads them to accept a celluloid image of New Mexico. The red scarf reappears in "Woman" as the "pathetic bit of a red tie" (55) that makes up part of the woman's riding attire, explicitly linking the woman and the tourist.

Yet however sympathetic students might be to Lawrence's promotion of Indian culture and to his criticism of Western culture, most cannot accept the ending. What bothers them is not just the human sacrifice but the representation of the woman as a passive accomplice. Described throughout as already dead, lacking any "will of her own" (45), the woman is seen nonetheless, by the narrator as well as the Indians, as willing, indeed desiring, her own sacrifice: "She knew she was a victim: that all this elaborate work upon her was the work of victimising her. But she did not mind. She wanted it" (67). The words of the date-rape defense strike home. My student Leo's response to the sacrifice is typical: "The last sacrificial scene is supposed to show the cosmic unity and balance, but instead it becomes another scene of male dominance through its allusion to rape," he writes. "The nakedness of the woman, the dark sacrificial stone, the 'four men holding her by the outstretched arms and legs,' the sun's last rays touching the 'shaft of ice,' and the impending insertion of the sacrificial knife into her body all serve to show male sexual dominance over the woman."[1]

Why must the woman be a victim, and why does she come to accept her impending death? She has no epiphany. She achieves no power, no insight. Indeed, during the ceremony that will end in her death, "no-one translated" (68). The woman "is only a means to an end," writes another student, Jennifer. "She has made the ultimate sacrifice for a man. Instead of making the sacrifice a noble action the woman agrees to submit to for the benefit of humanity, Lawrence uses the sacrifice as a power trip for men, proving that he is anything but a feminist." Such observations move us from interpreting the meaning of the story in terms of Lawrence's notion of cosmic unity to interrogating the notion of womanhood that informs his representation of that vision. I ask my students, "What in the culture lies behind this sacrificial narrative and the representation of the woman and the Indians on which the narrative's emotional and ideological effects depend?"

To begin to answer this question (one that with varying particulars we return to throughout the course as we study other texts from the 1920s and 1930s), we go through the story noting the adjectives and imagery used to describe the woman, the Indians, and the land, as well as the kinds of oppositions set up between the races and between the sexes. The woman is described as "dazed," "void," and "dead" (39, 40), that last adjective linking her to the strip-mined land, the "thrice-dead little Spanish town" near her home, and the dead silver market (39). The woman's conscious development, we are told, has been arrested since marriage; she is morally held down by her husband (40). Such characterizations suggest her passivity and powerlessness and provide evidence (as do Freud's writings) of the oppressive effects of patriarchy on the psychology and moral capacity of women. Like Freud, Lawrence could be seen to critique the construction of woman in patriarchy.

Yet the woman is also "assured" (a word repeatedly used to describe her), "proud," "spoilt," and "foolhardy" (40, 45, 46), suggesting that her character flaws are partly responsible for her fatal destiny. It is her assertion of her independence and her rebellion against her "invincible slavery" (40), against being kept in a "walled-in" adobe house (39) as if womanhood were a "protected occupation" (Woolf, *Room* 40), that initiates the action of the story. She "had *harassed* her husband into letting her go riding with him" (my emphasis); later she forces her male servant to *yield* to her "peculiar overbearing" insistence that she go out riding alone; and she *silences* her young son when he questions her defiance of conventional gender roles: "Am I *never* to be let alone?" (43). Although the narrative in no way defends those conventional roles—in fact, it challenges them—the woman's triumph over the men in her life can itself be read as an effect of the sexual imbalance that needs to be restored through the woman's ritual sacrifice. "Her ordinary personal consciousness" eventually succumbs to the "passional cosmic consciousness" of the Indians' religious vision (64). In other words, "Woman" at once challenges certain conventional gender differences (e.g., women are property, husbands masters) and mobilizes others (e.g., women should be passive, men active) in the service of a new sexual philosophy. As one student, Aniko, observes, the Indians—while preparing to sacrifice the woman—give her "a nice little home, a pretty blue dress, some flowers, and a puppy." "This is frighteningly similar," Aniko continues, "to a wife beater trying to make up for his violence by buying his wife flowers. Signifying their patriarchal powers, the Indians sit with the woman in 'fatherly solicitude.' The relevant word is 'fatherly,' reestablishing hierarchical values"—and infantilizing the woman.

The Indians are described variously as "marvelous," "mysterious," and "timeless" and as "unsanitary," "indecent," and "cunning" (42), depending on whether the romanticized or the racist view of the natives is being invoked. These opposing views are attributed to a specific character, as in Lederman's racist dismissal of the Indians as "lowdown and dirty," all of them "more or less alike," and the young visitor's "peculiar vague enthusiasm" for this ancient and mysterious people (42). My students see that Lawrence resists both views. But what about adjectives and attitudes that are not tied to a specifiable narrative voice? "Savage," the adjective or appellation most commonly applied to the Indians, links the divergent views of Lederman and the young visitor as well as the narrator's descriptions of the Indians and their religious ceremonies. Along with "barbaric," "wild," "terrible," "fierce," "inhuman," and "impersonal," "savage" recurs throughout the narrative. Clearly the term establishes a fundamental contrast between civilized and ancient man. For example, in contrast to the "civilized" men (the husband, son, and servant), the Indians never yield to the woman's demands. Their relentless nature, their calm self-assurance without self-consciousness, and their "powerful physical presence" without sex consciousness establish their difference from and superiority to westerners, who are highly "self-conscious" and "sex-conscious" (58, 59). But whose perspective are we getting in such passages? Where do these notions of savages come from?

The uncertainty over who is speaking in passages like those cited above leads many students to accept these insistent characterizations as neutral ones. While most students in my women's studies class are quick to pick up on any disparaging representation of the woman, many take the descriptions of the Indians at face value. Adjectives such as "proud," "foolish," and "childish" used for the woman clearly represent to students a specific, and specifically sexist, attitude toward women, yet the adjectives used for the Indians are seen as merely descriptive. For many students, Indians *are* proud, whereas the woman's pride signals a particular point of view, specifically a masculine point of view that disparages independent-minded women. My challenge is to get students to ask how certain representations of Indians and women come about and to question how such representations can become so ingrained in our cultural imagination that we can take them for granted as natural.

An answer begins to emerge when we examine another pair of adjectives used to contrast the woman and the Indians. The woman is frequently described as "white," the Indians as "dark" or, more particularly, "black." Students commonly take these terms as simply physical descriptions, rarely noting their persistent and even peculiar use. For example, observing the young Indian who guards her, the woman notes:

> He seemed to have no sex, as he sat there so still and gentle and apparently submissive, with his head bent a little forward, and the river of glistening black hair streaming maidenly over his shoulders.
> Yet when she looked again, she saw his shoulders broad and powerful, his eyebrows black and level, the short, curved, obstinate black lashes over his lowered eyes, the small, fur-like line of moustache above his blackish, heavy lips, and the strong chin, and she knew that in some other mysterious way he was darkly and powerfully male.   (58)

Once the persistent use of "black" is pointed out to students, they pick up on the identification of blackness with the Indians in this and other descriptive passages. Because maleness for Lawrence is an elemental force, not an individual attribute, blackness suggests not a racial category but a primal spiritual state.

After noting how Lawrence uses blackness in "Woman," we turn to an earlier passage, also presenting the woman's observation of her Indian captors, that provides a telling example of how whiteness functions in the story:

And the elder men, squatting on their haunches, looked up at her in the terrible paling dawn, and there was not even derision in their eyes. Only that intense, yet remote, inhuman glitter which was terrible to her. They were inaccessible. They could not see her as a woman at all. As if she *were* not a woman. As if, perhaps, her whiteness took away all her womanhood, and left her as some giant, female white ant. That was all they could see in her.   (49)

Whiteness absorbs or eliminates womanhood. The woman's race is first noted at the moment she asserts herself against the servant who would confine her to the home and to the social conventions that limited women's freedom of movement: "'I shall go alone,' repeated the large, placid-seeming, fair-complexioned woman" (43). Later she identifies herself as a "lady" (46) and is insistently identified by the narrator as American (45). Whiteness is linked not with a primal femaleness, as blackness represents primal maleness, but, more precisely, with class and national differences that must be overcome.

Coupled with adjectives linking the woman to the impoverished land exploited by the colonizing westerners, the woman's whiteness comes to stand for, and ultimately comes to be sacrificed for, conventional middle-class femininity and Western colonization. The woman is whiteness personified; the Indian is maleness personified. Lawrence establishes an opposition between whiteness (gendered feminine) and maleness (racialized as black). Understanding Lawrence's sexual philosophy in racial terms can help account for the troubling ending. The woman's sacrifice guarantees, in the words of the last line of the story, "the mastery that man must hold, and that passes from race to race" (71). "This line is important," writes my student Leo. "Since the opinion of 'the woman' has been irrelevant throughout the story, it is Lawrence who is commenting on the needed distribution of power. Men *must* hold the 'mastery,' and the sacrifice of the woman serves as a blood bond between men." That blood bond is specifically between men of different races, *between* men and *across* races. My students rarely pick up on this point, partly, I believe, because of the nature of the course, women's studies, which leads them to focus on sexual rather than racial differences, and partly because of their tendency to see gender and race as separate, and separable, attributes. The racialization of sexual difference in this story prepares students to understand the gendering of racial differences in other works we study.

My teaching of "Woman" seeks to contextualize Lawrence's representation of the woman and the Indians in terms of other discourses and literature of the time. Before moving on to other primary texts that can help us understand how Lawrence's sexual philosophy is sustained by racial representation, we discuss selections from Marianna Torgovnick's *Gone Primitive*, especially the first chapter, "Defining the Primitive." Here students reencounter Lawrence's descriptive terms for the Indians in the context of the ideology of primitivism, according to which natives are childlike, libidinous, violent, dangerous, timeless, mysterious, natural, and free. "The ensemble of these tropes," writes Torgovnick, "however miscellaneous and contradictory—forms the basic grammar and vocabulary of what I call primitivist discourse, a discourse fundamental to the Western sense of self and Other" (8). Whereas the primitive conceived of as childish, irrational, and libidinous, a "dark" force to be feared, was feminized in many cultural productions of the time (later we discuss Freud's essays of the 1930s in which he refers to female sexuality as the "dark continent"), Torgovnick argues that Lawrence "masculinized" or "phallicized" the other dominant representation of the primitive, as powerful and assured, a "noble savage" to be emulated (159). However much Lawrence may criticize elsewhere both racist and romantic views held about natives, however much he may modify conventional notions of so-called primitive peoples, his story depends on primitivist tropes for some of its emotional force and import.

Primitivism is a concept we return to with Freud's essays on female sexuality, Nella Larsen's *Quicksand* (1928), Fannie Hurst's popular melodrama *Imitation of Life* (1933) and John Stahl's 1934 screen adaptation, Cedric Gibbons's 1934 film *Tarzan and His Mate*, and *Chasing a Rainbow*, a PBS documentary on Josephine Baker. Tracing primitivist iconography through various cultural productions of the 1920s, 1930s, and 1940s shows students how pervasive such representations were and enables students to see how Lawrence both reproduces and refigures these dominant tropes.

For example, although Lawrence promotes women's emancipation from moral enslavement to men, his story, like Edgar Rice Burroughs's Tarzan stories, in Torgovnick's words, "seems designed as a cautionary tale in the wake of suffrage for . . . women" (67), as does Hurst's *Imitation of Life*. Lawrence's 1928 column in the *Evening News*, "If Women Were Supreme" (retitled "Matriarchy" when it appeared in *Phoenix II*), captures the same anxiety that motivates Burroughs's and Hurst's plots. The editorial describes working women as the "silk-legged hordes" who "settle like silky locusts on all the jobs" and "occupy the offices and the playing-fields like immensely active ants" (549). However mocking Lawrence's tone may be, this editorial registers a pervasive cultural anxiety of the time to which Lawrence himself was obviously not immune.

Just as Lawrence's laudatory views of Indians can convince students that Indians naturally embody a primal, more genuine sexuality, so his defiance of conventional notions of women (e.g., his depiction of a woman who rides away without turning back to wave to her son and who never once thinks of her children during her months of captivity), coupled with his seductive prose, leads some students to ignore or elide Lawrence's more troubling representations of female sexuality. Teaching "Woman" alongside contemporaneous writings on female sexuality can lead students to dismiss Lawrence's views on sexuality as readily as they dismiss Freud's. However, my goal is to move students from agreeing or disagreeing with Freud or Lawrence to understanding the cultural force of Freud's ideas and the cultural matrix within which Lawrence's writings on sexuality were produced. The young Indian's story of the sun and moon, for example, defies Western notions of gender and identity and yet relies on gendered notions of sexual difference ("Woman" 65). "In attempting to break from shallow conventions of gender," my student Aniko writes, "Lawrence reaffirms fundamental stereotypes. In the Indian's sun and moon story about how the world works, the hot active sun is male, the cold, passive moon female. The sun is supposed to be kept happy," she writes; "the moon is supposed to be kept quiet" (see "Woman" 61). Despite Lawrence's desire and lifelong effort to break with and subvert conventional gender notions of his day, Lawrence also inevitably, simultaneously, writes within the cultural tropes available to him, which necessarily uphold these notions.

Teaching "Woman" apart from its broader cultural contexts risks perpetuating certain values as natural (Indians are proud, women are passive) and setting up a false choice between two mutually exclusive views (Lawrence as gynocritic or gynophobe). But precisely because a cultural criticism approach challenges accepted values and reading practices, it can also provoke resistance. While many of my women's studies students have been well prepared for my pedagogy by their interdisciplinary course work in the program, others find the range of material they are asked to negotiate daunting, while still others resist reading literature in other than aesthetic terms. Such resistance provides yet another opportunity for presenting the insights of cultural criticism. Lawrence's privileged place in the literary canon, from F. R. Leavis's writings in the 1940s to the 1979 *Norton Anthology of British Literature*, along with reigning formalist methodologies of that time, has contributed to the profound hold that gender hierarchy has on the Western imagination and on the conception of modernism. This does not mean that we should stop teaching Lawrence or that we should reject formalism; on the contrary, it means teaching Lawrence or formalism with greater awareness of "the role our own practice—in this case, teaching—plays in reproducing or subverting the dominant cultural formation" (Poovey 620). A cultural criticism approach to "Woman" seeks to account for the values we bring to our teaching as well as the values Lawrence brings to his writing and our students bring to their reading.

NOTE

[1]My thanks to my students Leo Dokshutsky, Jennifer Kostolansky, and Aniko Grandjean, whose papers I quote from by permission. I have lightly edited their writing for coherence and clarity of reference.

Using Student Resistance and Our Own in Teaching *The Captain's Doll*: Toward a Pedagogy of Affect

Cynthia Lewiecki-Wilson

> [T]eaching . . . must . . . *testify*, make something *happen*,
> and not just transmit a passive knowledge . . . believed to
> be known in advance.
> —Shoshana Felman, "Education and Crisis;
> or, The Vicissitudes of Teaching"

The interactive teaching and learning model of critical-writing pedagogy has strongly influenced my teaching, whether in a literature, women's studies, or writing class. By engaging only the content side of learning, teachers do a disservice to students, merely transmitting the already known. Such teaching constructs students as passive, empty vessels (Freire), relegating them to the position of the colonized other. Passive learning does not teach students to become agents of their learning.

I teach Lawrence's novella *The Captain's Doll* in a cultural studies class thematically focused on an inquiry into how representations affect us. We explore the historical, cultural, semiotic, and affective dynamics of representations—not just the representations we find in literature (and in nonliterary texts and cultural images) but also those we make of our own responses, such as:

> That book really changed my life!
> I hated it; it was *so* boring.
> I loved reading this, but it disturbed me.

While the dominant pedagogy in the academy discounts the value of students' affective responses, I hope to persuade you that attending to such responses is important and that engaging and questioning affect is intellectually serious and ethically responsible. We need a pedagogy of affect, one that challenges the pedagogy now in the ascendancy. This being so, I start off by explaining why a feminist has reason to fear, yet should take on, the project of engaging affect.

In "Emotion and Pedagogic Violence," Lynn Worsham argues that family, workplace, and school teach us the codings of emotion and the places for expressing and restraining it (121–22). These codings sustain patriarchal gender relations and the gendered division of mind and body, reason and emotion, as well as the projection of these categories onto others of different races and classes as essential characteristics. Worsham points out that emotion is coded as part of the signifying system of gender differences (men/reason, women/emotion) and as an organizing principle in the gendered division of labor (women are still the predominant providers of emotional nurturance).

Under the dominant pedagogy, teaching is valued less than scholarship and aligned with the subordinate side of the binaries, with the female, emotion, the body, the personal, and the particular. Scholarship—disembodied labor claiming reason, accuracy, and truth—is coded masculine. And the differing valuation assigned to the labor of teachers and scholars often extends to the different ways they use texts. Thus, on the one hand, scholars appropriate others' texts for their own authorial use, producing signed and owned products, which in turn positions them competitively by circulating and representing them in a scholarly market. On the other hand, in the feminized position, teachers use texts for purposes constrained more by situational pressures (the course, the students, and the institution).

Teachers usually do not claim sole authorship for their syllabi or teaching practices, nor do representations of their teaching usually circulate. Lacking an "objective" product, an authored representation, teaching tends to disappear in the professional circulation of signs through which status is determined. Therefore feminists do indeed have some reason to be suspicious of a pedagogy that engages affect or focuses on it. Their understandable fear is that such a pedagogy would inevitably have them attend to the subjective or emotional and thus risk reproducing the devaluation of women under patriarchy (women teachers as emotional caretakers).

What I am proposing, however, is a pedagogy not of emotion but of affect. And I am thinking in particular here of the theoretical distinction Brian Massumi makes between "affect" and "emotion" in "The Autonomy of Affect." Massumi points out that "affect is more often used loosely as a synonym for emotion," but he separates the two terms by arguing that emotion, while conventionally associated with subjectivity, is "an intensity owned and recognized"; affect, by contrast, is an intensity neither owned nor recognized and is "thus resistant to critique" (88). For instance, Massumi sees affect rather than the more mental construct ideology at work in contemporary media images, which are designed to have an impact on viewers before or despite analysis.

Whereas emotion pertains to a signifying system, Massumi theorizes that affect is a part of a bodily system through which sensations run, resonate, and feed back, potentializing knowledge making (96). This system of affective response is necessary to, and a substrate of, the production of meaning and volition (90) but operates "differentially in relation" to language (86). Research studies confirm the "primacy of the affective," meaning that an image itself, rather than its meaning, induces a strong response. As Massumi explains, "it would appear that the strength or duration of an image's effect is not logically connected to the content in any straightforward way. This is not to say that there is no connection and no logic. . . . [The] strength or duration of the image's effect could be called its *intensity*" (84–85).

Differentiating affect from emotion is one strategy for escaping the dominant pedagogy. As expressions of emotion, student responses will always seem unimportant and idiosyncratic, since emotion is already captured by the ideology that assigns it subordinate value as nonuniversal and nonobjective. But affect—uncaptured emotion that is, as Massumi says, "unqualified," "not ownable or recognizable," "resistant to critique" (88), but "nevertheless highly organized and effectively analyzable" in its consequences (107n2)—is intellectually challenging, requiring students to recognize and analyze what is yet unnamed. In studying their affective responses, students become agents who are actively constructing their emerging knowledge.

Massumi's rethinking of the mind-body relation—his determination to see mind and body, and meaning and affect, not as opposites but as resonating, interconnected systems (94) and his desire to think across the human-nonhuman divide, an impasse dominating language-based postmodern theories—is similar in some ways to Lawrence's. See, for example, M. Elizabeth Wallace's tracing of a Lawrentian epistemology of emerging knowledge, which she finds implicitly rendered in Lawrence's fiction and likens to the philosopher Michael Polyani's view "that all knowing is a [largely tacit] skill that can never be fully detached from the person performing it" (Wallace, "Circling Hawk" 106). And though, as Wallace points out, Lawrence consistently—in all his writing—emphasizes "the bodily roots of knowledge" in his lifelong "attempt to revise" our modern belief in distanced, objective thought (105, 108), his fictional representations of the process of coming to knowledge are especially memorable. He portrays affect as crucial to emerging knowledge: a character will respond intensely to an object or an image (e.g., the panel depicting the Creation of Eve that Will Brangwen carves in *The Rainbow*), then register a sense of emerging knowledge, not yet completely accessible to consciousness, but intuitive, tacit, or felt (on "felt sense" see Gendlin; Perl). Such scenes of encounter stress the importance of affective intensity (as opposed to known emotions) in growth. Once the object or image has served its purpose, it is often violently destroyed or burned (see also young Paul's response to the doll Arabella in *Sons and Lovers*). These striking images and events burn themselves into readers' memories.

In the final lines of *The Captain's Doll* we are told that Hannele wants to burn a picture of the doll she made of Captain Hepburn, the doll itself no longer being available. Set after the First World War in defeated Germany, in Rhineland and Tyrol, *The Captain's Doll* concerns the relationship of a former German countess, Hannele (Johanna) zu Rassentlow, and a married British officer, Captain Alexander Hepburn. Hannele is an artist, whose art is of a particularly female type: she creates works, like dolls and cushion covers, with fabric, needle, and thread. *The Captain's Doll* fits my purposes here because of its historical and cultural setting, because the characters are engaged in representation making, and because Lawrence dramatizes their struggle toward emerging knowledge through their affective responses and resistances.

In class we begin discussion of *The Captain's Doll* by cataloging a chain of representational images, starting with images of concrete objects, then moving to linguistic representations, like metaphors and similes, that deploy images in describing a character and then on to displaced representations of representations. There is the doll Hannele makes, of course, the exact replica of the captain, accurate in every detail, and the doll reproduced and recontextualized in Worpswede's still life (118). These are object images. There are also linguistic representations of this painting in newspaper reports and characters' representations of their view of the doll. Mitchka expresses its finished, closed quality: "Exactly him. Just as finished as he is. Just as complete. He is just like that: finished off" (76). Hannele represents the doll as her "puppet" (78) and later a "barren" and "dead" puppet (90). Hepburn himself says of the doll, "you've got me" (79).

This last group—comprising characters' representations of their affective responses to the image—emphasizes the capture or closure of fluidity, vitality, or potential change in fixed representations, in things. Lawrence wrote in *Fantasia of the Unconscious*, "the nearer a conception comes towards finality, the nearer does the dynamic relation, out of which this concept has arisen, draw to a close. To know, is to lose. When I have a finished mental concept of a beloved, or a friend, then the love and the friendship is dead" (91). In effect, in the first half of the story, the captain *is* his doll.

There are also many instances of representational images used to figure a character's affect. Captain Hepburn's face is "like a mask," "deep-graven," with "a fixed look—as if carved half grotesque in some glossy stone," his hair "changeless" (81). And Hannele's affective response to the captain is figured in an image: she associates his smile with "the fixed sadness of monkeys, of those Chinese carved soapstone apes" (82). Mrs. Hepburn looks like one of Hannele's dolls (95), with her odd crumpled face, costume-like dress, and tinkling jewelry (86). If she is like a puppet in her jerky little movements and the way she plays a role, "as a heroine in a romance" (99), she also seems to see herself as a puppet master, inviting Hannele to tea and pulling not-so-subtle strings in an orchestrated ruse of a threat. The text makes clear that Mrs. Hepburn also pulls her husband's strings, represents and misrepresents him to others, and ventriloquizes his voice, appropriating him and speaking for him in embarrassing ways—for example, "my husband is a greedy man, a greedy man" (96). Mrs. Hepburn also represents herself in other roles: "more of the woman than the mother," "rather old-fashioned," Irish—"and we Irish can't help it"—"able to sympathise" (99). Indeed, "her terrible bits of connubial staging" (105) crudely reveal the appropriation and misappropriation and the aggressive violence involved in acts of representing self and other. They also prepare for the ensuing struggle between Hannele and Alexander in the second half of the story.

But before that struggle commences, Captain Hepburn must get rid of his wife. In explaining his marriage and his wife to Hannele, Hepburn turns the power of descriptive figuring on his wife: she once was a "gentle soul," "a fairy . . . condemned to live in houses" (110), a "delicate creature" taken out of its habitat and taught "to perform tricks" (110, 111), an Irish sprite "cooped up" and "tombed in" (111), a bird in a cage (112). These descriptions suggest an essential and natural original vitality corrupted and perverted by capture and justify the story's solution: let the caged spirit escape through the open window to find its freedom. The narrative turns the violence of representation making on her, enacting a reversal of that which she had used against her husband.

Free of his wife, the captain's affective vitality seems released: "His face seemed different, more flexible" (110). Hepburn is more autonomous and disconnected from others. "The emotional flow between him and all the people he knew and cared for was broken, and for the time being he was conscious only of the cleavage" (113–14). Hannele's rupture with him had occurred even earlier: having seen him with his wife, "the charm was gone" (107). As Hannele struggles against disillusion, she ponders his identity. Is he "really" the truth of her experience, "the queer, delicate-breasted Caesar of her own knowledge" (108), or is he the wife's doll? (As Hepburn admits at the close of the novella, "if a woman loves you, she'll make a doll out of you . . . in her mind. [My wife] had her doll of me right enough" [151].)

Reminding students that *The Captain's Doll* is itself a representation, I ask them to discuss whether they, as readers, want to close off this story by capturing it in a single interpretation. We compare our assumptions about literary stories and our affective responses to them with our assumptions about and responses to other kinds of representations. Do we have similar assumptions about visual art (and this brings us back to the doll and the Worpswede painting), TV sitcoms, films, advertisements, and why or why not?

Students explore their responses to the first part of the story through writing and then compare these in discussion. Generally, most of my students are sympathetic to Countess Hannele's situation, and they find ample evidence in the text to support their view. We discuss how our social locations, values, and beliefs contribute to our affective responses. The students I teach come from working-class families, and they identify with Hannele as the underdog, for example, because they identify with her class position as a poor, displaced war refugee at the mercy of the monied British wife. Although many of my students think of themselves as conservative Christians, most do not find the story's marital infidelity shocking; they consider the adulterer (Captain Hepburn) more at fault than they do the mistress. We discuss how students' responses rest not only on class identification and religious views, but also on assumptions about gender: men are responsible, commanding moral agents, while women are passive; women are more physically and socially vulnerable than are men (hence students' sympathy with Hannele); wives are somehow at fault when their husbands stray (patriarchy's blaming of women and its higher valuation of men). We discuss too how several of these assumptions contradict each other.

Of course, I want my students to be active reading subjects, aware of how readers construct as well as question meanings, of how meaning is negotiated and depends on a reader's location, knowledge, and purposes. My hope is that a pedagogy of affect can help students attend to and analyze how representations that arouse their affective responses and resistances influence them as readers.

The idea that reader response elicits merely personal expression and is therefore not valuable because it is not universal or factual is fairly widespread. Yet when students' affective responses and resistances are themselves made a text of the course, discussed, compared, and analyzed, it becomes apparent that most responses are not personal or original. Studying their own responses over time and comparing theirs with classmates', students quickly see general patterns. (This shouldn't surprise them or me, since Massumi argues that intensity has a social element, the conserved trace of past actions as tendencies [91].) My student Sharon Cottle, who has given me permission to quote from her journal, notes the following:

> One of the big patterns that I see when I read my own and others' responses is that we all say we like to read things which we feel give us a connection to the story. I like to be able to relate myself to the main character of whatever is going on in the story. If the connection isn't there, I find that I lose interest in whatever it is I'm reading. When we read each other's journals, I found these comments: "I like reading books dealing with similar problems that I have to face, so I can get an idea of the actions that other people take." "When I looked back through my journal, I noticed I tend to relate or respond to stories or writings with my own experiences."

As students write, share, discuss, and reflect on their responses, I ask them to consider the following questions: Why do we have the responses we do? Where do they come from? How are our responses similar and different? What makes them so? In what ways are our responses connected to our histories and culture? Do readers respond to a text or an image as a whole or to only part of the text or image? Are responses necessarily connected to the content? What particulars trigger our responses? Why do we resist certain images or parts of texts, even while perhaps assenting to the overall work?

Postmodern theories of language predict, actually, that the language of response, like other language uses, will not be original but will be constructed out of the differential relations of the always already available. Influencing what we can pin down in language, our affective responses are composed of embodied tendencies and incipiencies that also, in part, circulate culturally. Students, in listening to and rereading their own and their classmates' responses, start to see and trace these cultural patterns. "It is the perception of this self-perception, its naming and making conscious, that allows affect to be effectively analyzed," Massumi claims (97).

Focusing on readers' affective responses brings resistance to the center of classroom inquiry. Resistance has long been recognized as an important component of classroom dynamics (Felman, "Psychoanalysis"; Finke; Wolff). Often resistance is theorized from psychoanalytic theory or from social-linguistic theory. Janice M. Wolff uses both in analyzing the "sedimented" ideology her students bring to their reading (485). She argues for "teacherly resistance" (491), consciously enacted in the margins of student writing, concluding that resistance can and does produce further writing. In "Knowledge as Bait: Feminism, Voice, and the Pedagogical Unconscious" Laurie Finke uses psychoanalytic concepts to probe the relation of resistance to silence. Teachers and students enact roles in classroom exchange, she argues. Students "play" the role of student by resisting knowledge, by "adopting a position of ignorance" and transferring to teachers the role of the one who knows (11). Both psychoanalytic and social-linguistic theories call for analysis of students' as well as teachers' resistances, and both point out that resistance is potentially, though not necessarily, productive. It can also be reactive. Worsham argues, for example, that "affective struggle" has "a negative moment" of "pure resistance and repudiation" (140).

In rethinking affect, I do not want to contest these theories of resistance; I want to build on them by adding the ideas of resonance and feedback. I'm thinking of affect as a frictional force, something like electric resistance, that produces energy. Only if our students can be encouraged to identify and return again and again to these frictional moments—and then to interrogate these moments, attempt to analyze them—can we hope for anything more than passive, superficial learning in our literature classrooms. Massumi conceives of these intense resistances as responsive pathways, not yet linguistic memories, not yet thought. Reflection could be considered not as looking inside a self but as a reflexive motion, an infolding or directional return provided by a feedback loop. Teachers can create such a loop by asking for reflective narratives of affective response and resistance. If higher functions like self-reflection are fed back through an affective system that operates by inhibiting or amplifying incipiencies and tendencies, then resistance is necessary to learning, and those higher functions don't really reside, as Massumi puts it, in "a mysterious container of mental entities" but "are present and active in that now not-so-'raw' domain" of the body (90). While affective potential is immanent in the body, it is also unbounded, "in contact with the whole universe of affective potential" (105). Instead of seeing student resistance either as personally defensive and politically reactive or as empowering and politically progressive, this model of the mind in the body suggests that learning is always an embodied process and that no learning can take place without the resistance of feedback loops. The model also suggests that while resistance may be foundational, it is not yet political.

After discussing the social construction of gender, the different consequences of gender location, and our different interested readings based on our own sympathies and locations, I bring up resistance and declare my own—as a feminist—to the conclusion of the story, to the captain's desire for Hannele to submit to him in marriage. And I ask students what elements of the story they resist. Usually they express few resistances to the plot up through the wife's death. Most students don't accept Mrs. Hepburn's death as an accident, but they also think it would be out of character for the captain to have killed her. Yet students don't resist the convenient turn of her death. In the face of their religious beliefs, especially, this seems odd, so I push them to inquire why they don't object. It quickly becomes clear that they want the plot to dispose of the wife so the two lovers can marry and live "happily ever after." Once students uncover their affective responses, they recognize that they want to read the story as a familiar romance narrative. I ask them to consider whether Lawrence manipulates his readers into the position of romance readers—or, as David Ellis suggests in his introduction to the Penguin CUP volume, into the position of readers of lighthearted, sophisticated comedy (something about the urbane tone Lawrence establishes warns us "not to enquire too solemnly into the circumstances of her [the wife's] removal from the scene," Ellis writes [Introduction xx]).

As we move into the second half of the story, we continue to track representational images and characters' affective responses to them. The captain proceeds by following traces of himself ever more dispersed in representations of representations. First, he finds his doll image looking out at him from a shop window in Munich, a "poor little devil" of a figure (117), suggesting a fetish containing a spell or curse. Does this cast Hannele into the role of witch, for making the doll? The shop girl only reluctantly becomes interested in the captain when he points out that he was the model for the doll. He is like a modern-day celebrity; his virtual self as image has affective priority over his actual self. Following the "trace" of the newspaper article (118), the captain buys the still-life painting of his doll with sunflowers and poached egg on toast, then goes to the Tyrol in pursuit of Hannele. She is engaged to marry Herr Regierungsrat, who himself seems a disillusioned illusionist, a representation-making accommodator to postwar conditions. He is planning to write a book; he talks and acts grandly, amid hopelessness. The Tyrol is filled with tourists playing roles, with peasants in costume, with young Germans heartily greeting one another and affecting mythic roles as they march up and down the mountains. "The young Tannhäuser, the young Siegfried, this young Balder beautiful strode climbing down the rocks, marching and swinging with his alpenstock" (131). *The Captain's Doll* portrays the affective history of the rise of Nazism. The climbers in their "ghastly fanged boots" (131) masquerade as mythic folk heroes, exuding a cult of physical superiority amid a disturbing undercurrent of anti-Semitism.

There are several places in the second half of the story where students note their resistance. Many find the anti-Semitism, although historically accurate, objectionable. No longer romance readers, students begin to read against the narrative as critical readers. We discuss whether the tone of the anti-Semitism changes. The self-justifying refrain, "Jews of the wrong sort" (118, 128), carelessly repeated, suggests that anti-Semitism is brazen and pervasive, if self-deceptive (what would "a Jew of the right sort" imply?). The tone seems to change, though, in the scene in which the "Jews from Vienna" (144) pretend to be "elegant Austrians out of popular romances" (145). Here the language is playful, yet while the tone may seem less harsh, the affective beliefs inscribed in the scene reveal hidden traces of anti-Semitic feeling. By likening the Jews to characters in novels, the text aligns them with the dolls and puppets of the story: with Mrs. Hepburn, with the captain's doll, with Herr Regierungsrat, as well as with the German folk dressed in their costumes and parading around the countryside.

Are the Jews being accused of not being realists or of being inauthentic, of pretending to be what they are not? Is the slur class based (the newly rich posturing as old gentry) or race based? We discuss the underlying assumptions of both possibilities. The class-based attack reveals (hidden) circulating affective beliefs about Jewish wealth, and class hatred does figure elsewhere in the story (see, e.g., 128). Even before such attitudes have been owned and understood as feelings, long before they are examined rationally, they do their damage covertly. Historically, their circulation was part of the instrumental strategy for the Nazi consolidation of power. And if this accusation is meant as a racial slur? Stating that the Jews pretend to be Austrian assumes that they aren't and couldn't be and represents the historically accurate trace of an affect that led to horrific consequences: the religious designation, Jew, coming to signify a unified racial construct and the emergence of a race-based concept of nationhood that would demand Jewish expulsion and genocide. Unpacking the affect of this one scene reveals a concrete history, illustrating another important definition of the word *affect*: "a strong feeling having active consequences" ("Affect").

Attending to the affect of representations, then, means not only coming to see, understand, and analyze the affective beliefs embodied in representations but also reflecting on the active consequences of those beliefs in the world. The common complaint against reader response, that it privileges the merely personal, neglects the frequently serious social effects of affect. Focusing on reader responses can be reading responsibly, and it requires us to read differently, not to produce a single authorized interpretation but to attend to variant readings, moments of difficulty and resistance, and possible contradictions in texts. For example, students also point to another reference to Jews in *The Captain's Doll*. The passage below either contradicts or qualifies the others; it suggests that the Jews, as unassimilated difference, check the impulses of the tendencies emerging and circulating in German culture:

> Certainly they were lords of the Alps, or at least lords of the Alpine hotels this summer, let prejudice be what it might. Jews of the wrong sort. And yet even they imparted a wholesome breath of sanity, disillusion, unsentimentality to the excited "Bergheil" atmosphere. Their dark-eyed, sardonic presence seemed to say to the maidenly-necked mountain youths: "Don't sprout wings of the spirit too much, my dears."   (140)

At this point, I often introduce information from Lawrence's life to show how close the story comes to his own experiences and responses (see, e.g., *Letters* 4:

32–33, 54–78). Some students want to explain the anti-Semitism in terms of Lawrence himself—it's there because he was anti-Semitic. This seems a good spot to ask whether we want to interpret the story in relation to Lawrence's life. The point is not to resolve this question but to discuss what is gained and lost by such a move and to consider different purposes and contexts for such arguments. I also mention, or read from, interpretations of *The Captain's Doll* that relate the story to Lawrence's other statements in the 1920s about the proper relations between men and women (see Ellis, Introduction; McDowell).

If students have worked hard enough, doing a number of short writings and discussing and comparing these in small groups and with the whole class, they are by this point aware that affective responses differ but often fall into patterns. Students have come to respect and take seriously the resistances and responses that we analyze and discuss. Do our class, race, or gender positions account for certain patterns? Some students also become enthusiastic about constructing variant interpretations, which we discuss and test. Does the variant reading jibe with the details of the text? What events and details does the reading explain or ignore? What are the consequences of such an interpretation? And we reconsider how our responses to textual details are connected to our own reading habits, social locations, interests, and purposes in using a text.

Resistance produces variant readings. Several years ago, during a small-group activity, four female students working together produced a memorable reading of the end of the story. All four were older, nontraditional students, who, not surprisingly, resisted the standard interpretation, that Captain Hepburn reestablishes his masculinity at the end through the recontainment of Hannele in a marriage to him based on obedience and submission. The students argued that the patterns of containment and release established in the first half of the story through the doll icon and especially its legs are reiterated in reverse in the second half. They connected the image of Hannele's body, particularly her legs, flickering underwater as she swims back to the shore, to the legs of the captain's doll:

> The captain was watching Hannele. With a white kerchief tied round her silky, brownish hair, she was swimming home. He saw her white shoulders, and her white, wavering legs below in the clear water. . . . The captain . . . watched Hannele. She swam slowly and easily up, caught the rail of the steps, and stooping forward, climbed slowly out of the water. Her legs were large and flashing white and looked rich, the rich, white thighs with the blue veins behind, and the full, rich softness of her stooping loins.   (124)

The students compared the color and image patterns here with those of the glacier, which Alexander tries, somewhat humorously and ironically, to conquer. The glacier, they noted, is characterized in terms of coldness, anger (126), darkness, and doom; described in terms of white and blue ("blue-purple intense darkness" [133]); and figured as the powerful and potentially destructive and creative feminine: "Hepburn was happy in that upper valley, that first rocking cradle of early water. He liked to see the great fangs and slashes of ice and snow thrust down into the rock, as if the ice had bitten into the flesh of the earth. And from the fang-tips the hoarse water crying its birth-cry, rushing down" (133). These students argued that the glacier represents pent-up energy, the dangers of capturing and closing off living vitality. The captain tries to dominate and surmount the glacier, but he only partly succeeds. He slides down and is left with burning, bleeding fingers. The students concluded that in ending with the burning of the picture, the story ironically affirms (burn or get burned) the release rather than the recontainment of the captured image.

If students were to read some of Lawrence's other work—say, comments on the education of women in *Fantasia of the Unconscious* or Rawdon Lilly's urgings of obedience and submission at the end of *Aaron's Rod*—and then return to *The Captain's Doll*, they might read the story as a statement about woman's submission to man. A pedagogy of affect does not necessitate making a choice between objective fact and subjective feeling but asks students to attend to Lawrence's shifting views and to reflect on different purposes for and ways of reading. Indeed, without the test of history and the world, there would be no way to critically examine affective beliefs and their consequences. Yet, after many encounters with students' responses to this story, I am now unable to read it without seeing the traces of their variant readings. What good variant readings demonstrate, I think, is the struggle for meaning we are always engaged in. When we make meaning, we grapple with language and formal signifying structures and the aggressive appropriation in our own and others' representations and responses. Struggling to make meaning is not just an issue of language but also an affective struggle of embodied response and resistance essential for becoming an agent of emerging knowledge.

"Learning to Squint" / the Critic as Outlaw: Teaching *Studies in Classic American Literature* as Cultural Criticism

Isobel M. Findlay and Garry Watson

> The law permits me to write, only I must write in a style
> that is not *mine*! I may show my spiritual countenance,
> but I must first set it in the *prescribed folds*! . . . You do
> not demand that the rose should smell like the violet, but
> must the greatest riches of all, the spirit, exist in only *one*
> variety? . . . *Grey, all grey*, is the sole, the rightful colour
> of freedom. Every drop of dew on which the sun shines
> glistens with an inexhaustible play of colours, but the spir-
> itual sun . . . must produce only the *official colour*! [The]
> modesty of genius does not consist in what educated
> speech consists in, the absence of accent and dialect, but
> rather in speaking with the accent of the matter and in the
> dialect of its essence. It consists in forgetting modesty and
> immodesty and getting to the heart of the matter.
> —Karl Marx, "Comments on the Latest Prussian
> Censorship Instruction"

We suggest to students that by the time Lawrence started to conceive his book on American literature in 1917, he must have felt much as Marx felt in 1842. It's true that the wording of the decree to which Marx was responding—according to which, for example, "the censorship should not prevent *serious and modest* investigation of truth, nor impose *undue* constraint on writers" (Marx 111; our emphasis)—was altogether milder than that of "England's official verdict" on *The Rainbow*, which made sure on 13 November 1915 that that novel "would not be available in Britain again for another eleven years." ("It was," pronounced Sir John Dickinson, the magistrate at Bow Street Court, "appalling to think of the harm that such a book might have done. It was utter filth, nothing else would describe it" [Kinkead-Weekes, *D. H. Lawrence* 282].) But still, Marx's words aptly describe something of the frustration Lawrence must also have experienced as a result of his own encounters with different kinds of censorship—including, for example, the unofficial kind that prevented *Women in Love*, which was substantially finished by the end of 1917 (391), from being published until 1920 (in the United States) and 1921 (in England). After all, the law *did*—theoretically, at least—permit Lawrence to write, but only if he did so in a style that was not his own; only if he wrote within the *"prescribed folds."*

Given, then, Lawrence's refusal to do so, one oughtn't to be too surprised to find him in 1917 looking hopefully toward (and getting ready to move to) the United States. Indeed, in retrospect, his interest in the United States almost seems as predictable as T. S. Eliot's departure from the States. Eliot, whose own idea of "educated speech" led him to judge that Lawrence suffered "from a lack . . . of the critical faculties which education should give, and an incapacity for what is ordinarily called thinking" (58), was moving in the opposite direction, toward deeper identification with England. In any case, in January 1917 we find Lawrence explaining that a friend has told him he "could quite easily get over to America if [he] could state a definite work that took [him] over" and he "want[s] to go" (*Letters* 3: 72, 73). In fact, Lawrence maintains that it is now "necessary" for him "to address a new public" and that he therefore "want[s] to go to New York and write a set of essays on American literature, and perhaps lecture" (73). And when we consider the exuberant way in which he outlined his agenda months later, in a letter to Amy Lowell, who he thought could help him (since her brother was president of Harvard and she could "touch the pulse of the *Yale Review* and things like that" [3: 155]), it is easy to believe that the necessity was genuine in the sense that without a public that would allow Lawrence to stretch himself as he does so effortlessly here, he would be lost:

> This is to say, with an eye to material things as well as spiritual: at last I am learning to squint:—I am doing a set of essays on "The Transcendental Element in American (Classic) Literature." It sounds very fine and large, but in reality is rather a thrilling blood-and-thunder, your-money-or-your-life kind of thing: hands-up, America!—No, but they are very keen essays in criticism—cut your fingers if you don't handle them carefully.—Are you going to help me to hold up the *Yale Review* or the *New Republic* or some such old fat coach, with this ten-barrelled pistol of essays of mine, held right in the eye of America? Answer me that, Donna Americana. Will you try to suborn for me the conductor of one of these coaches?—Never say nay.—Tis a chef-d'oeuvre of soul-searching criticism.   (3: 156–57)

Here, we would suggest, is a nice example of a writer inventing his style, his own style (or, rather, one of his styles), as he goes along. And, whatever else is to be said about the combination of irony, irreverence, and sheer fun, this style is strikingly different from—and much more colorful than—the serious, digni-fied, sober, and authoritative style one usually associates with criticism (or, as students are quick to agree, with the kind of academic writing we expect from them).

In the circumstances, then, it seems entirely appropriate to find Lawrence arguing, in the first version of what later became the opening chapter of *Studies in Classic American Literature*, that "[n]ow we must learn to think in terms of difference and otherness" (*Symbolic Meaning* 17)—because if readers do not learn to do this, then the prospects for a writer as genuinely different as

Lawrence are clearly hopeless. But, of course, even if Lawrence had his own
writing somewhere in the back of his mind, what he was mainly thinking of was
the kind of challenging difference and otherness he detected in such "familiar
American classics" as Hawthorne, Poe, Whitman, and Cooper (16), as well as in
such unfamiliar ones as Melville, who was "almost unknown to Americans" at
the time (Arnold 102). It seems likely that this quality of difference attracted
Lawrence to these writers in the first place and made him want to write about
them. So it is important to emphasize to students how odd Lawrence's approach must have appeared, since what seemed most obvious about the first
four of these writers was precisely their familiarity. Hence, no doubt, their
charm, which made it possible to regard them "with indulgence" and to treat
American literature—Harvard offering one course in the subject at the time—
as "a small branch or province of English literature" (Lawrence, *Symbolic
Meaning* 16–17). It seems fair to say that no one before Lawrence had seriously
considered that there might be something so radically new in the writings of
these nineteenth-century Americans that it would be as difficult for cultivated
twentieth-century readers to detect as "the infant cry of Tertullian, Augustine,
Athanasius, the great saints of the African church" must have been for those
"orthodox Romans" who were so intent on "judging from the standards of Virgil
and Cicero and Tacitus" that they failed to perceive the "incipient newness" (16).

So much, then, by way of describing the kind of context we think needs to be
established if one plans to teach *Studies in Classic American Literature* in
courses either on American literature or on cultural theory (to mention only the
two most obvious choices, apart from courses on Lawrence). As for a course on
American literature, Frank Kermode is not exaggerating when he calls *Studies*
"a powerful enough book to change the ways in which a nation reads its classics"
(95)—because, through the influence of the book's "many avowed disciples"
(Colacurcio 488), that is exactly what it has done. Thus, for example, in the
"very personal book," *Love and Death in the American Novel*, Leslie Fiedler
promotes forms of reading that take readers out of "the state of torpor" that is
their "cultural security," while he risks charges of "impiety" and "grossness" and
acknowledges his debt to Lawrence for being "closest to the truth" and for affirming in "an appropriate passion and style" that "duplicity and outrageous-
ness" mark "those American books ordinarily consigned to the children's shelf
in the library" (ix, x, xiii). In a similar vein, while writing about American literature's "agitated desire to make a world in which tensions and polarities are fully
developed and then resolved" (x), Richard Poirier claims that Lawrence wrote
"probably the crucial study of American literature" because "Lawrence was
himself by temperament an 'American' writer working within the conventions
of English literature" (37). And, more recently, in Donald Pease's reexamina-
tion of American Renaissance writings, Lawrence's book once again occupies a
crucial role, this time for the way it allows Pease "to call attention to what is
missing in modern commentary on the period" (48).

It is tempting to say, in the light of Lawrence's influence, that it ought to seem odd *not* to teach *Studies* in a course on America's classic literature of the last century. Leaving this point aside, however, what about the possibility of teaching this book in a cultural theory course? Such a course presents instructors with a splendid opportunity both to teach how "to think in terms of difference and otherness" and to study the book's guiding principle—"Never trust the artist. Trust the tale" (8)—a dictum that "is indeed," as David Lodge has nicely put it, "a cardinal principle of modern hermeneutics, from Freud and Nietzsche to Lévi-Strauss" ("Reading").

To help our students grasp the significance of the distinction Lawrence makes between the "artist" and the "tale," we instructors can direct them first to the argument he mounted in 1925 on behalf of the novel. He claims that in the novel "[e]verything is true in its own time, place, circumstance, and untrue outside of its own place, time, circumstance" ("Morality" 172). Whereas you "can fool pretty nearly every other medium"—"you sweep the ground a bit too clear in the poem or the drama, and you let the human Word fly a bit too freely"— Lawrence insists that "in a novel there's always a tom-cat, a black tom-cat that pounces on the white dove of the Word, if the dove doesn't watch it; and there is a banana skin to trip on; and you know there is a water-closet on the premises. All these things help to keep the balance" ("The Novel" 181). In other words, we can trust the novel for the same reason we can trust the tale: because they are both composed of "art-speech," which Lawrence maintains "is the only truth." While an "artist is usually a damned liar, . . . his art, if it be art, will tell you the truth of his day. And that is all that matters." So when we read a tale or novel like *The Scarlet Letter*, we can choose between what the "artist," that "sugary, blue-eyed little darling of a Hawthorne has to say for himself" and "the impeccable truth of his art-speech" (*Studies* 8). Or as Lawrence put it elsewhere, "All vital truth contains the memory of all that for which it is not true" (*Letters* 2: 247). Students are usually intrigued by but finally unwilling to accept Lawrence's claim that the novel offers a unique opportunity to ensure that "*all* things [are] given full play" ("Why" 198)—they rush to defend other genres against what they see as Lawrence's attack. But it's worth asking them to debate what it would mean for a novelist to resist the temptation to put a "thumb in the scale" and "pull down the balance to his [or her] own predilection" and if the resulting novel or tale might be able to offer us our best access to "vital truth," the kind found only in art-speech and only when we respect "the trembling instability of the balance" and allow it to assert itself ("Morality" 172).

Students should then be asked to consider Lawrence's explanation for why Benjamin Franklin thought the particular version of "a perfect citizen" he concocted would serve as "a pattern to America":

> He thought it simply was the true ideal. But what we *think* we do is not very important. We never really know what we are doing. Either we are materialistic instruments, like Benjamin, or we move in the gesture of

creation, from our deepest self, usually unconscious. We are only the actors, we are never wholly the authors of our own deeds or works. IT is the author, the unknown inside us, or outside us. The best we can do is try to hold ourselves in unison with the deeps which are inside us. And the worst we can do is to try to have things our own way, when we run counter to IT, and in the long run get our knuckles rapped for our presumption.

(*Studies* 26)

This could be an account—decades before the French offered theirs—of the death of the author, and it obviously asks to be pondered in conjunction with Lawrence's advising us to trust the tale rather than the artist. But what on earth are we to make of "IT"?

Students stand a better chance of making sense of Lawrence's answer to this, which Lawrence has already provided in the preceding chapter, if they follow the reasoning by which he arrives at it—a process of reasoning that in turn gives rise to new questions concerning his views on freedom. Lawrence begins by providing an example of the kind of lie that justifies his trying to save the American tale from the American artist. If we were to ask artists why they or their ancestors came to North America, the artists would say, Lawrence assures us, that it was "in search of freedom of worship" (9; just for fun, we survey our students, before they read *Studies*, to see how many answer as Lawrence predicts). That this answer is plainly false, Lawrence claims, is shown by "the history of New England during the first century of its existence." Lawrence gives equally short shrift to the idea that the United States is "the land of the free": "Why, if I say anything that displeases them, the free mob will lynch me, and that's my freedom. Free? Why, I have never been in a country where the individual has such an abject fear of his fellow countrymen." So why *did* the Pilgrims come? "They came largely to get *away* . . . away from themselves. Away from everything. That's why most people have come to America, and still do come" (9). And while that's "all very well" in its way, escaping oneself and one's circumstances "isn't freedom" but a "hopeless sort of constraint. It is never freedom," Lawrence insists, "till you find something you really *positively want to be*" (9–10). Or, if such escape *is* freedom, it is the kind he associates with what he calls the "negative ideal of democracy" (14), which is to say that it is negative freedom.

This, at any rate, is how Pease understands Lawrence's argument in the discussion he devotes to Lawrence early in his book *Visionary Compacts*:

Modern liberalism, the ruling ideology in Lawrence's culture and our own, emphasizes an individual's struggles against the conformity demanded by his fellows, thereby demoting civic covenants to the status of contracts and the "spirit of place" to a cultural superstition. But Lawrence believed modern liberalism to be a form of negative freedom, the desire merely to be free *from* a variety of constraints, whether of European tyrants, constrictive legislation, or, more pervasively, the past itself. (6)

Now while our undergraduates are apt to find freedom from various constraints unproblematically positive, the reason Pease values Lawrence so highly is that he credits Lawrence with carefully distinguishing this "negative freedom from what freedom meant in America's classics" (6). In this respect, Pease argues, Lawrence differs decisively from "most modern interpreters of the American canon," who have tended to see the American classics not as "an *antidote* to the negative freedom at work in modern existence" but as "an *example* of [it]" (7; our emphasis).

As Pease sees it, most critics of the American Renaissance make the mistake of assuming that its writers adhere to a revolutionary mythos that "sanctioned a notion of negative freedom" and "produced citizens who believed in nothing but opposition—to family, environment, cultural antecedents, and even their former selves" (x, ix). His own view is that before the Civil War, "Hawthorne, Whitman, Emerson, and in very different ways Melville and Poe searched for forms of cultural agreement more lasting than the mere opposition to a past sanctioned by the Revolutionary mythos" (ix). Perhaps. But, in any case, students can be asked what evidence Pease could provide to persuade us that this was also Lawrence's view of these writers. He offers a slightly abbreviated version of the following passage, which we quote in full:

> Men are free when they are in a living homeland, not when they are straying and breaking away. Men are free when they are obeying some deep, inward voice of religious belief. Obeying from within. Men are free when they belong to a living, organic, *believing* community, active in fulfilling some unfulfilled, perhaps unrealized purpose. Not when they are escaping to some wild west. The most unfree souls go west, and shout of freedom. Men are freest when they are most unconscious of freedom. The shout is a rattling of chains, always was.   (*Studies* 12)

This may give us Lawrence's definition of "positive freedom" (9), but to what extent can such freedom be found in America's classics? The question seems particularly suited for classes on American literature, and we won't pursue it here. Instead, we propose to say something about two other questions this passage raises.

What does Lawrence mean by an "organic" community? And how should we understand the paradoxical equation of positive freedom and obedience? Both questions seem to us appropriate for students of cultural theory to consider. Let's take the second first. What does Lawrence have in mind when he speaks of "[o]beying from within"? The answer is soon forthcoming, and it simultaneously answers our earlier question about what he means by "IT." According to Lawrence, there are two forms of "IT": an old form that he associates with the "mastery" of "kingship and fatherhood," as these were to be found in the European Renaissance, and a new form that is made up of "the deepest *whole* self of man, the self in its wholeness, not idealistic halfness" (13). With this distinction in mind, we have students look at the following explanation:

> If one wants to be free, one has to give up the illusion of doing what one likes, and seek what IT wishes done.
> But before you can do what IT likes, you must first break the spell of the old mastery, the old IT.
> . . . The true liberty will only begin when Americans discover [the new] IT, and proceed possibly to fulfil IT. (13)

In other words, true, or positive, freedom is to be found when we obey "the deepest *whole* self," understood as a "multitude of conflicting [selves]" (15). Or, at least, this seems to be *one* possible view of this form of freedom, which is associated with the tale, while the other, negative, kind is now associated with the "vulgarly cocksure" (13) artist, or would-be author.

But if, as Pease would have it, Lawrence is to be read as the champion of the kind of positive freedom that can be found only in a community, how should we interpret Lawrence's ironic treatment of Franklin's preoccupation with "social man" (19) and of the idea of "a perfect citizen" (26)? We think this shows not that Pease is wrong but that he is only half right. Lawrence is both a champion and a critic of positive freedom. And, as for negative freedom, there are things he admires in it, as well as things he dislikes about it.

On the question concerning the term "organic" to describe the community Lawrence values, the main point we make in cultural studies classes—besides strongly recommending Anne Fernihough's discussion of the subject in the opening two chapters of her book *D. H. Lawrence: Aesthetics and Ideology*—is that Lawrence could hardly have been using the term to promote what he elsewhere refers to as "the ideal of Oneness, the unification of all mankind into the homogeneous whole"; he makes it quite clear that in his view that ideal "is done away with" ("Democracy" 78). We suggest that it is possible to get some idea of the kind of community he does promote in *Studies* from such claims as the one he makes at the beginning of the chapter on Edgar Allan Poe: "the old white psyche has to be gradually broken down before anything else can come to pass" (70). It's true that much about Lawrence's ideal community remains uncertain; students should discuss, for example, whether or not Lawrence envisages it as a democracy. On the one hand, he insists that "the nucleus of a new society" Cooper dreamed "in his immortal friendship of Chingachgook and Natty Bumppo" is "*beyond* democracy" (59; our emphasis). But, on the other, Lawrence does make a point of ending *Studies* with "the exultant message of American Democracy," the "true democracy, where soul meets soul, in the open road" (187, 186).

Students may conclude that the only thing that is certain here is Lawrence's willingness to embrace change. Thus at the end of the eleventh chapter—which might form the basis of an interesting classroom discussion, particularly when read in conjunction with Saul Bellow's angry attack on Cecil M. Brown's black power reading of it in 1971—we find Lawrence interpreting the sinking of the *Pequod* in *Moby Dick* to mean that "the great white epoch" is "doomed." And students are struck with how he accepts this possibility ("I accept my doom as a sign of the greatness which is more than I am") with equanimity. What interests him—we would say, characteristically—is the question, "what next?" (169).

We close by emphasizing two issues our students frequently raise. First, although *Studies* reveals a radical Lawrence, in it Lawrence discusses no women, working-class, aboriginal, or black writers. While we point out in class that the politics of canon had already by 1920, as Lawrence understood, "shoved down into oblivion" those books that did not replicate the dominant American success story, books that, he argued, needed to be republished (Preface 267), we also admit that the situation today is obviously very different. The work that was done in the 1980s and 1990s has, on the one hand, considerably expanded our sense of the canon while, on the other, simultaneously put in question the very notions of both "classic" and "American" literature (Jay). We ask students simply to reflect on whether they believe Lawrence's *Studies* might help us to read creatively some of the writings that have been recently discovered or rediscovered, and we indicate how the book's theory still challenges and equips us to read attentively at a time when some of *Studies'* basic assumptions—about great literature and the nation—are themselves being challenged.

Second, when we remind students of the frustration Lawrence shared with Marx—as a result of Lawrence's experience of the politics of literacy, of the polarized thinking and restricted repertoire of permissible styles of reading and writing that repressed difference—students consider this frustration in the light of their own writing experience, of the influence of current style manuals, communications texts, and works of cultural criticism that have defined a crisis now thought of in the United States as "the National Problem, the Communications Problem" (Lanham 1). They are quick to see that if questions concerning the extension of literacy—whose literacy and in whose interests?— constituted a defining moment in the struggles for cultural and political authority, legitimacy, and representation that took place both in the nineteenth century (Vincent) and in the modernist era (Bourdieu), something similar might be said of questions concerning the alleged decline of literacy today.

For the sake of convenience, we take E. D. Hirsch as representative of those defining such a cultural crisis. His "ethics of readability" depend on what he calls "the principle of linearity" (136–37). His model of style and readability and his claims to universality rely heavily on gendered notions of directness, penetration, and pointedness (what feminist scholars call masculinist discourse) and on the careful categorization and separation of different classes of writing: the separation of literary and nonliterary, for example, and the careful classifying of forms of legitimate expression. Whose interests, students begin to ask, are served by the separation of expository, argumentative, descriptive, and narrative prose? Whose stories get circulated as the natural and authoritative forms of truth, while, say, aboriginal storytelling becomes a form of folklore or just another perspective? or while gay or feminist or anticolonial voices are represented as forms of political distortion or cultural marginality? In Hirsch's model language that differs from the norm disturbs efficient communication, and social determinants of style are mere background, even though Hirsch purportedly registers a "progressive tendency in the general history of languages" that moves "towards increasing efficiency of communication in all genres of writing" (8). Students find it liberating to realize that Hirsch proposes not a universally true notion of style but a powerful one that has a particular history.

This influential model of style and readability relies for its authority on incompletely disclosed assumptions and renders illegitimate style that diverges from the norm—in other words, the style of much social exchange as well as of the literature we value. The protective colors, *"[g]rey, all grey,"* the de-energizing sameness of a monochrome world, leave no place for the dialect variations of the demotic voice or for Lawrence's "words fly[ing] like dust into your eyes and grit between your teeth, instead of like music into your ears" (*Fantasia* 66). Students identify with Lawrence's frustration over the world's concern with "outside tidiness" in writing and the critics' compulsion to "tidy [him] up": "I can't bear art that you can walk around and admire. . . . An author should be in among the crowd, kicking their shins or cheering them on to some mischief or merriment" (*Letters* 5: 200–01). In contrast to models designed to preserve the status quo and proposed by "the proper high-brow Romans" of our day (*Studies* 7), Lawrence's *Studies* offers instructors an opportunity to demystify reading and writing as a preliminary to reforming them and to opening up risks in both writing and thinking for our students.

The Resurrection of Pan:
Teaching Biocentric Consciousness and Deep Ecology in Lawrence's Poetry and Late Nonfiction

Keith Sagar

When I began to write criticism of Lawrence in the 1950s, in the heyday of F. R. Leavis, nothing could have seemed more natural and virtuous. We were all genuinely excited by Lawrence, who spoke directly to us about our most urgent concerns. Of course, each of us found different things to admire in Lawrence, but one thing we all admired was the refreshing sanity of his attitude toward sex—his willingness to speak frankly about it so that it was no longer a "dirty little secret" (Lawrence, "Pornography" 177). Now, with the advantage of hindsight, we can see that we made too much of sex in Lawrence. It was partly his own fault—he did call himself a "Priest of Love" (*Letters* 1: 493). But we only partly understood what he was saying about sex (we ignored, for example, the religious implications of the word *priest*) and allowed the sexual content to distract us from other equally important elements in his work.

Lawrence contributed to the revolution of the 1960s, but when the dust settled in the 1970s, sex ceased to be the all-important matter it had been. However, teachers of my generation were still teaching Lawrence as though we expected our students to be just as excited by Lawrence on sex as we had been in the 1950s. Our students found it hard to see what all the fuss was about.

Those of us teaching Lawrence in the third millennium need to focus student attention differently. That so much is still being written on Lawrence testifies to his continuing ability to challenge and excite readers. The battle is still raging over whether Lawrence is essentially feminist or antifeminist. Current critical theory has useful contributions to make to the study of Lawrence, and the major novels can still yield new meanings. There is now more interest than ever before in the nonrealistic fiction, the nonfiction, and the poetry. If we are interested in the nature and workings of the creative imagination, Lawrence has as much to offer as Blake or Coleridge. And if we are interested in myth and comparative religion, again there is a rich field in Lawrence.

Lawrence does address himself to the most urgent problems of our world in a way that ought to excite the young, and the great challenge to critics and teachers of Lawrence today is to demonstrate this. It seems to me that the most urgent problem of all is the destruction of the natural environment, and here, of course, Lawrence was far in advance of his time. He was interested in conservation, but much more important is his perception that the prime function of the creative imagination is to reestablish the connection between self and not-self, between the human being and the cosmos. Late in his life, Lawrence speculated that a disastrous change in human consciousness had taken place about 600 BC, when "the immediate connection with the cosmos was broken."

> Man and the cosmos came out of touch, they became, in a sense, enemies. Man set himself to *find out* the cosmos, and at last to dominate it. Henceforth the grand idea was no longer the living sway of the cosmos over man, through the rule of kings. Henceforth it was the dominion of man over the cosmos, through the collective effort of Mind.
>
> (*Apocalypse* 196)

In *Etruscan Places* (written in 1927) Lawrence claims:

> The old religion of the profound attempt of man to harmonize himself with nature, and hold his own and come to flower in the great seething of life, changed with the Greeks and Romans into a desire to resist nature, to produce a mental cunning and a mechanical force that would outwit Nature and chain her down completely, completely, till at last there should be nothing free in nature at all, all should be controlled, domesticated, put to man's meaner uses.   (130)

At different stages of his life, Lawrence used different names for the lost religious consciousness and for the living universe it is in touch with. One of those names was Pan.

All poets, by virtue of the creative imagination, are capable of recovering something of this vision that Lawrence believed to be the only true religion. It is what Blake meant by "Fourfold Vision" and Coleridge by his claim that "we are all one life." Far from dismissing it as lunacy, we now dignify it with such terms as *holistic thinking* (Lawrence defined thought as "a man in his wholeness wholly attending" ["Thought," *Complete Poems* 673], *biocentric consciousness* (which takes life itself rather than the human species to be the primary concern), and *deep ecology*.[1]

The elements of Lawrence's vision were there from the start—his love of nature and his ability to activate the response of others to it, his hatred of urban ugliness and mechanization, his respect for the life of the body and its feelings. But it took his marriage, the break with his past and with England, and the outbreak of war to make these elements cohere into what Lawrence called a metaphysic. In "The Crown" (written in 1915) Lawrence discusses the two eternities—the Christian eternity, which is ahead, and the pagan eternity: "If I look at the eternity behind, back to the source, then there is for me one eternity, one only. And this is the pagan eternity, the eternity of Pan. This is the eternity some of us are veering round to, in private life, during the past few years" (299). This is perhaps Lawrence's first use of Pan in this large sense, not as specific local god or as the sinister, rather Gothic and literary figure of some of his short stories, or as a way of idealizing the virility of some of his heroes, but as all the pagan gods rolled into one, the Pan of pantheism: "Pan, All: what you see when you see in full" (*St. Mawr* 65).

Why a dissatisfaction with the present should have caused Lawrence to veer toward the pagan eternity of Pan is explained by Jung: "The unsatisfied yearning of the artist reaches back to the primordial image in the unconscious which is best fitted to compensate the inadequacy and onesidedness of the present" (*Spirit* 82–83). Jung sees the reactivation of these primordial images as one of the most valuable tasks the artist can perform: "He has plunged into the healing and redeeming depths of the collective psyche" (105). "Whenever the collective unconscious becomes a living experience and is brought to bear upon the conscious outlook of an age, this event is a creative act which is of importance for a whole epoch" (98).

Before the First World War Lawrence's work was anthropocentric, concerned almost exclusively with human relationships, with nature as a background—a lively and prominent background, but a background nonetheless. But the war put a sword through the side of his belief in humanity and a human future. The news from the front and the moral debacle at home combined with his ill health, marital problems, and the persecution of Lawrence and his work by the authorities to produce a misanthropy verging on madness. Lawrence was later to call this period of his life his "nightmare," and the novel that came out of it, *Women in Love*, could well be described as "a nightmare of mental disintegration and spiritual emptiness" (Hughes 130; see below 155–56). The hero, Birkin, imagines a future world cleansed of humanity, "just uninterrupted grass, and a hare sitting up" (127).

What saved Lawrence's sanity in these worst days was his deepening faith in the nonhuman world as a source of health and wholeness. He wrote on 30 April 1915, "What massive creeping hell. . . . It isn't my disordered imagination. There is a wagtail sitting on the gate-post. I see how sweet and swift heaven is. But hell is slow and creeping and viscous . . . as is this Europe now—this

England" (*Letters* 2: 331). In the years that followed, Lawrence's fiction suffered from his loss of belief in people. You can't have novels without people. But you can have poems without people. Lawrence's greatest work of the immediate postwar period was his finest collection of poems, *Birds, Beasts and Flowers*. His misanthropy was in one sense a sickness but in another a healthy purging of his hitherto anthropocentric vision and of what was left of his youthful anthropomorphic attitude to nature. Man now appears on the scene, if at all, as the intruder, the aberration, who in the presence of the sacred can think of nothing better to do than to try to kill it (or, in psychological terms, refuse to acknowledge it, drive it into the seething darkness of the unconscious).

Lawrence had an almost occult insight into the being of nonhuman creatures, even into the spirit of landscapes. But in the best poems of *Birds, Beasts and Flowers*, having gone further than any other English poet into the nonhuman life mode, Lawrence has to acknowledge the essential unknowability of it and stand silent in the presence of gods not his (see "Fish"). One of those gods, Lucifer—brightest of angels, now exiled to the underworld but "due to be crowned again" ("Snake")—Lawrence linked with Pan. According to Jung, when God cast Lucifer out of heaven, he cut off a vital part of himself, his link with the world of the flesh; he repudiated nature itself.

Of course, Lawrence's pantheism was very different from Wordsworth's. Lawrence also believed in impulses from vernal woods (or rather from the bristling, turpentiney, lightning-scarred pine tree outside the door of his New Mexico ranch) but not that such impulses took the form of private moral lessons. As soon as he was able, Lawrence took himself to some of the least comfortable and least processed environments on earth and exposed his pantheism to the spirit of those places—to the lava-streaked slopes of Etna, the steaming jungles of Ceylon, the Australian outback, the deserts of the American Southwest. At last he settled on a ranch high in the New Mexico Rockies. These places are inimical to man, the intruder, whose attempts to import a human scale of values seem both ridiculous and doomed. Man can live in these places, but only man racially and religiously adapted, with the aid of rituals and consciousness evolved over thousands of years. The wilderness does not need man (Wordsworth's landscape loses all meaning without man, whose mind invests it with meaning, virtually creates it).

The challenge for Lawrence was now to find a way to write about people, in fiction, without surrendering the newly won biocentric vision. And what, more than anything else, enabled him to do this was his closeness, from 1922 to 1925, to the Indians of the American Southwest. Here Lawrence found, for the first time, a way of life that seemed to him truly religious:

> To the Indian there is no conception of a defined God. Creation is a great flood, for ever flowing, in lovely and terrible waves. In everything, the shimmer of creation, and never the finality of the created. Never the distinction between God and God's creation, or between Spirit and Matter.

> Everything, everything is the wonderful shimmer of creation, it may be a deadly shimmer like lightning or the anger in the little eyes of the bear, it may be the beautiful shimmer of the moving deer, or the pine-boughs softly swaying under the snow.   (*Mornings* 61)

It is not simply nature worship, for Pan is fierce and bristling, sometimes malevolent, with the power to blast, and "among the creatures of Pan there is an eternal struggle for life, between lives" ("Pan in America" 29). It seemed to Lawrence that among the Indians the oldest Pan, who had died in Europe at the birth of Christ, was still alive. The Indians had rituals to enable them to handle the potent, potentially destructive, energies of Pan. For the European there must be a death to the old false consciousness followed by a resurrection equally painful, to a new and deeper reality—the stark, sordid, beautiful, awe-inspiring reality of Pan, which Lawrence himself was now wrestling with on his pack-rat infested, lightning-scarred, but certainly not god-forsaken ranch in the Sangre de Cristo Mountains. The finest fictional fruit of the new vision was *St. Mawr*, in which the bored heroine, Lou, is persuaded by a stallion as Evangelist to flee the City of Destruction, to renounce Vanity Fair in favor of another, spiritually vibrant world in the Delectable Mountains of New Mexico, there to become a priestess of Pan.

It seemed to Lawrence, however, that the religion of the American Indians had specifically evolved in forms suitable to their race and place. Europeans, with their very different culture and consciousness, could find invaluable clues there but would need a different life mode. In Lawrence's attempt to resurrect Pan in Mexico in *The Plumed Serpent*, Pan is too closely delimited by the spirit of a harsh and bloodthirsty land. As Lawrence began to long for the softer, greener, more feminine spirit of Europe, Pan came to seem atavistic and too oppressively male. Pan's world came to seem like an ending rather than a new beginning. Of Kate, the heroine of *The Plumed Serpent*, Lawrence says, "Her world could end in many ways, and this was one of them. Back to the twilight of the ancient Pan world, where the soul of the woman was dumb, to be forever unspoken" (312).

Lawrence returned to Europe in 1925 to continue his quest and in the spring of 1927 embarked on a tour of the Etruscan sites with his American Buddhist friend Earl Brewster. There, in the flaked and faded frescoes of the underground tombs of the Etruscans, Lawrence found what he had been seeking: evidence that it had been possible, if only for a century or two, before Etruria came under the heel of the Romans, for a European people to get themselves into a right relation with nature. His long pilgrimage had brought him at last to these tombs, and in them he found vivid human life of perfect awareness and relatedness, without the crippling dualism of mind versus body, male versus female, human versus nonhuman, physical versus metaphysical, life versus death. Lawrence's effort, in his last years, is to respiritualize the world. The Etruscans confirmed for him what he had always known: that it is futile hubristic perversity to seek the life of the spirit apart from the given world, for God is in everything that lives and nowhere else.

The female protagonists of so many of Lawrence's fictions are perhaps projections of his own distressed anima, the subjugated feminine component in his psyche, which he is seeking to release from the male hegemony or, rather, to reconcile with a chastened animus. James Hillman argues that the successful introjection of the anima in a man "does not mean acquiring the characteristics of the other gender: rather it means a double-consciousness, mercurial, true and untrue, action and inaction, sight and blindness, living the impossible oxymoron, more like an animal who is at once superbly conscious in its actions and utterly unconscious of them" (125). So, in *St. Mawr*, Lou imagines a regenerate man:

> A pure animal man would be as lovely as a deer or a leopard, burning like a flame fed straight from underneath. And he'd be part of the unseen, like a mouse is, even. And he'd never cease to wonder, he'd breathe silence and unseen wonder, as the partridges do, running in the stubble. He'd be all the animals in turn, instead of one, fixed, automatic thing, which he is now, grinding on the nerves. (62)

Lou is not, however, to be identified with Lawrence. Her romantic expectations still, at the end, compel her to blind herself to the pack rats and the squalor and to cast a glamor over the universe.

The Etruscans worshipped the phallus and the lingam. Lawrence tried to embody this aspect of their consciousness in *Lady Chatterley's Lover*. In letter after letter Lawrence insisted to his friends that *Lady Chatterley's Lover* was a phallic, not a sexual, novel. Few of them, I imagine, could see any difference. What Lawrence was trying to draw attention to was the religious symbolism, for a phallus is the male organ in its function as fertility symbol. Lawrence at this time frequently used the term *phallic consciousness* to mean simply the opposite of mental consciousness—that is, phallic consciousness was any instinct or intuition or desire or knowledge that bypassed the tyranny of the intellect. Phallic consciousness is the opposite of "sex in the head," but it also signifies any premental consciousness, not only sexual. In *A Propos of* Lady Chattterley's Lover, Lawrence tried to explain the distinction:

> If England is to be regenerated [it] will be a phallic rather than a sexual regeneration. For the phallus is only the great old symbol of godly vitality in a man, and of immediate contact.
>
> It will also be a renewal of marriage; the true phallic marriage. And still further, it will be marriage set again in relationship to the rhythmic cosmos. . . . For the truth is, we are perishing for lack of fulfillment of our

greater needs, we are cut off from the great sources of our inward nourishment and renewal, sources which flow eternally in the universe. Vitally,
the human race is dying. It is like a great uprooted tree, with its roots in
the air. We must plant ourselves again in the universe. . . . [The] two great
ways of knowing, for man, are knowing in terms of apartness, which is
mental, rational, scientific, and knowing in terms of togetherness, which
is religious and poetic. The Christian religion lost, in Protestantism finally,
the togetherness with the universe, the togetherness of the body, the sex,
the emotions, the passions, with the earth and sun and stars.

(328, 330, 331)

Of course, since these words were written, science has changed a good deal and
is now centrally concerned with systems, interactions, and interdependencies,
with the "knowing in terms of togetherness" that Lawrence associated primarily
with religious and poetic forms of knowing. The Gaia hypothesis, for instance,
sees the earth as a living organism and "postulates that the physical and chemi-
cal condition of the surface of the Earth, of the atmosphere and of the oceans
has been and is actively made fit and comfortable by the presence of life itself."
In this view, living creatures and the earth cannot be understood apart from
each other; parts of the Earth organism (like the Amazon rain forests) are "vital
organs" that, "if disrupted, could cause the whole Earth (Gaia) to malfunction"
(Devall and Sessions 123, citing Lovelock 121).

Similarly, when Lawrence speaks of sex and marriage, he is thinking of their
connection with the earth; at those moments, he is always also necessarily
speaking of what we have come to call ecology, the relation between people and
the natural environment, which he called the cosmos or circumambient universe. Ecology was, for Lawrence, a matter of a different consciousness, a
wholeness, an atonement, a being in touch. And of all the ways of being in
touch that our civilization has almost killed off, perhaps one that can give us an
inkling of that consciousness is sex.

Any form of regeneration must be preceded by a death—the death of the old
false consciousness, an ego death. The Elizabethans called orgasm the little
death, because it seemed to them the only experience short of actual death
where the soul escapes from the hard shell of self to meet and touch the not
self. The phallus is in this sense a bridge not only between man and woman but
also between self and cosmos. This, then, is what Lawrence meant when he
wrote in 1927 that "the phallus is a great sacred image; it represents a deep,
deep life which has been denied in us, and still is denied" (*Letters* 5: 648). And
in his last work, *Apocalypse*, he wrote, "The phallus is the point at which man is
broken off from his context, and at which he can be re-joined" (181).

Deep ecology in this sense, is Lawrence's primary theme, the underlying
unity and coherence of his entire oeuvre. His contribution to it constitutes his
greatness and his continuing centrality. Even as Lawrence neared death he
poured his life into everything he wrote, into fictions such as *The Escaped Cock*

(formerly known as *The Man Who Died*), where the risen Christ-become-Osiris (a resurrected, humanized Pan) repudiates his former mission and sacrifice in favor of "the greater life of the body" in the phenomenal world: "From what, and to what, could this infinite whirl be saved?" (120).

Lawrence's later fiction contains some of the most wonderful descriptions of the natural world in our literature, but the late poems—like "Demiurge"—are perhaps even more charged with his sacramental vision:

> They say that reality exists only in the spirit
> that corporeal existence is a kind of death
> that pure being is bodiless
> that the idea of the form precedes the form substantial.
>
> But what nonsense it is!
> as if any Mind could have imagined a lobster
> dozing in the under-deeps, then reaching out a savage and iron claw!
>
> Even the mind of God can only imagine
> those things that have become themselves:
> bodies and presences, here and now, creatures with a foothold in creation
> even if it is only a lobster on tip-toe.
>
> Religion knows better than philosophy.
> Religion knows that Jesus was never Jesus
> till he was born from a womb, and ate soup and bread
> and grew up, and became, in the wonder of creation, Jesus,
> with a body and with needs, and a lovely spirit.
>
> (*Complete Poems* 689)

Lawrence's lifelong critique of Christianity was simultaneously an appreciation of its anti-Greek insistence on incarnation and on the sacramental nature of wine, bread, and marriage. He continued to explore these ideas to the end of his life, and their fullest theoretical expression is in *Apocalypse*. In an early draft, Lawrence's vision of the future is bleak:

> The triumph of Mind over the cosmos progresses in small spasms: aeroplanes, radio, motor-traffic. It is high time for the Millennium. And alas, everything has gone wrong. The destruction of the world seems not very far off, but the happiness of mankind has never been so remote. . . . How they long for the destruction of the cosmos, secretly, these men of mind and spirit! How they work for its domination and final annihilation! But alas, they only succeed in spoiling the earth, spoiling life, and in the end destroying mankind, instead of the cosmos. Man cannot destroy the cosmos: that is obvious. But it is obvious that the cosmos can destroy man.
>
> (199, 200)

In the final version of *Apocalypse* Lawrence managed to rekindle a spark of hope. Here are the last words of his last work:

> What man most passionately wants is his living wholeness and his living unison, not his own isolate salvation of his "soul." Man wants his physical fulfillment first and foremost, since now, once and once only, he is in the flesh and potent. For man, the vast marvel is to be alive. For man, as for flower and beast and bird, the supreme triumph is to be most vividly, most perfectly alive. Whatever the unborn and the dead may know, they cannot know the beauty, the marvel of being alive in the flesh. The dead may look after the afterwards. But the magnificent here and now of life in the flesh is ours, and ours alone, and ours only for a time. We ought to dance with rapture that we should be alive and in the flesh, and part of the living, incarnate cosmos. I am part of the sun as my eye is part of me. That I am part of the earth my feet know perfectly, and my blood is part of the sea. My soul knows that I am part of the human race, my soul is an organic part of the great human soul, as my spirit is part of my nation. In my own very self, I am part of my family. There is nothing of me that is alone and absolute except my mind, and we shall find that the mind has no existence by itself, it is only the glitter of the sun on the surface of the waters.
>
> So that my individualism is really an illusion. I am part of the great whole and I can never escape. But I *can* deny my connections, break them, and become a fragment. Then I am wretched. What we want is to destroy our false, inorganic connections . . . and re-establish the living organic connections with the cosmos, the sun and earth, with mankind and nation and family. Start with the sun, and the rest will slowly, slowly happen.   (149)

Wordsworth himself was unable to sustain his pantheism against his adulation of "the mind of man." In the year of Wordsworth's death, 1850, Tennyson published *In Memoriam*, with its prophetic rejection of Darwinian nature:

> Arise and fly
> The reeling Faun, the sensual feast;
> Move upward, working out the beast,
> And let the ape and tiger die.
> (465)

Perhaps Earl Brewster had quoted these lines to Lawrence when Lawrence replied:

> But the point is I don't *want* the tiger superseded. Oh, may each she-tigress have seventy-seven whelps, and may they all grow in strength and

shine in stripes like day and night, and may each one eat at least seventy
miserable featherless human birds, and lick red chops of gusto after it.
Leave me my tigers, leave me spangled leopards, leave me bright cobra
snakes, and I wish I had poison fangs and talons as good. I *believe* in
wrath and gnashing of teeth and crunching of cowards' bones.

(Letters 3: 719)

Lawrence was pushed to such shrillness by his sense that both religion and
rationalism were ranged against him. In 1894 T. H. Huxley claimed in the
"Prolegomena" to *Evolution and Ethics* that the purpose of education was "the
application of [man's] intelligence to the adaptation of the conditions of life to
his higher needs." To this end he must be "perpetually on guard against the cosmic forces, whose ends are not his ends, without and within himself." He concluded, "That which lies before the human race is a constant struggle to
maintain and improve, in opposition to the State of Nature, the State of Art"
(44–45). In Lawrence's adulthood that was still the received wisdom and had
become the basis of our entire industrial society. Pantheism meant either something archaic or something to do with the Wordsworthian pieties. It had nothing to do with the realities of modern life—and was certainly not a serious
option as a religion for the twentieth century. Lawrence took it upon himself to
make it so. It was a Herculean task at a time when, as Lawrence writes in *St.
Mawr*, nature seemed to be disappearing under the "century-deep deposits of
layer upon layer of refuse" (151), when the machine seemed to have triumphed
utterly, when H. G. Wells and the majority for whom he spoke complacently assumed that history was the story of humanity's progress toward the triumph of
mind over both nature and human nature.

Perhaps this notion of history was still received wisdom as recently as 1969,
when Patricia Merivale ended her book *Pan the Goat-God: His Myth in
Modern Times* with the statement that "later writers [than Lawrence] have
taken no interest in the Pan-Christ dialectic, or the closely related theme of the
death of Pan, or the Romantic transcendental Pan" and that "Pan is unlikely to
become a literary fashion or a public myth again" (218, 228). Lawrence is assumed to be the last Romantic in this respect, the last writer to try to take Pan
seriously. Yet within a year Ted Hughes, reviewing a book on ecology, was in-
voking Pan in exactly Lawrence's sense:

> When something abandons Nature, or is abandoned by Nature, it has lost
> touch with its creator, and is called an evolutionary dead-end. According
> to this, our Civilization is an evolutionary error. Sure enough, when the
> modern mediumistic artist looks into his crystal, he sees always the same
> thing. He sees the last nightmare of mental disintegration and spiritual
> emptiness. . . . But he may see something else. He may see a vision of the
> real Eden, "excellent as at the first day," the draughty radiant Paradise of
> the animals, which is the actual earth, in the actual Universe: he may see

> Pan, . . . the vital, somewhat terrible spirit of natural life, which is new in every second. Even when it is poisoned to the point of death, its efforts to be itself are new in every second. This is what will survive, if anything can. And this is the soul-state of the new world. But while the mice in the field are listening to the Universe, and moving in the body of nature, where every living cell is sacred to every other, and all are interdependent, the housing speculator is peering at the field through a visor, and behind him stands the whole army of madmen's ideas.   (129–30)

Though the madmen are still at the helm, Gaia is now a public myth, a public reality, again—"[b]ecause this is what we are seeking: something that was unthinkable only ten years ago, except as a poetic dream: the re-emergence of Nature as the Great Goddess of mankind, and the Mother of all life" (Hughes 133). What our students will see—if we teach the full range of Lawrence's work, not just the fiction but also the poetry and the late nonfiction—is that Lawrence may be at the beginning, not the end of an era, and what is now called deep ecology is but the latest name for Pan.

NOTE

[1] The term *deep ecology* was coined by Arne Naess in 1973 and taken up by George Sessions (and many others). In *The Turning Point*, Fritjof Capra comments on the distinction drawn by Sessions between deep and shallow ecology:

> Whereas shallow environmentalism is concerned with more efficient control and management of the natural environment for the benefit of "man," the deep ecology movement recognizes that ecological balance will require profound changes in our perception of the role of human beings in the planetary ecosystem. In short, it will require a new philosophical and religious basis. Deep ecology is supported by modern science, and in particular by the new systems approach, but it is rooted in a perception of reality that goes beyond the scientific framework to an intuitive awareness of the oneness of all life, the interdependence of its multiple manifestations and its cycles of change and transformation. When the concept of the human spirit is understood in this sense, as the mode of consciousness in which the individual feels connected to the cosmos as a whole, it becomes clear that ecological awareness is truly spiritual.   (458)

In *Deep Ecology*, Bill Devall and Sessions cite Lawrence's "Pan in America" as a source of the deep ecology perspective (83) and mention (213n4) the essay's reprinting (as "The Death of Pan") in Lorne Forstner and John Todd's collection of ecophilosophical essays.

Lawrence and Rites of Passage

Langdon Elsbree

I teach Lawrence by using the three-stage model of ritual found in Arnold Van Gennep's *The Rites of Passage*. (I particularly rely on chapters 1, 2, 3, and 6.) This paradigm, supplemented by Victor Turner's later development of it, is one excellent way of understanding Lawrence, whether in a semester-long seminar on him, a survey of British writers, or a short unit.[1] While Van Gennep was by no means the first scholar to study the rituals of traditional societies, he was the first to order a vast body of ethnographic accounts of such rites into an intelligible pattern, enabling anthropology and other disciplines to move beyond the study of individual rituals to the study of ritual itself as a phenomenon. In bare outline, his model is simple: (1) the separation of persons or groups from the social order, (2) the transitional or liminal passage, and (3) the incorporation of persons and groups back into the social order, with a new status or identity.

In one of his most suggestive passages, Van Gennep writes, "For groups, as well as for individuals, life itself means to separate and to be reunited, to change form and condition, to die and to be reborn. It is to act and cease, to wait and rest, and then begin acting again, but in a different way" (189). Van Gennep's description of this cycle also describes a fundamental ideal of growth throughout Lawrence's fiction and poetry. In fact, in Lawrence's work the failure to change form and condition, to die and be reborn, to act and rest, and then to begin acting again but in a different way usually occasions a diagnosis of whatever it is that retards, warps, inhibits, or destroys.

Whatever the rebirth—Mabel Pervin's in "The Horse-Dealer's Daughter," Paul Morel's defiance of extinction in the final lines of *Sons and Lovers*, or the speaker's in *Look! We Have Come Through!*—Lawrence builds toward this mysterious and essentially religious phenomenon, including the trauma, suffering, and uncertainties about the future that accompany it. By contrast, whether it is the speaker's fear of "one of the lords of life" in "Snake" (*Complete Poems* 351), Gerald Crich's paralysis and dying in the snow and ice in *Women in Love*, or Elizabeth Bates's bitter realization of failed connection with her dead husband in "Odour of Chrysanthemums," Lawrence stresses the conditions that result in denial, loss, and psychic self-mutilation. Common to these examples is Lawrence's foregrounding of passages and transitions, where the drama of change embraced or rejected is the test of whatever is vital or deadening in persons, classes, and cultures. Lawrence characteristically employs the liminal or middle stage of ritual, where persons and groups are no longer one thing but are not yet another. It is the stage where the values at stake and the implications of choice and new identities emerge and where transformation is either embraced or retreated from. The liminal is Lawrence's chosen turf because it alone focuses on the conditions of change.

While Van Gennep believed that the liminal stage was central to rites of passage (as the stage where the values at stake defined whatever was positive or negative in the self), the first stage—separation—is usually the most obvious to an outside observer. Whether marked by the shaved heads and prescribed garb of military rookies (or novitiates of a religious order) or by the orientation period for college freshmen, this stage makes the decisive break between a person or persons and the "normal," or given, social order. However, once the break has occurred, we find ourselves—often immediately—in the second stage. In Lawrence's work, the move from first stage to second is especially swift. Thus in the opening chapter of *The Rainbow*, "How Brangwen Married a Polish Lady," Tom is separated from the usual life around him by his drifting, drinking, and loneliness; Lawrence initiates the second phase, liminality, when Tom sees Lydia Lensky and exclaims, "That's her" (29). Similarly, in "The Woman Who Rode Away" Lawrence divides the "Californian girl from Berkeley" (40) from her uxorious, work-driven husband, her family, and their ranch when a visitor wonders aloud about the Indians living in the mountains, virtually simultaneously initiating the woman's quest to visit the Chilchui.

In Lawrence, the second stage is often a quest or journey, one of the purest examples of the liminal. Lawrence typically makes the separation quickly so that he can get into the dramatic issues, as in the opening stanza of "The Ship of Death," beginning "Now it is autumn" and leading up to "And it is time to go" (*Complete Poems* 716). Even when the narrative is not precisely a quest, few of Lawrence's major contemporaries have a more sharply honed talent for separating the protagonists and initiating the rite of passage that becomes their life or a significant part of it—note, for instance, in *Sons and Lovers*, the rapidity with which Lawrence isolates Gertrude and Walter Morel at the dance where they meet and fall in love.

Liminality is the most complex of the three stages in Lawrence's fiction, and, for that matter, in most fiction. Betwixt and between, identity in flux, the person or group traverses the passage—or fails to for reasons that become the grounds for the analysis by narrative. In the homology between rites of passage and narrative structures, the liminal is the threshold between past and future. (A fairly recent historical development, adolescence as a social, psychological, and legal category, is one obvious instance of the liminal.) In Lawrence especially, liminality is the medium of change. By liberating characters to be other than they have been, it directs their energies toward this otherness; thus when Tom encounters Lydia he is not only startled out of his solitude but also led by her otherness toward courtship and marriage.

Put in other terms, the liminal is the space where authorial imagination finds opportunities for freedom and play. These opportunities manifest themselves in Lawrence's criticism, a genre not always associated with liminality. In *Studies in Classic American Literature*, for example, while sorting out his ambivalence about the contrary impulses in Whitman's poetry of merging and death on the one hand and democratic openness to life on the other, Lawrence suspends the finality of judgment as he moves back and forth between these impulses. This liminal space allows Lawrence to test each impulse and his thoughts about it while discovering his case for Whitman's being the truly representative American poet, the only begetter of the heroic message of American life and letters. Only at the end, when Lawrence concludes his argument, does he complete his own ritual passage, his encounter with Whitman (187). Even in the essay on *The Scarlet Letter*, where Lawrence has made up his mind about the novel (wrongly, I think)—"a sort of parable, an earthly story with a hellish meaning" (89)—he pauses to open up a liminal space and play with the possible meanings of the letter: "Adulteress. Alpha. Abel, Adam. A. America" (95). In other critical contexts, such as those of "Why the Novel Matters" and "Morality and the Novel," Lawrence exalts the novel's liminality, its spaciousness to accommodate all living relationships and moments, its freedom in principle to give all things full play, provided the novelist avoids rigging things by parti pris.

There is often a sinister or minatory atmosphere in the liminal settings where Lawrence chooses to accelerate ritual passages into trials by combat, frenzied contests, virtually apocalyptic visions of death in life or of death as the price of life. In *The Fox*, Bailey Farm, a sanctuary Banford and March struggle to preserve, is violated by Henry and the escalating, unequal battle for possession of March, his monomaniacal love finally winning her person if not her soul. In "The Rocking-Horse Winner," the home of the child Paul is haunted by voices saying, "There must be more money!" (230); the climactic ritual passage occurs in the child's bedroom, his liminal space, where his mother discovers him obsessively rocking and driving himself to pick the derby winner, only to die shortly afterward of brain fever. In *Women in Love*, the Alps become the liminal isolation, the cold beauty of whiteness and apartness, where Gerald, Gudrun, Birkin, and Ursula complete the long transitional passages they have made separately and together. Heightening the deadly battle of wills between Gerald and Gudrun is Loerke, a nihilistic spirit, a liminal figure of despairing freedom who survives without illusions or human connections, with only the rituals of his work.

But other modes of liminality in Lawrence's fiction are, initially at least, exhilarating and liberating. In "Tickets Please," the excitement, danger, and romance of the tram lend freedom and pride to Annie and the other women conductors who ritually thrive on controlling hymn-singing colliers, cheaters evading the ticket machine, and other challenges to their authority. In *The Rainbow*, the Marsh Farm is the liminal space where Anna Brangwen flourishes during her childhood. Once Lydia and Tom's child is born, Anna no longer has the anxious burden of supporting her mother and can begin her passage of becoming an independent, playful, and forgetful little girl.

In these and similar liminal spaces, one meets a Lawrence who relishes the thrust and parry of wit and idiom and who gives free play to characters absorbed by and growing through the felt textures, routines, and surfaces of daily life. Too often slighted by critics, his acute comic eye celebrates unconstrained human energies and vitality. Frequently (perhaps too frequently), the apocalyptic lurks just offstage—in "Tickets Please," Annie and the other women John Thomas has used turn into maenads when they attack him and seem bent on dismembering him, punching his ticket, so to speak. But the affirming liminal spaces demonstrate a different side of Lawrence's sensibility, a side that, though deeply wounded by the First World War and its disruptive social consequences in England and elsewhere, was never entirely repressed. To read *Etruscan Places* (based on his experience in 1927 but published posthumously) is to discover this side of Lawrence in his wholehearted love of the ritualized, now long vanished Etruscan civilization.

Incorporation, the final stage of ritual passage, would appear to have a simplicity like that of separation. The conferring of the PhD, the awarding of varsity letters, the commissioning of officers are all public ceremonies signaling a person's completion of a ritual passage and inclusion, with altered status or identity, in a group. However, this third phase tends to be more complicated in narrative structures than in rites of passage. Incorporation provides the symbolic frame indicating that the action of the passage is over and that a new relationship or equilibrium exists between the person and the group, but narratives often thwart this expectation. The claims of the individual and the social order may be at odds; the social order may prove a dungeon with no escape. There may not even be a social order to incorporate the person. Alternatively, the person may be overwhelmed and left numb by the passage itself (like Lydia long after the death of her first husband in *The Rainbow*). For Lawrence, this last stage is far more problematic than the first two. Often he concludes with the liminal still intact, and we are left with two characters—like Ursula and Birkin in *Women in Love*, the priestess and the Christ figure in "The Man Who Died," or Connie and Mellors in *Lady Chatterley's Lover*—who are transformed, but hardly within a community, more in the limbo that liminality sometimes is.

Given Lawrence's belief that the process of living and growing has no end beyond itself, his aversion to closure makes artistic and philosophical sense. It was enough that some of his couples could say the equivalent of *Look! We Have Come Through!* even as other unknown passages remained ahead.

Van Gennep's concern with earlier rites as well as Turner's with modern forms of liminality and the postmodern "liminoid" create a context in which to place Lawrence's search for adequate ritual (Turner, *Ritual* 52–55).[2] I take Lawrence's preoccupation with ritual as given. Ritual informs his intuitions about the human body as the primary source of our knowledge of the sacred. It underlies his sensitivity to customs—of the English class system, of Hopi dancers, or of Mexican Indians on market day—and to the spirit of place. One has only to recall his days in Italy, England, the American Southwest, Ceylon, and Australia to feel the presence in his works of the quest for renewal by ritual. But however fascinated Lawrence was with traditional societies and their rites, he did not finally believe them to be adequate for his time: "The truth of the matter is, one cannot go back. Some men can: renegade. But Melville couldn't go back . . . and I know now that I could never go back. Back towards the past, savage life" (*Studies* 144). Later, as a sympathetic concession, he adds, "We can take a great curve in their direction, onwards. But we cannot turn the current of our life backwards . . . towards their soft warm twilight" (145). Analogies between their rituals and ours, yes; the exploration of earlier rites and myths, most decidedly yes. But the end of such exploration for Lawrence must lead back to the present—the "magnificent here and now of life in the flesh [that] is ours, and ours alone, and ours only for a time" (*Apocalypse* 149).

Briefly put, Lawrence assumes that the liminal is the contemporary crisis of growth or death, and his goal is the discovery of ways to transcend rootless modern liminality and ossified social forms. Without question, he was often drawn in his more patriarchal and dogmatic moments to conservative rituals and myths, dying gods, undying archetypes, and the stasis of unchanging models—the stuff of James Frazer's *The Golden Bough* and the like.

Alien cultures, their rituals and symbols, offered Lawrence one kind of liminality. Turning to his own roots, the English materials, we find that, from *The Rainbow* on, a main theme concerns traditional rites of passage. They can be empty, imprisoning, or dying. The necessary rupture with the past creates the liminality in the lives of Ursula, Birkin, and many others. This break produces uncertainty and fear (Ursula's decision to marry Anton). It can drive persons to fossilized retreats and roles (Anton to the military and India). But it also occasions the possibility of new freedom and being (Ursula's vision of the future at the end of *The Rainbow*). To exorcise the deadly rites of traditional class, sexual, and social identities, Lawrence typically devises his own rites and passages, often the most energized and mythopoetic places in his fiction. These include Tom Brangwen's death, the harvesting and dance scenes, and Ursula's confrontation with the horses in *The Rainbow*; Birkin and Gerald's wrestling, Gudrun's cataleptic writhing before the cattle, and Gerald's extinction in the snow in *Women in Love*; the face probing in "The Blind Man"; the trial by combat in *The Fox*; the deaths and rebirths enacted at the pond and later at the house in "The Horse-Dealer's Daughter"; and the priestess of Isis anointing the scarred wounds of "The Man Who Died." This list is merely indicative, not inclusive.

Lawrence's primary achievement in these and other such ritual sequences is creating a liminal space, a set of narrative brackets, where characters may touch their unrealized selves and one another. This liminality is frequently marked by violence, an essential feature in many of Lawrence's ritual transitions. As the story "You Touched Me" suggests, for someone to admit to being touched by another person means recognizing a double violation.[3] The first is the violation of the class, social, or sexual conventions one has tried to live within, what Lawrence calls "the walled security, and the comparative imprisonment, of the established convention" ("Study of Thomas Hardy" 21). The second violation is the shock of the unknown—coming into consciousness with the other person, existing in the liminal present, and facing the unimaginable transitions of the future. We see this, for instance, in the last lines of "The Horse-Dealer's Daughter" when Fergusson tells Mabel "I want you, I want you" but does so with "that terrible intonation which frightened her almost more than her horror lest he should *not* want her" (152).

In effect, Lawrence's rhythms, language, and narrative dynamic naturally assume the form of ritual progression. He often constructs or climaxes his shorter fictions with a single ritual of touching, for instance, Elizabeth's washing the body of her dead husband while she faces the waste of the past and the grimness of her future in "Odour of Chrysanthemums," the mutual violations in "The Blind Man" when Maurice and Bertie touch each other's faces, and the violent struggles in "Tickets Please" and "Samson and Delilah." In the novels, individual rituals punctuate the longer liminal passages of the major characters toward life or death. At times, substantial parts of or whole chapters build around a single ritual, as in "The Cathedral" and the final chapter (the horses) in *The Rainbow* and in "Sisters" (the wedding), "Rabbit," and "Gladiatorial" in *Women in Love*.

In short, the imaginative creation of rites that expel the deadly or enhance the vital is the artistic challenge Lawrence took on, even during the last years of his life. He acknowledges the necessity of "ancient forms" for daily life when, in *A Propos of* Lady Chatterley's Lover, he says that only through the rituals of dawn and noon; of kindling fire and pouring water; of the moon, seasons, procession and dance, the great events of the year, can we return to "vivid and nourishing relation to the cosmos and the universe" (329)—while simultaneously acknowledging that ancient forms alone cannot suffice.

What are the limitations or risks of relying on Van Gennep's model? I have encountered at least two. The first is the danger of the model's becoming an empty formula that levels all Lawrence's works and makes them boringly alike. Of course, any perspective risks this. Van Gennep's model should be seen not as a totalizing approach but as one organizing principle in much of Lawrence's work—not in all of it.

The second danger is the nullification of whatever is dubious, objectionable, or even odious in Lawrence—for instance, some of his views about power, whether in sexual relations or political leadership. But to find reprehensible his uses of the rituals of power in, say, *The Plumed Serpent* still necessitates the recognition of their presence (hard to escape in any event).

One can avoid these dangers in the classroom simply by clarifying Van Gennep's model and applying it to a few works but considering other Lawrence works without reference to it. Further, if students choose to work with Van Gennep's model in their papers for the course, urge them to show how and why the model fits by specifying the particular context, dramatic conflict, and values at stake. Van Gennep is not equally relevant to all Lawrence's interests by any means; thus some degree of pluralism is not just literary tactfulness but also honesty.

An anthropology originating in Van Gennep (and reaching fruition in Turner) provides us with effective ways to understand the challenge Lawrence confronts us with in his criticism and poetry as well as in his fiction—the challenge to transform ourselves and to face the violence to body and soul that transformation may require. From the time Lawrence began his own liberation, in his rewriting of *Sons and Lovers*, until his death, he and Frieda, living uncertainly and marginally on three continents, sustained one long ritual passage where liminality was the condition of his freedom. His continuing quest in both his life and his art resisted closure in its various forms. For Lawrence closure meant incorporation into the existing social order. And that, for him, meant tragedy.

NOTES

[1]See Elsbree, chapters 1–4, for discussions of the homology between rite and story and of Van Gennep and liminality. I have drawn on these chapters for this essay.

[2]As the indexes in most of Turner's major works show, Turner honors his indebtedness to Van Gennep and builds on his pioneering work. What the index in *From Ritual to Theatre* does *not* show is Turner's indebtedness to Lawrence; but Lawrence is referred to by name (13), his concept of "man alive" is mentioned (13, 23, 46), and his concept of the "trembling instability of the balance" is alluded to (44). See also Turner's discussion of "communitas" (41–45) and "social drama" (9–12), both applicable to Lawrence's fiction. Two of Turner's many other books should also prove useful: *Dramas, Fields, and Metaphors* and *The Anthropology of Performance*.

[3]In his introduction to *"England, My England" and Other Stories*, Bruce Steele retitles "You Touched Me" as "Hadrian" because he believes Lawrence preferred the latter (xlii). I have retained "You Touched Me," however, because the story was first published with this title and because the title so effectively epitomizes one of Lawrence's central preoccupations.

Sea and Sardinia: If You Can
Teach Only One Lawrence Text

Howard Mills

I've been spoiled rotten. For nearly thirty years at an English university and in three of four exchange years on American campuses, I've been able to teach single-author courses on Lawrence—at the graduate and undergraduate levels. So it will seem ungrateful if I look back on the pitfalls of such courses, especially when (as usual) they are constructed chronologically. But the positive and major part of this essay explains why any survey of Lawrence's works would do well to give prominence to, and even begin with, the Italian travel books and to give priority to the one that is the middle of the trio and comes from the middle of Lawrence's oeuvre: *Sea and Sardinia*. I suggest further why that work could effectively represent Lawrence in any course that can find room for only one of his books.

The surveys of Lawrence I've taught have always included the three travelogues reprinted in Anthony Burgess's omnibus paperback *D. H. Lawrence and Italy* (first published in the United States in 1972).[1] The first and last of the travelogues were endowed with central or pivotal roles by virtue of their positions in Lawrence's development: *Twilight in Italy* as an early stepping-stone from *Sons and Lovers* to the wartime fiction, *Etruscan Places* a late pointer to *Lady Chatterley's Lover* (the concept of touch) on the one hand and to the author's death on the other. But although one of my coteachers, David Ellis, early wrote about *Sea and Sardinia* as a test case for reading Lawrence on Lawrence's own terms ("Reading"), we were long traditional enough about what was mainstream Lawrence to entitle a seminar on Lawrence's "Introduction to [Maurice Magnus's] *Memoirs of the Foreign Legion*" as an interlude in the onward-going purposiveness of our program, and I fancy we treated the Sardinia book similarly.

Now that I've come to find the idea of an author's own ongoing purposiveness bogus and constricting, I believe that even the travel books, written in the first person and drawing on the author's actual travels, can best be appreciated by ignoring cross-references to the author's life or personality. So what I'd do today in teaching Lawrence is break free of both chronology and biographical context by starting right off with *Sea and Sardinia*. I follow the view of Burgess's centenary study (1985) that "it is the outstanding travel book, the most charming work he ever wrote, conveying the taste and colour of life with that daring in which Lawrence excelled" and—therefore—"by far the best introduction to his oeuvre" (*Flame* 143). The recent biography by Mark Kinkead-Weekes (long another of my coteachers) agrees: "This is one of the most delightful of Lawrence's books, to which those who have never read him (and for that matter those prepossessed against him) should be sent first of all" (*D. H. Lawrence*

622). In promoting *Sea and Sardinia* to the start of the course, I'd hope that its charm, daring, and lack of "a palpable design on us" (Keats's phrase for Wordsworth's overdidactic poems [832]) would color students' approaches to other texts. My further motive for discussing it first parallels Lawrence's own motive for going to Sardinia: the book, like the country, offers what Burgess calls an "unspoilt pocket of strangeness" (Introduction ix). Although much of the book's comedy derives from the ways the narrator was proved wrong, he went to Sardinia because it "is like nowhere. . . . [It] has no history, no race, no date, no offering. . . . [It] lies outside; outside the circuit. . . . [T]here is an un-captured Sardinia still. It lies within the net . . . but it isn't landed yet. And the net is getting old and tattered. A good many fish are slipping through" (3). One thinks of Lawrence's maxim about nailing down the novel and Catherine Carswell's reminder that Lawrence "is like Joey in the Punch and Judy Show. He will not 'stay put'" (*Savage Pilgrimage* viii). *Sea and Sardinia* doesn't bear its chronological-biographical context heavily on its back.

"Comes over one an absolute necessity to move," the book's first sentence tells us (1). If academic critics, comfortably settled in their department chairs, scold Lawrence for restlessness ("Why can't you sit still like I do?"),[2] students are immediately engaged. And it's the young who respond also to stylistic mo-bility—to the opening chapter being on the move in its modes of writing. They'll see that the two-page opening rhapsody on Etna gives way to rapid mut-terings as guidebooks are flipped through ("Where then? Spain or Sardinia . . . Sardinia then. Let it be Sardinia" [3]). Then the muttered rehearsal of things to be done twixt sleep and wake "at this unearthly hour" constantly fuses with the poetic glimpses out of the corner of an eye more intent on the clock, the tea-kettle, and the train schedule. Thus: "Under the lid of the half-cloudy night sky, far away at the rim of the Ionian sea, the first light, like metal fusing. So swallow the cup of tea and a bit of toast. Hastily wash up . . ." (4). ("Stream of con-sciousness?" ventures someone who's just started *Ulysses* and thinks of Bloom rescuing the burnt kidney.)

It's then a small step to see how the chapter's so-called ideas—or, rather, its voluble, volatile narrator's—don't sit still but slip, slide, even perish. Even the one that most appalls students, the advocacy of a swift hanging for the hangdog-faced convict, is swiftly undermined: "seeing the pair of convicts, I must re-member again Oscar Wilde on Reading platform, a convict. What a terrible mistake, to let oneself be martyred by a lot of canaille. A man must say his say" (11). As for the grand opening idea of Etna, which tends to dominate published accounts of the book, it subsides into a kind of whimsy. Are we invited to take seriously what Burgess calls the "good bad Lawrentian logic" (*Flame* 146) of this: the Sicilians emit "a relentless physical familiarity that is quite bewildering to one not brought up near a volcano"? The dodginess increases as Lawrence adds, "This is more true of the middle classes than the lower," and then pushes his luck with, "The lemon-trees, like Italians, seem to be happiest when they are touching each other all round"—an observation surrounded by Marvellian surrealism ("Women, vague in the orchard under-shadow, are picking the lemons, lurking as if in the undersea") and by the pure whimsy of a mind idling as the journey drags out ("So many lemons! Think of all the lemonade crystals they will be reduced to! Think of America drinking them up next summer" [8]). Then comes a blank, a typographical gap, and perhaps a sleep, before the passenger sits up again and takes notice of a different stretch of the line. In the journal-like layout of this book, blank spaces separate entries of anything from five lines to five pages, the blanks representing a lapse of time or interest after which the mind gets up and sets off in a fresh direction. The thing to look for is not an authorial expression of ideas but the narrator-traveler's rhythm of rumination. The central part of this opening chapter is best thought of as a railway poem like Philip Larkin's "Dockery and Son" or similarly described train journeys in *A Passage to India*—a representation of how the mind works, or idles, during passive travel. (A brilliant description of this effect occurs in Geoff Dyer's *Out of Sheer Rage* [45–46].)

I've been running together excerpts and observations that have come up in several groups' responses to one seminar exercise, a cooperative analysis of the opening chapter. Who can say whether such analysis is a matter of pulling the chapter together or pulling it apart? Behind the onward movement of a day's journey, the unifying principle seems to be disunity. Anaïs Nin pointed out the paradox by saying that "Lawrence has no system, unless his constant shifting of values can be called a system: a *system of mobility*" (14).

While I referred just now to cooperation, discussion is more often combative. For an average group contains both totalizers and disintegrationists,[3] those who pull together and those who pull apart, and the life of a discussion comes from setting them against each other and then sitting back to enjoy the fireworks. An appropriate exercise to this end is to ask each student to contribute a paragraph that he or she feels reflects some central thread or recurrent characteristic of the book; the others will provide some context—or contrasts. One student felt she'd struck thematic pay dirt by choosing the second paragraph of "To Nuoro"—"The roads of Italy always impress me" (121). A totalizer could refer us to a consonant, equally resounding affirmation back in chapter 1: "The Italians have made wonderful roads and railways" (13). But a disintegrationist's eye might run down that early page and quote the paragraph on the interminable delays of the *coincidenza* at passing places on the single-track railroad. ("Clerks away ahead joyfully chalk up our hours of lateness. . . . All adds to the adventurous flavour of the journey, dear heart" [13]). We return to the Nuoro chapter, and somebody points out that such all-inclusive talk of Italy and its roads menaces the elsewhere affirmed polarity of Sardinia versus either Sicily or the Italian mainland. Then turn the page and the admiration crumbles anyway. Will roads and railways crumble away, the narrator muses—and answers himself with "I rather hope so" (122).

Someone's eye roams further and finds a similar U-turn in the ensuing section on Italy, the past, and self-discovery: "And then—and then . . . ," it swivels

(123). Equally abrupt is the change of gear from such momentous matters to this: "If one travels one eats. We immediately began to munch biscuits, and the old peasant . . . began to peel himself a hard-boiled egg. . . . With calm wastefulness he peeled away the biggest part of the white of the egg with the shell—because it came away so" (123–24). By chance another student's chosen passage, from the end of the previous chapter ("To Sorgono"), has this old man starting his first-ever trip on a bus and thinking the bus was under way "since the door was shut" (120). The book itself displays a cheerful, pointless "calm wastefulness" like that of this same old man peeling his egg.

I believe now that I could bring out this lively diversity better if I sprang *Sea and Sardinia* on students at the outset, before they were preconditioned by earlier books and before the dead hand of diagnostic critics fell on them. Students' easily aroused if usually unjustified unselfconfidence makes them over-impressed by critics whose titles seem to suggest that they offer the total picture—and Lawrence seems to inspire a remarkable number of these, everything from Eugene Goodheart's *The Utopian Vision of D. H. Lawrence* to Mary Freeman's *D. H. Lawrence: A Basic Study of His Ideas*.

For instance, my students are apt to turn to the recent *Study of D. H. Lawrence's Italian Works* (to quote its subtitle), Jill Franks's *Revisionist Resurrection Mythologies*. The book helps insofar as it shows how different the three travelogues are. But it hinders insofar as its procedure is to identify globally and a priori the quintessential Lawrentian concerns and judge the works accordingly. So *Sea and Sardinia* gets a low grade because those concerns are veiled, and "Lawrence only excels when his writing contains some hope of resurrection in the body. When he omits to write about sex with some belief in its restorative powers, there is a tremendous sense of something missing" (121). Still, the search for resurrection takes the form of the "classically Lawrentian" quest for "an undivided self," a desire that "colors all of his ethnological judgments" (122)—which Franks illustrates by a paragraph from the "Mandas" chapter that contrasts the Sardinians' "one downright mind" with a Sicilian's "dozen minds" (80–81).

A class could treat that paragraph from "Mandas" as if it were one student's contribution to my "choose a sample" exercise and thus discover that Franks's choice is (like the adjacent, longer paragraph on bread, which Franks ignores) one incidental part of an extended episode, re-created with all the resources of imaginative fiction, in which the narrator and the "q-b" (the queen bee, as this book calls Frieda) try to relate to three particular Sardinians. The episode is expansively, even self-indulgently, humorous—especially the trio's "soup-swilkering," which reflects Lawrence's playful linguistic inventiveness as well as his squeamishness (confirmed by a childhood reminiscence):

> And they fell on their soup. And never, from among the steam, have I heard a more joyful trio of soup-swilkering. They sucked it from their spoons with long, gusto-rich sucks. The *maialino* was the treble—he

trilled his soup into his mouth with a swift, sucking vibration, interrupted by bits of cabbage, which made the lamp dither again. Black-cap was the baritone; good, rolling sucks. And the one in spectacles was the bass: he gave sudden deep gulps. All was led by the long trilling of the *maialino*. Then, suddenly, to vary matters, he cocked up his spoon in one hand, chewed a huge mouthful of bread, and swallowed it down with a smack-smack-smack! of his tongue against his palate. As children we used to call this "clapping."

"Mother, she's clapping!" I would yell with anger, against my sister. The German word is schmatzen.

So the *maialino* clapped like a pair of cymbals, while the baritone and bass rolled on. Then in chimed the swift bright treble.   (78–79)

If students find it difficult to hear the play of sound in the language (here or elsewhere in *Sea and Sardinia*), the excellent unabridged cassette recording of the book may help. (See part 1, "Materials," in this volume.)

The humor moves on to the English tourists' gushing enthusiasm for Sardinia over Sicily, met with the Sardinians' "immense sarcasm" (79) and their disconcerting information that the innkeeper, with whom the q-b has already had an inane exchange about socialism, is Sicilian. (That exchange, incidentally, hardly squares with the view of Sardinians or of socialists expressed in the paragraph Franks chose.) The wish to break through the Sardinians' "invisible screen" (78) of separateness conflicts both with the narrator's preference elsewhere for Sardinian self-containedness over Sicilians' physical intimacy ("they pour themselves one over the other like so much melted butter over parsnips" [7]) and with his prevailing wish to fend off would-be conversants. And the lecture on bread is undercut by the "delicate little generosity" of "the black-cap" in sending up to their room one of his wonderful white loaves (82).

If the immediate context—and the preceding Dickensian fun with the wayward lantern (76–77)—makes the paragraph Franks highlights seem uncharacteristically (for this chapter especially) nagging and insistent, wider-ranging counterchoices make it also inconsistent. David Ellis reminds us that Lawrence's famous dictum that "everything is true in its own place, time, circumstance" carries the consequence that everything will be less true when those variables change ("Here" 113). If on a particular evening in Mandas Lawrence is against Sicilians' dozen minds, later on a particular morning (back on the mainland) he rejoices that "in an hour one changes one's psyche. The human being is a most curious creature. He thinks he has got one soul, and he has got dozens. I felt my sound Sardinian soul melting off me. I felt myself evaporating into the real Italian uncertainty and momentaneity." So he promptly and defiantly reaches for one of the earlier chapters' prime targets: "I perused the 'Corriere.' . . . I like Italian newspapers because they say what they mean" (181).

Another long-range connection—or disjunction—would be with those passages that show Lawrence hating national generalizations when they are turned on him ("they hate one's Englishness, and leave out the individual" [51]; "I am not England. I am not the British Isles on two legs" [48]). Other passages show Lawrence trying to stereotype and getting it wrong: earlier, in chapter 1, on the platform "the only one that is absolutely like a rare caricature is a tall stout elderly fellow with spectacles and a short nose and a bristling moustache, and he is the German of the comic papers of twenty years ago. But he is pure Sicilian" (7). Or they show him finding his bluff called about his admiration for southern "naturalness": it depends where you sit when someone is sick on the train (a "natural" woman is conscious enough to change seats, putting Lawrence in the firing line). The couple with the maid "don't fuss" when she throws up in the train: they "are just not upset. Not half as upset as we are. Their naturalness seems unnatural to us." But then comes one of the book's several slaps in the eye *from* the q-b[4]—"the q-b says it is largely stupidity" (16), a thought that had, however, slipped into Lawrence's own description of the woman who has "that queenly stupid beauty of a classic Hera" (14). And when nobody clears the vomit away, Lawrence swivels to feel "a bit chary of this 'nature,' in the south" (16). A similar check to any inclination to mythologize comes with the indulgent southern parents of children that "have been sick all day" but slobber over "a lemon-milk-orange-tea-sugar-biscuit-cake-chocolate mess. This inordinate Italian amiable patience with their young monkeys is astonishing. . . . Till at last one sees the southern Holy Family as an unholy triad of imbecility" (40, 41).

As far as critical commentary on *Sea and Sardinia* goes, I don't believe any more than Lawrence did in virgin minds, "like a blank white sheet on which nothing is written" (*A Propos* 308). But I would like to persuade students that there's ample critical stimulus (to support or refute) in Burgess's short introduction, which at worst wastes only ten minutes to read. However, my students are usually in a hurry to lose their perceived virginity. The only thing to do is to give them back their independence by bringing home the fact that the critics rarely agree. A sheet of excerpts (the briefer the better) will show students that they must steer their own course between, for example, Franks's disappointment that "the numenosity of experience" is lacking (118) and Burgess's delight that, "lacking in surprising events," the book's "magic lies in what the power of poetic observation can do to the ordinary" (Wordsworth's enterprise, not Coleridge's; *Flame* 144).[5] Another large question is whether to take as straight the incidents of impatience and anger and therefore what tone to attribute to the book. Franks finds the book full of "overabundant anger," its tone "bitter, caustic and disillusioned" (120, 117); she sees Lawrence writing "his travel experience as he receives it, as a slap in the face of his own ideals" (118), but she doesn't see him making comic capital out of this. In contrast, Kinkead-Weekes thinks that "the comic tones are struck from the start" and that "it is the comic self-characterisation that keeps reducing the discomforts of the journey to a comically grumbling undertone" (*D. H. Lawrence* 623, 622). A related question is whether the contradictions we have noted are hapless or intentional. John Middleton Murry says that "in no single book of Lawrence's is his inward uncertainty and division more naively exposed. . . . [It] seethes with weak and childish contradictions" (*Son* 161, 164), whereas Burgess hears another tone and sees a more artful form of self-mockery: the book "is a wonderful self-portrait and it shows Lawrence at his most attractive. . . . Part of the remarkable piquancy lies in the wonderful open generosity of the eye [of the narrator] that misses nothing and its contrast with the Lawrence [as character in the narrative] who so easily gets fed up with everybody" (*Flame* 144, 149).

It's no concern of mine which way majority opinion goes in a class: the important thing is not where it arrives but that it travels. Only if it gravitated toward the general idea of intentional mobility would I drop into the conversation a few alternative ways of describing that. I might recall two unpretentious phrases from the "Study of Thomas Hardy": "fair play all round" and "sheer play of being free" (89, 32). The first might sum up the book's balance of matters high and low ("It's all life," the q-b admonishes the grumbling narrator [99]); the second indicates travel as a positive joy (not Franks's fearful "flight and escape" [118]), Lawrence's playing fast and loose in entertaining discrepant views, and his free linguistic playfulness. Or I might quote this passage from "Study"—"Every work of art adheres to some system of morality. But if it be really a work of art, it must contain the essential criticism on the morality to which it adheres. And hence the antinomy, the conflict necessary to every tragic conception" (89)—and, I'd ask students, to every *comic* conception too? Is *Sea and Sardinia* a comedy in that sense?

But perhaps students should balk at the suggestion of a formalized conflict. It's no coincidence that, whenever in particular works Lawrence stops wanting to teach (never mind preach or nag), he also turns his scorn on "systematised messes." In *Etruscan Places*, he protests that "the experience is always spoilt" by "crazy attempts to co-ordinate and get into a fixed order that which has no fixed order and will not be co-ordinated. . . . Why must all experience be systematised? . . . Why can't incompatible things be left incompatible?" (114).

Blurring biography and literary creations is one way to produce the "systematised messes" Lawrence hated. Burgess expresses a common view when he says that Lawrence's work should be read "in an order dictated by the vicissitudes of his life" (*Flame* x). I've come to disagree strongly, preferring to take the point of Burgess's gathering together the three Italian travelogues and of offering the middle piece as the best introduction to Lawrence's work—and one sure to quicken the appetite for more.

NOTES

[1] I use in teaching and quote throughout this paper Burgess's collection, which includes *Twilight in Italy*, *Sea and Sardinia*, and *Etruscan Places*. The three books have been published individually in Cambridge and Penguin CUP editions. These editions print a previously unpublished final chapter to *Etruscan Places* and correct errors in earlier texts (e.g., "the tombs, like bulbs, were underground" [*Sketches* 13] for "the bulbs"

in Burgess [6]). In the case of *Sketches of Etruscan Places* Burgess omits the forty-four photographs collected by Lawrence, which are included in the CUP edition. Mara Kalnins's edition of *Sea and Sardinia* usefully emphasizes the breaks between sections by restoring the horizontal lines, to accompany the blank spaces, that occur in the typescripts prepared for and corrected by the author but not in early editions or in Burgess. But I see no drawbacks to Burgess's texts serious enough to outweigh the advantage of price. In Burgess each work has separate pagination.

[2]"Why can't one sit still?" Lawrence himself asks ruefully in the face of that "absolute necessity to move." Relevant here is George Orwell on Tolstoy's impatience with Shakespearean mobility: "Clearly he could have no patience with a chaotic, detailed, discursive writer like Shakespeare. His reaction is that of an irritable old man who is being pestered by a noisy child. 'Why do you keep jumping up and down like that? Why can't you sit still like I do?' In a way the old man is in the right, but the trouble is that the child has a feeling in its limbs which the old man has lost" ("Lear" 294). The Lawrence of *Sea and Sardinia* has a feeling in his limbs that many of his critics sound as if they never had.

[3]I borrow the first term from Anne Fernihough, whose *D. H. Lawrence: Aesthetics and Ideology* combats both the idea of Lawrence's work as homogeneous and the idea that Lawrence's political viewpoint suppresses "an endless confusion of differences" (Lawrence qtd. in Fernihough 186).

[4]I stress *from* because the q-b is usually the butt of humor: "slap in the eye *for* the q-b!" (my emphasis), the narrator elsewhere half winces, half exults when she asks a "touristy question" (28).

[5]In *Biographia Literaria*, Coleridge says that Wordsworth was "to give the charm of novelty to things of every day, and to excite a feeling analogous to the supernatural, by awakening the mind's attention from the lethargy of custom, [removing] the film of familiarity" (7).

Picking Up "Life-Threads" in Lawrence's Mexico: Dialogism and Multiculturalism in *The Plumed Serpent*

Virginia Crosswhite Hyde

In the essay "America, Listen to Your Own" (1920), D. H. Lawrence urges that we "pick up the life-thread" from Native American peoples—"the Red Indian, the Aztec, the Maya, the Incas" (90). But his Mexican novel *The Plumed Serpent* (1926), attempting to illustrate this process, is taught only rarely, to my knowledge: it appears but sporadically in courses in mythology, twentieth-century British (or American) literature, and even Lawrence as a major figure; for it carries a great weight of political and feminist condemnation, is equally weighty in length, and seems to many to be in a side current of Lawrence's achievement. But it contains some of the most luminous scenes in all of Lawrence. It interconnects well with selections from *Quetzalcoatl*, its independent first version (finally published in 1995); with essays from *Mornings in Mexico* (1927); with Lawrence's drawings of a Pueblo Indian ceremony that influenced the dance in *The Plumed Serpent*; and even with a few poems like "Spirits Summoned West" and "Men in New Mexico," from *Birds, Beasts and Flowers*, of 1923 (*Complete Poems* 410–12, 407–08).[1] And it can be seen to represent a particular watershed and redirection of Lawrence's thinking, as he continues the female quester (like Ursula, or Alvina of *The Lost Girl*) in the more mature form of Kate Leslie, gives prominence to her ideas through her viewpoint, and brings several Mexican Indians to the fore in a multicultural plot about an agrarian-based movement restoring the native gods of Mexico. The curious fact is that the novel has seldom been discussed in this light despite its obvious pertinence to indigenous "Third World revolutions in our time" (Paik 204).

One hears of Lawrence's leadership period as if it were a monolithic block of time in which misogynistic, masculinist, and even imperial or protofascist attitudes were static and unchanging. But this treatment does not explain the radical shift from male protagonists—in *Aaron's Rod* (1922), *Kangaroo* (1923), and *The Boy in the Bush* (1924)—to a female "central surrogate" in all the American fiction (Clark, *Dark Night* 13): *Quetzalcoatl* (written in 1923); *St. Mawr*, "The Princess,"and "The Woman Who Rode Away" (all written in 1924); and *The Plumed Serpent* (written in 1924 and early 1925). (This is where the poem "Sprits Summoned West," calling on all the women the author has lost in his life, can be a useful transitional text.) Nor does the totalizing treatment of this period recognize the overtures toward racial harmony in the interracial marriage of *The Plumed Serpent*. Finally, the leadership label, though it describes one aspect of this novel, underestimates the novel's rich multiplicity, the eclectic voices that represent not just a formal dialogic device but also an approach to multiculturalism. If some of these points remain arguable, all the better: students then have the opportunity to observe an active phase of criticism and perhaps even canon formation. Lawrence is stronger for the questioning and constructive critics, inside and outside Lawrence studies, who have engaged with his views.

Luckily, recent scholarship has shed new light on the direction of Lawrence's ideas and methods in this period, and contemporary criticism has suggested new ways of reading Lawrence. Many critics are now in agreement that he seems to have created his own independent theory of dialogics, with some similarities to that of Mikhail Bakhtin (1895–1975),[2] in Lawrence's 1925 essays on the novel as a form, almost all belonging to the months immediately following *The Plumed Serpent* and therefore having special relevance to the fiction of that time (Hyde and Clark).[3] In the essay "Why the Novel Matters," Lawrence states (possibly even anticipating criticism of his Mexican prophet Ramón), "Let us have done with the ugly imperialism of any absolute" (196). According to the same essay, the "whole" is "a strange assembly of apparently incongruous parts, slipping past one another," allowing a character a state of ongoing contingency that is always relative to everything else (196). This is the kind of space that characters of *The Plumed Serpent* maneuver for themselves, sometimes resulting in moments of grace in which the author (or a character) may transcend biases and limited ideas. Such moments call for Lawrence's well-known advice about "art-speech": "Never trust the artist. Trust the tale" (*Studies* 8).

Of course, Lawrence had little of what we call political correctness—and students should know this at once—but in America he confronted the big topics that concern American students (and others) today: not only the sterility he saw in the modern industrial society (hence the value he placed on the brilliant landscapes of the Southwest) but also male and female relations, race relations, and class relations. Although he is often associated with authoritarian ideas and a utopian concept of natural aristocracy (Mensch 207–52; Freeman 189–207), Lawrence was actually unusual in his time in seeing the core and clue of Mexico not in its Europeanized elite in both church and society but in its vast Indian population: to Kate, for instance, "Mexico meant the dark-faced men in cotton clothes and big hats: the peasants, peons, pelados, Indians" (75). Moreover, *Quetzalcoatl* shows an awareness of the Indians' colonial (and postcolonial) tragedy. If any people on earth have reason to feel abused, states Lawrence, the Mexican Indians have: "Mexico, the treasure house of the world, and the peons used as nothing more than spades to dig the treasure out, for four centuries" (113–14). While these masses possess a void of unfulfillment (*The Plumed Serpent*, too, describes the "uncreated" look in their eyes [77]), there is a great pit of self-loss inside the oppressors. In the "attempt to overwhelm and convert the dark men," says Lawrence, "the white man has lost his own soul, collapsed upon himself" (44). Lawrence's response to Mexico was complicated and ambivalent (Rossman, "D. H. Lawrence").

Broad contextualization is fitting for any Lawrence assignment, for his readers always need an awareness of the big picture, and nowhere is this truer than in his Mexican works. Some students particularly enjoy the search for details beyond the text; others are content with a brief overview. The appendixes and notes in the Cambridge and Penguin CUP editions of *The Plumed Serpent* assist substantially not only with Mexican history and Aztec mythology but also with significant sections that were deleted from the novel at the last minute. The publication of *Quetzalcoatl* more than seventy years after its creation (Martz, Introduction) also answers some of the obstacles to assigning Lawrence's Mexican writings. Of course, the novelist did not live to see the worst abuses of European Fascism, but *Quetzalcoatl* contains an emphatic statement against it by Cipriano, the Zapotec Indian general who, but for his repudiation of Fascism, is the work's most dangerous character: "Fascism won't hold against the lust for anarchy which is at the bottom of the Fascisti themselves. The Fascisti only live because they think they can bully society. It is a great bully movement, just as communism is a bully movement" (248).

Quetzalcoatl escapes many of the charges of misogyny that confront the final novel—charges that Kate Leslie is dominated by the neo-Aztec leaders, especially by her husband Cipriano—for Kate Burns (prototype of the later character) never marries in Mexico, nor does she finally commit herself to the budding theocracy. In the unfinished version, she mocks men who ask to be identified as ancient gods—Ramón as Quetzalcoatl and Cipriano as Huitzilopochtli—and refuses, commonsensically, to assume the role of a goddess with them. Above all, she scoffs loudly at Cipriano's proposals: "Am I going to give my soul to Cipriano Viedma? . . . Be, in short, his slave-woman . . . with no soul of my own? Am I going to do that? . . . I am *not!*" (285).

In short, Kate Burns sometimes delights the reader with sturdy defenses of her individuality, finally packing to go home to Europe. But a new set of questions soon arises. Should one want her to reenter the world she has already declared empty and doomed? Worst of all, what about the personal racial prejudice that makes marriage to Cipriano unthinkable?—"There was a gulf between him and her, the gulf of race, of colour, of different aeons of time" (312; cf. 318). This significant racial issue reaches its resolution in *The Plumed Serpent* when Kate Leslie marries Cipriano—the major difference between the two versions. But perhaps this marriage does make all the difference. It may represent only a flexible, passing triumph (we will never know Kate's future beyond the last chapter), but, though almost never remarked on, it is one of the big achievements of the final Mexican novel.

Perhaps even more difficult for the teacher than these problems of context is the problem of the length of *The Plumed Serpent*. Using it even in an all-Lawrence course, I found that it consumed unexpected weeks because, containing poetry and multiple philosophical stances, it is slow reading. In the light of these complexities, I suggest that, when a course allows for a unit (but not a full semester) on Lawrence in America, a cross section of short works can be most rewarding. This kind of reading assignment can introduce works from a variety of Lawrence's genres, even artwork, that bear on one or more of the same themes. A unit might include his 1924 essay "Dance of the Sprouting Corn" (Mornings in Mexico 54–61 [Heinemann]), one or both of the illustrations he sketched for it, the poem "Men in New Mexico" (written in 1922) or "O! Americans" (written in 1924; *Complete Poems* 774–80), and two or more chapters of *The Plumed Serpent* (like the seventh, "The Plaza," and the last, "Here!")—all are deeply interrelated, and all make use of Indian dance rituals Lawrence observed in New Mexico and Arizona. For an even shorter expenditure of time—say, less than a week—"The Plaza" and one poem can show some of Lawrence's best work. The teacher may hesitate to limit materials so stringently, but students should be encouraged to read more widely with the promise that "The Plaza" is a crossroad of nearly all the big issues in the novel and will surely lead to broader discussion.

The works I have selected (and other combinations could easily be chosen) deal with how rituals allow access to forgotten ways of life and open the senses to sources of energy in the surrounding universe. According to Lawrence, vital primordial knowledge still exists in certain ancient ceremonies (like those of the Pueblo Indians). "We must go back to pick up old threads," thinks Kate Leslie in *The Plumed Serpent*, speaking for modern white "civilization" in the wake of its massive industrialization, loss of faith, disconnection from nature, and devastating warfare (the First World War being less than a decade past). "We must take up the old, broken impulse that will connect us with the mystery of the cosmos again, now we are at the end of our own tether" (138). The weaving metaphor recurs as Cipriano tells Kate that people (and nations) actively weave their souls as if creating an Indian blanket: "It is very nice while all the wools are rolling their different threads and different colours, and the pattern is being made," but the product loses its interest when "finished." Thus the Navajo blanket makers leave a space for "their soul to come out, at the end" (234). This celebration of life's unfinished, dynamic quality is in keeping with Lawrence's aesthetic of continuous renewal, his aversion to stasis—an aesthetic that makes his works a series of experiments with possible lives, often outside the mainstream of a "finished" modern society. In *The Plumed Serpent*, as in *Mornings in Mexico*, Lawrence employs dance, the most mobile art, to illustrate life with its "threads" flying and open-ended, part of a great free play of being, yet touching ritualistically on the motions of others.

In the chapter "The Plaza" most of the novel's "threads" form cross connections. Kate is the observant quester as she visits the village marketplace of Sayula and becomes first a witness to ceremonies about Quetzalcoatl's return to Mexico and then a participant in an Indian dance that gives access to "the most ancient and everlasting soul of all men, where alone can the human family assemble in immediate contact" (126). This dance contrasts with the shallow "butterfly twitching" (115) of the effete Europeanized visitors from the city.

While they "gyrate *à la mode*," without direction, the Indian dancers form dynamic interactive patterns—concentric "wheels" revolving in different directions but in precise relation to each other, an inner wheel of women and an outer one of men, the two wheels representing the "greater womanhood" and "greater manhood" in which the individual participants transcend their everyday selves. Kate joins in, learning to tread the earth rhythmically, contacting its depths, while one of the men holds her hand "softly, loosely, but with transcendent nearness," forming with her one of the numerous couples who participate. A delicate "spark of contact lingering like a morning star"—that which mediates between opposites like dusk and dawn—links the two dancers without any violation of their own very different identities and, indeed, without speech or further contact; yet they become part of "the ocean of the great desire," the "greater, not the lesser sex" (131). Lawrence was dubious about logocentricity despite the fact that words form his medium (Schneider), and here he creates not a voice exactly but a distinctive presence in this unknown partner. The dancers are described as if linked to the cosmos itself: "the waters over the earth wheeling upon the waters under the earth" (131) echoes Genesis 1.7–8 about the second day of Creation. As Marianna Torgovnick notes, it is unusual to retain the separate sexes in the ecstatic oceanic experience (165), but Lawrence remains an essentialist in this respect, differentiating them even at such a moment of oneness. Here the chapter can represent and draw in larger concerns about the novel.

Although the reader never learns the name of Kate's plaza companion, he is an important character linking her at this time to the native people in the plaza and elsewhere. The episode somewhat prefigures her later marriage to Cipriano, in which the two, "at twilight, between the night and the day," are pledged to each other in the morning star (329). Shortly after dancing with the unknown man, she learns from Ramón's wealthy first wife that news of Kate's dance "with the Men of Quetzalcoatl" has already spread. Carlota, a representative of upper-class Spanish Mexico and its Catholic Church, is shocked: "But, Señora, why did you do such a thing? Oh why?" (156). Even earlier, when Kate initially traverses Lake Sayula, she is similarly identified with Quetzalcoatl's people, first when an Indian man emerges from the water and asks for a tribute to the old lake gods and next when her boatman pulls a "little cooking-pot" from the lake, giving her this "ollita of the gods," which may once have held offerings to the ancient god Quetzalcoatl (95, 94). In the eyes of such men, followers of the new movement, there is none of the "uncreated" emptiness Kate fears in some of the other Indians' gazes (77); there is, rather, "the morning star, or the evening star" (92), indicating the men's solidarity, faith, and self-worth based on the restoration of their local gods.

When, later, boatmen frighten Kate, she breathes the "higher power" (106) or "Great Breath" (108) in the lake atmosphere and establishes "the communion of grace" with them by sharing oranges and sandwiches (107). Kate's servant Juana—who takes her to the plaza and dances there herself—similarly links Kate with the local people. Furthermore, at Kate's wedding to Cipriano, Ramón not only points out the sacred star-bonding between the two marrieds but also adds, "And the star that is between *all men and all women*, and between all the children of men, shall not be betrayed" (331; my emphasis). I believe it is Kate who takes this injunction most to heart (despite her awareness of noble lineage and in the face of Ramón's continuing assumption of his own leadership). The wordless plea of the Indian people—"*The blood is one blood*"—urges on Kate "the primeval oneness of mankind," and she even undergoes "a slow, organic process" of bodily change for a contact that "her innermost blood" has sought, though unconsciously (417, 413).

Another issue raised by "The Plaza" is woven inextricably into other sections of the novel: the extent to which the men dominate Kate. Is it an indication of male dominance that the "waters under the earth" (131) appear to represent the women? This is a common reading (see Daleski 240–51; Woodman), sometimes combined with the facts that Kate's nuptials seem to identify her with earth (329) and that Cipriano is cast as the dominant partner in their sexual relations (422). This claim that Kate is forced into sexual passivity is sometimes countered by a description of Kate, in lovemaking, "like a fountain gushing noiseless and with urgent softness from the volcanic deeps" (422). Whatever her experience, it is "dark and untellable," beyond "conscious 'satisfaction'" (422)—and yet, in some sense, quite active, as in tantric practices (Parmenter 313–14; Doherty). Of course, Kate's submissiveness outraged Kate Millett in *Sexual Politics* (1969), as it troubled Simone de Beauvoir before her (1949) and has disturbed others since.[4] Torgovnick agrees that Kate's sexuality becomes passive; nonetheless, when considering Lawrence's use of "the primitive" and his refusal to exploit, stereotypically, the "orgiastic" in this regard, she states (in 1990) that "we can modify the anger in Millett's critique to a new understanding of, and even sympathy with, Lawrence" (168).

The novel itself counters the male sky myth, in a number of ways, and students may consider them in response to a series of questions. How important is it that Kate (in "The Plaza") chooses her dance partner rather than the other way around? This question raises an issue applying to the novel as a whole: How significant is it that the viewpoint character, the one with (arguably) the most agency and awareness, is a woman, and how does this affect the hierogamous myth, which links the heavens with the male mind and the earth with the female body? In the novel at large, does the myth fit Kate and Cipriano—or would a reversal of the myth fit them more closely? Kate is eventually identified as the goddess Malintzi, a name recalling not only a historic figure but also, linguistically, the goddess Malinalxoch (Hyde and Clark 143). How does Kate's place in the pantheon, on a par with the male gods, affect the sky myth? A term used by Ramón's second wife, Teresa—"God as woman" (433)—may prove relevant or at least provocative. In the Aztec myths told in *The Plumed Serpent*, the Creator appears to be both man and woman, possessing a womb (125).

Students will be interested to know that the native dance in "The Plaza" is partly modeled on real-life Pueblo rituals that Lawrence describes in essays like "Dance of the Sprouting Corn." One of his drawings of this dance shows how the male dancer takes the lead, with his female partner in close alignment just behind him. The essay confirms these positions in the corn dance (still enacted today), but another essay, "Indians and Entertainment," notes that women take the lead on some occasions, as in the "deer dance" (Mornings in Mexico 50 [Heinemann]), and explains a round dance that may also influence the one in "The Plaza." Some students may even prefer "Dance of the Sprouting Corn" to the fiction, for the essay projects a nonfictive authenticity; certainly, it offers possibilities for comparative papers or short writing assignments as well as discussion. Similarly, the poems "Men in New Mexico" and "O! Americans," referring in part to such rituals, raise searching questions about conditions for American Indians. Is Lawrence justified in transposing an experience from the New Mexico Pueblo to the Mexican village? Should an account of native rituals be expected to conform to values of another lifestyle—those, for example, of the reader or even of the author? When writing about another culture, can a writer ever avoid appropriating it for purposes alien to it? These considerations raise further issues about contacts between indigenous and other lifestyles (on this topic see also Thompson's essay in this volume).

In the final chapter, the novel's "threads" form a loose mesh (perhaps like the Navajo blanket with its hole for the soul's escape) as diverse characters live in fairly close contact with one another. Kate's claim that she must return to Europe creates some suspense, but the title of the chapter—"Here!"—indicates that she will remain "here" (in Mexico) with her husband. Lawrence, perhaps reluctant to resolve the novel's dialogic play, remained unsure about the end of Kate's story, furiously revising most of the chapter, then withholding its telling name until the very last moment. The title spotlights the immediacy of present time and place in the last pages. They are full of different forms of life coexisting side by side, everything being delicately evanescent and relative (and yet related) in a motile evocation of a springlike day. A virtual curtain call brings into one chapter Kate, Teresa, Ramón, Cipriano, a farmer, working peons, a boatman, a singer from the Quetzalcoatl movement, Kate's "mozo," and animals as vibrantly alive as any in all of Lawrence. Even the air seems "mysteriously alive, with a new Breath," but Kate feels "out of it" (431). The chapter illustrates the way life changes moment by moment as Kate's mood shifts from a particularly quarrelsome interlude, gradually catches life's flame, and warms again to relationships.

Student discussion might focus on Lawrence's choice to cancel a flood of denunciations that Kate aims at Ramón in the chapter's next-to-last draft (contained in a Penguin appendix and in the Cambridge critical apparatus). Students may well determine that she is combative enough without the denunciations, needling Ramón about his "Quetzalcoatlian" moods (428; cf. 427, 430), accusing Teresa of slavelike "submission" to Ramón (434; cf. 412), and refusing to tell Cipriano when (or if) she will return from Europe: "*Quién sabe!*—Who knows!" (437). She seems at one point to renew her old pride in noble blood (436). Even the usually mild Teresa is forced to state that Kate is "fighting all the time" (434). A similar opposition between Birkin and Ursula in *Women in Love* (1920) causes David Lodge to find dialogic complexity in that novel ("Lawrence"), but Kate's relation to her companions, men and women (and to herself and her author), is often as confrontational as it is dialogic, in Lawrence's own sense. One effect of all these clashes in *The Plumed Serpent* is to affirm the variety of human nature, for the individuality that Kate values is, it seems to me, revealed as one necessary side of a person—though not the complete identity (see 389–90). Ramón appears, for once, barely able to carry on his mission because of his human "vulnerability" (427). Teresa proves to have deep reserves of pride and even sarcastic wit. Kate is "a soldier among women" (434), whom not all husbands would welcome. And Cipriano, whose "doom" is the wordless impassivity that masks his emotions for Kate, has "already released her" (437). There is a great deal of truth in Margaret Storch's point that Kate's function is "to be changed" (*Sons* 165), but much in Kate's character is irreducible, not just part of the "hard and finished, accomplished" self that is dispensable (429); and yet Kate is desired, as the book's last lines emphasize. She is the bearer of a critical intelligence that survives intact through the conclusion.

As Kate reconsiders her plan to leave Mexico, she recognizes anew the glamour of a gendered universe, for the "greater sex" can "fill all the world with lustre" (439). Some students may notice the verbal connection between the chapters "The Plaza" and "Here!" Both refer to the "greater sex." Through the wheels of "greater manhood" and "greater womanhood" in the earlier dance, "greater sex" seems to link the dancers to the cosmos itself. In the conclusion, it exists in the frieze-like tableau of a grand "spangled" bull, "dappled like the sky," following his mate into a *canoa* on the lake (431, 432). It is there in a roan horse, "prancing along the shore"; in "white and yellow calves, new and silky . . . skipping"; and in a bushy black ass foal, born in the night, learning to stand near its mother. Kate, knowing that "all the dark aeons" must be coming to life in the new creature, recognizes the dance of life even in the foal's first awkward movements: "Already it dances!" she tells its keeper (435). And the "greater sex" even flashes in the eyes of chance acquaintances, perhaps ultimately relating all living things. Students may well wonder what Lawrence means by "sex" in this sense, and a lengthy discussion may follow.

By the time Kate is ready to reconcile with Cipriano, she understands how much she will lose if she leaves him, for the two are balanced complements to each other. Likewise, she sees clearly how much he will lose (let go) by letting her go. Until their last parting, she had felt certain that he would not "let go"— unlike most things in life, including her past husbands, that "let you down" (70) or let go of one (see Hyde and Clark 142). She is therefore hurt that he has "released her" without a word on her announcement of departure—has let her down, let go of her. This, I believe, is the meaning of the novel's last line before

Lawrence altered it when proofreading. In this penultimate version, Kate addresses Cipriano with the words of a French song that seem to dismiss him, to
accuse him of some form of desertion: *"Le gueux m'a plantée là!"* 'The rascal
left me standing there!' (Penguin CUP 462). This is how the volume very nearly
ended. But the substitute line, as published, resonates with earlier passages on
love and commitment, making it possible to read the line as a statement of trust
and hope: "You won't let me go!" (444). Kate has just been planning how to re-
lent only "as far as I need, and no further" (439). But she relents enough to
make the taciturn Cipriano more eloquent on the subject of love and desire
than is Rupert Birkin in *Women in Love*. In Spanish, Cipriano says, *"Te quiero
mucho! Mucho te quiero! Mucho! Mucho!"* (444) ("I love you very much! I desire you very much! Very much! Very much!") (my trans.; see also Hyde and
Clark 140–42). What more did Ursula ever want to hear from Birkin? Just as
the highly verbal Kate has previously learned the value of silence (from the
wordless dance partner, for example, and Cipriano's still touch), Cipriano now
recognizes the importance of words—an episode indicating, perhaps, that Kate
influences him beyond her expectations. Students may analyze in some detail
just who is leading whom in this conclusion.

Kate's influence is more exigent than I have yet indicated, for Cipriano has
appeared in more disturbing circumstances, deplored by discerning critics like
L. D. Clark (*Dark Night* 97–98), Jean-Paul Pichardie (271), and others: I think
of the execution of criminals Aztec-style in the strange chapter "Huitzilopochtli's Night." But Cipriano's dangerous side is apparently mitigated by Kate's
presence. While Cipriano is cast as a war god, the goddess in *Quetzalcoatl* is
termed "the woman of peace" (218), and Malintzi in *The Plumed Serpent* is said
to dispense the green leaf of mercy to commute a death sentence. Cipriano has
told Kate of "two spirits" within him—one "like the dry season," bringing a fiery
power urge, and one "like the early morning in the time of rain," a time of tenderness that he identifies with her (186). She is linked symbolically with the
rain that heals the hot, dry land until a virtual Atlantis seems to return, like "the
world before the Flood" (415).

These considerations bring us to the song embedded in the final chapter; unlike many of the Quetzalcoatl songs, which contain didactic or doctrinal elements, this song is a simple celebration of the morning star, the symbol of unity
that has already figured prominently in the plaza dance and Kate's wedding.
(Indeed, Ramón as Quetzalcoatl has the morning star as his special sign.)
Although not specifically designed to keep Kate from leaving, the song is one of
reconciliation, a kind of romantic serenade. "My way is not thy way, and thine is
not mine," it admits, but these two discrete directions can meet like the dark
and light at dawn: "Let us separately go to the Morning Star, / And meet there."
The sexual essentialism, like the dance imagery from "The Plaza," is resumed:
"A man cannot tread like a woman, / Nor a woman step out like a man." Nonetheless, "Be with me there, my woman / Be bodily there" (441). Students may
consider how this imagery of unity may relate to the statement in a previous

chapter that the "only step" to "the new world" must arise from a "marriage" of "the old blood-and-vertebrate consciousness [of the Indian] with the white man's present mental-spiritual consciousness" (416, 415). It is a common view that Lawrence, in this novel, wants "blood . . . consciousness" to overwhelm the "mental-spiritual" faculty. But why, then, does the text refer to "the *two* great human impulses," giving the victory to the two together: "Not the rider on the white horse: nor the rider on the red" (418; my emphasis)?

Finally, the teacher may resort again to the big picture, seeking (rather tenuously) to sum up Lawrence's Mexican period. Paul Eggert points out this writer's "chameleon" tendency "to experiment" beyond the bounds of a single text; for, even after the formal completion of one work, "its concerns [are] only gradually resigned, mixing intertextually with the next book review, poem, short story, or novel" ("Comedy" 134, 145). This hint should remind us of other works in Lawrence's Mexican period. "The Woman Who Rode Away," written between the two versions of *The Plumed Serpent*, can be seen as an "experiment" with some of the same details, an exploration of one tragic alternative plot (Wallace, "Circling" 113–15). It exists in its own right, of course—and I view it as a work of irony (Hyde, "To 'Undiscovered Land'" 184–86)—but it can also be identified as a piece in the larger context provided by contiguous works, including the happier conclusion of *The Plumed Serpent*.

Another example of crossover from one work to another concerns the servants in *The Plumed Serpent* and *Mornings in Mexico*. Soon after Kate's marriage, the housekeeper Juana—who has provided a window to the working-class Mexicans—drops out of the novel, for Kate moves to a new home and is accompanied from it to the last meeting place by a young "mozo." Readers feel Juana's absence because, with her oppositional, "bottom-dog" (110) viewpoint, Juana supplies some of the novel's diversity and even, according to Rebecca Carpenter, "counterbalances Don Cipriano" in her tendency to keep Kate's feet on the ground (123). Juana's characterization stands out as one of Lawrence's most notable portraits of an individual of her class—warm and loyal yet worldly-wise and insolent all at the same time. But Lawrence was developing another significant representative of the working class in the essay "The Mozo" (Mornings in Mexico 23–35 [Heinemann]), written contemporaneously with late parts of *The Plumed Serpent*. The essays in the *Mornings* volume show a progression somewhat paralleling that from *Quetzalcoatl*, with Kate's repudiation of marriage to "a dark, Indian Mexican" (318), to the interracial union in *The Plumed Serpent*. Despite Lawrence's onetime idealization of the "Red Indian," the essays' narrator takes a detached or even satiric stance at his first authentic Indian dances, shifting to deeper engagement in later accounts like "Dance of the Sprouting Corn"; and in "The Mozo," an essay with a Christmastime setting like the one ending *The Plumed Serpent*, Lawrence can identify closely with the young Zapotec Indian servant who has suffered torture rather than be inducted into mass military service: the Indian emerges as an individual—"like myself," Lawrence says (33). This final insight is despite the writer's earlier assumption of superiority, for he initially finds a "gulf" separating them (8). I see these conclusions as culminations of Lawrence's long struggle with ambivalent views; if these conclusions represent a momentary victory (and students may want to explore whether they do or not), the victory is nonetheless a noteworthy one on the trail of the "life-thread" in Lawrence's America.

NOTES

[1]*D. H. Lawrence and New Mexico*, in paperback, includes the essays on Native Americans, poetry of the period, *St. Mawr*, "The Princess," "The Woman Who Rode Away," and more; provides helpful commentary between selections; and reproduces photographs and artwork (including *Corn Dancers*).

[2]On Bakhtinian methods in Lawrence, see Lodge, "Lawrence"; Eggert, Introduction 11–13 and "Comedy" 134–37; Hyde and Clark; Hyde, Introduction xxx; Fleishman, " 'He Do the Polis' " and "Lawrence"; and Stewart, "Linguistic Incantation."

[3]See also Hyde, Introduction xv, xxxi; Clark, "Reading"; Steele, Introduction, D. H. Lawrence, "*Study*" xlvii–1; and Worthen, *D. H. Lawrence and the Idea of the Novel* 152–67. The essays are "Art and Morality," "Morality and the Novel," "The Novel," "Why the Novel Matters," and "The Novel and the Feelings." A sixth essay on the novel as a form, "The Future of the Novel" (published earlier as "Surgery for the Novel—or a Bomb") belongs to 1923.

[4]There is a great range of feminist responses to this novel. See, e.g., Kate Millett 398, 410; Beauvoir 223; Apter; Gilbert, *Acts* 193–242; Hyde, " 'Lost' Girls" 111–14 and *Risen Adam* 173–206; Laird, *Self* 148–95; Nixon 205; Ruderman 142–53; Siegel, *Lawrence* 10–11, 186; Storch, *Sons* 157–78 and " 'But Not the America' "; and Torgovnick 159–74. See also Rossman, " 'I Am the Call,' " esp. 304.

COURSE-CONTEXT SKETCHES

Teaching Lawrence's Tortoise Poems as a Sequence

David Ellis

Readers "will look round for poetry," wrote Wordsworth near the beginning of his Advertisement, or Preface, to *Lyrical Ballads*, "and will be induced to enquire by what species of courtesy these attempts can be permitted to assume that title" (1). Because of their apparent lack of form, a similar inquiry is often provoked by Lawrence's poems. The absence in them of immediately recognizable patterns gives the impression of someone speaking thoughts as they occur, without premeditation or care for artistic effect. Hence R. P. Blackmur's claim that in the later work, the art of Lawrence's poetry exists only "at the minimum level of self-expression" (255).

Instead of being a justification for presenting them casually, this impression the poems often make has seemed to me a reason for doing the opposite and led to my decision to print the tortoise poems on their own in 1982 (*Tortoises*). I wanted to ensure that at least six of Lawrence's poems were in no danger of losing the benefit of that slight initial pause and narrowing of attention which most of us accord automatically to whatever is self-evidently poetic to the eye or ear. That Lawrence's poetry isn't has always lent credence to Blackmur's complaints. Since Blackmur's essay first appeared in 1935, many critics have pointed to the skill with which Lawrence varies his tone, controls rhythm by alteration in line length, and employs such traditional resources of the poet as assonance, alliteration, and repetition. But moving in that direction means being trapped within Blackmur's terms, and the eventual outcome is always the kind of sterile quarrel over definitions Dr. Johnson was trying to avoid when—in the last paragraph of his "Life of Pope"—he wrote, "If Pope be not a poet, where is poetry to be found?" (230). Pope and Lawrence are very different figures, so the most appropriate equivalent observation might be that if all the people Blackmur knew expressed themselves as well as Lawrence, when was there ever a man so fortunate in his friends?

The tortoise poems have not been well served by the anthologies or by the recent English edition of the *Complete Poems*, which (welcome though it certainly is) functions like a crowded art gallery in its capacity for exciting in all but the specialist feelings of satiety and confusion. Lawrence originally meant these six poems to appear on their own and as a sequence. According to Harry T. Moore, the tortoise poems were written in the late summer of 1920 when, with Frieda in Germany, Lawrence was living in or near Florence (*Priest* [Heinemann] 417). By December of the following year, they had been published in New York by Thomas Seltzer. But in England they did not appear on their own and in what Lawrence, referring to the Seltzer edition in a letter, called a "chap-book" form (*Letters* 4: 174). In 1923 Lawrence had them incorporated instead into the first English edition of *Birds, Beasts and Flowers*, where they made up the major part of the section on reptiles (in the distinguished company of "Snake"). That placement may have been appropriate in strictly zoological terms, but the tortoise poems do not quite seem at home under such a heading, and the nature of their presence in *Birds, Beasts and Flowers* has encouraged compilers of anthologies to believe that individual tortoise poems could be printed separately. The favorite of the anthologists is the first ("Baby Tortoise"). Given the compulsion they are under, that choice makes some sense, but there is at least one popular anthology where the poems are represented by the last ("Tortoise Shout"), a choice that makes no sense at all.

To anyone who reads the tortoise poems through, it must be obvious that they do form a genuine sequence and need to be read and taught as such. How else, for example, to appreciate the continual emphasis in the first five on the tortoise being "voiceless" and "dumb" or understand the significance of the cross that it is described as bearing in the second? Together these poems offer a self-contained and circumstantial version of the Fall from self-sufficiency into dependence and from wholeness into division.

In the first three, it is above all the unselfconsciousness with which the baby tortoise braves the world that prompts Lawrence's envy and admiration. "No one ever heard you complain," he says (352),[1] so that although the reader may be led to give as much additional stress to the pronoun *you* as when reading *thee* in "No hungry generations tread thee down" ("Ode to a Nightingale"), the effect is antithetical in the two poems: a manifestation of self-pity in Keats's poem but an implied general protest against that unamiable human characteristic in Lawrence's. Yet the baby tortoise, as well as being a defiant, unselfconscious individual, is for Lawrence the representative of his species and, like Keats's nightingale therefore, immortal by courtesy of a Romantic logic fortunate to have escaped the attention of the Royal Society for the Prevention of Cruelty to Animals. The notion that tortoises have been setting out on their life's journey for some time now—"Fulfilled of the slow passion of pitching through immemorial ages / [Their] little round house in the midst of chaos" (354)—helps Lawrence imagine the first stirrings in the creature before him as the beginning of life in this world (as of course they are for the tortoise). What he then celebrates is the period in the tortoise's life before the promptings of the sexual instinct drive it into a need for relation. By implicit reference to the Bible story (to that golden age before humankind knew sex), and with another twist of Romantic logic, it is as if this period—hardly any longer, one would have thought, for the first tortoise than for this latest representative—were being brought to its catastrophic end for the first time and that there had been eons rather than months when the tortoise could be found "[w]andering in the slow triumph of his own existence" (358).

Thanks largely to *Lady Chatterley's Lover*, Lawrence enjoys a popular reputation as the joyful celebrator of sexual union. The poems show how some of Gudrun's thoughts on the matter, or Connie's in a bad mood, could also be his. This is the sexual act seen from the outside, in a different species, of course, but with a human application that is evident. (See the reference in "Lui et Elle" to the tortoise's "adolescence" [361].) The poems convey a painful sense of how the tortoise is left exposed by sex, "[t]his grim necessity from within" (363): brought out of his shell, with a consequent loss of independence and dignity.

It would be foolish to deny that, in all this, the point of view is aggressively male. Lawrence is nothing if not open about his prejudices, and at least we are offered insights into the reasons for them. So much (for example) does he himself come off second best in his encounter with the female tortoise at the beginning of "Lui et Elle" that it is not surprising to find out how fervent he is later in his support of the male. That this female is so much larger than her partner encourages Lawrence to imply a certain resentment against her for being the cause of the male's abandonment of his singleness. But as one of the women characters from the novels might have said, without the female, singleness is something the male would never have had in the first place. And the same voice might have added that since the poem never suggests the female tortoise makes any effort to attract the male (the naturalists tell us she is in fact the victim of rape), it often seems as if Lawrence would be willing to blame a plate-glass window for the way a bird flies into it.

Apart from one or two positive notes struck toward the end of the sequence, the story the poems tell would seem almost entirely painful were it not for the humor of Lawrence's sardonic, specifically Midlands voice. Although this humor would not be enough to save Lawrence in every quarter, it might soften the attitude of any women readers disgusted with the poems because they feel (as of course does the women observer in "Lui et Elle") that Lawrence's point of view is a trifle biased. And the humor needs to be insisted on in rebuttal of that familiar charge of too much intensity, brought with quasi-automatic frequency against almost everything Lawrence wrote. Actually, although the poems contain several moments that anticipate the dramatic change of register in their finale, they are for the most part humorously philosophical in tone. (There was always a part of Lawrence capable of being amused by the world without any diminution in his native earnestness.)

Rather than for their intensity, therefore, the poems might more reasonably be criticized for the disdain Lawrence exhibits in them for decorum in either its literary or social sense. "The same cry from the tortoise as from Christ, the Osiris-cry of abandonment," reads the third line from the end of the last of them (367). Some readers are likely to find such collocations ludicrous or even shocking, especially after they have been made aware that the idea of sex as crucifixion was suggested to Lawrence in part by the sight of the male tortoise spread-eagled on the back of its mate in the act of copulation. But the person who sees religion in everything will feel no qualms about importing everything back into religion, and the association of Christ with Osiris is not the casual, haphazard gesture Blackmur seems to think it is (as anyone familiar with Lawrence's "The Man Who Died" can testify). In these poems, Christ represents the suffering involved in dying into a new life, but for Lawrence, Osiris is equally important as a symbol of the self-division sex brings. To put them together, in defiance of decorum, shows either freedom of spirit or damned bad form, according to one's point of view.

My own will be self-evident, yet to criticisms of the kind hinted at above, to disgruntled women readers or purists of one sort or another, the best defense will in any case always be the reminder that what really matters here are the tortoises: that the dominant impression these poems leave is of the distinctiveness of tortoise life. To say that, of course, is to modify only slightly the received wisdom on all the poems in *Birds, Beasts and Flowers*. What is usually said of this collection is that, by turning in it to the natural world and being able, therefore, to exercise an extraordinary gift for perceiving what Vivian de Sola Pinto once risked calling the "divine otherness of non-human life" (12), Lawrence was able to distance himself or escape from experiences that in *Look! We Have Come Through* (1917) had proved too pressingly autobiographical. There is a great deal of truth in this argument. Yet it would be wrong to over estimate any human being's capacity for perceiving our fellow inhabitants of the world as other, even when they happen to be fish (see Lawrence's remarkable poem "Fish"). It is in the nature of perception and language that the characteristics of birds, beasts, and flowers should be seen by analogy or contrast with ours. Thus not only the tortoise's "wimple" or "trousers," but also Lawrence's amazement in "Tortoise Family Connections" (356–58) at its lack of family feeling.

For all that, for all his transference of human characteristics to tortoises and his exploitation of them for the expression of private fears, the common view that Lawrence forces us to realize the special nature of each form of life is surely right. What we are made to see of the tortoise in these poems has implications for the human condition (how else but in relation to ourselves can we see it?); but these do not obscure the vividness of the notation, the memorable way this strange mixture of insect, animal, reptile, and bird is brought before us.

More than any other writer, Lawrence has the power to make us feel ashamed of ever believing that the torpid shell in the backyard is flattered by its status as a pet. He adds a further degree of force to the distaste we might already feel at hearing of those container trucks that arrive in the English Channel ports each carrying around seven thousand tortoises, some dying from shock and others from having been accidentally impaled as they were packed into orange boxes. "And do not call the tortoise unworthy because she is not something else," writes the poet to whom Lawrence's poetry probably owes more than it owes anyone else, in his "Song of Myself" (Whitman 75). But Lawrence goes further than Whitman does by showing the tortoise as far too individual and fascinating a creature to require any apology.

One may be attracted or repelled by Lawrence's poetry, but it is worth saying that one is almost never baffled. Unlike Eliot and Pound, who seem to have written in anticipation of the expansion in university education and the corresponding need for material that experts could be expert on, Lawrence is rarely obscure. There is a consequent difficulty in, and possible impertinence about, any kind of annotation or commentary in one's teaching of him. To attempt to argue skeptics into a conviction that Lawrence is a good poet, when all the evidence for making their own decisions is at hand in the poems themselves, would be absurd. If we nevertheless feel some natural, human prompting to prejudice the issue, the clearest sign will be in our determination to teach the complete sequence of tortoise poems as Lawrence originally hoped his readers would see them.

NOTE

[1]Unless otherwise indicated, all page references for quotations from Lawrence's poetry are from D. H. Lawrence, *Complete Poems*.

The Tuning of "Piano"

Keith Cushman

"Piano," one of Lawrence's most widely anthologized poems, exists in two distinct versions. The poem first appeared in *New Poems* (1918), Lawrence's fourth collection of poetry. But an earlier version, titled "The Piano," exists in a notebook Lawrence used while a student at Nottingham University College from 1906 to 1908. The text of the earlier version is readily available in *The Norton Anthology of English Literature* (7th ed.) and in *The Complete Poems of D. H. Lawrence*.

The striking differences between the two texts lead to lively classroom discussion, especially if the instructor can refrain from remarking too early that in revising "The Piano" into "Piano," Lawrence transformed a diffuse, sentimental, not quite coherent poem into a sharply focused, emotionally complex poem. Students seem eager to define and talk about the emotions Lawrence is evading in "The Piano" but powerfully articulating in "Piano." In the process, they come to understand a looser (non-Yeatsian) variety of modernist poetic form and come to terms with a sort of poetry rooted in emotional integrity and honesty (a Lawrentian sort of poetry).

If time permits, students can be directed to the classic consideration of "Piano" found in I. A. Richards's *Practical Criticism: A Study of Literary Judgment*, published in 1929 while Lawrence was still alive (and thus one of the earliest introductions of Lawrence into the academy). Richards discusses his students' various responses to the poem. Most of the students condemned "Piano" on the grounds of sentimentality (99–112, 241–54). In 1977 the Advanced Placement English Examination printed the texts of "The Piano" and "Piano" and required students to write an essay explaining what characteristics made "Piano" the better poem. Holly Laird's "The Poems of 'Piano'" provides a detailed interpretation of the poem's compositional evolution. (For other discussions of the poem, see de Sola Pinto 7–8 and Gilbert, *Acts* 47–49.)

Students will note that the dramatic situation in both texts is the same. "Softly, in the shadows, a woman is singing" to the poet, a young man ("The Piano"). The woman seems to be romantically interested in the poet, but the music triggers a childhood memory in him. He remembers "sitting under the piano" as a boy on Sunday evenings while his mother played and he pressed her feet. Both texts are structured around the conflict between present/adulthood/ "woman . . . singing to me" and past/childhood/mother. But the two poems resolve this conflict quite differently.

Students comment on the obvious fact that Lawrence has pared the five stanzas of "The Piano" down to the three of "Piano," but they may need help seeing that in the process Lawrence has focused the poem more effectively to emphasize the poet's inner struggle. I point out that the eliminated first stanza of "The Piano" is filled with nonfunctional detail:

Somewhere beneath that piano's superb sleek black
Must hide my mother's piano, little and brown, with the back
That stood close to the wall, and the front's faded silk, both torn,
And the keys with little hollows, that my mother's fingers had worn.

Even worse, the notion that the mother's piano is somehow, somewhere, there all along spoils the drama of the situation in which the mother's piano is conjured up only when the present-day woman, accompanied by the "great black piano," sings to the poet.

The fourth stanza of "The Piano," also eliminated, is devoted to the poet's "sister at home in the old front room / Singing love's first surprised gladness." Lawrence must have intended to introduce a third variety of love, the sister's sweet first love, to contrast with the singer's seductive come-on and the boy's innocent mother love. Students come to agree that this was one variety of love too many for a short poem. This stanza also jarringly intrudes on the poem's developing drama.

Asking students to analyze the changes Lawrence made from stanza 3 of "The Piano" to stanza 2 of "Piano" is the key to this classroom exercise. In "The Piano," "The full throated woman has chosen a winning, living song / And surely the heart that is in me must belong / To the old Sunday evenings." The tentativeness of that "surely" reveals Lawrence's uncertainty about what shape and meaning to give to the experience he is describing.

But in "Piano," "In spite of myself, the insidious mastery of song / Betrays me back, till the heart of me weeps to belong / To the old Sunday evenings at home." Here Lawrence charges the situation emotionally and dramatically, for the speaker is *resisting* being carried back to the past by the music. He is betrayed back in spite of himself, and the mastery of song is "insidious." (Leavis's analysis of the complex movement of the poem—contrasted with Tennyson's "Tears, Idle Tears"—argues that this speaker's resistance is a striking example of the crucial link between "Thought and Emotional Quality" in poetry [*Living Principle* 75–80].) Students are able to identify the poet's complicated feelings here. As an adult he should be responding to the woman singing (seductively) to him "in the dusk," rather than retreating imaginatively to childhood and the secure, womb-like space he occupied "sitting under the piano, in the boom of the tingling strings / And pressing the small, poised feet of a mother who smiles as she sings."

In "The Piano" the woman is rather melodramatically "singing me a wild Hungarian air / And her arms, and her bosom, and the whole of her soul is bare." The poet is able to withstand the temptation of the past as "this music's ravaging glamour" devours his mother's tunes. The present-day woman conquers. But in "Piano" the singer "burst[s] into clamour" "in vain." The "ravaging glamour" of the woman's singing is transformed into "The glamour / Of childhood days" as the poet acknowledges precisely what is at stake. His "manhood" is "cast / Down in the flood of remembrance," and he weeps "like a child for the past."

Although "Piano" openly and honestly displays sentimental feeling, it is not a sentimental poem. (Students can see this quickly in a useful contrast X. J. Kennedy sets up between "Piano" and Eliza Cook's "The Old Arm-Chair" [658–59].) The sentiment is part of the poet's inner struggle, a struggle that centers in a confusion of sexual identity. He perceives his imaginative journey to the cozy haven of his remembered childhood as a humiliation, a betrayal of his sense of adult masculinity ("manhood").

I share with students an early letter in which Lawrence remarks that "it is the hidden *emotional* pattern that makes poetry, not the obvious form" (*Letters* 2: 104) and argue that in "The Piano" he seems to be evading that "hidden *emotional* pattern," perhaps because it was rather too close for comfort. However, the revised text, "Piano," subtly, stirringly creates a complex emotional movement. Through classroom comparison of the two versions of the poem, students see more than Lawrence's radical improvement of his poem: they also glimpse that artistic discovery and self-discovery are sometimes indistinguishable.

Lawrence and Freud on Dreams: Loosing versus Trapping *The Fox* in the Classroom

Louis K. Greiff

Like many of Lawrence's texts, *The Fox* is likely to disturb and disappoint today's undergraduate readers encountering it for the first time. This response can occur even when those readers are English majors freely choosing an advanced elective given over to the study of Lawrence's work. Ethical objections prove constant in beginning discussions of *The Fox*, most prominently against Henry's willed murder of Banford and, closely related, against Henry's and the narrator's assumed sexism and contempt for lesbians or, as students see it, their mutual disgust at feminine intimacy of any sort. Aesthetic problems arise with initial discussions of *The Fox* as well—the implausibility of events (like Banford's murder by tree); the perceived eccentricity, even downright silliness, of the characters and their actions (March especially); and always the story's unexpectedly troublesome ending. The "long tail" that Lawrence appended to *The Fox*, in fact, seems to resist completion by undergraduate readers much as it resisted completion by the author himself.

A teacher's challenge with this text is, as always, to invite exploration in place of either condemnation or conversion to a cause—also to avoid dissecting "The Fox" and nailing his hide to the blackboard in favor of letting him loose in the classroom just to see what happens. A worthwhile strategy of liberation I've found in teaching *The Fox* begins by calling attention to March's two dreams at least temporarily without regard to anything else in the text. Armed with dream theories from Lawrence's own *Fantasia of the Unconscious* and from Freud's *On Dreams* (short enough to be read in its entirety), students can generate imaginative and convincing interpretations of March's dreams with little or no intrusion from their teacher. Ironically, Freud proves more helpful here than Lawrence does: Freud's observations on recurring dream imagery, on "dream work" (process), on the dreamer's motives, and on the special status of nightmare ("anxiety dream") all come alive in March's sleeping imagination (16, 60).

It's difficult, at the outset of such discussion, to avoid the unavoidably phallic tail of Lawrence's dream fox, especially since to the dreamer herself "it seemed his brush was on fire" (*Fox* 20). Once past this, however, students begin moving in more promising and less obvious directions. They perceive that the steps in Freud's dream work—dramatization, condensation, displacement, and final ordering—all clearly play out in March's dreams. Her visionary fox is quickly identified in class as a Freudian condensation, half fox and half Henry, or as an even more complex condensation of animal and vegetable—part human, part fox, and part sheaf of grain, "yellow and bright, like corn"—with all three organic entities conflated into a single, and singing, sexual figure (20). On the basis of such specific observations, it's not difficult for students to conclude that March's first dream exactly conforms to the Freudian formula for dream motivation—the disguised fulfillment of a repressed and forbidden erotic wish (*On Dreams* 59). The disguise seems most revealing in March's first dream, as the fiery foxtail brushes her mouth or, in Freudian terms, as tail and mouth displace male and female genitalia and as pain displaces the sexual pleasure that March both anticipates and desires.

While March's second dream reflects many of the same elements as her first (girl meets fox), it's a darker and far more troubling vision. Students know at once, of course, that it's a nightmare since March awakens from it suddenly and in tears. Prodded by Freud's insistence that nightmares are wish fulfillments too—the repressed wish now being insufficiently disguised and directly threatening the dreamer—students have speculated that March dreams Banford dead because March really wants her dead. A good question to raise at this point is why the fox figure (ever-sexual albeit now skinned) appears in a thanatic as well as an erotic dream. One intriguing response to this has been that as March covers Banford's body with the fox skin, she acts out Freud's notion that a dreamer always condenses "either-or" into "and" (*On Dreams* 28). March's wish, in other words, is to be rid of Banford by any means possible—by death if necessary or, even less likely, by Jill's becoming involved with a fox or man of her own. Knowing Jill, March also knows that this last desperate wish is hopeless or, in the illogical eloquence of sleep, that

> all she could find . . . was a fox skin. She knew that it wasn't right, that this was not what she [Jill] could have. But it was all she could find. And so she folded the brush of the fox, and laid her darling Jill's head on this, and she brought round the skin of the fox and laid it on top of the body, so that it seemed to make a whole ruddy, fiery coverlet, and she cried and cried and woke to find the tears streaming down her face.   (40–41)

While March's dreams end suddenly and permanently right here, a discussion of textual dreaming in *The Fox* should not. The questions that turn a class from limited to all-inclusive issues can, in fact, be raised precisely at this point. Do the same strategies employed to reveal March's dreams, for instance, also account for the text as a whole? Does *The Fox* itself function like one of March's sleeping visions writ large, thus revealing the covert fulfillment of repressed and forbidden authorial desires? Such questions usually invite heated and imaginative responses from students. Among the varied conclusions students have reached, one has recurred frequently enough to be termed Lawrence's "atavistic wish." Given a world in which human complexity is compounded (or confounded) by modernity—the First World War, the irreversible evolution of sexual roles and relationships—*The Fox* may dream out Lawrence's wish for a far older and more primitive alternative. It may longingly envision a return to the hunt not only as a means of livelihood but also as a seductive model for human activity in general and for male activity in particular.

Approaching *The Fox* as a triply condensed hunting dream (literally of foxes, erotically of mates, and thanatically of enemies) helps account for the work's ethical difficulties yet by no means excuses them. The same approach also helps students come to terms with the strangeness of *The Fox*—its implausibility of character and event as measured by realistic standards, yet hardly by the standards of any dream a student or teacher is able to recall and willing to recount in class. Finally, if *The Fox* is read as dream inscription, its ending can be approached as Lawrence's awakening from the temptations of his own fantasy. This perspective helps account for the difficulty of the work's "long tail," the ending's function, even its departure in style and substance from everything else in the text. If Lawrence proves honest in *The Fox* by dreaming out his forbidden wish, he proves doubly honest at the close by admitting its impossibility. As the story ends, Henry and March cease to be predator and prey, dream fox in pursuit of dream rabbit. They emerge from these strange disguises as a man and woman painfully conscious, like Lawrence himself, of their troubled past and even more uncertain future.

Teaching "The Prussian Officer" with the Help of Daniel Stern and Jessica Benjamin

Phyllis Sternberg Perrakis

In "The Prussian Officer" students can see Lawrence for the first time getting conscious hold of an understanding that was latent in *Sons and Lovers*—the importance of preverbal modes of experiencing the self and an awareness of how language, and the relation to culture it brings, can introduce or strengthen a false and excessively self-conscious form of identity. Indeed, "The Prussian Officer" is built around the conflict between preverbal and verbal senses of self: the orderly, Schöner, seems much more comfortable with his preverbal, instinctual self, while the captain, Hauptmann, relies almost entirely on his rigid, self-conscious, verbal self.

Students are quick to point out that the conflict between the two men (and between these two modes of knowing the self and relating to the other) breaks out when the captain kicks the orderly. However, they may need help realizing that both men lose their usual ways of adapting: the captain loses control of his emotions and gives way to a previously unknown instinctual violent self; the orderly, lacking the verbal resources to admit or articulate what has happened to him, experiences an intense sense of isolation and humiliation.

If students have read *Sons and Lovers*, they appreciate knowing that at the time of writing "The Prussian Officer" Lawrence had begun reassessing his family dynamics, particularly his relationship with his parents. He began to understand and value his inarticulate father, the despised brute of his childhood, differently. Lawrence's growing awareness of conflict between a preverbal self and a self-conscious, verbal self finds lifelong expression in his astonishing ability to suggest (to articulate—insofar as possible) the workings of the inner selves of relatively inarticulate characters.

"The Prussian Officer" provides students with a particularly clear example of the conflict between the preverbal and verbal senses of self. Since students are often troubled and puzzled by the violence of the story, Daniel Stern's discussion of core and verbal senses of self in *The Interpersonal World of the Infant* proves useful. Stern's analysis can help students better understand the oppositional natures developed in the tale. Schöner's "free and self-contained" movements and the unthinking confidence with which his "young, brown, shapely peasants' hands grasp the loaf or the wine-bottle" (*"Prussian Officer"* 3) testify to his ease with a core level of self that Stern argues is first developed in the early months of life when the infant becomes aware of "itself as a coherent, willful, physical entity" separate from the mother (26). The orderly's "expressionless eyes, that seemed never to have thought," attest to his inexperience with a more self-conscious mode of self identity (3).

Conversely, Hauptmann's strict suppression of his instincts and feelings and his excessive mental consciousness point to an overly developed verbal sense of self, the mode of relating an infant achieves in the second year that allows the child "to objectify the self, to be self-reflective, to comprehend and produce language" (Stern 28). Although Hauptmann "knew himself to be always on the point of breaking out," he rigidly controls his "passionate temper," and his mental discipline reigns supreme (4). However, his discomfort with his physical self, suggested by his inability to find satisfaction with a woman, leaves him irritable and frustrated.

After a brief introduction to Stern's theory, students notice how the captain, physically awakened to his nonverbal self against his will by Schöner, tries to master the newly stirred instincts by dominating the orderly. I add that the captain also tries to force from his orderly some form of what Jessica Benjamin calls recognition—"that response from the other which makes meaningful the feelings, intentions, and actions of the self" (Benjamin 23). Schöner, however, is determined not to acknowledge any personal element in his contact with the captain and in this way protects himself from conscious submission to Hauptmann.

Gradually their interaction causes each man to act out of his less-developed sense of self. Students easily see that the captain attempts to break through the orderly's refusal to grant him recognition by physically abusing Schöner. But they are less likely to observe that the captain's dominance is not fully asserted and the orderly is not fully forced into submission until Hauptmann extracts from the younger man the admission that Schöner had been writing poetry "[f]or my girl" (8). Schöner is violated more by Hauptmann's invasion of his newly asserted and vulnerable verbal sense of self than by the captain's vicious kicks.

Forced to acknowledge the captain's power over him, the orderly feels stripped of agency and independence. Unable to reach out to others or exercise his autonomy, the young man's core sense of self is damaged as he feels himself "coming to pieces, disintegrated" (10). The captain, conversely, feeling "pleased" and "proud," reasserts his personal control over Schöner by singling the orderly out from the "common subjection" in which all the soldiers in the company were united (12). But when Hauptmann commands Schöner to fetch his lunch, he adds, unwisely, "Quick!" (13). I ask students why that one extra word might be especially dangerous. They usually mention its echoes from the final sentence of *Sons and Lovers* and its Lawrentian connotations of inner vitality, as well as its more realistic effect here, of adding insult to injury. I suggest that the word "quick" helps awaken the orderly's sense of independent core selfhood, and I direct students to the evidence for this in the text: while physically obeying the order, Schöner finds "hard there in the centre of his chest was himself . . . not to be plucked to pieces" (13).

What students struggle with most, however, is that to reverse the master-slave relationship begun by the captain the orderly must kill the man who he feels is threatening his autonomy; having become half of a "split unity" (Benjamin 65), Schöner, whether master or slave, seems unable to survive alone. I find both Stern's and Benjamin's work helpful here in emphasizing that only a new mode of relating, one that integrates the verbal and preverbal senses of self and incorporates the "delicate balance" (Benjamin 12) between self-assertion and mutual recognition of the independence of the other could have allowed the captain and Schöner to coexist. The story's bleak ending suggests, I tell students, just how fraught with anxiety the attempt to discover such a new mode, by integrating into the self previously underdeveloped aspects of one's identity, can be. Stern's theory can help students understand the extremity of this anxiety—and thus the violent resolution of Lawrence's tale.

"I Don't Like England Very Much, but . . .": The Construction of Englishness in "England, My England"

Tim Middleton

I teach Lawrence's "England, My England" to first-year cultural studies students in a module that explores the construction of national identity in England in the period from 1900 to 1950. Lawrence's story provides a way into many of the tensions associated with proclaiming adherence to English national identity in the early twentieth century. By means of subtle narrative focalization, it both partakes in and critiques the (often rather mournful) mythmaking that informs works as apparently diverse as W. E. Henley's *For England's Sake*, Edward Thomas's *The Heart of England*, Ford Madox Ford's *England and the English*, and, in the postwar period, Ernest Raymond's *Tell England* and A. G. Macdonnell's *England, Their England*. As David Gervais argues, Lawrence, unlike many commentators on the state of the nation in the early twentieth century, has the "rare ability to evoke the pathos of modern England without succumbing to nostalgia for some 'land of lost content'" (87).

In what follows I adapt exercises that I use at different points in the workshops offered on the module: where it seems appropriate, I offer contextualizing remarks regarding what each task aims to achieve and how I get students to work on it. These are introductory activities intended to initiate debate and discussion: students work in small groups on one activity for about thirty to forty-five minutes before reporting back to the whole seminar group.

Exploring Englishness

I ask students to read Lawrence's letters to Collings, 22 July 1913 (2: 46–47), and Lady Asquith, 9 November 1915 (2: 431–32), and then to work on one of the following activities:

> To what extent is Lawrence's characterization of the English in the letter to Collings figured in the character of Egbert? Discuss one or two examples.
>
> Do Lawrence's remarks about English women inform the character of Winifred? Discuss one or two examples.
>
> Summarize Lawrence's argument in the letter to Lady Asquith about what is happening to England. Does this England belong to a certain class? Is the England Lawrence refers to here the same as the one with which Egbert is identified? Note any similarities and differences and comment on them.
>
> To what extent can the family relations at the heart of "England, My

England" be seen as a representation of the wider state of the nation as diagnosed by Lawrence in his letter to Lady Asquith?

"England, My England": Place and "Structures of Feeling"

This activity involves students working more closely with the text. It assumes some initial work on cultural geography (e.g., Agnew; Keith and Pile, esp. 1–40) as well as familiarity with Raymond Williams's notion of a "structure of feeling" (*Long Revolution* 64, 57–88). The activity is as follows:

> "England, My England" has three locations: Crockham Cottage, London, and the battlefields of Flanders. Comment on the function of each in the story with reference to J. Agnew's remarks on the meaning of place.

I usually get students to work in small groups on one location, tracking references and descriptions and beginning to build up an account of the feelings and behaviors associated with each location. I hope students will work on how London and Flanders as sites of modernity are contrasted to Crockham. More acute students will point out that Egbert's emotional investment in Crockham Cottage is compromised by the reliance on money from Winifred's father; they may also note that Crockham and Flanders are both places of savagery. In the wider context of the module, I get students to consider the ways in which the regional divide between southern and northern England functions in the story since this opens up issues around the ongoing construction of "the South Country" as the site of the "real" England (see Giles and Middleton 73–103).

"England, My England": Subjectivities

These activities let students use their knowledge of the text to come up with a range of passages relating to the construction of subjectivity. The activities assume some basic work on discourse theory and on Mikhail Bakhtin's notion of dialogics (e.g., Holquist; D. Macdonell).

> "England, My England" probes the shifting perception of the ways of being associated with such roles as Englishman, father, craftsman, and soldier.
>
> a) Compare Egbert and Godfrey Marshall as Englishmen and as fathers: note major similarities and differences.
> b) Egbert seems to inhabit many different roles: for example, gardener, lover, dabbler in the arts, father, soldier. Choose two of these roles and comment on the extent to which they are in tension.

c) Compare the family backgrounds of Egbert and Winifred. What differences in the characters' value systems might stem from their upbringing?

What shapes or informs how characters react or act at specific moments in the story? Consider in particular Winifred's attraction to Egbert (7–8) and her feelings after the birth of the children (11–12); Godfrey's attitudes toward his son-in-law (9, 15–16); Egbert as gardener (5, 9, 24–25); and Egbert's decision to join up (27–28) and Winifred's reaction to it (29–30).

These activities encourage debate and discussion on many passages in the text and ask students to undertake some intellectually challenging work questioning the notion of Englishness (both individual identity and national identity) and how it is constructed.

Sons and Lovers and Book History

A. R. Atkins

I teach book history with final-year honors undergraduates in a specialist course called The Novel and the British Book Trade, 1830–1914. The course aims to help students understand historically some of the material and sociological conditions in which novels were produced in the first eighty years or so of machine printing. We look at early Victorian works published in weekly parts, serial and three-decker novels, and the single-volume hardbacks that dominated the industry from the mid-1890s. Students are expected to become familiar, through study of critics like N. N. Feltes, Andrew Blake, and Peter Keating, with developments such as the achievement of international copyright agreements between Britain and the United States; the introduction of the Monotype machine and the Net Book Agreement in the United Kingdom; the recurring debates over the viability of cheap books and the need for censorship; and the growth of formal contracts, royalty agreements, and literary agents. They are also encouraged to relate these topics to more conventional, literary readings of the novels.

Sons and Lovers is well suited to such a course because of its complex, protracted composition and publication and what might be called its protomodernist qualities. The first two-hour seminar focuses on the novel as commercial artifact and on the series of events that led to the production of the first edition. I use Mark Schorer's facsimile edition and articles by Helen Baron ("Mrs. Morel," "Sons," "Surviving Galley Proofs") for examples of how Lawrence created the novel from a palimpsest of material and for examples of Edward Garnett's cuts and of changes made for reasons of censorship, house style, and so on by Duckworth and the printers. A student presentation looks at the format of the first edition and how it was advertised and reviewed, comparing it with other books published by Duckworth and other firms that year. We conclude by considering the merits of the two distinct editions now in print (see part 1, "Materials," in this volume) and the importance of historical knowledge in reaching editorial and critical interpretations.

The second seminar addresses a variety of topics, depending on the group's interests. One possibility is the effect of Garnett's cuts on the novel, both formally and stylistically, and what they reveal about his attitudes and about roles in prewar literary culture. Another examines the relations among art, gender, and history in the novel and in Lawrence's career. Some students adapt work by Baron ("Jessie Chambers' Plea") to argue that Paul is simply Lawrence's masculinist mouthpiece, relentlessly asserting a free artistic subjectivity that explicitly resists attempts by women to attain an equivalent sense of professionalized self. Such conclusions are challenged, however, by persistent reminders of how Paul's identity is determined (or overdetermined) by his society and its dominant modes of production: despite all his phases of artistic vision (on these see Kushigian; Atkins; and Laird, *Self*), Paul ends the novel working as a clerk (a copyist, like his brother William) and designer for Liberty's (a real firm, but one whose name is replete with ironies).

These issues are not just formal or psychological but relate directly to the course's book-history concerns. Students are invited to compare Paul with Lawrence's understanding of his own position as an author. Paul Eggert's groundbreaking argument that Lawrence was split in *Sons and Lovers* between "an ambitious but only half-understood literary experiment on the one hand, and a countervailing, articulate literary fashion on the other" ("Opening" 43), helps students realize that analysis of a novel's themes and structures can be closely related to the novel's identity as a commercial artifact and a locus of cooperation, conflict, and change between different agents in print culture. Early on, according to Jessie Chambers (62), Lawrence aspired to be like William Blake, writing and making books by hand for private patrons (and merely "helped" by a wife); later on, he struggled with the constraints and opportunities of mainstream publishing, sometimes dreaming of making a thousand a year, sometimes plotting to use private-press publication as the best means of securing a sympathetic readership (Worthen, "Expensive Edition"). Much has been written about Sylvia Beach and *Ulysses* and about the freedom offered to Virginia Woolf by the Hogarth Press; the class concludes with some reflection on how the history of literary modernism might be rewritten if more attention were paid to the careers of Lawrence, Dorothy Richardson, or the Sitwells.

Teaching *Sons and Lovers* in a Global Context in South Africa: Colonialism and Modernity

James M. Phelps

My students at the University of Zululand come largely from educationally disadvantaged backgrounds stemming from political disruptions, demoralized teachers, violence, underfunded schools, and damaged school infrastructure—all set within a context of rapid cultural transformations. Traditional rural upbringings are changing to modern urban ones. Thus the intellectual potential of many students has often been inadequately cultivated during their crucial formative years. These disadvantages, which make any university-level teaching challenging, are frequently complicated by an anti-Eurocentrism that also affects the teaching of Lawrence. But despite these difficult conditions, some good work is accomplished, and Lawrence holds his own under the circumstances.

I attempt to relate *Sons and Lovers* to the historical and contemporary context from which my students have come. By the middle of the nineteenth century, when in Bestwood "a sudden change took place" and the "gin-pits were elbowed aside by the large mines of the financiers" (9), the first Europeans had arrived in southeastern Africa, the country of the Zulu people, and the period of colonization had begun. There are parallels between the social changes resulting from the modern age that Lawrence pictures in *Sons and Lovers* and those that occurred in Zululand and are still affecting my students today.

Lawrence, in the opening pages of *Sons and Lovers*, contextualizes his story of growing up in a modern working-class home in historical, social, and economic terms. He clearly contrasts the ancient rural life of Nottinghamshire and Derbyshire—where the "ruined priory of the Carthusians" and "Robin Hood's well" are integral to the scene and where the preindustrial "cottages of the [gin-pit] coal-miners in blocks and pairs here and there, together with the odd farms and homes of the stockingers, straying over the parish, formed the village of Bestwood" (9)—with the modern industrial age unleashed by the capitalist development of the coal mines. If the colonial and modern experience in Zululand is recognized as generic with and flowing from the expansion of the modern industrial economy seen in *Sons and Lovers*, my students are often better able to relate the conflicts in the Morel family to their own lives.

In *Sons and Lovers*, characters are caught in various processes of alienation: feeling, particularly sexual feeling, is set at odds with intellect; the working class is alienated from the middle class; and the natural world is divided from and exploited by the industrial mining economy. As these processes interweave, so the world in which the sons grow up distorts them. William never escapes being a victim of this distortion and dies tragically young as a result. Paul is likewise a victim, but as he suffers he begins to recognize that his problems arise in part from influences outside himself; and though he deeply needs the sensitive spiritual companionship of both mother and Miriam Leivers, he increasingly realizes that he would have to sacrifice his emerging sexual being if he were to persist in these relationships and grant them the highest value. As Lawrence unfolds Paul's struggles to set himself free, he develops a penetrating critique of modern society.

At the University of Zululand the BA degree takes three years to complete. In the final year two major subjects are chosen: about thirty-five percent of our students choose English as one of their majors. I teach Lawrence's *Sons and Lovers*—the one twentieth-century English novel English majors are required to study—to students in the second semester of their third year.

The issue in *Sons and Lovers* that first catches hold of the students' imaginations is the relationship between Mr. and Mrs. Morel. The patriarchy of traditional African culture persists despite many cultural changes. It is breaking down, however, so the conflict between husband and wife arouses intense identification. My young, urbanized women students strongly identify with Mrs. Morel; their male counterparts sympathize with her too, since often their mothers have been the ones who have especially encouraged their educations. But there are always some young men very much on Mr. Morel's side, identifying with him both as a man and as a working-class man. These opposing sympathies set up opportunities for class discussions.

However, the highly complex exploration of modern dissociated sensibility embodied in Paul and the struggles he has in love with Miriam and Clara are more difficult for my students. Romantic love and relationships chosen by individual men and women are modern phenomena. Arranged marriages were the norm in Zulu culture, and polygamy is still common. In modern urbanized conditions, love leading to marriage does now occur, but relations between men and women are in a fluid state—a context obviously contributing to the way my students identify, or fail to identify, with the situations and characters in *Sons and Lovers*. Nevertheless, the sons' relationships with the mother and father and with the first girlfriends always fascinate my students—partly, I suspect, because they are mixed with the issue of the transition from working class to middle class. My students identify strongly both with the mother, who believes in the importance of an education as a way out of the working class, and with Lawrence, the son of an almost illiterate father but a more educated mother—because many come from similar backgrounds.

In teaching *Sons and Lovers* at the University of Zululand, I have found that the best teaching advice comes from Lawrence (a teacher once himself) through Birkin in *Women in Love*: clear emphasis of key elements, as Birkin advises in teaching about flower fertilization in the "Class-room" chapter, is essential. In addition to the political, economic, and historical elements described above, I ask my students to focus on Lawrence's use of the interloper (literally, one who "leaps between") in *Sons and Lovers* (Lawrence uses this figure else-

where, of course—for example, in *Women in Love* and in *Lady Chatterley*).
This focus offers a way of examining not only the intrusion of first William and
then Paul into their parents' relationship but also the interloping of Miriam into
the relationship between Paul and his mother and later of Clara into the relationship between Paul and Miriam. (The interloping of Paul into the relationship between Clara and Baxter Dawes is highlighted when students consider
the role of the interloper in this novel on a larger scale: the intrusion of industry
into rural England and of industrial England into other cultures.) Lawrence's
psychology of interpersonal dynamics in the family—similar to certain contemporary psychologies that practicing psychologists increasingly favor over the
Freudian approach—is also illuminated by the interloper plot analysis. Finally,
I recommend to my students Michael Black's little book on *Sons and Lovers*
and Helen Baron and Carl Baron's introduction to the new Penguin edition of
the novel: both are short, well-written, and treat the new uncut edition of the
novel.

A few of my students have given permission for me to reproduce here extracts from their responses to the following essay assignment:

> The struggles in love of Paul Morel might appear to some as far removed
> from the experience of young people in South Africa today, but this is not
> so. What is your reaction to this statement? Carefully select incidents in
> the novel to substantiate your views. Make particular reference to what
> you consider common or different experiences of modernity.

Students' responses were written in September 1996; usage and tense errors
have not been corrected.

> The situation we find Paul Morel in is evident in South Africa. Through
> urbanization and industrialization people were separated from their fam-
> ilies. People would move from the rural areas to urban areas searching for
> jobs. A man would only come home once a month, or after six months.
> The children will be raised by the mother alone, and they won't have a
> balanced adulthood. Because of their closeness with their mothers they
> would use them as role-models when choosing wives. The same goes for
> Paul Morel who is brought up by his mother because the father is work-
> ing in the mines. Although he comes home every day, he is too tired to
> control the house.   (Thulisile G. Maphungela)

> Young South Africans have also undergone such hardships. For instance,
> with the growth of the mining industries, when the fathers go to the
> mines the mothers become heads of their families. . . . Thus, this leads to
> the shift from the father to the mother. When they [the children] are to
> express affection to their father, they experience conflict. (Wesley Canham)

The struggles in love of Paul Morel are not as far removed from the experience of young people in South Africa as some might think. For example, I speculate that many mothers are possessive and dominant over the lives of their children, particularly boys. Boys are expected to take a lead in family matters. In other words, boys are often expected to look after the little ones and mothers after the death of fathers. This kind of life affects young men tremendously. For instance, when a boy becomes mature and is expected to get married, a mother becomes more possessive and jealous, because she believes he will be taken away from her, just like Mrs. Morel believes "she [Miriam] carries him [Paul] off from me" (230), and that her share, either financially or socially, will be threatened, just as Mrs. Morel thinks of Miriam: "She's not like an ordinary woman, who can leave me my *share* in him" (230; student's emphasis).   (Tholinhlanhla X. Zulu)

Clearly, my best students find that *Sons and Lovers* provides useful insights into English culture as well as into South Africa's cultural transformations and students' own family and maturational problems. They respond to *Sons and Lovers* with an immediacy unlikely in turn-of-the-twenty-first-century Europe or North America. Too often we teach *Sons and Lovers* only in the context of Eastwood and the mines, but that Lawrence is taught worldwide in an educational environment of great diversity should inform our teaching of this novel in particular. The context of Paul Morel's struggle is a matter not just of cultural conditions in England at the time of Lawrence's upbringing and education but also of England in the world, including the extension of the conflicts between the working and middle classes into the colonial domain. The novel both describes and critiques ideological hegemonies of Lawrence's time—a time that in many ways continues to be our own.

Teaching the Case of the Subversive Novel: The Role of Contemporary Reviews in *The Rainbow* Trial

Wayne Templeton

On 13 March 1915, Sir Charles Matthews, director of public prosecutions, ordered the destruction under the Obscene Publications Act (1857) of all copies of D. H. Lawrence's recently published novel *The Rainbow*. This state of affairs was reached because during the First World War Lawrence dared openly to criticize war, imperialism, industrial capitalism, education, marriage, democracy, and, by implication, literature. But pressure was not brought to bear on the judiciary from, as one might expect, the military establishment, Parliament, or the Church of England; rather, the ban was achieved as a direct consequence of hostile critics—reviewers of the novel—two of whom, James Douglas and Clement Shorter, were the prosecution's leading witnesses.

In studying *The Rainbow*, students benefit from examining a number of contemporary reviews; these reviews help contextualize the novel's suppression as one example of the Georgian reaction to modernism. Other examples abound; in the United Kingdom alone, Thomas Hardy, a precursor to modernism, was censured all his life. Joyce's *Ulysses* was banned, as were Lawrence's *Lady Chatterley's Lover* and Radclyffe Hall's *The Well of Loneliness*. Compton Mackenzie's *Extraordinary Women* was almost prosecuted, and certainly E. M. Forster's *Maurice* would have been had its author not withheld publication for many years.

Students also need to expand their understanding of how and why the censorship of literature proceeds, and even, perhaps, to learn how to anticipate that progress. I suggest to them that there are three categories of literature: popular, scholarly, and subversive. In the early twentieth century, they were distinguished as, respectively, popular, Edwardian, and modernist. While popular literature is simple (nonliterary, nonilluminating, denotative, concrete, literal, moral, and explicit) and scholarly works are complex (or at least more complex—literary, reflective, abstract, connotative, figurative, and implicit), both are largely noncritical of and in fact acquiescent to political hegemony; that is, they are politically conservative, often reactionary and conventional, even derivative: in Eric Auerbach's terms, mimetic as opposed to revelationary.

Subversive literature, however, is critical of hegemony, often countercultural, experimental, original, creative, and, as a result, complex, difficult, ambiguous, and invariably perceived, initially at least, as hostile. If we were to define each literary category as either simple or complex and either uncritical or critical, we would have simple-uncritical (popular) literature, complex-uncritical (highbrow, scholarly, or Edwardian) literature, and complex-critical (subversive, or modernist) literature. (One would find simple-critical literature in political pamphlets and certain children's stories, although even the latter, like parables, might be considered complex-critical literature.)

Critics also fall into three categories: the populist, the conservative scholarly (or what Terry Eagleton terms "sage"), and the radical. The populists would not normally have been concerned with a work like *The Rainbow*, shunning it at the outset because of suspicions of lofty goals, abstractions, and the poetic use of metaphors. They would have preferred, in 1915, to review the stirring new Edgar Rice Burroughs tale, *Tarzan of the Apes*, or John Buchan's spy thriller, *The Thirty-Nine Steps*. But a few populist critics were made curious enough by the publicity of *The Rainbow* to read and then comment on Lawrence's new work. Typical of these was the anonymous reviewer in the *Westminister Gazette* who was perplexed rather than outraged by the novel (Rev. of *The Rainbow*), as was Gerald Gould, who confessed, "I simply cannot imagine what Mr. Lawrence was about to write *The Rainbow*. I believe it has been accused of impropriety, but to me the most improper thing about it is the punctuation." As for the rest of the novel, in Gould's view it consists "almost entirely of fleshy people in paroxysms of emotion . . . which signify nothing" (66).

Conservative critics, while perhaps in 1915 acknowledging something of Lawrence's talent, also believe in the status quo and the need for rules and standards and see themselves as the guardians of public morality on constant watch for literature that is immoral, seditious, indecent, obscene, libelous, prurient, or nihilistic. And for them *The Rainbow* was an abomination, an insult to every decent human being alive, a work to be banned immediately. Robert Lynd, writing in the *Daily News*, denounced the work as "a monotonous wilderness of phallicism." Clement Shorter, editor of the conservative literary magazine *Sphere*, compared Lawrence with the "lurid" French writer Zola, whose novels are "child's food compared with the strong meat contained in . . . *The Rainbow*. . . . There is no form of viciousness, of suggestiveness, that is not reflected in these pages. I can only suppose that Mr. Methuen [the publisher] . . . for some reason failed to read this book in manuscript. . . . I can find no justification whatever for the perpetration of such a book."

Even harsher was the criticism of James Douglas, of the *Star*, who later became editor of the *Sunday Express*. "There is no doubt," he wrote, "that a book of this kind has no right to exist. It is a deliberate denial of the soul that leavens matter. These people [in the novel] are not human beings. They are creatures who are immeasurably lower than the lowest animal in the Zoo. There is no kindness in them, no tenderness, no softness, no sweetness. They are maladies of the mind, growths upon the brain, diseases more horrible than the good honest diseases known to the pathologist." And they certainly are not literary figures, for literature does not exist "to serve as a clue to the deepest haunts of hell." This "is insanity, the chilly, creeping madness of the sensualist who destroys the godlike mind by wearing out the senses in vain pursuit of all the imps of grossness. . . . Art is not anarchy. It is our servant, not our tyrant. The artist is not his own law-giver. He must bow before the will of the generations of man."

And finally: "The wind of war is sweeping over our life, and it is demolishing many of the noisome pestilences of peace. A thing like *The Rainbow* has no right to exist in the wind of war." Douglas was the prosecution's leading witness.

In 1857, Ernest Pinard, prosecuting attorney at the obscenity trial of *Madame Bovary*, made a point similar to Douglas's concerning the "laws of literature" necessary to ward off anarchy: "Art without rules," Pinard intoned, "is art no longer; it is like a woman who would shed all her clothing. To impose upon art the single standard of public decency is not to enslave but to honor it" (Kendrick 110). Pinard reminds us, notes Bradford Mudge, that "certain novels, like certain women, are more dangerous than others" (95); this is because they— both novels and women—are subversive; they subvert the standards, the moral codes, the status quo, and, most dangerous, they threaten the hegemony dependent on the status quo. And the critics, as apologists of that hegemony, align themselves with the judiciary and the clergy as defenders of those standards.

There were also radical critics in 1915, but not many. One was Helena Swanwick, writing in the *Manchester Guardian*; another, later to become a friend of Lawrence, was Catherine Carswell, who praised *The Rainbow* for being complex, beautiful, and subversive, a book "rich in emotional beauty and in the distilled essence of profoundly passionate and individual thinking about human life. . . . It betrays, moreover, the hand of a master writer. There are passages here . . . which must rank with the best work done by great novelists of any age. But for himself Mr. Lawrence is aiming at something quite different and distinct from mere good fiction . . . ; love in our modern life, instead of being a blessed, joyous, and fruitful thing, is sterile, cruel, poisonous, and accursed. . . . The modern world, according to Mr. Lawrence, is mad and sick and sad because it knows not how to love."

In a similar vein J. C. Squire, writing in the *New Statesman* under the pseudonym Solomon Eagle, stood virtually alone in criticizing the prosecution of *The Rainbow* and the reviewers who had so clamored to draw the novel to the attention of the authorities. But critics such as these had great difficulty being heard because they could not be published in newspapers and magazines with comparatively large numbers of subscribers (Carswell, who worked for the *Glasgow Herald*, was fired the day after her review was mistakenly published [Draper 100]). This is because, as Edward Herman and Noam Chomsky have meticulously delineated, large newspapers and magazines, in common with the advertisers on whom they depend, are equally a part of and submissive to the standards set by the political-cultural hegemony. They are also businesses working in partnership with publishers for whom the market represents the public will (witness the phenomenon of the bestseller). Newspapers cite subscription figures, which are directly related to the amount they can charge advertisers. These communication networks are, of course, not only in the business of making money but also in the business of building power, of forging and protecting political alliances.

Herman and Chomsky's propaganda model predicts the conditions under which one can anticipate corporate media's hostility, condemnation, and distortion or even omission of the truth in their efforts to maintain the status quo; these conditions include the need to support a government friendly to the media should they be under attack from elsewhere and the concomitant needs to silence critics of the government and to defend themselves. The propaganda model also includes the observation, which one can verify in reading the reviews hostile to *The Rainbow*, that criticism is invariably emotionally charged and bitter, conveying a sense of moral outrage and condemnation. Interestingly, this outrage is hyperbolic when the issue is relatively minor; when confronted with serious issues, the press is more inclined to silence. And here I would point out that some of the larger contemporary review publications—the *New York Times Book Review*, for example, and the *Athaeneum*—did not even review *The Rainbow*. These omissions involve what Chomsky terms the "obligation of silence" (81), a refusal to discuss issues that lie "beyond the conceivable" (165), issues such as hostile political criticism that are deemed illegitimate to expose. In such reactions, Chomsky says, we can see "the real issue lurking behind the barrage of rhetoric [or the silence]: it is the need to protect the ideological institutions . . . from analysis" (160). Chomsky's observation corresponds to Terry Eagleton's that all media-generated social discourse occurs within a public sphere that "acknowledges no given rational identity beyond its own bounds, for what counts as rationality is precisely the capacity to articulate within its constraints" (15)—which are ostensibly moral but ultimately hegemonic.

In reviews of *The Rainbow*, all this is remarkably clear. Reviewers lashed out at Lawrence for his "viciousness," his "suggestiveness," his "brutality," the "liberties he takes"; a few actually mentioned the war, but as Mark Kinkead-Weekes notes in his introduction to the novel "war-fever alone will not explain what happened. What else was responsible for the hysteria?" (lxx). He cannot say, but I think it clear that in the face of Lawrence's provocative criticism of the very fabric of British life—democracy, marriage, industrial capitalism, education—the critics could only focus on lesser evils.

Emile Delavenay has suggested that neither the authorities nor the critics sharing their worldview could address the disturbing issues Lawrence raised because of the embarrassing questions a discussion of the issues might have provoked. These issues would be of particular relevance during a trial. What happened was that following a rash of harsh reviews "practically inviting police intervention," the novel was seized and a trial date set (Delavenay 236). However, Detective-Inspector Albert Draper, of the Criminal Investigation Department of New Scotland Yard, made it clear to Methuen, Lawrence's publisher, that the trial "*would not be heard in a public court*" and that "*the author had no right to appear in the matter*" (238; Delavenay's emphasis), or at least that is what Methuen told Lawrence. Delavenay suggests that the publishing house may have been particularly acquiescent "in the hope of saving [its] own reputation from any slur, by complying with the suggestions of Inspector Draper." If that was the intention, Methuen was successful, for in addition to not having its author and his legal counsel in the courtroom, it was saved the ignominy of personal criticism. Indeed, the firm of Methuen was praised by Sir Hubert Muskett, the solicitor for Scotland Yard, as "a publishing house of old standing and the highest repute" and by Sir John Dickinson, the magistrate, as having "dealt with the matter with the strictest propriety" (239).

"The venom of the prosecuting solicitor and of the magistrate was thus saved for the absent author" (239), against whom they had acted "for the protection of public morals and public decency." *The Rainbow*, they said, was a "disgusting, detestable and pernicious work. . . . *Although there might not be an obscene word found in the book*, it was in fact a mass of obscenity *of thought, idea*, and *action*" (240; emphasis mine)—this attack despite the fact that the home secretary, Sir John Simon, had said in a public statement that "the publishers and not the author were the defendants" (241). In a private memorandum addressed to New Scotland Yard, Simon had made reference to Lawrence's wife, Frieda Weekley Lawrence, born Frieda von Richthofen, cousin of the famous Manfred von Richthofen, the First World War flying ace nicknamed the Red Baron. (Delavenay also notes the high level of official involvement in this case. Normally the home office was not involved, nor were the upper echelons of Scotland Yard. Even the prosecuting solicitor, Muskett, senior partner of Wontner and Sons, handled only the most important cases [241].)

While this may seem an extreme case, I believe it is not. Then as now, in the United Kingdom and elsewhere, the status quo attempts to suppress radical criticism of itself and does so most effectively when it can avoid having to admit there is any criticism and when a body of conservative artists and critics supports its efforts, in part through the implication that the suppression has to do not with art but with bad art. Radical critics are those who rescue this subversive literature from anonymity. These critics, born, in Terry Eagleton's words, of a struggle against "the absolutist state" (10), recognize the need for the canon to continue to expand. They also perceive in experimentation the possibility of innovative techniques developed to foster successful communication of new subject matter in a rapidly changing though continually repressive world, and they define literature as always subversive, critical of the status quo, and complex to the degree necessary to contend with complex subjects, problems, themes, and methods of characterization. Literature in these terms is ambiguous, reflecting an ambiguous world; it is ironic, connotative, and figurative, in ways and to a degree that popular writing is not and cannot be, for popular literature serves different purposes, as does highbrow, or scholarly, literature. And the difference here in critical terms is that conservative critics, writes Anthony Easthope, perceive literature "on the basis of *the frozen syllabus* . . . , a representation of the historical past as an ideal order, always already completed. Symptomatic of this is the degree to which [conservative] literary studies ignores the contemporary" (168). This view of literature is another facet of the obligation of silence, and if it had been permitted to exist unchallenged, we would probably now not have *The Rainbow*—or *Ulysses, Lady Chatterley's Lover, The Diviners, Catcher in the Rye*, or *The Handmaid's Tale*.

Toasting and Caroling in *The Rainbow*:
Dramatic Rituals in the Classroom

Virginia Crosswhite Hyde

Recognizing the power of gesture, ritual, and cult lore, D. H. Lawrence, more than most other writers, sought heterogeneous means of communicating with his audience—branching out from prose into prose poetry, poetry and song, chant and ritual, drama, and other arts. Some or all of these can become part of the classroom experience. When teaching *The Rainbow*, I ask the students to look for scenes that might be staged or presented as dramatic rituals; but other texts work as well.

The wedding toast and chivaree for Anna and Will Brangwen make especially good examples, for they concern communal experience that is perhaps best conveyed by a group rather than by a solitary reader. Chapter 5 ("Wedding at the Marsh") stands almost alone in creating the novel's impression that the Brangwens are located within a living society; the farm scenes generally feature isolated individuals or the nuclear family, but the wedding scenes bring together a broad spectrum of neighbors and relatives. Starting with the signing of the church registry, several students may move on to some of the rhythmic toasts:

> *(Scene: Inside the honeymoon cottage.)*
>
> TOM.   Fill your glasses up, an' let's have it all over again.
>   Hearth an' home, an' may ye enjoy it.
> FRANK.   Bed an' blessin,' an' may ye enjoy it.   (127)

As the presentation proceeds to Tom's speech about the "married soul" (129), it maintains humor while launching issues that the class may later discuss:

> TOM.   There's very little else on earth, but marriage. .... In heaven there is no marriage. But on earth there *is* marriage, else heaven drops out, and there's no bottom to it.
> FRANK'S WIFE. Just hark you now. ....
> ALFRED.   It's the brandy.   (128–29)

An angel must be "more than a human being," asserts Tom, thus leading to his claim that the soul of man and woman together form "an angel" to "rise united at the Judgment Day" (129). The entire conversation is a chantlike ritual, and Lawrence's characteristic repetition, of which students sometimes complain, reveals itself as a function of this evocative form. The lines are even close to metrical verse at times, from iambic pentameter ("There's very little else on

earth, but marriage") to some loose combination of anapests and dactyls: "It'll
not be the soul of me when I was a lad: for I hadn't a soul as would *make* an
angel then" (129). The class will understand several features of Lawrence's art
and thought all the better after this exercise: the poetic and dramatic elements of his art, the mystique of the physical soul, the combination of the sexual and the sacred, and the high value Lawrence places on relationship—not
only the one between the married couple but also the one among members of
a community.

This sense is furthered by the traditional singing wake that follows soon after
the toasts, with the singers standing outside the honeymoon cottage and the
young marrieds watching from the bedroom:

> *(Scene: Later, outside the honeymoon cottage.)*
> ALFRED.   We'd better leave 'em alone.
> TOM.   Nay nay. We'll carol 'em, for th' last time.
> *(Sound effects: Fiddles and piccolo.)*
> ELEVEN TIPSY MEN (singing).   "In the fields with their flocks abiding."
> *(Inside, Anna starts up and listens.)*
> WILL (*inside*).   It's the wake.
> ANNA (*looking out*).   It's Dad.
> WILL.   And my father.
> ANNA.   Aren't they silly?   (133)

The focus on the text that is required by this dramatic treatment ensures that
the students notice tones, dialects, gestures, settings, and even sound effects.
Of particular note is the shift of location from the outside to the inside of the
cottage, symbolizing the changing of the generations from that of the fathers to
that of the young couple—the transitional link between Ursula and the ances-
tral Brangwens. In some ways, a shift is even occurring from one entire worldview to another, but not without connections.

Additional insights can arise from research projects resulting in short reports
that explain the meaning of the wake, provide the text of the carol the men sing,
or explain the reference to "the old mystery play of St. George," which the
group discusses in the interim between the toast scene and the serenade (130).
Both the mystery play and the caroling are Christmas activities, not especially
wedding customs, and are thus among the annual seasonal activities that
Lawrence later discusses in connection with the third Brangwen generation
(259–61). Referring the students to this later echo reveals to them the importance of historical and cultural continuity in this novel—and adds a new dimension to the novel's employment of repetition—so that they can begin to look for
other recurring rhythms and motifs themselves.

Examining the Stylistic Diversity of *The Rainbow* and *Women in Love* in an Honors Seminar on Criticism and Research Methods

Jack Stewart

In my third-year honors seminar on criticism and research methods, I situated *The Rainbow* historically between nineteenth-century norms of the novel and emergent modernism, relating changes in the social world to Lawrence's concept of the new woman. *The Rainbow's* symbolic structure absorbs students' attention. The wavelike succession of generations and the parallelism of moonlight scenes call for careful distinctions to be made between the experiences of different characters in the ongoing process of self-formation. Since I wanted students to orient themselves to the language of the novel, I emphasized its diversity of stylistic modes, ranging from mythic symbolism in the opening chapter and "The Cathedral" through ritualism in the stacking of sheaves and Anna's pregnant dance to realism in "The Man's World" and "The Widening Circle," followed by expressionism and futurism in "The Bitterness of Ecstasy" and closing with visionary symbolism in the final chapter.

Contexts for Lawrence's language of the unconscious were found in biblical and Jungian symbolism and for his visual imagery and verbal rhythms in contemporary European art movements. Required readings included selections from *The Portable Jung* ("The Structure of the Psyche," "Aion: Phenomenology of the Self," "Marriage as a Psychological Relationship," and "On the Relation of Analytical Psychology to Poetry") and James Frazer's *The Golden Bough*. Lawrence's reading of Frazer's *Totemism and Exogamy* and Edward Tylor's *Primitive Culture* together with Lawrence's articulation of a blood-consciousness antithetical to mental consciousness were noted, as was his concept of allotropism deriving from his response to futurism (*Letters* 2: 470, 182–84, 593). The study of ritual, myth, archetype, and symbol provided a fruitful context for *The Rainbow*, which was the focus of seminar discussion, oral reports, and a research essay of five thousand words plus documentation of secondary sources. In developing theses students were asked to adopt a particular critical approach. I found that an interactive approach to the novel, combined with readings in psychology and mythology, stimulated student interest and learning.

In teaching *Women in Love* in the same seminar, I asked students to read simultaneously Mikhail Bakhtin's *The Dialogic Imagination*. The focus this time was on narrative discourse, particularly rhetorical strategies, dialogic interplay of voices, and contextualization of an author's speech within a character's. The dual approach was challenging as students struggled to assimilate Bakhtin's theory to Lawrence's practice. Some students were able to make relevant connections and to view the novel and its narrative techniques with new critical insight; others found their understanding of Bakhtin clarified when they applied his concepts to Lawrence's novel. Close parallels were also found between Bakhtin's concepts of heteroglossia, polyphony, and dialogic discourse (*Dialogic Imagination* 262–63, 275–79, 259–422) and Lawrence's convictions that "[the] novel is the highest complex of subtle interrelatedness that man has discovered" and that "[m]orality in the novel is the trembling instability of the balance" ("Morality" 172).

Given the complexity of *Women in Love*, I selected a series of scenes in which the class could look closely at language and see how certain words, like *knowledge* and *knowing*, become dialogized by recurring in various contexts and in the speech of conflicting characters. I found that focusing on the following examples had heuristic value: Gudrun's "knowing" the wedding guests as "a finished creation" in "Sisters" (14) (as distinct from the novel's—and life's—openendedness); Birkin's diatribe against Hermione's "lust for power, to *know*," and his invocation of "the great dark knowledge you can't have in your head" in "Class-room" (42, 43) as against Sir Joshua Malleson's rational knowledge that is liberty—"[in] compressed tabloids"—in "Breadalby" (86); Birkin's occult knowledge of "the lotus mystery" through copying a drawing of Chinese geese in the same chapter (89); Gudrun's sexual knowledge of Gerald's being through concentrating on phallic water-plants in "Sketch-book" (119); Birkin's intuitive knowledge of the symbiotic flows of creation and dissolution in "Water-Party" (173); Gerald and Gudrun's carnal knowledge of each other's sadomasochistic impulses in "Rabbit" (242) and her tactile knowledge of his "living, radio-active body" in "Death and Love" (332); the African fetishes' "mystic knowledge in disintegration and dissolution" in "Moony" (253); and Birkin's knowledge of potency in "the deepest physical mind" and the lovers' initiation into mysteries of darkness, silence, and touch, a paradoxical "knowledge which is death of knowledge, the reality of surety in not-knowing," in "Excurse" (318, 319). (For a fuller discussion of knowledge in this novel see Stewart, "Dialectics.)

Women in Love is the most challenging and rewarding of Lawrence's works to teach, but it is more difficult to teach continuously and as a whole than *The Rainbow* is. Zeroing in on individual scenes (such as the Arab mare episode) or on a constellation of scenes, such as "Rabbit," "Moony," and "Gladiatorial," can, however, highlight Lawrence's ritual action and symbolic language, while the dialogic approach tends to highlight contrasting viewpoints and values.

Virginia Woolf's complaint that Lawrence makes insistent demands on the reader, "so that I don't escape when I read him," is not an idle one (*Writer's Diary* 188). His power to make the reader see and think invites an engagement not only with the text and its contending voices but also with other minds, a kind of interaction that a research seminar uniquely provides.

"More Likely to Be the End of Experience": *Women in Love*, Sati, and the Marriage-Plot Tradition

Rebecca Carpenter

Women In Love is an effective focal point for a course on the evolution of the marriage-plot tradition in British literature. Inviting students to explore the differences between nineteenth-century marriage-plot novels and *Women in Love*, which clearly rejects both the structure and the assumptions of such novels, helps students understand what is modern about this novel.

The opening scene of *Women in Love* immediately announces itself as a departure from the marriage-plot tradition. The conversation between Ursula and Gudrun recalls and defies the many scenes in which Jane and Elizabeth Bennet exchange confidences. Students immediately remark that Ursula and Gudrun could not have concluded that marriage is "[m]ore likely to be the end of experience" (7) if they had been nineteenth-century marriage-plot heroines. As the novel goes on, students enjoy analyzing Birkin's attempt to redefine the terms of marriage and Ursula's modification of his terms, the homoerotic relationship between Birkin and Gerald, and Gerald and Gudrun's destructive relationship. Many students admire and identify strongly with either Birkin or Ursula and become strongly invested in the success of their relationship.

Students just beginning to read this novel frequently complain that it is difficult to understand the rapid and dramatic emotional changes Lawrence's characters undergo. In my opening lecture, I tell students that one of Lawrence's modernist techniques is to give us minute-by-minute snapshots of characters' emotional states. I suggest that we have all at moments felt extreme irritation with or even hatred toward those whom we love (this usually gets nods of agreement). Some students also have trouble with Birkin's abstract expressions, like "star equilibrium" (319) and "strange conjunction" (148). Close readings of "Mino" (ch. 13), "Moony" (ch. 19), and "Excurse" (ch. 23) help students become more comfortable with Birkin's language.

For example, after a first reading of "Mino," many of my students think that Birkin doesn't want to love Ursula, that he wants sex without commitment, or that he isn't interested in Ursula's emotions. They are confused by Birkin's seeming rejection of love. I point out that Birkin wants to pledge himself forever to Ursula. I then turn their attention to Birkin's statement that he wants "an equilibrium, a pure balance of two single beings—as the stars balance each other" (148). I ask students to consider the kind of love relationship that Birkin had with Hermione and to compare it with the kind of love he wants with Ursula. Students are usually able to make good sense of Birkin's desires after considering the problem in this context. They note that Birkin doesn't want a love that obliterates either partner's personality; he doesn't want the kind of clingy and dependent and manipulative relationship he experienced with Hermione.

I then point out Lawrence's references to sati in the novel. Lawrence clearly knew about the practice of sati—the act of widows casting themselves on their husbands' funeral pyres in India; he explicitly mentions this custom in "The Industrial Magnate" chapter. After Gerald Crich takes over his father's business, he stops the practice of providing coal to widows. Many of these women's husbands died in the mines or from diseases brought on by long hours in the pit, but Gerald refuses to acknowledge any obligation to the widows. He dislikes the mere thought of these extraneous, needy women who accepted this charity from the family business for years and wonders, "Why were they not immolated on the pyre of the husband, like the sati in India?" (230).

Later in the novel, Lawrence employs sati metaphorically to describe domestic life. In "Flitting" (ch. 29) Lawrence describes a "wintry afternoon" (372) when Ursula and Gudrun return to their own personal heart of darkness, the house in Willey Green in which their family lived. As they inspect their old home, there are repeated images of "papery" imprisonment (e.g., "a cell would have been lovelier"; "walls . . . dry and papery"; "[W]ere they standing . . . suspended in some cardboard box?"—"a sense of intolerable papery imprisonment in nothingness" [372–73]). Ursula's eyes focus on the hearth, a symbolic site in the home, traditionally considered its heart, around which the family gathers. Ursula finds herself drawn toward the pieces of paper she sees lying under the grate. When she looks more closely, she realizes that she is looking at pictures of women, charred representations of her own sex:

> In the hearth was burnt paper, and scraps of half-burnt paper.
> "Imagine that we passed our days here!" said Ursula.
> "I know," cried Gudrun, "It is too appalling. What must we be like, if we are contents of this!"
> "Vile!" said Ursula. "It really is."
> And she recognized half-burnt covers of "Vogue"—half-burnt representations of women in gowns—lying under the grate.   (372)

These discarded, burnt images of women suggest what Lawrence believed marriage and domesticity could do to women—and perhaps could particularly do to women who wanted to be in vogue or who devoted their lives to tending the hearth and keeping the home fires burning while their husbands did their duty to god and country. Such women wound up being sacrificial victims, barely recognizable versions of the colorful women they once were, symbolically trapped under the grate rather than seated by it. Victorian mythologies held that women relished their domestic duties. In this scene, Lawrence suggests that domesticity kills women, mars their potential, turning them into charred fragments (cf. Sargent, "The Lost Girl," on the way the care of Manchester House comes close to killing Alvina; see Lawrence, *Lost Girl* 62). Ursula and Gudrun recognize the need violently to reject this kind of life. Lawrence thus invokes the trope of sati to further his rhetorical attack on Western culture and justify his call for a new kind of relationship between man and woman.

I point out to students that sati played an important and far from innocent role in the imperial discourse of Lawrence's time. As Lata Mani has established, sati was often invoked as a justification of continued British rule in India; colonial administrators cited incidents of "the barbarity of Hindu males in their coercion" (97) and used it to legitimate England's moral authority. Obviously, a people that engaged in such savage customs was not ready for self-rule (88–126). In *Women in Love*, Lawrence implies that marriage in Victorian England is the spiritual equivalent of sati (and thus that the West could claim no real moral superiority over the East in this respect): marriage too demands that women destroy themselves, that they stifle themselves and immolate their natural independence. Ursula and Gudrun regard the home, which was traditionally held to be women's sphere and sanctuary, with disgust and horror; the home is a trap they wish to escape.

My course, Marriage in the Modern Era, is a lower-division course, so I limit myself to five or six texts; teachers of more advanced students will want to select a more ambitious list. Possible texts include Jane Austen's *Pride and Prejudice*, Charlotte Brontë's *Jane Eyre*, Mona Caird's *The Daughters of Danaus*, Thomas Hardy's *Jude the Obscure*, E. M. Forster's *Howard's End*, Evelyn Waugh's *A Handful of Dust*, Doris Lessing's *Martha Quest*, Hanif Kureishi's *The Buddha of Suburbia*, and Julian Barnes's *Talking It Over*. These novels allow students to see how twentieth-century novelists have modernized, modified, and rejected the Victorian marriage-plot tradition.

Looking at *Women in Love* in the context of this tradition, my students are always delighted and surprised to note that unlike many other twentieth-century novelists, Lawrence manages to recuperate the idea of marriage and retain an ideal of love. While authors like Waugh, Kureishi, and Barnes depict modern marriage in a cynical light, Lawrence shows Birkin hoping that one can be reborn through committed love:

> I don't *know* what I want of you. I deliver *myself* over to the unknown, in coming to you, I am without reserves or defences, stripped entirely into the unknown. Only there needs the pledge between us, that we will both cast off everything, cast off ourselves even, and cease to be, so that which is perfectly ourselves can take place in us.   (147)

Many of my students have lived through painful divorces, and even those who have not live in an age of divorce, an age simultaneously sentimental and cynical about love and marriage. My students enjoy Lawrence because he makes them think about love and gives them a way to believe in love again.

I am consistently impressed by my students' discussions of what seems modern about *Women in Love*—by their ability to make sense of its emotional content and of its critique of traditional Victorian relations between the sexes as a form of spiritual sati for women, by their ability to appreciate the qualities of Lawrence's prose and Birkin and Ursula's attempts to rewrite marriage for the modern era.

Unlearning Europe: Postcolonial Questions for Teaching *The Plumed Serpent*

Theresa Mae Thompson

Students probably need more help with historical context and with postcolonial theory in reading *The Plumed Serpent* than in reading any other Lawrence novel. An early question the teacher should raise is, should we assume that the power to transfigure another culture, to assert authority over its languages, beliefs, and aesthetics, arises always and solely with the invading, colonizing peoples. Certainly when the colonized turn the tables and "invade" the original invader, the issue gets more complicated. As Edward Said points out, "cultures actually assume more 'foreign' elements, alterities, differences, than they consciously exclude. . . . [Who] in Britain or France can draw a clear circle around British London or French Paris that would exclude the impact of India and Algeria upon those imperial cities?" (15).

But what do we find when we examine interactions between indigenous populations and invading Europeans and Americans of European descent? Of course, it would also be impossible to draw a circle around Mexico City and isolate that which is only Spanish, but the balances of power there were different from those in London and Paris. The five-hundred-year American holocaust occurred and in many ways continues to devastate Mexican populations. What can be explored in the classroom, however, is Homi Bhabha's theory of hybridization, which states that the cultural and genetic intermingling that occurs between colonizers and the colonized creates sites of excess. These sites can turn "the discursive conditions of dominance into the grounds of intervention" for the indigenous population against descendants of colonizing and imperialist populations (35). Studying *The Plumed Serpent*—in which Lawrence focuses on the concerns of disenfranchised natives and mestizos in Mexico—students can explore exactly this kind of intervention.

At the beginning of the twentieth century, the greatest fear of imperial nations centered on the idea of such hybridization. While the fear often focused on a eugenics discouse of white racial degeneration, all primary discourses surrounding colonization sought to prohibit the European colonist or visitor from extended contact with native populations. As Ann Laura Stoler argues, in the 1920s "fears of physical contamination [merged] with those of political vulnerability. . . . Thus, whites in the colonies adhered to a politics of exclusion that policed their members as well as the colonized" (357). Of course, it was during the 1920s that D. H. Lawrence lived in Mexico and New Mexico and was thus—in the terms Stoler describes—at risk of "contamination" from native populations.

Despite the strong presence of European religions, languages, economic structures, and social practices in the area, the novel Lawrence wrote while living there, *The Plumed Serpent*, asserts a position completely antithetical to the white-supremacist eugenics discourses gaining power in Europe and the United States during the same period. The novel contemplates the hybridization of cultures, races, religions, and histories in Mexico and the Southwest and imagines indigenous populations regaining power and control over the Americas by a resurgence of tribal religion and practice.

The narrative of *The Plumed Serpent* explores, and sometimes conflates, Pueblo and Aztec spirituality from an outsider perspective, that of a forty-year-old British widow, Kate Leslie, who is visiting Mexico. Kate embarks on a quest for psychical and spiritual renewal in a Mexico inhabited by a people nearly somnolent as a result of the material and spiritual effects of the European invasion. The revolution occurring in Mexico, Kate rapidly learns, is not just another military act of aggression but also a revolt of the Mexican soul. Ramón Carrasco and Cipriano Viedma, presented as simultaneously mortal men and incarnations of the Aztec gods Quetzalcoatl and Huitzilopochtli, respectively, direct the Mexican revolution. These men, particularly Cipriano, both frighten and attract Kate. She fears that their revived and revised Mexican spirituality will become more and more her own quotidian reality, erasing her sense of identity. Nevertheless, her quest for renewal becomes allied to the renewal of the native pantheon.

Students should be encouraged to debate whether or not *The Plumed Serpent* straightforwardly appropriates and manipulates sacred Mexican rituals and mythologies. Does it revamp native spirituality to create a Lawrentian vision of the ideal "primitive" state? Certainly such an act would erase the experiential reality of the indigenous cultures, and many modern and postmodern novels do participate in such erasure, which, as Diane Elam argues, "is not an accidental lapse [but] the structural corollary of the imperialism of modernism's claim to write a history that can be, in principle, universal, whose 'meaning' is unaffected by the site of its inscription." Is Lawrence's construction of both the past and the possible future in *The Plumed Serpent* "unaffected by the site of its inscription" (100)? Does it claim to be universal history?

Students should be assigned Lawrence's essay "New Mexico," in which he claims:

> New Mexico was the greatest experience from the outside world that I have ever had. It certainly changed me forever. Curious as it may sound, it was New Mexico that liberated me from the present era of civilization, the great era of material and mechanical development. Months spent in holy Kandy, in Ceylon, the holy of holies of southern Buddhism, had not touched the great psyche of materialism and idealism which dominated me. . . . But the moment I saw the brilliant proud morning shine high up over the deserts of Santa Fé, something stood still in my soul, and I started to attend.   (142)

In New Mexico, Lawrence continues, it is "easy to understand that the Aztecs gave hearts of men to the sun. . . . Ah, yes, in New Mexico the heart is sacrificed to the sun and the human being is left stark, heartless, but undauntedly religious" (143).

Clearly, Lawrence is moved by finding at last a people he can truly call religious. Can students find any evidence in the novel to show that the Pueblo (particularly Hopi) rituals and stories, the Aztec poetry, myths, and histories Lawrence uses from this colonized world—or even the land or landscape itself—ravage and colonize Lawrence's aesthetic and philosophical vision? In the same essay, Lawrence reveals his awareness that the religiousness of the place and the people has been and continues to be disrupted by European contact and that native contact with European peoples has had almost entirely negative results. He recognizes that, when examined from "the angle" of white civilization, the Pueblo people surrounding him in New Mexico "*may* be thoroughly objectionable" (144). However, he rejects this angle as much as an Anglo tourist can, finding in everything the Pueblos do away from their interaction with white people an unforgettable level of religious and spiritual practice, particularly in "the dance, so quiet, so steadily, timelessly rhythmic, and silent" (145).

Once students learn that Lawrence read many of the contemporary anthropological studies of the Southwest and Mexican tribes and that he deliberately uses oral storytelling traditions such as chant, repetition, stereotypes, and agonistic intonations to build the strong religious fervor underlying the Mexican revolution in the novel, they can be asked to consider the influence of Pueblo and Aztec traditions on specific hymns and scenes. For instance, the overblown melodrama of Cipriano's screaming "Die!—die!—die!" to the nearly unconscious, ailing Carlota, flinging his "sinisterly-flaming sarape" over his face as he "blew out of the room" with "only his black, glittering eyes" visible (347), makes more sense if considered in the light of Walter Ong's study of oral traditions in which "outsize figures" are needed "to organize experience in some sort of permanently memorable form" (70). Further, the spiritual point of the passage—that Carlota, emblematic of the oppressive Spanish and Catholic presence in Mexico, must die if the native gods are to return, flourish, and help Mexicans regain their power (and that Cipriano, as the general of the returning Aztec deities, is therefore Carlota's arch enemy)—probably only becomes available to students if they are able to read the scene as native myth rather than as realist fiction.

Students should also be encouraged to compare passages in the early version of the novel (*Quetzalcoatl*) with passages in the final published one, especially since Lawrence planned "to expand the whole work by developing its mythological dimensions, with the result that *The Plumed Serpent* is nearly twice the length of *Quetzalcoatl*" (Martz, "*Quetzalcoatl*" 290; see also Hyde, "'Lost' Girls"). For instance, Lawrence makes significant changes to a native dance scene in the town plaza. The dark Mexican drummers, natives with little or no European heritage, are placed contrapuntally to images of urban Mexicans who, in trying to be part of the European culture that has for so long dominated Mexico, have painted their faces "the white of a clown or a corpse" before going out for a night on the town (*Plumed Serpent* 114). The painted faces of the urban Mexicans are, of course, revelatory of how invading Europeans have colonized Mexican cultural practice. But students might want to investigate the role of spiritual Pueblo and Mexican *koshari*, ritual clowns who, "by making fun—obscene fun—of all that is most sacred," remonstrate against the loss of spiritual connection with the earth and thus remind the Pueblo of the significance of the sacred (Tyler 194). Lawrence received some of his understanding of native myths, including those shaping the plaza scene and the scene in which Catholic relics are removed from the Sayula church, from Lewis Spence's *The Gods of Mexico*, which he read in 1924. Students thus might find fruitful paper topics by reading selections from Spence and exploring and then evaluating the selections' possible impact on or embodiment in the novel.

Finally, students should reflect on the implications of the fact that in the earlier version, as Kimberly VanHoosier-Carey notes, Kate "has little contact with Cipriano, she does not marry him or have a sexual relationship with him, she does not take on the role of Malintzi, and in general, she has little connection to the other characters except that of repository for explanations of their ideas and symbols" (105). Kate's transformation reveals a strong shift in Lawrence's consciousness concerning race relations. In the earlier version, the English heroine, Kate Burns, rejects marriage to her lover because he is an Indian (see the section of the early manuscript in the Penguin CUP edition, 458–60). She says, "The change is too great. I can't make it. I can't change my race. And I can't betray my blood" (458). Yet, by the final version of *The Plumed Serpent*, Kate comes to the dark-skinned Cipriano of her own free will, pleading for his love and devotion (444). The blending of eros and agape, erotic and spiritual love, in this passage is warmly reciprocated by Cipriano, but the real transformation occurs in Lawrence's vision. Something in Lawrence has altered regarding ethnic and racial relations—an alteration unlikely in the fascist context of European thought during the 1920s.

The novel transcends the European cultural context in many ways, among them in its apparently effortless assumption, as in Pueblo spirituality, that gods interact with human beings as part of the material world, not as separate forces. Ramón (as Quetzalcoatl), Kate (as Malintzi), and Cipriano (as Huitzilopochtli), like dancers wearing kachina masks, unproblematically embody both the human and the deity at the same time.

That is to say, unproblematically from a Pueblo or Aztec perspective, perhaps. The critical struggle to read the code of *The Plumed Serpent* often relies on Western-biased paradigms and one-sided visions of cultural interaction. Yes, Lawrence does appropriate native mythologies, sometimes with great inaccuracy, in *The Plumed Serpent*, but those sacred narratives do not act passively in this process. They also infiltrate Lawrence's vision of the future and transform it. The depictions of native spirituality in this novel reveal more than a simple appropriation of native culture or the inscription of European beliefs on indigenous beliefs and practices; they reveal the inescapable entanglements between cultural narratives that occur in twentieth-century literature (see Krupat 14).

The Plumed Serpent reflects the commingled world cultures of the twentieth century, cultures made up of, yet distinct from, the original component cultures. In the culture wars, as in all wars, no one remains untouched; everyone is forced to shift ground before the salvos of the other. In *The Plumed Serpent* the sacred space constructed between Lawrence's vision and the practices of southwest native populations provided a site that enabled the deconstruction—albeit fleeting and sometimes illusory—of dominance and submission models of cultural interaction.

Teaching *Lady Chatterley's Lover*

Louis L. Martz

In teaching *Lady Chatterley's Lover*, faculty members and students should concentrate on the second version instead of the third and final one, since version 2 is both a more attractive and a more subtle novel. Version 2 is now available in a Penguin edition under the misleading title *John Thomas and Lady Jane*, British slang terms for the male and female sexual organs—misleading because these names occur only in the final version (for which Lawrence indeed suggested this title). In the third version Lawrence, released from censorship (by publishing privately) and writing in wretched health (only two years before his death), made drastic changes in characters, language, and tone to create a more vehement protest against the conventions and practices of British society. As a result, in version 3 the use of what Lawrence calls "the taboo words" is greatly increased, and the sexual episodes are longer and more detailed. These differences become clear if we compare the two versions of the famous episode in which the lovers run out naked in the rain and later decorate their bodies with flowers (ch. 12 in version 2; ch. 15 in version 3). Lively debate can arise from considering the way in which Mellors (in version 3) shifts from King's English to the local dialect, in which he uses "taboo words."

At the same time, a narrative voice, angry and strident, frequently intervenes to direct and comment on the action of version 3. This voice is especially evident in Lawrence's treatment of Clifford, the wounded and impotent husband, who in version 2 has been viewed with sympathy as a victim of the war but who now in version 3 is hardened into an image of upper-class arrogance and a self-centered quest for power. One can see this process at work by comparing the two versions of the episode where Clifford has trouble managing his motorized chair (ch. 11 in version 2; ch. 13 in version 3).

In version 2 the harshness of industrial conditions, along with the problem of relations between the classes, is presented through the figure of Parkin, the gamekeeper-lover, a poorly educated man of the laboring class who speaks in the local dialect. His acute sensitivity, which he regards as a female element in his nature, sets him at odds with the ugliness of industrial society. In version 3 Parkin is transformed into Mellors, a self-reliant man well educated in a grammar school who speaks King's English most of the time and has been an officer in the war with experience in India and Egypt. Mellors can thus become a spokesman for Lawrence's denunciations of contemporary English society and its sexual attitudes, as in Mellors's notorious attack—arising from his memories of Bertha Coutts—on female sexuality (ch. 14). Since Mellors is described several times as "almost a gentleman," the class difference between the lovers is diminished; as a result the great scene near the end of version 2 (ch. 15) where Connie visits Parkin in the working-class home of a friend is totally removed from version 3. This scene, one of the best that Lawrence ever wrote, painfully reveals the distance between the classes as Connie unwittingly makes one misstep after another, such as calling her lover Parkin instead of Mr. Parkin. The scene is climactic and essential in version 2, since it shows the grave difficulty of attempting to bring together the now bitterly opposed classes, a situation in which the wounded and defeated Parkin must be rescued by the love and understanding of Connie. The pathos—one might almost say the tragedy—of version 2 thus arises from watching the efforts of two sensitive human beings to transcend the strictures of a dying and oppressive society.

In version 2 the lovers are constantly associated with a pastoral landscape, as in the closing pages of chapter 11: "And they both walked in silence, in the freshness and the stillness of the half-awake wood, whose trees stood around like presences, like witnesses, among the mist of bluebells." One should compare this with the parallel conclusion of chapter 14 in version 3, where the landscape has almost completely disappeared. In version 2 the actors move with the seasons from autumn to autumn, whereas in version 3 this seasonal movement is fragmented and the function of the landscape is attenuated. In many ways version 3, while producing a great deal of polemical and satiric power, coarsens the atmosphere of version 2, as in the early introduction in version 3 of the unpleasant character Michaelis (chs. 3 and 5) and Connie's crude affair with him.

The basic difference between the two versions—or rather the two novels—is brought home in the ending of each work. In version 3, Mellors's voice (in a four-page letter) dominates the conclusion; a significant contrast is the poignant scene that concludes version 2, where Parkin and Connie attempt a final embrace in the woods of Annesley Park. If version 2 is taught, selected passages from version 3 provide excellent materials for class discussion and for student papers. Some students may decide to read all of version 3 on their own. Such comparisons provide a valuable exercise in critical reading. (For further detail on reading the two versions together, see Martz, "Second Lady Chatterley.")

The third version of *Lady Chatterley* is available in the new Penguin CUP edition (1994), based on the new Cambridge University Press edition (1993), both edited by Michael Squires. The earlier versions of the novel have been brought out by Cambridge University Press (as *The First and Second Lady Chatterley Novels*, 1999) but will not be subsequently published by Penguin. Students might want to look at Frieda Lawrence's favorite version, *The First Lady Chatterley*. A detailed comparison of the three versions is given by Michael Squires in *The Creation of* Lady Chatterley's Lover. For other comparisons of the three versions see John Worthen, *D. H. Lawrence and the Idea of the Novel* (ch. 10); Philip M. Weinstein's "Choosing between the Quick and the Dead"; and Peter Scheckner, *Class, Politics, and the Individual* (ch. 4). An effective appraisal of the weaknesses of version 3 has been given by Ian Gregor in *The Moral and the Story* (ch. 8). Suggested reasons for these weaknesses are given by Worthen (*D. H. Lawrence and the Idea of the Novel* 110–16), where Worthen concludes, "In the second version of *Lady Chatterley's Lover* [Lawrence] had written his greatest novel of the 1920's; a fitting successor to *Sons and Lovers*, *The Rainbow* and *Women in Love*" (116).

Team-Teaching Lawrence
in a Culminating Senior Seminar

Carol Peirce and Lawrence W. Markert

At the University of Baltimore, the final senior course required of English majors is called Seminar in English: The Modern Tradition. The catalog description reads as follows:

> A culminating close examination of a major twentieth-century work or author in the light of modern literary traditions. Through panels and group discussions, the students will relate the work or author, as a touchstone, to other writings of past and present. Emphasis will be placed on independent research culminating in a critical, creative, or professional project. Subject matter may change from year to year.

Peirce has taught this seminar on her own, centering on Lawrence Durrell's *Alexandria Quartet* and using Lawrence's *Women in Love*, Joyce's *Portrait of the Artist*, and Proust's *Swann's Way* as background texts. With Markert, however, she has several times team-taught this senior seminar on Lawrence, focusing on four major works in four units as described below.

1. *Sons and Lovers*: The Psychological Trap (3 weeks)
   D. H. Lawrence, *Sons and Lovers*, *Fantasia of the Unconscious*, and *Psychoanalysis and the Unconscious*
   Sophocles, *Oedipus the King*
   Shakespeare, *Hamlet*
2. *The Rainbow*: The Growth of the Poet's Mind (3 weeks)
   D. H. Lawrence, *The Rainbow*, "The Crown," and "Study of Thomas Hardy"
   Nietzsche, *The Birth of Tragedy*
   selected Romantic and symbolist poets
3. *Women in Love*: The Turn of the Novel (3 weeks)
   D. H. Lawrence, *Women in Love*
   Arnold Bennett, *Anna of the Five Towns*
   Thomas Hardy, *Tess of the D'Urbervilles*
4. *Lady Chatterley's Lover*: Myth, Ritual, and the Final Statement (2 weeks)
   D. H. Lawrence, *Lady Chatterley's Lover*, *Apocalypse*, and *A Propos of Lady Chatterley's Lover*
5. Seminar Papers (3 weeks)

As we study Lawrence in depth, we look at other authors in other genres (drama, poetry, fiction): ancient Greek drama and myth; Celtic and northern mythology; the English Renaissance and Shakespeare; the nineteenth-century Romantic poets and their inheritors, the symbolists; twentieth-century fiction, art (including some of Lawrence's own paintings), and poetry—emphasizing at every point those works we know Lawrence to have read, seen, or been influenced by. We intend this seminar both to form a culminating study of literature for our students and to allow them to give serious consideration to a major twentieth-century writer in a rich historical, literary, artistic, and cultural context.

Team-teaching works particularly well in a course on Lawrence, an author who stresses again and again—in all his writing from his novels to his letters—the free, equal, and necessary interrelations between opposites. We expected that our different life situations (older woman, younger man) and backgrounds (Peirce in Shakespeare, mythology, New Criticism; Markert in modernism, psychology, philosophy, semiotics) would lead to lively classroom exchanges; and both our planned and unplanned disagreements created freedom for our fifteen students to voice their own opinions much more openly.

The strategy we worked out for our first unit was a game of point counterpoint in which we presented *Sons and Lovers* as two different novels: Peirce introduced it as the culmination of the traditional novel, while Markert advanced the idea that it was something completely new, the beginning of a new symbolist novel. This debate opened up many discussions about form and style and left students with the lasting impression of Lawrence's position in the history of the novel, straddling the gap between the traditional novel and the experimental.

Our different training and perspectives allowed us to handle other recurring perplexities in teaching Lawrence, such as students' frequent difficulty with the elaborateness of Lawrence's language. Markert's interest in semiotics and poetic language led to one kind of examination of Lawrence's style, while Peirce could compare Lawrence's prose richness with that of Donne and other Elizabethans.

Crucial to the success of such a team-teaching arrangement, we believe, is the commitment of both faculty members to participate fully in each class meeting, always to be present even if the other colleague is responsible for initiating discussion or introducing background works on a particular day. From our disagreements, we sought to demonstrate that in literary study there is never a single right or definitive interpretation and that specifically in Lawrence respect for the interplay of opposites is central. With that agreement established between us, we found ourselves learning as much as our students did as we team-taught Lawrence in the nest of works described above.

"Man-for-Man Love": *David,*
the Bible, and Gender Construction

Raymond-Jean Frontain

D. H. Lawrence's *David: A Play* (1926) is central to a three-week unit on the biblical David and the construction of masculinity in an upper-division course titled The Bible and Gender Construction in Western Culture that I teach in an interdisciplinary gender studies program. Few writers lend themselves so well to discussion of gender issues as Lawrence does, and his absorption in the language and imaginative values of the Bible—particularly as regards sexual relations—is rivaled perhaps only by James Baldwin, with whom I pair Lawrence in my course.

Lawrence returned repeatedly to the idea of the biblical David's covenant with Jonathan, to David's assertion that his love for Jonathan was "passing the love of women" (2 Sam. 1.26, King James Version), and to David's subsequent desolation after the loss of Jonathan (see Frontain "Bible," "James Baldwin," Rev. of *D. H. Lawrence*, "Ruddy"). In *Studies in Classic American Literature*, while reflecting on "the progression of merging" in Walt Whitman's poems, Lawrence observes:

> For the great mergers, woman at last becomes inadequate. For those who love to extremes. Woman is inadequate for the last merging. So the next step is the merging of man-for-man love. And this is on the brink of death. It slides over into death.
> David and Jonathan. And the death of Jonathan.
> It always slides into death.
> The love of comrades.
> Merging. (178)

Lawrence's reference to the love of David and Jonathan is unexpected in a discussion of Whitman, but it reveals a great deal about Lawrence's view of Whitman's "mystery of manly love, the love of comrades" (*Studies* 177), "man-for-man love." Indeed, the covenantal relationship shared by David and Jonathan, Jeffrey Meyers suggests, is the model for male love in Lawrence's fiction, as opposed to the Greek homosexual ideal contained in Plato's *Symposium*, which Meyers claims was used by "practising and more reticent homosexuals" of Lawrence's day (135). The covenant between David and Jonathan both sanctifies and invests with the moral authority of the Bible the need for "a man friend, as eternal as you and I are eternal" that Rupert Birkin describes to Ursula in the final scene of *Women in Love* (481).

In my course, we come to Lawrence's *David* only after reading and discussing the David narrative contained in 1 and 2 Samuel and the opening chapter of 1 Kings and after analyzing the interpretive choices made by Donatello and Michelangelo in their sculptural representations of David as the slayer of Goliath (see Frontain, "Ruddy"; Howard). Lawrence's concern with gender issues is clear in the opening scene of his play, which I ask students to read looking for evidence of how Israelite society in the play seeks to control the gender identity of its members and whether and to what extent Lawrence seems to accept or to disagree with Israelite construction of gender. Discussion the first day concerns two issues raised in that first scene: Is Agag a king even when, in defeat, he is tied to a post in his enemy's courtyard, and what kind of husband not only should, but actually will, Michal accept? Michal conflates these issues when she deliberately mistakes her father's presentation of the war spoils, pretending that Agag is present only as her suitor. The comment that Michal is "too much among the men" (10) when she should be indoors spinning wool with the women alerts the reader to her unorthodox gender behavior and to her potentially unorthodox expectations in a mate.

We spend the remainder of week 2 discussing the relationship of David and Jonathan. Lawrence juxtaposes the masculine self-sufficiency of Saul and Eliab (21) with David's desire to be filled with God the way that a woman is filled sexually by a man (40), reversing traditional gender expectations and suggesting that, as biblical narrative repeatedly asserts, the Lord does not judge as humans do. It is even suggested that Saul's acting in routinely masculine ways prevents him from remaining a fit instrument of the divine (35). David's receptivity to and commitment to the Lord, however, prevents him from being fully available emotionally to Jonathan. In the scene dramatizing the Bible's poignant observation that "the soul of Jonathan was knit with the soul of David, and Jonathan loved him as his own soul" (1 Sam. 18.1), Lawrence causes David to qualify his response to Jonathan's free acknowledgment of love (41–42). Clearly, Lawrence's David is close to Michelangelo's: beautiful, he attracts others to him but remains finally unavailable. One key issue we discuss in class is why Jonathan can enter into his extraordinary covenant with David (62–64) but cannot follow him at the end of the play (127–28).

In the final week on this unit, we turn to James Baldwin's novella *Giovanni's Room* (1956). Discussion of the differences between Baldwin's and Lawrence's constructions of male love relationships are telling. In the novella, David is unable to accept his love for Giovanni (Italian for Jonathan) because of David's fear of being rendered effeminate; his covenant with Giovanni is defeated by his inability to challenge the social construction of gender that Lawrence's *David* renders meaningless. Likewise, the sexual nature of David's involvement with Giovanni in Baldwin's work highlights the absence of explicit eroticism in Lawrence's *David* and asks the class to reconsider how Lawrence understood a "man-for-man love" that complements man-for-woman love yet ultimately transcends it. Further, the agonized self-scrutiny of Baldwin's David emphasizes by contrast the emotional removal of Lawrence's David, who trusts finally only in the Lord.

The relationship of Baldwin's David with Hella serves as a useful foil to the relationship of Lawrence's David with Michal in that Hella's desire for a traditional life as wife and mother counterpoints Michal's refusal to stay among the women and spin wool. A game I like to play in class is asking how the balance of one work would be affected by the presence of a character from another work. Would Baldwin's David feel differently about the possibility of heterosexual marriage if he were paired with Lawrence's Michal rather than with Hella?

One paper topic I suggest to students is an examination of Lawrence's concern with the David-Jonathan relationship in his other works (I guide students to the references summarized in Frontain, Rev. of *D. H. Lawrence*, and to Kaye on Lawrence's conflicted attitude toward homosexuality). I have also had substantial student essays juxtaposing Lawrence's construction of masculinity in *David* with the dramatic treatments of the David story by André Gide (*Saul*, 1903) and David Pinski (*King David and His Wives*, 1919), two nearly contemporary plays, copies of which I leave on reserve. (Students need little guidance in analyzing the extraordinary sensuality of Lawrence's dramatic language as they compare the erotic nature of relationships in these three plays.) And for a third paper topic, I quote John Worthen's observation that Lawrence risked things in the plays that he would not risk in other genres (*D. H. Lawrence: The Early Years* 282), and I ask students to analyze specifically what he risks in his delineation of gender roles and relationships.

I have found that Lawrence's play provokes excellent discussion of how a later text can simultaneously reflect and challenge the Bible's understanding of masculinity as well as how it might use the Bible in the attempt to alter contemporary social construction of gender.

Teaching Lawrence's
Early Plays with His Early Prose

Hans-W. Schwarze

D. H. Lawrence's eight plays—*A Collier's Friday Night* (1909), *The Widowing of Mrs. Holroyd* (1910, revised 1913), *The Merry-Go-Round* (1911), *The Married Man* (1912), *The Fight for Barbara* (1912), *The Daughter-in-Law* (1913), *Touch and Go* (1918), and *David* (1925)—and two play fragments, *Altitude* (1924) and *Noah's Flood* (1925), have almost been neglected so far. Not many people know about them, critics hardly mention them, and research has been sporadic and has often contained errors. The publication of the plays by Cambridge University Press (edited by Hans-W. Schwarze and John Worthen) in 1999 may result in their receiving more (and long overdue) attention in the classroom.

In my course on Lawrence, students need to become familiar with the living conditions, social environment, and attitudes of one hundred years ago, and Lawrence's early plays are invaluable in this process. I start with some of Lawrence's early short stories: "Odour of Chrysanthemums," "Daughters of the Vicar," "The Miner at Home," and "Strike-Pay." If time allows, we also read *Sons and Lovers*. I ask students especially to consider the use of the Midlands accent and dialect words in these works; the dramatization of "Odour" in *The Widowing of Mrs. Holroyd*; the social classes, domestic rituals, and working conditions (e.g., in "Miner"); and the miners' pastimes (e.g., in "Strike-Pay").

This introductory phase of the course is followed by our reading and discussing of Lawrence's early plays. In the past I have used the collection first published by Penguin in 1969: *A Collier's Friday Night, The Daughter-in-Law,* and *The Widowing of Mrs. Holroyd*. The book's introduction by Raymond Williams is one of the best surveys and critical assessments of the plays available and also offers many questions and hints for class discussion.

Lawrence's early plays depict a succession of representative events and stages of family life in a mining community at the turn of the century; they show daily life, the joys and sorrows linked with courting, marriage, and eventually death in the family. Students will recognize that Lawrence treats his characters with reverence, profound tenderness, and truthfulness. Since plays are written to be performed, students especially benefit from giving practiced or even impromptu renderings of specific scenes in class, struggling to do justice to the dialect. Analysis and discussion should be supported by an introduction to the contemporary theater with the help of Ian Clarke's *Edwardian Drama*. The extent to which Lawrence's early plays did not conform to contemporary standards will become obvious.

Ideally, performances of the plays as television productions should be available for the course: *Collier's* (BBC, 1976), *Daughter-in-Law* (BBC, 1985),

Widowing (ITA, 1961; PBS, 1974; BBC, 1995). However, as there are copyright problems still to be solved, copies of these productions are not easily accessible. A selection of reviews of the 1968 season of these plays in London is available in Keith Sagar's *D. H. Lawrence Handbook* (283–328). The course certainly helps students appreciate Lawrence's early plays as the work of—as Philip French put it—"A Major Miner Dramatist." And these early plays also give students a memorable historical and cultural context for studying and hearing the voices of the characters in Lawrence's fiction.

Lawrence's Poetry and Expository Prose: Writing with Power and the Canons of Comp

Gordon Harvey

Once students of freshman writing have learned that they can achieve power by being objective, reasonable, and transparent, they can usefully be set to read some of Lawrence's nonfiction, which achieves power by refusing to be any of these. Lawrence can function as the exception that challenges, complicates, and ultimately vivifies the rule.

To illustrate: consider the rule of objectivity—the principle that one can most vividly bring a phenomenon before a reader by rendering it as exactly as possible in its objective otherness. To complicate this rule I use Lawrence's poems on animals. I first give the rule some color by having students read passages from Lawrence that testify to its human (not just its rhetorical) truth. I use excerpts from the conclusion of "Odour of Chrysanthemums" ("She had denied him what he was" [198]) and five or six other passages in prose and verse (see p. 65, par. 2, in this volume) that state in different ways the importance of recognizing otherness. Students read these passages in the first class alongside "Fish," a poem that rejects Lawrence's own projecting, anthropomorphizing impulse ("I had made a mistake. / I didn't know him." [338; line 109]).

Simply asking what these passages have in common and what they might have to do with "Fish" generates lively discussion. But the heart of the exercise comes next. Having adduced the idea that respect for otherness entails a refusal to project one's own desires, moods, and associations onto, or to abstract an essence from, someone or something, students then read Lawrence's representations of animals in poems like "Kangaroo," "He Goat," "Bat," "Hummingbird," and the tortoise sequence. These pieces work precisely by projecting onto the animals an essential character derived from Lawrence's moods, associations, desires. The witty epithets and metaphors along with the moody addresses to the animals express the imagination and feelings of the perceiver—surely not the objective otherness of the animals. Indeed, the descriptions seem aggressively subjective. (This same apparent contradiction between principle and practice can be considered by having students read Lawrence's wonderful essay "Indians and Entertainment," which, after strongly asserting that white attempts to describe Indian consciousness are doomed to be false—"to express one stream in terms of the other . . . is false and sentimental. . . . [A] man cannot belong to both ways" [55]—launches into an unabashed representation of Indian consciousness during dance.)

Some students will say that there really isn't a contradiction here, since in poetry the focus must always be the feelings of the poet—a discussable but finally untenable view. Others will happily pronounce Lawrence a hypocrite. But to the question, Why then should we read this? thoughtful students will admit to finding the poems, while certainly full of the Lawrence persona, also strangely evocative of the animal in question. The kangaroo is there, present in the poem, as it isn't in a neutral, factually accurate description in an encyclopedia or zoology textbook—an example of which can be brought in for comparison, as can Dickens's memorable satire on the "adequate" definition of a horse in chapter 2 of *Hard Times*. What emerges in discussion of this comparison is the Blakean idea that we don't perceive something in its distinctness unless we perceive it with the imagination. In Lawrentian terms, it's the idea that accurate-seeming description—description that brings out the singular otherness of its object—is vivid by virtue of being an individual's apprehension, an act of imaginative contact making that engages us in a more than cerebral way. Students can at this point be given excerpts from one of Lawrence's critiques of the merely visual, camera-eye standard of reality in art—as against a reality of relationship (e.g., "There is nothing to do but maintain a true relationship to the things we move with and amongst and against" or "the eye sees only fronts, and the mind on the whole is satisfied with fronts. But intuition needs all-roundedness, and instinct needs insideness" ["Art" 167; "Introduction to These Paintings" 579]).

Students test out this view by considering closely a number of descriptive passages from prose by Lawrence and other writers: essays, autobiography, books of anthropology, psychology, literary criticism, even novels. It's easiest to control this last part of the sequence if the teacher brings in the readings, but it's more fun if students find and bring in passages that seem to them evocative. Either way, the question students must ask themselves is what makes vivid description vivid. And the answer usually turns out to be not factual completeness or a transparent, impersonal rendering but rather some evidence of the perceiver's presence—some sense of the effect that the object has on a particular person and some selecting or abstracting, by that person, of a unified or essential effect.

Reading Lawrentian description and pondering the slipperiness for any writer of the objective-subjective distinction make students see passages of ordinary prose in an engaged way and make them see anew the principle—really the challenge—of accuracy in describing. A similar complicating and refreshing can go on for the canons of reasonableness and transparency in analytic writing, this time using selected essays and articles by Lawrence. Like the animal poems, Lawrence's prose arguments get much of their power from forbidden sources—from being nonreasonable and nontransparent. I have students compile, based on the semester so far and my comments on their essays, a list of qualities that make for persuasive essay writing. These usually include sticking to a single thesis; not repeating oneself; having a clear and tight progression of thought; supplying concrete facts and evidence for claims; being calm, trustworthy, and fair (e.g., by making balanced concessions to other viewpoints and qualifying one's position); maintaining a consistent and serious tone; and writing in a way that doesn't call attention to itself and especially not to one's mood or personality. Lawrence's prose—from longer essays in history, psychology, and literary criticism to short opinion pieces—doesn't follow these rules. And yet one is irresistibly drawn along by it. Is this because such writing is merely entertaining, pleasant because not to be taken seriously as "truth"? This dichotomy between truth and entertainment lurks in most student minds and needs bringing into the open; doing so inevitably complicates the idea of being persuaded. Or does stating something in a nonboring, not merely cerebral way—and keeping a reader constantly engaged—require an enactment of the writer's personal relationship with the material that in turn requires some stretching of the usual rules of academic persuasiveness and definitions of truth? Again, I ask students to bring in some passages of writing that they honestly enjoy, admire, or feel deeply convinced by and to try to say what makes the reader attend.

NOTES ON CONTRIBUTORS

A. R. Atkins has held an Izaak Walton Killam postdoctoral fellowship at the University of Alberta and has taught at the Universities of Reading and Bristol. He is editor of the Oxford World Classics edition of Lawrence's *"The Prussian Officer" and Other Stories* (1995).

Donald Buckley is associate professor of biology and director of instructional technologies in the School of Health Sciences, Quinnipiac University. A geneticist who has studied plant life in Sri Lanka and Costa Rica, he has been a moving force in science education and computer-aided pedagogy at both regional and national levels.

Rebecca Carpenter is assistant professor of English at Western Maryland College; she specializes in modern British literature and postcolonial studies. Her articles have appeared in several journals, including *Conradiana, D. H. Lawrence Review, Etudes Lawrenciennes*, and, most recently, the *Minnesota Review*. She is currently investigating representations of male failure in twentieth-century British literature.

Pamela L. Caughie is professor of English and director of women's studies at Loyola University, Chicago. She is author of *Virginia Woolf and Postmodernism* (U of Illinois P, 1991) and *Passing and Pedagogy* (U of Illinois P, 1999), which contains a version of the Lawrence essay included here. She is editor of *Virginia Woolf in the Age of Mechanical Reproduction* (Garland, 1999).

Keith Cushman is professor of English at the University of North Carolina, Greensboro. He has written or edited five books on Lawrence. He is associate editor of the *D. H. Lawrence Review* and past president of the D. H. Lawrence Society of North America. He has received the Harry T. Moore Award for Lifelong Contributions to and Encouragement of Lawrence Studies. He and Earl Ingersoll are coeditors of a forthcoming collection of new essays titled "D. H. Lawrence: New Worlds."

David Ellis is professor of English literature at the University of Kent, Canterbury. His Lawrence work includes introductions to the new Everyman editions of *Sons and Lovers* and *Women in Love* (Knopf, 1991, 1992); coauthorship (with Howard Mills) of *D. H. Lawrence's Non-fiction: Art, Thought and Genre* (Cambridge UP, 1988); and the third and final volume of the new Cambridge biography of Lawrence, *Dying Game* (1997).

Langdon Elsbree is professor of English emeritus at Claremont McKenna College. He has coauthored editions of the *Heath Handbook* and published *The Rituals of Life* (Kennikat, 1982) and *Ritual Passages and Narrative Structures* (Lang, 1991). He has written essays on dance and ritual in Lawrence, edited forums on teaching Lawrence, and frequently reviewed for the *D. H. Lawrence Review*.

Maria Aline Seabra Ferreira is associate professor in the English department at the University of Aveiro. She has published principally on D. H. Lawrence and Angela Carter. Her most recent articles include "Myth and Anti-myth in Angela Carter's 'The Passion of New Eve'" in *Journal of the Fantastic in the Arts* and "An-Other Jouissance: Secular and Mystical Love in Kate Chopin's 'Two Portraits'" in *Literature and Psychology*. Her main interests are women's studies, psychoanalysis, and literary theory.

Isobel M. Findlay is assistant professor at the University of Saskatchewan, where she received a 1998 teaching award. Her current research includes cultural and communications theory, D. H. Lawrence, law and literature, and a book-length study of Chartism. She is coeditor (with L. M. Findlay) of *Realizing Community: Multidisciplinary Perspectives* (U of Saskatchewan, 1995); general editor of *Introduction to Literature*, 4th ed. (Harcourt, 2000); and coauthor (with J. Y. Henderson and M. L. Benson) of *Aboriginal Tenure in the Constitution of Canada* (Carswell, 2000).

Raymond-Jean Frontain is professor of English and interdisciplinary studies at the University of Central Arkansas, where he teaches a course on the Bible and gender construction. Most recently he edited *Reclaiming the Sacred: The Bible in Gay and Lesbian Culture* (Haworth, 1997).

Sandra M. Gilbert is professor of English at the University of California, Davis, and author of *Acts of Attention: The Poems of D. H. Lawrence* (1972; 2nd ed., Southern Illinois UP, 1990). Her latest publications include *Wrongful Death: A Memoir* (Norton, 1995), *Ghost Volcano: Poems* (Norton, 1995), and *Kissing the Bread: Selected Poems, 1969–1999* (Norton, 2000). Most recently she has edited *Inventions of Farewell: A Book of Elegies* (Norton, 2001), and she is currently at work on a book entitled "Death's Door: Mourning, Modernity, Poetry."

Louis K. Greiff is professor of English and division chairperson at Alfred University. His current research combines a long-standing interest in Lawrence with a recent interest in film adaptation. His book *D. H. Lawrence: Fifty Years on Film* is forthcoming in 2001 (Southern Illinois UP). His previous publications include work on Lawrence as well as other major modernists, on cinematic adaptation, and on Vietnam-related literature and film.

Gordon Harvey is associate director of the expository writing program at Harvard University. He writes about topics in Renaissance and modern poetry and poetics and in composition. He is author of *Writing with Sources* (Hackett, 1998); his contextual teaching materials on Lawrence described in this volume (as well as on several other authors) will be published by Bedford.

Virginia Crosswhite Hyde is professor of English at Washington State University, Pullman. She wrote *The Risen Adam: D. H. Lawrence's Revisionist Typology* (Pennsylvania State UP, 1992) and is editing the Cambridge edition of Lawrence's *"Mornings in Mexico" and Other Essays*. She coedited (with L. D. Clark) the Penguin CUP edition of *The Plumed Serpent* (1995) and has published articles on Lawrence, Yeats, Florence Farr, Auden, Browning, Kafka, and George Eliot.

Mark Kinkead-Weekes is professor emeritus at the University of Kent, Canterbury, which he helped to found. He is author of the second volume of the recent Cambridge biography of Lawrence, *D. H. Lawrence: Triumph to Exile, 1912–1922* (1996), and editor of the Cambridge edition of *The Rainbow* (1989). He wrote the introduction and notes for the Penguin CUP edition of *Women in Love* and has also written books on Samuel Richardson and William Golding and articles on British, American, African, and West Indian writers.

Cynthia Lewiecki-Wilson is associate professor of English and affiliate of the women's studies program at Miami University, Middletown, where she teaches writing, literature, and women's studies. She is interested in theories of writing and difference—including those of gender, race, nationality, and disability—and has published articles and a book on writing and pedagogy. She is author of *Writing against the Family: Gender in Lawrence and Joyce* (Southern Illinois UP, 1994).

Lawrence W. Markert is vice president for academic affairs at Hollins University. He is author of various articles and books on late-nineteenth- and early-twentieth-century British literature and culture, including *The Bloomsbury Group: A Reference Guide* (Hall, 1990), *Arthur Symons: Critic of the Seven Arts* (UMI, 1988), and *Riddle and Incest: Poems* (New Poets Series, 1974).

A. A. Markley is assistant professor of English at Penn State University, Delaware County. He has published essays on a variety of nineteenth-century British works and has written on homosexuality and homosocial desire in Mary Shelley's fiction, the poetry of William Morris, and the novels of E. M. Forster. He has edited, with Gary Handwerk, William Godwin's novels *Caleb Williams* and *Fleetwood* (Broadview, 2000) and is currently serving as volume editor for the forthcoming *Mary Shelley: Literary Lives and Uncollected Writings* (Pickering).

Louis L. Martz is Sterling Professor of English emeritus at Yale University. His latest book is *Many Gods and Many Voices: The Role of the Prophet in English and American Modernism*, which includes essays on *Quetzalcoatl* and *The Second Lady Chatterley*, as well as a chapter on the relation between HD and "DH" (U of Missouri P, 1998). He has edited Lawrence's *Quetzalcoatl* (Black Swan, 1995) and both the *Collected Poems* and the *Selected Poems* of HD (New Directions, 1983, 1988). He has published five books on poetry of the seventeenth century, the best known being *The Poetry of Meditation* (Yale UP, 1954) and *Milton: Poet of Exile* (Yale UP, 1980, 1986).

Jorgette Mauzerall is assistant professor of English at Fort Valley State University. Her doctoral dissertation is a study of D. H. Lawrence, entitled "The Body of Culture: Decadence and Gender in the Novels of D. H. Lawrence." She has contributed to the *D. H. Lawrence Review* and published in the *ADE Bulletin* an article on teaching.

Tim Middleton is head of English studies at the College of Ripon and York, St. John. He teaches and has published on gender and national identity in modern and postmodern British and American fiction. He is coauthor of *Writing Englishness, 1900–1950* (Routledge, 1995) and *Studying Culture* (Blackwell, 1999).

Howard Mills has recently retired from the University of Kent, Canterbury, and moved to Boulder, Colorado, where he now teaches part-time at Colorado College and the University of Colorado. Among his books are *D. H. Lawrence's Non-fiction: Art, Thought, and Genre* (coauthored with David Ellis; Cambridge UP, 1988) and *Working with Shakespeare* (Barnes, 1993).

Carol Peirce is professor of English at the University of Baltimore. She has recently given papers at two Lawrence conferences and published an article in a collection of essays on Lawrence's relation to Lawrence Durrell. She coedited two issues of *Twentieth Century Literature* on Durrell (1987) and is coeditor of *Deus Loci: The Lawrence Durrell Journal*.

Phyllis Sternberg Perrakis teaches in the English department at the University of Ottawa and is the president of the Doris Lessing Society. Besides writing articles on Doris Lessing, Margaret Atwood, and Alice Munro, she is associate editor of *D. H. Lawrence: The Cosmic Adventure* (Borealis, 1996) and the editor of *Spiritual Exploration in the Works of Doris Lessing* (Greenwood, 1999).

James M. Phelps, born and educated in South Africa, completed his MA on Lawrence's short fiction at the University of Natal, Pietermaritzburg, and his DPhil "The Interloper Plot in the Novels and Other Works of D. H. Lawrence" (1997) at the University of York. He is senior lecturer in English at the University of Zululand.

Charles L. Ross is professor of English at the University of Hartford. He is author of *The Composition of* The Rainbow *and* Women in Love: *A History* (UP of Virginia, 1979) and *Women in Love: A Novel of Mythic Realism* (Twayne, 1991). He is also editor of *Women in Love* (Penguin, 1982) and coeditor (with Dennis Jackson) of *D. H. Lawrence: New Versions of a Modern Author* (U of Michigan P, 1995).

Keith Sagar is former reader in English literature at the University of Manchester. He is author or editor of over twenty books, most of them on D. H. Lawrence or Ted Hughes. These include *The Art of D. H. Lawrence* (Cambridge UP, 1966), *D. H. Lawrence: A Calendar of His Works* (U of Texas P, 1979), *The Life of D. H. Lawrence* (Pantheon, 1980), *D. H. Lawrence: Life into Art* (U of Georgia P, 1985), and *The Laughter of Foxes: A Study of Ted Hughes* (Liverpool UP, 2000).

M. Elizabeth Sargent is associate professor of English and writing coordinator at the University of Alberta. She is (as M. Elizabeth Wallace) editor of *Part-Time Academic Employment in the Humanities* (MLA, 1984). She publishes on the teaching of writing and on Lawrence. Her work has appeared in the journals *College English*, *ADE Bulletin*, *Profession*, *Women's Review of Books*, and the *D. H. Lawrence Review* and in the books *The Challenge of D. H. Lawrence* (U of Wisconsin P, 1990), *D. H. Lawrence in Italy and England* (Macmillan, 1999), and *Writing the Body in D. H. Lawrence* (Greenwood, 2001).

Hans-W. Schwarze is senior lecturer in English at Tübingen University. He has published on modern English drama and theory of prose fiction. He teaches courses in Shakespeare, nineteenth-century prose, and twentieth-century prose and drama. He is coeditor (with John Worthen) of the Cambridge edition of *The Plays*, by D. H. Lawrence (1999).

Carol Siegel is professor of English at Washington State University, Vancouver. She is author of *Lawrence among the Women: Wavering Boundaries in Women's Literary Traditions* (UP of Virginia, 1991), *Male Masochism: Modern Revisions of the Story of Love* (Indiana UP, 1995), and *New Millennial Sexstyles* (Indiana UP, 2000). She has written the introduction to the Penguin CUP edition of Lawrence's *The Lost Girl* (1995) and is coeditor of the interdisciplinary journals *Genders* and *Rhizomes*.

Luba Slabyj is a doctoral student at the University of Alberta. She is completing a dissertation entitled "Father-Daughter Desire in *The Rainbow*, *King Lear*, and *Silas Marner*."

Jack Stewart is professor emeritus of English at the University of British Columbia. He is author of *The Vital Art of D. H. Lawrence: Vision and Expression* (Southern Illinois UP, 1999), a member of the editorial board of the *D. H. Lawrence Review*, and president of the D. H. Lawrence Society of North America. He has written numerous essays on Lawrence, especially on *Women in Love*. His recent articles on Lawrence and the visual arts include "Metaphor and Metonymy, Color and Space, in Lawrence's *Sea and Sardinia*" (1995); "Landscape Painting and Pre-Raphaelitism in *The White Peacock*" (1997–98); and "Color, Space, and Place in Lawrence's *Letters*" (2000).

Wayne Templeton is professor of English at Kwantlen University College. He is author of *States of Estrangement: The Novels of D. H. Lawrence, 1912–1917* (Whitston, 1989). His recent publications include two essays on Euramerican perceptions of the American Southwest—"'Indians and an Englishman': Lawrence in the American Southwest" and "Xojo and Homicide: The Postcolonial Murder Mysteries of Tony Hillerman"—and an essay on the genesis and effects of Lawrence's tuberculosis, "D. H. Lawrence: Illness, Identity, and Writing." He serves on the editorial board of the *D. H. Lawrence Review*.

Theresa Thompson is assistant professor at Valdosta State University, where she teaches twentieth-century British and postcolonial literature. Her publications include "Confronting Modernist Racism in the Post-colonial Classroom: Teaching Virginia Woolf's *The Voyage Out* and Leonard Woolf's *The Village in the Jungle*," in *Re: Reading, Re: Writing Re: Teaching Virginia Woolf* (Pace UP, 1995); *Stephen King and the Representation of Women* (Greenwood, 1998), a collection of critical essays, coedited and introduced with Kathleen Margaret Lant; and "'Negotiating the Divide': Mapping Global Feminism" (2000).

Garry Watson is professor of English at the University of Alberta. He is author of *The Leavises, the "Social," and the Left* (Bryn Mill, 1976). His recent publications include essays on political correctness, in *English Studies in Canada*; on Melville and Conrad, in *Conrad, James, and Other Relations* (Maria Curie Skłodowska U, 1998); on the western, in *Cineaction*; on Lawrence and religion, in *Etudes Lawrenciennes* (2000); and on Lawrence and the abject body, in *Writing the Body in D. H. Lawrence: Essays on Language, Representation, and Sexuality*, edited by Paul Poplawski (Greenwood, 2001).

SURVEY PARTICIPANTS

Antony Atkins, freelance Web designer and editor, *Oxford (UK)*
Ralph Behrens, *University of Central Arkansas* (emeritus)
Jonathan Bolton, *Auburn University, Auburn*
Gerald Butler, *San Diego State University*
Rebecca Carpenter, *Western Maryland College*
Pamela L. Caughie, *Loyola University, Chicago*
Cheng Lok Chua, *California State University, Fresno*
Barry Cullen, *Middlesex University, London (UK)*
Langdon Elsbree, *Claremont McKenna* (emeritus)
Anne Fernihough, *Girton College, Cambridge (UK)*
John Ferns, *McMaster University (Canada)*
Maria Aline Seabra Ferreira, *University of Aveiro (Portugal)*
Isobel M. Findlay, *University of Saskatchewan (Canada)*
Raymond-Jean Frontain, *University of Central Arkansas*
Louis K. Greiff, *Alfred University*
Eric Haralson, *State University of New York, Stony Brook*
Gordon Harvey, *Harvard University*
Richard A. Hocks, *University of Missouri, Columbia*
Virgina Hyde, *Washington State University, Pullman*
Mara Kalnins, *Corpus Christi College, Cambridge (UK)*
W. J. Keith, *University of Toronto (Canada)*
Wiestaw Krajka, *Maria Curie Sklodowska University (Lubin, Poland)*
Jeraldine Kraver, *Michigan State University*
Matt Leone, *Colgate University*
Cynthia Lewiecki-Wilson, *Miami University*
A. A. Markley, *Penn State University, Delaware County*
Louis L. Martz, *Yale University* (emeritus)
Jorgette Mauzerall, *Fort Valley State University*
Tim Middleton, *College of Ripon and York, St. John (UK)*
Donna Miller, *University of Bologna (Italy)*
Howard Mills, *University of Kent, Canterbury (UK—emeritus)*
Carol Peirce, *University of Baltimore*
Phyllis Sternberg Perrakis, *University of Ottawa (Canada)*
James Phelps, *University of Zululand (South Africa)*
Charles L. Ross, *University of Hartford*
Michael Ross, *McMaster University (Canada)*
Hans-W. Schwarze, *Tübingen University (Germany)*
Marion Shaw, *Loughborough University, (UK)*
Carol Siegel, *Washington State University, Vancouver*
Jack Stewart, *University of British Columbia (Canada)*
Wayne Templeton, *Kwantlen University College (Canada)*
Theresa Thompson, *Valdosta State University*
Kathryn Walterschied, *University of Missouri, Saint Louis*

Nicole Ward-Jouve, *University of York (UK)*
Joyce Wexler, *Loyola University, Chicago*
John Worthen, *University of Nottingham (UK)*
George Zytaruk, *Nipissing University (Canada*—emeritus)

WORKS CITED

Works by D. H. Lawrence

Note: If both Penguin and Cambridge University Press (CUP) editions of a Lawrence text are cited in this volume, both are listed. If only a CUP edition is cited, the CUP entry will note if a Penguin edition is available. If a Penguin edition is cited, the entry will note if it is a CUP edition. Penguin editions do not include CUP textual apparatus, introductions, or notes, but they do include the CUP text of Lawrence's work and have identical pagination. For more information on editions, see pages 7–9 in "Materials."

Aaron's Rod. 1922. Ed. Mara Kalnins. Cambridge: Cambridge UP, 1988. (Penguin, 1996).

"Adolf." 1920. *"England, My England" and Other Stories* 201–08.

"America, Listen to Your Own." *Phoenix* 87–91.

Apocalypse and Other Writings on Revelation. 1931. Ed. Mara Kalnins. Cambridge: Cambridge UP, 1980. (Penguin, 1995).

A Propos of Lady Chatterley's Lover. 1930. *Lady Chatterley's Lover* [and] *A Propos of* Lady Chatterley's Lover 303–35.

"Art and Morality." 1925. *"Study of Thomas Hardy" and Other Essays* 163–68.

"An Autobiographical Sketch." *Phoenix II* 592–96.

Birds, Beasts and Flowers. 1923. *Complete Poems* 275–414.

"The Blind Man." 1920. *"England, My England" and Other Stories* 46–63.

"Books." *Phoenix* 731–34.

The Captain's Doll. 1923. *The Fox, The Captain's Doll, The Ladybird* 73–153.

"Chaos in Poetry." *Phoenix* 255–62.

The Collected Letters of D. H. Lawrence. Ed. Harry T. Moore. 2 vols. London: Heinemann, 1962.

The Complete Poems of D. H. Lawrence. Ed. Vivian de Sola Pinto and F. Warren Roberts. New York: Viking, 1971. Harmondsworth: Penguin, 1977. [Same pagination.]

The Complete Short Novels. 1982. Ed. Keith Sagar and Melissa Partridge. New York: Penguin, 1990.

The Complete Short Stories. Vol. 2. New York: Viking-Compass, 1961.

"The Crown." 1925. *"Reflections on the Death of a Porcupine" and Other Essays* 251–306.

David: A Play. 1926. *Plays* 433–525.

"Democracy." 1919. *"Reflections on the Death of a Porcupine" and Other Essays* 61–83. *Phoenix* 699–718.

D. H. Lawrence and Italy: Twilight in Italy, Sea and Sardinia, Etruscan Places. Ed. Anthony Burgess. New York: Viking, 1972. New York: Penguin, 1997. [Same pagination.]

D. H. Lawrence and New Mexico. Ed. Keith Sagar. Paris: Alyscamps. 1995.

D. H. Lawrence on Education. Ed. Joy Williams and Raymond Williams. Harmondsworth: Penguin Education, 1973.

"D. H. Lawrence's 'Odour of Chrysanthemums': An Early Version." Ed. James T. Boulton. *Renaissance and Modern Studies* 13 (1969): 4–48.

"England, My England." 1915 version. App. in *"England, My England" and Other Stories* (CUP) 217–32.

"England, My England." 1922. *"England, My England" and Other Stories* 5–33.

"England, My England" and Other Stories. Ed. Bruce Steele. Cambridge: Cambridge UP, 1990.

"England, My England" and Other Stories. (CUP). Ed. Bruce Steele. Introd. and notes by Michael Bell. New York: Penguin, 1995.

"Enslaved by Civilization." *Phoenix II* 578–81.

The Escaped Cock. Ed. Gerald M. Lacy. Los Angeles: Black Sparrow, 1973. (See also *The Man Who Died*).

Etruscan Places. 1932. New York: Viking, 1957. Also in *D. H. Lawrence and Italy* 1–115.

Fantasia of the Unconscious. 1922. Psychoanalysis 51–225.

The First and Second Lady Chatterley Novels. Ed. Dieter Mehl and Christa Jansohn. Cambridge: Cambridge UP, 1999.

The First Lady Chatterley. Foreword by Frieda Lawrence. 1944. New York: Penguin, 1973.

"Fish." *Complete Poems* 334–40.

"Foreword to *Sons and Lovers*." *Sons and Lovers* (CUP) 467–73. *Letters*, ed. Huxley, 95–102. Tedlock 22–29.

"Foreword to *The Collected Poems of D. H. Lawrence*." *Phoenix* 251–54. *Complete Poems* 849–52.

"Foreword to *Women in Love*." *Women in Love* 483–86. *Phoenix II* 275–76.

The Fox, The Captain's Doll, The Ladybird. 1923. Ed. Dieter Mehl. Cambridge: Cambridge UP, 1992. (Penguin, 1994).

"The Future of the Novel." (Formerly "Surgery for the Novel—or a Bomb"). 1923. *"Study of Thomas Hardy" and Other Essays* 151–55.

"German Books: Thomas Mann." *Phoenix* 308–13.

"Hadrian [You Touched Me]." 1920. *"England, My England" and Other Stories* 92–107.

"Her Turn." 1913. *"Love among the Haystacks" and Other Stories* 128–33.

"The Horse-Dealer's Daughter." 1922. *"England, My England" and Other Stories* 137–52.

"Hymns in a Man's Life." *Phoenix II* 597–601.

"Indians and Entertainment." Mornings in Mexico *and* Etruscan Places 52–64.

"Introduction to *Memoirs of the Foreign Legion*." *Phoenix II* 303–61.

"Introduction to *The Dragon of the Apocalypse*." *Phoenix* 292–303.

"Introduction to These Paintings." *Phoenix* 551–84.

"John Galsworthy." *"Study of Thomas Hardy" and Other Essays* 209–20.

John Thomas and Lady Jane. New York: Penguin, 1977.

Kangaroo. 1923. Ed. Bruce Steele. Cambridge: Cambridge UP, 1994.

Lady Chatterley's Lover. 1928. *Lady Chatterley's Lover* [and] *A Propos of* Lady Chatterley's Lover. Ed. Michael Squires. Cambridge: Cambridge UP, 1993.

Lady Chatterley's Lover [and] *A Propos of* Lady Chatterley's Lover. (CUP). Ed. Michael Squires. New York: Penguin, 1994.

Last Poems. 1932. *Complete Poems* 685–728.

The Letters of D. H. Lawrence. Ed. Aldous Huxley. London: Heinemann, 1932.

The Letters of D. H. Lawrence. Vol. 1: 1901–13. Ed. James T. Boulton. Vol. 2: 1913–16. Ed. George J. Zytaruk and James T. Boulton. Vol. 3: 1916–21. Ed. James T. Boulton and Andrew Robertson. Vol. 4: 1921–24. Ed. Warren Roberts, James T. Boulton, and Elizabeth Mansfield. Vol. 5: 1924–27. Ed. James T. Boulton and Lindeth Vasey. Vol. 6: 1927–28. Ed. James T. Boulton, Margaret H. Boulton, and Gerald M. Lacy. Vol. 7: 1928–30. Ed. Keith Sagar and James T. Boulton. Cambridge: Cambridge UP, 1979–93.

Look! We Have Come Through! 1917. *Complete Poems* 189–274.

The Lost Girl. 1920. (CUP 1981). Ed. John Worthen. Introd. and notes by Carol Siegel. New York: Penguin, 1995.

"Love among the Haystacks" and Other Stories. Ed. John Worthen. Cambridge: Cambridge UP, 1987. (Penguin, 1996).

". . . Love Was Once a Little Boy." 1925. *"Reflections on the Death of a Porcupine" and Other Essays* 329–46. *Phoenix II* 444–59.

"Making Pictures." *Phoenix II* 602–07.

"The Man Who Died." St. Mawr *and "The Man Who Died."* New York: Vintage, 1953. (See also *The Escaped Cock*).

"Matriarchy." *Phoenix II* 549–52. Rpt. in Scott 224–27.

"The Miner at Home." 1912. *"Love among the Haystacks" and Other Stories* 123–27.

"Morality and the Novel." 1925. *"Study of Thomas Hardy" and Other Essays* 171–76.

Mornings in Mexico *and* Etruscan Places. New York: Penguin, 1960.

Mornings in Mexico *and* Etruscan Places. London: Heinemann, 1970.

"New Mexico." *Phoenix* 141–47. Also in *D. H. Lawrence and New Mexico* 103–05.

New Poems. London: Secker, 1918.

"Nottingham and the Mining Countryside." *Phoenix* 133–40.

"The Novel." 1925. *"Study of Thomas Hardy" and Other Essays* 177–90.

"The Novel and the Feelings." 1936. *"Study of Thomas Hardy" and Other Essays* 201–05.

"Odour of Chrysanthemums." *English Review* 8 (June 1911): 415–33.

"Odour of Chrysanthemums." *"The Prussian Officer" and Other Stories*. London: Duckworth, 1914.

"Odour of Chrysanthemums." *"The Prussian Officer" and Other Stories*. Ed. Atkins. App.: Ending of "Odour," 1911 *English Review* version. 224–27.

"Odour of Chrysanthemums." 1914. *"The Prussian Officer" and Other Stories* (CUP) 181–99.

"Odour of Chrysanthemums." 1914. *Selected Short Stories*. New York: Dover, 1993. 108–24.

"On Being Religious." *Phoenix* 724–30.

"Pan in America." *Phoenix* 22–31.

Phoenix: The Posthumous Papers. 1936. Ed. Edward D. McDonald. New York: Penguin, 1978.

Phoenix II: Uncollected, Unpublished and Other Prose Works by D. H. Lawrence. Ed. Warren Roberts and Harry T. Moore. London: Heinemann, 1968.

The Plays. Ed. Hans-Wilhelm Schwarze and John Worthen. Cambridge: Cambridge UP, 1999.

The Plumed Serpent. 1926. Ed. L. D. Clark. Cambridge: Cambridge UP, 1987.

The Plumed Serpent. (CUP). Ed. L. D. Clark. Introd. Virginia Hyde. Notes by Clark and Hyde. New York: Penguin, 1995.

"Poetry of the Present" (as "Introduction to the American Edition of *New Poems*"). *Phoenix* 218–22. *Complete Poems* 181–86.

"Pornography and Obscenity." *Phoenix* 170–87.

The Portable D. H. Lawrence. 1947. Ed. Diana Trilling. New York: Viking, 1985.

Preface. *Bottom Dogs*. By Edward Dahlberg. *Phoenix* 267–73.

"The Princess." *St. Mawr and Other Stories* 157–96.

"The Proper Study." *Phoenix* 719–23.

"The Prussian Officer" and Other Stories. 1914. Ed. John Worthen. Cambridge: Cambridge UP, 1983. (Penguin, 1995).

"The Prussian Officer" and Other Stories. Ed. Antony Atkins. Oxford: Oxford UP, 1995.

Psychoanalysis and the Unconscious. Psychoanalysis 1–49.

Psychoanalysis and the Unconscious *and* Fantasia of the Unconscious. Introd. Philip Rieff. New York: Viking, 1960.

Quetzalcoatl: *The Early Version of* The Plumed Serpent. Ed. Louis L. Martz. Redding Ridge: Black Swan, 1995.

The Rainbow. 1915. Ed. Mark Kinkead-Weekes. Cambridge: Cambridge UP, 1989.

The Rainbow. (CUP). Ed. Mark Kinkead-Weekes. Introd. Anne Fernihough. New York: Penguin, 1995.

"Reflections on the Death of a Porcupine" and Other Essays. Ed. Michael Herbert. Cambridge: Cambridge UP, 1988.

"The Rocking-Horse Winner." 1926. *"The Woman Who Rode Away" and Other Stories* (CUP) 230–43.

"Samson and Delilah." 1917. *"England, My England" and Other Stories* 108–22.

Sea and Sardinia. 1921. Ed. Mara Kalnins. Cambridge: Cambridge UP, 1997. (Penguin, 1999). *D. H. Lawrence and Italy* 1–205.

Selected Critical Writings. Ed. Michael Herbert. New York: Oxford UP, 1998.

Selected Letters. 1950. Ed. Richard Aldington. New York: Penguin, 1996.

The Selected Letters of D. H. Lawrence. Ed. James T. Boulton. Cambridge: Cambridge UP, 1996.

"She Said As Well to Me." *Complete Poems* 254–56.

"The Ship of Death." *Complete Poems* 716–20.

Sketches of Etruscan Places *and Other Italian Essays*. Ed. Simonetta de Filippis. Cambridge: Cambridge UP, 1992. New York: Penguin, 1998.

"Snake." *Complete Poems* 349–51.

Sons and Lovers. 1913. Ed. Helen Baron and Carl Baron. Cambridge: Cambridge UP, 1992.

Sons and Lovers. (CUP). Ed. Helen Baron and Carl Baron. New York: Penguin, 1994.

Sons and Lovers. Introd. Howard J. Booth. Ware, Hertfordshire: Wordsworth, 1999.

Sons and Lovers. Introd. Geoff Dyer. New York: Modern Library, 1999.

Sons and Lovers. Introd. David Trotter. New York: Oxford, 1995.

Sons and Lovers: *Text, Background, and Criticism*. Ed. Julian Moynahan. Viking Critical Edition. 1968. New York: Penguin, 1977.

"The State of Funk." *Phoenix II* 565–70.

St. Mawr. 1925. St. Mawr *and Other Stories* 19–155.

St. Mawr *and Other Stories*. Ed. Brian Finney. Cambridge: Cambridge UP, 1983. (Penguin, 1997).

Studies in Classic American Literature. New York: Penguin, 1977.

"Study of Thomas Hardy." 1936. *"Study of Thomas Hardy" and Other Essays* 3–128.

"Study of Thomas Hardy" and Other Essays. Ed. Bruce Steele. Cambridge: Cambridge UP, 1985.

The Symbolic Meaning: The Uncollected Versions of Studies in Classic American Literature. Ed. Armin Arnold. Fontwell: Centaur, 1962.

Three Plays by D. H. Lawrence: A Collier's Friday Night, The Daughter-in-Law, The Widowing of Mrs. Holroyd. New York: Penguin, 1969.

"Tickets Please." 1919. *"England, My England" and Other Stories* 34–45.

Tortoises. Ed. David Ellis. Canterbury: Yorick, 1982.

Twilight in Italy. 1916. Twilight in Italy *and Other Essays*. Ed. Paul Eggert. Cambridge: Cambridge UP, 1994. (Penguin, 1997). 85–226. *D. H. Lawrence and Italy* 3–168.

The Virgin and the Gipsy. New York: Penguin, 1970.

The White Peacock. 1911. Ed. Andrew Robertson. Cambridge: Cambridge UP, 1983. New York: Penguin, 1995.

"Why the Novel Matters." 1936. *"Study of Thomas Hardy" and Other Essays* 191–98.

The Widowing of Mrs. Holroyd. Three Plays 147–200.

"The Woman Who Rode Away." 1925. *"The Woman Who Rode Away" and Other Stories* (CUP) 39–71.

"The Woman Who Rode Away" and Other Stories. 1928. Ed. Dieter Mehl and Christa Jansohn. Cambridge: Cambridge UP, 1995.

"The Woman Who Rode Away" and Other Stories. (CUP). Ed. Dieter Mehl and Christa Jansohn. Introd. N. H. Reeve. New York: Penguin, 1996.

"Women Are So Cocksure." *Phoenix* 167–69.

Women in Love. 1920. Ed. David Farmer, Lindeth Vasey, and John Worthen. Cambridge: Cambridge UP, 1987.

Women in Love. (CUP). Ed. David Farmer, Lindeth Vasey, and John Worthen. Introd. and notes by Mark Kinkead-Weekes. New York: Penguin, 1995.

Books and Articles

"Affect." Def. 1b. *American Heritage Dictionary of the English Language.* 3rd ed. 1992.

Agnew, J. "Representing Space, Scale and Culture in Social Science." *Place/Culture/ Representation.* Ed. James Duncan and David Ley. London: Routledge, 1993. 251–71.

Apter, T. E. "Let's Hear What the Male Chauvinist Is Saying." *Lawrence and Women.* Ed. Anne Smith. London: Vision, 1978. 156–77.

Arnold, Armin. *D. H. Lawrence and America.* London: Linden, 1958.

Atkins, Antony. Introduction. D. H. Lawrence, *"The Prussian Officer" and Other Stories* (Oxford) xii–xxix.

Auden, W. H. "D. H. Lawrence." *"The Dyer's Hand" and Other Essays.* New York: Random, 1962. 277–95.

Auerbach, Eric. *Mimesis: The Representation of Reality in Western Literature.* Trans. William Trask. New York: Doubleday, 1953.

Bakhtin, Mikhail. *The Dialogic Imagination: Four Essays.* Ed. Michael Holquist. Trans. Caryl Emerson and Holquist. Austin: U of Texas P, 1981.

———. "Discourse in the Novel." Bakhtin, *Dialogic Imagination* 259–422.

Balbert, Peter, and Phillip L. Marcus, eds. *D. H. Lawrence: A Centenary Consideration.* Ithaca: Cornell UP, 1985.

Baldwin, James. *Giovanni's Room.* New York: Dial, 1956.

Baron, Helen. "Jessie Chambers' Plea for Justice to 'Miriam.'" *Archiv* 137 (1985): 63–84. Rpt. in *Journal of the D. H. Lawrence Society* 4 (1987–88): 7–24.

———. "Mrs. Morel Ironing." *Journal of the D. H. Lawrence Society* 1 (1984): 2–12.

———. "*Sons and Lovers*: The Surviving Manuscripts from Three Drafts Dated by Paper Analysis." *Studies in Bibliography* 38 (1985): 289–328.

———. "The Surviving Galley Proofs of Lawrence's *Sons and Lovers.*" *Studies in Bibliography* 45 (1992): 231–51.

Baron, Helen, and Carl Baron. Introduction. D. H. Lawrence, *Sons and Lovers* (Penguin, 1994) xv–xlv.

Barthes, Roland. "The Death of the Author." 1968. *Image/Music/Text.* Trans. Stephen Heath. New York: Hill, 1977. 142–47.

Beaty, Jerome, and J. Paul Hunter, eds. *Norton Introduction to Literature.* 7th ed. New York: Norton, 1998.

Beauvoir, Simone de. *The Second Sex.* 1949. Trans. and ed. H. M. Parshley. New York: Vintage, 1974.

Belenky, Mary, et al. *Women's Ways of Knowing.* New York: Basic, 1986.

Bellow, Saul. "Culture Now: Some Animadversions, Some Laughs." *Modern Occasions* 1.2 (1971): 162–78.

Benjamin, Jessica. *The Bonds of Love: Psychoanalysis, Feminism, and the Problem of Domination.* New York: Pantheon, 1988.

Bennett, William J. *The Devaluing of America: The Fight for Our Culture and Our Children.* Nashville: Nelson, 1994.

Berger, John. *Ways of Seeing*. London: BBC and Penguin, 1972.

Bersani, Leo. *Homos*. Cambridge: Harvard UP, 1995.

Beynon, Richard. *D. H. Lawrence:* The Rainbow *and* Women in Love. Cambridge: Icon, 1977.

Bhabha, Homi. "Signs Taken for Wonders: Questions of Ambivalence and Authority under a Tree outside Delhi, May 1817." *The Post-colonial Studies Reader*. Ed. Bill Ashcroft, Gareth Griffiths, and Helen Tiffen. New York: Routledge, 1995. 29–35.

Birkerts, Sven. "Perseus Unbound." *Literature: The Evolving Canon*. Ed. Birkerts. Boston: Allyn, 1996. 1632–36.

Black, Michael. *D. H. Lawrence:* Sons and Lovers. Cambridge: Cambridge UP, 1992.

———. *D. H. Lawrence: The Early Fiction: A Commentary*. London: Macmillan, 1986.

Blackmur, R. P. "D. H. Lawrence and Expressive Form." *Form and Value in Modern Poetry*. Garden City: Doubleday-Anchor, 1952. 253–67.

Blake, Andrew. *Reading Victorian Fiction: The Cultural Context and Ideological Content of the Nineteenth-Century Novel*. New York: St. Martin's, 1988.

Booth, Howard J. Introduction. D. H. Lawrence, *Sons and Lovers* (Wordsworth) ix–xx.

Booth, Wayne. "Confessions of a Lukewarn Lawrentian." *The Company We Keep: An Ethics of Fiction*. Berkeley: U of California P, 1988. 436–57. Rpt. in Squires and Cushman 9–27.

Boulton, James T. "D. H. Lawrence's 'Odour of Chrysanthemums': An Early Version." *Renaissance and Modern Studies* 13 (1969): 4–48.

Bourdieu, Pierre. "Flaubert's Point of View." *Critical Inquiry* 14 (1988): 539–62.

Brown, Keith, ed. *Rethinking Lawrence*. Philadelphia: Open UP, 1990.

Buber, Martin. *Between Man and Man*. Trans. Ronald Gregor Smith. New York: Macmillan, 1965.

———. "Dialogue." 1929. Buber, *Between Man* 1–39.

———. "Elements of the Interhuman." 1957. *The Knowledge of Man: A Philosophy of the Interhuman*. By Buber. Ed. Maurice Friedman. Trans. Friedman and Ronald Gregor Smith. New York: Harper, 1966. 72–88.

———. "The History of the Dialogical Principle." Buber, *Between Man* 209–24.

Burgess, Anthony. *Flame into Being: The Life and Work of D. H. Lawrence*. New York: Arbor, 1985.

———. Introduction. D. H. Lawrence, *D. H. Lawrence and Italy* vii–xiii.

Butler, Judith. *Gender Trouble*. New York: Routledge, 1990.

Capra, Fritjof. *The Turning Point*. London: Fontana, 1983.

Carpenter, Rebecca. "'Bottom-Dog Insolence' and 'The Harem Mentality': Race and Gender in Lawrence's *The Plumed Serpent*." *D. H. Lawrence Review* 24–25 (1996): 119–29.

Carswell, Catherine. Rev. of *The Rainbow*, by D. H. Lawrence. *Glasgow Herald* 4 Nov. 1915: 4.

———. *The Savage Pilgrimage: A Narrative of D. H. Lawrence*. London: Secker, 1932.

Chambers, Jessie. *D. H. Lawrence: A Personal Record by E. T.* 1935. New York: Cambridge UP, 1980.

Chasing a Rainbow. Dir. Christopher Ralling. PBS, Feb. 1992.

Chodorow, Nancy. *Feminism and Psychoanalytic Theory*. New Haven: Yale UP, 1989.

———. *The Reproduction of Mothering: Psychoanalysis and the Sociology of Gender*. Berkeley: U of California P, 1978.

Chomsky, Noam. *Necessary Illusions*. Boston: South End, 1989.

Chopin, Kate. "The Story of an Hour." *"The Storm" and Other Stories*. Ed. Per Seyersted. Old Westbury: Feminist, 1974. 163–65.

Cixous, Hélène. "Sorties." Cixous and Clément 61–132.

Cixous, Hélène, and Catherine Clément. *The Newly Born Woman*. 1975. Trans. Betsy Wing. Minneapolis: U of Minnesota P, 1986.

Clark, L. D. *Dark Night of the Body: D. H. Lawrence's* The Plumed Serpent. Austin: U of Texas P, 1964.

———. Introduction. D. H. Lawrence, *Plumed Serpent* (CUP) xix–xlvii.

———. *The Minoan Distance: The Symbolism of Travel in D. H. Lawrence*. Tucson: U of Arizona P, 1980.

———. "Reading Lawrence's American Novel: *The Plumed Serpent*." *Critical Essays on D. H. Lawrence*. Ed. Dennis Jackson and Fleda Brown Jackson. Boston: Hall, 1988. 118–28.

Clarke, Ian. *Edwardian Drama: A Critical Study*. London: Faber, 1989.

Colacurcio, Michael J. "The Symbolic and the Symptomatic: D. H. Lawrence in Recent American Criticism." *American Quarterly* 27 (1975): 486–501.

Coleridge, Samuel. *Biographia Literaria*. Ed. James Engell and W. Jackson Bate. Vol. 2. Princeton: Princeton UP, 1983.

Cowan, James C. *D. H. Lawrence: An Annotated Bibliography of Writings about Him (1909–1975)*. 2 vols. Dekalb: Northern Illinois UP, 1982–85.

Crick, Brian. *The Story of "The Prussian Officer" Revisions: Littlewood among the Lawrence Scholars*. Retford, Eng.: Brynmill, 1983.

Cushman, Keith. *D. H. Lawrence at Work: The Emergence of "The Prussian Officer" Stories*. Charlottesville: UP of Virginia, 1978.

Daleski, H. M. *The Forked Flame: A Study of D. H. Lawrence*. Evanston: Northwestern UP, 1965.

Delany, Paul. *D. H. Lawrence's Nightmare: The Writer and His Circle in the Years of the Great War*. New York: Basic, 1978.

Delavenay, Emile. *D. H. Lawrence, the Man and His Work: The Formative Years: 1885–1919*. Trans. Katherine M. Delavenay. Carbondale: Southern Illinois UP, 1972.

Devall, Bill, and George Sessions. *Deep Ecology*. Salt Lake City: Smith, 1985.

Dinnerstein, Dorothy. *The Mermaid and the Minotaur: Sexual Arrangements and Human Malaise*. New York: Harper, 1976.

Doherty, Gerald. "The Throes of Aphrodite: The Sexual Dimension in D. H. Lawrence's *The Plumed Serpent*." *Studies in the Humanities* 12 (1985): 67–78.

Dollimore, Jonathan. *Sexual Dissidence: Augustine to Wilde, Freud to Foucault*. Oxford: Claredon, 1991.

Douglas, James. Rev. of *The Rainbow*, by D. H. Lawrence. *Star* 22 Oct. 1915: 4.

Draper, R. P., ed. *D. H. Lawrence: The Critical Heritage*. London: Routledge, 1970.

Dyer, Geoff. Introduction. D. H. Lawrence, *Sons and Lovers* (Modern Library) xi–xix.

———. *Out of Sheer Rage: Wrestling with D. H. Lawrence*. New York: North Point, 1997.

Eagle, Solomon [J. C. Squire]. "Current Literature: Books in General." *New Statesman* 20 Nov. 1915: 161.

Eagleton, Terry. *The Function of Criticism: From* The Spectator *to Post-structuralism*. London: Verso, 1984.

Easthope, Anthony. *Literary into Cultural Studies*. London: Routledge, 1991.

Eggert, Paul. "Comedy and Provisionality: Lawrence's Address to His Audience and Material in His Australian Novels." Eggert and Worthen 131–57.

———. Introduction. Eggert and Worthen 1–18.

———. "Opening Up the Text: The Case of *Sons and Lovers*." Brown 38–52.

Eggert, Paul, and John Worthen, eds. *Lawrence and Comedy*. Cambridge: Cambridge UP, 1996.

Elam, Diane. *Romancing the Postmodern*. New York: Routledge, 1992.

Eliot, T. S. *After Strange Gods*. London: Faber, 1934.

Ellis, David. *D. H. Lawrence: Dying Game, 1922–1930*. Cambridge: Cambridge UP, 1997.

———. "Here and Now in Sardinia: The Art of Lawrence's Travel Writing." Ellis and Mills 98–119.

———. Introduction. D. H. Lawrence, *The Fox, The Captain's Doll, The Ladybird*. (CUP). Ed. Dieter Mehl. New York: Penguin, 1994. xiii–xxx.

———. "Reading Lawrence: The Case of *Sea and Sardinia*." *D. H. Lawrence Review* 10 (1977): 52–63.

Ellis, David, and Howard Mills. *D. H. Lawrence's Non-fiction: Art, Thought and Genre*. Cambridge: Cambridge UP, 1988.

Ellis, David, and Ornella De Zordo, eds. *D. H. Lawrence: Critical Assessments*. 4 vols. East Sussex: Helm, 1992.

Elsbree, Langdon. *Ritual Passages and Narrative Structures*. New York: Lang, 1991.

Felman, Shoshana. "Education and Crisis, or, The Vicissitudes of Teaching." *American Imago* 48.1 (1991): 13–73.

———. "Psychoanalysis and Education: Teaching Terminable and Interminable." *Yale French Studies* 63 (1982): 21–44.

Feltes, N. N. *Literary Capital and the Late Victorian Novel*. Madison: U of Wisconsin P, 1993.

———. *Modes of Production of Victorian Novels*. Chicago: U of Chicago P, 1986.

Fernihough, Anne. *D. H. Lawrence: Aesthetics and Ideology*. Oxford: Clarendon, 1993.

———. Introduction. D. H. Lawrence, *Rainbow* (Penguin) xiii–xxxiv.

Fetterley, Judith. *The Resisting Reader: A Feminist Approach to American Literature*. Bloomington: Indiana UP, 1978.

Fiedler, Leslie. *Love and Death in the American Novel.* New York: Criterion, 1960.

Finke, Laurie. "Knowledge as Bait: Feminism, Voice, and the Pedagogical Unconscious." *College English* 55 (1993): 7–27.

Fish, Stanley. *Is There a Text in This Class?* Cambridge: Harvard UP, 1980.

Fleishman, Avrom. "'He Do the Polis in Different Voices:' Lawrence's Later Style." Balbert and Marcus 162–79.

———. "Lawrence and Bakhtin: Where Pluralism Ends and Dialogism Begins." Brown 109–19.

Ford, Ford Madox. *England and the English.* New York: McLure, 1907.

———. "D. H. Lawrence." *Portraits from Life.* Boston: Houghton, 1937. 70–89. Rpt. in Nehls 1: 106–21; Beaty and Hunter 310–12, 314.

Ford, George. *Double Measure.* 1965. New York: Norton, 1969.

Forstner, Lorne J., and John H. Todd, eds. *The Everlasting Universe: Readings on the Ecological Revolution.* Lexington: Heath, 1971.

Foucault, Michel. *The Use of Pleasure.* 1984. Trans. Robert Hurley. New York: Vintage, 1986. Vol. 2 of *The History of Sexuality.*

Franks, Jill. *Revisionist Resurrection Mythologies: A Study of D. H. Lawrence's Italian Works.* New York: Lang, 1994.

Frazer, James G. The Golden Bough: *A New Abridgement from the Second and Third Editions.* Ed. Robert Fraser. World's Classics. New York: Oxford UP, 1994.

———. *Totemism and Exogamy.* 4 vols. London: Macmillan, 1910.

Freeman, Mary. *D. H. Lawrence: A Basic Study of His Ideas.* Gainesville: UP of Florida, 1955.

Freire, Paulo. *The Pedagogy of the Oppressed.* 1971. Trans. Myra Bergman. New York: Continuum, 1990.

French, Philip. "A Major Miner Dramatist." *Critical Essays on D. H. Lawrence.* Ed. Dennis Jackson and Fleda Brown Jackson. Boston: Hall, 1988. 214–16.

Freud, Sigmund. *Moses and Monotheism.* 1939. Harmondsworth: Penguin, 1990.

———. *On Dreams.* 1901. Trans. James Strachey. New York: Norton, 1980.

———. "The Question of Lay Analysis." 1926. *The Standard Edition of the Complete Psychological Works of Sigmund Freud.* Trans. James Strachey. Vol. 20. London: Hogarth, 1975. 177–258.

———. "The Uncanny." *The Standard Edition of the Complete Psychological Works of Sigmund Freud.* Trans. James Strachey. Vol. 17. London: Hogarth, 1964. 217–52.

Frontain, Raymond-Jean. "Bible." *Gay and Lesbian Literary Heritage.* Ed. Claude J. Summers. New York: Holt, 1995. 92–100.

———. "James Baldwin's *Giovanni's Room* and the Biblical Myth of David." *CEA Critic* 57.2 (1995): 41–58.

———. Rev. of *D. H. Lawrence: A Biography,* by Jeffrey Meyers. *James White Review* 11.1 (1993): 23.

———. "'Ruddy and Goodly to Look at Withal': Drayton, Cowley, and the Biblical Model for Renaissance Hom[m]osexuality." *Cahiers Elisabéthains* 36 (1989): 11–24.

Fuss, Diana. *Identification Papers*. New York: Routledge, 1995.

Fussell, Paul. *The Great War and Modern Memory*. New York: Oxford UP, 1975.

Gallop, Jane. *Around 1981: Academic Feminist Literary Theory*. New York: Routledge, 1992.

Gendlin, Eugene. *Focusing*. New York: Everest, 1978.

Gervais, David. *Literary Englands: Versions of "Englishness" in Modern Writing*. Cambridge: Cambridge UP, 1993.

Gide, André. *Saul*. *My Theatre: Five Plays and an Essay*. Trans. Jackson Matthews. New York: Knopf, 1952. 3–107.

Gilbert, Sandra M. *Acts of Attention: The Poems of D. H. Lawrence*. 1972. 2nd ed. Carbondale: Southern Illinois UP, 1990.

———. "Afterword: D. H. Lawrence's Uncommon Prayers." Gilbert, *Acts* 193–242.

Gilbert, Sandra M., and Susan Gubar. *No Man's Land: The Place of the Woman Writer in the Twentieth Century*. Vol. 1: *The War of the Words*. Vol. 2: *Sexchanges*. New Haven: Yale UP, 1988–89.

Giles, Judy, and Timothy Middleton, eds. *Writing Englishness, 1900–1950: An Introductory Source-book on National Identity*. London: Routledge, 1995.

Gilligan, Carol. *In a Different Voice*. Cambridge: Harvard UP, 1987.

Goodheart, Eugene. *The Utopian Vision of D. H. Lawrence*. Chicago: U of Chicago P, 1963.

Gould, Gerald. Rev. of *The Rainbow*, by D. H. Lawrence. *New Statesman* 23 Oct. 1915: 66–67.

Graff, Gerald. *Beyond the Culture Wars*. New York: Norton, 1992.

———. "Other Voices, Other Rooms: Organizing and Teaching the Humanities Conflict." *Teaching the Conflicts: Gerald Graff, Curricular Reform, and the Culture Wars*. Ed. William E. Cain. New York: Garland, 1994. 17–44.

Gregor, Ian. *The Moral and the Story*. London: Faber, 1962.

Greiff, Louis. *D. H. Lawrence: Fifty Years on Film (1949–1999)*. Carbondale: Southern Illinois UP, 2001.

Haraway, Donna. "Situated Knowledges: The Science Questions in Feminism and the Privilege of Partial Perspective." *Feminist Studies* 14 (1988): 575–99.

Harris, Janice H. "Lawrence and the Edwardian Feminists." Squires and Cushman 62–76.

———. *The Short Fiction of D. H. Lawrence*. New Brunswick: Rutgers UP, 1984.

Hartman, Geoffrey. "The Fate of Reading Once More." *PMLA* 111 (1966): 383–89.

HD. *Bid Me to Live*. 1960. Redding Ridge: Black Swan, 1983.

Henley, W. E. *For England's Sake: Verses and Songs in Time of War*. London: Nutt, 1900.

Herman, Edward S., and Noam Chomsky. *Manufacturing Consent: The Political Economy of the Mass Media*. New York: Pantheon, 1988.

Hillman, James. *Anima—An Anatomy of a Personified Notion*. Dallas: Spring, 1985.

Hirsch, E. D. *The Philosophy of Composition*. Chicago: U of Chicago P, 1977.

Hogarth, Paul. *Escape to the Sun: Travels in the Footsteps of D. H. Lawrence*. Nottingham: Djanogly Art Gallery, U of Nottingham Arts Centre, 1996.

Holbrook, David. *Where D. H. Lawrence Was Wrong about Woman.* Cranbury: Associated UP, 1992.

Holquist, Michael. *Dialogism: Bakhtin and His World.* London: Routledge, 1990.

Homans, Margaret. *Bearing the Word: Language and Female Experience in Nineteenth-Century Women's Writing.* Chicago: U of Chicago P, 1986.

Howard, Richard. "The Giant on Giant-Killing." *Fellow Feelings.* New York: Atheneum, 1976. 53–55.

Hughes, Ted. *Winter Pollen: Occasional Prose.* Ed. William Scammell. London: Faber, 1994.

Hurst, Fannie. *Imitation of Life.* New York: Collier, 1933.

Huxley, Aldous. Introduction. D. H. Lawrence, *Letters* (ed. Huxley) ix–xxxiv. Rpt. in D. H. Lawrence, *Selected Letters* (Penguin) 5–31.

Huxley, T. H. "Prolegomena." Evolution and Ethics *and Other Essays.* New York: Appleton, 1929. 1–45.

Hyde, Virginia. Introduction. D. H. Lawrence, *Plumed Serpent* (Penguin) xv–xxxv.

———. "'Lost' Girls: D. H. Lawrence's Versions of Persephone." *Images of Persephone: Feminist Readings in Western Literature.* Ed. Elizabeth Hayes. Gainesville: UP of Florida, 1994. 99–120.

———. *The Risen Adam: D. H. Lawrence's Revisionist Typology.* University Park: Pennsylvania State UP, 1992.

———. "To 'Undiscovered Land': D. H. Lawrence's Horsewomen and Other Questers." *Women and the Journey: The Female Travel Experience.* Ed. Bonnie Frederick and Susan McLeod. Introd. Frederick and Hyde. Pullman: Washington State UP, 1993. 171–89.

Hyde, Virginia, and L. D. Clark. "The Sense of an Ending in *The Plumed Serpent.*" *D. H. Lawrence Review* 25 (1993–94): 140–48.

Hynes, Samuel. *A War Imagined: The First World War and English Culture.* New York: Atheneum, 1991.

Iida, Takeo. *The Reception of D. H. Lawrence around the World.* Fukuoka, Jap.: Kyushu UP, 1999.

Imitation of Life. Dir. John Stahl. Universal, 1934.

Irigaray, Luce. *An Ethics of Sexual Difference.* 1984. Trans. Carolyn Burke and Gillian C. Gill. Ithaca: Cornell UP, 1993.

———. *I Love to You: Sketch of a Possible Felicity in History.* Trans. Alison Martin. New York: Routledge, 1996.

———. *The Irigaray Reader.* Ed. Margeret Whitford. Oxford: Blackwell, 1991.

———. "Questions to Emmanuel Levinas" 1990. Irigaray, *Irigaray Reader* 178–89.

———. *Speculum of the Other Woman.* Trans. Gillian C. Gill. Ithaca: Cornell UP, 1985.

———. "Wonder: A Reading of Descartes, *The Passions of the Soul.*" Irigaray, *Ethics* 72–82.

Jay, Gregory S. "The End of 'American' Literature: Toward a Multicultural Practice." *College English* 53 (1991): 264–81.

Johnson, Samuel. *Lives of the English Poets.* Vol. 2. London: Everyman, 1925.

Joyce, James. "The Dead." *Dubliners.* New York: Dover, 1991. 119–52.

Jung, Carl. *The Portable Jung*. Ed. Joseph Campbell. Trans. R. F. C. Hull. Harmondsworth: Penguin, 1976.

———. *The Spirit in Man, Art and Literature*. Trans. R. F. C. Hull. London: Routledge, 1966. Vol. 15 of *The Collected Works of C. G. Jung*.

Kahn, Coppelia. "The Hand That Rocks the Cradle: Recent Gender Theories and Their Implications." *The (M)other Tongue: Essays in Feminist Psychoanalytic Interpretation*. Ed. Shirley Nelson Garner et al. Ithaca: Cornell UP, 1985. 72–88.

Kalnins, Mara. "D. H. Lawrence's 'Odour of Chrysanthemums': The Three Endings." *Studies in Short Fiction* 13 (1976): 471–79.

Kaye, Richard. "D. H. Lawrence." *Gay and Lesbian Literary Heritage*. Ed. Claude J. Summers. New York: Holt, 1995. 438–40.

Keating, Peter. *The Haunted Study: A Social History of the English Novel, 1875–1914*. London: Secker, 1989. London: Fontana, 1991.

Keats, John. Letter to John Hamilton Reynolds. 3 Feb. 1818. *The Norton Anthology of English Literature*. Ed. M. H. Abrams. 6th ed. Vol. 2. New York: Norton, 1993. 832–33.

Keith, M., and S. Pile, eds. *Place and the Politics of Identity*. London: Routledge, 1993.

Kendrick, Walter. *The Secret Museum: Pornography in Modern Culture*. New York: Penguin, 1987.

Kenndy, X. J. *Literature: An Introduction to Fiction, Poetry, and Drama*. 4th ed. Boston: Little, 1987.

Kermode, Frank. *D. H. Lawrence*. Fontana Mod. Masters. London: Fontana, 1973.

Kinkead-Weekes, Mark. *D. H. Lawrence: Triumph to Exile, 1912–1922*. Cambridge: Cambridge UP, 1996.

———. "Eros and Metaphor." *Lawrence and Women*. Ed. Anne Smith. London: Vision, 1979. 101–21.

———. Introduction. D. H. Lawrence, *Rainbow* (CUP) xix–lxxvi.

———. Introduction. D. H. Lawrence, *Women in Love* (Penguin) xiii–xxxii.

———. "The Marble and the Statue: The Exploratory Imagination of D. H. Lawrence." *Imagined Worlds: Essays on Some English Novels and Novelists in Honour of John Butt*. Ed. Maynard Mack and Ian Gregor. London: Methuen, 1968. 371–481.

———. "The Shaping of *Look! We Have Come Through!*" *Presenting Poetry*. Ed. H. Erskine Hill and R. A. McCabe. Cambridge: Cambridge UP, 1995. 214–34.

Kristeva, Julia. *Desire in Language: A Semiotic Approach to Literature and Art*. Ed. Leon S. Roudiez. Trans. Thomas Gora, Alice Jardine, and Roudiez. New York: Columbia UP, 1980.

———. "Oscillation between Power and Denial." Trans. Marilyn A. August. *New French Feminisms*. Ed. Elaine Marks and Isabelle de Courtivron. Amherst: U of Massachusetts P, 1980. 165–67.

———. *Strangers to Ourselves*. Trans. Leon S. Roudiez. New York: Columbia UP, 1991.

Krupat, Arnold. *Ethnocriticism: Ethnography, History, Literature*. Berkeley: U of California P, 1992.

Kushigian, Nancy. *Pictures and Fictions: Visual Modernism and the Pre-war Novels of D. H. Lawrence*. New York: Lang, 1990.

Laird, Holly. "The Poems of 'Piano.'" *D. H. Lawrence Review* 18 (1985–86): 183–99.

———. *Self and Sequence: The Poetry of D. H. Lawrence.* Charlottesville: UP of Virginia, 1988.

Landow, George. *The Dickens Web.* Watertown: Eastgate, 1992.

———. *Hypertext: The Convergence of Contemporary Critical Theory and Technology.* Baltimore: Johns Hopkins UP, 1992.

Landow, George, and Jon Lanestedt. *The "In Memoriam" Web.* Watertown: Eastgate, 1992.

Lanham, Richard. *Style: An Anti-textbook.* New Haven: Yale UP, 1974.

Larkin, Philip. "The Explosion." *Collected Poems.* London: Faber-Marvell, 1988. 175.

Larsen, Nella. *Quicksand.* 1928. Quicksand *and* Passing. New Brunswick: Rutgers UP, 1986.

Lawrence, Frieda. *Not I, but the Wind.* 1935. *Frieda Lawrence.* By Rosie Jackson. London: Harper, 1994. 97–196.

Leavis, F. R. *D. H. Lawrence, Novelist.* 1955. London: Chatto, 1964.

———. *The Living Principle: "English" as a Discipline of Thought.* New York: Oxford UP, 1975.

Lerner, Laurence. *The Truthtellers: Jane Austen, George Eliot, and D. H. Lawrence.* New York: Schocken, 1967.

Levinas, Emmanuel. *Ethics and Infinity: Conversations with Philippe Nemo.* 1982. Trans. Richard A. Cohen. Pittsburgh: Duquesne UP, 1985.

———. "Ethics as First Philosophy." Levinas, *Levinas Reader* 75–87.

———. *The Levinas Reader.* Ed. Sean Hand. Oxford: Blackwell, 1989.

Levy, Mervyn. *Paintings of D. H. Lawrence.* London: Cory, 1964.

Littlewood, J. C. F. *D. H. Lawrence I: 1885–1914.* British Council Pamphlet. London: Longman, 1976.

———. "Lawrence's Early Tales." *Cambridge Quarterly* 1 (1966): 107–24.

Lodge, David. "Lawrence, Dostoevsky, Bakhtin: Lawrence and Dialogic Fiction." Brown 92–108.

———. "Reading and Lessons." Rev. of *The Story of the Stories,* by Dan Jacobson, and of *The Art of Biblical Narrative,* by Robert Alter. *Times Literary Supplement* 5 Nov. 1982: 1207.

Lovelock, James. *Gaia: A New Look at Life on Earth.* New York: Oxford, 1979.

Luhan, Mabel Dodge. "Plum." *Lorenzo in Taos.* New York: Knopf, 1932. 245.

Lynd, Robert. Rev. of *The Rainbow,* by D. H. Lawrence. *Daily News* 5 Oct. 1915: 6.

Macdonell, Diane. *Theories of Discourse: An Introduction.* Blackwell: Oxford, 1986.

Macdonnell, A. G. *England, Their England.* London: Macmillan, 1933.

Mailer, Norman. *The Prisoner of Sex.* Boston: Little, 1971.

Mani, Lata. "Contentious Traditions: The Debate on *Sati* in Colonial India." *Recasting Women: Essays in Indian Colonial History.* Ed. Kumkum Sangari and Sudesh Vaid. New Brunswick: Rutgers UP, 1990. 88–126.

Mansfield, Katherine. *Letters of Katherine Mansfield.* Ed. J. Middleton Murry. New York: Knopf, 1929.

———. *Novels and Novelists*. Ed. J. Middleton Murry. New York: Knopf, 1930.

Marks, Elaine. *Marrano as Metaphor: The Jewish Presence in French Writing*. New York: Columbia UP, 1996.

Martz, Louis. Introduction. D. H. Lawrence, Quetzalcoatl ix–xxxi.

———. "*Quetzalcoatl*: The Early Version of *The Plumed Serpent*." *D. H. Lawrence Review* 22 (1990): 287–98.

———. "The Second Lady Chatterley." *Many Gods and Many Voices: The Role of the Prophet in English and American Modernism*. Columbia: U of Missouri P, 1998. 183–208.

Marx, Karl. "Comments on the Latest Prussian Censorship Instruction." Trans. Clemens Dutt. *Marx/Engels: Collected Works*. Vol. 1. New York: International, 1976. 109–31.

Massumi, Brian. "The Autonomy of Affect." *The Politics of Systems and Environments, Part II*. Spec. issue of *Cultural Critique* 31 (1995): 83–109.

McDowell, Frederick P. W. "'The Individual in His Pure Singleness': Theme and Symbol in *The Captain's Doll*." Squires and Cushman 143–58.

Mensch, Barbara. *D. H. Lawrence and the Authoritarian Personality*. New York: St. Martin's, 1991.

Merivale, Patricia. *Pan the Goat-God: His Myth in Modern Times*. Cambridge: Harvard UP, 1969.

Meyers, Jeffrey. "D. H. Lawrence and Homosexuality." *D. H. Lawrence: Novelist, Poet, Prophet*. Ed. Stephen Spender. New York: Harper, 1973. 135–46.

Miliaras, Barbara. "The Collapse of Agrarian Order and the Death of Thomas Brangwen in D. H. Lawrence's *The Rainbow*." *Etudes Lawrenciennes* 3 (1988): 65–77.

Miller, Donna R. "'This Pulsing Frictional To-And-Fro:' The Function(s) of Lexico-Grammatical Reiteration in D. H. Lawrence." *Lingua e Stile* 24 (1989): 467–83.

Millett, Kate. *Sexual Politics*. Garden City: Doubleday, 1970.

Millett, Robert W. *The Vultures and the Phoenix: A Study of the Mandrake Press Edition of the Paintings of D. H. Lawrence*. Philadelphia: Art Alliance, 1983.

Mohanty, S. P. "Us and Them: On the Philosophical Bases of Political Criticism." *Yale Journal of Criticism* 2.2 (1989): 1–31.

Moore, Harry T. *Poste Restante: A Lawrence Travel Calendar*. Berkeley: U of California P, 1956.

———. *The Priest of Love: A Life of D. H. Lawrence*. New York: Farrar, 1974. London: Heinemann, 1974.

Moore, Harry T., and Warren Roberts. 1966. *D. H. Lawrence*. New York: Thames, 1988.

Moynahan, Julian. *The Deed of Life*. Princeton: Princeton UP, 1963.

———, ed. *D. H. Lawrence's* Sons and Lovers: *Text, Background, and Criticism*. Viking Critical Edition. 1968. New York: Penguin, 1977.

Mudge, Bradford K. "The Man with Two Brains: Gothic Novels, Popular Culture, Literary History." *PMLA* 107 (1992): 92–104.

Murry, John Middleton. *D. H. Lawrence: Son of Woman*. London: Cape, 1931.

Naess, Arne. "The Shallow and the Deep Long-Range Ecology Movement: A Summary." *Inquiry* 16 (1973): 95–100.

Nehls, Edward, ed. *D. H. Lawrence: A Composite Biography*. 3 vols. Madison: U of Wisconsin P, 1957–59.

Nelson, Ted. *Literary Machines*. Sausalito: Mindful, 1992.

Nin, Anaïs. *D. H. Lawrence: An Unprofessional Study*. Chicago: Swallow, 1964.

Nixon, Cornelia. *Lawrence's Leadership Politics and the Turn against Women*. Berkeley: U of California P, 1986.

Norton Anthology of English Literature. Ed. M. H. Abrams et al. 7th ed. New York: Norton, 2000.

O'Connor, Frank. *The Lonely Voice: A Study of the Short Story*. New York: Harper, 1985.

Ong, Walter J. *Orality and Literacy: The Technologizing of the Word*. New York: Routledge, 1982.

Ortner, Sherry. "Is Female to Male as Nature Is to Culture?" *Woman, Culture, and Society*. Ed. Michelle Zimbalist Rosalda and Louise Lamphere. Stanford: Stanford UP, 1974. 67–87.

Orwell, George. "Lear, Tolstoy and the Fool." 1947. Vol. 4 of *The Collected Essays, Journalism, and Letters of George Orwell*. Ed. Sonia Orwell and Ian Angus. New York: Harcourt, 1968. 287–302.

——. *The Road to Wigan Pier*. New York: Harcourt, 1958.

Paglia, Camille. *Sexual Personae: Art and Decadence from Nefertiti to Emily Dickinson*. New York: Vintage, 1991.

Paik, Nak-chung. "Reflections on *The Plumed Serpent*." *D. H. Lawrence Studies* (D. H. Lawrence Society of Korea) 1 (1991): 184–210.

Parmenter, Ross. *Lawrence in Oaxaca: A Quest for the Novelist in Mexico*. Salt Lake City: Smith, 1984.

Pease, Donald E. *Visionary Compacts: American Renaissance Writings in Cultural Context*. Madison: U of Wisconsin P, 1987.

Perl, Sondra. "Understanding Composing." *Landmark Essays on Writing Process*. Ed. Perl. Davis: Hermagoras, 1994. 99–105.

Pichardie, Jean-Paul. *D. H. Lawrence: La tentation utopique: De Rananim au Serpent Plumes*. Rouen: U de Rouen, 1988.

Pinski, David. *King David and His Wives*. *Great Jewish Plays*. Trans. Joseph C. Landis. New York: Equinox, 1974. 161–215.

Pinto, Vivian de Sola. "D. H. Lawrence: Poet without a Mask." D. H. Lawrence, *Complete Poems* 1–21.

Poirier, Richard. *A World Elsewhere: The Place of Style in American Literature*. New York: Oxford UP, 1966.

Pollnitz, Christopher. "Craftsman before Demon: The Development of Lawrence's Verse Technique." Brown 133–50.

——. "'Raptus Virginis': The Dark God in the Poetry of D. H. Lawrence." *D. H. Lawrence: Centenary Essays*. Ed. Mara Kalnins. Bristol: Bristol Classical, 1986. 111–38.

Poovey, Mary. "Cultural Criticism: Past and Present." *College English* 52 (1990): 615–25.

Poplawski, Paul. *D. H. Lawrence: A Reference Companion*. Westport: Greenwood, 1996.

————. *The Works of D. H. Lawrence: A Chronological Checklist.* Nottingham: D. H. Lawrence Soc., 1995.

Preston, Peter. *A D. H. Lawrence Chronology.* New York: St. Martin's, 1994.

Raymond, Ernest. *Tell England: A Study in a Generation.* London: Cassell, 1922.

Rev. of *The Rainbow*, by D. H. Lawrence. *Westminster Gazette* Oct. 1915: 3.

Rexroth, Kenneth, Introduction. *D. H. Lawrence: Selected Poems.* New York: Viking, 1968. 1–23.

Rich, Adrienne. *Of Woman Born: Motherhood as Experience and Institution.* New York: Bantam, 1977.

Richards, I. A. *Practical Criticism: A Study of Literary Judgment.* New York: Harcourt, 1929.

Roberts, Warren. *A Bibliography of D. H. Lawrence.* 2nd ed. Cambridge: Cambridge UP, 1982.

Rolph, C. H., ed. *The Trial of Lady Chatterley: Regina vs. Penguin Books Limited.* New York: Penguin, 1990.

Ross, Charles. *The Composition of* The Rainbow *and* Women in Love: *A History.* Charlottesville: UP of Virginia, 1979.

————. "Electronic Editing and the Death of the Critical Edition." *The Literary Text in the Digital Age.* Ed. Richard Finneran. Ann Arbor: U of Michigan P, 1996. 225–31.

Rossman, Charles. "D. H. Lawrence and Mexico." Balbert and Marcus 180–209.

————. "'I Am the Call and You Are the Answer': D. H. Lawrence and Women." *D. H. Lawrence Review* 8 (1975): 255–330.

Ruderman, Judith. *D. H. Lawrence and the Devouring Mother: The Search for a Patriarchal Ideal of Leadership.* Durham: Duke UP, 1984.

Sabin, Margery. *The Dialect of the Tribe: Speech and Community in Modern Fiction.* New York: Oxford UP, 1987.

Sagar, Keith. *D. H. Lawrence: A Calendar of His Works.* Austin: U of Texas P, 1979.

————, ed. *A D. H. Lawrence Handbook.* Manchester: Manchester UP, 1982.

————. *D. H. Lawrence: Life into Art.* Athens: U of Georgia P, 1985.

————. *The Life of D. H. Lawrence.* New York: Pantheon, 1980.

Said, Edward W. *Culture and Imperialism.* New York: Knopf, 1993.

Salgado, Gamini, and G. K. Das, eds. *The Spirit of D. H. Lawrence: Centenary Studies.* London: Macmillan, 1988.

Sargent, M. Elizabeth. "*The Lost Girl*: Re-appraising the Post-war Lawrence on Women's Will and Ways of Knowing." *D. H. Lawrence in Italy and England.* Ed. Mara Kalnins. London: Macmillan, 1998. 176–93.

————. "The Wives, the Virgins, and Isis: Lawrence's Exploration of Female Will in Four Late Novellas of Spiritual Quest." *D. H. Lawrence Review* 26 (1995–96): 227–48.

Sargent, M. Elizabeth, and Garry Watson. "D. H. Lawrence and the Dialogical Principle: 'The Strange Reality of Otherness.'" *College English* 63.4 (2001): 409–36.

Scheckner, Peter. *Class, Politics, and the Individual: A Study of the Major Works of D. H. Lawrence.* Rutherford: Fairleigh Dickinson UP; London: Associated UP, 1985.

Schneider, Daniel J. "Alternatives to Logocentrism in D. H. Lawrence." Widdowson 160–70.

Schorer, Mark. Sons and Lovers: A Facsimile of the Manuscript. Berkeley: U of California P, 1977.

Schweickart, Patrocinio P. "Reading Ourselves: Toward a Feminist Theory of Reading." Gender and Reading: Essays on Readers, Texts, and Contexts. Ed. Elizabeth A. Flynn and Schweickart. Baltimore: Johns Hopkins UP, 1986. 31–62.

Scott, Bonnie Kime, ed. The Gender of Modernism: A Critical Anthology. Bloomington: Indiana UP, 1990.

Sedgwick, Eve Kosofsky. Epistemology of the Closet. Berkeley: U of California P, 1990.

Sessions, George. "Shallow and Deep Ecology: A Review of the Philosophical Literature." Ecological Consciousness. Ed. Robert C. Schultz and J. Donald Hughes. Washington: UP of America, 1981.

Shapiro, Karl. "The Unemployed Magician." A D. H. Lawrence Miscellany. Ed. Harry Moore. Carbondale: Southern Illinois UP, 1959. 378–95.

Shorter, Clement. Rev. of The Rainbow, by D. H. Lawrence. Sphere 23 Oct. 1915: 104.

Showalter, Elaine. Sexual Anarchy: Gender and Culture at the Fin de Siècle. New York: Viking, 1990.

Siegel, Carol. "Floods of Female Desire in Lawrence and Eudora Welty." D. H. Lawrence's Literary Inheritors. Ed. Keith Cushman and Dennis Jackson. London: Macmillan, 1991. 109–30.

———. Introduction. D. H. Lawrence, Lost Girl (Penguin) xiii–xxx.

———. Lawrence among the Women: Wavering Boundaries in Women's Literary Traditions. Charlottesville: UP of Virginia, 1991.

Simpson, Hilary. D. H. Lawrence and Feminism. De Kalb: Northern Illinois UP, 1982.

Smith, Anne. "A New Adam and a New Eve: A Biographical Overview." Lawrence and Women. Ed. Smith. New York: Barnes, 1978. 12–48.

Spence, Lewis. The Gods of Mexico. London, 1923. Rpt. as The Myths of Mexico and Peru. Toronto: General Publishing, 1994.

Spilka, Mark. The Love Ethic of D. H. Lawrence. Bloomington: Indiana UP, 1955.

Sproles, Karyn Z. "Teaching Sons and Teaching Lovers: Using Lawrence in Freshman English." D. H. Lawrence Review 19 (1987): 330–36.

Squires, Michael. The Creation of Lady Chatterley's Lover. Baltimore: Johns Hopkins UP, 1983.

Squires, Michael, and Keith Cushman, eds. The Challenge of D. H. Lawrence. Madison: U of Wisconsin P, 1990.

Steele, Bruce. Introduction. D. H. Lawrence, "England, My England" and Other Stories (CUP) xix–li.

———. Introduction. D. H. Lawrence, "Study of Thomas Hardy" and Other Essays xix–liv.

Stern, Daniel N. The Interpersonal World of the Infant: A View from Psychoanalysis and Developmental Psychology. New York: Basic, 1985.

Stewart, Jack F. "Dialectics of Knowing in Women in Love." Twentieth Century Literature 37 (1991): 59–75.

———. "Linguistic Incantation and Parody in Women in Love." Style 30 (1996): 95–112.

Stoler, Ann Laura. "Making Empire Respectable: The Politics of Race and Sexual Morality in Twentieth-Century Colonial Cultures." Dangerous Liaisons: Gender,

Nation, and Postcolonial Perspectives. Ed. Anne McClintock, Aamir Mufti, and Ella Shohat. Minneapolis: U of Minnesota P, 1997. 344–73.

Storch, Margaret. "'But Not the America of the Whites': Lawrence's Pursuit of the True Primitive." *D. H. Lawrence Review* 25 (1993–94): 48–62.

———. *Sons and Adversaries: Women in William Blake and D. H. Lawrence.* Knoxville: U of Tennessee P, 1990.

Swanwick, Helena M. Rev. of *The Rainbow*, by D. H. Lawrence. *Manchester Guardian* 28 Oct. 1915: 5.

Tanner, Tony. Rev. of *D. H. Lawrence: Triumph to Exile, 1912–1922*, by Mark Kinkead-Weekes. *Times Literary Supplement* 23 Aug. 1996: 4.

Tarzan and His Mate. Dir. Cedric Gibbons. MGM, 1934.

Tedlock, E. W., Jr. *D. H. Lawrence and* Sons and Lovers: *Sources and Criticism.* New York: New York UP, 1965.

Tennyson, Alfred. *Tennyson: A Selected Edition.* Ed. Christopher Ricks. Berkeley: U of California P, 1989.

Thomas, Edward. *The Heart of England.* London: Dent, 1906.

Todorov, Tzvetan. "A Dialogic Criticism." *Literature and Its Theorists: A Personal View of Twentieth-Century Criticism.* 1984. Ithaca: Cornell UP, 1987. 155–68.

———. *Mikhail Bakhtin: The Dialogical Principle.* 1981. Minneapolis: U of Minnesota P, 1984.

Torgovnick, Marianna. *Gone Primitive: Savage Intellects, Modern Lives.* Chicago: U of Chicago P, 1990.

Trotter, David. Introduction. D. H. Lawrence, *Sons and Lovers* (Oxford) vii–xxxiii.

Turner, Victor Witler. *The Anthropology of Performance.* New York: Performing Arts Journal, 1986.

———. *Dramas, Fields, and Metaphors: Symbolic Action in Human Society.* Ithaca: Cornell UP, 1974.

———. *From Ritual to Theatre.* New York: Performing Arts Journal, 1982.

Tyler, Hamilton A. *Pueblo Gods and Myths.* Civilization of the Amer. Indian Ser. 71. Norman: U of Oklahoma P, 1964.

Tylor, Edward B. *Primitive Culture.* 1871. 6th ed. 2 vols. London: Murray, 1920.

Van Gennep, Arnold. *The Rights of Passage.* Trans. Monika B. Vizedom and Gabrielle L. Caffee. Chicago: U of Chicago-Phoenix, 1960.

VanHoosier-Carey, Kimberly. "Struggling with the Master: The Position of Kate and the Reader in Lawrence's *Quetzalcoatl* and *The Plumed Serpent*." *D. H. Lawrence Review* 25 (1993–94): 104–18.

Vincent, David. *Literacy and Popular Culture: England 1750–1914.* Cambridge: Cambridge UP, 1989.

Wallace, M. Elizabeth. "The Circling Hawk: Philosophy of Knowledge in Polanyi and Lawrence." Squires and Cushman 103–20.

———. "'Study of Thomas Hardy': D. H. Lawrence's 'Art Speech' in the Light of Michael Polanyi's *Personal Knowledge*." Diss. U of Kent, Canterbury, 1974.

Watson, Garry. "'The Fact, and Crucial Significance, of Desire': Lawrence's *Virgin and the Gipsy*." *English* 34 (1985): 131–56.

―――. "The Real Meaning of Lawrence's Advice to the Literary Critic." *University of Toronto Quarterly* 55.1 (1985): 1–20.

Weinstein, Philip M. "Choosing between the Quick and the Dead: Three Versions of *Lady Chatterley's Lover.*" *The Semantics of Desire: Changing Models of Identity from Dickens to Joyce*. Princeton: Princeton UP, 1984. 224–51.

Whelan, P. T. *D. H. Lawrence: Myth and Metaphysic in* The Rainbow *and* Women in Love. Ann Arbor: UMI Research P, 1988.

Whitman, Walt. *The Complete Poems*. Ed. Francis Murphy. Harmondsworth: Penguin, 1975.

Widdowson, Peter, ed. *D. H. Lawrence*. Longman Critical Readers Ser. New York: Longman, 1992.

Williams, Raymond. Introduction. D. H. Lawrence, *Three Plays* 7–14.

―――. *The Long Revolution*. London: Penguin, 1965.

Williams, William Carlos. "An Elegy for D. H. Lawrence." *The Collected Earlier Poems of William Carlos Williams*. New York: New Directions, 1951. 359–61.

Wolff, Janice M. "Writing Passionately: Student Resistance to Feminist Readings." *College Composition and Communication* 42 (1991): 484–92.

Woodman, Leonora. "D. H. Lawrence and the Hermetic Tradition." *Cauda Pavonis* ns 8.2 (1989): 1–6.

Woolf, Virginia. "Memories of a Working Woman's Guild." *"The Captain's Death Bed" and Other Essays*. New York: Harcourt, 1950. 228–48.

―――. *A Room of One's Own*. New York: Harcourt, 1929.

―――. *A Writer's Diary*. Ed. Leonard Woolf. London: Hogarth, 1953.

Wordsworth, William. *Wordsworth's Literary Criticism*. Ed. Nowell C. Smith and Howard Mills. Bristol: Bristol Classical, 1980.

Worsham, Lynn. "Emotion and Pedagogic Violence." *Discourse* 15.2 (1992–93): 119–48.

Worthen, John. "A Biography." Poplawski, *D. H. Lawrence: A Reference Companion* 3–93.

―――. *D. H. Lawrence*. New York: Arnold, 1991.

―――. *D. H. Lawrence: A Literary Life*. London: Macmillan, 1989.

―――. "D. H. Lawrence and the 'Expensive Edition Business.'" *Modernist Writers and the Marketplace*. Ed. Ian Willison, Warwick Gould, and Warren Chernaik. Basingstoke: Macmillan, 1996. 105–23.

―――. *D. H. Lawrence and the Idea of the Novel*. Totowa: Rowman, 1979.

―――. *D. H. Lawrence: The Early Years, 1885–1912*. Cambridge: Cambridge UP, 1991.

―――. Introduction. D. H. Lawrence, *Lost Girl* (CUP) xix–liv.

―――. Introduction. D. H. Lawrence, *"Prussian Officer" and Other Stories* (CUP) xix–li.

―――. Rev. of *Sex in the Head: Visions of Femininity and Film*, by Linda Ruth Williams. *Journal of the D. H. Lawrence Society* (1996): 74–77.

Young, Jane Jaffe. *D. H. Lawrence on Screen*. New York: Lang, 1999.

Žižek, Slavoj. *Enjoy Your Symptom*. London: Routledge, 1992.

Index of Lawrence's Works

Index of Names

Modern Language Association of America

Approaches to Teaching World Literature

Joseph Gibaldi, series editor

Achebe's Things Fall Apart. Ed. Bernth Lindfors. 1991.

Arthurian Tradition. Ed. Maureen Fries and Jeanie Watson. 1992.

Atwood's The Handmaid's Tale *and Other Works*. Ed. Sharon R. Wilson, Thomas B. Friedman, and Shannon Hengen. 1996.

Austen's Pride and Prejudice. Ed. Marcia McClintock Folsom. 1993.

Balzac's Old Goriot. Ed. Michal Peled Ginsburg. 2000.

Baudelaire's Flowers of Evil. Ed. Laurence M. Porter. 2000.

Beckett's Waiting for Godot. Ed. June Schlueter and Enoch Brater. 1991.

Beowulf. Ed. Jess B. Bessinger, Jr., and Robert F. Yeager. 1984.

Blake's Songs of Innocence and of Experience. Ed. Robert F. Gleckner and Mark L. Greenberg. 1989.

Boccaccio's Decameron. Ed. James H. McGregor. 2000.

British Women Poets of the Romantic Period. Ed. Stephen C. Behrendt and Harriet Kramer Linkin. 1997.

Brontë's Jane Eyre. Ed. Diane Long Hoeveler and Beth Lau. 1993.

Byron's Poetry. Ed. Frederick W. Shilstone. 1991.

Camus's The Plague. Ed. Steven G. Kellman. 1985.

Cather's My Ántonia. Ed. Susan J. Rosowski. 1989.

Cervantes' Don Quixote. Ed. Richard Bjornson. 1984.

Chaucer's Canterbury Tales. Ed. Joseph Gibaldi. 1980.

Chopin's The Awakening. Ed. Bernard Koloski. 1988.

Coleridge's Poetry and Prose. Ed. Richard E. Matlak. 1991.

Dante's Divine Comedy. Ed. Carole Slade. 1982.

Dickens' David Copperfield. Ed. Richard J. Dunn. 1984.

Dickinson's Poetry. Ed. Robin Riley Fast and Christine Mack Gordon. 1989.

Narrative of the Life of Frederick Douglass. Ed. James C. Hall. 1999.

Eliot's Middlemarch. Ed. Kathleen Blake. 1990.

Eliot's Poetry and Plays. Ed. Jewel Spears Brooker. 1988.

Ellison's Invisible Man. Ed. Susan Resneck Parr and Pancho Savery. 1989.

Faulkner's The Sound and the Fury. Ed. Stephen Hahn and Arthur F. Kinney. 1996.

Flaubert's Madame Bovary. Ed. Laurence M. Porter and Eugene F. Gray. 1995.

García Márquez's One Hundred Years of Solitude. Ed. María Elena de Valdés and Mario J. Valdés. 1990.

Goethe's Faust. Ed. Douglas J. McMillan. 1987.

Hebrew Bible as Literature in Translation. Ed. Barry N. Olshen and Yael S. Feldman. 1989.

Homer's Iliad *and* Odyssey. Ed. Kostas Myrsiades. 1987.

Ibsen's A Doll House. Ed. Yvonne Shafer. 1985.

Works of Samuel Johnson. Ed. David R. Anderson and Gwin J. Kolb. 1993.

Joyce's Ulysses. Ed. Kathleen McCormick and Erwin R. Steinberg. 1993.

Kafka's Short Fiction. Ed. Richard T. Gray. 1995.

Keats's Poetry. Ed. Walter H. Evert and Jack W. Rhodes. 1991.

Kingston's The Woman Warrior. Ed. Shirley Geok-lin Lim. 1991.

Lafayette's The Princess of Clèves. Ed. Faith E. Beasley and Katharine Ann Jensen. 1998.

Works of D. H. Lawrence. Ed. M. Elizabeth Sargent and Garry Watson. 2001.

Lessing's The Golden Notebook. Ed. Carey Kaplan and Ellen Cronan Rose. 1989.

Mann's Death in Venice *and Other Short Fiction*. Ed. Jeffrey B. Berlin. 1992.

Medieval English Drama. Ed. Richard K. Emmerson. 1990.

Melville's Moby-Dick. Ed. Martin Bickman. 1985.

Metaphysical Poets. Ed. Sidney Gottlieb. 1990.

Miller's Death of a Salesman. Ed. Matthew C. Roudané. 1995.

Milton's Paradise Lost. Ed. Galbraith M. Crump. 1986.

Molière's Tartuffe *and Other Plays*. Ed. James F. Gaines and Michael S. Koppisch. 1995.

Momaday's The Way to Rainy Mountain. Ed. Kenneth M. Roemer. 1988.

Montaigne's Essays. Ed. Patrick Henry. 1994.

Novels of Toni Morrison. Ed. Nellie Y. McKay and Kathryn Earle. 1997.

Murasaki Shikibu's The Tale of Genji. Ed. Edward Kamens. 1993.

Pope's Poetry. Ed. Wallace Jackson and R. Paul Yoder. 1993.

Shakespeare's King Lear. Ed. Robert H. Ray. 1986.

Shakespeare's Romeo and Juliet. Ed. Maurice Hunt. 2000.

Shakespeare's The Tempest *and Other Late Romances*. Ed. Maurice Hunt. 1992.

Shelley's Frankenstein. Ed. Stephen C. Behrendt. 1990.

Shelley's Poetry. Ed. Spencer Hall. 1990.

Shorter Elizabethan Poetry. Ed. Patrick Cheney and Anne Lake Prescott. 2000.

Sir Gawain and the Green Knight. Ed. Miriam Youngerman Miller and Jane Chance. 1986.

Spenser's Faerie Queene. Ed. David Lee Miller and Alexander Dunlop. 1994.

Stendhal's The Red and the Black. Ed. Dean de la Motte and Stirling Haig. 1999.

Sterne's Tristram Shandy. Ed. Melvyn New. 1989.

Stowe's Uncle Tom's Cabin. Ed. Elizabeth Ammons and Susan Belasco. 2000.

Swift's Gulliver's Travels. Ed. Edward J. Rielly. 1988.

Thoreau's Walden *and Other Works*. Ed. Richard J. Schneider. 1996.

Voltaire's Candide. Ed. Renée Waldinger. 1987.

Whitman's Leaves of Grass. Ed. Donald D. Kummings. 1990.

Woolf's To the Lighthouse. Ed. Beth Rigel Daugherty and Mary Beth Pringle. 2001.

Wordsworth's Poetry. Ed. Spencer Hall, with Jonathan Ramsey. 1986.

Wright's Native Son. Ed. James A. Miller. 1997.

MEMOIRS OF DR EDUARD BENEŠ

BY EDUARD BENEŠ
MY WAR MEMOIRS

BY GODFREY LIAS
BENEŠ OF CZECHOSLOVAKIA

MEMOIRS OF
DR EDUARD BENEŠ

*From Munich to New War
and New Victory*

TRANSLATED BY GODFREY LIAS

GREENWOOD PRESS, PUBLISHERS
WESTPORT, CONNECTICUT

Library of Congress Cataloging in Publication Data

Beneš, Edvard, Pres. Czechoslovak Republic, 1884–1948.
  Memoirs of Dr. Eduard Beneš.

  Translation of Paměti.
  "The present volume is the first of three which the
late President Dr. Eduard Beneš intended to write ...
only one of the three volumes was completed."
  Reprint of the 1954 ed. published by Allen & Unwin,
London.
  Includes index.
  1. Czechoslovakia—Foreign relations. 2. Europe—
Politics and government—1918–1945. 3. Beneš, Edvard,
Pres. Czechoslovak Republic, 1884–1948. 4. Czechoslo-
vakia—Presidents—Biography. I. Title.
[DB2191.B45A3613 1978]   943.7'03   78-16354
ISBN 0-313-20592-2

First published in 1954. Translated from the Czech
original.

Reprinted with the permission of George Allen & Unwin
Limited

Reprinted in 1978 by Greenwood Press, Inc.
51 Riverside Avenue, Westport, CT. 06880

Printed in the United States of America

10 9 8 7 6 5 4 3 2 1

INTRODUCTION

THE present volume is the first of three which the late President Dr. Eduard Beneš intended to write as a continuation of his earlier Memoirs published between the two world wars. He felt it to be his duty to give the people of Czechoslovakia an account of his stewardship of their affairs while he was in exile from the time of the disaster of Munich—their twentieth century Battle of the White Mountain for which many of them held him to be responsible—down to his return to Prague at the end of the second World War and the triumphant re-establishment of Czechoslovakia within its original boundaries. The series was to have been at once a justification of his own handling of the affairs of the Czechoslovak State during this critical period and a review of the work of his colleagues and opponents so that their countrymen could see where praise and punishment were due and could also set a clear course for their Fatherland towards a prosperous and secure future.

Only one of the three volumes was completed. While Dr. Beneš was compiling the second, battling with increasing physical disabilities as he did so, the Communist Party of Czechoslovakia staged its long-projected and well-planned *coup d'état* of February 25th, 1948. The strains and stresses of this grievous blow, comparable to those he had undergone at Munich, completed the undermining of his health. He left the Presidential Castle, the Hradčany, on February 29th never to return. On June 7th, 1948, he resigned and on September 3rd, 1948, he passed away at his country home at Sezimovo Ústí. Though Volume Two was never finished a comprehensive draft of it is in existence setting forth in full detail Dr. Beneš's account of the Munich crisis. As for Volume Three it is only known that Dr. Beneš planned to include in it the inner history of the final phase of the war from the time when the Provisional Government of Czechoslovakia left London for Moscow and later established itself at Košice in East Slovakia behind the lines of the Soviet armies which were slowly forcing the retreating Germans westwards out of Czechoslovakia and towards their final débacle.

The first part of the Memoirs starts with a recapitulation of the events which led to Munich, skips Munich itself and goes on to deal with the period between Munich and the moment when the Provisional Czechoslovak Government was about to leave London for Košice. Chronologically speaking, most of the volume should follow, instead of preceding, the account of Munich. But from the political standpoint, it was obviously desirable to inform the Czechoslovak Nation as soon as possible what had been done in their name abroad while they themselves were under Nazi domination. They had themselves experienced Munich and its effects. But they were almost entirely ignorant of the steps which Dr. Beneš and his collaborators had taken outside Czechoslovakia to neutralise the effects of Munich. If the Communists had not seized power, and if he himself had been well enough, Dr. Beneš would next have rubbed in the lesson of Munich in the hope of averting a repetition of that disaster. Finally, he intended to give the Nation the political background of the military liberation of the country—how the so-called Košice programme came to be adopted as the common political programme of the Coalition Government, what the relations were between that Government and the Russians and between the different political parties of which the Government was made up.

The first volume was published in Prague in the autumn of 1947, and some 250,000 copies were sold in the six months before the Communist *coup d'état*. Soon after this arbitrary act, all the published works of President Beneš, and of his predecessor, President Masaryk, were withdrawn from the bookshops. Within one year these two founders of the democratic Czechoslovak Republic were branded as traitors and their names execrated —cautiously at first and then with growing, and insolent, outspokenness. In less than four years, the National Independence Day—October 28th— which marked the consummation of the years of struggle under their leadership before and during the first World War, had been reduced to the anniversary of Nationalisation in 1945. Officially, National independence now dates not from 1918 but only from May 9th, 1945, the day on which units of the Red Army allegedly 'rescued' Prague from the Germans. Actually, of course, the Red Army never rescued Prague. It simply arrived the day after the last German forces had been overpowered by a detachment of the army of General Vlasov, the Russian commander who went over to the Germans after his capture and recruited several divisions for them from among his compatriots. Some of the Vlasov troops were stationed near Prague when the citizens of the capital rose against the Germans on May 5th, 1945, and they hoped by changing sides again even at the last moment to avert their inevitable punishment. So they threw themselves into the fighting on the side of the Czechs and by May 8th German resistance had ended. Marshal Koniev's soldiers reached Prague on the following day when the fighting was over. But it is their entry into the capital which the Czechs and Slovaks are now forced to commemorate regardless of the fact that if the independence of Czechoslovakia really dates only from the end of the second World War, every prior international act, including the country's treaty of alliance with the U.S.S.R. in 1943, has no validity. It may be added that nearly all the actual leaders of the Prague rising were not Communists but supporters of President Beneš. They have either been executed like General Kutlwašr, who directed it, or imprisoned or have had to flee their country in order to save their lives.

One of President Masaryk's favourite sayings was: 'A lie has short legs'. And the motto of the Czechoslovak Republic was and still is: 'Truth prevails'. Sooner or later, truth will certainly catch up with these and other Communist distortions of Czechoslovak history. According to the Communist version now current, Dr. Beneš, like Professor Masaryk before him, was an imperialist agent, a life-long enemy of the Soviet Union and, therefore, an enemy of the Czech and Slovak 'masses'. Needless to say, the accusation is nowhere borne out by the writings of either. So far as Dr. Beneš himself is concerned we see him in these Memoirs as a sincere friend of the West who is also hoping for the ultimate triumph of Socialism. He is constantly urging the importance of friendly relations with the Soviet Union. The present Soviet-Czechoslovak Alliance on which the relations of the Czechoslovak 'People's Democracy' and the U.S.S.R. are still based is his work. We see him also as a convinced advocate of public ownership of all the means of production though he stresses his desire that this should come about gradually through evolution and the freely-expressed wishes of the electorate instead of by violent revolution and dictatorial methods. Furthermore he constantly reiterates his firm belief in the possibility of the peaceful co-existence of different types of regime in terms which should be entirely acceptable to Moscow. It is true that occasionally the Memoirs also show signs of increasing apprehension about Communist intentions. Dr. Beneš more than hints his belief that they intended to stage 'a violent revolution' and warns them plainly that 'they must impose some restraint on themselves' (p. 285). He goes on to quote Pushkin: 'Remember, young world, that the best and most permanent changes are those which have their origin in a moral improvement without any commotion at all.' And he evidently was not sure whether the Anglo-Soviet Alliance of 1942 would continue to operate after the war. The Czechoslovak-Soviet treaty of December, 1943, he said 'was intentionally and consciously linked to the Anglo-Soviet Treaty of May 26th, 1942. *At the time**I firmly believed that this treaty would continue in operation after the war ended. Was I right or wrong?' (p. 285).

His fears of a possible Communist revolution were realised almost

*My italics. (Tr.).

before the ink in which he expressed them was dry. From the moment that Stalin forced the Czechoslovak Government to withdraw its acceptance of the invitation to attend the Marshall Plan Conference in Paris in July, 1947, it was clear to him as to everyone else that Czechoslovakia was no longer a free agent. The latent crisis finally came to a head in the following February when the hasty action of the non-Communist Ministers in resigning from the Government played into the hands of the Communists. Some of these Ministers who are now in exile have stated that President Beneš knew and approved of their decision to resign. I have very good reasons for believing that this is incorrect. If they informed him of this intention they can only have done so in terms which left with him the impression that they simply intended to stay away from meetings of the Cabinet until the Communists accepted the decisions of the majority of the Ministers. This of course the Communists never had any intention of doing. The coup had to take place. It could only have been prevented by the use of force. With the Russians close at hand and the West holding aloof, President Beneš, as at the time of Munich, decided that force would be the greater of two evils. In these circumstances the resignation issue is not of great practical importance except in so far as it throws light on the political acumen of those concerned. In this respect it can only be stated that the judgment of the Czechoslovak people immediately after the event was much less unfavourable to President Beneš than to his Ministers. When he died, less than seven months later, they wept, mourning him as the one man in their country who could have saved democracy and freedom had he received sufficient support. Were they right or wrong?

Throughout his life, right up to and even after the day when he found himself for the second time faced with the impossible task of standing alone against a ruthless dictatorship, Dr. Beneš was an optimist. He never accepted Munich as final. Though nearing his end, he did not accept the Communist coup of February, 1948, as final either. But by that time, so far as he was concerned, the zest for a fight had gone out of him. But he kept his conviction that the Communist regime of force would not last for ever.

During the war, of course, the President's combativeness was still gloriously alive. We see him in his Memoirs starting to get ready for the coming fray even before he left Czechoslovakia a few weeks after Munich. Soon he is in the United States discussing the situation with Roosevelt, with Cordell Hull, with Sumner Welles. He fired his first broadside when Hitler broke his pledged word and occupied Prague on March 15th, 1939. Sure that war would soon break out, Dr. Beneš returned to London in the summer and, equally convinced that Hitler would be beaten, because both the United States and the U.S.S.R. would ultimately be forced to fight the Nazis, he threw all he had into the allied cause, including that gallant little band of Czech and Slovak airmen who contributed materially to the defeat of the Luftwaffe in the Battle of Britain. But except for a passing reference here and there, Dr. Beneš says nothing in this volume about the military side of the war; nothing about the exploits of the Czechoslovak forces, nothing about his own personal experiences during the bombing of London. The only military event which moved him to depart from his unwritten rule was Stalingrad on which he comments with a certain naïveté which betrays not simply that he had no real conception of what a battle is actually like but also—perhaps for the only time in his writings—that he had a heart and human emotions as well as a brain.

Though Dr. Beneš gave his book the somewhat cumbrous sub-title of *From Munich to New War and New Victory*, its real theme is the revocation of the Munich settlement. In bringing this about, Dr. Beneš can claim both sole credit and complete success in almost every respect except one—he was quite unable to secure a *modus vivendi* between the Czech and German inhabitants of the country. Whose fault this was is best left to the reader to decide. The real issue between Dr. Beneš and Wenzel Jaksch, the Sudeten German Social Democratic leader, concerned the right of secession—a right which even President Lincoln refused to concede when faced with a similar demand. The German minority—President Beneš wholly rejected the word Sudeten—demanded complete autonomy within the Czecho-slovak State. The Czechs, under the leadership of the President, held this to mean that at any moment the Germans could walk out on their partners and adhere to the German Reich. They saw no secure future for a State so constituted. They therefore insisted on a unitary State in which the will of the majority was to prevail though minorities were to have full cultural rights and equal opportunity (as well as responsibility) with the majority. The Germans flatly rejected the idea of a unitary State because they had no faith in Czech promises of equality.

The gap could not be bridged. The Czechs could not forget that the German population of Bohemia and Moravia had provided the excuse for Munich. The Germans could not forget either that the Czechs had not always treated them as equals in the period between the two world wars or their own relationship to the Germans of Germany. In these circum-stances it was inevitable that in the end the Czechs should demand the expulsion, or 'transfer' of the great mass of the Germans. Dr. Beneš makes it clear that the British, French and American Governments, as well as the

Soviet Government, agreed to this policy. In the parallel case of the
Magyar minority in Czechoslovakia, on the other hand, there was no such
agreement although the problem was almost precisely similar. Some of the
Magyars were driven out of Slovakia before the Allies intervened. Others
were exchanged at a later date for Slovaks in Hungary. But most of the
Magyar inhabitants of Slovakia are still there. But of the 3,500,000 Germans in the Republic at the end of the war only some 250,000 now remain.

This volume of Memoirs deals with the political negotiations which led
to the transfer of these unfortunate people. It shows the steps by which the
lone figure of the ex-President in exile gradually built up a Government
round him and negotiated once again as President of his country with the
three great figures of the war, Roosevelt, Churchill and Stalin. If the
author goes into seemingly unimportant details and not infrequently
repeats himself, let it be remembered that he was clearing his reputation
as a statesman in the eyes of his own people, not those of the world.

It should perhaps be emphasised that though the only possible translation
of the Czech name for this book, Paměti, is Memoirs, the volume is not
really autobiographical and contains comparatively few reminiscences or
impressions. Its purpose is to vindicate the author's statesmanship by giving
an account of his thought processes during the period of his fight against
Munich and by recounting the various concrete steps by which revocation
was accomplished and the Czechoslovak State re-established within its
former frontiers. It was written by a professed Czechoslovak rather than a
Czech, and for Czechs and Slovaks, especially the former. Dr. Beneš's
literary style, as even his countrymen will readily admit, is often hard to
follow. He takes liberties with syntax and grammar and his sentences are
sometimes so long that their character and direction change before they
come to an end. Thus their meaning is not always to be grasped at the first,
or even a second, reading. Nor, of course, does the Czech language re-
semble English either in its construction or its metaphors. It has, for
example, no definite or indefinite article. It has fewer tenses than ours as
well as more cases. I have therefore felt it necessary, and permissible, to
take many liberties of my own with the original in order to make the book
conform as far as possible to English standards of composition. But I hope
I have succeeded in preserving the author's sense and meaning when—or
rather, by—departing from literality. I am encouraged in this hope by the
fact that I have had the benefit of several most competent helpers, some of
whom must unfortunately remain anonymous at present for reasons which
need no elaboration. I may, however, express my gratitude quite openly
to Professor R. Betts of the School of Slavonic Studies, who has checked

both my translation and my explanatory notes with meticulous and generous care. I am, of course, solely responsible for the views expressed in this introduction, and in my own notes.

My thanks are also due to the workers at the Royal Institute of International Affairs and the Conservative Research Department for kindly discovering the original English texts of a number of unpublished official documents which it seemed desirable to reproduce in their original form rather than to re-translate them into English from the Czech. The American Department of Information has rendered the same service in respect of certain documents appertaining to events which took place in the United States. Mention should also be made of my secretary, Mr. W. Krasser, who deciphered my often illegible handwriting with almost uncanny accuracy. Last but not least I wish to pay tribute to my wife who unfailingly supported our flagging energies by administering to our internal economy just when sustenance was needed.

Vienna, June, 1953   GODFREY LIAS

CONTENTS

CHAPTER I

THE GATHERING STORM

1. *How the Peace of 1919 was Gradually Lost*

AS early as 1921–22, only two or three years after the signing of the Treaty of Versailles, when Germany had got over her defeat in 1918, there began in Europe a great and exciting drama: the fight for the revision of the Versailles Peace. It was one of the greatest and most dramatic struggles in the political history of Europe. It ended in a new tragedy, vast and destructive: the second World War.

This struggle first centred round reparations. It began soon after the fixing of the precise amount of German payments in May, 1921, and ended in a victory for Germany and the liquidation of its reparations debt at the Conference of Lausanne, which opened on July 2nd, 1923. There, German reparations were reduced from 132,000,000,000 to 3,000,000,000 marks, and while the conference was actually in progress, Reichs Chancellor Franz von Papen told his friends and acquaintances that Germany would not pay even a penny of that sum.

Next followed the disarmament clauses of the peace treaty. The struggle concerning these began in Geneva after the signing of the final protocols of the Locarno Treaties of October 16th, 1925,[1]* when it was decided to call a conference at which the manner and measure of general disarmament for all States were to be fixed. It ended on October 14th, 1933, also in Geneva, when Germany left the Disarmament Conference, and then, on March 16th, 1935, revived the Reich's Army. Finally, there came the revision of the territorial clauses of the Versailles Treaty in the years 1932-33 when, on Mussolini's initiative, the so-called Four-Power Pact was concluded (March 18th, 1933). The war against Abyssinia followed, paving the way for Hitler's annexation of Austria and for Munich. This revision culminated in the second World War.

The object of the struggle for the revision of the peace treaties was to bring about a complete change of the whole European situation. The Versailles Treaty had given predominance on the European Continent to Great Britain and France, their friends and smaller allies. The threefold attack on the treaty was for the purpose of abolishing this predominance on the Continent and to transfer it to the other side. As I have just said:

*See notes at the end of each chapter. (Tr.).

Territorial changes began to be discussed in earnest in the years 1932-33, in other words, at the moment when Hitler came into power in Germany, thus adding to the authoritarian regime which already existed in Central Europe—Mussolini's Fascist dictatorship—another and much more dangerous one: the German Nazi dictatorship.

On March 18th, 1933, Mussolini proposed to the British Premier, Ramsay MacDonald and to Sir John Simon, during their visit to Rome, the conclusion of the Four-Power Pact which, besides pushing the League of Nations into the background, provided for the *secret* establishment of a so-called European directorate of the Western and Central European Great Powers, with the Soviet Union excluded. The territorial revision of the peace treaties was expressly proposed. From diplomatic conversations at that time, it appeared that this revision was to affect especially the Little Entente States and Poland. France and Great Britain were to withdraw from their positions on the Continent to their colonial empires. In Central and Eastern Europe the Fascist powers, Germany and Italy, were to decide alone and effectively. The internal policy of both Fascist Powers was sharply anti-Socialist, as well as anti-Communist, so the Four-Power Pact was automatically not only revisionist, but also in its whole substance directed against the U.S.S.R.

The Four-Power Pact, as is well known, was actually signed in Rome on July 15th, 1933, but its ratification did not take place, not only because of the resistance of the Little Entente and Poland, but still more because of the indignation of democratic public opinion in France and England which felt instinctively that such an agreement could serve only to strengthen the two Fascist dictatorships and establish their supremacy on the European Continent.

Whatever our opinion about the course of this struggle for the revision of the peace treaties, in a certain sense it was a normal development. After every war the defeated party tries to wipe out its defeat, either by political and diplomatic means, or by a new war. This has ever been the law of history and of international politics and the process will be repeated, even after the second World War. It was more than usually certain that this would happen with a nation like the Germans. Indeed, from the very beginning they never made any secret about it, although official Germany continued to utter platitudes about the necessity of keeping peace and its desire for friendly co-operation with its former adversaries. Hitler's *Mein Kampf*, published in 1925 and 1927, and the utterances of other nationalists and militarists were officially represented to Allied public opinion as the eccentricities of opponents of the 'moderate' German Government, which, at the same time, however, used them to extort further concessions from the allies.

To everybody who knew Germany and the Germans and, indeed, to everybody who carefully watched Germany after 1920, it must have been clear that a long period of struggle over the peace treaties *was beginning* and that its result would be either a certain balance and final co-operation between victors and vanquished, or another great war. Czechoslovak policy never doubted this and had no illusions about it. The numerous declarations which I made as Minister for Foreign Affairs and as President, in Parliament and in other places, are clear proof of this, as were also my incessant efforts for peace and for the establishment of peace safeguards in Europe, and my unremitting aim of establishing the safety of the State which I pursued during all the twenty years of the First Republic.

If, therefore, we look back at Czechoslovak foreign policy between the two wars, we can, in my opinion, definitely state that it was not only animated by a full understanding of what was happening and what was going to happen, but also that it single-mindedly and consistently followed an undeviating course with perseverance and resolution. On the one side, we were always at work in the interest of peace—ready to co-operate with our adversaries, to come to terms with them in a friendly manner and, where it was necessary, to make such concessions as occasion demanded to the defeated, so that they could be reconciled with the new international order. On the other side, we made all efforts to build up guarantees of collective security, and to strengthen the League of Nations, but at the same time, we prepared for defence in case of a conflict.

That was the sense of our policy at Geneva, of our policy at Locarno. We made a number of concessions at the conferences on reparations, disarmament and economic co-operation. Such, too, was the aim of our conciliatory and moderate policy towards a democratic Germany in general. We never did, and never could, exclude the possibility of good neighbour relations with a really democratic and peace-loving Germany, if such a Germany should exist. At this point, I refer to the book of Dr. Kamil Krofta:* *From the period of our First Republic* (published in 1939 during the German occupation), which truthfully shows how we went to the extreme of concession to conciliate Weimar Germany.

We had, of course, to count with the second eventuality, too : *namely, that our and our allies' policy of conciliation would be unsuccessful.* We reckoned, that as long as reactionary Germany and its friends felt weak, they would

---

*Dr. Krofta was Dr. Beneš's successor as Foreign Minister when Dr. Beneš became President in succession to Professor Masaryk. (Tr.).

B

choose the road of gradual advance to new positions and of feigned co-operation. But there would come a time when there would have to be an end to concessions and the victors in the first World War would have to state clearly that this or that could not, and might not, be done. If Germany should ever consider the time to be ripe and herself to be nationally and militarily strong enough, it would adopt new methods: threats, violence and finally war. From the moment when the Fascist dictatorship in Italy joined the Nazi dictatorship in Germany, there could be no more doubt about this development.

Today, after the second World War, let us take heed. Exactly the same procedure—adapted to changed conditions—will be repeated again.

As proof that our pre-Munich policy thus correctly interpreted developments in Europe, I will quote here my declaration of October 31st, 1933, in the Chamber of Deputies and in the Senate, on the subject of foreign policy. Cautiously (as was necessary in an official statement) I outlined the meaning and aims of the Nazi revolution and the start of Hitler's Third Reich:

'Until the arrival of the present regime in Germany, fourteen years of post-war European policy have been taken up with the struggle to secure peace in Europe on the basis of the Paris Peace Treaties. During this period, it became clear to all, even in the camp of the former victorious powers, that it would not be possible to hold the defeated nations in a position of permanent inferiority, and that agreement between the two camps must be gradually prepared. The change must be brought about peacefully and the respective positions be adjusted so that, by a process of gradual compromise, a new peace organisation of Europe will finally be reached.

'*The German National-Socialist revolution has interrupted this gradual development.* In my opinion, the final aims and ideals of Stresemann's policy were, broadly speaking, not much different from the final aims of the policy of present-day Germany. The two differed only in their external manifestations and procedure and in the better understanding of the aims, efforts and needs of the rest of Europe, which exercised a passing influence on the tactics and methods of Stresemann's Germany.

'Ever since the unification of the German nation in modern times, especially after the revolution of 1848, German policy has had a Pan-German basis. The Reich of Kaiser Wilhelm followed this policy as well as present-day Germany. Europe must reckon with this as a fact and must prepare itself accordingly.

'*But present-day Germany considered the pace and methods of Stresemann's*

Germany for the realisation of German national aims, as too slow. It has therefore broken away from this line of development and begun to use more radical methods. The consequence is that nearly all European countries have *been taken by surprise by the sudden expansion of German national dynamism.* Some of them are also frightened by it. They have become aware of a change in German strength, which, seemingly, they expected to take place only later, and they have begun to draw political conclusions and arrange their policy and tactics accordingly.'

Germany's international aims and the whole European problem were fully understood in our country from *the moment of the arrival of Nazi Germany.* I was personally well aware of the inevitable alternatives—that the two sides would either definitely agree to a peaceful development in Europe, or would collide in a dreadful conflict. I wanted our State—just in the centre of the colliding interests : a new State, not yet firm enough in tradition and evolution, not yet fully known to the world—to be firmly anchored at the moment when there would be either an agreement or a conflict, to be prepared and to emerge successfully either from diplomatic negotiations, or even from a war.

For this reason, I tried—as far as was in our power—to keep the camp of the Allies of 1918 in being, that is to say, Great Britain, France and their Allies of the first World War—so that they could continue in unity and co-operation as long as possible. I also strove to maintain our alliance with France and the States of the Little Entente. I was convinced that a peaceful compromise would be possible only if Germany at the critical moment should see itself opposed by a coalition of States, and would not succeed in disturbing these alliances so as to be able to fight for its aims against each of us separately and with one after the other. This was also the *main reason* why I tried systematically from 1922 to 1938 and again during the second World War to secure co-operation and agreement between Western Europe and the Soviet Union.

When Nazi Germany left the Disarmament Conference and the League of Nations in October, 1933, *I had to admit to myself that this was probably the end of the policy of seeking general agreement and that we in Europe were being driven almost irresistibly into a terrible conflict.* The representative of Germany on the Disarmament Conference, Ambassador Nadolny, frankly admitted this in reply to a direct question I put him at the time of his departure from Geneva in October, 1933. He added, that Hitler's decision to withdraw from Geneva was 'madness and the beginning of a terrible fresh tragedy and another dreadful disaster for Germany'.

The development of Nationalism and Nazism in Germany confirmed this diagnosis. Its unconcealed expansionism, expansive pan-Germanism, the clear uncompromising declaration of war to the death against every shade of democracy: the deliberate utilisation of all Germans abroad as revolutionary organisations against the States in which they lived: the systematic propaganda for a Central European 'Lebensraum' and about the 'Herrenvolk': the bestial anti-semitism and 'primitivism' which distinguished Germany's so-called 'Führer', whose vulgarity made him the exact personification of the whole doctrine and of the new German regime —all these things made it clear to me that there were no more *two political camps*, defeated Germany and the victorious allies, but two fundamentally differing and irreconcilable worlds, the opinions, aims, ideals and legal conceptions of which were fundamentally opposed to one another. I was sure that in the end these two worlds would clash.

In addition, as I saw it, was the problem of the Soviet Union. On which side would it finally be ranged ? I never agreed with the policy of the Western democracies, which for so many years isolated the Soviet Union and excluded it from co-operation in Europe and in the world. It seemed to me that victory would go to the side to which the Soviet Union ultimately gave its support. I therefore tried systematically, and *before it was too late*, to incline it towards the ranks of the European democracies. For years I carried on this struggle both at home and abroad, and, as is well known, the fight was a hard one.

Professor Masaryk and I had categorically rejected already during the first World War, the policy of intervention against the Soviet Union. Our principle in post-war European policy was not to isolate the Soviet Union, but to try for co-operation and thus bring about an agreement between the U.S.S.R. and the rest of Europe. We did this partly because we always held that without the participation of the Soviet Union there would be neither balance nor real peace in Europe and the world and partly because we feared that the Western European policy of isolating the Soviet Union would push it, if perhaps only tactically and temporarily, into an agreement with Germany against the rest of Europe, which could have been extremely dangerous at that time for the whole future of Europe. And for us, for Czechoslovakia, this would have spelt mortal danger.

We entered into diplomatic relations with the Soviet Union in 1922 at the Conference of Genoa and right up to 1938 we consistently did our utmost to maintain a policy of friendly co-operation, in spite of the strong opposition of our right-wing parties. From the moment the Soviet Union also recognised the dangerous possibilities of a supremacy of the Fascist dictatorships in Europe and changed its attitude, tactics and behaviour towards theWestern democracies and the League of Nations, we also did our utmost to bring the Soviet Union and the Western Democracies into direct alliance with one another and with ourselves. Treaties of alliance between the Soviet Union and France, and between the Soviet Union and Czechoslovakia were in fact concluded in 1935. I wish to stress that neither during the first World War nor during the years up to 1938, nor up to the present day* were we ever animated by any ideological motives of *internal policy*.

Our conviction that an agreement with the Soviet Union *was essential, was always based exclusively on considerations of international policy* and the maintenance of peace in Europe as a whole.

We therefore considered it a great triumph of our peace policy and that of Europe, when the Soviet Union joined the League of Nations on September 18th, 1934, and together with France and ourselves began to carry out a consistent policy of collective security, finally concluding treaties of mutual aid with France and ourselves and non-aggression pacts with the other two members of the Little Entente and Poland. Personally, I knew conditions in the Soviet Union on the whole quite well. I knew that for some time the regime had been very strong and that the talk and propaganda about a possible internal revolution from whatever side were either naïve nonsense or exaggerated and deliberate propaganda; I knew also that its military strength was great, well organised and was still growing.†

Finally, I knew by 1935 that the two Five-Year Plans had essentially changed the economic structure of the Soviet Union, so that it had become one of the greatest industrial States in Europe. My journey to Russia between June 6th and 17th, 1935, fully confirmed this impression.

I want to stress especially that, having in view the possibility of an impending conflict with Germany, we tried with full sincerity and, at that time, with the full consent of all the parties in the government, to round off this aspect of Czechoslovak foreign policy in the years 1932–33 by an agreement with Poland. Today, it is already known that in September, 1932, at Geneva, I offered Colonel Beck, the Polish Foreign Minister, a political agreement which was to pave the way for a military treaty. He promised to consider the matter and let me have his views in due course. When there was no answer, we repeated the offer in the Spring of 1933,

*These words were written in 1947. (Tr.).

†In 1937, the Soviet administration and army were purged of pro-German elements, thanks in part to the disclosure of their activities by Dr. Beneš—see Author's Note 8 (Chap. I), page 47. (Tr.).

after Hitler had been nominated Chancellor of the Reich, this time through the Polish Minister at Prague, W. Grzybowski. When even this produced no answer, I instructed our envoy in Warsaw, Dr. V. Girsa, to repeat the offer once more. Again there was no reply. *But on January 26th, 1934, the well-known—and fateful—Polish-German Treaty was signed in Berlin*, a step which substantially enabled Germany to make ready for the attacks launched in 1938–39. Marshal Pilsudski apparently realised that a policy of agreement with democratic Czechoslovakia was incompatible with the undemocratic and a-social tendencies of his semi-Fascist regime which was supported by the Polish aristocracy and reaction.

To these fundamental principles of our pre-war foreign policy, I should like to add that it was always governed by the principle of the indivisibility of European peace and by the ideal of collective security as expressed in the Covenant of the League of Nations to which we always remained faithful. We did so because we believed these principles to be ethically right and because we felt that they ought to become the whole basis of future international intercourse. Moreover, after the first World War the League of Nations was a really great political and moral force, which stood for the *peaceful* reconciliation of the interests of the Great Powers and mutual co-operation and maintenance of the balance of power.

If a policy of firmness and principle had been followed at that time, it would have been possible to have made the Geneva institution into a great instrument against all aggression. It would therefore have been a sin not to have used this instrument and not to have tried to build it up into a permanent and strong institution. That did not mean, of course, as many of my opponents at that time declared, that we believed *blindly* in the effectiveness of the League of Nations in all circumstances and that I was placing all my hopes on it. Our whole system of alliance proved that our attitude to the League was never uncritical.

Finally, I wish to explain that our policy of constructing the Little Entente was merely the expression of our conviction that in every future European crisis, semi-feudal Hungary, as it emerged from the first World War, would, for social and national reasons, automatically gravitate to the side of German imperialism and Prussian reaction and turn against its three smaller neighbours. Any attempt to establish some other combination, with Hungarian participation—like the attempts of reactionary Poland to reach an agreement with the Horthy regime—would, on our part, have been futile if not indeed ridiculous so long as Hungary did not change socially. And when Fascism took root in Italy and Nazism in Germany, a permanent alliance of the three reactionaries, the Italian, the

German and the Hungarian, was inevitable, though, for Hungary, this meant in the end a new and great catastrophe. In the circumstances then obtaining, the Little Entente, in the form we gave to it, was the natural and indeed the only possible alliance for the three States concerned. Any deviation from this alliance by a member meant that it was digging its own grave. *An essential pre-requisite for success was, of course, that social conditions in Yugoslavia and Rumania should gradually change*—at any rate, by degrees. I was always aware of the fact that if this did not happen, it would be such an inner weakness of the whole Little Entente that in the end it would disrupt the alliance.

I must emphasise that this concept of European international policy and the acceptance of systematic co-operation with the Soviet Union against aggression and reaction in Germany, necessarily involved Western Europe's understanding the need for some adaptation of its social policy to conditions in the Soviet Union, which had gone through a revolution, and conversely, that the Soviet Union as well should seriously think of a similar adaptation of Soviet political and revolutionary conditions to the concepts of *political* freedom in Western Europe. Failing this, it was essential that these systems should at least tolerate one another. For me this meant that Western Europe would be forced to evolve towards a visibly progressive and really democratic social and economic policy and that the Western European bourgeoisie would have to make considerable social and economic concessions to the workers and socialistically-minded people. It seemed to me that European, and indeed world, peace necessitated this and that it would be worth it.

It was from this standpoint also that I regarded Czechoslovakia's internal and foreign policy. I considered that my country must move in this direction gradually, step-by-step and by a process of evolution; that this was, and would be, quite simply one of the pre-requisites of international security and of the very existence of our State. I kept constantly before me the fact that the permanence of the Czechoslovak State was dependent on the existence of a democratic, progressive, socially mature and steadily developing Europe. In such a Europe, I thought, we will always maintain our freedom. In a reactionary Europe which supports Fascism and kills or squanders democracy, freedom and progress, we will always be in danger. It was in this sense that the words of Masaryk applied to us : The existence of States depends upon the ideas which gave them birth.

My policy was the systematic and consistent application of these principles—hence my never-ceasing struggle in internal policy. Actually, from the moment of my return from the Paris Peace Conference in September,

1919, I was always in some kind of opposition in internal policy. This was why the pre-Munich right-wing parties were always trying to get rid of me.

These then were the fundamental principles of our foreign policy after 1919–21 and especially in the period 1932–38, when Nazism came into power in Germany.

2. *The Events Which Led to Munich—Our Efforts to Save Ourselves*

(a) Hitler's first attempt to disorganise Europe—
Hitler's Treaty with the Poland of Pilsudski

The acute international crisis out of which the real disintegration of post-war Europe sprang, started as early as 1931 with the renewal of the Sino-Japanese conflict which quickly came to Geneva. In Europe, the crisis first manifested itself in the deepening conflicts inside Germany and in the German elections of 1932 in which the Nazis gained such successes that Hitler was able to seize power in January, 1933. The far-reaching consequences of this event were soon felt throughout Europe, especially at the Disarmament Conference in Geneva, where they culminated—as I have already mentioned—in the departure of Germany from the Conference and, later, from the League of Nations. The conflict between Germany and the rest of Europe was now plainly visible and from that moment it was never out of the picture of European policy.

The Four-Power Pact, the direct precursor and model for the Munich agreement of 1938, not only did not lessen the European crisis, but made it even more acute and widespread than it had been before, especially when the Treaty itself inevitably fell through in the autumn of 1933 in consequence of the resistance of the Little Entente and Poland and especially because of the opposition of public opinion in France and Great Britain.[1]

Poland's ill-considered, arrogant mark of defiance, the German-Polish Treaty of January 26th, 1934, caused a further deterioration. The Poles started negotiations with Hitler in the autumn of 1933 as a Polish answer to the Four-Power Pact, which was peculiarly unfavourable, if not actually hostile, to Poland. The German-Polish Treaty was one of the fateful compacts and dire events which characterised this period. It increased the tension between France and Poland, caused fresh tension between ourselves and Poland and between the Soviet Union and Poland. In addition, it accelerated the already patent withdrawal of France from the whole of Central Europe. This, in turn, facilitated the establishment of those French cliques of Laval, Bonnet and Petain which were to lead to the negotiations for an agreement with Hitler and so to Munich, the dreadful fall of Poland and finally to the capitulation of France itself in June, 1940.

When the Polish Minister, Mr. Grzybowski, came to me on January 28th, 1934, to announce the signing of the German-Polish Treaty, I said to him substantially:

'I consider the signing of your treaty with Germany to be a great blow to the present European policy. It means that you are helping Germany not merely to stop discussing disarmament, but to turn definitely to gradual rearmament. It means that you are leaving the Geneva Front and are enabling Germany to justify its anti-Geneva policy of expansion. This connection you have made with Germany in fact will have far-reaching consequences. The whole so-called French system of European security has been undermined and a common Eastern front against German aggression has been made impossible.'

Minister Grzybowski argued that the signing of the Four-Power Pact had forced Poland, in its turn, to seek its own security, and that France and Great Britain had to be taught that Poland could go its own way. To this I answered that it was a way which could only lead to the strengthening of Germany and its preparations directed against Poland and Czechoslovakia. Grzybowski replied that the Poles knew very well that Germany was preparing to attack them, but that the treaty would anyhow not last ten years and would perhaps induce France to take more account of Poland. It would also gain time for Poland itself to make better preparations for the conflict with Germany.

I replied that this calculation was based on false premises. I said that Germany, too, needed time for its preparations for its expensive, murderous undertakings and would be protected in these plans by the treaty with Poland. Seeing that Germany was twice as strong as Poland, it would gain correspondingly more from the respite, would be better able to prepare itself and would then go against us all.

Meanwhile, Mussolini continued his policy of expansion in the Balkans and Africa. In October, 1934, he was the chief backer of Pavelić in his preparations for the murder of King Alexander of Yugoslavia and at the same time he himself prepared his war against Abyssinia. After the death of Barthou when Laval became Minister for Foreign Affairs, Mussolini began to intrigue in Paris to get Laval's consent for the Abyssinian adventure. He succeeded. Hitler took advantage of the situation to make another important move in the extension of his power. In March, 1935, he deliberately violated Germany's disarmament obligations and changed over from extensive but secret arming to the public declaration that he was rebuilding the German army.

It seemed as if this critical development would be halted when the Assembly of the League of Nations on October 7th and 10th, 1935, decided in favour of sanctions against the Italian invasion of Abyssinia. The initiative in this matter was taken by Great Britain, which, in spite of the systematic̄ sabotage carried out by Laval, backed the Geneva institution with unaccustomed determination through the mouth of the Foreign Secretary, Sir Samuel Hoare. I personally gave full support to the League of Nations and, as President of the Assembly of the League, I assisted Sir Samuel Hoare without reservation and substantially in his efforts to apply sanctions against the aggressor. I was therefore much criticised at home by our right-wing parties.

But this momentary resistance to the despots was soon compromised, partly because Laval refused to apply the sanctions consistently and partly because of his ultimate agreement with the very British Foreign Secretary, Sir Samuel Hoare, who had first obtained sanctions at Geneva and then, reversing his original standpoint with incredible haste, consented to the partition of Abyssinia between Mussolini and the Emperor of Abyssinia even before the war had ended. Though the resistance of public opinion in Great Britain to this unhappy agreement led to the resignation of Sir Samuel Hoare on December 19th, 1945, chaos in Europe was increased by this incident and soon afterwards confusion became even worse confounded when, in July, 1936, the Spanish Fascist generals revolted against the Spanish Republic with the help of Hitler *and* Mussolini, to which the Western democratic States responded with unbelievable weakness.

The negotiations between the Great Powers about the Spanish Civil War in 1936 and 1937 (the revolt against republican Spain had broken out on July 18th, 1936) and especially the proceedings of the London Non-Intervention Committee, confirmed the impotence of the Western Powers to stop Fascist aggression against the Spanish Republic. Indeed, it was already clear that Fascism and Nazism held the political initiative and were in a position to disrupt the influence of the democracies on the Continent of Europe. All this happened in spite of the fact that from the time of the Spanish War, the Soviet Union began to intervene directly and more actively in the quarrels of the Western and Central European powers.

Meanwhile, on March 7th, 1936, Hitler, by occupying the left bank of the Rhine, struck *one of the last, decisive blows* against European peace. At that time, Czechoslovakia was ready to enter the conflict against Germany at the side of France, and according to all the signs, so also was Poland.

We told the French Minister in Prague clearly that we would follow France, in accordance with our treaty obligations, if she should draw the logical conclusion from Hitler's act. Hitler had violated the Treaty of Locarno with its so-called Rhine Pact which gave international authority to France and Great Britain in this specific case to go to war immediately.* The Western democracies could have stopped Germany and its criminal policy in time. In my opinion, Czechoslovakia was in duty bound to go with them and would have done so. But nothing happened.

Here, France committed the most fatal error the results of which were felt throughout Europe. It failed to act according to a treaty *which had been concluded for this very contingency, in full agreement with Germany, whose signature the Treaty actually bore.* The Western democracies acted on this occasion with inexplicable weakness, irresolution and the most frivolous lack of foresight. According to official British and French sources, the responsibility must be placed personally on the French Premier, M. P. E. Flandin. It is said that he was afraid of the social consequences of war in view of existing internal conditions in France and that at all the British-French-Belgian meetings in Paris and London at which the answer of the Powers to Hitler's occupation of the left bank of the Rhine was discussed, he therefore prevented resort to military measures against Germany in accordance with the Locarno Treaty. This fatal step on the part of French policy was the ultimate and *direct* cause of the decay and tragedy of France. From it, derived Munich and the French capitulation of June, 1940. In March, 1936, France deserted itself and it was so much the easier for it to desert *us* in September, 1938. Its own capitulation in 1940 and its consequent degradation were merely the direct consequence of its former error.

Hitler's speech on the occasion of the occupation of the left bank of the Rhine, in which he declared that the other provisions of the Locarno Treaties remained in force and that Germany was ready to agree with all its neighbours on co-operation, non-aggression and mutual respect for frontiers, completed the process of political decomposition in Central Europe. Europe now knew for certain that France and Great Britain were not prepared to intervene energetically to prevent further violations of a treaty so important for them and for Europe as the so-called Rhine Pact signed at Locarno.

Beck's Poland hinted with cynical and malicious glee that it was now clear how right Poland had been to conclude its treaty with Germany in January, 1934. France (it was pointed out) was not even defending itself.

*Without waiting for League approval. (Tr.).

How then could Poland count on France defending Poland in accordance with their alliance. Now that Germany was once more a mighty lord in Europe, Poland had been able to come to terms in time, whereas these other States would find it difficult to secure its favour ! Had Polish policy been right or wrong ?

In Yugoslavia, too, the policy of turning away from France was much strengthened. Prince Paul and his Prime Minister, Stojadinović, soon felt able to make a direct approach to Berlin. We already sensed this unmistakably at the beginning of June, 1935, at the Conference of the Little Entente in Bucharest and on the occasion of my journey to Rumania.[4] Prince Paul clearly hinted that he was no longer counting much on Western Europe.

Rumanian policy was much shaken. The Bulgarian Fascists rejoiced and Austria soon realised what a successful German coup against the West could mean, because immediately afterwards the subversive activity of German Nazis inside Austria itself and just across the border of the Reich against Austria increased to such an extent that Chancellor Schuschnigg was forced willy-nilly to sign the well-known agreement with Hitler of July 11th, 1936.

This almost unopposed violation of Austrian independence was not only the first blow, but also a decisive one.[5] Inside Austria it made Nazism a legal movement. In the Reich it made possible the most impudent penetration by Nazism into internal Austrian affairs and led to the establishment of the first Quislings in Europe. To Hitler it gave an international cloak, under cover of which he could calmly prepare the internal nazification of Austria and thereby its bloodless annexation.

(b) Hitler's disruptive offers of an Agreement with Czechoslovakia

In this situation Hitler thought that the time was also already ripe for an attempt to win Czechoslovakia over. His plan had two aspects: one, international and the other, internal. In the international field he would offer us a similar treaty to his treaty with Poland. His object was to drive a wedge between us and France (and Western Europe in general): to compromise us in the eyes of the Soviet Union and to isolate us internationally, so that we should automatically fall into the orbit of his policy.

In interior policy, the plan was to repeat what he had done in Austria: that is, to induce us to accept an agreement by which Nazism was to be legalised in Czechoslovakia and to use the treaty as a cloak under which to penetrate the ranks of our Germans, break up their political organisations and disrupt their active co-operation with the Czechoslovak Government and nazify them completely so that they would carry out Hitler's wishes in Czechoslovakia. Either he would use our nazified Germans simply to annex the so-called Sudeten regions at a suitable moment, or he would use those same treacherous elements to establish his direct or indirect rule over the whole Republic. The Germans would remain in the Republic, enter the Government in agreement with Berlin and gradually permeate the whole structure of the State.

In accordance with this plan, Count Trauttmannsdorff (then a high official of Hitler's Minister, Seldte) contacted our Berlin envoy in autumn, 1936, and told him that two of Hitler's trusted henchmen would like to go to Prague to talk with the President of the Republic* on the lines of Hitler's speech after the occupation of the left bank of the Rhine, in which he stressed Germany's readiness to reach agreement with all her neighbours. They wished, he said, to ascertain whether such an agreement would be possible with Czechoslovakia. The discussions were to be carried out in an atmosphere of great secrecy. They would, he declared, be simply an exchange of views between the two heads, in which the Ministers for Foreign Affairs would not participate—in particular, Minister Neurath was to be kept in ignorance of the matter. Only after everything had been agreed would the Ministries for Foreign Affairs be asked to draft and conclude a formal agreement.

I answered that I would receive Hitler's representatives to hear their point of view and that I would answer their questions immediately.

On November 13th, 1936, they arrived in Prague. They were Count Trauttmannsdorff, formerly an Austrian aristocrat and Czechoslovak citizen (his brother had an estate in Czechoslovakia, in Horšův Tyn), and Dr. Haushofer, the son of the well-known Bavarian authority on international politics, Professor Haushofer, who was later executed by Hitler. They once more stated the object of their visit: Hitler would like to agree with me personally on a new policy of friendship between our two States, sign some kind of pact of non-aggression like that with Poland, and remove the barriers of mutual distrust which the past had raised between us. This, they said, would mean the recognition of Czechoslovakia's frontiers and a final agreement that the two States would not go to war with one another. Hitler, they went on, wished to negotiate this treaty with me alone and they added in his name a number of flattering compliments. Meanwhile, they were to request me to observe absolute secrecy both

*Dr. Beneš succeeded Professor Masaryk as President on December 18th, 1935 (Tr.).

internally and internationally. They asked for an immediate answer to the question whether the President of the Czechoslovak Republic was ready, in principle, to start such negotiations and whether he considered that a treaty of such a nature between Germany and Czechoslovakia was possible. They concluded by telling me that after taking back an answer to these fundamental questions, they would return to Prague with the relative instructions and proposals in order to start concrete negotiations.

I answered at once that I was not against negotiations of such a nature and that I would welcome an agreement between Germany and Czechoslovakia. However, I could express myself more concretely only after I knew in greater detail on what principles an agreement would be based. As to the proposed procedure, I observed that, though I did not refuse to discuss these matters myself if the Reich's Chancellor expressly desired it, I could not, as a constitutional President, do this without the participation of the Minister for Foreign Affairs and that I should also have to inform the Prime Minister. I therefore asked the two negotiators not to leave Prague without visiting and informing the Foreign Minister, Dr. Krofta. For the rest, they could of course rely on the matter remaining absolutely secret while it was in the phase of diplomatic discussions. On the following day they visited Minister Krofta and informed him of the substance of the discussions. Then they returned to Berlin.

At the beginning of December, 1936, Hitler's two negotiators asked our Minister in Berlin to arrange another visit to Prague. I received them at the Presidential Castle in Prague on Friday, December 18th, 1936. The discussions were very thorough and, on my side, absolutely frank. Our talk lasted nearly seven hours and by the time it ended I was already in no doubt about what Hitler really wanted.

Trauttmannsdorff and Haushofer placed before me Hitler's proposal that Germany and Czechoslovakia should sign a declaration or treaty, similar to the Polish-German Treaty of January 26th, 1934 (or an analogous treaty of non-aggression) which would put the relations between our two countries on quite a new basis, namely, that Czechoslovakia and Germany should in no circumstances go to war with one another.⁶ It would also mean, they said, German recognition of the existing Czechoslovak frontiers. Though in the Reich and with Hitler himself there was much interest in the Czech Germans, the Führer, they intimated, considered an agreement to be possible in this question too. So far as Germany was concerned, it was only a question of the Germans in Czechoslovakia having some 'cultural autonomy' so that they could freely profess and cultivate their German nationality. If this were granted, Germany would not be interested in supporting the efforts of our German politicians to gain territorial autonomy.

In essence, therefore, what Hitler wanted was, from the international standpoint, a treaty similar to that with Poland which would weaken our treaties of alliance with France and the Soviet Union and our obligations to the League of Nations (as in the case of the Polish Treaty) and from the internal standpoint, some such declaration as he had signed with Austria on July 11th, 1936, which would enable him to penetrate and corrupt our German citizens (as in Austria) and to infiltrate Nazi doctrines into them from the Reich—with all that this process entailed.

I answered first the point about our Germans. I said I could not negotiate about this question with any foreign agents. It was a purely internal Czechoslovak question. This was the line I had taken with Stresemann at Locarno in October, 1925: I could discuss in a friendly way with delegates of a foreign power any internal Czechoslovak question, including our German question, with Reich Germans. *But I could not negotiate about it with them* nor accept in such a matter any official obligations whatsoever. From this standpoint, I was ready, if they wished, to tell them how I regarded the problem of our Germans and to explain our policy and future plans. But no more.

At the request of Hitler's two emissaries, I then explained the whole problem in detail: how we saw it and how we wanted to solve it; what our Germans had got already, what in my opinion they were still to get, in what way their rights had perhaps not been honoured yet and in what they —and also their friends in Germany—were wronging us. I spoke clearly, openly, without mental reservations and without regard to diplomatic forms.

To their question (which voiced the views of the Henlein party) whether the whole Czechoslovak nationality policy did not aim at enabling the Czechs to seep into and penetrate the German frontier regions in Czechoslovakia, to permeate them and so gradually to contract the German areas, I answered that the process certainly did exist, but that it involved a special sociological problem. It was the result of the general political and economic development of Czechoslovakia. The movement of the Czechs in this direction was an irresistible urge deeply rooted in the historical and economic background of the last two centuries and must be accepted as a fact. The so-called Czechisation of our German territories was an automatic and natural exchange and mingling of the German and Czech population, the exact converse of the process had gone on in former centuries in the opposite direction when Germans had displaced Czechs, often by violent means. It was an irresistible process, which, in these modern days could be seen wherever a nationally mixed territory was being industrialised on the edge of a less highly developed agricultural area. Already under Austrian rule, this process had developed swiftly. Our own German territory had been industrialised with the help of the Austrian government and bourgeoisie and the new industries had necessarily been manned by elements from the neighbouring Czech agricultural regions. *What was happening therefore was no deliberate policy initiated by an independent Czechoslovakia.* It was a natural modern sociological process and nothing could be done about it.

But the Czechoslovak Government, I assured them, was not planning a violent Czechisation of our German regions. In any case, no substantial change of the ethnical frontier could be expected in view of the maturity of both races. Any shifting of the frontier between the Czech and German elements in Bohemia and Moravia could only be brought about by force, by war. I went on: 'But we do not want a war. Nevertheless our Germans and also you in the Third Reich are well aware that our national frontier would automatically and necessarily shift somewhat more to the Northward if it should come to a new war and we should win. If, on the other hand, you were the victors, we know equally well *that you wish to take as much of our territory as possible and drive all Czechs out of our so-called German regions.* We are aware of that and we are preparing for it'. I spoke with such frankness that they seemed somewhat surprised.

With regard to the non-aggression treaty with Germany, I explained that the German proposal would necessarily involve Czechoslovakia's denouncing her treaties with France and the Soviet Union and leaving the League of Nations. But the Czechoslovak Government was resolved to honour its obligations in every case. No other course was open to it. Hitler's emissaries at once answered with an ironical smile, that 'signing a treaty with Germany certainly meant no such thing'. Poland had not acted in this manner. All that Germany would require was 'that Czechoslovakia, in case of a war between Germany and the States in question, would simply not put those treaties into operation'.

I was astonished at their explanation and still more so at their shameless cynicism in proposing a deliberate and premeditated violation of signed treaties.

After a short discussion in which I stated that in these circumstances an agreement would not be possible, the two negotiators asked me whether with my long experience at Geneva in formulating agreements and declarations of various kinds, I could not make some proposal of my own. I at once replied that it would be better to place an agreement between Czechoslovakia and Germany on a basis which did not affect our existing commitments and so would be lasting. A new agreement should, in my opinion, be based on the existing German-Czechoslovak treaty of arbitration signed at Locarno on October 16th, 1925, which the Government of the Reich had officially declared to be still in force, first, on March 7th, 1936 (after the occupation of the left bank of the Rhine) and twice again later. We would accept such a treaty which would broaden the agreement of Locarno and would rule out war between Czechoslovakia and the German Reich on the understanding that all disputes would be settled in accordance with the Locarno treaty of arbitration. I offered to prepare the text of this new treaty and send it to Berlin.

Both delegates accepted this proposal' and at my request they again spoke to Dr. Krofta, to whom they expressed their satisfaction about our discussions. But they never returned to Prague and did not even answer my proposal when it was sent to Berlin. The rupture of the whole negotiations was later explained by Berlin as having been due to an 'indiscretion' by Czechoslovakia. It was declared that the matter had come to Neurath's ears and that he opposed an agreement with Czechoslovakia. This 'indiscretion' was, as a matter of fact committed by the Czechoslovak Prime Minister, Dr. Milan Hodža, in a talk with the Yugoslav envoy. But according to another version, when Trauttmannsdorff accidentally met the Austrian Minister, Marek, in Prague, he dropped a hint about the matter to him; Marek transmitted it to Vienna and from Vienna it went to Berlin and so to Neurath.

But the real truth was that my concept of the treaty was not at all acceptable to the rulers of the Third Reich. It did not change the political orientation of Czechoslovakia, it did not cancel or compromise our alliances with France and the Soviet Union and it did not change our view of the principle of the indivisibility of peace or of European collective security. Nor did it offer fresh possibilities for the legal penetration of German Nazism into our country. On the contrary, it was intended to emphasise the necessity of not interfering with our democratic way of life and to prevent the very thing that Hitler's offer was designed to bring about.

To sign such a treaty with Czechoslovakia would not have suited Hitler, the radicals of the Nazi party in the Reich or of those in Czechoslovakia. They therefore considered the negotiations to have failed.

I received unofficial confirmation of this from Berlin in the second half of January, 1937, together with a very confidential hint that Hitler was

c

now engaged in other negotiations, which, if successful, would probably also affect us considerably,[8] and that the resumption of our talks must therefore be postponed till later. We at once gave our allies a brief account of these negotiations and how they had ended. But in the spring of 1937, Goebbels began a systematic and continuous campaign of hatred and revenge against Czechoslovakia, thus showing that Berlin, having failed to persuade us to accept its proposed agreement, had embarked on different tactics: agitation, terror and deliberately prepared violence. No definitive reply ever came from Berlin, either then or later.

I consider this interesting episode of the time when we were next-door neighbours of Nazism to be extremely characteristic, not only of Hitler and his regime, but also of the whole period of deliberate 'appeasement' by the Western Powers at the expense of their friends at the very moment that Hitler was preparing for war against them and planning the destruction of his weaker neighbours one by one. But I wish to stress again that I had correctly gauged Hitler's plans by which he was preparing 'Munich'[9] and that we remained unflinchingly faithful to our policy even when the other countries of Central Europe succumbed one after the other to the fear evoked by the increasing vehemence of German Nazism.

(c) Disruptive Nazi and Fascist Policy is Successful in Poland and Yugo-
    slavia—
    Our Reply

By the end of 1947, the Spanish Republic had fallen, internal dissensions in France had multiplied after the fall of the Popular Front and the international impotence of France and of Great Britain was now established. The Sino-Japanese war had been renewed in a new and most bitter form in the summer of 1937 (July 8th) and new quarrels had resulted at Geneva. In Central Europe, Hitler's Germany had been pursuing its systematic tactics of disruption since the end of 1936, concentrating especially on compassing the internal dissolution of Schuschnigg's Austria. The Hungarian Prime Minister had paid official visits to Warsaw and Berlin where there were open talks about plans for the disruption of Central Europe and especially about the partition of Czechoslovakia. Gömbös—whose visit to Warsaw was on October 21st, 1934—boasted mockingly of this in the lobbies of the Hungarian Parliament after his return from Warsaw, quoting cynical remarks by Pilsudski and Beck about Czechoslovakia. Meanwhile, Prince Paul and his Prime Minister Stojadinović, had been negotiating with Mussolini and Hitler from the end of 1936 until January, 1938, when decisive steps were finally taken to lead Yugoslavia into the camp of the Fascist Powers. Finally, the systematic campaign which Goebbels had been conducting against Prague since the beginning of 1937 was being actively and maliciously aided and abetted by Beck's Poland and Horthy's Hungary.

Thus, the Fascist Great Powers were already advancing, the Western democracies were in full retreat and the whole continent of Europe was in a state of gradual dissolution. Spain, France, Poland, Austria, Yugoslavia, Rumania, Bulgaria and Greece were all to a greater or less degree infected internally by the Fascist plague.

By the spring of 1938, disruption had gone sufficiently far to enable Hitler, on March 12th, to invade Austria (undermined as it was by the Nazis) and incorporate it in the Third Reich without provoking anything more than a few platonic protests. These had not even ended when, in May, preparations began for the planned attack on Czechoslovakia.* To this we answered, as is well known, by our mobilisation of May 21st, 1938.[10] Thereupon began a new critical period which was to decide the fate of Europe and of the world—perhaps for a long time.

Czechoslovak foreign policy had been watching all these developments with growing apprehension and uneasiness. I was afraid of this process of dissolution and asked myself where it would lead and how it would end. Right up to the signing of the Munich Treaty by the Great Powers I did not personally abandon my obstinate hope which buoyed me up in my consistent resistance to Nazism that the day-to-day deterioration of the situation would, in spite of all appearances, be arrested by timely and determined action and that a new European war could still be avoided. I therefore did everything in our power, as was but our duty, to avert this catastrophe.

Already, in 1931, we had called the attention of the members of the League of Nations in Geneva to the necessity of real courage to stop the expansion of Japan before it was too late, pointing out that otherwise the Geneva institution would receive a grave, perhaps a mortal, blow. In 1932, watching the development in Germany, I warned the Italian representative at Geneva, Baron Aloisi, that Italy should change its policy and not support Hitler's advent to power, or else the avalanche could not be stopped by anybody in Europe and would bring Central Europe, to say nothing of Italy itself, into ruin. At the same session of the League of

*At the time of the Anschluss with Austria, it had been officially announced that Germany had no more territorial demands to make in Europe. (Tr.).

Nations, as I have already stated, I had a long, private and earnest conversation with the Polish Foreign Minister Beck, who attended for the first time, and in the course of this I proposed a complete revision of our relations, including an agreement for the neutralisation of our common frontier and the preparation of future military co-operation, in order to present a common front against coming events from Germany.*

At the same time I had a talk with Chancellor Brüning at Geneva. He warned me that the Allies must make fresh concessions and give full Great-Power status to Germany or else Hitler would come into power. I declared, apparently to his great surprise, that under the circumstances then obtaining in Germany I was reckoning on Hitler's coming into power in any case. I explained to him, and subsequently to Minister Curtius, why this was bound to happen.

Before that, however, in July, 1932, when I returned to Prague from the Disarmament Conference at Geneva where I had the function of general Rapporteur and could therefore penetrate into the minds of the different delegations of the Great Powers, I immediately assembled the whole Czechoslovak General Staff[11] in the presence of the Minister for National Defense, Bradáč, and made a statement to the following effect: ' . . . In spite of all our efforts for the success of the Disarmament Conference at Geneva, everything I have already seen and heard there inclines me to the second eventuality† and *I am obliged to call your attention to this fact.* If the Conference fails—and it very probably will—a dreadful crisis is inevitable. First it will be political and then, immediately afterwards, there will be the danger of war. *I give you four years. The crisis will probably come in 1936 or 1937. By that time the Republic must be fully prepared militarily.*'

After the end of the session of the Assembly of the League of Nations in October, 1932, I received highly confidential information at Geneva that at the 'Volta' Conference which was held in Rome at the same time, Hitler's delegates and Mussolini had agreed on large-scale preparations for the so-called revision of the peace treaties. In reality this was the first move to bring about the destruction of the smaller Central European States and the first step towards the Four-Power Pact. I therefore went straight to Belgrade from Geneva to warn King Alexander of this plot. I explained my fears about the future of Europe and stressed the Italian and German danger. We agreed as a counter-move on even closer co-operation between our two States and a more energetic policy by the Little Entente. In agreement with him, I accordingly proposed in January, 1933, the so-called

*i.e. the advance of Hitlerism. (Tr.).

†i.e. that the Conference would fail. (Tr.).

Organisational Pact of the Little Entente to unite and range us even more closely against the impending action of Rome and Berlin.

When I got back to Prague, I quickly prepared the text of this treaty and sent it to King Alexander at Belgrade as well as to Foreign Minister Titulescu at Bucharest. It was signed on March 16th, 1933, at Geneva, just at the very moment when Ramsay MacDonald and Sir John Simon were leaving Geneva for Rome to receive from Mussolini the draft Four-Power Pact, which Berlin and Rome intended to be the instrument for a complete change in the balance of power in Europe and which was particularly directed against the smaller Central European States.

In the autumn of 1933, after strenuous negotiations with the French Foreign Minister, Paul-Boncour, we succeeded in rendering the Four-Power Pact harmless, but the process of Europe's dissolution was not halted.[12] In October, 1933, Germany left the League. Soon afterwards, Hitler for the first time turned to Prague and through various intermediaries sounded us out on the subject of securing a bilateral treaty of non-aggression with Germany. When he discovered after inquiry through a third party that we had flatly rejected his overtures and had loyally informed Paris, London, Warsaw, Belgrade and Bucharest, Hitler turned to Warsaw, where he was more successful.

In mid-January, 1934, when I returned once more to Geneva and met Colonel Beck there on January 20th, I asked him—as I had reliable reports from Moscow of negotiations between Berlin and Warsaw—whether it was true that Poland was negotiating a bilateral treaty with Germany. I had also instructed our Minister in Berlin, Mastný, to find out the facts from the Polish Ambassador in Berlin, Lipski. I actually had in my pocket a telegram containing quite precise details about the whole negotiations. But Beck told me to my face that they were not true.

A few days later, on January 26th, the well-known Polish-German treaty between Hitler and Pilsudski was signed. Soon afterwards a campaign against us began in the Polish press. It was so violent that the German Minister in Prague, Dr. Koch, considered it necessary to come to me personally and assure me that Germany had nothing to do with it and that nothing of the kind had been agreed upon when the German-Polish treaty was concluded.

We in Prague defended ourselves against the approaching catastrophe as best we could. One means to this end was to establish co-operation with the Soviet Union and its direct participation in European and League affairs. Ever since 1927, when Commissar M. Litvinov came to Geneva for the first time to take part in the session of the Preparatory Committee for Disarmament, I had never ceased to try to establish friendly and permanent contact with him and his colleagues and to work with them towards a general exchange of views which would lead to a rapprochement. I emphasised the main principles of our policy, the first and most important being that Czechoslovakia was convinced that without the participation of the Soviet Union in European, and particularly, Central European affairs, Germany would again be supreme in Europe and would endanger European peace. After the establishment of the League Committee for the Liquidation of the Sino-Japanese conflict in the years 1931 and 1932 and after the convocation of the Disarmament Conference we continued these talks as well as our co-operation with the Soviet Union. My endeavours at that time to persuade the Soviet Union to take an active part in the League were chiefly supported by France. Into this period falls first the journey of Herriot to Moscow and then Paul-Boncour's plans for direct negotiations with Moscow.

It seems that the Four-Power Pact was the deciding factor in finally making Moscow begin negotiations to enter the League of Nations which the Soviet Union ultimately did on September 18th, 1934. At that time, as President of the League Council, I was able, in co-operation with Barthou and Eden, to give material assistance towards the successful solution of the difficult problem of obtaining immediately a permanent seat in the Council of the League of Nations for Moscow, thus assuring the entry of the Soviet Union into the League.*

With the support of the Soviet Union, systematic work to secure peace against the plans of the Fascist Powers at once began at Geneva. Barthou and Litvinov—with my co-operation—drafted the well-known 'Eastern Pact' for mutual aid against an aggressor in Central and Eastern Europe which was to be signed by France, Germany, the Soviet Union, Poland and Czechoslovakia. One of the objects of this pact was to make impossible what later actually happened when Poland turned against us and the Soviet Union while the Munich Agreement was in preparation. The 'Eastern Pact' was never signed because of the united resistance of Hitler's Germany and Beck's Poland. All that remained was the Franco-Soviet Agreement of May 2nd, 1935, and the Soviet-Czechoslovak agreement (signed at Prague on May 16th, 1935), which was ratified in June, 1935, during my first journey to Moscow.

Nevertheless, I considered the entrance of the Soviet Union into the League of Nations in September, 1934, to be a triumph of the policy of

*The chief problem was to circumvent the efforts of less qualified States to obtain the same status as the U.S.S.R. (Tr.).

peace and the signing of the French and Czechoslovak treaties with the Soviet Union to be the beginning of a new French and Czechoslovak policy which would link the Soviet Union with Western Europe and establish direct co-operation between East and West. *This I held to be quite indispensable if the expansion of Hitler's Germany to the East and thus also to the West was to be stopped.*

But the assassination of King Alexander on October 9th, 1934, which also caused the death of Barthou, again threw Europe into great confusion. This event was followed by a fatal and irremediable change in the internal and foreign policy of France, as well as of Yugoslavia. And though for some time Barthou's successor, Laval, seemed to continue the policy of co-operation with the Soviet Union, he soon began to embark upon a two-faced policy, also approaching at the same time Mussolini and indirectly Hitler. His grandiose intrigues and gambles eventually culminated in the disastrous capitulation of France in June, 1940, and the treasonable adventures of Petain and Laval in the years 1940–44.

After Christmas, 1934, Laval went to Rome where he negotiated with Mussolini about a new policy in Central Europe. He hinted that he would have no objection if Italy should transfer her expansion from Europe to Abyssinia. He did go to Moscow in May, 1935, to sign the treaty with the Soviet Union—an inheritance of the policy of Barthou—but he interrupted his journey in Berlin, where he hinted that the treaty should not be taken seriously:[18] Laval's object in concluding the Treaty was simply to use it as a means of pressure to enable him to come more easily to an agreement with Hitler. *Broadly speaking, the death of Barthou and the coming to office of Laval must be considered as the final collapse of the post-war policy of France.* At that moment France placed itself on a slippery slope and took all Europe with it. In spite of the energetic and well-meant attempt of the Blum government to arrest its decline, France was now sliding irresistibly and unmistakably down towards its capitulation in 1940.

(d) The Sanctions against Italy—The last Attempt of the Western Democracies to resist

We tried desperately but in vain to stop this general deterioration and the violent Fascist aggression by taking strong action at Geneva in September, 1935, against Italy's attack on Abyssinia and by imposing sanctions. So far as Great Britain was concerned, it was the last attempt to resist the violence of the Fascist Powers. As I have already mentioned, Sir Samuel

Hoare[14] placed Great Britain more resolutely behind the League of Nations than that country had ever been before.

But it was a swan song. A few months afterwards, Sir Samuel Hoare agreed with Laval about the partition of Abyssinia and therewith about the liquidation of sanctions. *Thus he began in the true sense of the word the subsequently notorious and fatal policy of so-called 'appeasement'.* First there came appeasement in the case of Abyssinia, then appeasement in the matter of the occupation of the left bank of the Rhine, then a continuation of appeasement in the matter of China, then appeasement in the Spanish Revolution, appeasement about Austria, and finally 'appeasement' in regard to Czechoslovakia leading to the agreement of the Great Powers at Munich.

Great Britain was the last country which openly submitted to this decadent process. Eden, who took over the Foreign Office after the forced departure of Hoare, at first resisted this development with all his strength. But when Neville Chamberlain came to power on May 28th, 1937, after the resignation of Baldwin, differences between him and Eden soon arose over Chamberlain's readiness to compromise with regard to new provocations by Fascist Italy, and Eden resigned on February 20th, 1938. The development of 'appeasement' as the official policy was then completed in Great Britain, too, and in a manner which was catastrophic for Europe and the world.

To this very cursory outline of the condition of the democratic Great Powers at the beginning of 1938 I wish to add the following:

The state of Great Britain's armaments and its war preparedness generally in the summer of 1938 was—apart from its permanent and considerable fleet—quite inadequate. Successive British governments had, it seemed, no right concept of what was really being prepared in Europe. They culpably neglected proper preparations for the Army and the Air Force. The plan for rearming the country, which was accepted in 1937 after the final failure of all the attempts Great Britain had made to come to an agreement with Germany about armaments, was hardly even in a preparatory stage in 1938. It is true that the production of weapons was beginning to accelerate but mass production had not yet begun. In comparison with other countries, its force was very weak, the number of anti-aircraft weapons was inconsiderable and air-raid precautions were in their infancy. Germany had very precise information about British unpreparedness and in September, 1938, during the Czechoslovak crisis Göring ironically gave the British Ambassador in Berlin 'fairly accurate details of the British Air Force and of the British A.R.P.'[15]

In so far as its army was concerned, France was better equipped than Great Britain, but in 1938 she also was quite unprepared for sudden war, especially a modern one. Its preparations could not compare with Czechoslovakia's. This is surely strange seeing that France was informed of our arrangements down to the minutest detail by General Faucher, the head of the French military mission in Prague, who every week attended the military conferences with the President of the Republic, and not only knew exactly what we were doing, but *why we did it*. Be that as it may, France was far from being up to date in the number and production of tanks; and had an inadequate air force and an entirely insufficient output of planes and air-raid defence weapons. On these matters, also, Germany was well informed.

The fact is that the state of armaments and war preparedness, that is to say, the total effective forces of the Western democracies at the beginning of 1938, corresponded accurately to their internal moral and political condition and the general decline of their prestige as Great Powers. On the other hand, the military preparations of Nazi Germany had been pressed on feverishly, systematically and in all departments *since the spring of 1935*, when from secret rearming its rulers had changed to open arming, and were rebuilding the old imperial army in its full strength and power.[16] In the autumn of 1938, Germany as a whole was incomparably better and more solidly prepared for war than both the Western Powers together.

3. *Our struggle to save ourselves in the last Three Years before Munich*

(*a*) Preparedness of our Army

After the failure of sanctions and the fatal Anglo-French acquiescence in the German occupation of the left bank of the Rhine there remained, it is true, our alliance with France, the treaty of the Little Entente, our alliance with the Soviet Union and the League of Nations. *But for the first time since the World War we were faced with the concrete, menacing question: In the moment of crisis, which of these treaties and guarantees could we really rely upon in this general and catastrophic decline of European democratic values and of the democratic Great Powers ?*

From 1937 onwards theories were disseminated in France and legal theses written (by Professor Barthelemy in *Le Temps*) according to which the Franco-Czechoslovak Treaty of Alliance had ceased to be valid because the Treaty of Locarno had become a dead letter.

The French Government, of course, never accepted this theory, because this would have involved releasing Great Britain from her obligations to

France. But the theory made a successful starting point for reactionary French circles in the development of their policy. The League of Nations received a blow which was nearly mortal when sanctions against Italy were abandoned on July 15th, 1936. And from that summer, the Little Entente also began to disintegrate—first Yugoslavia and then Rumania began to follow the same path.

I was, on the whole, well aware of the general situation in Europe at this period when President Masaryk resigned and when I was elected his successor after a certain internal crisis.* It was clear to me that in accepting this high office, I was going into very stormy seas and that we would have to reckon with this fact in framing our future policy. In every direction I looked, I could sense that Europe was plunging towards a great conflict and that we especially would not escape as the spark that caused the ultimate explosion would surely come from Germany. I therefore decided in the first place to redouble our efforts to bring our army to a high pitch of perfection. To this task I dedicated myself with greater energy and devotion than to anything else before.

My first and principal reform was to establish a Supreme Council for the Defence of the State, consisting of the chief ministers and representatives of the various parties in the Government. We improved the organisation of the Ministry of National Defence; we delimited the competence of the General Inspector of the army and of the Chief of the General Staff more clearly; we established inspectorates for the various weapons, especially the air force, and we defined the rôles of the various district commands and the corps commands, even nominating the commanders in case of war.

Under my chairmanship, the Supreme Council for the Defence of the State took all necessary measures in regard to the permanent frontier fortifications and the financing of that great, and in every respect successful, enterprise which was at least as efficient as the Maginot Line and in some respects surpassed it. For three whole years I had regularly and systematically discussed and settled with our military experts the more important questions concerning the readiness of our army, in my capacity as Supreme Commander of the armed forces of the Republic. The law for the defence of the State and other necessary legislation were prepared; the Officers'

*President Masaryk resigned on December 9th, 1935, and Dr. Beneš was elected as his successor on December 18th, 1935, by 340 votes out of 440. The 'inner crisis' was due to difficulties raised by the right-wing parties in the Coalition Government which were dissatisfied with Dr. Beneš's foreign policy and his socialistic tendencies. In the actual voting, there were 20 votes for Professor Nemec and 76 blank papers, most, if not all of which came from the Henlein Party. Four persons were absent (Tr.).

Corps of the army was strengthened and fully equipped; we provided the army with weapons of all kinds and motorised it in so far as it was possible in our country at that time; we established armoured units and developed our air force on an adequate scale.

At that time we were also supplying the armies of our two allies in the Little Entente. We delivered war material and equipment on credit to Yugoslavia and Rumania to the value of thousands of millions of crowns and began to fit out their armies systematically.

It is a fact that in the late summer of 1938, our army, *in spite of all its deficiencies, which I did not conceal from myself, was at the time of the Munich discussions,* one of the best in Europe and that it was fighting fit in its morale as well as in its equipment—as our two mobilisations, in May and in September, demonstrated. Our officers' corps was in no way inferior in technical ability. Nor did the lessons of the second World War in the fields of military science and practice necessitate any material alteration in our military organisation, training and theory.

I was always proud of the fact that in these three years the Czechoslovak Republic did more in this direction than any other democratic State in Europe and that when we mobilised in September, 1938, the Republic was properly prepared for war—with two exceptions—one of these was in the sphere of civil air-raid defence where we could not surmount all difficulties including the petty quarrels of the two ministries concerned. The other was the unfinished state of the fortifications on our Southern frontier with Austria. I have sometimes been told that all these costly preparations were futile and that we could not use them at the time of Munich. Even if that were so, what would have been said to us all and to me personally both at home and abroad, if we had been as unprepared in 1938, as for example France and Great Britain? In any case, our fighting spirit, which up to that time had not been sufficiently cultivated, was increased and strengthened during those three years to meet the situation which developed in Europe. This was of great value to us during the second World War and still is today, especially with regard to our officers !*

(*b*) My Journeys to Rumania, Yugoslavia and France

My second task was to strengthen and to save what could be saved of our alliances in the growing disintegration of Europe. I made preparations

*Since the communist *coup d'etat* in February, 1948, practically all the army officers to whom President Beneš was referring have either been retired or imprisoned. Many have been hanged. Some have escaped this fate only by fleeing abroad (Tr.).

for three official journeys in my capacity as President of the Republic: to Rumania, Yugoslavia and France. I went to Rumania on the occasion of the Conference of the Little Entente, held on June 6th and 7th, 1936. I was surprised to see that a rift was already clearly visible in the Little Entente's ranks. The Yugoslav Regent, Prince Paul, opposing the Rumanian Foreign Minister, Titulescu, as well as the Czechoslovak Foreign Minister, Dr. Krofta, and myself, rejected every proposal which in our opinion could strengthen the Little Entente community with regard to the approaching crisis. Prince Paul excused his attitude by referring to the uncertainty which existed about France and Great Britain. He passionately recounted to me various slanders against Titulescu and attacked our Minister in Belgrade, Dr. Girsa, of whom he said that he was too much given to listening to the views of the Yugoslav opposition.

Still more serious was Yugoslavia's open refusal of closer co-operation in face of the disruption of Europe brought about by Germany. This occurred when the Yugoslav Prime Minister, Milan Stojadinović, came to see me on September 12th, 1937, in Topolčianky and Bratislava, where one of the regular sessions of the Little Entente was being held. *In agreement with Paris, I proposed to the other two members of the Little Entente that our separate treaties of alliance should be consolidated into one single treaty, operative in respect of all States* and that this should be followed by the conclusion of a treaty of alliance between the Little Entente as a whole and France.* Stojadinović began by talking about other matters, went on to make excuses and ended by simply rejecting the proposal. The Rumanian Minister for Foreign Affairs, Antonescu, who was in Topolčianky at the same time told me that Rumania would accept the proposal if Yugoslavia did so too. I have no documentary proof that he already knew what Stojadinović's views were, but I think he did, because I had previously instructed Dr. Krofta to communicate the plan in writing to both the other members of the Little Entente before the meeting and Antonescu had been able to talk to Stojadinovič (who had come to the meeting in Slovakia via Bucharest) and therefore must have known that his condition would ruin my whole plan.

The game Prince Paul was playing was indeed already perfectly clear in the summer of 1937. He wanted to join the Berlin-Rome Axis against the axis of France of the Popular Front and the Soviet Union. This policy took a more or less official aspect when it became known that he was paying frequent visits to Germany, that he was in contact with Berlin through his brother-in-law, the Bavarian Count Toerring-Jettenbach and *that he was*

*The Little Entente was only operative against Hungary (Tr.).

(secretly, for the time being) negotiating with Mussolini. The opposition inside
Yugoslavia was openly criticising these activities and Prague and Bucharest received confidential information on the subject. In the end, it was
expressly confirmed to me personally by the Yugoslav Minister in Prague.
The Yugoslav Minister in Paris, Murić, spoke quite cynically about the
matter.

When I was certain that the secret negotiations of Prince Paul and Dr.
Stojadinović with Mussolini threatened to disrupt the Little Entente and
complete the disruption of Central Europe I decided to try to stop this
development by paying an official visit to Belgrade and making a personal
intervention. Prince Paul and Mussolini, fearing that my journey would
hinder their secretly prepared agreement, deliberately postponed my visit
and speeded up the signature of their treaty. Only after it had been concluded and signed on March 25th, 1937 (it was ratified with unusual speed
as early as March 27th), did I get a hesitating and rather bashful invitation
to visit the brotherly Yugoslav Nation. Perhaps it was expected that the
coolness of the invitation would deter me from my journey. But world
peace was at stake and I therefore went to Belgrade without hesitation for
the official visit which was fixed for April 5th to 7th.

I was received with rejoicing by the Yugoslav people, but the Yugoslav
dictators and those soldiers who had been so enthusiastic about the Little
Entente before were both curt and embarrassed. During the talks, I was
confirmed in my opinion that the leaders and official Belgrade were already
whole-heartedly on the other side. They told me—Stojadinović in particular read me a long lecture on the subject on the second day of my visit—
that if there should be a new war between the Great Powers, Yugoslavia
would not be able to take part in it and would remain neutral under all
circumstances. I asked if they could seriously believe for a single moment
that in view of the geographical position in which they were situated they
could avoid participation in a war in which Germany and Italy were
involved. I added that in Prague we had no such naïve illusions.

But what I was told was a clear indication that in order to guard itself
against a conflict between Germany and Italy on the one side and France
on the other, Yugoslavia intended to make agreements with what was
subsequently to become the Axis. Yet in spite of this the Yugoslav dictators assured me that they were remaining faithful to the Little Entente
even though they would not conclude any new treaties with us. Such were
the circumstances in which I paid my first very disagreeable and even
painful visit to Yugoslavia in 18 years.

From my talks with Prince Paul and with the opposition (and with delegates of the Yugoslav Sokol)* I perceived not only a change in the orientation of foreign policy, but also a quickly progressing internal decomposition disguised by Stojadinović's superficial Fascist authoritarianism and pompous and affected arrogance.

I asked myself whether this meant that Yugoslavia was irretrievably lost for us in the approaching crisis.[17] After my return to Prague, however, I did not send quite so pessimistic a report to Paris. I was still hoping that the new political orientation of Yugoslavia, namely, its going over to the Axis, would be delayed by my journey.† But I was soon convinced that the whole process was continuing—by this time with the addition of Hungary to the plot.

Nevertheless, I tried for the third time to stop this development—when 'Führer' Stojadinović came to the funeral of President Masaryk in September, 1937, I talked with him for four hours in the Presidential Castle. I reproached him sharply for violating the obligations of the Little Entente when he concealed his negotiations with Mussolini, hypocritically coquetted with the Hungarians and negotiated with Hitler behind our back. He excused himself very insincerely. I explained to him that the European crisis was rapidly approaching, that I was doing all I could to ensure that France and the Soviet Union—which were and would be our powerful allies—should be prepared for it together with ourselves, that in the end there would come a catastrophic defeat for Germany and the rest. But I added that we all would have to hold out and stand faithfully together. Finally he was—sincerely or insincerely ?—moved, touched and tears even came into his eyes. But he confessed that he had been invited to pay a political visit to Berlin. I asked him emphatically, and urged him, not to go. He did not promise anything, however, and ultimately went to Berlin on January 17th, 1938. At Karinhall, he boastfully made friends with Göring and *finally made him a secret promise that Yugoslavia would not oppose the 'Anschluss' with Austria and would not interfere in a conflict between Germany and Czechoslovakia but would remain neutral* . . .

Yugoslavia did remain neutral so long as it suited Germany and Italy. From 1940 Berlin began to exert pressure on Yugoslavia to make a formal adherence to the Axis and contribute directly to the war of Germany against Great Britain. At that time I was already able to deliver to the

*A large contingent of Yugoslav Sokols participated in the Sokol Festival in Prague in the following summer, when tension between Czechoslovakia and Germany was growing daily, and received a rapturous welcome from the spectators (Tr.).

†The official statement issued in Belgrade at the end of the visit spoke of 'the harmony of views, and unity of policy and aims, of the two kindred peoples which remain inseparably linked in the future.' (Tr.).

Yugoslav Minister in London, Subotić, the plans which Berlin and Rome had prepared in advance for the partition of Yugoslavia. (I received these plans in London through our excellently working underground organisation at home, which had obtained them direct from sources inside the German General Staff in Berlin.) Such was the reward Mussolini and Hitler had prepared for Prince Paul's and Stojadinović's services! Even earlier, during his official journey to Berlin in April, 1939, Prince Paul had himself heard from Hitler that after the German victory and the introduction of the New European Order, Yugoslavia would not have to trouble either about an army of its own or about a foreign policy. Germany would take care of such matters.

Shortly before his fall at the beginning of the year 1941, Prince Paul complained to his Minister in Ankara, whom he had called home in a critical situation because of new pressure from Berlin: 'I have already done everything Berlin wished me to do. We left the Little Entente, we dissolved the Balkan Entente, we have conformed to the policy of Berlin in everything—what else in God's name does Hitler want of us?' Not long afterwards he learned directly and officially of all the plans of Hitler and Mussolini and he could at last understand the whole tragic situation into which his policy had brought Yugoslavia.

Such was the moral and political catastrophe which overwhelmed everyone who deserted the path of right and began to come to terms with Hitler in this threatening European maelstrom. In excusing themselves for having done so, some might argue that even we who remained faithful to our principles were nevertheless not saved from Nazi occupation by our fidelity. Yes, but what an enormous moral difference lies between us! Our official policy had been warning the world for years, and right to the last moment it had stood firm in desperate opposition against capitulation to Fascism and finally it was forsaken by nearly the whole world. When our Nation had been sacrificed and thrown to the mercy of Nazism, our people, step-by-step, rose again and rallied finally in unanimous resistance! What an example for the future of the Nation!

I only wish to make it clear that in the years 1936–38 Czechoslovak policy rightly diagnosed what was the matter in Europe. It did everything, really everything, to retrieve the situation of Czechoslovakia, of its friends and of all Europe in face of Fascist gangsterism and pan-German Nazism and of war itself. *In that period when the European and world crisis was approaching, there was no State in Europe which could have a clearer conscience of doing its duty towards its Nation and its friends than the Czechoslovak Republic under the presidency of Masaryk and myself.*

In saying this, I do not want to assert, of course, that everything was as it should be in Czechoslovakia. There were among us influential persons and important political circles either without the slightest conception of the real situation in Europe, or egotistically unwilling to understand what was at stake, what was coming and what was to be and must be done. Some of them—they were few—coquetted with Fascism and admired Hitler's methods. They went to Berlin and then reported at home how they had found 'order' there and how 'Germany was prosperous and flourishing'. From 1935, these people were thinking in terms of co-operation with Henlein or even preparing it and they were turning up their noses about everything that happened in the 'Hrad' (President's Castle). They understood later what was the matter, when it was already too late and after the war the Nation dealt with nearly all who had doubted.*

My official journey to France had been agreed upon for June, 1938. But meanwhile the course of events in France showed that Paris, too, was definitely moving towards 'appeasement'. The critical moment came after April 10th, 1938, when the Daladier Government took office with Georges Bonnet as Minister for Foreign Affairs. It deliberately steered French policy away from France's Central European alliances. I soon realised this when, at the beginning of June, 1938, our Legation in Paris was officially asked by the Quai d'Orsay to postpone my visit to Paris, the date of which had already been fixed. The reason given was that one of the items on my programme was the unveiling of a memorial for the Czechoslovak Army in France in 1918 at Darney, in the presence of President Albert Lebrun. We were informed that Berlin would consider this a provocation.

During all those exacting and exhausting negotiations (from 1935 onwards), I tried my utmost to steer a straight course with the Soviet Union on one side and France on the other. On June 4th, 1936, after the French elections which resulted in the formation of the government of the Popular Front, the new Premier, Léon Blum, had sent me a message that France would never again behave with such weakness as his predecessor had done at the time of the occupation of the left bank of the Rhine and assured me that his Government would be strong and firm towards Germany and that we might count on this.

This was really France's last stand. The Foreign Minister, J. Paul-Boncour, sent me a number of messages in the same strain. He tried

---

*President Beneš is here referring to the so-called 'Retribution Decrees' under which those who had collaborated with the Germans were tried and sentenced. A number of alleged collaborators who joined the Communists just before the end of the war were not however brought to trial, and some of course had managed to escape abroad (Tr.).

especially to re-establish the Eastern front of the Little Entente and he also tried to win over Poland. On the direct intervention of Paul-Boncour, Leon Noël, then French Ambassador in Warsaw, came to me in Prague to ask whether he could assure Warsaw that Czechoslovakia would carry out its Locarno obligations towards France if Poland were attacked by Germany and France went to its aid. In agreement with Foreign Minister Krofta, I answered categorically 'yes': that Czechoslovakia would intervene with arms at the side of France and Poland in the spirit of its Locarno obligations. Paul-Boncour then assured me that he would try to force Warsaw to undertake the same obligation in case of a German attack on Czechoslovakia. Noël really attempted to do this, but in vain. *Warsaw did not answer.*

Nevertheless, I tried again to reach an agreement with Poland in these years while the crisis was developing. When in mid-August, 1936, the Chief of the French General Staff, General Gamelin, passed through Czechoslovakia on his way to Poland, I sent General Faucher* to see him in his train and give him a *written* invitation to the Polish Government to the effect that having in view the serious situation and the fact that a European crisis was well on the way, we should start preparations for Polish-Czechoslovak military co-operation. General Gamelin spoke about the matter to the President of the Polish Republic and General Smigly-Rydz and handed them the offer which General Faucher had delivered to him. He received the evasive answer that he, a soldier, must understand that this was primarily a political question. There was no further answer. When, as Marshal, Smigly-Rydz returned General Gamelin's visit to Paris on September 6th, 1936, he was asked by French spokesmen, at our request, to say what Poland would do in the case of a German attack on Czechoslovakia. They received the very curt answer that Poland was bound to Czechoslovakia only through membership of the League of Nations and the obligations which resulted therefrom.

Nevertheless, Léon Blum, in agreement with Prague, made another attempt to win back Belgrade and *proposed, with our explicit consent, a treaty of alliance between France and Yugoslavia.* This was politely refused like the offer Minister Krofta had made, with the knowledge of Paris, at Topol-čianky on September 12th, 1936, when we invited our two partners in the Little Entente to change our separate alliances into a general alliance of the countries of the Little Entente with France.

Even the journey of Yvon Delbos, Minister for Foreign Affairs in the

*Head of the French Military Mission in Czechoslovakia. See page 27 (Tr.).

D

Chautemps' Government which succeeded Léon Blum's, to Warsaw, Bucharest, Belgrade and Prague in December, 1937, failed to halt the process of deterioration. *Central Europe—with the exception of Czechoslovakia—had no longer a common policy with France.*

By the summer of 1937, it was clear from what had happened that on the Continent of Europe only France, Czechoslovakia and the Soviet Union remained in favour of determined and consistent resistance to the onslaught of the Fascist Powers and France was already wavering as a result of the subversive activities of her reaction. Great Britain at that time was withdrawing into its island shell. On June 18th, 1935, it had concluded a unilateral naval agreement with Germany, which was advantageous for Great Britain. Later, on April 16th, 1938, it signed quite a number of 'appeasement' treaties with Italy, which came into force on November 16th, 1938. Belgium, seeing the general trend in Europe and being deprived of its chief safeguards under the Locarno Treaties by Hitler's occupation of the left bank of the Rhine, returned on April 24th, 1937, to its former useless policy of neutrality. It renounced the alliance with France and Great Britain and on October 13th, 1937, accepted from Germany the treacherous and worthless signature of a treaty promising to respect Belgian integrity. Thus, everyone in Europe was spinelessly, if resignedly, running away from the fight for the defence of democracy and was 'safeguarding' himself alone by means of blind negotiations with perfidious Hitlerite Germany and dictatorial Italy.

In these moments of apprehension, trouble and anxiety, I asked myself again and again just where all this could end. I had sufficient diplomatic experience and understanding of the historical logic of great events to see that Europe was hastening to its doom as a result of universal selfishness. It will be easy to understand my feelings in the years 1936–38 when I directly sensed how, step-by-step, the life work of Masaryk and myself was collapsing and the world was gliding down into the abyss.

(c) The Last Steps of France to her Fall at Munich

Such was the situation which faced the Czechoslovak Republic in March, 1938—that is, just before the last act but one of the violent Fascist and Nazi policy of destroying Europe, namely, the annexation of Austria. It seemed to me virtually certain that the annexation of Austria was the immediate prelude to a Second World War. In May, 1928, on my first post-war visit to Berlin, I had told State Secretary von Schubert and Minister Stresemann that if Austria were annexed by Germany, whether by violence or not, they could expect with certainty that within six months there would be a great European crisis out of which would come a new European war. (Our Minister in Berlin, Dr. Chvalkovský, was present at that conversation and took it down). Stresemann who was already seriously ill made written comments on this talk—he lay in his bedroom at the time and sent the whole paper to the various leading officials of his Ministry. *It was said* that he gave a warning against such a step. After my departure from Berlin our conversation leaked out. It was untruthfully reported (and used as a propaganda weapon against me) that I had threatened Berlin with a European war. I purposely repeated this Berlin conversation to the German Minister in Prague, Eisenlohr, in 1936–38 on several occasions as a warning when Neurath began to declare the Austrian question to be a 'Familienangelegenheit'. Within six months after the annexation of Austria the crisis came—the crisis in which Czechoslovakia was the stake. And from that crisis the second World War developed inevitably.

At the time of the Austrian crisis I was waiting to see what the Great Powers, France and Great Britain, were going to do, and whether Austria or some other country would turn to the League of Nations. It is necessary to point out that it was the duty of each member of the Council of the League of Nations to file a complaint against Germany at Geneva. When in 1931 Brüning and Curtius attempted the 'Anschluss' and *Czechoslovakia was a member of the Council,* we at once turned to Geneva as well as to Paris and Rome with a protest and an appeal. The whole question had necessarily to come before the League immediately afterwards. But in 1938 all Europe was already so far gone that Geneva as an instrument of European democracy was already dead. This was proved on several other occasions before the League itself closed down during the war. It only came to life once during this period when, in December, 1939, thanks to the extraordinary activity of the Secretary-General J. Avenol and the ministers Daladier and Bonnet and the vigorous intervention of the American Ambassador Bullitt, the League took action against the Soviet Union over its war against Finland. (The Soviet Union was expelled from the League of Nations on December 14th, 1939.)

After the annexation of Austria in April, 1938, the progress of France towards 'appeasement' culminated in a political development which I have already mentioned. When the government of Chautemps fell on April 9th, Edouard Daladier was entrusted with the formation of a new Cabinet. On forming his new Government he first invited Paul-Boncour to a talk and discussed with him the question of his taking over the Ministry for

Foreign Affairs. Paul-Boncour sketched to him the principles of his well-known traditional policy: collective security, Geneva, alliance with Great Britain, co-operation with the Little Entente and, if possible, with Poland and therewith a new strengthening of the unity with Allied Central Europe and finally strong emphasis on the Franco-Soviet Treaty.

Daladier declared he would think it over. Then he called Georges Bonnet and listened to his programme which was already based on what was called 'appeasement'—that is, on the policy of reserve in Central European, Eastern European and Spanish affairs, on a plan for agreement with Fascist Italy, on the execution of a cautious, distrustful policy towards the Soviet Union and on turning French policy primarily towards France itself and its great colonial Empire. At the same time the French Right, led by Flandin, warned Daladier that they would give no support to his Government if Paul-Boncour became Minister for Foreign Affairs.

On the next day Daladier told Paul-Boncour on the telephone that he had given the Foreign Ministry to G. Bonnet. This was the first unequivocal and official withdrawal of France from Central European affairs, the first clear and outspoken renunciation of a policy which France had followed for nearly twenty years.

Was this a definitive expression of the consciousness of the weakness of France in a crisis? Was this another grave proof of the increasing internal decomposition which progressed still further after the fall of the Popular Front? Was it the fear of war and of its social consequences in a France internally disrupted? Or was it merely the renewal of the former policy of the Four-Power Pact which already in 1933 had advocated for France and Great Britain the same concept: a withdrawal to their own colonial empires and the abandonment of the so-called continental policy (especially in Central Europe) which Daladier had explicitly accepted as early as 1934, giving Mussolini and Hitler the right to expand into Central Europe, the Balkans and eastward against the Soviet Union?

Actually, it was all of these things. *It was the prologue to Munich and also to the capitulation of France in 1940.*

Daladier was a man who for many years had never forgotten to point out whenever occasion offered that he had not been at Versailles, that he was not responsible for the Peace Treaties of 1919, that it was necessary to accommodate oneself to the new developments, that France could not make itself responsible for the disordered Central European States. His extremely adverse and contemptuous, even sneering, remarks about Poland and Rumania were at that time everywhere known and notorious in the Paris salons. He surrounded himself in his Cabinet with a number of known defeatists. Some of them were old and disillusioned pro-Austrian adversaries of the post-war allies in Central Europe, especially of democratic Czechoslovakia (de Monzie!—who had been the advocate of Hungarian noblemen in their lawsuits against Czechoslovakia before international courts in the matter of landed estates). Frivolous, immoral and politically corrupt persons were among his associates.

Georges Bonnet was known as ever ready for compromise. To him any means was good enough provided it helped him get what he wanted. He was, in the worst sense of the word, a typical politician. His normal practice was to have several—at least two—policies at once; to give as Minister written and telegraphic instructions correctly in line with public or official declarations by the Government and at the same time verbal orders in quite the opposite sense which disavowed his own public declarations or instructions sent in writing. In the country with which he was negotiating he would have an official envoy for the first policy and a confidential agent for the second so that he could speak to everybody as it suited him at the moment. He considered the former basic policy of French alliances as nothing more than a stock of props to make use of in any way that circumstances dictated.

Afraid of the social and revolutionary consequences of war in France, Bonnet was *a priori* against any decided or war-like resistance to Hitler's policy of expansion. At most he would have liked to see war between Nazism and Bolshevism. If he ever spoke of remaining faithful to us or to signed treaties, it was only because he thought for a while that such declarations might deter Germany from a *'fait accompli'* by a surprise coup which would unchain a sudden war. He did not speak in such terms because he was really prepared to put our treaty of alliance with France into effect.

This was the background when we had our first serious conflict with Germany on May 21st, 1938. Daladier, and especially Bonnet, and the British Government too, had been given definite proof on that occasion that we were prepared to fight if attacked and that therefore—if they did not intervene in time in one way or another—there really would be a war which France would have to enter in accordance with its treaties with us the moment Hitler committed an act of violence against us. From that moment Georges Bonnet worked feverishly to frustrate our determined policy and to render our military defences untenable at any cost. For this he had a number of supporters in Daladier's Cabinet. I shall return to this subject in greater detail in my book dealing with the events which led up to the agreement of the four Great Powers at Munich.

(d) We and the Soviet Union work together to save peace—Munich

Thus in April, 1938, when the Daladier-Bonnet administration took office in France, we and the Soviet Union were politically isolated in Europe *in basic and determined anti-Fascism and anti-Nazism.*

Our co-operation with the Soviet Union after the conclusion of our treaty of 1935 was, in general, normal, lasting and consistent. Politically we were in regular contact with one another and our loyal exchange of views on the general situation was never interrupted. We were thus able to establish a certain degree of co-ordination in our respective policies.

Already on May 30th, 1935, I had agreed that a Czechoslovak military delegation led by the chief of our Air Force, General Fajfr, should pay an official visit to the Soviet Union. Thus started our first air co-operation with Moscow. In August of the same year a delegation of the Soviet army, led by General Shaposhnikov, participated in our first large-scale manœuvres, saw our whole armaments industry and prepared the way for our deliveries of essential armament material to the Soviet Army.

In September a delegation of the Czechoslovak Army led by the Chief of the General Staff, General Krejčí, left for the main manoeuvres of the Soviet Army. They returned literally surprised, and, from a military point of view, even enthusiastic about what they had seen in the Soviet Union. General Krejčí declared after his return that the 'Red Army, its discipline, its high morale and its mechanised equipment were a fresh inspiration for every Russian', adding that 'the energy of the Government, its unprecedented efforts, as well as the strength of the Russian soldier, call for the admiration of every military expert'. At that time the West did not accept our valuation of the Soviet Army and its possibilities. But this merely encouraged us to fix our eyes more steadily on the Soviet Union and to try to get to know and understand it.

In October, 1935, a group of Soviet journalists paid an official visit to Czechoslovakia. On that occasion, I myself as Minister for Foreign Affairs and the Soviet envoy, Alexandrovskij, both spoke in very clear terms about our new Treaty of Alliance, which *'was to stop the preparations of those nations in our vicinity which are ready to disturb the peace by large-scale military adventures and to try to subdue their peace-loving neighbours'.* Similar declarations and manifestations of various kinds followed with increasing frequency in the years 1936 and 1937 coupled with practical co-operation in the sphere of aviation, armaments and the mutual exchange of political and military information. This gave German, Polish and Hungarian propa-

gandists an increasing number of pretexts for scurrilous attacks on Czechoslovakia and for attempts to bring us into discredit in the eyes of the
Western European Powers as the 'chief propagators of Bolshevism in
Europe'. But we really had no other aim than to prevent by all means at
our disposal the outbreak of a second World War which Germany with
her policy and ideological and material preparations was visibly preparing
to unchain.

Our views about developments in Germany and also in Western Europe
were already at that time essentially the same as those of the Soviet Government though Moscow undoubtedly viewed the European scene far more
pessimistically than did Prague. In agreement with Moscow we tried on a
number of occasions to establish closer political and military co-operation
between the West and the Soviet Union. So, for example, in 1938, we
were asked by the Soviet Minister in Prague to help to induce the West
(especially France) to give active help in equipping the Soviet Navy with
some special weapons. I intervened. I repeated my request. I stressed the
importance of this help but I had no success whatsoever. I was forced to
conclude that those in power in France clearly did not want to help.

In view of the feverish war preparations of Germany we did all that
could be done so far as Moscow and Prague were concerned. As already
indicated, we agreed to deliver considerable quantities of certain special
weapons from our armament factories, weapons which the Soviet Army
especially needed and could not get from France or anywhere else. But
what was still more important, we also agreed, at my request, on the
exchange of temporary military missions to examine our joint preparations for defence and mutual aid and to co-ordinate preparations in all
necessary points. In the summer of 1937, another Soviet military mission
inspected all our frontier fortifications, our chief armament factories and
our air force. As a result, other measures were taken and agreements concluded, especially in connection with Soviet air assistance in case of a
German attack on Czechoslovakia (an extension of our air-fields was also
agreed, but at the time of Munich this had not been finished). During the
visit of Colonel Fr. Moravec* to Moscow in 1938, an agreement was
reached about the exchange of military and intelligence information.

After the visit of the Soviet Mission to Czechoslovakia, a similar
Czechoslovak military mission, led by General Husárek, was sent to the
Soviet Union. The members were shown everything we needed to know:

*Colonel, afterwards General, Moravec was Director of Military Intelligence of the
Czechoslovak Forces in Great Britain during the war. After the Communist Revolution
of February, 1948, he left Czechoslovakia and is now in America (Tr.).

the state of Soviet preparations for the defence of Soviet territory, the state of preparedness of their armament industry, and especially also the state of the Soviet Army and Air Force. The written report of our military mission on the condition and preparations of the Soviet Army was not only valuable then and in 1938, but much more so later, during the second World War when it helped us to estimate Soviet military preparedness for the European war, the military possibilities of the Soviet Union and Soviet military policy in general after 1941.

By the spring of 1938, and from then to September, I believe everything that the international situation and our mutual relations made possible under the Czechoslovak-Soviet Treaty of 1935 was actually done. I confess that some of our commitments which we had undertaken and which were still in course of preparation could not be entirely carried out by September, 1938 (as, for example, our new fortifications along the Austrian frontier).* There were several energetic but unsuccessful attempts by Soviet diplomacy to organise a conference of military experts of the General Staffs in the critical period before Munich to exchange views on the common defence of West and East Europe against a Fascist attack. *On my special instructions we were always ready and fully prepared for such a conference, but right up to the end of September, 1938, we never succeeded in getting the French, British and other States to agree.*

After our mobilisation in May, 1938, I permitted our Chief of Staff, General Krejčí, to approach General Gamelin direct in writing with an offer to go to Paris to discuss concrete measures about the co-ordination of an eventual Czechoslovak and French mobilisation. After some time, General Krejčí received a written answer from General Gamelin to the effect *that in such a matter he could only do what his Government ordered, and that at the moment he had had no instructions on the subject.*

Our soldiers received no further message, nor were they invited to Paris. Thus we learned shortly before the Munich crisis that *the French army either did not want or was unable to make any such preparations.* The French High Command knew exactly what the attitude of the Daladier-Bonnet Government was. General Gamelin could surely have given such an answer only after consultation with his Minister of War, Edouard Daladier.

In September, 1938, therefore, we were left in military, as well as in political, isolation with the Soviet Union to prepare our defence against a Nazi attack. We were also well aware not only of our own moral, political and military preparedness, but also had a general picture of the condition of Western

*See pp. 28, 29 (Tr.).

Europe; as well as of Nazi Germany and Fascist Italy, in regard to these matters.*

At that moment indeed Europe was in every respect ripe to accept without a fight the orders of the Berchtesgaden corporal. When Czechoslovakia vigorously resisted his dictation in the September negotiations with our German citizens, we first of all received a joint note from the British and French Governments on September 19th, 1938, insisting that we should accept without amendment the draft of a capitulation based essentially on an agreement reached by Hitler and Chamberlain at Berchtesgaden on September 15th. When we refused, there arrived from France and Great Britain on September 21st an ultimatum accompanied by emphatic personal interventions in Prague during the night on the part of the Ministers of both countries and repeated later in writing. We were informed that if we did not accept their plan for the cession of the so-called Sudeten regions, they would leave us to our fate, which, they said, we had brought upon ourselves. They explained that *they certainly would not go to war with Germany just 'to keep the Sudeten Germans in Czechoslovakia'*. I felt very keenly the fact that there were at that time so few in France and Great Britain who understood that something much more serious was at stake for Europe than the retention of the so-called Sudeten Germans in Czechoslovakia.

The measure of this fearful European development was now full, precipitating Europe into ruin. Through three dreadful years I had watched the whole tragedy unfolding, knowing to the full what was at stake. We had resisted desperately with all our strength . . .

And then, from Munich, during the night of September 30th our State and Nation received the stunning blow: Without our participation and in spite of the mobilisation of our whole Army, the Munich Agreement—fatal for Europe and the whole world—was concluded and signed by the four Great Powers—and then was forced upon us.

But about this I shall report to the Nation in another volume.†

*It seems clear from this sentence, which was evidently worded with great care, that President Beneš had no illusions about the possibility of resisting Hitler in 1938 if the Western Democracies refused to fight.

†This was never finished (Tr.).

NOTES TO CHAPTER ONE

[1]The Locarno Treaties were signed in London on December 1st, 1925.

[2]Perhaps there will be another opportunity to tell more about my discussions with Colonel Beck, the Polish Foreign Minister, at Geneva in the spring of 1933 when we almost reached full agreement about common action between the Little Entente and Poland against the Four-Power Pact. We agreed that Colonel Beck should pay a visit to Prague and we also agreed on future procedure as well as to try to reach a full Czechoslovak-Polish understanding. The next Polish Minister in Prague, Edward Raczynski—who succeeded Mr. Grzybowski—rendered very effective help.* But after an exchange of telegrams between Beck and Warsaw, there came from Warsaw—probably from Marshal Pilsudski himself—the uncompromising answer: 'never', and the discussions ended forthwith. This seems to mark the beginning of the preparations for the final change of Polish policy towards Germany. It was said that Pilsudski had then developed the theory that Poland was more and more becoming a Great Power and so both could and must show France that it could follow an independent policy.

[3]On January 28th, 1934, I sent the following circular cable to our Legations in which I summarized this conversation and informed them of our views:

'With regard to the Polish-German treaty I am sending you this information on our attitude:

1. We were informed by our Minister in Berlin immediately after the publication of the German-Polish communiqué of November 15th, 1933, that negotiations were in progress and that the two parties intended to express German-Polish relations in the form of a treaty in the spirit of that communiqué. Information has reached us that the new relationship would be expressed in the form of a 'Declaration'. On January 19th, 1934, our Minister in Warsaw informed us that a treaty was being prepared and that certain circles asserted that two of the conditions were that Poland should disinterest itself in regard to Austria and should refrain from concluding a treaty with Czechoslovakia. On the same day I had a conversation with Minister Beck at Geneva but he said nothing about negotiating and signing any declaration.

2. On January 27th, the Polish Prime Minister at Prague informed me officially on behalf of his Government that:

(a) The Polish Government stresses that nothing has been discussed between the Polish and German Governments except what was covered by the text of the Declaration. To my question whether the Declaration was signed on the conditions mentioned under (1) above, he replied that the communication he had received on the subject indicated a negative answer but that he would transmit my question to his Government.

(b) The Declaration was only the continuation of negotiations based on the communiqué of November 15th, 1933, and an expression in writing of what had then been said orally.

*Count Raczynski was afterwards Foreign Minister in General Sikowski's Government in exile. He is now living in England (Tr.).

(*c*) The Declaration was an appendix to Locarno concerning frontiers and apart from which the whole basis of Polish policy in regard to its other treaties and the League of Nations remained unchanged.

3. Our attitude to this affair is as follows:

(i) The Declaration has advantages and disadvantages but we do not believe that it will be observed either in respect of its terms or duration. It is certain that Warsaw errs if it believes the question of frontiers to be in abeyance for ten years. I believe that, in the clause about the solution of political, economic and cultural questions, the Germans, either explicitly or by means of a mental reservation, have reserved the right to discuss the question of the frontiers in bilateral negotiations and that therefore in the Declaration itself there is already the germ of future disputes.

(ii) The advantages of this agreement *for Germany* are as follows:

(*a*) Hitler's Germany has broken the ring of isolation.

(*b*) Germany, which needs time for internal consolidation and to arm, benefits more from this respite than Poland.

(*c*) The agreement indirectly concerns the authority of the League of Nations and therefore serves the aims of those who are against Geneva.

(*d*) The most serious consequences will be that the agreement will be used against France in the disarmament discussions as a proof of German love of peace and therefore as a means of pressure on France to make concessions.

(iii) It is necessary to wait to see what effect this agreement will have on France's policy towards Germany and whether it will impel France towards an agreement with Germany and to concessions in the matter of disarmament. If so, new difficulties would arise with Poland, which does not want to disarm in any case and especially does not want to accept the MacDonald plan. But Poland expects that the Great Powers will not agree on disarmament, that therefore it will not have to disclose its own disinclination for disarmament and that it will thus be able to avoid a dispute with Germany on this issue. Disputes about armaments in Poland's opinion will be limited to the Western Powers. Whether this view is correct will appear in the near future.

4. Our policy remains unchanged. Our efforts for a rapprochement with Poland continue. For our part we are quite sincere; we offered a treaty of eternal friendship and in conversations with Beck at Geneva I again went into all matters in detail. Now we will simply wait.

5. I expect Germany will find some means of intimating that it is willing to enter into the same kind of agreement with us as with Poland. Though we will not reject *a priori* the possibility of talks, we will show no initiative and will not ask for anything. We have no frontier or other disputes with Germany and we therefore need not do what Poland has done now. But if there should be talks or negotiations on whatever subject, we will do nothing without the Little Entente and without loyally discussing matters with France beforehand. Similarly towards Germany our behaviour in this respect will of course be loyal and open. But we could not accept anything which either directly or indirectly impairs the authority of the League of Nations.

6. The fact that Germany's hands will be somewhat freed towards Austria does not alarm us at the moment. Perhaps this fact will help to clear up Italian policy and underline the truth that the Austrian problem has really become a European problem and is not merely a problem for us and France. This may hasten a European solution.

7. In Moscow, the Polish-German rapprochement naturally arouses distrust.

To what degree this declaration is an error for Polish and European policy will probably appear very soon. We must not be misled by public statements or declarations in the press.

E.B.

⁴It is worth mentioning that my conversations with King Carol from 1945 onwards made clear to me his unconcealed admiration for the policy of Hitler and for Hitler's person. King Carol himself openly imitated Mussolini in his methods and internal policy —sometimes even in minute details. But he tried sincerely to remain faithful to the policy of the Little Entente as long as possible.*

⁵I discussed very reservedly with Schuschnigg during his earlier visit to Prague (January 17th, 1936) the possibility of mutual aid against Nazi Germany. I received the impression that Austria did not dare to enter into such an arrangement.

⁶As was proved during the Nuremberg Trials, the Germans as early as 1937 had made precise military plans and calculations for attacking Czechoslovakia, which shows the value of Hitler's negotiations for permanent peace with Czechoslavakia ! The technique was to have been the same as Hitler later used against all his victims.

⁷The text of the draft treaty which I prepared and sent to Berlin, is as follows:

The President of the Czechoslovak Republic and the Führer of the German Reich, desirous of contributing to the maintenance of general peace in Europe and in the same degree resolved to maintain peace between Czechoslovakia and Germany by securing the peaceful settlement of disputes which may arise between the two States,

Recognising that the rights of States cannot be changed without their consent and mindful of the fact that the sincere observance of the rules for the peaceful settlement of international disputes enables the two States to solve the problems which might divide them without the use of force,

Have decided to reaffirm and to extend the Treaty of October 16th, 1925, between the Czechoslovak Republic and the German Reich, and for this purpose have appointed as their respective plenipotentiaries:

the President of the Czechoslovak Republic,

Mr........................

The Führer of the German Reich,

Mr........................

who after exchanging their full powers, found to be in good and due form, have agreed on the following articles:

*Rumania was the only one of Czechoslovakia's Allies which mobilised at the time of Munich (Tr.).

Article One

The High Contracting Parties reaffirm the principles which animated them when they concluded the Treaty of October 16th, 1925,* and pledge themselves to continue to observe the terms of this Treaty.

Article Two

Each of the High Contracting Parties shall respect the sovereignty of the other Party and its full and undisturbed execution within the whole State territory and undertakes not to interfere in the internal affairs of the other Party. As such are declared to be all matters which under international law are left to the exclusive competence of individual States including the form of their political and social organisation.

Article Three

The High Contracting Parties undertake to continue in good neighbourly relations which they will develop, deepen and strengthen.

Article Four

The High Contracting Parties pledge themselves to extend and develop their economic co-operation and trade relations. To this end they will in particular enter into negotiations for a new trade agreement on a more lasting and broader basis.

Article Five

The High Contracting Parties undertake to solve all current disputes arising from their political, economic, cultural and other relations in a friendly spirit through diplomatic channels.

Article Six

This Treaty, the Czechoslovak and German texts of which shall have equal validity, shall be ratified and the instruments of ratification shall be exchanged as soon as possible in Berlin/Prague. The treaty shall become effective immediately after the exchange of the instruments of ratification and shall remain in force under the same conditions as the Treaty mentioned in Article One of the present Treaty.

In faith whereof the plenipotentiaries have signed this Treaty and have hereto affixed their seals.

Done at Prague/Berlin in the Czechoslovak and German languages on . . . . 1937.

[8] As a slip of the tongue by Trauttmannsdorff had unwittingly revealed, these negotiations were with the anti-Stalin clique in the U.S.S.R., Marshal Tukhatchevsky, Rykov and others. Hitler expected these negotiations to be successful and he was therefore not interested in bringing the discussions with us to a speedy conclusion. If the attempt to disrupt the Soviet Union had succeeded, the whole situation in Europe would have been transformed, but Stalin prevented this just in time. I at once informed the Soviet Minister at Prague, Alexandrovsky, of what I had learned from Berlin about the Mastný-Trauttmannsdorff talks.

[9] I reasoned as follows: Either Hitler really means what he says, in which case his offer is a sign of extreme weakness and we must therefore avoid compromising ourselves as

*One of the Locarno series (Tr.).

Poland has done; or it is an infamous fraud, in which case it is still more important for us not to depart from our policy, the honesty of which will be an asset to us.

[10]Details will be given in my book on the Munich Crisis.

[11]General S. Ingr was then on our General Staff and took part in this conference.*

[12]The whole affair was shrouded in strict secrecy at Geneva. But I nevertheless learned of it in time and I had two long talks with MacDonald—on March 13th and again on March 17th, on the day of MacDonald's and Simon's departure for Rome—and warned him emphatically about Mussolini and his plans. It was in vain; MacDonald and Simon returned to Geneva and then went back to London with the draft of the Four-Power Pact already in their pockets.

[13]Laval's meeting with Göring, who was visiting the grave of Pilsudski in Cracow on May 18th, 1935, was of importance in this connection for it was a means of starting one of Laval's famous negotiations.

[14]Now Lord Templewood.

[15]See *Failure of a Mission*, London, 1940, by Ambassador Sir Nevile Henderson, p. 152.†

[16]Great Britain gave direct help to Hitler in these rearmament plans when it confirmed and legalized his violation of the disarmament clauses of the Versailles Treaty by the conclusion of the British-German Naval Treaty of June 18th, 1935.

[17]Immediately after my journey to Belgrade the leaders of the Yugoslav opposition issued this declaration:

'For some time now there has prevailed among our people a growing apprehension that Mr. Stojadinović is changing the direction of the foreign policy of our Nation, founded on our alliance with France and the countries of the Little Entente and on friendship with Great Britain and the countries of the Balkan Entente. The events of the last three months prove that these apprehensions are very well founded. Abandoning the foreign policy we have hitherto pursued—a policy which has been and remains the expression of the real convictions of our people, the Stojadinović Government is leaning towards the "Berlin-Rome" Axis and aligning our foreign policy with that of Rome and Berlin with the object of separating Yugoslavia from her allies.

'The régime of Stojadinović first began to weaken the Little Entente. When at Milan, Mussolini supported the revision of Hungary's frontiers, a storm of protest rose from our allies, the Rumanians and Czechoslovaks. Our Government not only did not protest, but took steps to prevent these protests being mentioned in our press. We

---

*Afterwards Commander of the Czechoslovak forces in Great Britain. He was regarded with suspicion by the Soviet Union and was retired from the army in 1946. He then became Czechoslovak Minister to Finland, a post which he resigned after the Communist *coup d'état* in February, 1948 (Tr.).

†The exact words used by Sir Nevile are: 'Fairly accurate details of the number of modern anti-aircraft guns we then possessed as well as of the unpreparedness of England's air defences generally.' (Tr.).

rejoice at every rapprochement with our brothers, the Bulgarian Nation, but we think the method chosen is not the right one. The treaty with Bulgaria not only does not guarantee the security of our frontiers but does not even mention the fact that our new relationship does not weaken our obligations arising from the Balkan Entente with other Balkan countries.

'We recognise the importance of good relations with Italy, our most powerful neighbour. But the treaty with Italy, which involves close political, and perhaps even military, co-operation, has been realised at a moment when Italy is in extremely strained political relations with our ally, France, and our friend, Great Britain. These States are discussing with Italy questions of the utmost importance for their countries and Italy has been strengthened in its negotiations by this treaty. France and Great Britain are being weakened—and with our help.

'The Government of Stojadinović has also adopted an attitude towards the League of Nations which changes our whole policy. Neither in the treaty with Bulgaria, nor in that with Italy, is there any mention of obligations arising from the Covenant of the League of Nations. The Italian press even stresses the fact that the agreement with Yugoslavia is outside the sphere of the League of Nations. Stojadinović takes the same attitude towards the League of Nations as Italy and Germany.

'The Government of Stojadinović is today pursuing a foreign policy over which the public has no control and without regard for the requirements and feelings of the Nation. Criticism of the activities of the Government is not permitted. There is a danger that our allies and friends may overlook the fact that the policy of the Stojadinović Government is only the expression of a small group of men now in power. The Nation is far from such a policy, and our allies and friends should not have any doubts on this matter.'*

[18] J. Paul-Boncour has authoritatively described this fatal change in French policy in his book *Entre deux guerres*, pp. 96, sqq.

*The correctness of this estimate was shown when Prince Paul's Government was overthrown and Yugoslavia, in spite of overwhelming odds, joined Great Britain in the fight against Germany and Italy (Tr.).

CHAPTER II

THE OUTBREAK OF THE SECOND WORLD WAR

1. *My Departure from Home—Beginning of the Second Liberation Fight abroad —America's interest in a country which had been prostrated by Munich*

ON October 1st, 1938—the day after the signing of the Munich Agreement —Marshal H. Göring officially informed Dr. V. Mastný, the Czechoslovak Minister in Berlin, that Germany could not allow me to retain the office of President of the Republic. He would, he declared, never negotiate with me. At the same time he hinted that if I did not resign immediately, Germany, in carrying out the Munich Agreement, would proceed against Czechoslovakia with the utmost ruthlessness.

A similar declaration was made to the delegate of our Ministry of Foreign Affairs, A. Heidrich,* by State Secretary Weizsäcker of the Berlin Foreign Office. Some members of our delegation which had gone to Berlin to take part in the discussions about the execution of the Munich Agreement reported to me in the same sense. Similar threats also reached me in Prague at the same time through unofficial channels and Dr. Jaroslav Preiss† on his return to Prague from Berlin brought me a message to this effect.

Nor was this all.

The whole Fascist network in Western, Central and Eastern Europe saw in the second President of the Republic a symbol of democratic and resolutely anti-Nazi policy, as well as the friend and political successor of Masaryk. It should be added that in the Berlin Sports Palace on September 26th Hitler himself had made a rude and ferocious attack on me in which he proclaimed me his implacable enemy and said plainly that it was a life and death struggle between him and me. He seldom spoke a truer word.

All this made me feel that it was necessary to go. To do so was in the best interests of the State, but it was also a means of expressing my personal opinion about the newly-created situation and of making an unmistakable protest against the Western European circles which had brought about the Munich 'appeasement'. In addition, I already sensed a change of mood at home.

*Mr. Arnošt Heidrich became the permanent head of the Czechoslovak Foreign Office in the Third Republic. He retained this post after the Communist Revolution of February, 1948, but later escaped from the country and went to the United States (Tr.).

†Chairman of the Živnostenská Bank (Tr.).

Accordingly, on October 5th, I announced my resignation in a letter to the new Government which I had previously nominated. Then in a broadcast speech I said farewell to the Czechoslovak people.[1] I spoke in studiously discreet and moderate terms, as the situation demanded, but seen in post-war perspective the speech was borne out by subsequent events. I asked my fellow-citizens to restrain their feelings in spite of the disaster which had happened to us, to abstain from recriminations and reproaches against other States, to avoid internal quarrels and not to lose either their self-confidence or their belief in the justice of our holy cause. I indicated that Munich was only the beginning: that other events would follow, that I would remain true to my principles and to democracy and that I would continue to work for the Nation elsewhere. Perhaps at that time only a few of my listeners clearly understood the meaning of my words. Again I thought of 'my plan' and the approaching war.

Wholly exhausted mentally and physically, with indescribable feelings in my heart and with heavy thoughts of the terrible political and moral upheaval which was convulsing Europe and would perhaps disrupt it completely, I departed with my family on October 6th, shortly after noon, from Prague Castle to Sezimovo Ustí in southern Bohemia. There I tried to recover from the heavy blows I had received during the previous year and especially during the preceding few months.

So that I should have time to prepare my future plans I intended to stay in my fatherland for several more weeks, at any rate until October 28th.* After that, I intended to leave either for Switzerland or for England and thence for the United States where on the offer of my American friends I had accepted the Chair of Sociology at Chicago University. But the tension between Prague and Berlin continued. The Berlin Government informed Prague that its plans concerning Czechoslovakia could only be of a provisional nature as long as I remained in the country; and the Prague Government, intimidated by the new threats from Berlin, sent me several special messages to Sezimovo Ustí, through Dr. J. Schieszl asking me to leave the country as soon as I could manage it. At the same time my nephew, Bohuš Beneš, arrived from London with earnest appeals and warnings from my friends there to leave the country as soon as I possibly could. So, in spite of the fact that I was far from well, I resolved to go to London as early as October 22nd, my chief reason being to avoid aggravating the position of the Government.

Before leaving the country I confided my opinions on the situation to my entourage in the President's Office and to some of my political friends,

*Independence Day (Tr.).

E

Prokop Drtina, Jar. Smutný, J. Jína, Zd. Chytil, Zd. Bořek-Dohalský, Dr.V. Girsa and others*, and warned them that the necessary preparations for the revival of the fight would have to be made. 'As soon as the second European war starts', I told them, 'we must again begin an all-round struggle, as in 1914. We will have to prepare the organisation of resistance at home, establish permanent contact with anti-Nazi Europe and organise an army at home and outside our frontiers for the fight against Germany on the side of the rest of Europe which will be forced to go to war in spite of the Munich treason—or rather because of it. A numerically strong political and military emigration will be needed and it must leave the country in time. Make all necessary preparations and without fail be ready by next year!'

In October, 1938, I expected the war to start not later than May or June, 1939—that is within about eight months after Munich. I was sure that it would be inaugurated by an attack against Poland which Germany was surely preparing to reward in this manner for Polish support to German policy during the previous years against us and France—especially during the Munich crisis. I expected, and fervently hoped, that post-Munich Czechoslovakia would still be to some extent independent when the war started.

After I reached London, Jan Masaryk and I discussed our future plans for co-operation. I also immediately organised an 'underground' connection with my country. Already in the second half of November the first political messenger from my Prague friends, Dr. Jaroslav Dràbek,† arrived in London. Other messengers followed regularly until my departure for America in February, 1939. Immediate effective help came from our Military Attaché in London, Colonel Kalla. I maintained active contact with my political friends at home and wrote hundreds of letters to them answering their numerous messages and questions to London, asking them to hold out, to be of good courage, not to give way to despair under

*Dr. Drtina, after working in President Beneš's Chancery in London during the war, became Minister of Justice in liberated Czechoslovakia. He incurred the enmity of the Communists and after being severely injured in a fall (in mysterious circumstances) from a window was put in Pankrac Gaol, but was afterwards released. Mr. Smutný was head of the President's Chancery during the war and became head of it when the Government returned to Czechoslovakia. He retired shortly after President Beneš died in September, 1948. He escaped abroad after the Communist *coup d'état* in February, 1945, and is now living in England. Of the others mentioned here, Dr. Dohalský was executed by the Nazis (Tr.).

†Dr. Drábek was a well-known Prague lawyer who acted as Public Prosecutor at the trial of Reichs Protektor K. H. Frank and various members of the Protectorate Government after the war (Tr.).

the impact of Munich, nor to faint-heartedness as a result of events at home in the so-called Second Republic. I wished by all means in my power to maintain a good morale at home and foster the hope of better times, so that war would not find us wholly unprepared.[2]

The development of political conditions in Czechoslovakia after Munich is well known: I was simply held responsible for Munich and all its consequences. The bitterest reproaches and most violent attacks were directed against me. It was so easy and convenient to put the whole responsibility on the man who in the fateful moment stood highest and therefore had the furthest to fall ! I had told myself from the outset that it was not the moment either to discuss these things or to look for the real culprits or to quarrel about what had happened. I therefore silently accepted this responsibility and told myself that I must resolutely and patiently bear it until the march of events made an explanation possible. So I never protested, never defended myself, never reproached anyone, either at home or abroad. I did not even criticise France or Great Britain, Poland or Yugoslavia for their suicidal policy.

I made it a rule for my future procedure—without regard to what was happening at home—not to criticise the post-Munich Government in public, but on the contrary to facilitate its heavy task, and thus mitigate troubles at home and party strife. I held it to be better on the whole for future developments that I should temporarily bear all the responsibility on my own shoulders. For the time being I made it a rule not to appear politically in public, to be silent and wait until it was clear to all that a war would soon break out. Until that time I wanted to organise channels of communication with my country and prepare a permanent underground connection with the homeland for use when war started. In this mood I wrote from London in November, 1938, answering a letter from Dr. Lad. Rašín. I analysed the whole problem of Munich and our new situation and I hinted at my plans for the future. From that moment I counted on him as my future resistance collaborator.[3]

From similar considerations sprang my letter of November 30th, 1938, to Dr. Emil Hácha.[4] I congratulated him on his election as President— wishing thereby to ease the position of the post-Munich Government so that it should not be thought in Prague that for the time being I had any intention of interfering with the internal policy of the Second Republic or of making the Government's position *vis-à-vis* Berlin more difficult. I also wanted to indicate how in my opinion a true democrat should behave in the interests of State and national discipline in the face of a decision of unfavourable destiny.

Finally, from these considerations, presentiments and preparations sprang also my letter of January 27th, 1939, which I sent to the Prague Government via the London Legation shortly before leaving for the United States to inform it of my intentions and plans and to draw its attention to what it was to expect and for what it had to prepare itself, the State and the Nation.

This letter which˙ was sent to Prague by the Chargé d'Affaires, K. Lisický,* Counsellor of our London Legation, was in the form of a discussion between him and me. I know for certain that it was received by Foreign Minister, Dr. Chvalkovský.

It ran as follows:

'1. Dr. Beneš stated that he was abstaining on principle from interfering in Czechoslovak internal affairs. He is keeping contact with his personal friends, answering the normal correspondence of all who write to him, but he does not intend to take part in internal political activities. Under present conditions he would regard the existence of various fronts directed against one another and fighting for power as out of tune with the situation. It is well that a second party† exists because this may serve to maintain the sympathy of the general public for us in Great Britain, France and America—a most necessary factor for our State if tension or even war should develop in Europe. It is necessary that both parties should assist one another in this situation. Dr. Beneš himself takes cognisance of one thing only: The State and its supreme interest. *Salus rei publicæ*; this must be today our only programme, one common to all.

'2. Similarly, as he resigned from the Presidency when he saw that in the new situation such a step was in the interest of the State, so he abstains, and intends to go on abstaining, from political actions which could bring difficulties to the Government in foreign policy. He is refraining from public pronouncements, interviews, articles, lectures and has refused to publish anything whatsoever lest this should be misused to the detriment of the State. He has given to his sojourn in England an entirely private character. It was devoted to the scientific preparation of

*Mr. Karel Lisický became Chargé d'Affaires of the Czechoslovak Legation in London when Jan Masaryk resigned after Munich.

†Shortly after Munich the numerous small political parties were consolidated into two: the Party of National Unity comprising Agrarians, Clericals, Small Traders and Fascists, and the Party of Labour comprising Socialists and the left wing section of the National Socialists. The Communist Party was declared illegal and a Decree was issued under which the Government's sanction was required before a new party could be formed. This prohibition remained in force when the Third Republic came into existence after the war (Tr.).

his future professional work at Chicago University or other American universities which have invited him to lecture. He intends to come back again to London in July for another visit with the object of preparing further scientific publications. (I may mention in this connection that Dr. Beneš has taken over the remainder of a lease of a small house in Putney, formerly let to his nephew, B. Beneš, an official of the information section of our Ministry.) While in America he will lecture on the development of democracy and its problems from the end of the eighteenth century to the present day. He will, of course, in the future as always, stand firmly for democracy, but he will remain on the theoretical field and if possible avoid touching upon actual events.

'3. Dr. Beneš is, of course, watching the development of the international situation with great attention. Having the opportunity to watch it from the broader forum which London provides, *he does not exclude the possibility of an acute crisis already breaking out in the spring* (1939), though the present paralysis of the West may still lead to another postponement of the conflict by further concessions to the totalitarian powers. In this case the conflict could come *later in that year* or in the *following year*, but Dr. Beneš does not exclude a paralysis lasting some years. He thinks the next stage of the attack will not be in the East,* but in a solution of the problem of the Mediterranean or even possibly in connection with the question of colonies.⁵ After this the East will again come on to the list. But even if some sort of agreement should be reached now, he thinks a final solution by armed conflict is almost *inevitable*. This conflict will come under conditions which will not be so favourable for the West as last autumn when the West refused to 'fight for the Sudetenland'. It will be necessary to utilise our present grave situation and 'neutrality' by conserving our forces as much as possible not only now but also during the further development of events. He considers a German victory in an armed conflict to be out of question as everything points to America again intervening in the war. Finally, a victory for the West presents the only hope of consolidating Europe socially with the help of Britain and America and preventing either complete chaos and social disorganisation or plain bolshevism, this time a German variety. There must be no illusions about the possibility of either the world, or Europe alone, accepting a German victory and consequent domination of practically the whole of continental Europe. This means that, if necessary, the war will be a very long one or there will be a whole series of wars.

*i.e. East Europe—in other words, Poland (Tr.).

'4. If war comes, it must be clear to everybody at home that there can neither be several sides nor several parties. Immediately, from the very beginning, it must be clear to everyone that the State's watchword is "Neutrality". The conditions under which the war starts and its future development have to decide our further course of action. Every action taken abroad must be precisely co-ordinated with all requirements of the Nation and of the State at home so that the complications of the present difficult position in which the Nation finds itself may not be unduly increased. For this reason Dr. Beneš would take no arbitrary steps on his own responsibility nor act without full agreement even in such a case.

'5. Dr. Beneš does not hold himself to be a political emigrant and does not exclude from his future plans a return to his country if this should be right or suitable. He would, of course, return with the consent of the Government as he does not in the least intend to aggravate its present situation, the gravity of which he fully recognises, and he fully appreciates the activity of the Government under these conditions.

'6. He does not count on any German goodwill towards our State. Nobody can have the least confidence in any future German undertaking with regard to the whole of South-Eastern and Central Europe: Poland, Yugoslavia, and the rest. It is impossible to count on a general reconciliation or peace so long as the present divergence of regimes and the present supremacy of the dictatorships continue to exist in Europe. Tension and fresh conflicts will arise. It is therefore in the interest of the State and Nation to act under German pressure in matters of internal and foreign policy only in the case of the direst necessity so that in future such acts shall not divide us and cannot be misused against us when conditions change.

'7. In any case, in the judgment of Dr. Beneš, we are approaching a period which will bring changes of no smaller compass, or political, social and economic importance, than those brought about by the World War. This opinion is now shared by the great majority of people in competent circles in Britain and France. Whether this will happen immediately or in this or the following year, or in the years to come, it is hard to say and nobody dares to risk a definite prophecy. But it is with such apprehensions that nearly all are looking towards the future. Some are still waiting for the fall of one or other of the dictatorships owing to their internal difficulties. Dr. Beneš thinks that, without impulse from outside, their downfall cannot come now.

'8. Therefore, in the opinion of Dr. Beneš, it is not necessary for our people at home to be downcast. Uncertainty, apprehensions, fear of war and of further political, social and economic commotions are universal: in France, Britain and especially also in the totalitarian States. So far as the immediate future is concerned. Dr. Beneš does not expect any miracles, or any specially favourable surprises for us. But he thinks that, whatever happens, our State and Nation can *in the end* emerge stronger from its present difficult situation and future troubles with its chief injustices corrected even though, like the rest of Europe, it may have to undergo grave times of *occupation, unwanted war and social commotions.* Because it is politically more advanced and its social structure more balanced and because it is so mature, it will rise sooner from disorder than other Nations.'

★ ★ ★

After Munich, pressure from Berlin and the feigned or real indifference of the other European States to the fate of the Czech countries completely isolated the Prague Government. This deeply affected the feelings of all our people. Dejected by what had happened, the people felt themselves abandoned by the rest of the world and delivered into the hands of the Berlin bandits. The post-Munich Government in Prague therefore looked —rightly or wrongly—for some kind of *modus vivendi* with Nazi Berlin. Moreover, most of its members did not believe that war was really just at the gates. Dr. Chvalkovský expressed this belief with insultingly cynical scepticism. I myself did not consider the security guarantee which the Western Powers gave to Czechoslovakia during the Munich crisis to be wholly worthless. I imagined that Nazi Germany—in its own interest— would show a certain, even if small, degree of respect for this pledge. I did not expect that the Germans would try to occupy Czechoslovakia by force until the eve of a real war or after it had actually begun.

And as I believed that war would begin with an attack against Poland not sooner than in the summer of 1939, I hoped to the last that Czechoslovakia would be able to rise again, at least partially, and at once take part in that war on the side of Poland, France and Great Britain—in spite of all that had happened between us and them in 1938. I wanted to dedicate all my work abroad first and foremost to the preparations for this eventuality so that we could enter a second World War against Germany as a direct participant, as a State with a regular Government, which, if necessary, would in certain circumstances go abroad in good time and transfer at least part of our original Army to the territory of one of the neighbouring States. Too well did I know from the war of 1914–18 the Calvary of winning step-by-step international recognition *ab initio* for a new revolutionary Government and State. I did not want us to have to go through this again in a new war. Unfortunately we did not escape having to do so because I had erred in a number of these assumptions and expectations. After systematic pressure from Berlin and a base, disruptive campaign— again carried out throughout the Republic with the help of our Germans —Hitler ordered Dr. Hácha and Minister Chvalkovský to Berlin on March 14th, 1939. In their political disorientation and through downright incapacity they allowed themselves to be forced by persuasions, threats and violence to sign a proclamation by which they placed the fate of the Czech Nation in Hitler's hands and tacitly recognised the separation of Slovakia which took place at that time. Hitler then used this declaration in his own way to establish the so-called Protectorate. But already on March 14th, 1939, before Hitler began these discussions with Dr. Emil Hácha in Berlin, the German forces had begun the invasion of Czechoslovakia which by that time was already nearly defenceless. One single regiment—the 8th Silesian regiment in Místek—valiantly attempted military resistance— without orders from Prague. Alas, this was the only attempt! The simultaneous journey of Tiso* to Hitler had already been treasonably prepared some time in advance. The separation of Slovakia and the act of treason against the Republic had been deliberately planned by some Slovak separatist leaders for months with the help of the Nazis and behind the back of Prague. Thus *with their full complicity* a Slovak protectorate was also established in those critical days.

I have no intention of occupying myself here in detail with what led up to March 15th. This is not one of the matters on which I could report to the Nation myself. The whole history of March 14th and 15th, 1939, was adequately disclosed and elucidated during the trial before the National Courts in Prague and Bratislava of the members of the so-called Czech Protectorate Government and the so-called Slovak Government which took place during the second half of 1946 and the beginning of 1947. And though, in 1939, I hesitated to draw final and definitive conclusions in public about what would happen at the end of this terrible crisis and war, one substantial and fundamental question on which my opinion never changed, nor will change, was already quite clear to me: in March, 1939, Dr. E. Hácha, our highest judge and lawyer, President of the State, and Dr. Chvalkovský, its Minister of Foreign Affairs, in their culpable political

---

*Monseigneur Dr. Tiso was subsequently President of the puppet Slovak State. After the war, he was arrested and hanged for treason in April, 1947, after a trial lasting over five months (Tr.).

narrowmindedness and ignorance *sacrificed the State both internationally and internally without having any right, authorisation or mandate to do so.* Tiso and his companions *at the same time deliberately committed base treason, infamously stabbing their own Nation in the back.* There are matters of law, and principles of political morality, which must not be *sacrificed at any price, not even for the sake of any supposed or real opportunistic political advantages whatsoever, nor under the most cruel threats and pressure.* For us, one such legal right and principle was, and is, our unified national State. A signature which surrendered the freedom of the State and accepted a Czech and Slovak Protectorate can be defended, justified or excused by nobody, by nothing and never.

The same is true of all our envoys and responsible diplomatic officials who were abroad, free and able to preserve the legal existence of the Republic but who either did not dare or failed to do so. It is true that the situation of our Legations was not everywhere the same. In some places it was easier—in countries where the Governments were anti-German and had the courage immediately to reject the violent action of Germany—in other places it was difficult and in a number of States wholly impossible. *If on the one hand, full credit is due to those who knew how to defend their offices and the interests of the Republic, then, on the other hand, those who failed in one or the other respect will have to answer for their actions* and explain their behaviour to our people and Government before the appropriate body which will be set up for this purpose.* The Nation has a right to know how its accredited representatives abroad behaved.

The guarantee given us by the Western Powers during the Munich crisis to compensate us for our temporary submission to force proved to be politically worthless on March 14th and 15th. *This was the second failure to honour a pledge and international obligation.* As a reason and excuse for this fresh non-observance of a freely accepted obligation, the first reaction of Paris and London after March 15th, 1939, was to cite the actions of our own citizens: Hácha's signature and Tiso's treason. This was only a very feeble and worthless excuse.

The whole outside world, including Paris and London, had no doubt that the Anglo-French undertaking to Czechoslovakia given when she accepted the Munich treaty, had again been broken. In particular, everybody saw that this was a new gangster crime of the typical Hitler variety, a new act of banditry, a new perjury. *So the Munich 'dictate' had been destroyed by its*

*Special Courts, known as 'People's Courts' were established after the war to deal with those who were accused of acts of commission or omission from the time of Munich onwards (Tr.).

own authors, through the non-observance of the solemn obligations which all four Great Powers had voluntarily undertaken, *had forced on us by irresistible pressure and then had themselves ignored*. In the whole history of mankind it is hard to find such a complete political fiasco—the fiasco of the whole Munich policy and 'appeasement' which collapsed when the truncated Czechoslovak Republic was forcibly occupied. But also in the whole history of Europe there is scarcely a precedent for such unprincipled behaviour by the Great Powers against a small friendly Nation which had done its utmost to fulfil its *own* obligations!

I remained in London till the end of January, 1939, intently watching international relations and events. Everything confirmed my conviction that Chamberlain's 'peace with honour' and 'peace for our time' were nothing more than totally illusory catch phrases. Meanwhile I was eagerly preparing my lectures for Chicago University and at the same time maintaining my underground connection with my country. My postal correspondence with friends at home was then so large that my brother Vojta Beneš—whom I met in London at Christmas, 1938, when he returned to Prague from the United States⁶—soon had to pass on to me a warning from the Prague Government that I should not aggravate its position and that I should stop it all. In London, meanwhile, I began to resume personal contact with some of my old friends and also with a number of old political acquaintances. I do not hesitate to say that all of them without exception—even if they did not always say so—showed embarrassment and shame at what had happened and what was still happening. French diplomacy had completely faded out after Munich and virtually did not exist. It continued to deceive itself and French public opinion by concluding a treacherous and fraudulent treaty with Germany which was signed in Paris by Ribbentrop on December 6th, 1938. British diplomacy was somewhat less reckless. Not wholly trusting Germany after the occupation of Prague and noting the subsequent steps against Poland, Great Britain negotiated an alliance with Poland which was announced in the House of Commons by Chamberlain on April 6th, 1939, and with Rumania and Greece, which he announced on April 13th, 1939.

Unfortunately, the actual military preparations of the two Great Powers for the steadily approaching war were of no great value—all the less so because they were accompanied by discussions for a fresh credit and economic agreement with Germany on March 15th, 1939, carried on by the President of the Board of Trade, Mr. Hudson. All the European dictatorships, Beck's in Poland, Metaxas's in Greece, Carol's in Rumania were to be helped. We are glad they got it and do not grudge it to them in the least. We simply remember with bitter irony that, only a short time before, it had been thought necessary for the Republic of Masaryk alone to be sacrificed to Hitler to purchase a few months of apparent peace with the result that all the smaller States of Europe had become gravely demoralised!

I announced that my university lectures in Chicago would start in February, 1939 and I made preparations accordingly for my departure to America. As I was almost certain that the general European crisis would begin about, and in any case not later than, the end of the summer, I booked a return passage on the ship in which we were leaving for America. At the end of January I was ready to leave for the United States.

My wife, Bohuš Beneš and I went on board the American ship *George Washington* at Portsmouth on February 2nd, 1939, for our voyage over the Atlantic. I finished my university lectures on the ship and considered the plan for my whole work in the United States. In America, as in London, I wanted to move very cautiously at the start. But what happened when I reached New York changed this plan considerably. Even before our arrival in New York harbour I was surrounded by a number of interviewers and journalists from New York. I was almost forced to speak on the American radio from the ship and to my surprise the police and civic authorities took me straight from the ship to the City Hall, to Mayor La Guardia.

And here was a fresh surprise: we were cheered by crowds of people in the streets, in the packed City Hall where La Guardia welcomed us in an emotional speech on the theme: 'Four representatives of two decadent European democracies and two violent dictatorships meeting at Munich decided that instead of politics they would perform common butchery. They laid a small, fettered State on their operating table and then with merciless treachery began to cut it up. Today we welcome the President of this State in New York. We assure him that we have not forgotten this act of butchery by the European Great Powers, that we value him according to his merits and that therefore here in the United States we will always assist his brave Nation. And we declare that this Nation will soon again rise to freedom and that its President will again return to his liberated country.'

This speech caused immediate excitement and on the next day alarm in the press. I saw that, if I wanted to carry out my original plan, it would not be possible to stay long in New York. Such a reception had encouraged us very much, but on the other hand it had for the time being made things difficult for me because I had to answer in the same or similar vein and that was not my exact intention. I therefore went on to Chicago as soon as I could. But there, too, we received much the same kind of welcome—especially from our compatriots.

I hurried through these demonstrations during the first few days of my stay in Chicago and then withdrew into greater privacy, preferring to invite important people one at a time and explain to them in detail the impressions, opinions and plans with which I had come from Europe. Then I contacted the University more closely, met its President, R. Hutchins, and a number of other colleagues (professors Quincy Wright, Ch. Merriam, Bernadotte Schmitt, Harper and others), all of whom showed great interest and real friendship. Then I began my university lectures.

While I was in London I had already accepted a number of offers to lecture at various universities as well as to important societies and organisations, political and non-political institutions, scientific and learned societies. All these lectures dealt with such problems as European democracy and its development, European dictatorships, social and economic conditions, questions of peace and war in Europe. For the time being I refused to speak about Munich. But such lectures gave me sufficient opportunity to stress the dangers of European developments, to warn that war was coming, to assess the harmful nature of European diplomacy and to show how fatal was the road along which the world had been travelling since Munich.

I remained in Chicago from the beginning of February until July, 1939. During this time my lecture tour took me right across North America from West to East and from North to South. I visited and lectured at all the important universities. A number of universities offered me honorary degrees, a number of others tried to tempt me to leave Chicago University. My wife and I visited the birthplaces or graves of George Washington, Jefferson, Lincoln, Wilson and wherever we went there were huge meetings and demonstrations at which not seldom ten, fifteen, even twenty thousand people took part. It was an immense work of propaganda for peace, democracy and Czechoslovakia; against what had happened in Munich. Only then I did fully understand how great were the moral assets which the Republic had built up during the twenty years of our existence and during our fight for democracy in 1938 by our faith in and fidelity to Masaryk's democracy, our endeavour to save peace, our dignified attitude towards Germany and Nazism. I confess to have made the fullest use of these moral and political assets during my six months in North America.

The fact that I had settled in Chicago—almost in the centre of the

United States—and that I had accepted a professorship at the university, won me access to the scientific and learned circles of the United States and was of real importance. At the same time it meant that I was right in the centre of the life of our compatriots* which automatically enabled me to help them towards a correct orientation during the coming war.

Next to the Munich period, this was one of the most active and at the same time one of the most fatiguing periods of my political life. But the moment war began, it bore the richest fruit in every direction. I would never have believed that all classes of the American population could show so much real interest in us and that such true selfless sympathy would be shown to a small State crushed by the policy of Munich.

There would be no end to telling all our experiences and how day after day in all American circles our hopes were revived and we were encouraged to fight for the liberty of our country: among scholars and scientists and in the universities, among workers and in other political circles, in the churches and religious centres, in social and economic organisations—the least they demanded was to hear my authentic views of what to expect in the immediate future—in the expert political circles of the two leading political parties, Democrats and Republicans, and last but not least in all official circles.

All this pointed to one conclusion: *in such conditions our cause cannot be lost and if within a measurable space of time a conflict in Europe should arise—* and it surely will—*we must do all in our power to win these great moral and political forces in the United States to the side of the victory of our truth†* and *never lose them again !*

2. *First Consequences of March 15th—Protests to the Powers and the League of Nations*

March 15th, 1939, which found me already in the United States, was, above all, a new and very hard blow for Great Britain and France, both morally and materially. Munich and the blunders of the Munich policy cost no other countries more dearly than it did these two States—unless it were Poland and Yugoslavia. I believe that in the final analysis it was more costly to them than to Czechoslovakia. In spite of the injustice which had been committed against us by nearly all the world, we had kept our honour and our rights and claims morally intact ! We had warned the

---

*About a third of the 1,500,000 people of Czech and Slovak origin in the United States live in Chicago (Tr.).

†The motto of the Czechoslovak Republic is: 'Truth prevails'. (Tr.).

whole world in time, officially and with the greatest emphasis, and we had mobilised our armed forces twice for our defence!

Alas, we had remained deserted and totally isolated in the hands of our ferocious and barbarous enemy.*

But the occupation of Prague was the real beginning of the second World War —March 15th, 1939, had to lead to it in the end. In spite of the desperate and pusillanimous efforts of official Paris and London, the world could not remain silent any more. And the weight of the war—which had been delayed by such dreadful (moral and material) sacrifices—was to be borne first and foremost by Paris and London!

At that time I was already in Chicago and beginning to lecture at the University. I got the first news of these tragic happenings on the morning of March 15th. It was a terrible blow for me: the whole foundation of my further plans in case of war had been already destroyed in time of peace. Independence, statehood, unity with the Slovaks, all seemed to be lost. The Germans in our country were masters everywhere and of everything! And the uncertainty about what the rest of the world, our people at home, our representatives abroad would do! And above all: what would happen if Hitler should delay the next blow against Poland and we would have to wait for years for the general war against Germany? Would our people at home hold out in that hell? Would they remain strong in their resistance and morally untouched?

What a dreadful prospect!

I considered for a long time what to do next. I could think of nobody else who in this moment should and could raise his voice in protest and act freely in the name of the Nation except the second President of the Republic who from this moment was truly in exile and who, through what had just happened at home, was again quite free to speak and act. By Hitler's crime, by this fresh British and French failure to keep their pledged word and by Hácha's signature to the protectorate I felt freed from all earlier obligations which I had temporarily imposed myself and from all that I had been forced to take part in by violence and pressure since September 19th, 1938. All these ceased to operate! The so-called *First Republic again existed legally!* And its voice had to make itself heard at whatever price!

This finally was my decision.

In this sense—though at that moment such things could not be spoken

---

*This is a tacit refutation of the Soviet Government's assertion that it had offered help which Dr. Beneš had refused. When this book was published in Prague, President Beneš was not able to speak openly on this subject (Tr.).

of fully and openly—I sent telegrams on March 16th to President Roose-velt, Prime Ministers Chamberlain and Daladier, to Maxim Litvinov and the President of the League of Nations' Council. I advocated the point of view that I had a right to send these protests because, as the second legally elected President of the Czechoslovak Republic, I had been forced by German violence to resign my office and to go into exile in defiance of right, justice and the Constitution and also because the events themselves prevented any other real and unfettered representative of the Czecho-slovak State and Nation from taking action.

The telegram which was sent on the morning of March 16th, 1939, read as follows:

'The Czech and Slovak people are victims of a great international crime. The people of Czechoslovakia cannot protest today and because of the happenings of the last month cannot defend themselves. Therefore I as ex-President of Czechoslovakia, address this solemn protest to you:

'Last September, the Franco-British proposals and a few days after-wards, the Munich decision, were presented to me. Both these docu-ments contained the promise of the guarantee of the integrity and security of Czechoslovak territory. Both these documents asked for unheard-of sacrifices by my people in the interest of European peace—these sacrifices were made by the people of Czechoslovakia.

'Nevertheless, one of the Great Powers which signed the Agreement of Munich is now dividing our territory, is occupying it with its army and is establishing a "protectorate" under threat of force and military violence.

'Before the conscience of the world and before history I am obliged to proclaim that the Czechs and Slovaks will never accept this unbear-able imposition on their sacred rights. And they will never cease their struggle until these rights are reinstated for their beloved country. And I entreat your Government to refuse to recognise this crime and to assume the consequences which today's tragic situation in Europe and in the world urgently requires.

'I am also sending this telegram to the President of the Council of the League of Nations referring to the relevant articles of the Covenant of the League of Nations, especially Article 10. I am convinced that no Member of the League of Nations will recognise this crime, and I hope that all Members of the League will in due time fulfil their obligations arising out of the Covenant.'[1]

Three days later—on March 19th, 1939—I made my broadcast speech to the American Nation from Chicago University which had asked me to do so from its platform. In this address I gave a short survey of the September (1938) crisis and declared among other things:

'Five months ago at the time of the so-called September crisis, pressure was exercised on Czechoslovakia to make an unheard-of sacrifice of its territory in the interest of peace. Irresistible pressure was exercised on our people not to fight for their liberty, independence and territorial integrity and thereby to save all the rest of the world from war. General pressure was brought against this small State to sacrifice itself for the peace of the world. And this people really sacrificed themselves. In return they got an assurance and a guarantee that the integrity of what remained of their national territory would be maintained. This small Nation made the sacrifice—as is well known—under pressure of the Munich decision to which it submitted only because four European Great Powers had signed in Munich an obligation to guarantee the security of the new State.

'But in spite of all these sacrifices, of all this self-restraint, in spite of all promises and guarantees by the Powers which had solemnly signed the Munich Agreement and in spite of Germany's promise to make no further territorial demands in Europe; in spite of the fact that by the Munich treaty and its consequences more than 1,200,000 citizens of Czechoslovak nationality had come within the boundaries of foreign States, the German Government has brutally violated its promises and obligations, invaded Czechoslovak territory, established a so-called protectorate and its rule of terror, secret police, political and religious hatred and persecution and the system of concentration camps, and after suppressing all freedom of the press, of speech and conscience and after establishing its Government of violence and inhumanity in this way, it has cynically claimed to have done all this in the name of peace in Europe.

'But I beg you not to forget that the events about which I am speaking do not concern Europe alone nor the nations of Central, Southern and Eastern Europe. They concern France and Britain, too, the Scandinavian Nations and also the United States. Nor is this all: the whole world is not only in danger of war but also in danger of the extermination of all concepts of real human morality, freedom, honour and decency. This is what is at stake! A society which goes on tolerating this state of affairs will be annihilated and will disappear.'

After declaring that the State, the Czechoslovak Republic, continued legally to exist, that German brutality could not annihilate it, I concluded as follows:

'I am convinced that my Nation, going through this fight courageously and proudly as ever in the past, will come out of it victoriously with the sympathy, appreciation and love of all the decent people of the world on its side. It has done so several times in its troubled history and there is no place more apt for this declaration of mine than the free country of Washington and Lincoln.'*⁸

In the morning of March 17th—a day after I had sent my telegram of protest to President Roosevelt from Chicago—Under-Secretary of State, Sumner Welles made an official statement which was announced to me early in the morning of the same day by telephone from Washington. In this he declared that:

*The full English text of this address is not available. But the following additional extract is of interest:

'Do not believe that it was a question of self-determination for a minority. From the beginning it has been a battle for the existence of the State. A dictatorship cannot tolerate freedom. A dictatorship can permit no liberty, no freedom, no democracy in its vicinity. It was and is and will be a battle for existence by a free Nation opposed by a totalitarian State which denies freedom. The latest move of the German dictatorship in the occupation of Czechoslovakia proves it.

'This last tragic event must now finally open the eyes of the whole world to the fact that the Czechoslovak Nation was from its beginning condemned by the dictators. With the subjugation of Czechoslovakia, freedom is being guillotined. And nobody in the United States or in the world should forget that the regime which is now attempting to kill freedom in Czechoslovakia is based on these three groups of conceptions:

'First of all, the regime does not recognise any obligations unless it is expedient for it to do so; it will fulfil no promise; it will respect no law; it will keep no pledge; it will show no tolerance, either political or religious; it will admit no right to property either of State or of individuals unless it considers it expedient to do so. And for every crime against human decency it will always discover a pretext.

'Second, the only principle on which this regime is based is the rule of force and violence. This regime can maintain no respect for the idea of right. It preaches that the only right is might—force and violence. If you look back through the pages of history you will find that this is the system which was always termed the age of barbarism. Today it would rule the world as the age of brute force.

'The third basis of this regime is the simple use of the old slogan "the end justifies the means". And in their minds that end means one thing only—the success of their rule of brute force, which is combined with the propaganda of lies which they have elaborated both internally and internationally as a weapon, and as a most important factor in maintaining this regime, and in deceiving the world as to their real intent.

'This whole theory has been made into a State system, a system which today undertakes to subjugate Czechoslovakia, a system which has begun to rule throughout my country and which tomorrow will extend its terrorism still farther.

'And the people of the United States and of what remains of free Europe must be prepared for a continuation and extension of this rule of brute force.'

F

'The Government of the United States has on frequent occasions stated its conviction that only through international support of a programme of order based upon law can world peace be assured.

'This Government, founded upon and dedicated to the principles of human liberty and of democracy, cannot refrain from making known this country's condemnation of the acts which have resulted in the temporary extinguishment of a free and independent people with whom, from the day when the Republic of Czechoslovakia attained its independence, the people of the United States have maintained especially close and friendly relations.

'It is manifest that acts of wanton lawlessness and of arbitrary force are threatening world peace and the very structure of modern civilisation.

'The imperative need for observance of the principles advocated by this Government has been clearly demonstrated by the developments which have taken place during the past three days.'

The Government of the United States included this declaration in its official Note of March 20th, sent to the German Chargé d'Affaires, refusing to accept the German Note of March 17th, 1939, which announced to the Government of the United States the establishment of a German Protectorate in Bohemia and Moravia.

On March 27th, President Roosevelt sent the following letter in answer to my telegram:

'DEAR DR. BENEŠ,

I have received your telegram of March 16th, 1939, regarding the tragic events of last week in Central Europe. I have followed these happenings with deep concern. While the Government of the United States has observed that the provinces of Bohemia and Moravia have been occupied by German military authorities and are now under the *de facto* administration of German authorities, it has not recognised the legal status of that situation. I need hardly add that I deeply sympathise with the Czechoslovak people in the unfortunate circumstances in which for the time being they find themselves.

Very sincerely yours,
FRANKLIN D. ROOSEVELT.'

Chamberlain answered on March 20th in a short telegram in which he referred to the fact that he had expressed the view of His Majesty's Government on the German invasion of Czechoslovakia in his speech at Birmingham on March 17th, 1939. On March 18th, Maxim Litvinov sent to the Czechoslovak Minister in Moscow a copy of the Soviet Note which had been delivered on the same day to the German Ambassador. In this Note he very decidedly rejected the whole of Nazi Germany's activities against Czechoslovakia.[9] From Daladier—in conformity with what had become his 'established tradition' in Czechoslovak affairs—there was no answer.

The British and French Governments answered the German Notes announcing the establishment of a German Protectorate in the Czech countries and in Slovakia only after the first step had been taken by the United States. Their official Notes, dated March 18th, rejected the German action and proceedings as contrary to the principles of international law and signed treaties.[10] The British answer stated expressly that H.M. Government were forced to consider the events of the past days to be a clear violation of the Munich Agreement and of the spirit in which the signatories of this Agreement had engaged themselves to co-operate for the peaceful solution of all European questions. The Note protested also against the changes carried out in Czechoslovakia by the military action of Germany and declared that in the opinion of the British Government these changes were lacking in any legal foundation whatsoever.[11]

Immediately after these events we agreed with Jan Masaryk and Envoy Vladimír Hurban on the next step. Soon after Munich, Masaryk had resigned from his office as Czechoslovak Minister in London. Just then he was on a lecturing tour in the United States and after the March events, with my approval, he immediately returned to London to work there. Meanwhile in London, K. Lisický, Counsellor of the Legation, Colonel Kalla, and Dr. Jan Gerke, Secretary of the Legation, in conjunction with the Foreign Office, had in critical days and under difficult conditions saved our Legation and had immediately reported this fact to us in Chicago. Afterwards, until the end of the war, Masaryk had the greatest and most successful share in our common resistance activity in Great Britain and America where he knew better than anybody else both the conditions and the people with influence. He did great service there for our national cause.

Vladimír Hurban, the Czechoslovak Minister in Washington, very decidedly and with the right political perception of the whole situation, refused to deliver the Washington Legation to the Nazi authorities on March 16th. He came at once to Chicago to visit me and placed himself and his office at the disposal of the second President of the Republic for the continuation of the fight. During all this crisis and also later on during the war he carried on his work in the United States very efficiently and success-fully, truly patriotically and in faithfulness to the Republic regardless of all consequences. Working very devotedly with him and afterwards with me were Dr. J. Papánek, the second loyal and unyielding Slovak in America, our Consul in Pittsburgh, and many others. In Chicago we immediately established the first provisional political centre of resistance which for the time being we called 'Action Abroad'.

Soon afterwards the leading representatives of the American Czechs and Slovaks in New York, Chicago, Cleveland, Pittsburgh and in Texas—the greatest part of the Czechoslovak community in the United States— began, with our approval and within the framework of their legal obliga- tions as American citizens, to concentrate all the endeavours of their central organisations in America in support of the new movement for the liberation of Czechoslovakia. They appealed to me to take the leadership of the second resistance liberation at once.[12] In London, Paris, Poland, Moscow and a number of other places similar movements began to form, too—spontaneously or prompted by us.

The organised work of the second resistance movement had begun.

From April, 1939, onward we gradually succeeded in uniting our main forces and organisations in the United States and Canada. We also imme- diately contacted most of the Czechoslovak diplomatic and consular missions—as many as had survived—and tried to unite for the approaching European war everything that had remained of the Czechoslovak State apparatus abroad in all other States.[13] From the United States—via London, Paris and Belgrade—we also established new and better con- nections with our country—connections, which, by the way, were never interrupted afterwards—and we urged *that the greatest possible number of soldiers and officers should go abroad without delay*. In particular, and in reply to an inquiry from home, I agreed to the coming of Generals Sergěj Ingr and Rudolf Viest.* Our political functionaries in Paris, who had their own connection with our homeland, were sending similar requests to their contacts at home.

An event of exceptional importance for us was the fact that a whole group of officers of the Czechoslovak military intelligence service in the Ministry of National Defence escaped from Prague to London with the principal part of their working material on the eve of the Nazi occupation. All these officers placed themselves at my disposal in a letter sent to

*General Ingr afterwards became Commander-in-Chief of the Czechoslovak Forces in Great Britain. After the war he was retired and became Minister at The Hague. After the Communist *coup d'état* in February, 1948, he remained abroad. General Viest was para- chuted into Slovakia at the time of Slovak rising in 1944. He was captured by the Germans and declarations made by him after his capture suggest that he thought he had been betrayed by the Russians. He was later released by the Americans who rejected the Czechoslovak Government's request to hand him over for trial as a collaborator (Tr.).

Chicago shortly after their arrival in London (March 14th, 1939). Later, under Colonel Fr. Moravec, they were to maintain an extremely active and never-interrupted contact with our country. Their work for the common cause began at once in co-operation with the British, and later with the French, Army. We considered the new status in Czechoslovakia after March 15th to be legally a state of war between Czechoslovakia and Germany. So we immediately began to work and fight against the bandits who had invaded our country.

On May 23rd the Council of the League of Nations met in Geneva for the first time after the German invasion of Czechoslovakia. I availed myself of this opportunity to register a second solemn protest against the German occupation. On May 13th I sent from Pittsburgh, where I had arrived on a lecturing tour, identical telegrams to the General Secretary of the League of Nations, J. Avenol, and to the Foreign Ministers of the three European Great Powers which were members of the Council of the League—Lord Halifax, G. Bonnet and V. Molotov. The text of the protest was:

'On March 16th after the military invasion of Czechoslovakia by Germany I sent you a declaration of protest and asked you to lay this protest before the President of the Council so that the proper steps could be taken in this matter. In view of the fact that the Council of the League of Nations is about to meet I beg to repeat this request adding at the same time this further protest:

'In consequence of the military invasion of Czechoslovakia and the establishment of a so-called German protectorate over the Bohemian and Moravian provinces, and over Slovakia, the Hungarian Government has occupied by force and at variance with its earlier obligations part of Slovakia and Subcarpathian Ruthenia and has forced the State and local authorities which owing to the crippling of Czechoslovakia were unable to resist successfully to consent to the occupation of the whole territory of Subcarpathian Ruthenia and part of Eastern Slovakia.

'In view of the fact that the principal Articles of the Covenant of the League of Nations as well as the commonly recognised principles of international law have thus been violated so shamelessly, in view of the fact that the Council of the League of Nations has been entrusted, by a special treaty guaranteeing local autonomy to Subcarpathian Ruthenia in the framework of the Czechoslovak Republic, with the supervision of the accomplishment of this guarantee—a right and duty accepted by the Council of the League of Nations and accomplished successfully and conscientiously for twenty years—in view of the fact that not only the rights of the Czechoslovak Republic and the Subcarpathian people but also the rights and duties of the Council of the League of Nations have thus been illegally destroyed and that this use of force must not be tolerated by any member of the League if a fresh humiliation of the League is not to ensue, and in view of the fact that this is a new blow directed at the League's existence, I am addressing myself to the President of the Council in my function as former President of the Czechoslovak Republic with the respectful request that this new crime against international law should not remain unnoticed and that with regard to the violated articles of the Treaty the matter should be put before the Council so that the necessary steps may be undertaken.

'I would like to add, that Czechoslovakia, *though legally continuing to exist*, has at present—in view of the fact of its being subjected to a rule of oppression and violence—no possibility to maintain its rights fully in Geneva. Therefore I hope it will be permitted to the former President of the Czechoslovak Republic who in the name of Czechoslovakia has co-operated with the League of Nations for seventeen years, who is devoted to the cause of maintaining and consolidating international peace and who has been elected President of the Assembly and on many occasions President of the Council of the League, to appeal to the Council asking not only for the protection of the rights of Czechoslovakia but also for protection of the rights of the League of Nations.

DR. EDUARD BENEŠ,
Professor of Chicago University.'

At the first confidential meeting of the Council of the League of Nations, M. Avenol announced that my telegram had arrived at Geneva. But he refused to have it officially discussed in the Council on the ground that the protest had been submitted in an irregular manner, that is to say, not by the Czechoslovak or another Government, but by a 'private individual'. The majority of the Council accepted this seemingly legal, but extremely unjust and humiliating point of view which was contrary to the spirit of the Covenant and especially to the rights and duties of the League of Nations. This was undoubtedly a case which fundamentally concerned the League of Nations itself, especially the Hungarian occupation of Subcarpathian Ruthenia of which the Geneva institution was co-guarantor. But the Soviet Ambassador in London, Ivan Maisky, acting on instructions from Moscow, told the meeting that in these circumstances the Soviet Government accepted the duty of submitting the protest to the League itself. The General Secretary was thus forced to place the Czechoslovak protest before the Council of the League for regular discussion.

In consequence of this discussion, our protest was to have come before the Council and Assembly of the League of Nations in September, 1939. But by September the European situation had completely changed. Germany had invaded Poland. Great Britain and France had declared war on Germany with all the consequences these events entailed. Finally the Soviet-German treaty was also signed. So neither the occupation of Czechoslovakia nor any of these new great events were ever discussed at all in Geneva. By then, the League of Nations was already lapsing into helplessness.

Immediately the Germans occupied our country, thousands of our officers and soldiers began to escape from Czechoslovakia going first to Poland, Hungary, Yugoslavia, Rumania, Turkey, etc., and thence to France. Our Paris Legation negotiated an agreement with the French Government which enabled our soldiers temporarily to enter the Foreign Legion so that in the event of war they could become the nucleus of an independent Czechoslovak Army which would be the legal continuation of the Czechoslovak Army at home. So all our *military* preparations were automatically centred on Paris.

At the same time there were preparations for special Czechoslovak military action in Poland under our Legation in Warsaw and our Consulate in Cracow in collaboration with General L. Prchala and other Czechoslovak officers who had succeeded in crossing the frontier into Poland in time. According to our global plan they were to be part of our political and military organisation in London and Paris. When the tension between Poland and Germany increased, General Sergěj Ingr from London and General Prchala in Warsaw tried to come to an agreement with the Polish Government. But even in those moments so full of fate for both Poland and ourselves the Polish Government was clearly determined to continue Colonel Beck's policy against Czechoslovakia and was boycotting our resistance movement in Western Europe and me personally. It would negotiate only with those of our people who declared themselves to be opposed to me and who offered a prospect of standing for a future policy which would almost have made us tributary to Poland. Accordingly, after the German invasion of Poland had begun on September 3rd, 1939, and after preliminary discussions with some of our political and military functionaries (chiefly with General Prchala), the Polish President issued a decree in Warsaw in which he agreed to the establishment of 'Czech' and 'Slovak' (not Czechoslovak) legions on Polish territory as parts of the *Polish* army. Without reference to us, General L. Prchala was then charged by *Polish military authorities* with the organisation of these legions.[14]

Meanwhile, after the Germans occupied Prague, the number of our political workers who began to assemble in Paris, London and the United States for the fight for the liberation of Czechoslovakia was growing daily and it was further strengthened by refugees who succeeded in escaping to Poland, Yugoslavia or Rumania. Among them were former ministers, deputies, senators, professors and especially officers and soldiers as well as the envoys and officials of those of our legations and consulates which had not been handed over to the Germans and the members of which were gradually reporting for the fight against Germany.

I have already mentioned that we had decided in Chicago on the first extensive and systematically organised action which should be taken against Germany when war broke out. Another important resolution of our American compatriots in this direction followed between April 18th and 20th, 1939, at a conference of the chief Czech and Slovak organisations in America—the Czech National Association, the Slovak National Association, and the Association of Czech Catholics—which met in Chicago and resolved to combine their forces for a new fight in a new joint organisation, the *Czechoslovak National Council of America*. Under the chairmanship of Professor J. Zmrhal they immediately afterwards offered their devoted and patriotic support to our liberation movement in so far as was compatible with the law and their duties as citizens of the United States. This was the first, speedy and successful beginning of the work of our American compatriots. Within one single month from March 15th, we had accomplished the unification of our main forces in America. In the first World War it had taken not months but years for this stage to be reached.

Our first and foremost task was to give our people some fundamental concepts for their fight against Germany—a programme which would be the basis of our whole fight. This was accomplished at the meeting of American citizens of Czechoslovak descent held in Chicago on June 8th, 1939, at the suggestion of our American Legionaries of World War I. War had not yet begun and American public opinion, as well as official Government circles, was very sensitive about acts which could be interpreted as agitation for war or for any other form of conflict with the totalitarian dictatorships. I had therefore to be extremely reserved and cautious in my remarks.

Nevertheless, even at that meeting I was able to say at least the most urgent things. I stressed that it would be a grave error to look at the events in Czechoslovakia which followed the Munich crisis and the German occupation without also having regard to what had happened and was happening all over the world. The European politicians had failed to assess the consequences of the development which began in 1932 when first Germany, later Italy and finally Japan definitely decided to annihilate the Peace of Versailles. What happened to us in 1938-39 was only the beginning and a small item among these consequences which were still going on and would continue to do so.

But, I went on, we were not bound by the Munich 'Diktat' and we had not and would not recognise the German occupation. We did not accept the Vienna arbitration award which took away further territory from us and which Hungary had recklessly violated as soon as it suited her. We did not and would not recognise March 14th and 15th: I pointed out in this connection that the occupation of the Republic on March 15th had not been recognised by any country except some of Germany's most intimate allies. *The Czechoslovak Republic therefore legally continued to exist,* and our international rights and obligations as between other States and ourselves were also still valid.

I further stressed that we could regard all this as constituting *a substantial legal basis for our struggle;*[16] that the negotiations before or after March 15th between Berlin and Prague which led to the establishment of the Protectorate over Czech and Slovak territory lacked any legal basis as they had been forced on us by violence and barbaric threats. The acts in question were simply acts against the Constitution, against the laws and were legally invalid because no representative of the so-called Second Republic had been authorized to perform them.

At the end of my speech I addressed a few special words to the Slovaks—whose compatriots at home had been cut off from the Czechs by the machinations of Hitler and the treacherous Tiso Government. I stressed that this too was treasonable, unconstitutional and illegal and that *we therefore regarded it as invalid.*

On this basis, I concluded, we would begin the fight for the liberation of our State and Nation. From this, we would draw all the legal and political conclusions!

3. *My Conversation with Franklin D. Roosevelt*

Before I left the United States, I visited Washington and, on May 28th, 1939, had a long conversation with President F. D. Roosevelt.

Our discussions came about in a peculiar manner. At the end of April, 1939, in Chicago I received a visit from an old friend from World War I, Hamilton Fish Armstrong, editor of the review *Foreign Affairs* and at that time President Roosevelt's regular adviser in matters of foreign policy. He was also the author of a good and analytically written book on the events which led to Munich.[16] He and I discussed the situation in Europe and when I had explained my views about the further course of events he insisted that I should go to see President Roosevelt as soon as possible. He offered to arrange a meeting. Some days later he told me in Chicago that I would shortly be received by Roosevelt in the President's private summer home and that for the time being this fact should remain entirely confidential.

I readily followed Armstrong's directions and Roosevelt then fixed May 28th, 1939, for the meeting. I was to go for lunch and the afternoon to Hyde Park some 70 kms. north of New York. I was accompanied by my American secretary, Ed. B. Hitchcock, the former European correspondent of *The Christian Science Monitor* of Boston. We stayed with Roosevelt for about three and a half hours during which time I had one of my most important conversations of post-Munich times. I had already met Roosevelt in World War I, when he was Under-Secretary of the Navy and in 1919 I negotiated with him the use of American ships for the repatriation of our soldiers from Siberia. He now showed himself to be an educated and far-sighted politician extraordinarily well-informed on world problems and on questions of European policy as well as on the general bearing of the Munich crisis. He was also very well informed on the whole about questions concerning the Soviet Union. He knew and understood its chief problems and, in particular, had long ago realised that it was absolutely necessary to solve the problem of bringing the Soviet Union into the framework of international policy if world peace was to be advanced and if the dictatorial regimes in Europe were to be defeated. Holding this point of view, he looked very critically on the France of Daladier and the Great Britain of Chamberlain. He saw very clearly why these two countries had decided to follow the policy of 'appeasement' and then of Munich. He rejected this uncompromisingly. Especially he condemned their impossibly opportunistic and undemocratic behaviour towards our country.

Roosevelt received me most cordially, greeted me as the President of the Republic and added that for him there was no Munich so that to him I was still the President. I saw at once that I could speak quite frankly and with full confidence. The conversation which followed was a determining factor in the framing of the whole of my future policy during the war. We spoke first of Munich. He asked me a number of questions. He wanted to know many details and some of the personal factors. He stressed especially that we had done well not to let ourselves be provoked into war with Hitler in the circumstances which existed in 1938. He considered that we would have suffered dreadfully. Western Europe did not want to help and America could not have done so. If the Soviet Union had intervened alone, he was not at all sure in the political conditions of those times how the whole affair would have ended.* Neither Western Europe nor America were in any sense prepared for the conflict either morally or materially. Indeed, Hitler would perhaps have attained his final goal more easily and sooner—at least temporarily.[17]

Then followed the most dramatic part of the conversation. Roosevelt asked me directly:

'Tell me frankly how you envisage the possible course of the political situation in Europe and how you think events will progressively develop.'

'War in Europe is to be expected already this year,' I replied. 'In my judgment it may break out any day after July 15th. Hitler is preparing for war very intensively and wants it. He will most certainly provoke it.'

'My military experts expect it later—not before the harvest has finished. But how do you imagine that Hitler will start the war?'

'Undoubtedly by an attack on Poland.'

'What will be its course?'

'War with Poland will move very fast. It will be a real "Blitzkrieg." Within two weeks the Germans will be in Warsaw and the whole Polish campaign will not last more than six weeks.'

The President expressed astonishment that I should take such a pessimistic view of the Polish capacity to resist. I justified my attitude by my knowledge of the thorough preparations of the German dictatorship and the total unpreparedness, lack of seriousness and empty megalomania of the Polish dictatorship which I had observed very clearly during the Munich crisis. I argued further that all Germans would march with enthusiasm against Poland. Against us this would not yet have been the case—some were still hesitating. And it would then have been easier for Western Europe too, because the Soviet Union would have intervened at the same time.

'And how do you envisage the further course of events?'

'Britain and France will be in the war. But this will not prevent the fall of Poland, because they too are insufficiently prepared. But Belgium and the Netherlands will also be involved in the war, and it seems Switzerland as well. That at least, is what I hear from Europe—direct from Germany.'

*The Soviet Union's treaty obligations to help Czechoslovakia only became operative if France acted too (Tr.).

My opinion was based partly on earlier reports about Hitler's plans, his concept of the 'Blitzkrieg' and his views about political and military morale and partly on direct reports received from Europe during the preceding weeks.

'And then?'

'It is necessary to reckon with the fact that after Czechoslovakia and Poland all other Central European States as far as Greece will also fall. Hitler will thus come face to face with the Soviet Union. His real objective is the Ukraine and the definite pushing back of the Soviet Union as far as possible to the East. I am fully confident that Great Britain will oppose this. What will happen in France, I cannot say. But I hope that in the end France, too, will pull itself together for real resistance.'

'What do you think the Soviet Union will do?'

'In the end it too will enter the war.'

'On whose side?'

'Of course, on *our* side. War between the Soviet Union and Germany is sooner or later quite inevitable. This springs necessarily from the Nazi and the Communist ideologies, from Hitler's conception of German national interests, from his concrete plans and from the character of the people who are in power in Germany.'

The President agreed. But then he asked me a number of questions about the Soviet Union: Whether the Soviet Union would be able to fight; whether its army and especially the Soviet officers' corps were in good shape—as to this he said he had a number of contradictory reports—whether the Soviet war industry and communications were functioning properly and whether they had enough technical equipment, etc.

I gave Roosevelt a long account of my experiences in the Soviet Union during my journey in 1935 including what I had seen myself and what had been reported to me in pre-Munich days by our soldiers about its latest preparations. I ended by expressing my opinion that it would be a *long* war, an all-in war, a really horrible war.

Roosevelt commented on my remarks and rounded them off with a series of comments and views of his own, based partly on information he had received and partly on his own experiences especially on the talks he had had with various Soviet representatives including Litvinov who, as People's Commissar for Foreign Affairs, had visited him during the negotiations in Washington for the normalisation of Soviet-American relations.

In the end we reached the most delicate question of all: what would the United States do? The President asked my opinion and I answered frankly:

'I think the United States will also have to enter the war in any case. Europe alone cannot win the war against Hitler. And even if the United States does not enter the fight against Nazism, Nazism will attack the United States. It is necessary not to forget that in Hitler and his companions, the rest of the world is up against real madmen who are out of their minds and capable of anything. Besides, the decay of the Western democracies has gone so far that, without the help of America, Western Europe cannot be rescued from present-day Germany.'

'How do you think America could help?' asked Roosevelt ultimately.

'Europe will need the unconditional help of your great financial aid. It will also need your industry, supplies of arms and ammunition, food and, of course, your ships. It cannot manage without these. I cannot say whether it will be also necessary to send soldiers. I do not know. I hope that perhaps they will not be needed.'

Finally we turned to our Czechoslovak affairs. I explained to the President that immediately war broke out I intended to establish a political and military organisation from our refugees, emigrants and all those who would be leaving our country. I said that at the proper moment I intended to establish an Army and a Provisional Government and thus to repeat in a new form what we had done in the First World War under the leadership of Masaryk. I added that at the outset our greatest difficulty would be the question of how to finance the whole movement.[18] I ended this lengthy explanation with the statement that when the question of recognising our revolutionary Government arose, I would turn for help to the President himself. And I added that I hoped my request would not be refused.

The President asked me to give him the chief points of my exposé in writing. He expressed the hope that events would take a satisfactory course and said:

'We have helped you once. We will help you again. Do remain in contact with me and let me know how your affairs progress.'

Then he asked for more detailed information of the circumstances in which the Masaryk Government had been recognised by the United States in World War I.

I left Roosevelt with the conviction that he fully understood the whole problem of the approaching war crisis in Europe; that he was aware of the part which the United States would necessarily be called upon to play; that he understood the problem of the two European dictatorships and also the position of the Soviet Union. From various allusions, especially while he was telling me in some detail of his talks with Litvinov, I realised that he was also aware of the universal social crisis which would inevitably spring from a new war and why therefore the Western democracies of Europe were afraid to go to war against Hitler at the side of the Soviet Union. Finally, I was sure that he would help us in every way he could.

As I have already said, this conversation was decisive—it contributed to the forming of my whole future policy which I built up from the beginning of World War II and during its progress. Before I left the President I again thanked him for the American attitude after the Nazi invasion of Czechoslovakia and asked him to maintain the same attitude in the future whatever might happen in Europe. I then ended the discussion by asking the President of the United States these three concrete questions:

(a) Can I take it for granted that the Government of the United States believes in the possibility of re-establishing an independent Czechoslovakia and that it intends to direct its future policy to this end ?

(b) In view of the fact that a new European war may soon break out, is the Government of the United States able, and does it intend, to maintain its present attitude of refusing to recognise the German occupation of our State, thus continuing the friendly policy towards Czechoslovakia which it has adopted hitherto ?

(c) If war should come, can we expect the eventual recognition of a Czechoslovak Government in Exile as well as help for the Czechoslovak liberation movement which of course would conscientiously respect the laws of the United States and its neutrality while the United States remained neutral ?

With regard to the first two questions the President immediately took a fully positive attitude. On the third question he expressed the view that the United States could certainly do as much for Czechoslovakia as during the war of 1914-18 but that a favourable decision in this particular question would depend on circumstances and the actual war situation. He added: 'You may be sure that in this war we will not do less for you than in the last war.'

On June 29th, 1939, just before my return to Europe, I also visited the Secretary of State, Cordell Hull. I gave him my opinion of the European situation and I raised the same questions about our affairs. I did not ask for an immediate reply as I was to get it on the following day—by arrangement with President Roosevelt—from Under-Secretary Sumner Welles who was to give me Roosevelt's final message. On that day I had a long conversation with Sumner Welles in our Legation in Washington in the presence of Envoy Vlad. Hurban. We discussed the events in Europe in detail and especially the development of German and Soviet policy. Sumner Welles again repeated in substance the assurances which President

Roosevelt himself had given to me during my visit to Hyde Park. On July 12th, 1939, I left the United States. I was hastening to Europe because I feared I might not arrive before Hitler attacked Poland.

4. *Great Britain, France and ourselves at the beginning of the War*

As I approached the shores of England, I considered how to begin my work in London. I remembered how we had been received in October, 1938: with embarrassment on the part of the political world and a strong hint from the Foreign Office that I should behave with very great reserve; with sorrow, mingled sometimes with indignation against British policy, on the part of all my own and Czechoslovakia's friends; with real understanding everywhere from ordinary people. One of the first to visit me in Gwendolen Avenue, Putney, and to express his contempt of the policy of the so-called democratic Powers, was H. G. Wells. I got a letter from Lord Robert Cecil. Old friends came to see me: H. Wickham Steed and Mrs. Steed, R. W. Seton-Watson and Mrs. Seton-Watson, Sir Walter Layton* and Lady Layton, the family of R. F. Fitzgibbon Young and Mrs. Young and many others. Now after my return from the United States these visits were repeated in greater number and with greater emphasis, with increased sympathy and attended by more important political conversations. Furthermore, a number of important journalists came to ask for interviews and articles. I was asked to lecture. Friends from the universities of Oxford and Cambridge also came to see me.

During the first week of my new sojourn in Britain, I again adopted an attitude of reserve as I had once more been warned by the Foreign Office that it would not be advisable to air our problems in public. But shortly after July 20th, Jan Masaryk and Wickham Steed told me that a special Parliamentary group intended to invite me to lunch and to make a small, intimate but, for the time being, private political demonstration to show that they had not forgotten Czechoslovakia or me. They told me that the demonstration would be sponsored by Winston Churchill and Anthony Eden but that all political parties would participate. All felt that the clouds were beginning to gather over Europe, that the political atmosphere was becoming more charged with electricity. It was commonly expected that something serious would soon happen. They did not want Munich to be forgotten.

I accepted the invitation to lunch on behalf of myself and my wife (and our Minister, Jan Masaryk). The date was fixed for July 27th, 1939, and

*Now Lord Layton, C.H. (Tr.).

the occasion took the character of a political demonstration for Czecho-slovakia. In the chair was Winston Churchill, that man of invincible energy and youthful, romantic spirit 'to whom Great Britain always ran as to a war-horse, whenever she was threatened by war'—as J. V. Stalin said of him to me later. About forty persons were present, politicians and men of affairs, and it can be said that around the table sat a great part of those who were at that time forming public opinion in Britain. Besides Winston Churchill and Anthony Eden the other politicians present included Lord Robert Cecil, Sir Archibald Sinclair, Arthur Henderson, Arthur Green-wood, leader of the Labour Party, Miss Megan Lloyd George, Lord Lytton, Lord Davies, Lady Violet Bonham-Carter (later chairman of the Liberal Party), the old Labourite J. R. Clynes, General E. L. Spears, Harold Nicolson, Sir Walter Layton, Professor R. W. Seton-Watson, Among the journalists were Wickham Steed, Gordon Lennox, Captain Liddell-Hart and many others. Speeches were made by Winston Churchill, Anthony Eden, Lord Robert Cecil, Sir Archibald Sinclair, Arthur Hen-derson, Harold Nicolson and Wickham Steed. I replied for our party.

In his opening speech, Churchill referred in terms of very warm appre-ciation of my political activity for more than twenty years and my work for peace and a decent policy in Europe in general, as well as to my self-denying behaviour during the crisis in 1938. He declared that there would be no peace in Europe so long as Czechoslovakia remained enslaved and he promised that he would always work to right the dreadful wrong which had been committed against us. He concluded: 'I do not know how events will develop. And I cannot say that Great Britain will now go to war for Czechoslovakia. *I only know for certain that the peace which still has to be established will not be made without Czechoslovakia.*' As he spoke these words Churchill was so deeply moved that his eyes filled with tears.

After Churchill had spoken I replied in a short speech. I thanked all present for the friendly reception accorded me after my return to England from the United States. I declared that in September, 1938, I had felt I could not stand alone against the will of the Western European Powers because I was convinced that this would have meant our speedy ruin under conditions which would have been very unfavourable to us. I reminded Anthony Eden of our talk in April, 1935, in Prague when standing before a great map of Europe in my ministerial office. I had informed him of the plans of Germany and already foretold exactly the possible chain of events which had actually come to pass in Europe. I added that when I had arrived in England in October, 1938, I had not got into touch with friends and acquaintances because I did not want to make the situation more difficult either for them, the British Government or the Government of the Second Republic. In America, too, I had maintained great reserve. I had abandoned this attitude only after German infamy had reached its height by occupying Prague and after my warnings had been proved true. At that point I had got into touch with American public figures including President Roosevelt, members of his Cabinet and of both political parties. I stated with satisfaction that I had found complete understanding in America for the Czechoslovak cause and that I now hoped to find a similar understanding in Britain, too. I asked all present not to forget the great and unmerited sufferings of the Czechoslovak people. This speech was received with warmest acclamations by all present.

Then Anthony Eden spoke. He identified himself, he said, with all that had been said by the two preceding speakers. He recalled his long co-operation with me in Geneva and 'the good advice he had so often received from me in Central Europe matters', and he fully confirmed that during his visit to Prague in 1935 he had been warned of what was being prepared in Germany. He too, solemnly declared that there was and would be no peace unless Czechoslovakia was liberated. Sir Archibald Sinclair (who a short time previously had courageously urged the re-establishment of Czechoslovakia at a public meeting) spoke for the Liberals. Deeply moved, he promised the co-operation and loyalty of all liberally-minded people in Britain to the ideals of democracy against Nazi dictatorship and he warmly praised the behaviour of our London Legation during the crisis of 1938. After him came Viscount Robert Cecil, well advanced in years, who declared in a speech which was classical in form and content that what Britain had done in September, 1938, was a 'shameful betrayal' of her whole great past and of all her present obligations to European democracy. He coupled this with moving reminiscences of President Masaryk and his meeting with him on various occasions.

Lord Lytton spoke in the same sense.

Young Arthur Henderson for the Labour Party associated himself with these speakers and declared that there were no differences between the political parties in respect of removing the injustice done to Czechoslovakia. He added that Great Britain would have to do her duty in solving the European political problems which were pending. In reply to a question from Steed who asked whether I could say something of my reception by official circles in America, I stated that I had been assured not only by President Roosevelt and State Secretary Cordell Hull but also by both political parties that America would never recognise the violence done to Czechoslovakia and that they had promised co-operation with the

European democracies in regard to future developments. All understood the sense of these declarations to be that what Neville Chamberlain ought now to do on Britain's behalf, Roosevelt and Hull had already done in America.

Churchill then closed the proceedings with a short address in which, after reminding us of the gravity of the moment, he summed up and stressed all that had been said.

By unanimous agreement, no special publicity was given to this occasion because tension was too great. I myself took the view that the difficult internal situation of Great Britain made it necessary to proceed cautiously. But the meeting was nevertheless a very important and characteristic sign of the general situation in Britain. What a change it denoted as compared with the conditions in London half a year previously when I was getting ready for my journey to the United States! How totally different was the comprehension of what was going on in Germany and on the European continent and how different was the present temper in the face of what had happened to British policy during the preceding year, especially in regard to the treatment meted out to Czechoslovakia! I at once saw clearly that in Great Britain also we could and must prepare to begin our fight for liberation and our work to overthrow German Nazism. It was for us an immensely encouraging moment!

When I arrived in London on July 18th, 1939, I found already at work: Jan Masaryk, Dr. Hubert Ripka, who on his own initiative had left our country immediately after Munich to begin political work in exile, Minister Smutný and Colonel Fr. Moravec. Shortly afterwards there came from Paris, General Ingr, General Viest and Dr. Outrata.* Reliable information which our London intelligence service received at that time from Czechoslovakia and Berlin convinced me that Germany would certainly begin its attack on Poland at the end of July or at the latest during August.

I therefore sought to collect around me at once as many collaborators as possible—it being my principle that a priori no honest patriot should be excluded from co-operation—and to unite our whole movement so far as this was then possible. My intention *was to establish the central seat of our resistance movement in London this time.*† I had also ascertained that important British political circles and British public opinion were fully aware of the gravity of European events and of the fact that the policy of 'appeasement' was visibly nearing its critical culmination. The British

*Dr. Outrata became Finance Minister in the Provisional Government (Tr.).

†In the first World War it had been established first in Geneva and then in Paris (Tr.).

'men of Munich', and of course even more those in Paris, still believed that the crisis between Poland and Germany would not lead to war and would at worst end with some 'second Munich'. They developed a really feverish activity in this direction.

Meanwhile more of our political collaborators had arrived in London from home. On July 20th, 1929, Dr. Milan Hodža came to me to London from Switzerland. We agreed—as I then thought easily—on the principle of our political co-operation. We concurred in the necessity of consistently fighting against Hitler and of re-establishing the Republic. We decided that we would not return to the past, would not discuss nor quarrel either about Munich or about our future internal affairs or about the new organisation of the State (Slovakia, Germans, etc.). This would be settled later when war began, while the war was in progress and especially after the war had ended—at home. I simply did not want to begin discussing matters which I feared would immediately give rise to dissension. Via Poland there arrived Monseigneur Jan Šrámek with the Consistorial Councillor František Hála,* Deputies Rudolf Bechyně, Dr. Jar. Stránský, Senator Vojta Beneš, the Slovak Deputy Ján Bečko, Deputy Fr. Uhlíř and many others who at once took their places in our joint political movement.

Our second important centre began to form in Paris soon after Munich partly around the Legation (Dr. Osuský†) and partly around the soldiers (Generals Ingr and R. Viest, Colonel Španiel, Col. Dr. Langer and others) and a number of politicians and journalists (Dr. H. Ripka, Minister J. Smutný, Dr. G. Winter and others). The Paris section was very active and prepared to renew the traditions of the struggle during the first World War. In these difficult moments it certainly did much good preparatory work. The Czechoslovak colony in Paris also worked well from the outset. At my request—following the intervention of our soldiers in Paris —Dr. Osuský came to London twice to discuss the situation and to make preparations for future co-operation between London and Paris. I regarded as our most important asset, however, the presence of our military intelligence service in London with a number of officers under Colonel Fr. Moravec together with a sufficient number of officers and soldiers in France with General Ingr and General Viest. To me these were a guarantee that when war started we could at once begin to organise the Czechoslovak liberation Army.

*Leaders of the People's Party when the war ended. Mgr Šrámek was the first Prime Minister of the Third Republic. Of the other persons named here, Rudolf Bechyně afterwards went into opposition to President Beneš (Tr.).

†A Slovak. Afterwards an opponent of President Beneš (Tr.).

Therefore, on September 3rd, when the German attack on Poland led to the declaration of war on Germany by Great Britain and France, it was clear to me that a great moment in world history had arrived—a moment which would have the most far-reaching consequences for the world.

For us, 11 a.m. on September 3rd was an extremely moving and stirring moment when in our small house in Putney we stood at the wireless set and listened with excitement to the broken voice of Neville Chamberlain announcing that at that very moment the British Ambassador in Berlin (it chanced to be Nevile Henderson—the second victim of Hitler's policy) was delivering the declaration of war.

Chamberlain's voice sounded really tragic and broken and fully indicated the whole tragedy of this moment and the dreadful error British diplomacy had lived to see after it had made so many moral and material sacrifices and sacrifices of prestige during its policy of seeking a so-called 'Peace with honour' with Hitler. In the whole history of world diplomacy there are few errors so fatal, so far-reaching in their consequences for all the world as this one !

Listening to the radio with my wife and myself, were Dr. Lobkowicz* and Mrs. Lobkowicz who by chance were visiting us. We listened, without uttering a word and deeply moved, to the whole speech of Chamberlain and to the British National Anthem which followed it. We stood, as it were, reverently, and speaking no word of comment. We felt all the terrible tragedy of the words of the British Prime Minister and were aware of that moment marking the beginning of dreadful suffering for the British Empire as well as of further unheard-of suffering for our own people. But at the same time we were aware, too, that this was the beginning of the fight for our new liberation and our first step after Munich towards our new independence !

On the afternoon of the same day we listened to the declaration of war by France. The voice of Daladier sounded even more broken, gloomy and tragic than that of the British Prime Minister. I could almost sense what that moment meant for France's leading man and could almost foresee how Daladier would himself ultimately react to all these events. That it meant his sad and final downfall was already clear to me !

Judging that our forces were ready for resistance and that in spite of all our differences we were sufficiently united, I sent on the same day—some hours after the declaration of war by Great Britain and France—telegrams to the Prime Ministers of Great Britain and the British Dominions, of

*Afterwards Czechoslovak Ambassador in London. His wife is Irish. They are now living in the United States (Tr.).

France and Poland, in which I simply stated that Czechoslovakia which legally continued to exist had been in a state of war with Germany since March 15th, 1939, and that it was automatically joining the Allies.

The text of the telegram was as follows:

'At this moment in which the British people are obliged to wage a war imposed upon Poland, Great Britain, and France by Nazi Germany, I wish to express to your Excellency, with deep and unalterable feelings of sympathy, the desire and decision of the Czechs and Slovaks to join your people without hesitation in this struggle for a free Europe.

'Our country is invaded and occupied by armed forces of Nazism and the whole Nation is suffering under inhuman terror and oppression. Its forces, however, both moral and physical, remain intact.

'We Czechoslovak citizens consider ourselves as being at war with the German military forces, and we shall march with your people till the final victory and the liberation of our Fatherland.'

On September 9th I received the following reply from Prime Minister Chamberlain:

'I gratefully acknowledge your Excellency's generous message of sympathy and support in this grave hour. The sufferings of the Czech Nation are not forgotten, and we anticipate that by the triumph of the principle for which we have taken up arms, the Czech people will be liberated from foreign domination.'

Similar replies arrived from the Governments of the British Dominions, Egypt and Iraq. *But there were no replies from the French or the Polish Prime Minister*. Both were still animated by the spirit of the pre-war policy of their countries and the policy of Munich, and took no cognizance of us— or at least (at that time) of me personally.

A week later, on September 19th, 1939—when our old friend Robert Bruce Lockhart who throughout the war rendered us such inestimable, friendly and devoted services had been appointed permanent and direct liaison officer between us and the Foreign Office—I began political negotiations with the British Foreign Secretary, Lord Halifax.

It was a typically British reception that I got from Lord Halifax at the Foreign Office. He himself, as is well known, had played an important part in the events which led to Munich. At the time of my call he was certainly well aware, as was also Neville Chamberlain himself, what a terrible defeat the Munich policy and therefore also their own had suffered as a result of the latest events of 1939. But Lord Halifax had enough personal courage to declare when he greeted me and before any political discussion had taken place: 'We in Great Britain are fully aware of our share in the responsibility for the destiny of your country and for your personal fate.' I answered: 'I thank you for those words, Lord Halifax. We will certainly return to this subject later. But today I would like to discuss how *we* can take part with you in this war.'

In the ensuing discussion at which Sir Orme Sargent was also present I did not again mention Munich. I only gave details of our future political and military plans. Finally I asked Lord Halifax to agree to the future establishment of a Czechoslovak political organ which would either take the place of a provisional Government or already be a Government. I explained that this committee would be the supreme organ of our whole diplomatic, political and military action. Above all it would be at the head of our Army which was already beginning to form in France and to some extent also in Britain.

Lord Halifax agreed in principle but deferred taking an actual decision. He asked me to continue with our preparations and our organising work and to keep the Foreign Office regularly informed of the progress of our work. The British Government would give us a definite answer later in accordance with the march of events and the future state of our movement. The conversation ended with a detailed discussion with Sir Orme Sargent of conditions in the 'protectorate' and the political and moral state of our Nation at home.

I would like to stress that in organising the movement we were from the beginning working on the principle that the authority of our Legations and Consulates in countries in which their official continuity had been secured, should not be infringed. This was not only to avoid any step which could weaken their existence or their position but also to secure for the liberation movement the use of their services and of their official status. This was a rather difficult question and there were often grave differences.

The reasons for these were easy to see. It was not clear whether France, Great Britain, the United States, the Soviet Union and others which continued to recognise our Legations after March 15th, 1939, were also prepared to accept the *continuity of our State*. They did not want to commit themselves in this matter, wishing to be able to decide for or against according to the progress of the war and their own interests. For instance, I knew positively that in the summer of 1939 Germany had urged the abolition of our Legation in London. Some circles in London were in favour of doing so. Even in August, 1939—at the request of Counsellor Lisický of the Legation—I had had to ask Lord Halifax in a special personal letter that our Legation should remain untouched.

Our foreign missions therefore had to be extremely careful. But the political movements—especially on the military side—were in general rather radical in their attitude towards Munich and its consequences and they tried to act from this standpoint. The Legations often felt endangered by this behaviour because radical demonstrations and conspicuous political and military decisions (which moreover were often directed against the British and French Governments) were followed by recriminations and warnings from the Governments concerned. On the other hand the Legations themselves showed a tendency to lead and govern the political and military movement or at least to play the most important and decisive rôle. But the direction of resistance and revolution 'officially' by the Legations led to a number of difficulties from which new conflicts arose. These quarrels disappeared in their more acute form only after a legal Government had again been recognised and the Republic had been fully re-established internationally.[19]

5. My Attempts to reach agreement with France—the Negotiations of Monseigneur J. Šràmek

On October 6th, 1939, at the very urgent request of General Ingr, Dr. Ripka and Dr. Outrata I left for Paris. Our Paris Legation and our military representatives had just finished rather difficult negotiations the outcome of which was an agreement with the French Government for the formation of our National Army in France under the control of a Czechoslovak Provisional Government. This provisional government, however, did not yet exist. Mention of it in this agreement was an indication that such a government might be established and recognised by the French Government at a later stage.

The agreement was signed—after certain internal controversies among ourselves—by Premier Daladier and Envoy Osuský on October 2nd, 1939. Ingr, Ripka and Outrata believed that immediately the army agreement was signed there would be negotiations for the establishment and recognition of the Government. They therefore asked me to make a point of being present. At their very urgent request I went to Paris—though not very gladly. I did not expect any favourable reception or negotiations. As it turned out, my trip was completely unsuccessful.

Before this, however, Monseigneur J. Šrámek had already gone to Paris from London in full agreement with me. We knew that the Daladier Government regarded me with great disfavour. Minister Šrámek, on the other hand, had some acquaintances in Catholic circles in Paris and General Ingr, Ripka and others thought he might have some influence, especially with Catholics (for example with Champetier de Ribes, then State Secretary in the Ministry of Foreign Affairs). These expectations proved to be correct. Šrámek, therefore, became our chief negotiator with the Daladier Government when the re-establishment of our relations with France was discussed. But for the time being not even Šrámek could obtain more than consent to the establishment of a Czechoslovak National Committee in France. According to Šrámek, Daladier—through Champetier de Ribes—had rejected the establishment of a Government and had opposed my taking part in our movement at all. He had expressed his confidence in Osuský, especially, had tried to bring about the participation of Dr. Hodža and had hinted that he would eventually accept somebody else instead of me as leader of our resistance movement. Šrámek himself had taken a firm stand. He had not deviated from our fundamental policy. He had expressed himself with great reserve about Hodža and had not yielded in the matter of my participation in the movement. As he had not been able to secure the formation of a Government, he had given only provisional consent after mutual consultation, to the establishment of a Committee to supervise the organisation of our National Army. The whole negotiation was extremely difficult and painful and in a certain sense all our people found it both disturbing and depressing.

Nevertheless the trip did at least give me the chance to thresh out all current matters concerning our movement with our military representatives and political collaborators in France and to contact French political circles. Among the French ministers and politicians whom I then met, I mention E. Herriot, G. Mandel, Y. Delbos, Reynaud, Queuille, Blum, Paul-Boncour, Ambassador L. Noel, Pierre Comert, General Faucher*, not to mention many other politicians, journalists, professors, and a number of older friends.

When I asked for an interview Daladier refused to receive me or to discuss any political questions whatsoever with me. Afterwards he reported on the matter to the French Government giving his reasons. Daladier and Bonnet and the majority of their colleagues were continuing to maintain a reserved and *de facto*, a *negative* policy towards Czechoslovakia in spite of what they had done against the vital interests of the Czechoslovak Nation in 1938 and in spite of the fundamental changes in the general European situation after Munich and after the outbreak of war.

In reality, as I ascertained quite positively in Paris and later in London, too, both still held to their previous line and were steadily going on with their Munich policy. They had been forced to come to the aid of Poland

*French military attaché in Prague at the time of Munich. (Tr.).

against their will. They had evidently wanted to repeat in the case of Poland in September, 1939, what they had done to us a year before and to bring about a 'second Munich'. They had wanted to avoid any action which in their opinion could impair France's relations with Germany and even more with Italy and Hungary. As early as September, 1939—that is to say from the very beginning of hostilities—their plan had been to induce Italy and Hungary to refrain from entering the war on Germany's side, to localise the whole conflict in this way and then to work for early negotiations for a premature peace with Germany and to turn Germany towards a conflict with the Soviet Union. In order to realise this aim, *they were ready to sacrifice Czechoslovakia once more and, in some new form, Poland also.* I am describing here objectively what I saw and how I understood their policy at that time.

In addition to these considerations, I personally was a symbol of pre-war Czechoslovakia (which they considered to be completely dead) and of Czechoslovakia's former policy, a symbol of hostility against Mussolini and, of course, against Hitler. They had thrown Czechoslovakia and *me personally* to the wolves—and this too did not make them like me *personally*. In their opinion, therefore, it was impossible to link the France they represented with my person. Until the fall of France in June, 1940, they never changed their attitude towards Czechoslovakia or to me. Our friends of those days—for example Mandel and others—also assured me that another reason why Daladier had refused to speak to me was because, after what he had done to Czechoslovakia, he did not dare to look me in the face. No wonder . . .

What I saw and heard at that time of what was happening in France convinced me that as long as France remained under the leadership of Daladier, Bonnet, de Monzie and a number of similar politicians and gerrymanderers she could neither win the war, *nor recover from her grave illness.*

My stay in Paris, a month after the beginning of war, gave me a very bad impression of the state of France. I did not conceal this from my friends and after a fortnight in Paris I returned to London suddenly and without taking leave. I made up my mind that I would not be able to return to Paris during the war and that I would have to rely mainly on the British Empire and the United States for the prosecution of the war, always believing at the same time that later on the Soviet Union would also fight on our side. Accordingly I adapted the attitude and policy of our movement to the sad, grievous and cruel French reality . . . Events proved that already at that time I had rightly estimated the situation of France—and the war as a whole.[20]

In accordance with its plans, the Daladier Government acted *to prevent the formation of a Czechoslovak Government.* It justified this attitude on dissensions in our ranks and on its refusal to have anything to do with me politically.[21] After very difficult negotiations it would only allow the formation of a Czechoslovak National Committee with very limited competence. It behaved even worse towards us than Tsarist Russia in the first World War. As I have already mentioned, these negotiations were carried out on our side by Monseigneur Šrámek with Champetier de Ribes.

During my stay in Paris we therefore agreed on the formation of the Czechoslovak National Committee with such political and military functions as the French Government approved. It was stressed to Šrámek that I must not be Chairman of the Committee.

I ought to add that the British Government which was watching these negotiations in Paris with a certain reserve had its special point of view in these matters. It too considered that, *for the time being* it would be premature to form a regular Czechoslovak Government. Nevertheless it expressly told Paris that it would be quite impossible to form a Czechoslovak Government without my participation as Paris would have liked to do. This point of view was conveyed to the French Ministry of Foreign Affairs while I was in Paris. But I only heard this myself from the British Foreign Office later (on February 10th, 1940).

Temporarily and willy-nilly we had to make do with the formation of the National Committee. By decision of the Committee I discussed its diplomatic recognition with the British Foreign Office after my return to London. The National Committee was recognised by the French Government on November 17th, and by the British on December 20th, 1939.

6. *The Paris National Committee and Our Emigration*

Though for the time being we only had a National Committee, we immediately began intensive and energetic work.[22] The National Committee established its seat in Paris which was the only place at that time in which it was possible to organise our Army with some prospect of success. I myself, while remaining in close contact and permanent co-operation with the Paris Committee, was organising our offices and our propaganda on British soil in London with the help of Jan Masaryk and Minister Smutný.

Under the firm and prudent leadership of its Paris Vice-President, Monseigneur Šrámek, the Committee without doubt obtained important results in France throughout its period of activity which lasted from November, 1939, to the fall of France in June, 1940. It succeeded in solving a number of difficulties in spite of the unfavourable atmosphere of nervousness, defeatism and political disfavour in Paris. General Ingr and General Viest were entrusted with the administration of military matters and after many difficulties succeeded in organising the first Czechoslovak Division in France. Dr. Eduard Outrata was charged with the administration of financial and economic matters; Dr. Osuský took care of foreign affairs; Dr. Ripka dealt with information and Dr. Slávik was responsible for the social welfare of the emigrants. It was the most difficult period of our work and when the number of our quarrels was the greatest. Ultimately, the whole of this period, and the activities of the Committee which was often much criticised, will eventually be examined in detail and justly appreciated.

Towards the end of 1939 and the beginning of 1940 the Socialist deputies František Němec and Bohumil Laušman came from Prague followed by Dr. Prokop Drtina, one of my nearest personal collaborators in the presidential office in Prague, deputy Joža David, Professor Vladimír Klecanda, Col. Hutník (Kudláček), Col. Chodský (Boček)* and a number of others. Most of them had taken part in the underground political activity at home. Some generals and hundreds of other officers escaped by various ways from Czechoslovakia at that time with the object of helping with the organisation of the Army in France. Among them were the generals Znamenáček (Cihák), Miroslav (Neumann), Nižborský (Hasal), Slezák (Vicherek), Ghak (Mézl) and Janoušek. Finally—also with a view to collaborating with us—there escaped the ministers Dr. L. Feierabend and Ing. Jaromir Nečas who had been in underground contact with me after the beginning of the war and before they left our country. In May, 1940, Ján Lichner, the Slovak Deputy and Minister in the post-Munich Government, left Slovakia. He got into touch with me while still on his way to Belgrade and was at once brought into our common work.†

A group of Czechoslovak Communists, among them some deputies and senators (Nosek, Hodinová, Valo, Beuer, Kreibich) who had left our country after Munich and had found asylum in England offered me their co-operation in the common fight as soon as I returned to Britain from the United States. We had a number of meetings which took a hopeful turn.

*The names in brackets were the real names and the others those taken during the war in the interests of relatives at home (Tr.).

†Mr. Lichner refused to leave Slovakia after the Communist Revolution and in 1950 was sentenced to 17 years' imprisonment on charges of treason, and espionage (Tr.).

But when the German-Soviet treaty was concluded on August 23rd, 1939, their attitude to the whole of our military and political activities became reserved. From that time they did not co-operate with us though our contact was never wholly interrupted. After the German invasion of the Soviet Union they renewed their former policy and co-operated unreservedly with us in the fight against Hitler.[22]

Until 1943 I was also in permanent and good contact with W. Jaksch, deputy of the German Social Democrats, and his political friends, as well as with other German political groups (Zinner, Lenk, Kirpalová, Kögler, Peres) who had left the country after Munich.*

Such was the composition of our Western political emigration in the spring of 1940. Everywhere we relied on those diplomatic and consular missions which continued to be recognised and had been preserved and on our military organisation which already had a solid basis and was accepted as serious evidence of our efforts and aims and the feelings of the whole Nation. But mainly, of course, we relied *on our daily and permanent contact with our country and on the resistance of the whole Nation at home against Germany.* The unheard-of terror which the Germans adopted against us at home from the outbreak of the war especially after October 28th and November 17th, 1939,† and the fact that the whole world knew that we abroad were only expressing what the Nation at home was feeling and doing—all this entitled us to come forward immediately and unequivocally in the spirit of the legal continuity of our State *as representatives and symbols of the fight of the whole Nation.*

In the spring of 1940—knowing that the Germans were preparing for the attack against Belgium and the Netherlands—I judged it to be time to put forward in London the question of the formation and recognition of a Czechoslovak Government on the soil of Great Britain, thus giving the Czechoslovak liberation movement the correct international, legal and political form. That day arrived after the fall of France when our Army had been evacuated and transferred to Britain and when the Czechoslovaks —as well as the Poles, Dutch, Belgians, Norwegians and Free French— made London their official headquarters and the chief centre of their Western political emigration.

*Dr. Jaksch and the other German leaders ceased to co-operate when Dr. Beneš and the Czechoslovak Provisional Government adopted the policy of expelling the German minority (Tr.).

†The date of the disturbances in Prague, November 17th, 1939, when Jan Opletal and two other students were buried was afterwards adopted as International Students' Day in their memory (Tr.).

NOTES TO CHAPTER TWO

[1]The text of this address appears in the Appendix.

[2]A typical letter was the one given below to Ing. Jaromír Nečas, former and subsequent Minister*;

DEAR COLLEAGUE NEČAS,

Thank you for your friendly letter. Yes, the time will come, the time for all of us who took the right road against evil and cowardice. In that certainty I am quietly and firmly preparing for our future work. We will meet again. There are no other alternatives than justice, truth, fair play on the one side; evil, violence, cowardice and betrayal on the other. We went the first way—we will continue in it. Kind regards to you and your wife—also from my wife!

Yours,
DR. EDUARD BENEŠ

London, October 30th, 1938.

[3]My answer to Dr. L. Rašín has been published in my book *Six Years of Exile and the Second World War*, pages 22-32.† Rašín's letter to me read as follows:

Prague, November 7th, 1938.

MR. PRESIDENT,

I could not bring myself to write to you at the time of your resignation from office. Then you left and again there was no opportunity for me to write. But now the development of our political situation and the attacks hurled against you, compel me to send you these few sincere and frank words.

It happened that I did not come frequently into contact with you until the days when the events drew to their tragic culmination. I regret this very much. From that morning of September 22nd when I saw you exhausted and desperate, I feared that the capitulation of the State would necessarily lead to your resignation. I feared that the idea of an independent and united Czechoslovak State which had been realised through so many sacrifices, efforts and lives, would break down. I, with a few of my friends, wanted to prevent this: to prevent the capitulation of the State by going to war even at the price of immense sacrifices, to prevent your resignation by forming a strong Government of courageous men even at the price of suppressing the political parties. I wanted to prevent demoralisation and preserve the moral ideals of the Nation—the ideals by which it lives—even at the price of Bohemia becoming Thermopylae and you Leonidas.

Things did not work out in this way and I do not want to return today to our conversations. If in these I have perhaps sometimes been too sincere and open, please bear me no grudge. I was actuated by one single desire: to save the independence and honour of the Nation and to preserve those moral values which had been accumulated during twenty years of independence. Today I would like to tell you something else. In my Party, very often quite alone, and in public almost alone, I am still defending your political standpoint which, as I understand it, was the concept of a truly free and independent State conforming to our evolution through a thousand years. From this

*Mr. Nečas died in London during the war when holding the office of Minister of State in the Provisional Government.

†Not available in English.

concept arose the risk of an armed conflict with Germany. My only reproach is that we did not face this danger when it became concrete. Evading the logical conclusion, we have deprived the logical premises of their validity. Perhaps I am wrong and perhaps I find it easier to take such a line than you who were responsible at that moment for hundreds of thousands of lives. But I am still convinced that conditions dictated after a war that has been lost would not be much worse than the conditions of a 'peace' which delivers a million Czech souls to extinction and slavery and delivers the State, now tri-partite instead of united, unconditionally to its neighbours. I do not know whence we shall be able to draw inspiration for national heroism.

Today they are looking for a scapegoat. I am sorry that what I warned you of is coming true: you alone are to bear the responsibility for everything that happened and all those cowards who hid behind you and your authority, who left the decision to you so that they themselves could shelve the responsibility of taking it, do not raise a finger to defend you and to admit their share of responsibility. To all these 'politicians' who were around you and with whom you supposed you would lead the State out of the catastrophe, and in whose loyalty you trusted, nothing is more welcome than the opportunity to divert the attention of the Nation from their own guilt by inciting it against you. I had and have no illusions about our political life. But I never thought that in a time so tragic for Nation and State there would be in our political life so little chivalry, responsibility and courage and so much baseness, cowardice and lack of character—such a desire to turn the national catastrophe to personal profit.

That is why I am writing to you, Mr. President. I would like to assure you that I have nothing in common with these agitations and attacks against you even if my own Party and its press are making them. The most reliable proof of the correctness of a policy is said to be its results. Of two catastrophes from which we could choose you have chosen the one which has happened. I would have chosen the other one—war. In this I did not agree with you. But I did not on that account lose my respect for your qualities and abilities and I am not ready to forget all the positive sides of your work for the Nation and State during a quarter of a century. With grief and sorrow I can see that by your resignation the idealistic generation which worked for the liberation of the Nation during the war at home and abroad is disappearing from our public life and that post-war materialists are getting a hearing whose aim is to make the Republic serve their personal advantage.

I wish you, Mr. President, enough rest and strength, and especially I wish for you that your wife should retain her strength and calmness—she who always so valiantly bore, with you, all good and evil and whom all who had the honour of knowing her remember with respect. I am happy that I, and my wife also, belong to their number.

With the expression of my profound respect,

I am, sincerely yours,

DR. LADÍSLAV RAŠÍN.

⁴My letter to Hácha read as follows:

London, November 30th, 1938.

MR. PRESIDENT,

I know well what grave tasks you will have as President of the Republic, and therefore I am writing to wish both for the Republic and yourself, that your election today may in these difficult times contribute to its full prosperity. You have done great services to our country as President of the Administrative Court by your great experience and knowledge and by your just and careful legal procedure often in the most delicate matters. That all at home have united to bring about your election only underlines this fact. I send you my best wishes for the success of your new work and I hope that the State and Nation may emerge from their present situation as soon, and in as good condition, as possible.

With the expression of my sincere respect,

DR. EDUARD BENEŠ.

P.S. In the rush of events it was not possible for me to answer your telephone call in the last days of the crisis. I had several times considered the procedure you suggested and had discussed it with Envoy Mastný. Perhaps it will be possible at a later date to tell why it could not be adopted.

DR. E. B.

In the last days of the Munich negotiations Dr. Hácha had expressed his opinion by telephone that I should interrupt negotiations with France and Great Britain and speak directly to Berlin. I do not know how he got this idea. When the crisis came to a head, I had considered all possible ways of saving the situation and I had—at least for a moment —thought of this possibility, too. But I rejected it without even allowing my thoughts to formulate the full consequences.

Hácha's answer, which reached me in London, read as follows:

Prague, December 10th, 1938.

MR. PRESIDENT,

Your kind letter has moved, but also stimulated, me in my task which I accepted with hesitation and the greatest self-denial as a hard burden which duty laid upon me. I was looking forward to a modest private life and to following up my old bent for literary work. The duties of my present office weigh very heavily on me as I am aware of my insufficiency. I am trying within the limits of my strength 'to make the best of it' and console myself with the hope that my functions will only have a transitory character and that they will be taken from me within a measurable space of time. I am aware of the fact that I shall be judged severely soon but contemporaries are perhaps never capable of just judgment.

I beg you to accept the expression of my sincere respect and my wish that you should enjoy the best of health.

DR. E. HACHA.

[5] After the visit of Chamberlain and Halifax to Rome on January 12th-14th, 1939, there were intensive negotiations for special treaties to give effect to the Italo-British appeasement agreement of November 16th, 1938.

[6] At that time I did not expect the events of March 15th and I therefore believed that my brother could safely return to Prague—at any rate for some time. But afterwards he had to take the risk of a very dangerous escape via Poland.

[7] I signed this telegram as 'former' President of the Republic because I felt that before the outbreak of war the situation was not ripe for an *immediate and public presentation* of the claim of legal continuity for the pre-Munich Republic. This happened soon after-wards. Some of my collaborators (e.g. Envoy Hurban*) asserted that already at that

*Czechoslovak Minister in Washington. (Tr.).

time I should have signed: '*second*' President of the Czechoslovak Republic and not 'former' President. People of bad will, they said, could use this designation against the theory of continuity. And later such people certainly did misuse it—as well as my letter to Hácha (see page 95).

[8]The full text of this address is in my book *Six Years of Exile and the Second World War*, pp. 39-46.

[9]For the full text of the Soviet Note see Appendix, pp. 296-7. The note explained the whole political and legal attitude of the Soviet Government. It was at that time a clear diplomatic, legal and political analysis of the real character of the German act of violence of March 15th.

[10]The French note was published in the French diplomatic documents, 1938-39 (Livre jaune), doc. number 76, 77.

[11]As I have already mentioned, the Soviet Union answered with a very firm Note and refused to recognise the annihilation of Czechoslovakia. It continued to grant all aid to the Czechoslovak Legation in Moscow and recognised its legal and diplomatic position until January 1st, 1940, when it changed its policy, having previously informed the Czechoslovak Envoy in Moscow on December 15th, 1939, that it would consider his functions to be at an end on January 1st, 1940.* Envoy Zdeněk Fierlinger left Moscow for Paris and London and joined our movement in Western Europe. I expected that this change of Soviet policy would prove only temporary and provisional. Therefore we did not protest. We waited patiently for the day when it would be possible for us to return to our joint policy and to renew our friendly diplomatic relations. That day came more than one and a half years later after Germany attacked the Soviet Union in June, 1941.

[12]I answered them in an address printed in the Appendix.

[13]During the following weeks many of our diplomatic and consular, political and military officials and functionaries announced their adherence to me one after the other. Altogether, their help was valuable and efficient. And though our situation at that time was very bad, especially financially, all of them gradually joined in the full work of resistance.

[14]We in London† were not in agreement with the spirit and tendencies of General Prchala's work though we had to submit to politically inescapable necessities in order to prevent differences in our resistance movement. We did not agree because General Prchala yielding to Polish wishes allowed the formation of 'Czech' and 'Slovak' legions, and because he and his friends asked for and received from the Polish Government of Col. Beck money for *political* activities and their personal subsistence. We also disapproved because for some time they refused to accept the principle of unity in our activities in West and East and wanted—to the detriment of the unity of our whole movement—to exploit the hostility of the Polish Government against me personally.

[15]In spite of the strong position held by the so-called 'men of Munich' in Britain and France at that time in Government, in Parliament and in public opinion, the international

*The change in Soviet policy followed the Soviet-German agreement and the partition of Poland (Tr.).

†Dr. Beneš returned to London from America on July 19th, 1939 (Tr.).

situation was developing in such a way that I already considered it possible to make an unequivocal denunciation of Munich and of announcing the principle of the legal continuity of our State in my first public pronouncement on the situation.

[16]Hamilton Fish Armstrong: *When There is no Peace*, London, Macmillan, 1941.

[17]Soon after my return to England an identical point of view was formulated by the Labour Party leaders, Arthur Greenwood and Arthur Henderson Jr., who at that time were not sure whether the situation in 1938 might not in the end have led to a European war directed only against the Soviet Union. However that may be, England, in their opinion, was not yet ready or sufficiently united internally to undertake war against Hitlerite Germany.

[18]This question was later solved justly and rightly in agreement with Great Britain.

[19]At this point the so-called 'Envoy-Theory' must be mentioned.

Our Envoy, or Legation official, who had remained in office after March 15th, 1939, and was still recognised by the Government to which he had been accredited, held himself to be and was in reality the last vestige of the authority of the Republic which *de facto* had been suppressed at home. This automatically gave him a very advantageous position compared with all other Czechoslovak citizens abroad whose legal position from the international standpoint was very uncertain. On account, particularly, of this exceptional situation, he had a politically very important position which meant much, and enabled him to do much, for the Republic in those difficult times. In particular, so far as the State was concerned he could serve as an important *starting point* for the new fight and as a basis for new political successes when the full political fight for liberation began afresh.

This aspect of our Legations had to be respected by us all. The difficulty lay in the fact that some envoys—in reality Dr. Osuský was the only one—formed their own conclusions and drew impossible deductions. They regarded all other political personalities as 'private' persons and themselves to be the only political representatives of the State and Nation. They claimed that this entitled them to some special position of leadership in the resistance movement, to the right of independent decisions about what should and should not be done, what a particular person should, or was allowed to, do and whether he should be admitted to this or that work or official position. At the beginning Dr. Osuský, for example (having in view the attitude of the French Government) opposed the formation of a central resistance organ. In particular he opposed on various grounds the formation of a collective political organ of the whole Nation which should have authority over everyone without exception. Dr. Osuský did not *publicly* develop this theory to its full extent and with all its implications. He merely hinted at it occasionally as, for instance, in an interview with the *Petit Parisien* in October, 1939. But he acted upon it to the full in respect of others wherever possible.

This caused us great difficulties for a long time. In practice, it meant that an envoy who enjoyed such an independence and who was not subordinated to a Government was in reality a Sovereign and could use his exceptional position according to his own judgment being neither controlled by nor subordinate to anyone. Moreover he had invaluable advantages in this serious time: diplomatic privileges, the right of cypher, passport visas wherever he wished to travel, access to the authorities, in some cases even financial means or the possibility of an income from Legation and consular functions, etc.

H

In cases of political disagreement with him we others were in a very disadvantageous position.

From the outset I regarded this as a danger to our whole movement. And I considered such behaviour on the part of an envoy to be not only an unwholesome sign but also as unpatriotic and an expression of very unpolitical thinking. Any envoy who adopted such a policy exposed himself to the possibility—very detrimental to the interests of the State— that he would lose all independence *vis-à-vis* the Government to which he had been accredited because by a mere stroke of the pen he could be eliminated whenever that Government chose. He was thus condemned to become a puppet in their hands and in their political manoeuvres. Correct, political, thinking should have made him recognise that his greatest interest was in the quickest possible establishment of a national, political centre and of a national authority above him with which he could co-operate and which he could support in his special position so as to prepare the new diplomatic recognition of the State. This is what, for example, our Minister in Washington, Vladimír Hurban, did with great correctness immediately after March 15th, 1939, when on March 19th he came to Chicago to agree with me about our future steps. A number of other officials also acted in this manner, gradually reporting for work in the resistance movement.

Having already some misgivings on this point immediately after March 15th, 1939, I first intended to establish a kind of board of political directors composed of our Envoys in London, Paris, Washington, Moscow and Warsaw as a first step towards the later formation of a recognised Government. Another reason for doing so was that at that time there were no other political personalities abroad and I hoped in this way to circumvent 'envoy difficulties' and disputes arising therefrom. Our Legation in Paris at once sent a negative answer giving as reason that the French Government did not want the establishment of such a centre and that if it were set up it would endanger the existence of our Legation in Paris. I have no doubt that the post-Munich Paris Government was against this step. At that time, or so it seemed to us, it was against everything I was doing abroad.

Again in Paris, this 'envoy theory' was also of some importance at a later stage when there were negotiations for the formation of the first Government and particularly on the subject of my exclusion from the leadership of the second resistance movement. The theory was again of great importance after the National Committee had been formed and a bitter personal quarrel developed between its members and Envoy Osuský. It continued to operate right up to the moment when the Czechoslovak Government was formed in London and recognised in July, 1940. It caused us much trouble and evoked a number of quarrels. But except Osuský no other Envoy either referred to it, or practised it.

[20]While in Paris I wrote my frank opinion of the situation in France to Ambassador Fr. Charles-Roux in Rome and to Senator Barbier of Darney who during my visit had further discussions with me about finishing the monument in Alsace for our soldiers from World War I.

[21]Dr. Osuský, who wanted to emphasize that I was unacceptable in France, wrote to me of the hostile way in which Daladier had spoken to him, confidentially, about my whole political activity and especially of my behaviour during the Munich crisis. The letter was intended to be an insult. It was meant to be an argument against my taking any part in our resistance movement. I brought it to the notice of Monseigneur Šrámek and later of our London Government.

[22]The original members of the Committee were: Beneš, Ingr, Osuský, E. Outrata, Ripka, Slávik, Šrámek and Viest. At the time the Committee was formed I asked that it should be put on record that the Committee would be enlarged when other politicians, especially those belonging to Socialist groups*, arrived from home and by Jan Masaryk representing our emigrants in Britain. During the negotiations for recognition of the Committee by Great Britain I announced this to the British Government in writing.

[23]Our Communist emigrants in the Soviet Union will be dealt with in the chapter on the Soviet Union. I expect that in course of time the Communists themselves will speak of the activities of this emigration.

*There were several Socialist parties in Czechoslovakia before the war, and two when the Czechoslovak Government returned to Prague after the war. These two were the Social Democrats and the National Socialists—the party to which Dr. Beneš himself belonged before he became President. At the general election in 1946, the National Socialist Party obtained more votes than any other except the Communist Party (Tr.).

CHAPTER III

THE FIRST GREAT CRISIS OF THE WAR: CAPITULATION OF FRANCE

1. *Rescuing the Czechoslovak Army from France*

FROM the beginning of April, 1940, we got daily reports from perfectly reliable sources in Prague and Berlin that Germany was preparing to attack France and Great Britain via Belgium and the Netherlands. Already at the outbreak of war I had no doubt that Germany was preparing a plan of this kind and would carry it out. I saw this attack as an inevitable development of the war. The German 'Drang nach Osten' must always be a 'Drang nach Westen' too. Unfortunately this fundamental element of German policy was, once again in 1938, not understood by the leading men of France and Great Britain and of the other European States. They had to pay dearly for it. And I do not conceal my fear that they will be ready to do the same again in the future because in politics, human stupidity and human egotism are inexhaustible.

After the attack on Norway in April, 1940, I considered that the invasion of Belgium and the Netherlands would provide a suitable occasion for obtaining international recognition of our Government through the good offices of the British Government and for establishing the whole legal and political organisation of the Czechoslovak Republic in exile thus gradually preparing the cancellation of what had happened at Munich. This mode of procedure would also serve the purpose of recalling to people's minds what had happened under the leadership of Masaryk at the end of the last war, in 1918.

I opened these negotiations on April 26th, 1940, in a conversation with Sir Alexander Cadogan, Permanent Under Secretary of State in the British Foreign Office. I asked for the consent of the British Government to the formation of a Czechoslovak Government on British soil, a Government composed of the members of the present (already recognised) Czechoslovak National Committee with additions which would make it as far as possible representative of all the political strata of the Czechoslovak people. In the beginning the British Government had some doubts. It also felt bound to France where the hostile attitude of the Daladier Government towards Czechoslovakia did not change until its fall on March 20th, 1940, though the formation of the Reynaud Government which followed created a situation which might have been regarded as a slight improvement so far as we were concerned.

In May, June and July these verbal and written discussions between the British Foreign Office and myself continued. There was a rather extensive correspondence in notes and memoranda—on our side they were given to the British Government through Bruce Lockhart—which clarified and finally solved all difficulties. At the end of June the recognition of the Government was decided upon and assured.

Meanwhile, on May 10th, 1940, the Germans had carried out their attack on Belgium and the Netherlands. There followed the German advance into France, the piercing of the front, the dividing asunder of the French and British Armies and the concentration of the British forces at Dunkirk. By the beginning of June it was, broadly speaking, clear to us in London that events were leading inexorably to the military breakdown of France.

Our first care was to rescue the Czechoslovak army in France for the further fight. It was clear to me that Great Britain could not, and would not, follow the example of France and that she would enter into no armistice negotiations with Germany. We therefore decided to do all in our power to rescue our soldiers from France and to ensure that all Czechoslovaks at home and abroad would remain allies of the British Empire without compromise, without hesitation and until the end, come what might. Our struggle was not inspired merely by the thought of who would win. It was an uncompromising moral struggle—a fight against evil with which for us there was, and could be, no compromise.

When it was quite clear that France was preparing to capitulate and when I ascertained that the Poles, too, would try to ship their army from France to England, I decided on June 18th, 1940, to send a letter to Anthony Eden, Secretary of State for War, in which I stressed that:

'As you know, we have in France our National Army. It consists now of one division and a special Czechoslovak air unit. Whatever may happen in France, the Czechoslovak National Committee will continue its present policy at the side of your country in the common fight against Germany and Italy. It is, therefore, of vital importance for us to rescue this Army at the time of the final evacuation of your Army from French territory. I am sure that this would be of great political importance from the general European political standpoint.

'In agreement with my political colleagues and the Commander of our Army in France we have carried through all necessary measures for rescuing our Army to continue the fight. I beg you and the British

Government to help us in these our endeavours. In present circumstances my direct connection with our soldiers in France is very difficult.
But if your military representatives in France would contact our Army
(which is now in the Agde camp near Montpellier in Southern France)
and its Commander-in-Chief, General Ingr (who is in Beziers, near
Agde), mutual agreement could be reached to take all necessary steps
for its rescue.'

On the same day I sent a similar letter to Sir Archibald Sinclair, Secretary
of State for Air, and intervened personally with politicians and officials in
the Foreign Office, the War Office and the Admiralty.

The official reply of both Ministers to my letter arrived immediately.
In those critical times these friends of Czechoslovakia fully understood the
political importance of rescuing our soldiers and gave us their sincere help. [1]

In London we were at the same time in constant communication with
our military command in France and we co-ordinated our action with the
negotiations carried on by General Ingr. For the British Government,
occupied as it was with the rescue of its great expeditionary force, this was
a period of immense strain. But we too, in those days, experienced
moments of something near to despair: in the military sense, all was at
stake.

At that time, the Czechoslovak Forces in France consisted of a relatively
numerous flying corps and one army infantry division. The airmen had
been sent to the front under General Slezak (Vicherek) immediately after
the outbreak of war and fought under the French flag and in French units.
On June 17th, the day of the capitulation, several hundreds were at the
front, some were in an instruction camp in Merignac, near Bordeaux, and
others were concentrated in Port Vendre. The British Broadcasting Cor-
poration made it possible for us to broadcast French and Czech appeals to
our airmen to concentrate and fly to Great Britain. In a short while, more
than 500 air personnel arrived safely in England. The rest reached England
after daring and adventurous flights and travels and after overcoming all
obstacles and traps set for them by the Germans as well as local difficulties
from the side of the French. Thus when the historic Battle of Britain began
six weeks later, our airmen could already play an important part in the
fight against the common enemy.

The Czechoslovak infantry division in France, the two regiments of
which were also at the front at the time of the capitulation, succeeded in
forcing its way to the Mediterranean after extremely difficult negotiations
and disputes which sometimes got very near to actual violence. General
Ingr remained ashore with a group of about 60 officers and devotedly

ensured the departure of the various units of the division. The French General Staff made no difficulties, but the local authorities gave no support whatever to our soldiers; transport connections and the French administrative apparatus were already in a chaotic state. It was also necessary to wait for the regiments to arrive direct from the front, and this created great difficulties. And so it was not possible to evacuate even a half of our soldiers in France. The part of the division which was rescued finally reached a Northern English harbour* in mid-July, 1940, after overcoming various obstacles.

On a small scale this adventure reminded us of our Siberian march in World War I. Some of our detachments had to save themselves via North Africa, others via Gibraltar, others even by way of Casablanca. Some of our airmen and soldiers escaped from France to Egypt or to Palestine and were brought to Great Britain many weeks later after very complicated travels.† The fight to save our small army and air force will remain one of the most dramatic events of our Western army units during the second World War. And the help the Czechoslovak soldiers and airmen received from the British Navy and the British authorities in their difficult situation, which often seemed to be quite hopeless, will be a lasting proof of the renewed friendship and solidarity of these two nations in their common fight against Nazism.

On July 14th, after the arrival of our units on British territory, Anthony Eden sent the following message to the soldiers of the Czechoslovak Army:

'As Secretary of State for War, and on behalf of all ranks of your comrades of the British Army, I extend to you a most cordial welcome upon the occasion of your arrival upon our shores. From these shores, from the high seas, from the air, and from every base of operations within the British Empire we have resolved with your valuable aid to attack and overwhelm the forces of our common enemy, and we are further resolved never to relinquish that sacred cause until your beloved Mother Country for which you have bled and suffered so long has been restored once and for all to her own sons and daughters.'

Our policy in these tragic four weeks—from the fall of France and the signing of the armistice to the rescuing of our Army and its transference to British soil—was based on the declaration which I broadcast to the people of Czechoslovakia in the Czech Lands and Slovakia on June 19th, two days after the French capitulation. In it I assured them that this was neither the end of the war nor a final victory of Germany. The British Empire

*Liverpool (Tr.).

†Some of them fought in the Western Desert and took part in the siege of Tobruk (Tr.).

would persevere in the fight to the end. We would march with it whatever should happen. But neither was France conquered and her resistance would continue. And America would intervene in the war, and the Soviet Union was aware that Central and Eastern Europe—and the Soviet Union with them—were now in greater danger than before. It would be the turn of them all. Therefore, there must be no doubts, no fears. The war, I said, was continuing and would continue till the final fall of Germany and Italy.[2]

2. *The British Recognition of the Provisional Czechoslovak Government*

During our negotiations for rescuing the Czechoslovak Army and Air Force I continued my conversations with the Foreign Office for the recognition of our Government. The arrival of Czechoslovak military forces in Great Britain gave to these conversations a new and firmer legal and practical basis. The formation and recognition of a Government became so to speak a necessity.

Soon after March 15th, 1939, I had worked out a legal basis for the military and political re-establishment of Czechoslovakia on French and British soil. In the years 1915 to 1918 we had worked in a similar way; but in the second World War, though our military forces at that time were much smaller than in 1918, we had a much greater claim and incomparably stronger reasons for being recognised, for becoming war allies and for enjoying again all the rights of an independent State fighting against Germany. Twenty years of liberty and all that had happened since September 19th, 1938, entitled us to this while on the British Empire and all others it imposed an enduring, weighty moral and legal duty until our liberation was complete.

This legal concept was based on the following fundamental principles:

1. Our State had legally never ceased to exist. No Czechoslovak must renounce this principle of continuity either in the internal or international sphere. All that had happened since September 19th, 1938, had happened illegally, unconstitutionally and had been forced on us by threats, terror and violence. We would never recognise it.

2. As in the last war, we will again create our National Army—even if it is only a small one—and incorporate it in the whole military action of the Allies. The Army will be independent, Czechoslovak and a continuation of our home army of republican days.

3. We will establish a Czechoslovak Government and strive for its recognition and we will incorporate ourselves politically and diplomati-

cally into the ranks of the fighting allied nations. We will establish our whole governmental and State apparatus on allied territory for the solution of all legal, administrative, economic and financial questions between the Allies and ourselves, thus fully re-establishing the Republic—for the time being, on foreign territory—not only legally, but also in fact, in international policy, with all the consequences for the nation at home.

4. We will organise all our political emigrants in an official, consultative, semi-parliamentary organ, to act as a control of the Government; organise, and discipline our political collaborators and soldiers and give to the whole movement, order, respect, coherence, and most important of all, a *democratic character and spirit*. At the same time we will thus secure the co-operation of the most reliable of our people either in military, political or official activities and thus demonstrate our political experience and maturity.

This sketch of our further work and the development of our movement I gave to the Foreign Office during our negotiations for the recognition of the Government. The presence of our brigade and our airmen on British soil was my last and most impressive argument. At the beginning of July we reached agreement on nearly all fundamental points. So on July 9th, 1940, I sent the following letter to Lord Halifax:*

'In my letter of December 20th, 1939, I had the honour of announcing to Your Excellency the formation of a Czechoslovak National Committee authorized to represent the Czechoslovak people and especially to do in the United Kingdom, in agreement with the Government of His Majesty, all that may be necessary to re-establish the Czechoslovak Army under the competence of His Majesty's Government in the United Kingdom.

'By your letter of the same day, the British Government recognised the Czechoslovak National Committee in the sense mentioned above.

'For some months the Czechoslovak National Committee has worked within its competence and responsibility and has organised the Army, which has now been evacuated from France and arrived in Britain. It also has fulfilled its duty both to the Czechs and the Slovaks suffering in the homeland, by organising their resistance against the common enemy at home, as well as abroad. It has prepared all that is necessary for the next phase of our fight for the liberation of our country from German occupation.

'This new phase is now beginning. In the new situation arising from the latest events in our country and in Europe generally, the National

*Original English text not available (Tr.).

Committee—in agreement with the Army, with all Czechoslovak political elements abroad, but especially in agreement with the clearly perceptible and unbreakable spirit of resistance of the immense majority of the whole population of our occupied country—has now decided to establish a Provisional Czechoslovak Government with a complete State organisation, so far at least as it can be established on British soil. I have been charged to announce to Your Excellency this important and decisive step of our fight for the liberation of our country.

'Having in mind the fact that the free Czechoslovak Nation itself will in full freedom fix all that is necessary for the re-establishment of the final organisation of the State after the end of the war, we have decided to constitute this provisional system of the State organisation as follows:

1. President of the Republic:
   Dr. Eduard Beneš, second President of the Czechoslovak Republic

2. Prime Minister:
   Dr. Jan Šrámek, the former Czechoslovak Deputy Prime Minister

   Members of the Government:*

Jan Bečko	Stefan Osuský
L. Feierabend	Eduard Outrata
General S. Ingr	Pauliny-Tóth or J. Lichner
Jan Masaryk	Hubert Ripka
Jaromír Nečas	Juraj Slávik
František Němec	General Rudolf Viest

3. Czechoslovak State Council: This will be established as a kind of provisional Parliament and will consist of representatives of the most important political and social tendencies in our country. It will act as a consultative and controlling organ, the activity and competence of which will be defined by special decree of the President of the Republic in agreement with the Government.

'Announcing these facts to Your Excellency I wish, above all, to thank the British Government cordially for all the help which they have given to the Czechoslovak National Committee in its political and military activity from the beginning of the war. Special gratitude is due to His Majesty's Government for their attitude after the events of March 15th, 1939, when they categorically refused to recognise the occupation of our country and continued to recognise our Czechoslovak Legation in its

*The Ministries to which they were allotted are given on p. 112 (Tr.).

political and legal privileges as well as the other legal Czechoslovak authorities in countries subordinated to the competence of His Majesty's Government in the United Kingdom. By so doing, they have solemnly emphasized the political and legal continuity of the Czechoslovak Republic.

'In establishing the Provisional Czechoslovak Government we therefore are continuing and building our State structure on the basis which has been preserved by the far-sighted policy and generous attitude of His Majesty's Government, animated by a sublime sense of justice and respect for international law and the sacred rights of the Nations to freedom and independence.

'In this spirit I turn to Your Excellency with the request for the recognition of the Provisional Czechoslovak Government, and I assure you that our State will always be deeply grateful for the help which the great British Nation has given to the Czechoslovak people in its temporary subjugation and in its present sufferings and privations.'

On July 18th, 1940, Lord Halifax replied as follows:*

'In your letter of July 9th, you have kindly informed me that the Czechoslovak National Committee intends to establish a Provisional Czechoslovak Government in this country and that you have been charged with the task of announcing this to me and of asking His Majesty's Government in the United Kingdom to recognise this Provisional Czechoslovak Government composed of the persons the names of whom you mention in your letter.

'I have the pleasure to be able to reply that His Majesty's Government in the United Kingdom are in principle ready to recognise the Provisional Czechoslovak Government so constituted and to facilitate its activity on the territory which is under the competence of His Majesty's Government in the United Kingdom. His Majesty's Government have taken notice of the fact that this Provisional Government is to be a representative government of the Czech and Slovak people and that it is intended that also the Czechoslovak State Council, which you mention in your letter, will be of fully representative character and will include the recognised Czech and Slovak leaders abroad, as far as they have not been included in the Provisional Government.

'On communicating this to you, I would like to make it clear that His Majesty's Government, in approaching this act of recognition, do not intend to engage themselves in advance to the recognition or future support in the fixing of whatever future boundaries in Central Europe.

*Original English text not available (Tr.).

I would also like to mention that it cannot be presumed that His Majesty's Government necessarily share your conclusion, drawn in your letter: namely, that by their attitude after the events of March 15th, 1939, His Majesty's Government have taken any particular attitude concerning the legal continuity of the Czechoslovak Republic. The acts of His Majesty's Government had the significance that they protested against the changes brought about in Czechoslovakia by German military action, and that they stressed that in their opinion these changes had no legal basis. The recognition of the Czechoslovak Legation in London was to signify this fact.

'By the recognition of the Provisional Czechoslovak Government there will arise, of course, some administrative, financial and other questions, which will have to be settled, e.g., the question of competence over the Czechoslovak military forces and over Czechoslovak non-military persons in this country and the question of the gold of the Czechoslovak National Bank. The competent London authorities will be glad to discuss these questions with you or your representatives, whenever it may be convenient to you. I would be glad to learn whether in your opinion the discussions of these questions should start already before the intended act of recognition or only after it.'

At the same time we reached agreement with the Foreign Office that I would take note of Lord Halifax's first answer in a special letter and that a public declaration of British recognition of the Czechoslovak Government would be issued.

This declaration was made by Winston Churchill himself in the House of Commons on July 23rd.[2] Two days previously, I had received a second letter from Lord Halifax as a further answer to mine of July 9th. It read as follows:

London July 21st, 1940

'YOUR EXCELLENCY,

In the light of exchanges of view which have taken place between us, I have the honour to inform you that, in response to the request of the Czechoslovak National Committee, His Majesty's Government in the United Kingdom are happy to recognise and enter into relations with the Provisional Czechoslovak Government established by the Czechoslovak National Committee to function in this country. His Majesty's Government will be glad to discuss with the representatives of the Provisional Government certain questions arising out of this recognition which require settlement.

Sincerely yours,

(Signed) HALIFAX'

3. The Creation of the Czechoslovak State Organisation Abroad

This was the first big and important step in the field of international law for the nullification of Munich and the German occupation arising from it. We at once put into effect all necessary measures within the framework of our political emigration and Army. As far as the restrictions of exile allowed, all laws, decrees, customs and administrative and other traditions of the First Republic became valid at once. Constitutional laws, especially, were fully respected from the outset as well as other laws as far as they could be applied abroad. The rights of the Czechoslovak Parliament were divided between the President, the Government and the State Council on the basis of existing conditions abroad and on the principle that every change of the constitutional or any other law must be only temporary for the period of the war and applied so as to come as near as possible to the spirit and letter of the Constitution and of home legislation. Where full continuity could be applied at once, it had to be applied without exception.

We naturally presumed that all our resistance activities would be submitted for approval at home after the war, and that, after revision in the light of conditions at home, they would receive political validity in postwar Czechoslovakia. We therefore decided that the principle of political and legal continuity of the Republic, beginning with the whole State structure must be applied systematically in the life of our emigrants, our citizens in exile and especially our Army.

By international act, I had again been recognised as President of the Republic in the sphere of international law. The Government and I had been recognised by the same act. *It was a great diplomatic success, a success in international politics*, that the Allies, as in the last war, had not only recognised our Government but at the same time the Head of the State. It was a great success in *internal* politics, and this meant a decisive consolidation of the emigration and Army and at the end of the war a *stabilisation of relationships till the end of the war*. And in our opinion it corresponded to our theory of the *legal continuity of the State*, of the invalidity of Munich and its consequences, the invalidity of my resignation as President and my departure from home—the invalidity in short of all that had happened to us after September 19th, 1938. The violation of the Munich Agreement by Germany and Hácha's signature to the protectorate in Berlin on March 15th, 1939, had in our view fully and automatically re-established the *status quo ante* Munich though this did not mean that we would simply revert to 1938 conditions at home after the war. To advocate another policy would *from the Czechoslovak point of view have been tantamount to treason.*[4]

When I resumed my Presidential functions which—on pressure from Berlin—I had to resign immediately after Munich,* I considered it my duty that my first act as President of the Republic should be the formal nomination of the new Government. In so doing I used the same procedure that had been observed by us in the historic Prague Castle during the twenty years before Munich throughout the terms of office of Masaryk and myself.

On the same evening,† therefore, I issued in the form of a letter, the following decree:

'DEAR DOCTOR ŠRAMEK,‡

'I nominate you Prime Minister. At the same time I nominate as members of the Government the following Ministers and Secretaries of State:

Deputy Jan Bečko§	State Secretary in the Ministry for Social Welfare
Minister Dr. Ladislav Feierabend	Minister of State§
Divisional Gen. Sergěj Ingr	Minister of National Defence
Minister Jan Masaryk	Minister of Foreign Affairs
Minister Ing. Jaromir Nečas	Minister of State§
Deputy František Němec	Minister for Social Welfare
Minister Dr. Štefan Osuský	Minister of State§
Dr. Eduard Outrata	Minister of Finance
Dr. Pauliny-Tóth	State Secretary in the Ministry of Finance
Dr. Hubert Ripka	State Secretary in the Ministry of Foreign Affairs
Minister Dr. Juraj Slávik	Minister of the Interior
Divisional Gen. Rudolf Viest	State Secretary in the Ministry of National Defence

*See page 50 (Tr.).

†July 21st, 1940 (Tr.).

‡Monseigneur Šramek, a Czech, remained Prime Minister until the formation of the so-called Košice Government in April, 1945, when he was succeeded by Mr. Zdenek Fierlinger. After the Communist *coup d'état* in February, 1948, Dr. Šramek and a colleague, Mons. František Hala, Minister of Posts, were arrested when trying to board an aeroplane which would have taken them illegally to Paris. They were interned in a Monastery where Dr. Šrámek is believed to have remained till the present. Mons. Hala is believed to have died in 1952 (Tr.).

§ i.e. without portfolio. The prefix 'Minister' either indicated cabinet rank in a pre-Munich administration or the head of a Legation (Tr.).

'We are continuing in the tradition of the First Republic, the Republic of Masaryk, and are preparing a new Republic which will adapt itself now to the events of the war and to *the new conditions which will arise after the war.* I believe that we will all carry out our duties harmoniously, worthily and courageously. Our first task is to organise the Army and to wage war and then to order all our affairs abroad: the choice of representatives, the welfare of refugees and emigrants, the appointment of officials, etc. And in all our acts we must keep always before us the need to maintain and strengthen unity, harmony and peace among us.

'Above all, our care will be directed to the prosecution of the war. We will wage war against our oppressors and enemies together with all our allies—whosoever shall join them during the war—accepting all the consequences, without compromise and to final victory.

DR. ŠRAMEK (*Signed*) DR. EDUARD BENEŠ'

Four members of the Cabinet were clearly Leftist,* four can be considered as members of the Right Wing,† the rest belonged politically to the centre. Five Ministers had already been members of Czechoslovak Governments before the war. Three had been Czechoslovak envoys—in London, Paris and Warsaw.‡ Two had been Generals of the pre-Munich Czechoslovak Army. Prime Minister Monseigneur Šrámek had been leader of the People's Party. He had been Minister many times and once Deputy Prime Minister. The Government consisted of eight Czechs and five Slovaks.⁵‖

Also on the same day I issued as President of the Republic another important decree concerning the establishment of a State Council as consultative organ for the Government and the President of the Republic. Later on October 15th, 1940, I issued the decree on the provisional execution of legislative power.

By these means the controlling and consultative functions of the State Council were fixed and it was established how legislation should be effected in our State organisation until the end of the war. As already mentioned, the establishment of the State Council was a direct consequence of the recognition of the Provisional Czechoslovak Government by the Government of Great Britain. It was agreed on my suggestion during the negotiations that, in the spirit of the democratic tradition of the First Republic, a political organisation should be constituted to unite our

*Bečko, Nečas, Němec, Ripka. (Tr.).
†Šrámek, Osuský, Pauliny-Tóth, Slávik. (Tr.).
‡Respectively Masaryk, Osuský and Slávik. (Tr.).
‖The Slovaks were Bečko, Osuský, Pauliny-Toth, Slávik and Viest. (Tr.).

whole political emigration and to exercise certain functions belonging to an elected chamber. For self-evident reasons it was impossible to establish on British soil a Parliament in the true sense of the word. We therefore had to replace it by an organ with limited competence, but sufficiently representative and able to act as a controlling and consultative factor with regard to the Government and to the State functionaries. Throughout the war, the State Council performed its duties well and it certainly did great service to our cause.*

On July 24th, 1940, three days after the British recognition, I broadcast from London my first political message to our country in my newly-recognised capacity. Appreciating the political and, from the international standpoint, legal importance of the recognition of the Government and the Czechoslovak Republic, I specially stressed that:

'Once again we have an internationally recognised new Government. Once again the international status of the Czechoslovak Republic has been recognised and again our State flag is legally flying everywhere in the world.

'Without recognising Munich or any of its consequences, we are advocating and will continue to advocate the principle that *the Czecho-slovak Republic, the Republic of Masaryk, continued to live and exist even after Munich*. For that reason, our whole legal system still continues in the sphere of international law and politics. *For us, my departure from office and country has no legal validity. For us, there was legally no destruction of the Republic. For us nothing done in our country by Nazi violence after March 15th, 1939, has any political or legal validity.*

'I solemnly declare these to be our political and legal principles and I want to stress *that they are valid for all citizens of our State and of our Nation—for Czechs, Slovaks, Germans and Ruthenians and all others at home. Furthermore, I declare to be non-existent and illegal everything that we have been forced to do illegally and unconstitutionally since September, 1938.*

'You are not bound by any promises, obligations and oaths which have been extorted from you. Every one of you, every civil servant, functionary of State or local government, every soldier, gendarme, policeman, state or private employee, every citizen of the Republic who, in whatever office or function, is, directly or indirectly under obligation to the Nazi régime is today freed from such obligations so far as in his soul and conscience he has ever considered them to be binding. In the moment when he is again able to act freely, or when he is called upon by his free Government, he will act as a free man, as a true, self-respecting, honourable and faithful citizen of the Czechoslovak Republic.

'When we began to organise for resistance abroad after Munich and when our soldiers began to assemble in Western Europe, that was an ebullition of our tortured humanity and of our national faith. It was the holy voice of our history which called aloud to us. *Therefore, dear friends, we are fighting and will go on fighting to the end.* Our past and our new future, Europe and the whole world and the whole history of mankind must see that in this fateful moment there are Czechs and Slovaks who did not submit and will not submit whatever happens. What is at stake is the Nation itself which is eternal—its honour, its dignity, its good name, its faithfulness to its own history.

'We have lived through two grave, fearful years. For a long while, we have been falling into the abyss and day after day heavy blows have rained upon us. *Today, the descent has ceased. We are starting upward again, we are on the way to victory.*'[1]

Immediately after the recognition of the Provisional Czechoslovak Government, Dr. Ripka and General Ingr started discussions with the British War and Air Ministries about the co-operation of our Army and Air Corps with the British Forces. Agreement was reached in the matters of the legal position of our Army, its technical organisation, its relations to British units and on the general question of its finances. The agreement was signed in the Foreign Office on October 25th, 1940, by Lord Halifax and Jan Masaryk.

At the same time there was signed in the name of the British and Czechoslovak Governments by Sir Kingsley Wood, Chancellor of the Exchequer, and Dr. E. Outrata, Czechoslovak Minister of Finance, a special financial agreement regulating the financing of our forces during the war and the right to dispose of the Czechoslovak gold, deposited with the Bank of England before Munich.* The whole Czechoslovak political

---

*The gold in question appears to have been the £6,000,000 held by the Bank of England on Czechoslovak account at the time of the German occupation of Prague, March 15th, 1939. This gold automatically passed into German ownership when the Czechoslovak National Bank came under German control but was still in London when war broke out.

The agreement, which is dated December 10th, 1940—not October 25th, as stated in the text—has not been published. It provided, *inter al* (a) that the whole of the Czechoslovak National Bank gold should be placed at the disposal of the British Government for the prosecution of the Allied war effort and that for this purpose the gold should be sold by the Custodian of Enemy Property in the United Kingdom to the Bank of England for sterling and (b) that the Provisional Czechoslovak Government should hold the British Government, the Bank of England and the Custodian indemnified against any claim in respect of the gold in question (Tr.).

and military activity during World War II has therefore been financed from our own funds which had either remained at our disposal from the days of the Republic or which were procured during the war by means of loans. The agreement also regulated the preparations for Anglo-Czechoslovak co-operation for the reconstruction of economic life in the Republic after the end of the war.

These two agreements with the British Government afterwards normalised the whole of our political and military activity in Great Britain and put in legal, political and financial order every aspect of our future regular co-operation as an ally, both *de facto* and *de jure*.

For the second anniversary of Munich, September 30th, 1940, I arranged with the British Foreign Office for a message to be sent to our people at home on this subject. For the first time, I asked for a clear British declaration to the effect that the Munich 'Dictate' no longer existed and that future British policy would work for its complete annulment. I discussed the whole question with Bruce Lockhart, who, since our recognition, was the official British representative with our Government. Though my draft of the message was not accepted textually by the British Government, it was a substantial political step towards the realisation of our national aims. The address was delivered on the second anniversary of Munich by Winston Churchill himself, who said:

'Today is the second anniversary of the Munich Agreement, a date which the world will always remember for the tragic sacrifice made by the Czechoslovak people in the interest of European peace. The hopes which this agreement stirred in the heart of civilised mankind have been frustrated. Within six months the solemn pledges given by the unscrupulous men who control the destiny of Germany were broken and the agreement destroyed with a ruthlessness which unmasked the true nature of their reckless ambitions to the whole world.

'The protection which Hitler forced upon you has been a sham and a cloak for the incorporation of your once flourishing country in the so-called Greater Reich. Instead of protection he has brought you nothing but moral and material devastation, and today the followers of that great and tolerant humanitarian, President Masaryk, are being persecuted with a deliberate cruelty which has few parallels in modern history.

'In this hour of your martyrdom I send you this message. The battle which we in Britain are fighting today is not only our battle. It is also your battle, and, indeed, the battle of all Nations who prefer liberty to a soulless serfdom. It is the struggle of civilised Nations for the right to live their own life in the manner of their own choosing. It represents man's instinctive defiance of tyranny and of an impersonal universe.

'Throughout history no European Nation has shown a greater will to survive than yours, and today again your people have given countless proofs of their courage in adversity. Here in Britain we have welcomed with pride and gratitude your soldiers and airmen who have come by daring escapes to take part with ever-increasing success in that battle for Britain which is also the battle for Czechoslovakia. And no less sincere is our admiration of those Czechs and Slovaks who on the home front are risking death, and worse than death, in order to foster resistance against a cruel and heartless oppressor.

'It is because we both are fighting for the fundamental decencies of human life that we are determined that neither our struggle nor your struggle shall be in vain. It is for this reason that we have refused to recognise any of the brutal conquests of Germany in Central Europe and elsewhere, that we have welcomed a Czechoslovak Provisional Government in this country, and that we have made the restoration of Czechoslovak liberties one of our principal war aims. With firmness and resolution, two qualities which our Nations share in equal measure, these aims will be achieved. Be of good cheer. The hour of your deliverance will come. The soul of freedom is deathless; it cannot, and will not, perish.'

4. Crisis attacks our Army and our Emigration

The months of June and July, 1940, were the most dramatic of our action abroad. To them belong the fall of France, the fight to rescue our Army in France and the decisive negotiations on the recognition of the Republic and the Government. Not since Munich had we experienced days and weeks of such tension. These were great and critical moments of the second resistance movement.

The fall of France had considerably demoralised a great part of our political emigration and a part of our army. The quarrels in our political action abroad—in the case of Dr. Osuský almost exclusively a personal one —were disguised by various petty political pretexts. They reached their climax in France at that time. Some French circles, seeing where events in France were heading from a military and political standpoint, were really fanning the flames of our difficulties and were making use of some of our people as informers and to split our ranks. The formation of dissident organisations under the title of a 'Czech' and a 'Slovak' National Council (as against the official Czechoslovak National Committee) on which they were working from the beginning of 1940, served only to nurture and propagate these quarrels.[8]

When the fall of France and her capitulation became a reality, our people in France were engulfed in a political and military chaos the only escape from which was to go to Britain. But this way out was one of the most difficult and hazardous. The members of the Paris National Committee, our other functionaries and officials in France arrived in London in the second half of June, much affected psychologically by these military and political events. Most of them were deeply depressed and some, indeed, even believed that the war was already lost and that we had reached the end. In many respects, these events reminded me of what had happened during the first World War in Russia in 1917-1918.

In the first moments after the fall of France our Army was in rather bad shape. The composition of our forces in France was very uneven. A great part were Slovaks, who had lived for long years in France. Events in Slovakia had so confused many of them that they had no enthusiasm either for the Army or their military duties, even though the French military authorities had consented to their being received into our Army as Czechoslovak citizens. Fully 48 per cent of the troops who came to Britain were of the intelligentsia. A considerable percentage were Jews and at the beginning a small number also came from among our Germans.*
Our officers were to a large extent young officers who had scarcely left the military academy. They were still inexperienced and quite unprepared psychologically for such abnormal conditions under which this partly voluntary, partly conscripted army lived and served. They were often unable to control fully and correctly such a heterogeneous unit with such very divergent ideas.

Furthermore, some of our officers possessed undemocratic tendencies. Here and there there were signs of anti-semitism; and the stories of German terror at home inevitably evoked in the Army fierce hatred of everything German. This naturally did not help to promote companionship with our German soldiers. Among the rank and file themselves, a considerable part was predominantly Socialist. There were also strong nationalist tendencies; later Communist tendencies manifested themselves too. Memories of Munich, of political fights at home—fights against political parties and individual politicians—further contributed to make the early period after the arrival of our troops in Britain a time of chaos, obscurity, disunion and sometimes even ideological derangement. The worst feature of all was that the Army, having been on the French front,

*The term 'Sudeten' is not recognised in Czechoslovakia (Tr.).

had undergone the difficulties of the evacuation and seen the terrible fall of the powerful French army. For a while it *felt itself to be part of that defeated army.* All this facilitated the disposition among the soldiers of a mood to listen to every kind of propaganda: German, Hungarian, defeatism, espionage. Such movements always had a political background. Moreover, on the part of some political circles—after the conclusion of the German-Soviet treaty—such activities were extremely penetrating. I think that the time has not yet come to occupy oneself in detail with all these cases, which in any event were not numerous, and to analyse them politically.*

This deeply influenced the morale of our soldiers who had come over to England. In short: *our Army, which had arrived in Great Britain, was experiencing a deep spiritual and moral crisis.* Indeed, that we only got half of our division from France to Great Britain, was partly due to the fact that some of our soldiers, considering the fight either lost or finished, saw no reason for further service. A number of them therefore—to their own loss—simply refused to leave France.

The most serious aspect of the matter was that a small section of soldiers who had been evacuated to England thought along similar lines when it arrived. This group provoked crises and quarrels. It lacked discipline and often excused itself (whether rightly or wrongly) by complaints about fascism and anti-semitism in our Army. Finally, this section refused to continue its military service and asked for its discharge. It should be added that identical or similar signs manifested themselves to the same or even a greater extent in the French, Belgian and especially the Polish forces in Britain. So far as we were concerned it constituted a serious crisis—the most difficult we had to experience in our Army in World War II.

I visited our soldiers immediately after their arrival in England, ascertained their situation, heard their complaints and tried to settle all difficulties amicably and by persuasion. But finally I was forced to proceed somewhat more resolutely. I gave permission to General Ingr to expel from our camp—from contact with those of our soldiers who were continuing to serve—all who refused to obey my call to fulfil their patriotic and military duties. We also agreed to the proposal of the British authorities that they should be segregated for a time in a special camp. Some of these soldiers were soon afterwards admitted into the British Pioneer Corps, but the greater part of them rejoined our Army in the following two years, after having thoroughly sobered down from these

*Until Hitler attacked the U.S.S.R., Czech and Slovak Communists opposed participation in the 'capitalist' war. A good many of them were sent to prison for subversive activities (Tr.).

aberrations or misunderstanding, and performed their military service excellently afterwards.

For a long time we were worried by the so-called 'officers' crisis'. This lasted in an acute form from the time of the arrival of our forces in Great Britain into the first half of 1943. The reason was, simply, that there were too many officers in proportion to the number of men. These officers—there were more than 400—could not get their proper rank in a less numerous military unit and therefore had to serve as simple soldiers and be treated and paid accordingly. The Poles, French, Belgians and others had the same problem. Everyone will understand that, humanly speaking, these officers were called upon for a great and continuous effort of self-denial and sacrifice. There were, of course, quarrels (especially as to who should and who should not be confirmed as officers), complaints, dissatis-faction, opposition to the leaders and eventually to the Government and the Ministry of National Defence.

All possible ways were tried to solve this crisis, but none brought satis-faction because every solution meant increased expenditure to which the British Government did not want to consent. So there were demonstra-tions of dissatisfaction among the officers which sometimes fell not far short of being serious violations of military discipline. There were even collective demonstrations which could have been termed 'plotting' and 'mutiny' against the Ministry or the Government. It was therefore some-times necessary to intervene energetically and—in spite of my understand-ing of such manifestations of moral or material dissatisfaction—rather severely.

Regularly all such occurrences took a political colouring either in the Army itself or in the political emigration. The 'opposition' and the malcontents among the political emigrants used them as a weapon against the Government or against the Minister of National Defence. People in our movement who were really seditious, for political or other reasons, also tried to gain ground for their aims in this sphere. The greatest danger was, of course, that such things were apt to place our whole Army and our movement in an unfavourable light before the British and the other Allies.

Thus there was much trouble and pain and many difficulties. It was finally overcome in 1942 and 1943, partly through the arrival of new soldiers, and partly by the reorganisation and the new duties of the whole unit and also by a change in the attitude of the British authorities to some of our demands.

For me, these moments in June and July, 1940, were rather critical and painful. I was just negotiating for the recognition of our Government and some of our newly-arrived soldiers were manifesting these moral and psychological symptoms! Happily, the overwhelming majority of the others soon showed their good qualities, and the airmen, without exception, behaved well, and participated immediately after their arrival in preparations for the Battle of Britain. However, similar sights could be seen in the other exiled armies on a much larger scale, so that these events ended without any great *political* consequences for us. But it must be said that *for the moment* this crisis gave quite a shock to the whole of our movement.

Finally, there were specially great difficulties over the formation of the Government. I had taken upon me the task—partly in accordance with the wish of the British Government, partly in order to keep as far as possible in line with conditions at home—to form a National Government which would be accepted and recognised by all. But I did not want to recognise the old party system lock, stock and barrel with all that this entailed. This was partly because the Army strongly disliked it, but also partly because I should not only have been involved in unending quarrels, but in addition, at the very outset of our action abroad, should have brought some unsavoury aspects of party strife at home into the whole political system erected outside our frontiers. But this meant that for a number of matters, activities and duties I had neither criteria, nor guide-posts so that I often had to take decisions myself—almost on an authoritarian basis—simply on my own opinion and judgment. Accordingly, in the spirit of the well-known and reprehensible practice of the First Republic, I was made personally responsible for everything and so there was a perpetual recrudescence of those pernicious and unpatriotic manifestations of bad party manners which we had experienced at home. When some people were personally dissatisfied with something, or when they wanted to extort something for their personal benefit, they used to threaten or attack me (sometimes with extreme lack of decency or political propriety) and thus disorganise the whole movement from above. *At the outset*, this was a rather common practice on the part of all dissatisfied persons in our political emigration. Later, it vanished nearly everywhere.

Even more important was the fact that in this question I also had considerable difficulties with the British Government. Without proper regard to the real conditions in our emigration and at home, they imposed on me the condition that a provisional Government would only be recognised *if I secured full unity of all our political currents and, of course, also those of the Slovaks.* I endeavoured to reach this impartially and impersonally. At that time it was a superhumanly difficult task. Some things I refused to do in spite of everything. The British only began to trust us fully when they themselves realised how subversive and selfish some of our emigrants were, how full of hatred, and withal politically inept or mistaken or quite incapable of co-operation. In some cases I myself considered the things done by them in exile at that time to be criminal and treasonable. For example, in July, 1940, a few days before our recognition by the British Government, some of our people who had just arrived from France where they had been doing their best to wreck our prospects, sent a memorandum to the Foreign Office declaring that I represented practically nothing and nobody and that I and our Government ought not to be recognised. Later on, some of our people repeated these intrigues with the object of preventing our getting full and definitive recognition, especially from the Government of the United States.

Be that as it may, in July, 1940, the moment arrived when the decisive step in all our work abroad was to be taken. And *at that moment* there were among us a certain number of people who disrupted, quarrelled, pursued their own selfish interests, intrigued, when such tragic and at the same time decisive events were in progress as the Fall of France and the arrival of our army and emigration in London! The slightest nervousness, intrigue and unpatriotic action could, in those uncertain times, have overthrown everything, or at least delayed it. The whole discussions on the formation of our Cabinet and the future consolidation of our movement were, therefore, extremely strained and in a sense nervous and unsure. In the end we were able to achieve all these aims but only with the utmost nervous exertion and with the utmost of our endeavours.

When, at last, the formation and recognition of the Government was announced on July 21st, I breathed again. The greatest obstacles existing hitherto had been overcome. The way to the consolidation of the Army, the emigration and our whole movement was open. It was not the end to difficulties, quarrels and political intrigues. These continued for two more years, the so-called Czechoslovak 'opposition' relying even at that early stage on the support, including the financial support, of official and unofficial *Polish* circles. This went on for as long as our recognition was not yet fully accorded by all the Allies, especially the United States. More accurately, it continued almost to the end of the war, when fresh differences arose between us and the London Poles with regard to the policy to be adopted towards the Soviet Union. The intention was to undermine the position of our Government and prevent our whole system from ever being consolidated. But the recognition of the Government in July, 1940, was the end of the most difficult and most uncertain period of our work abroad.

5. Full Recognition of Czechoslovakia by Great Britain

After the recognition of the Provisional Czechoslovak Government on July 21st, 1940, our political and military activity on British soil moved rapidly and on the whole successfully. We soon had organised a civil and military administration in London and a complete diplomatic service in the rest of the world. Then we at once set ourselves the following important and concrete tasks: to transform 'provisional' recognition into a *definitive one*, thus regaining our pre-Munich international status and equality in international law with all the other independent allied States. And then, above all, the second task: *the revocation of Munich.*

Our State and national organism was functioning normally, so to speak, from October 28th, 1940, when after two years of German oppression we again celebrated our State Holiday and Independence Day freely on British soil with new hopes for the future and with the same ceremonies as we had celebrated it in Prague Castle during the twenty years of the First Republic. Even so, and despite the recognition of the Government—because it was merely 'provisional' recognition—the international and diplomatic position of the Czechoslovak Republic remained equivocal in some respects. We had to cope with this fact daily. Differences of status kept cropping up between the position of Czechoslovakia and that of the other allied States.

From the beginning of 1941, therefore, we began to discuss these questions with the British Foreign Office which soon agreed that it was necessary to put an end to uncertainties and discriminations and introduce a definitive legal order into our whole position. Essentially this meant the *legal* removal of the consequences of the Munich treaty and the German Occupation.

To secure this, it was necessary to achieve recognition of the following facts:

(*a*) The Government of the Czechoslovak Republic must be placed on the same legal basis as other allied Governments-in-exile and the Republic must get the same international status as before the crisis of 1938.

(*b*) In view of other political and military developments both in the world as a whole and in Czechoslovakia the 'provisional' period of the Czechoslovak Government was coming to an end because the whole population in the Czech Lands and perhaps about 80 per cent in Slovakia had identified themselves unconditionally with the Allies against Germany and with the Czechoslovak Government in London.

(c) The logical consequence of these two facts both legally and politically must be accepted: the unrecognised so-called Government of President Hácha in Prague was non-existent according to international law. In Prague, Hitler and his administration governed *de facto*, not any Czech government-in-captivity. In any case, neither the Protectorate itself nor any Czech Protectorate Government had been recognised legally by the British Empire or other allied and neutral states.

(d) Similarly in international law there did not exist an independent Slovakia because the so-called Slovak Government had not been recognised by any of the Allies and was substantially in the hands of Germany. According to international law therefore the separation of Slovakia and Subcarpathian Ruthenia from the Czech Provinces did not exist so far as the Allies and ourselves were concerned.

A discussion which the Foreign Minister, Jan Masaryk and I had with Foreign Secretary Anthony Eden on April 10th, 1941,[*] was conducted in this spirit. We discussed general international and military questions and agreed that the German campaign in the Balkans and the Mediterranean and the one which was imminent in the Near East with its direct or indirect menace to the Soviet Union in its later phases must have far-reaching effects on the international situation. We stressed to Eden that at this precise moment and in these circumstances, it might well have great importance for other countries if the Czechoslovak question were taken a step further. The smaller nations which were attacked would see in this very act what were the present and future aims of British policy. Thus Britain's determination to liberate Europe from Nazi oppression would again be confirmed and stressed.

On April 18th, 1941, I handed Eden a memorandum on these lines, stressing the following points, among others:

(a) Full diplomatic recognition *de jure* for the Czechoslovak Government, thus solving the question of the legal continuity of the Czechoslovak Republic.

(b) The appointment as a consequence of this recognition of a British Minister Plenipotentiary to the Czechoslovak President and Government and a Czechoslovak Minister to the King and the British Government. (Up to this time there had only been a British 'delegate'—Bruce Lockhart.)

(c) The Czechoslovak Republic, its President and Government to receive the same legal and political status from the standpoint of international law as the other fully recognised allied Governments in London.

[*]Mr. Eden succeeded Lord Halifax as Foreign Minister on December 23rd, 1940.

(*d*) The officially recognised titles to be used in future: the Czecho-slovak Republic, the President of the Czechoslovak Republic, the Government of the Czechoslovak Republic, the Legation of the Czechoslovak Republic. All future agreements signed with the Czecho-slovak Republic to be concluded in the name of the Czechoslovak Republic, as before September, 1938.

(*e*) The provisional character of the Czechoslovak Government to be regarded in future as an *internal* affair of Czechoslovak democracy, signifying that the existing Czechoslovak Government would imme-diately after the war conform to the rules of the democratic Czecho-slovak Constitution. Meanwhile, from the international standpoint the Czechoslovak Government to cease to be provisional.

In May and June, 1941, these questions were frequently discussed between us. There emerged difficulties both of a political and a legal character. In some British circles there was hesitation arising from the growing list of German victories, the uncertainty of the international situation and the rapid changes in Central Europe, in Germany itself and especially in the Soviet Union, whose entrance into the war we had been confidently expecting since January and February, 1941, in spite of the scepticism of the British and all around us. (I had had reliable reports of German preparations for the attack on Russia as early as January, 1941.)* But at last, by the end of June, after repeated interventions and discussions with the Foreign Office, *all our negotiations for full recognition were success-fully concluded.* When, after the entry of the Soviet Union into the war, we embarked at the beginning of July on a swift and successful discussion of our affairs with Russia, the British War Cabinet during the first half of July decided to take the necessary legal steps to regulate the whole of our problem. On July 18th, 1941, Minister Anthony Eden called for Jan Masaryk and handed him the following Note:°†

> *Foreign Office, S.W.1,*
> *July 18th, 1941*

DEAR MINISTER,

In a memorandum delivered on April 18th to Mr. Lockhart for His Majesty's Government in the United Kingdom, Dr. Beneš formulated demands in the matter of Anglo-Czechoslovak relations.

These demands were discussed also on the basis of a further letter from Dr. Beneš of May 28th and the exchange of views which followed

*See pp. 147–150 (Tr.).

†Original English text not available (Tr.).

especially with regard to the present situation in Czechoslovakia. I am sincerely glad that in consequence I am now able to inform you that His Majesty the King has decided to accredit an Envoy Extraordinary and Minister Plenipotentiary with Dr. Beneš as President of the Czechoslovak Republic. And His Majesty's Government will welcome a similar nomination if the Czechoslovak Government wishes to take such a step.[10]

This decision further signifies that His Majesty's Government now consider the legal position of the President and Government of the Czechoslovak Republic to be identical with the position of the other allied Heads of State and Governments now residing in this country and that in future in the official designation of the Czechoslovak State Organisation the terms Czechoslovak Republic, President of the Czechoslovak Republic, Government of the Czechoslovak Republic, Legation of the Czechoslovak Republic, etc., will be used. His Majesty's Government also accept that agreements concluded in future with your Government shall be negotiated in the name of the Czechoslovak Republic.

His Majesty's Government have taken note of the communication contained in paragraph II, 6 of Dr. Beneš's memorandum of April 18th, that the 'provisional' nature of the Czechoslovak Government shall in future be understood only as an internal matter of Czechoslovak democracy and that the term signifies that the present Czechoslovak Government will immediately after the war conform to the enactments of the democratic Czechoslovak Constitution.

The memorandum of Dr. Beneš of April 18th, has also raised the question of the legal continuity of the Czechoslovak Republic. The arguments developed in the memorandum show this to be a somewhat complicated question. The attitude of His Majesty's Government was expressed in the letter of my predecessor to Dr. Beneš, of July 18th, 1940, and His Majesty's Government wish to leave this question for subsequent consideration at the appropriate moment.

To prevent a possible misunderstanding, I beg to inform you that His Majesty's Government maintain the view expressed in my predecessor's letter in the matter of territorial questions, that is to say, they undertake no obligation by the present Note to recognise or to support any future frontiers whatsoever in Central Europe.

To His Excellency   I am, yours sincerely,

Mr. Jan Masaryk, C.B.E.   (*Signed*) ANTHONY EDEN

From the point of international law and international politics this British Note was of great importance for Czechoslovakia. Even if it did not expressly accept our point of view of the Republic's legal continuity and of our pre-Munich frontiers, it fully opened the way for a solution of both these questions in future discussions and it definitely restored to the Republic its full former international status. This was most important at that moment. In the matter of frontiers, too, we were placed in the same position as all other Central European States—including allied ones, such as Poland and Yugoslavia. At that time the British Government took the line—and later reaffirmed its attitude to the United States—that frontier questions must be decided *definitely and jointly* only at the Peace Conference.

NOTES TO CHAPTER THREE

[1]Eden's answer read as follows:*

'London, June 19th, 1940.

'DEAR FRIEND,

'I am really grateful for your letter of June 18th as I am well aware of the necessity of preserving your National Army, especially in so critical a time. The present situation in France makes the question of the evacuation extremely pressing.

'Yesterday and today I have undertaken everything possible to carry out this evacuation. The Foreign Office has given instructions to our Ambassador to contact Gen. Ingr for organising the greatest possible evacuation and the Admiralty has carried out all necessary measures. The Ambassador has also been instructed to try to reach agreement with the French for evacuation of the Czech Division from one of the Mediterranean ports.

'As long as the situation in France remains so unstable, one, unfortunately, cannot foresee how far these measures will be successful. But be assured that we will do all in our power to fetch your National Army to Britain.'

[2]This address is printed in my book *Six Years in Exile and the Second World War*,† on pp. 84-87.

[3]This declaration is printed in the Appendix.

[4]I therefore considered, and I still consider, as nothing else than treason the action of some of our emigrants who for mere personal reasons afterwards propagated among our political emigration and in our Army—and even among the British and Americans—the 'theory' that I was not the 'legal' President, thereby seeking to hinder the normalisation and consolidation of our conditions abroad *vis-à-vis* our own people and the Allies. I hold

*Original not available.
†Not available in English (Tr.).

this opinion the more strongly because these people while trying to mould events in accordance with their own calculations and while hoping for developments which accorded with their wishes and opinions, had nevertheless recognised our new legal and political situation by their acts and had even been ready to accept *various positions and offices at my hands as President of the Republic.*

⁵Later, another Minister of State was nominated: Jan Lichner.* Dr. Pauliny-Toth did not take office.

⁶(a) The Decree of the President of the Republic of July 21st, 1940, on the establishment of a State Council as an advisory body of the Provisional State Organisation of the Czechoslovak Republic, read as follows:

Paragraph One

A State Council is hereby established as an advisory body to the President of the Republic and as an auxiliary organ of control within the Provisional State Organisation of the Czechoslovak Republic.

Paragraph Two

The State Council has a maximum of 40 members, nominated individually by the President of the Republic for a term of one year. The mandate of a member of the State Council lasts for this time unless it is withdrawn at the instance of the President of Republic or of the State Council itself on a proposal of the Discipline Committee (Paragraph 8), or unless the member himself resigns it.

Paragraph Three

An official of the Movement abroad or a member of the forces who is nominated member of the State Council shall, if he accepts the mandate, be granted indefinite leave by his superior officer in order to be able to perform his functions.

Paragraph Four

The Chairman and three Vice-Chairmen of the State Council are appointed by the President of the Republic. The President calls and closes the sessions of the State Council. A member of the State Council has the right to take part in its deliberations only after having notified the President of the Republic that he accepts the mandate and having taken the following oath in writing.

'I promise on my honour and conscience to be faithful to the Czechoslovak Republic and its provisional State Organisation recognised on the soil of our Ally, Great Britain, and I promise to carry out my duties conscientiously and impartially, to fulfil the tasks which the common fight for the complete liberation of our country imposes upon a member of the State Council, and to persevere in the war against Nazism and its accomplices till final victory.'

Paragraph Five

To the President of the Republic appertains the final approval of the Rules of Procedure agreed upon by the State Council, and the approval of later changes and amendments.

*Also a Slovak (Tr.).

Paragraph Six

A member of the State Council, if also a member of the Government, may exercise his right of membership in the State Council, but shall abstain from voting. The Chairman of the State Council has the right to invite members of the Government to take part in meetings in order that they can give any explanations asked for by members of the State Council.

Paragraph Seven

The State Council is bound to give to the President of the Republic or to the Government within a fixed time an advisory report on any question or matter put before it by the President of the Republic or the Government, but it can also on its own initiative report to the President of the Republic or the Government on all branches of State activity.

Paragraph Eight

On the proposal of the Discipline Committee, the State Council can cancel the mandate of a member if it reaches the conclusion that he is unworthy. It has the duty to report such decision without delay to the President of the Republic.

Paragraph Nine

The members of the State Council shall receive due compensation* for performing their duties.

Signed: Signed:
DR. ŠRAMEK   DR. EDUARD BENEŠ

(*b*) The Decree of the President of the Republic of October 15th, 1940, on the provisional execution of legislative power, read as follows:
At the suggestion of the Government I decree:

Paragraph One

As long as it shall not be possible to carry out the provisions of the second chapter of the Constitution of February 29th, 1920, on the legislative power, the President of the Republic shall with the approval of the Government perform the tasks imposed on him by paragraph 64, sections 1 and 3 of the Constitution for which the consent of the National Assembly is necessary.

Paragraph Two

Regulations, the purpose of which is to change or annul existing laws or to make new ones shall, during the life-time of the Provisional State Organisation be issued whenever necessary by the President of the Republic on the proposal of the Government in the form of Decrees which shall be countersigned by the Prime Minister or the Minister entrusted with this execution.

Paragraph Three

The entire Government is entrusted with the execution of this decree which enters into force on the day of its signature. Signed in London by the President of the Republic on October 15th, 1940.

Signed: Signed:
DR. ŠRAMEK.   DR. EDUARD BENEŠ

*Their salary was £600 a year, free of tax (Tr.).

[7] The full text of this address is printed in my book *Six Years of Exile and the Second World War*, pp. 88–92.

[8] The whole scheme was inspired and led by Dr. Milan Hodža* who wanted in this way to secure his membership in the National Committee and in the forthcoming London Government as he himself personally confessed to me. An overwhelming majority of the members of the London Government, the State Council and our emigration were opposed to him at that time. Only with the greatest effort did I finally succeed in getting their consent to my nominating Dr. M. Hodža as a member of the State Council and as one of its vice-Chairmen. The intention was to bring him officially into the ranks of the liberation movement. He accepted the nomination but never carried out his mandate.

[9] Further details of all these negotiations are given in *E. Beneš: Studies and Essays presented on his Sixtieth Birthday*† (Prague, 1947, J. R. Vilímek) in the article by R. H. Bruce Lockhart: 'Some Private Recollections.' Lockhart took a very active part in these negotiations.

[10] On the British side, Mr. Philip B. B. Nichols was nominated and on our side, Dr. Max Lobkowicz.

*Dr. Hodža, a Slovak Protestant, was Prime Minister before Munich. After his quarrel with Dr. Beneš he went to America where he died in 1944.

†Not available in English (Tr.).

CHAPTER IV

THE GREAT CHANGE IN THE WORLD WAR : THE SOVIET UNION, ATTACKED BY GERMANY, PARTICIPATES IN THE STRUGGLE

1. *Volte Face in Soviet Policy*

NAZI Germany's attack on the Soviet Union, begun by Hitler on Sunday, June 22nd, 1941, fundamentally changed the whole international and military situation in Europe and the world.

I do not intend to examine here *in detail* the policy of the Soviet Union from Munich to the beginning of the German-Soviet War. I will mention only the most necessary facts. Even today it is still a delicate question. The events preceding Munich and between Munich and the Soviet Union's entry into World War II have been used, and in a certain sense also misused, against Soviet policy both before and after Munich. I will only repeat that before Munich the Soviet Union was prepared to fulfil its treaty with France and with Czechoslovakia in the case of a German attack.*

The treaty between the four Western and Central European Great Powers concluded in Munich on September 29th, 1938, was quite rightly considered by the Soviet Government to be not only a desertion of Czechoslovakia but also a desertion of the whole European policy of collective security founded on the Geneva obligations of France and Great Britain. Moreover the exclusion of the Soviet Union from all pre- and post-Munich discussions was equivalent—in the Soviet view—to an attack against the Soviet Union and to an attempt to secure its complete isolation. Moscow *rightly* feared that this fatal step could soon lead to a military attack by Germany against the Soviet Union.

Furthermore, the Soviet Union interpreted the Munich policy of France and Great Britain as a voluntary surrender by these States of their traditional influence in Central Europe—as the abandonment of the Central European sphere to the exclusive influence of Nazi Germany and Fascist Italy the logical inference being that Hitler's Germany was being put face to face with the Soviet Union. In view of the ideology of the Nazi Third Reich it seemed that the inevitable conflict with the Communist Soviet Union would not be long delayed. Already at the time of the

The U.S.S.R. was not obliged to go to war with Germany on Czechoslovakia's behalf unless France did so. (Tr.).

131

Munich crisis the League of Nations had clearly shown that it was non-existent as a political force and equally clearly the Western Powers no longer took it into account. Indeed, Chamberlain had already said as much in the House of Commons on March 8th, 1938.

For this reason I did not turn to the League of Nations before Munich—to the surprise of some of our friends in France and Great Britain. I was afraid I should damage rather than help the Czechoslovak cause by doing so. I simply did not believe that France and Great Britain, in the condition they were then in, would back our anti-Nazi policy in Geneva. On the contrary I feared that they would permit a solution—*a legal one confirmed moreover by an international institution*—which might later prove a serious and indeed fatal stumbling block for our cause if Germany used it to the full against us. I therefore decided not to risk such a step which could have reversed the whole future course of events to our complete disadvantage.

Thus, in my opinion, the Soviet Union no more than ourselves could expect anything from Geneva in the sphere of collective security. Developments before and after Munich—the recognition of the Italian Empire in Africa by Great Britain and France, acceptance of the occupation of Austria, Czechoslovakia and Albania with only platonic protests—were clear proof that France and Great Britain had fully capitulated to Germany and Italy and that they had simply—though not formally—accepted, and in fact recognised, the Italo-German claims in Central Europe and South-Eastern Europe.

The immediate question for all Europe, therefore, and especially for the Soviet Union, was: what would be Germany's next move after Munich. Logically, its quarrel with Poland for the so-called Danzig Corridor came first and this again brought up the question of how this problem would affect the policy of France and Great Britain. For the Soviet Union this question meant a fresh decision about the direction of its future policy and the definite crystallization of its final reaction to the whole European crisis.

The diplomatic archives on this fatally decisive moment of European and world policy are not yet *fully* accessible so that a historically *exact and documented* answer cannot yet be given to the relevant questions which at present can only be considered on the basis of somewhat unclear or uncertain assumptions. I myself will only record what I have either lived through myself and therefore know for certain, or at any rate believe I know for certain, or what I deduce logically from facts already known. I do not assert that these facts are either complete or fully decisive. I am not giving the complete history *but only making a contribution to it.*

As I judged the situation at the time, France, even after the occupation of Czechoslovakia, was resolved not to resist Germany and to leave Poland also to its fate. This is shown by the fundamental turn given to French policy by Prime Minister Daladier after April 10th, 1938, when after a comprehensive discussion and review of French foreign policy with J. Paul-Boncour he refused to admit him into his Government and nominated Georges Bonnet as Minister for Foreign Affairs.[1] On the other hand, Great Britain began to prepare for resistance with some vigour soon after Munich and later, shortly after the occupation of Czechoslovakia, she concluded guarantee defence treaties with Poland, Rumania and Greece.

In these circumstances, the Soviet Union was uncertain either of the future path of French policy or of a firm and unwavering British policy, although it was—seemingly—directed against the expansion of Hitlerism. So it decided to follow a policy which would bring the greatest *momentary* security to itself and which would grant it the greatest possible freedom of deciding its future behaviour in accordance with its own interests and the march of events. In the existing state of uncertainty this meant boldly carrying on negotiations on two different fronts—with the Western Powers and Germany at the same time or first with one and then with the other— as happened at the beginning of the summer of 1939.

The new policy was inaugurated by a change in the Soviet Ministry for Foreign Affairs: 'Tass' announced on May 4th, 1939, that Litvinov had at his own request resigned as Commissar for Foreign Affairs and that he had been succeeded by the President of the Council of People's Commissars, Viatcheslav Molotov. France and Great Britain were then offered an agreement based on a clear and decisive policy to stop German expansion on condition that, in the case of a conflict with Germany, the Soviet Union was to be allowed to occupy the Baltic States and its Army would be granted the right of passage through Polish territory. On these terms the Soviet Union was ready to participate with all its strength in a future conflict with Germany.

I do not wish at this stage to go into the question whether one or the other party to these negotiations had some special motive and plans or whether either of them was sincere or insincere. It is known that Moscow criticised the Western Powers for not sending sufficiently important personages to conduct the negotiations thus giving the impression and even the conviction that these Powers did not seriously want a treaty with the Soviet Union against Hitlerite aggressiveness. I am only concerned with hard facts and the results of the negotiations.

Poland which was—indirectly—a partner to these negotiations, categorically refused to consent to the demands of the Soviet Union regarding Poland and thus made an agreement between the Western Powers and the Soviet Union on this basis impossible. As I knew Col. Beck and the whole Polish regime, I had taken their attitude on this point for granted. In view of the Polish attitude the Soviet Union refused to accept an anti-German obligation of a nature which would not have enabled it to deploy all its forces for its full defence in the event of war. It therefore insisted on the conditions it had laid down. So, in the summer of 1939, the possibility of a firm agreement between the Western Powers, Poland and the Soviet Union with the object of decisively stopping Hitler's Germany from further European expansion had definitely ended.

I followed these negotiations—I was at that time in Chicago—with extreme anxiety. It was clear to me that they would determine how soon the European war would begin so that the fate of our country was also involved. From our point of view it was advantageous that the war—if it came—should break out soon and that the European 'marasmus,' during which the German occupation at home would work fearful moral and material destruction, should end as quickly as possible. In April, 1939, I got into touch with the Soviet Ambassador in Washington, Umansky. During the following months I gave him detailed information based on my reports from Europe and especially from Germany and home, and I was in general kept well informed by him about the future policy of the Soviet Union during these negotiations. Umansky was the only Ambassador of the Great Powers in the United States who after Munich and even after March 15th, 1939, remained quite openly in contact with me and supported me whenever possible.

Just at that time there were negotiations about whether a Czechoslovak pavilion would be allowed at the New York Exhibition. This question gave rise to a small diplomatic battle. Our pavilion had been announced and prepared before the occupation of Czechoslovakia. The United States had not legally recognised our occupation ; they therefore consented to our pavilion being officially and ceremonially opened. The Mayor of New York, La Guardia, took the matter up and helped Envoy Hurban and me in every possible way and the pavilion was opened on May 31st, 1939. On that occasion, in agreement with Washington, I was still acting together with Minister Hurban in the capacity of an official Czechoslovak representative—to the great discomfiture of the diplomats of the European Powers. The State Department was officially represented at this function, but of the diplomatic corps only Umansky took part officially in the opening of our pavilion. On the same day he invited me personally and received me himself when I paid a ceremonial visit to the Soviet pavilion. This caused a great sensation. And so far as we were concerned, of course, it served its purpose.

Shortly afterwards the Moscow negotiations for an anti-German treaty reached their dramatic culmination. As I have already mentioned, I had expected that nothing in the world would induce Minister Beck to yield to the Soviet demands in any form whatever especially as he already had the British guarantee treaty in his pocket. According to the British view the proposed anti-German treaty was in fact merely to involve the simple accession of the Soviet Union to the Anglo-Polish treaty of guarantee without any serious discussion of the more important Soviet demands and without conditions.

In another conversation with Umansky I again discussed these questions in detail. At his request I gave him a detailed written analysis for Moscow of the European situation *vis-à-vis* Germany and the negotiations between the Soviet Union and the Western Powers. Not long afterwards Umansky told me that he had received a telegram from Molotov to the effect that the negotiations between the Western Powers and the Soviet Union had definitely broken down.

I cannot say of my own personal knowledge by what means, on whose initiative and by what intermediary the negotiations which followed for the German-Soviet treaty of August, 1939, were undertaken. According to Stalin's declaration, the initiative for the negotiations and the project of a treaty came from the Germans. Already in May, 1939, my own attention had been drawn from Prague and from Moscow to *economic* negotiations between Germany and the Soviet Union. I received a message from Prague at Chicago that, soon after the occupation of Czechoslovakia, the Germans had seized the Škoda Works at Plzeň and found there all the documents concerning deliveries of armament material to the Soviet Union—to which as President of the State I had indirectly given my consent. They immediately decided not to interrupt these relations and to continue the deliveries. Soon afterwards I received information from Moscow that Ing. Hromadko of the Škoda Works had accordingly been sent to Moscow. Immediately afterwards I got reports originating from Hromadko himself, partly about conditions at home, partly about the Soviet-German economic negotiations.

Rightly or wrongly I drew very far-reaching conclusions from these indications. I foresaw the Soviet-French-British negotiations as definitely wrecked and I concluded that the Soviet Union would now take a quite independent political position based solely on what from the most realistic standpoint it might regard as being of direct benefit *to itself* in the sense of promoting the security of *its own* State. Assuming that it was not sufficiently prepared for war, it would do what it could to put off being involved in war as long as possible—at the same time preparing for war as feverishly as possible. That was my estimate of the situation.

In addition, as I had a reasonably good knowledge of Soviet doctrine, ideology and practice, I was sure that it would not lose sight of *its own* final revolutionary aim and the *ultimate* aim of Communist principles, even if this should force it into seeming or real illogicalities in its procedure and even if its policy should give the West the impression either of oft-repeated '*salta mortale*' (i.e. unexpected, sudden and sensational changes of policy and tactics) or of a-moral Macchiavellism.

In short: *I reckoned that the Soviet Union, after the rejection of its clear offer of an anti-German treaty to preserve world peace (which it was ready to carry out), would first turn right away from the Western Allies and would temporarily, at least, sit on the fence as between the Western Powers and Hitlerite Germany.* From the point of view of the world the explanation would be simply the interest of the Soviet State. Ideologically and from the standpoint of international Communism the line would be that it was necessary in case of war to keep the way open for the subsequent social world revolution which—as Communists then held to be certain—would be joined even by the *German* proletariat. These were my conclusions at that time.

Thus, through a microscope, as it were, I followed step-by-step every development of Soviet policy, even the smallest. When I returned to London from America early in the morning of July 19th, 1939, General Ingr and Colonel František Moravec brought me news from Germany of very active negotiations between Germany and the Soviet Union. I ordered Colonel Moravec to take all possible steps to get more detailed reports about these negotiations from Germany.[1]

Between August 10th and 12th, 1939, we got further important reports through the same channels. So far as *Germany* was concerned the decisive moment in the Soviet-German negotiations was the night of 3rd to 4th August. That night a meeting took place in Berlin in the Foreign Office, in which Ribbentrop, Göring, Goebbels, Keitel, Jodl and others took part to decide whether Germany should accept and sign the treaty with the Soviet Union or not. Hitler was in Berchtesgaden and took part in the conference by telephone, being permanently connected with the room in which the conference was taking place and directly with those who took part in it getting at the same time a report on the discussions from Ribbentrop.

It emerged from these discussions that Berlin had not negotiated through its Ambassador in Moscow, Count Schulenburg, but had already sent a special negotiator to Moscow, Ing. Hilger (Commercial Attaché of the German Embassy in Moscow holding the rank of Counsellor). When the conference was held he had just returned from Moscow and he gave those present at the meeting in the Foreign Office conclusive reports on the position of the negotiations with the Soviet Union. The discussions lasted into the morning hours of August 4th with Hitler all the time participating by telephone. Finally Hitler agreed and the German negotiator was able to take his answer back to Moscow by plane on the same morning (August 4th).

Accordingly, from August 12th, 1939, when this report from Berlin reached me in London I was sure that in a short time the sensational news would be announced to the public that a German-Soviet agreement had been concluded. At the same time our intelligence service received—from the same German sources—detailed reports of the development of the conflict between Germany and Poland concerning Danzig. We got details of the concentration of armies, of diplomatic manoeuvres, propaganda tricks, etc. The moral of all these reports was, *be prepared—that the critical time would be August 26th-27th, when the German-Polish conflict would probably start.*

In these circumstances I resolved to visit the Soviet Ambassador in London, Ivan Maisky, as soon as possible and discuss all these questions with him. This was my first meeting with a man of incontestably high political qualities with whom, afterwards, I systematically maintained good political relations during the whole of the war and with whom— time and again at decisive moments—I sincerely exchanged opinions on the development of the general situation. We always helped one another in a friendly manner. On this first occasion I wrote to Maisky and asked him to receive me. He invited me to lunch and we had a long discussion at the Soviet Embassy. By a coincidence the invitation was for August 23rd, 1939, the same day in the morning of which the London newspapers sensationally announced the arrival of Ribbentrop in Moscow and pub- lished the contents of the German-Soviet treaty which was to be ostenta- tiously signed in Moscow by Ribbentrop.

As is known, this news came to the world like a bombshell. Known, too, are the passionate polemics, discussions, quarrels, interpretations and mutual recriminations which immediately afterwards reverberated through the world. The events round which these endless polemics ranged are for many not quite clear even today and at the time were extremely surprising and really sensational for the whole of the Western world and America.

2. *The German-Soviet Agreement and Its Consequences For Our Movement*

Throughout my first discussion with Maisky I myself took all these events for granted. I had already been informed of them by our intelligence service and I had had reports from Germany that we must count on a German-Polish conflict in a very short time. Keeping all the events of the preceding weeks in their logical sequence at the back of my mind, I concentrated in my discussions with Maisky on the future developments. The interpretation of the treaty, its meaning, motives, wisdom and competence —all these things no longer interested me so much and I did not express any judgment or opinion on them. For the time being it was decisive for me that this meant war against Poland—and therefore against Great Britain and France—by Hitler's Germany and that the events which I had predicted to Roosevelt in Washington three months previously had come to pass. The principal lesson, so far as I was concerned, was that we had reached *a great turning point in world policy, the beginning of the downfall of the whole Munich policy and particularly of Germany and that the real and fateful fight for our new liberty and existence was about to begin !*

The conversation with Maisky touched all these matters. We discussed them for a long time and from various points of view. When I left Maisky, I had formed several sufficiently clear conclusions and impressions:

(*a*) Maisky did not agree with my view that the German-Soviet treaty meant that the Germans wanted to start their war against Poland at once and that they were, to all intents and purposes, fully prepared for it. He regarded with suspicion my authentic reports from Germany about the near outbreak of war and believed that war would probably not begin at once. Neither France, nor Great Britain, he considered, would fight and Poland alone would not dare to do so. '*Probably there will be a second Munich :* France and Great Britain have forced one Munich on Europe at your expense, probably they will force another on Europe at the expense of Poland !' Such, as I gathered from the hints he let fall, was the opinion of Ivan Maisky at that moment. He was extremely sceptical of my view that Great Britain would not stand for a second Munich.

(*b*) He was very reserved about the future policy of the Soviet Union. He said nothing definite about what the Soviet Union would do if war broke out between the powers. But I gathered from his remarks that he thought events would *in the course of time force his country, too,* to take part in such a war. When and how, he declined to say. My impression when I left was that the Soviet Union would try to remain neutral as long as possible so that when the war was nearing its end with both sides exhausted the Soviet Union could intervene decisively and bring about an automatic solution of European problems by means of social revolution.[1]

My conversation with Maisky was the second decisive conversation—after that with Roosevelt—which helped me to direct my whole policy in this war. I took it for granted that for a certain length of time we would have to be prepared for the neutrality of the Soviet Union. We would have to watch events carefully, give nothing away to anyone and be ready for a possible change later. From this standpoint I again confirmed my instructions given in my letter of June 26th, 1939, to Envoy Slávik while I was in America to the effect that our soldiers in Poland must be prepared to retreat into the Soviet Union in case of a Polish defeat and try to remain there until they should again be able to intervene.

Furthermore I understood the logic from the Soviet point of view when, shortly after the outbreak of the Polish war and the smashing of Poland by the 'Blitzkrieg', the Soviet Union decided to occupy the Eastern part of pre-war Poland and gradually to establish its military and strategic bases in the Baltic States. For me this was not merely a question of an occupation of territory claimed by the Soviet Union. Above all, it was the question of occupying advantageous positions which would as far as possible render the Soviet Union secure *in the event of its later participation in the world struggle.*

On September 19th, 1939, Maisky returned my visit at my Putney home and we again discussed the events of the preceding four dramatic weeks. The Soviet Army was already on the march into Lithuania and Eastern Galicia and Maisky wanted to know my impressions of the situation as I saw it from my British environment. He asked me, especially, how our people at home would regard the Soviet action. I did not conceal the fact that even though I personally was doing my best to view the Soviet's action with full understanding, at home its whole behaviour—especially the treaty with Germany—would have a very depressing effect. But at once I stressed to him the necessity for the Soviet Army reaching our frontier. 'Indeed, I do not know in detail', I added, 'how conditions will develop at home, but for the future it is necessary for the Soviet Union to remain the neighbour of ourselves and Hungary. After this new war we must be neighbours of the Soviet Union directly and permanently. *For us this is one of the lessons of Munich !* The question of Subcarpathian Ruthenia will be solved between us later and we surely will agree !'

We then examined the map together and Maisky assured me that it certainly would be the aim of the Soviet Union to establish itself somewhere on the line of our Slovak frontier because it was already concerned about what Germany, Poland and Hungary might do later. 'However matters end we two will surely agree on our common frontiers at the end of the war without any noisy quarrels and without crises'—thus I closed this second conversation which only confirmed me in the conclusions I had drawn from my first conversation with Maisky.

This whole dramatic phase of Soviet policy left me, as can well be imagined, quite calm, though impatiently expectant, nor did it move me, in spite of the vehement and permanent polemics in public on its sense and substance.

Perhaps this is the proper place to recall an important moment of the discussions with our Communists during that period. When I went to Paris at the beginning of October, 1939, for the negotiations on the eventual establishment of the Czechoslovak Government and on the organisation of our Army on French soil—negotiations which, as I have recounted already, ended in almost complete failure—Deputy J. Šverma* visited me on October 10th, 1939. With him was to have come also Dr. Vl. Clementis, but the latter—as I was told at the time—had just been arrested by the French police and Šverma came alone, secretly, through a back entrance of the hotel because he, as well as I, was closely watched by the police. I knew him well. He was a valiant and resolute man and proved this by his whole behaviour during the war. In 1935—together with Deputy R. Slánský†—he had led the negotiations with me on behalf of the Communist Party about my first election as President.

He was quite well informed of the pre-war conditions in France in 1938 and 1939 and also of the conditions in our colony there. He saw my difficulties with the Daladier group and, on the ground that all was lost, tried to persuade me to leave the West and make my way to Russia. He linked our liberation exclusively with a great *revolutionary* victory of the Soviet Union and considered that I should also accept this orientation. He thought that it would be necessary to turn all our liberation activities in this direction. Shortly after this conversation he set out on his return home and then to the Soviet Union.

*Mr. Švermá lost his life during the Slovak rising in 1944. His widow, Marie Švermová, rose to the position of Deputy Secretary-General of the Czechoslovak Communist Party after the war. About 18 months after the Communist *coup-d'état* of February, 1948 she was denounced as a spy and arrested. Mr. Švermá's companion, Dr. Clementis, became Foreign Minister after Jan Masaryk's death in 1948. He was later sentenced to death as a spy. (Tr.).

†Later Secretary-General of the Czechoslovak Communist Party. In November, 1951, he was arrested on a charge of being a spy in the pay of Western imperialists. He was tried in November, 1952, and hanged a few days afterwards (Tr.).

I explained my view of the situation to him. I considered it essential not to leave the West and to ensure that while the Soviet Union was taking no active part in the war our whole movement in the West should accommodate itself to the situation and avoid the possibility of becoming split. For me, the question was to prepare and to secure at *whatever price the unity of our whole liberation movement*. He objected that conditions in the West would ultimately push me to the right wing—would estrange me from the Soviet Union and drag me into the waters of reaction. Against this opinion I stressed that it would be a mistake to leave matters in the West to our emigrants who were only aligned with Osuský, Hodža and others, that it was essential from the outset to give our whole liberation movement a correct progressive, all-national and uniting line, and of course a world line, too—that is to say, a Western and Eastern line simultaneously —because this second World War was already and would remain a world, and revolutionary, war and the Soviet Union would quite certainly be forced into it at a later stage. Moreover, we must not forget that we would very possibly be interested in maintaining co-operation between West and East in the final phases of the fight against Hitler.

Besides (I argued on), for me it was not a question of my personal situation. If conditions at the outset in France and Great Britain should develop in such a way that I should be forced to make concessions to people and to events which afterwards—when the Soviet Union in one way or another entered the war—could not be co-ordinated with developments either in the Soviet Union or at home and might threaten to split our whole national liberation movement, then I would be ready to stand aside and leave the leadership to others. It was not a question of securing for myself any personal position in the movement or in the new Republic after the war. For me, it was a question of State and Nation. For the time being I considered that my most important duty was to try to direct our cause so as to secure the unity of the whole liberation movement not only in Great Britain and France but also in *America and the Soviet Union and to preserve it in all circumstances*.

This conversation with Deputy Šverma brought home to me the difference between my estimate of the development of the war and that of *our* Communists under the influence of the *Russian* Communists. We were both convinced that the Soviet Union, in spite of signing the treaty with Germany, would enter the war. But the Communists seemed to believe that it would be possible to delay this till the very end of the war. Seemingly it was in order to be able to intervene only at the end of the war that the Soviet Union had signed the treaty with Germany—thus gaining time.

Further, it intended to intervene in a mainly, or even exclusively, revolutionary sense at the moment when both sides were too exhausted to defend themselves successfully against a social revolution. *In addition the Communists considered that at such a time they would in any case succeed in bringing about a revolution in Germany.*

For my part, though I did not entirely exclude this possibility, which was in line with the real political aims of Bolshevik doctrine and ideology, *I was more inclined to believe that the Soviet Union could be drawn into the conflict earlier by one side or the other, even against its will, and I therefore did not consider that its participation in the war was necessarily very far distant.* At the same time I also considered other eventualities including the question of what would happen if the whole doctrine of Communism were not fully implemented. *In particular I almost wholly ruled out the possibility of their succeeding in drawing the German workers into revolution especially in alliance with the workers of the other Nations.* For this reason I did not think that the participation of the Soviet Union in the war would only be *revolutionary.* I felt that whether it wished it or not, the Soviet Union's intervention would be on a military basis—that is to say it would take part in the war in pursuit of power just as any other State. I also anticipated *that the Soviet's endeavours to keep neutral as long as possible* would be very intense—and at the same time extremely difficult—and that the Soviet Union would have to make great sacrifices to Germany in order to maintain this policy.

In addition, I could not bring myself to believe that the Western Powers and Germany would not see through these calculations and act accordingly. It was certain that by now both were sufficiently acquainted with Communist theories, especially the Lenin-Stalin theory of imperialist war and proletarian revolution, *and that they would therefore make their own plans to prevent the realisation of these Communist aims.*

To me, this meant that one side or the other would do all it could *to push the Soviet Union into war as soon as possible in a way which would give them the greatest possible military advantage. That they would simply look on while the Soviet Union made its military preparations for a world social revolution, seemed to me highly improbable.* I also had the feeling that the Hitler regime was already shaping its internal policy on this basis and especially that it was doing its utmost to prevent the participation of the German workers in any kind of revolution. In fact, if Moscow let itself be lulled by this hope, it would perhaps have an unpleasant surprise later on.

I did not extend my discussion with Deputy Šverma to the details of all these questions but our conversation brought these problems and contingencies clearly to my mind and, when I returned to London from Paris, I often used to return to these questions in my talks with Communists and Soviet diplomats in order to check whether my views were correct. I also realised that the Soviet Union's theories about the development of the war would have a decisive influence on the attitude of Communist Parties in the various States (e.g. in France) *and also on the attitude and ideology of our Communists at home and abroad in relation to the war*. It did not surprise me, therefore, when I got from home and elsewhere reports about the reserved, not to say negative, attitude of the Communists towards our national liberation movement during the first years of the war.

To these influences, opinions and calculations, perhaps even instructions, I imputed the decision of our London Communists in August and September, 1939, to retreat into the background—after having participated with considerable ardour in the initial stages of the fight for liberation—and to abstain from direct participation in our movement from the moment of the conclusion of the German-Soviet treaty. I attributed to the same causes the ever-increasing hostility of a section of our London and American Communists towards us. The latter soon afterwards began to stress the theory of imperialist war and to tar both the warring sides, the Western European and the German side, with the same brush. They put about the theory that our movement abroad waited on British imperialism and British capitalist war efforts, spoke of 'our common guilt' in the Munich capitulation and so on. At that time this section of our Communists also began to issue leaflets against us, in London. For example, on the pattern of British pamphlets against the British 'Men of Munich,' they issued a pamphlet 'Guilty Men of Czechoslovakia' in which they pilloried our so-called 'collaboration with Hitler' specifying not only that of Dr. Hácha but our whole movement abroad even including myself.

Similar reports soon began to reach me from my Prague friends' about Communist propaganda at home on the above lines. In particular, I received through underground channels some resolutions of the executive Committee of the Party published in their illegal Party newspaper and disseminated in Prague secretly, underground. From these resolutions of the underground leadership of the Party I noted that this particular Communist line reached its culmination at the end of 1940 and the beginning of 1941—six months before the Soviet Union was drawn into the war. Clearly the Communists did not as yet envisage a German attack on the Soviet Union. During the first months and years of the war the Executive Committee of the Czechoslovak Communist Party also seems to have accepted the erroneous belief of the Russian Communists that the Soviet

Union might be able to remain neutral for a long while—perhaps until the end of the war.* And, of course, it was also animated and actuated by the assumption that a world revolution would take place at the end of this 'imperialist conflict.'

On this basis and in line with Soviet directives, our Communist Party also worked out its moves in our internal policy and in relation to our whole liberation movement at home and abroad.[5] *It is true that it continued to resist Hitlerite Germany and also carried out, as far as it was able, its uncompromising resistance to the Germans at home.* But it kept its full independence, did not join other resistance groups at home and held aloof from our liberation movement abroad.

In my reports to the homeland, at that time and later, I warned our resistance groups not to let themselves be misled, but also wherever possible not to let this behaviour interrupt their co-operation with the Communists. On the contrary, they should re-establish relations and try to keep all-national unity at any price. I never excluded the probability that the Soviet Union would be drawn into the war comparatively soon and that then the Soviet Union—and with it our Communist Party—would be forced to change its attitude. When this actually happened in June, 1941, the policy of the Communist Party[6] did change to co-operation with Great Britain and the United States as well as with the progressive and democratic elements in the various Nations, and therefore also with us.[7]

And so this conversation with J. Šverma provided me with additional confirmation of the correctness of my calculations concerning the development of events in the East. And it forced me to continue to the full my cautious attitude based as it was not only on the unitary synthesis I had conceived about the world war and the future revolution which would probably result—in the form, too, which I anticipated—but also on my view that the *early* entry of the Soviet Union into the war, possibly even against its own will, was inevitable.

3. *Progress of the Soviet Union towards Participation in the War*

As soon as the Soviet Union began to stress its neutrality I concentrated almost exclusively on France, Great Britain and America, being convinced that this policy of neutrality would temporarily prevent any development whatsoever of our work in relation to the Soviet Union. The new Soviet propaganda about the 'Imperialist' war of the capitalist powers helped to confirm my deductions. The progress of the war at the beginning of 1940,

*As in the case of Japan (Tr.).

the German invasion of Norway, Belgium, and the Netherlands and above all the fall of France (the suddenness and speed of which greatly surprised, as it seemed to me, even the Soviet Union) all these events considerably strengthened my thesis.

The effect of these developments was to drive the Soviet Union still further into *neutrality*. In the second half of December, 1939, the Soviet Government had already announced to our envoy, Zd. Fierlinger, that his mission in Moscow must be ended. The envoy then left for Paris and, later, for London. We had expected this decision because as early as September 16th, 1939, the Soviet Union *had recognised the Tiso Government de facto and de jure* and had entered into diplomatic relations with it. Tuka sent a mission to Moscow and addressed compliments there from time to time. The Soviet Government, which wanted to be informed about what was happening in and around Slovakia, also sent its mission to Bratislava. After envoy Fierlinger's return to Paris I asked him for a detailed report about our position in the Soviet Union and about the way the situation had developed after Munich. Besides sending this report to me Fierlinger also gave a copy on April 20th, 1940, to the Paris National Committee. I drew the same conclusions from this report as from my other reports about Soviet policy. I was not wrong.

In addition, I gave much attention to the way in which the Soviet Government emphasized the '*insignificance of these various formalities,*'—the description envoy Fierlinger told me had been applied to the recognition of Slovakia, the abolition of our Legation, etc. when he left Moscow. It was clear that the Soviet Union was bribing Germany to prolong the period of neutrality. Consequently, in spite of all these events, which for our people at that time were very depressing events, I again said in my broadcast address to the homeland when France fell that I was convinced that the fall of France did not mean the end of the war and that I was still counting on the intervention in the war of the 'great eastern factor'—the Soviet Union.* I always retained this conviction.

The breaking out of the Soviet-Finnish war on November 30th, 1939, seemed to me a very significant event which fitted exactly into my interpretation of the future course of world events. I interpreted it as showing that the Soviet Union, regardless of the German-Finnish alliance and Germany's general policy, was consistently and undeviatingly pursuing its aim of wishing to protect itself against Germany both territorially and strategically. At the same time, it was ready to bear all the consequences of its actions: expulsion from the League of Nations and the attempts of Daladier to draw France and Great Britain into some form or other into action against the Soviet Union. The object of this manoeuvre was in line with Daladier's earlier plan. France was to disengage itself from the war against Germany and Germany's activities were to be diverted towards an attack against the Soviet Union, at the same time agreeing to make peace with the Western Powers.

These considerations confirmed my conviction that the Soviet Union was ceaselessly preparing for war and trying to guard itself against all possible eventualities to which war might give rise. I also held the view that this was nevertheless a very risky policy for the U.S.S.R. I therefore warned all my collaborators to remain always very reserved in their political attitude towards the Soviet Union. I told them to wait patiently without compromising themselves either with one side or the other and not to be influenced in any way by the very active anti-Soviet propaganda which was being carried on at that time in the West and in America in regard to the Soviet war against Finland.

Finally, at the end of 1940 I decided to test in the U.S.S.R. itself my conjectures as to the future development of Soviet policy. Our envoy having left Moscow, I wanted to investigate the possibility of sending a special unofficial representative to the Soviet Union for the purpose of maintaining permanent contact and informing us of the development of the situation *vis-à-vis* the progress of the war and at the same time informing the authorities in the Soviet Union of our own situation. I chose for this task Col. Heliodor Pika★ of the General Staff and Ing. Klučka, who at that time were both working for us in Rumania. Col. Pika left in October, 1940, going first to Constantinople where he was in permanent contact with the Soviet intelligence service. There our delegates were several times visited by a high officer from Moscow and ultimately our delegation was admitted into the Soviet Union without difficulty, thus becoming our first link between London and Moscow after the interruption of our diplomatic relations.⁹

As I wanted to find out what the Soviet Government thought of our current military activities I asked for information about the way they were treating our soldiers belonging to the unit of Lt.-Col. L. Svoboda† who had crossed into the Soviet Union after the fall of Poland. I ascertained that

★Col. Pika was hanged in 1950 by the Communist Government of Czechoslovakia after having been found guilty of spying for the Western Powers while he was in Moscow (Tr.)

†Lieut.-Col., later General, Svoboda became 'non-Party' Minister of Defence after the war. In 1950, he was replaced in that capacity by Dr. Alexei Čepička, the late President Gottwald's son-in-law, in order to facilitate the reconstruction of the Czechoslovak Army on the Soviet model. General Svoboda then became chairman of the Youth Movement and made a Vice-Premier but has taken little part in politics (Tr.).

these soldiers were placed in a temporary camp in the Ukraine, that they were reasonably treated, that there was no interference with their internal affairs and especially that they were subjected to no propaganda which would in the slightest degree have had an unfavourable effect on our activity in the West and on our national aims in general. I asked the Soviet authorities through Ambassador Maisky and Colonel Pika whether they could not send some of these soldiers to the West (to join our army in Great Britain). Even in this direction there came a positive answer and, actually, within a few weeks the Soviet Union helped to transport two detachments of our soldiers from Russia to the Near East where the British took them over and afterwards sent them to our military units in Great Britain.

These two developments left me in no doubt as to the situation. But it was necessary to proceed, on our side, with the utmost discretion and not by our negligence to cause the Soviet Union any difficulties in respect of its neutral position towards Germany. We succeeded. *And so from the beginning of 1941, my political calculations became an absolute conviction—after I had checked them with the probable Soviet plans.* I was sure that the participation of the Soviet Union in the war against Germany was in reality only a *question of time.* It was simply a question whether it would take place according to Communist suppositions, that is to say, not before the end of the war and in the form of a revolution and with the help also of German Communists (which I never ceased to doubt) or whether it would happen in accordance with my own expectations and opinion, in the near future and not simply on the revolutionary plane. The reports I received from Germany, soon brought me to the conclusion that in the end the deciding factor would be the Germans themselves, that is to say, Hitler, and not Stalin.

Our future actions were based consistently on this standpoint—especially in regard to our policy towards Poland. Towards the end of January, 1941, I asked the Premier of the Polish émigré Government, General Wladislaw Sikorski, to inspect our military units in Britain. He arrived on the eve of the military festivities of our Army on January 26th and spent the night with us at Aston Abbotts.

At that time we were already negotiating a Czechoslovak-Polish agreement for the final settlement of our mutual relations. It was therefore a very suitable occasion for a thorough discussion of the whole problem of the war which took the form of a conversation lasting till the early hours of the following day. For me the first question was to agree on a common policy towards the Soviet Union. I told General Sikorski frankly and clearly how I saw the situation: that we must reckon with the early participation of

L

the Soviet Union in the war against Germany, make our plans on this basis, come to terms with the Soviet Union about the military direction of the war and regulate our conception of the whole World War II in mutual agreement.

Sikorski's reaction to my exposition rather surprised me and showed me once more how difficult it would be to reach an agreement between us and the Poles—even in the case of General Sikorski. He rose and began to pace nervously about the room. Then he came to a halt in front of me in an almost military attitude and declared with extreme gravity: '*What you are saying would be a catastrophe for us all.*'

Nevertheless we discussed in detail every aspect of the Soviet Union's entry into the war. There was a clear line of cleavage between our standpoints. Sikorski counted on a kind of repetition of the first World War: Great Britain would hold out in the fight against Germany; it would get the help of the United States which would later enter the war and would help France to its feet again. Essentially in the second World War also the issues of war and peace would be decided by the United States and Great Britain. Poland therefore must be orientated only to them.

Later when the Soviet Union was attacked by Germany and was fully engaged in the war, Sikorski (and with him all Poles) added to this theory the opinion that Germany in its victorious march would first smash the Soviet Union and that afterwards the United States and Great Britain would smash Germany and would then together with Poland construct a victorious peace. At the time of our talk (that is to say, on January 26th, 1941) Sikorski considered himself to be in a state of war not only with Germany but also with the Soviet Union and he was not willing even to consider any suggestion that he should make preparations for an agreement with the Soviet Union while there was still time.

I pointed out to him that Great Britain alone—remembering that the United States was not yet actually at war with Germany—and perhaps even Great Britain and the United States together at some later date would not be able to control the course of the war throughout the world without the Soviet Union. I stressed the geographical situation of our two countries and my conviction that especially we Poles and Czechoslovaks, being on the far side of Europe, could not win the European war without the Soviet Union. I did not convince him.

We returned to this discussion several times in personal conversations later on. Sometimes Jan Masaryk, Dr. H. Ripka and the then Polish Minister for Foreign Affairs, Ed. Raczynski also took part and we had quite heated arguments. But Sikorski never changed his point of view essentially, not even when, a year later, after the German attack on the Soviet Union, he went to Moscow and began serious negotiations with Stalin for a Soviet-Polish treaty. His chief aim then was to get tens of thousands of Poles out of the Soviet Union and to add them to his Army in the West. The other 'London' Poles were even more uncompromising in their concept of World War II. As is well known, the matter ended with the break-up of the Polish front in London during 1943 and 1944.

This conversation with Sikorski—and a number of other conversations during the Polish-Czechoslovak negotiations[10]—led me to realize the fundamental difference between us. I therefore remained very cautious during all our negotiations with the London Poles and did not depart from the line which I was convinced was the only right one for us and would prove to be so. I held to my view and during the course of our negotiations with the Poles, I tried with the utmost sincerity first with Sikorski and then with Mikolajczyk, to influence them in their own interest as well as ours, to try in time to come to a real agreement with the Soviet Union.

Not long afterwards reports which reached me from Prague fully confirmed my expectations. The Soviet Union was still trying to postpone its participation in the war as long as possible. But when Hitler in the Battle of Britain in the autumn of 1940 failed to break British resistance and force it to sue for peace, he was obliged to resolve a dilemma which for Germany was really desperate: what was he to do if Britain should continue its resistance, strengthened more and more by the help of the United States and if the preparations of the Soviet Union either to enter the war or to evoke a great social revolution should increase to a maximum intensity?

For Germany these were catastrophic prospects and Hitler, actuated by his character and his lack of education, immediately made his fatal and amateurish decision, expecting in his political narrow-mindedness that he would get out of this situation somehow in the end. The United States not being in the war, he decided that the time was opportune for an attack on the Soviet Union to break its strength before this could be sufficiently developed, thus nipping in the bud its war preparations and its plan to enter the war and stage a revolution later on. At the same time he hoped that it would be possible to convince the Western Powers that the Soviet Union was planning a European and world revolution and to induce them to make peace with Germany and give him a free hand in the East. Pétain's France was without doubt ready to do so.*

At the beginning of March, 1941, Col. Moravec brought me reports

*Hess's arrival in Scotland on May 10th, 1941, has an obvious bearing on this theory (Tr.).

that Germany was seriously preparing for its attack on the Soviet Union. At the same time we got full details of the German preparations to solve the Yugoslav question and of an agreement between Mussolini and Hitler for the partition of Yugoslavia between Germany and Italy. I at once passed all these reports on to the Yugoslav envoy in London, Subotić, and warned Belgrade of what Rome and Berlin were preparing. This, of course, had, and at that time could have, no influence on the policy of Prince Paul. Long before Munich, he was already on the other side of the barricade, and therefore also opposed to us. Moreover, the Cvetković Government had already for a long while been negotiating with Hitler for Yugoslavia's accession to the Axis pact and its adhesion was publicly announced on March 25th, 1941. By that time Yugoslavia was already completely in Hitler's clutches and could not extricate itself—in spite of the attempts made later by revolutionary Yugoslavia to come to an agreement on Soviet help. Immediately afterwards, on March 27th, 1941, the revolution against Prince Paul broke out and Peter II was proclaimed king. The German invasion of Yugoslavia began soon afterwards on April 6th, 1941. In a short while, Peter II with all his entourage and the Government arrived in London.

But our reports of German preparations against the Soviet Union became increasingly numerous[11] until at the beginning of March we got such precise statements in London as: '*The campaign against the Soviet Union is said to have been definitely decided upon;* as soon as Germany has finished the Yugoslav campaign, i.e. in the first half of May at the latest, the German attack on the Soviet Union will begin; it is reported in Berlin that all the necessary military arrangements have been made and there has already been a conference of all the higher commanders of the German Eastern front at which the opening moves of the campaign were precisely determined and explained; the date of the "Kriegsbereitschaft" (alert) for the whole Eastern front is said to have been fixed for May 15th; some technical details of the military plan of the whole Eastern campaign were appended to this report'.

This was one of those solemn moments of the war which moved me the most. It was so fateful that at first I did not even dare to pass the news on immediately in *all* details to the Allies though in due course I told the essence of the matter to all, to the British, the Americans and the Soviet Union. To Winston Churchill I announced it under somewhat dramatic circumstances.

I had invited Churchill to visit our brigade in Leamington on April 19th. At noon of the same day, before reviewing our troops, we were invited for lunch by Mr. Ronald Tree, M.P. Besides Churchill and some other British guests and Czechoslovak soldiers, the American Ambassador Harriman and the commander of the American Air Force, General Arnold, were also present. After lunch we began to discuss the future course of the war and I had an opportunity to develop in detail to these political and military authorities the whole question of the German attack on the Soviet Union and to express my firm conviction that the participation of the Soviet Union in the war had been already decided in principle. '*Exactly when and how this will happen will not be decided by Stalin but by Hitler*'—this was how I described the situation on that occasion.

Winston Churchill, as he told me later, had just received similar reports from the United States of Hitler's preparations for his attack on the Soviet Union. My reports had sharpened, confirmed and rounded off his information. At that moment Great Britain was *alone* in the war against Germany. It suffered much and put forth its whole strength to hold out against the German assault. It can be imagined how Churchill received my reports and opinion! During the discussion he returned three times to the question: 'And you believe that the Soviet Union will really fight, that it will hold out, that its officers' corps is of a sufficiently high calibre?' I assured Churchill that I had full confidence in the Soviet Union and its power to hold out against a German assault.

After lunch we drove to our Army in Churchill's car and discussed in detail the state of the Red Army: its preparedness, its morale, the condition of the officers' corps. This last question especially—the memories of Tukhatchevsky and the officers' purges of 1936 and 1937 were still alive—constantly occupied Churchill's mind. And he added other questions concerning the moral and political state of the Soviet population, the country's economic preparedness, communications, etc. I tried honestly and truthfully to dispel his doubts and to strengthen and confirm his hopes.

I appreciated all his questions when I learned soon afterwards what reports Churchill was getting about the Soviet Union, partly from the British Intelligence Service, partly—indeed especially—from *Polish* sources in London. In general it can be said that they were unanimous: 'If a German-Soviet war should come the Soviet Union will be liquidated within eight to ten weeks'. This was how the British Intelligence Service formulated its opinion, and the Polish Intelligence Service said the same. After the attack on the Soviet Union had begun, Goebbels' propaganda service directly and indirectly, openly and secretly put identical reports in circulation.

On all these matters, and on my belief in the necessity for future co-

operation between the West and the Soviet Union in the prosecution of
the war, I systematically informed Bruce Lockhart who had worked with
us and helped us in the first World War during our* sojourn in Russia.
Bruce Lockhart agreed with Masaryk's policy of non-intervention in the
affairs of the Soviet Union at that time and was its exponent among the
British. After the war—before taking up journalism—he was for some
years attached to the British Legation in Prague. There he was our devoted
friend. And, in the second World War when he again entered the Foreign
Office, he was first of all put in charge of our affairs about which he was
well informed. He was also in close touch with the affairs of nearly all Slav
nations. Thus he was able to render us many valuable services. He deserved
well in fact in respect of British-Czechoslovak relations. I was in contact
with him several times a week; and especially in those troubled moments
of the attack of Hitler's Germany on the Soviet Union, he appreciated the
course of events correctly and endeavoured to influence British policy
accordingly.

Through him I gave the Foreign Office my opinions and frequent items
of information about the situation in Germany and Central Europe and
on the possible trend of Soviet policy. When the German attack against
the Soviet Union approached, I was particularly anxious that the British
reaction to this great event should be the right one, in line with conditions
on the Continent and *especially with the Allied and our own aims and interests
and also with the interests of the Soviet Union itself.* I cannot say to what
extent these opinions really swayed British circles when the given moment
arrived. In any case they had a quite considerable influence.

It is a fact that in those fateful days (June 21st and 22nd, 1941) we,
through the headquarters of our Government in London, were in uninterrupted contact with Bruce Lockhart—and through him as intermediary
with the Foreign Office and with Prime Minister Winston Churchill until
the moment when Churchill on the evening of June 22nd, 1941, delivered
his great broadcast speech in which he announced to the world that from
this moment Great Britain and the Soviet Union were Allies for the overthrow of Germany, Hitler and Nazism and everything connected with
them.

4. *Germany's Attack on the Soviet Union and the Renewal of the Soviet-Czechoslovak Alliance*

It is clear, therefore, that after Munich I did not allow myself to be misled
by the *seeming rapprochement* of Germany and the Soviet Union. I
_____
*i.e. that of the Czech legionaries (Tr.).

knew both States and their political and ideological orientation quite well. From the beginning I excluded the possibility that any agreement between them could be sincere or permanent. It could only be a temporary development and necessity, dictated by opportunist and tactical considerations in the case of both the partners. Conversely, it was clear to me that there was and must be an unbridgeable ideological abyss between these two implacable doctrines—that in the end they must clash with all the revolutionary consequences which must inexorably follow. *I was especially sure of this in the case of Germany.*

So I did not change my opinion, *not even when it seemed*—and was the generally accepted view—that, before Germany started the war in 1939, Germany and the Soviet Union had reached an implicit or explicit agreement on Poland, the Baltic States, Bessarabia and finally even on Finland to the benefit of the Soviet Union. I was therefore quite firm in my expectation that the conflict of the two ideologies would lead to a German-Soviet conflict. I awaited this with absolute certainty and did not hide the fact either from my British friends, or from British, American, Soviet or other officials.[11]

This point of view determined my attitude towards the Soviet Union immediately after Munich. The basic policy of the Soviet Union towards Czechoslovakia, before Munich and shortly after it, was shown by its behaviour at the time of the crisis of September, 1938, both by the Note which Foreign Commissar M. Litvinov addressed to Germany on March 18th, 1939, after the occupation of Prague and finally by Soviet Ambassador Maisky's intervention on behalf of Czechoslovakia at Geneva as late as May 23rd, 1939. Even when the Soviet Government after signing the German-Soviet Pact in August, 1939, first took a *somewhat passive attitude* towards us and finally from January 1st, 1940, definitely ceased to recognise the Czechoslovak Legation in Moscow, maintaining a strictly neutral attitude towards us, I adopted a passive and waiting attitude towards this new Soviet policy. This did not in the least mean that I regarded the Soviet Government's behaviour as entirely right or that I fully agreed with it. But as always, so also on this occasion, I did fully respect the actions of an independent State, which is and always must remain the sovereign judge of its tactical moves in foreign policy and especially in matters involving war. I therefore waited until events should ripen and bring about a change of Soviet policy.

From March to April, 1941—as I have already mentioned—we were regularly getting from both Berlin and Prague not only systematic reports about the German preparations for war against the Soviet Union but also information indicating how the German General Staff itself was imprudently and quite incredibly underestimating the value of the Soviet Army. It reckoned that the whole 'Blitz-Campaign' against the Soviet Union would last about sixty days at most, prepared its quislings for Kiev, Minsk and for Moscow and expected, that some time in September—after the liquidation of the Soviet Union—it would be able to devote its whole attention once again to Western Europe either with a peace offer or with a threat to invade Great Britain.

Our own reports on the Soviet Army were quite different. In 1938 already—but especially after the fall of France—I learned that the condition of the Soviet Air Force and armaments industry was satisfactory though not fully built up, that the equipment was sound and the preparations for defence solid and that the morale of the common Soviet soldier remained excellent. Of course, I took it for granted that at the beginning of hostilities there would be important German successes, but I was equally sure that after them the war would be substantially protracted and that great German disappointments were in store. In general I considered that in the existing conditions, a German attack against the Soviet Union was simply a German suicide. In my broadcast of June 24th, 1941, I clearly explained my attitude and my views for those at home in Prague.

On Sunday 22nd, when the crossing of the Soviet frontier by German armies was reported, we in London were all in a state of extreme tension and expectation as to how Great Britain and the United States would react. Churchill's speech broadcast on the evening of the same day dispelled all our apprehensions and uncertainty though even after he had delivered it, I had to convince other British political and military circles time and again of the necessity of marching together with the Soviet Union in the interest of us all unconditionally and to the end. It is clear, in fact, that Churchill's address remains one of the most important documents of the second World War.

Churchill said *inter alia* :

'At 4 o'clock this morning Hitler attacked and invaded Russia. All his usual formalities of perfidy were observed with scrupulous technique. A non-aggression treaty had been solemnly signed, and was in force between the two countries. Then, suddenly, without a declaration of war, without even an ultimatum, the German bombs rained down from the sky on the Russian cities. The German troops violated the Soviet frontiers, and an hour later the German Ambassador, who until the night before was lavishing his assurances of friendship, almost of alliance, on the Russians, called upon the Russian Foreign Minister to tell him that a state of war existed between Germany and Russia.

'Thus was repeated on a far larger scale the same kind of outrage against every form of signed compact and international faith which we had witnessed in Norway, Denmark, Holland and Belgium . . . and which Hitler's accomplice and jackal Mussolini so faithfully imitated in the case of Greece.

'Hitler is a monster of wickedness, insatiable in his lust for blood and plunder. Not content with having all Europe under his heel, or else terrorised into various forms of abject submission, he must now carry his work of butchery and desolation among the vast multitudes of Russia and Asia.

'I have to make a declaration. Can you doubt what our policy will be ? We have but one aim and one single irrevocable purpose. We are resolved to destroy Hitler and every vestige of the Nazi regime. From this nothing will turn us—nothing. We will never parley, we will never negotiate with Hitler or any of his gang.

'Any man or State who fights against Nazism will have our aid. Any man or State who marches with Hitler is our foe. That is our policy, and that is our declaration. It follows, therefore, that we shall give whatever help we can to Russia and to the Russian people. We shall appeal to all our friends and Allies in every part of the world to take the same course and pursue it as we shall, faithfully and steadfastly to the end.

'We have offered to the Government of Soviet Russia any technical and economic assistance which is in our power and which is likely to be of service to them. Hitler wishes to destroy the Russian power because he hopes that if he succeeds in this he will be able to bring back the main strength of his Army and Air Force from the East and hurl it upon this island, which he knows he must conquer or suffer the penalty of his crimes.

'His invasion of Russia is no more than a prelude to an attempted invasion of the British Isles. He hopes no doubt that all this may be accomplished before the winter comes, and that he can overwhelm Great Britain before the fleets and air power of the United States will intervene. The Russian danger is therefore our danger and the danger of the United States, just as the cause of any Russian fighting for his hearth and home is the cause of free men and free peoples in every quarter of the globe.

'Let us learn the lessons already taught by such cruel experience. Let us redouble our exertions and strike with united strength while life and power remain.'

We accepted Churchill's appeal immediately for Czechoslovakia.[13] On the following day President Roosevelt, Cordell Hull and Sumner Welles for the United States expressed their agreement with Churchill's policy of full aid to the Soviet Union in its resistance to Nazi Germany. On July 13th, 1941, the British-Soviet treaty was signed in which both States pledged general and mutual help against Hitler's Germany and agreed not to sign either a separate armistice or a separate peace with Germany. Soon afterwards the other Allies, one after the other, made their similar declarations. Poland, the Netherlands, Yugoslavia and Greece all fully accepted the basic principles of British-Soviet political and military co-operation against the Axis Powers.

As already mentioned, I broadcast from London on June 24th to the Nation at home. In it I explained how and why the German attack against the Soviet Union came about, how this was a suicidal act on the part of Germany, how in spite of initial successes Hitler would suffer dreadful catastrophes in the Soviet Union, how we had expected this development and that therefore our policy during Munich and afterwards had been right. Our former relations with the Soviet Union of 1938 were fully restored by these events. Our victory and the reversal of Munich must now be regarded as assured and the whole Nation persevere with re-doubled vigour in its fight against Germany.[14]

I at once renewed contact with the Soviet Ambassador, Ivan Maisky, who informed me on July 5th, 1941, that he had an official communication from Moscow for me. On the same day similar communications were sent by Maisky to the Polish and Yugoslav Governments. I visited him on July 8th. In discussing our mutual relations Maisky explained the point of view of the Soviet Government as follows: The Soviet Union stands for the independence of Czechoslovakia and does not intend to interfere in any way with the internal affairs of the Czechoslovak Republic which solely concern the Czechoslovak people. The Soviet Government is ready to renew immediately diplomatic relations with the Czechoslovak Government in London. To my inquiry whether the Soviet Government would accept our former envoy, he replied that if it was the wish of the Czechoslovak Government, the Soviet Union would agree to the return of Minister Fierlinger to Moscow. At the same time the Soviet Ambassador informed me that his Government would permit the establishment of Czechoslovak military units on the Soviet front if this was the wish of the Czechoslovak Government.

I asked the Ambassador that the verbal accord we had reached in this conversation should be put in writing. He replied that he would have to ask Moscow first. On the basis of instructions from Moscow he then sent me a letter on July 16th, 1941,[16] with which he enclosed the draft Soviet-Czechoslovak agreement. It read as follows:

'The Government of the Union of Soviet Socialist Republics and the Government of the Czechoslovak Republic have agreed to sign the following treaty:

'1. The two Governments have agreed immediately to exchange Ministers.

'2. The two Governments mutually undertake to aid and support each other in every way in the present war against Hitlerite Germany.

'3. The Government of the Union of Soviet Socialist Republics consents to the formation on the territory of the Union of Soviet Socialist Republics of national Czechoslovak military units under a commander appointed by the Czechoslovak Government in agreement with the Soviet Government. The Czechoslovak military units on the territory of the Union of Soviet Socialist Republics will operate under the direction of the High Military Command of the Union of Soviet Socialist Republics.

'4. The present agreement comes into force immediately after its signature and is not subject to ratification.

'5. The present agreement is drawn up in two copies, each of them in the Russian and Czechoslovak languages. Both texts have equal force.'

On the following day, the Czechoslovak Minister for Foreign Affairs informed the British and also the Polish and Yugoslav Governments, with both of which Ambassador Maisky had already discussed similar proposals. We at once began concrete negotiations and on July 18th, 1941—the day on which the *final* regulation of our relations with the British Government was also reached—we concluded our new treaty of alliance with the Soviet Union. It was signed at the Soviet Embassy in London by Ivan Maisky in the name of the Soviet Union and by Jan Masaryk in the name of the Czechoslovak Republic.

As I had informed my country in my broadcast from London on June 24th, the relations between our two States thus returned to the pre-Munich situation and the old friendship. The Soviet Union which had so resolutely and from the beginning opposed Munich and which had rejected March 15th, 1939, with the same resolution, *dealt in this decisive moment the death blow to Munich and all its consequences,* because it *immediately recognised the Republic again in its pre-Munich status,* fully and definitely and without any restrictions or conditions.

NOTES TO CHAPTER FOUR

[1]See pp. 38 sqq.

[2]I must mention at this point that our intelligence service which at that time was in the charge of Colonel Frant. Moravec on behalf of General Ingr, was quite first-class during the first period of the war. From the time of the First Republic it had, both in the Republic and in Germany, a magnificent net of intelligence agents among the German soldiers themselves, and especially among anti-Nazi Germans. In this way, until 1942 (up to the time of the purge after the shooting of R. Heydrich) we received from Germany—often direct from the German General Staff—reports which were a source of great astonishment to the British and which were of immense usefulness in the guidance of our liberation movement abroad. I feel it my duty to stress this fact. And I am anxious that it should be assessed by all of us at its true value. The military information so gained was at that time transmitted from the Republic to London by the radio transmitters of the 'UVOD' (Center of Military Resistance) together with politically important information of its own. Later, transmitters were worked by parachutists from Britain. I shall deal with this great achievement of our resistance movement at home in detail in the next volume of these 'Memoirs'. Without this permanent contact with our country, uninterrupted even during the greatest German terror and maintained at the price of the greatest sacrifice, our Movement abroad would not have gained many of the successes which were granted to it.

[3]Before I visited Maisky I had already sent the following report to my friends in our underground movement in Prague on August 21st (see *Six Years in Exile and the Second World War*, p. 61):

'London, August 21st, 1939

'1. According to our information, war must be expected in the period between August 20th and 30th, with August 26th-27th the crucial days. Of course, in view of the efforts being made in London and in Paris to avoid a general war at nearly any price, one must be prepared for desperate efforts to preserve peace up to the last moment. But matters have already gone so far that war can now be avoided only by a *near miracle*. Therefore be prepared for everything.

'2. We have information that the Protectorate will be abolished. Even in that case it would now be superfluous to stage a revolt or demonstrations which would involve massacres and premature terrorism. It would be better to take our stand on the political fact that when war starts what happens in the Czech countries and in Slovakia is not our responsibility.

'3. At the outset of hostilities, *we expect considerable German successes.* A considerable part of Poland will probably be occupied and the Poles will be pushed back into a position difficult to defend. The operations on the Western front will, it seems, not move very fast so that a quick and effective counter-offensive cannot be expected. Hitler, by the way, is calculating on these lines.

'4. You must not let yourselves be depressed by these events nor lose your optimism and courage. The Western Powers will no longer be able to give way and make peace with Germany after the war has lasted a few weeks, being satisfied with some impossible compromise. In this respect, both the British and French public will be obdurate. So far as the Soviet Union is concerned, we cannot yet say what its final attitude will be, *but in the end it will assuredly fight against Germany and will uphold and support us politically.*

'5. Your general line from the outset, therefore, until we can give you more information, must be restrained and non-committal . . . Continue to make all preparations for passive resistance . . . and do not neglect other possibilities, so that everything may be ready in time for all emergencies.

'6. Here in London we shall at once begin our full political, diplomatic and military activity. We shall wholeheartedly join the front against Germany and against the dictatorships. Until now, while London and Paris have always kept the way open for possible negotiations with Berlin and Rome, we have not been free and have had to restrain ourselves. Now everything will be easier. Nevertheless, *do not expect miracles, especially not immediate ones. Do not expect we shall win any great successes—do not even expect far-reaching promises.* Perhaps events will soon force France and Great Britain to declare themselves on our side. But possibly even now—especially so long as those guilty of Munich are in power—they will for some time avoid open and far-reaching obligations.

'7. Our military activities will presumably proceed sufficiently fast. In France negotiations are in an advanced stage; in Poland matters are getting complicated* . . . From our standpoint it is a question of order and unity. Being in a common war front with Poland, we want to agree and co-operate loyally with her.

'8. Either as an outcome of the fighting or as the result of negotiations in the case of disorganisation in Germany, *the restoration of Czechoslovakia is today already a certainty.* For the time being, of course, not even we ourselves can say under what exact conditions and within what boundaries. The fight on these issues is about to begin and it will depend exclusively on the way the war develops, on the situation under which peace is achieved, what will happen also on our territory, who will be in the war and who will keep out of it. It is self-evident that we will have to start cautiously. Our demands will for the time being be put forward with reserve and then we will gradually try as resolutely as possible for the *attainable maximum.*

'9. Come what may, therefore, do not let yourselves be confused—especially not by some of our tactical moves and declarations nor by the propaganda of our opponents—in the course of the struggle. Also do not let yourselves be misled by any declaration made by one or other of the Powers at the beginning of the war. Things are not clear to them. We have not yet been able to discuss anything with them concretely, because up to now they have all regarded us as war-mongers and some of those holding responsible positions have sought for an agreement with Germany even at the price of sacrificing us, Poland and others. Now things will be different. So do not let any event whatsoever discourage you. Do not believe anything to be final. Do not assume that any declaration, any initial failure, any unfavourable action against us or any similar thing will decide our ultimate fate and prevent the course of events from turning to our advantage. We are convinced *that the development of the war will carry matters far, very far* and that the whole of Europe will emerge much changed. For us this can mean only *a change for the better and the final triumph of our national cause.*

'Yours

Dr. E. B.'

⁴Dr. Vladimir Krajina especially distinguished himself by his tenacity and courage, giving us the most reliable information about the conditions in the so-called Protectorate in general and about the Protectorate Government.

*General Prchala and the émigré group in the West were at cross purposes (Tr.).

⁵See the resolution of the Executive Committee of the Communist Party of Czecho-slovakia of December 15th, 1940, sent to me in London from Prague by my friends and fellow-workers (Dr. Vladimir Krajina and his collaborators). From this I will give the following extracts:

'The second imperialist war has already lasted for fourteen months and there is still no end to be seen of it. Though a number of States, among them even mighty France, have lost their independence, the result of the war remains uncertain. While Germany, together with Italy, is trying to become masters of the European Nations which were formerly under the influence of Anglo-French imperialism, Great Britain, supported by the United States of America, still remains ruler of the seas and of immense colonies. *The United States of America*, which represent the most powerful imperialist colossus with the greatest economic and financial resources and the most developed industrial technique, are today the most dangerous factor in the development of the war. Specu-lating on becoming the heir of the British Empire, threatened with ruin and fearing the increase of German imperialist power, the United States are inciting Britain to continue the war, are using the war to win supremacy over South America, are inciting yet more European Nations to enter the war together with their competitor Japan and they are evoking an atmosphere of inevitable war in the Pacific. They try to misuse the just national liberation war of the Chinese Nation and make it an instru-ment of their own imperialist expansion in the Far East. The United States of America are trying to cause enmity between Germany and the Soviet Union in order to turn the expansion of German imperialism towards the East while themselves remaining out of the war and thus to win advantages over their competitors Great Britain, Germany and Japan, decide the war in their own favour and save the capitalist world order . . .

'The *Soviet Union* which has considerably grown politically, militarily and terri-torially during this imperialist war, represents today a force which in conjunction with the revolutionary movement of the international working-class and the oppressed nations will decide the result of the war. The Soviet Union which maintains neutrality and is carrying out an active policy of peace is attentively watching the forces of both imperialist camps and their war plans in all parts of the world, is influencing nations not to pull the chestnuts out of the fire for either imperialist bloc, is making impossible the preponderance of either bloc and is thereby preventing the danger of an imperialist victory of one or the other party to the conflict. Soviet-German friendship represents the corner-stone of the international situation against which the imperialist and anti-Soviet plans of the Anglo-French bloc have already been dashed to pieces and against which the ciminal intentions of the United States of America are now dashing them-selves to pieces. **The historical importance of the journey of Comrade Molotov to Berlin is based on the fact that, on the basis of the continuation of friendly relations between Germany and the Soviet Union, this journey frustrated the plans of the United States to spread the war and turn it towards the East. The U.S.S.R. will continue to use the differences between the imperialists to strengthen its own position and will watch for the arrival of the right moment for the final disruption of capitalism. On the basis of its peace policy, the U.S.S.R. continually earns greater sympathy among all nations especially among the working people of the great German Nation.***

*It is not clear whether the special emphasis on various passages of the resolution are those of President Beneš or the resolution itself (Tr.).

'The whole capitalist world is breaking into two immense war camps the battle between which threatens all mankind with an immense catastrophe. Both camps, while locked in a cruel struggle for the repartition of the world, have until now always kept back from decisive strokes for fear of a proletarian revolution involving the fate of the whole capitalist system and in the hope that some solution will be found at the expense of the U.S.S.R. But this hope is dwindling in consequence of the depth of inter-imperialist differences and in consequence of the steadily growing and already crushing strength of the U.S.S.R. and its wise policy of neutrality. *The imperialist chain is being stretched to breaking point and the near future will show which link as the weakest will be the first to give way. The revolution of the working-class and of the oppressed nations following in the footsteps of the great Socialist October Revolution represents the only real way out of the abyss of the present war* . . .

'All attempts of the occupants to break the resistance of the *Czech Nation* by furious terror, demagogy and with the help of a handful of traitors, have failed. Tension still exists between the ruling regime and the people. Goebbels' speeches addressed to the Czech Nation are partly a confession of failure and partly an attempt to win the Czech Nation to obedience by new means. These new means consist in promising the Czech Nation future advantages if it abandons its fight for liberty, if it accepts its fate and takes part at the side of Germany in building its own prison in Hitler's "New Europe". The German regime counts on the anti-proletarian class interests of that part of the local bourgeoisie which, after the fall of France, sees German capitalism as the saviour of the capitalist system. The Czech bourgeoisie in the true spirit of its history has now arrived at the rôle of *grave-digger* of its own Nation . . .'

'The changes which took place in the international situation after the break-up of the Anglo-French bloc have also caused a number of changes in the Czech political arena. After the defeat of France, Beneš, together with the Czech bourgeois-socialist émigrés, has placed himself still more in the service of British imperialism and is bolstering the disappointed ranks of his followers by inculcating faith in the United States of America. The resurrection of the old coalition in the form of a Czech émigré 'Government' is a complete disclosure of his plans to re-establish the capitalistic rule of the Czech bourgeoisie and at the same time a new manifestation of the total political decrepitude of the political representatives of the Czech bourgeoisie. The co-operation of Beneš with the bankrupt Polish aristocrats for the foundation of a Czechoslovak-Polish anti-German and anti-Soviet State tributary to Britain, the chasing of Czech citizens into the British imperialist army, the description of the first imperialist war as a liberation war of Nations and of the present war as its ideological continuation and culmination, the participation in Anglo-American intrigues against the U.S.S.R.—all these things make Beneš and the émigrés he leads an agency of Anglo-American capitalism in the Czech ranks, extremely hostile to the interests of the Czech national liberation fight and most dangerous. This group is a permanent threat that the Czech Nation will be fatally misused and led into a tragic collision with the German revolutionary workers and with our chief hope and support, the Socialist Fatherland of all workers, the Soviet Union. The illusions of the broad masses in the United States and their lack of comprehension of the imperialist character of the policy of Britain and America are exploited by Beneš's followers for a new activity : in the spirit of directives from abroad they agitate for the victory of the Anglo-American bloc as a supposed condition for our liberation, they continually propagate absurd chauvinist incitements, they are sowing hatred among the Czech population against German workers clad in military uniforms, and they are awakening distrust against the policy of the U.S.S.R.

Their activity is quite incompatible with the interests of the Czech national liberation fight and the service they are rendering to national capitalism in the mendacious guise of national heroes must be unmasked without pity . . .

'The KSČ (Communist Party of Czechoslovakia) which has overcome initial vacillations in evaluating the policy of the Anglo-French bloc and of Beneš is fulfilling its mission as leader of the Czech working-class and the Czech Nation honourably and successfully under the severest persecution. Only the KSČ explains to the working people the real meaning of the present war and the way out. Thanks to the KSČ all attempts of the Czech agents of Berlin have completely failed and the influence of Beneš has decreased considerably. Thanks to the KSČ, the majority of the Czech working people stand loyally at the side of the Soviet Union and reject the slanders disseminated by the Beneš group and the Social Democrats. Thanks to the KSČ, the capacity of the Czech working people to resist the anti-German chauvinist agitation of the Beneš following is growing and the working people resolutely resist the anti-semitic incitements of the Hácha group. Under the leadership of the KSČ, the working people are taking the first steps towards the opening of the fight for a part of their demands. The Party successfully leads in a number of campaigns especially in the anti-war campaign on the first anniversary of the outbreak of war and the campaign on the occasion of October 28th and November 7th. The party has won into its ranks many members of the socialist parties. *Only the KSČ in spite of insane terrorism and great persecutions has maintained its organisation and leadership underground and is continuing its active work.*'

⁶Later, in quieter and more stable times, it will be necessary to consider all the resolutions and the various publications of the Soviet Communist Party and the Communist Parties of the other Nations in detail, analyse them scientifically and objectively, compare them carefully with the progress of the war and show to what extent their doctrine was sound and what fundamental mistakes of policy or doctrine have been committed.

⁷Proof of this change is the declaration of the Executive Committee of the Communist Party of Czechoslovakia of June 23rd, 1941 (published at the time in an illegal number of the party paper *Rudé Právo*), the text of which also was sent to me in London by our underground workers at home (again Dr. Vladimir Krajina). It was a complete reversal of policy and read as follows:

'*Proclamation of the Executive Committee of the Communist Party of Czechoslovakia.*

'On June 22nd there spread through the whole world like wildfire the news that barbarian, bloody German Fascism has committed a new, unheard of crime—that it has treacherously attacked the Union of Soviet Socialist Republics. The land of victorious Socialism, the land of freedom, progress and culture, the land to which the hope of all oppressed and enslaved peoples is turning has been attacked!

'It has been attacked because Hitlerism, that slave-driving, most barbaric regime in history, has reached the desperate conclusion that it cannot maintain its rule of murder, violence and oppression over the German Nation, over all the oppressed nations of Europe, that it cannot expand this rule throughout the world nor conquer mankind so long as there stands that strong bulwark, the support and hope of all the oppressed, the symbol of mankind, the U.S.S.R.

'The criminal attack by the gigantic, rapacious Fascist hordes, armed with all modern means of warfare, against the U.S.S.R. has started the last phase of the mad and desperate onslaught on mankind.

'The hearts of millions throughout the world are beating more quickly. A single wish, a single and imperturbable conviction, a single thought has passed through all minds and united all thoughts: this last dreadful criminal attempt must be and will be broken. This crime must be the last.

'The Czech people never felt more unitedly, deeply and strongly that indivisible and fundamental relationship, that fateful connection of our Nation with the Nations of the U.S.S.R. than they do today. To every honest Czech it is clear that the greatest, most stupendously fateful battle of all history which is being waged in the East by the Red Army against the hordes of Fascist beasts, is also a battle for our future, for our destiny, for our liberty. Our Nation will never forget that at the time of Munich, when we were betrayed and deserted by all, the U.S.S.R. alone called upon the whole world to go to our rescue. Today it is for our freedom that the sons of the peace-loving, brotherly Nations of the U.S.S.R. are laying down their lives. To them, our dear brothers, our good friends and comrades we tender our respect, our admiration, our love. The heart of our whole Nation beats in unison with theirs. To them turn the eyes and hopes of all the oppressed nations of Europe. *They, the heroic vanguard of mankind, will be victorious.* They will win because they are armed not only with the most modern weapons but also with that greatest and most powerful of all weapons: the knowledge that they are fighting for justice, for truth, for liberty and brotherhood among men and nations, for a better future for mankind. They will win because even today there stand behind them the fettered and enslaved German working people. They will win because the whole progressive world is ranging itself at their side for the struggle. All nations of the world, and at this moment even a greater number of the Governments of these nations, especially of the most mature nations, among them America and Great Britain, have realised that the most dangerous common enemy of all nations and races, the enemy against whom all the forces of the whole world must unite, is Hitler's Fascism.

'No initial success of the Hitler hordes, made possible by the very treachery of the attack, can change in any respect the early and final decision. Fascism will be conquered and pulled out by the roots—will be swept away once and for always from the face of the earth! The Czech Nation must be prepared for the last decisive fight for our existence, our freedom and our future. The hour of our liberation is approaching. The chief order of the day is the iron unity of the whole Czech Nation, of all its strata without exception. Let us form a mighty block of granite into which the treacherous monsters of the enemy of humanity, Hitler, will not be able to advance—a block upon which all attacks—moral or physical—of the Hitler barbarians and their allies, the scum of the Czech Nation, will be broken.

'Let us gather inseparably and firmly around the backbone of our Nation, around the working-class which in the factories and on the railways holds today that most important weapon, the general strike and which, at the moment it is given the order, will deal the bloody regime its first mighty blow!

'Today let us remain quiet with the maximum of caution. Let us forge our unity of steel against Fascism! Long live the unity of steel of the whole Czech Nation against Fascism! Long live the Soviet Union, its famous Red Army, our Ally!

'The Central Committee of the Communist Party of Czechoslovakia.'

[8] My exact words were: After the present collapse of the resistance of the French Army, conditions in Central and Eastern Europe will not remain as before. In the further stages

M

of the struggle fighting will again be transferred to that field. *Moreover, the Soviet Union is aware that Nazi Germany and Fascist Italy have their plans to destroy it and to overwhelm everything eastward and south-eastward of the German frontiers'.*—Printed in my book, Six Years of Exile and the Second World War, p. 86.

⁹At the beginning of October, 1940, I sent to Colonel Pika in Bucharest new instructions in case he was forced to leave Rumania suddenly. These especially concerned our future co-operation with the U.S.S.R. It was at the time that the 'Iron Guard' came into power in Rumania and when the Germans were already in the country to train and prepare the Rumanian Army against the Soviet Union on the invitation of the Antonescu Government.

Col. Pika and his group managed in dramatic circumstances to escape from the Gestapo and to reach Constantinople with the help of Rumanian officials (October 16th, 1940). In Turkey, Col. Pika was in permanent contact with the Soviet representatives and went with Ing. Klučka to Moscow via Odessa at the end of April, 1941.

¹⁰I shall deal with these negotiations in detail in the next volume of the *Memoirs*.*

¹¹We received uninterrupted information of Germany's readiness for war with Russia, particularly from Prague, from our underground workers, civilians, members of Gen. Ingr's intelligence service who even had Germans among their informants. Ministerial Councillor Dr. J. Papoušek, Col. J. Balabán and Zdeněk Bořek-Dohalský especially distinguished themselves in this connection. Moreover, Ukranian emigrants, though they sometimes made fantastic reports, nevertheless revealed much. Some information also arrived from our Communists in Prague.

¹²In my speech of December 11th, 1940, to the Czechoslovak State Council—speaking of the meaning of the second World War—I stressed this point of view and declared that we must build our own policy on this basis. At that time I formulated my opinion cautiously but clearly enough for those who knew the conditions and both ideologies:

'In reality, therefore, the present war is in all its main problems a continuation of the war of 1914-1918 and it is quite unimportant whether the pretext for starting it was the German minority in Czechoslovakia or the Danzig question or anything else. In it there are the same problems, the same interests, the same battles on all their grandiose scale. The only change is that they have developed. The historic fight has reached a further, more advanced stage. The questions are posed more precisely, more radically and their final radical solution has become inevitable. The real question is whether the political victory will be won by democracy or dictatorship—Nazi totalitarianism and State absolutism. In the field of foreign policy the question is whether there will be an equalisation and more permanent balance between the Great Powers and a secure existence for the small States and Nations—whether the barbarism, inhuman and criminal Fascist and pan-German nationalism will really be liquidated definitively, too, and whether the final political, social and economic victory will rest with Fascism or Communism or with political Democracy, because it has had the courage to perform two essential tasks:

'1. To seek a more resolute solution of its internal social and economic problems and to march courageously forward into social and economic democracy;

*Not completed (Tr.).

'2. To revise everything in its own system that has, politically, not proved beneficial or has directly failed to change whatever needs redress in Parliamentarism and the party system and to carry out whatever reforms are needed to make its State administration more efficient and successful.

'Whatever the result of this struggle, we are today in the midst of a war which, as the continuation of the last war, will bring a deeper and more far-reaching general change than its predecessor. Politically, as well as socially and economically, the times which we are living through are and will be very revolutionary. At the end of the present war and during the years immediately following, we will be faced with conditions which will mean changes in the political, social and economic systems comparable perhaps to those which occurred in Europe after the French Revolution. That it will not be easy, that there will be fierce fights and difficult situations, that everywhere in Central Europe and in every direction we will have more difficult conditions to cope with after this war than after the last war and that it will be essential for our State after this war politically, socially, economically and morally to maintain even more carefully than before reasonableness, circumspection and balance—all this is self-evident.

'In my opinion, therefore, the war of 1939 is no turning-point. From the period 1914-1918 through the twenty years' fight between democracy and dictatorship in Europe, past Fascism and Hitlerism to the attack on Czechoslovakia, past Munich to the war with Poland, France and Great Britain and on, finally, to the fall of France and to the present gigantic fight of British democracy (which, though it will win and preserve its Empire, will have to face great and various changes of a revolutionary character on the European continent) all this is one immense, straight and unbroken line. Throughout, paying no heed to any party groupings and actuated solely by the interests of the State, I have stood always in one place. I have never moved from it and I do not have to move from it even today. It is the path of progress, expressing the ideals of political and moral, social and economic democracy. Once more in this renewal of the great fight for a new Europe and a new world, it must inevitably triumph.'

When I showed this speech to Šrámek as Prime Minister and Rud. Bechyně as Chairman of the State Council before the meeting of the State Council, both urged me to change the text on the ground that the Great Britain of that time (autumn 1940!) could not swallow such a revolutionary speech and that it would injure our Movement. Later, I toned down some other more radical remarks especially those which concerned Great Britain.

[13] On June 23rd, 1941, I sent the following telegram to Churchill:*

'June 23rd, 1941

WINSTON CHURCHILL,
    10 DOWNING STREET.

Your address yesterday will always be remembered as an act of great statesmanship. The Czechoslovak Government in London and the Czechoslovak people at home will follow your leadership and your call with complete loyalty and firmness till final victory is reached.

Yours truly,
EDUARD BENEŠ.'

*English text not available (Tr.).

Churchill's answer arrived some days later and read:*

'I thank you for your telegram about my broadcast speech. I know very well that we can count on the Czechoslovak Government and the Czechoslovak Nation which is resolved to help us in realising our common aim with all means at its disposal.

Sincerely yours,

WINSTON CHURCHILL.'

[14]This address is printed in my book *Six Years of Exile and the Second World War* (pp. 120-126).

[15]The following is the text of Ambassador Maisky's letter:

'London, July 16th, 1941.

'DEAR MR. PRESIDENT,

'On the instructions of my Government I put forward to you the enclosed draft agreement which is to regulate the relations between our two countries until the end of the war. The draft is in Russian. I think it unnecessary to translate it into English since you understand Russian and since it is intended that the authentic text of the agreement shall be in the Russian and Czechoslovak languages.

'If you have no objections to this draft, I am authorised by my Government to sign it immediately; and we can arrange its signature without delay. If you wish to propose any changes I would first have to report back to Moscow.

'I would be much obliged if you could give me your answer as soon as possible.

'Sincerely yours,

I. MAISKY.'

On the same day, with the concurrence of Minister Jan Masaryk, I sent Maisky the following answer:

'July 16th, 1941.

'DEAR MR. AMBASSADOR,

'My sincerest thanks for your letter of July 16th, 1941, and for the draft of an agreement between the Soviet Union and the Czechoslovak Republic. Fundamentally the draft agreement contains everything we discussed a week ago.

'Tomorrow I will make all necessary arrangements with J. Masaryk, Minister for Foreign Affairs, and I think there will be no objection to dealing with the matter in such a way that the agreement can be signed without delay. Mr. J. Masaryk will sign the agreement on behalf of the Czechoslovak Government.

I am, Mr. Ambassador,

Yours sincerely,

DR. E. BENEŠ.'

*English text not available (Tr.).

CHAPTER V

WAR AND THE UNITED STATES

1. *The United States in World War II*

A T the same time that Hitler came to power in Germany, Franklin Delano Roosevelt became President of the United States (he assumed office on March 4th, 1933). One might almost say that this was a dispensation of Providence.

President Roosevelt was a sincere democrat and a farsighted practical politician. I already knew him quite well from the time of Wilson during the first World War. He knew how to surround himself with helpers who like him perceived the danger threatening the whole civilised world from the German desire for supremacy and new territory. The Nazi teaching of the superiority of the German race and the brutal expansiveness of Japanese imperialism were even physically repulsive to him and were fundamentally contrary to his whole being. Therefore he had already become a consistent opponent of all Fascism and Nazism at the time when the Western democracies, from inner disruption or incomprehension, were retreating before violence and were carrying out the policy of so-called 'appeasement'. He was also fully aware of the depth of spiritual decline which was apparent during the last pre-war years of European politics.

His attitude was exemplified by his speech at Chicago on October 5th, 1937, in which he said:

' . . . The present reign of terror and international lawlessness began a few years ago.

'It began through unjustified interference in the internal affairs of other nations or the invasion of alien territory in violation of treaties; and has now reached a stage where the very foundations of civilisation are seriously threatened . . .

'Without a declaration of war and without warning or justification of any kind, civilians, including vast numbers of women and children, are being ruthlessly murdered with bombs from the air . . . Nations claiming freedom for themselves deny it to others.

'Innocent peoples, innocent nations, are being cruelly sacrificed to a greed for power and supremacy which is devoid of all sense of justice and humane considerations . . .

' . . . If we are to have a world in which we can breathe freely and live in amity without fear—the peace-loving nations must make a concerted effort to uphold laws and principles on which alone peace can rest secure.

'The peace-loving nations must make a concerted effort in opposition to those violations of treaties and those ignorings of humane instincts which today are creating a state of international anarchy and instability from which there is no escape through mere isolation or neutrality.

'Those who cherish their freedom and recognise and respect the equal right of their neighbours to be free and live in peace, must work together for the triumph of law and moral principles in order that peace, justice and confidence may prevail in the world. There must be a return to a belief in the pledged word, in the value of a signed treaty. There must be recognition of the fact that national morality is as vital as private morality . . . It is, therefore, a matter of vital interest and concern to the people of the United States that the sanctity of international treaties and the maintenance of international morality be restored . . . The questions involved relate not merely to violations of specific provisions of particular treaties; they are questions of war and peace, of international law and especially of principles of humanity . . . It is true that the moral consciousness of the world must recognise the importance of removing injustices and well-founded grievances; but at the same time it must be aroused to the cardinal necessity of honouring sanctity of treaties, of respecting the rights and liberties of others and of putting an end to acts of international aggression . . . If civilisation is to survive the principles of the Prince of Peace must be restored. Trust between nations must be revived.

'Most important of all, the will for peace on the part of peace-loving nations must express itself to the end that nations which may be tempted to violate their agreements and the rights of others will desist from such a course. There must be positive endeavours to preserve peace.

'America hates war. America hopes for peace. Therefore, America actively engages in the search for peace.'

No wonder, that in his declaration of war against the United States in December, 1941, Hitler referred to this speech in his characteristic and uncultured manner.

Actuated by these moral principles and views about political morality, Roosevelt tried to mediate in the Czechoslovak crisis of September, 1938, but without result. His attitude to the violation of what was left of Czechoslovakia in March, 1939, was inspired by the same motives.

Here I will briefly mention only how he tried to help the Allies from the time of the outbreak of war in Europe to the moment when Japan suddenly attacked the United States and America therefore entered the second world conflict. As a result of Japan's action, Germany and Italy also declared war on the United States.

The neutrality legislation of the United States prohibited the delivery of war material to parties waging war. In April, 1937, there was a change according to which the President of the United States was authorised to allow the export of war material if the buyer paid for this material in advance and carried it in his own ships. This regulation, known as 'Cash and Carry' was valid for two years only and its validity ended on May 1st, 1939, shortly before the war started. When, therefore, on September 5th, 1939, the Government of the United States proclaimed its neutrality in the European war, which had then begun, Roosevelt signed the neutrality law without the 'Cash and Carry' clause. But it was clear to President Roosevelt that the unprepared democracies would urgently need help against the perfectly equipped aggressor. Already in his message to Congress of January 4th, 1939, he had expressed his apprehension that the neutrality legislation of the United States as then formulated would give aid to the aggressor and refuse it to his victim. He referred to this speech when he asked Congress on September 21st, 1939, to amend the neutrality law and, especially, to abolish the general arms export embargo and to reintroduce the 'Cash and Carry' clause. These changes were accepted after lengthy discussions and from November 4th, 1939, when President Roosevelt signed the new bill, Great Britain and France were able to get war material from the United States for their own requirements and so far as their financial resources permitted. Though this aid was considerable, especially when after some hesitation the United States also allowed the sale of the most modern types of weapons, it was nevertheless limited by the buying power and the currency reserves of the buyers. After the fall of France practically the only buyer was Great Britain.

On November 28th, 1940, Lord Lothian, the British Ambassador at Washington, disclosed at a press conference that British currency reserves in the United States were nearly exhausted and asked for further help. Shortly afterwards, on December 18th, 1940, President Roosevelt explained his plan of 'Lend-Lease.' He justified this on the ground that Great Britain would get more aid without incurring an immediate financial burden though at the same time the United States was also arming.

According to this plan which he laid before the Senate and House of Representatives as a Bill on January 11th, 1941, after beginning his third term as President, the President of the United States was to be authorised to allow war material to be made and sold to Governments named by him or to lend it to them or to exchange it or make it available to them in other ways. In addition the President was to be authorised to supply foreign Governments with certain military information and to give permission for foreign war material to be repaired in the United States. In practice, this meant that damaged British ships could be repaired in the harbours and docks of the United States. The law, which was passed on March 11th, 1941, after some minor changes, was rightly regarded as a law to provide aid for Great Britain and after it was passed President Roosevelt was justified in saying that 'the greatest industrial nation of the world has become an arsenal of the democracies'.

The validity of this law, which originally was to expire on June 30th, 1943, lasted to the end of the war and its scope was gradually extended to all countries defending themselves against aggression. All the Allies therefore benefited from it, including the Soviet Union, which is also greatly indebted to this law.

The United States also helped the Allies in another direction. It was not only a question of deliveries but also of their arriving safely at their destination. Germany hindered this by the submarine war which was countered by Great Britain by the system of convoying ships and guarding the convoys with warships. The British Navy was overstrained after the fall of France and lacked escort vessels. Roosevelt therefore assigned 50 destroyers to Great Britain on September 3rd, 1940, in exchange for the lease of some British islands to the United States for 99 years for the construction of naval and air bases. In the existing legal conditions, this system of lease for the construction of the bases which proved very valuable when the United States entered the war was the only one which could be used for quick and effective help.

Nor was this all. On July 8th, 1941, Roosevelt announced that American naval units had landed in Iceland and taken over its protection. On July 20th, 1941, he declared that it was necessary to ensure the safety of the supplies for the American forces in Iceland and Greenland, and he therefore ordered that U.S. ships carrying supplies to these islands should be guarded en route by warships not only against an actual attack but also against a threat of attack.

This meant, in practice, that the United States took over the protection of convoys nearly to the coast of England and in this way they guarded an important part of the British traffic routes. A final step—the greatest assistance which could at that time be given to Great Britain—was taken by the United States on November 14th, 1941. On that day the House of Repre-

sentatives passed another amendment to the Neutrality Law allowing U.S.
merchant vessels to carry war material to British ports. At that period, the
United States delivered to Great Britain 50 per cent of their production of
war material and transported it to Great Britain.

After the attack on the Soviet Union, Roosevelt's most important
contribution was his joint declaration with Churchill, the so-called
Atlantic Charter of August 14th, 1941, every paragraph of which contra-
dicted the principles of policy practised by the Axis Powers.

All laws concerning aid to Great Britain and, later, to the Allies, meant
bitter fights for Roosevelt and his collaborators—sometimes in difficult
conditions. The year 1940 was a year of failure for the Allies and in the
second half of the year Great Britain stood quite alone in the fight against
Germany and Italy. In the United States it was the year of the presidential
election during which President Roosevelt had to occupy himself with
special American conditions and questions and had to consider the
American public which was influenced by isolationists and their propaganda which (as Germany was counting upon) fell on good ground among
certain sections of American public opinion. Roosevelt was obliged to
conduct the fight against isolationist propaganda, and against barren absolute neutrality in which Hitler was interested, as perseveringly as the fight
for arming the United States. He knew that the United States had to
prepare for the moment when they would be forced to take an active part
in the war. This danger arose immediately after the conclusion of the
Three Power Pact in Berlin on September 27th, 1940, when Germany,
Italy and Japan jointly threatened united opposition to the United States if
the latter should stand in the way of the programme of expansion of the
three signatories. Roosevelt's far-sighted efforts secured results in this field,
too. On September 16th, 1941, he was able to sign the law on general
military conscription according to which it was possible to call up nearly
17 million men between 21 and 35 years of age for the defence of the
United States.

To Roosevelt's unceasing efforts and his practical policy the United
States and the whole civilized world owe the fact that when Japan,
modelling itself on the Fascist States, attacked the United States (December
7th, 1941, Pearl Harbour) and when Germany and Italy followed Japan's
action by declaring war (December 11th, 1941), the United States in spite
of the opposition of the isolationists and the advocates of absolute neutrality
were prepared both morally and materially to throw themselves into
the war and carry it through to a victorious end together with their
Allies.

2. The United States and Munich

The attitude of the United States of America to Czechoslovakia during the second World War was characterised by a policy based upon a certain kind of legal continuity. During and after the crisis of September, 1938, the American public was extraordinarily disturbed by all that happened, by the actions of the European Great Powers against Czechoslovakia, and especially by the way in which this European crisis was solved by the Munich Agreement. The American press published very detailed reports on the events of those days, the broadcast gave them quite extraordinary attention and the real sympathies of American public opinion were undoubtedly *always* on our side.

When I went to the United States in February, 1939, I found that in a number of important matters the American public was more solidly and objectively informed about the events of Munich than public opinion in France or in Great Britain where the information released to the public was intentionally and tendentiously coloured by the policy of 'appeasement.'[1]

But it seemed—this is now clearly established by official documents—that official circles in Washington were seriously divided in their views about the September crisis and that therefore there was a considerable degree of uncertainty. There can be no doubt that *some* circles in Washington were resolutely *against* the policy of appeasement as practised by most of Europe against the German and Italian dictators *and especially against the way in which the policy was carried out* and of course, its results and consequences. In particular, this was the attitude of President F. D. Roosevelt himself.

But it is equally true that other circles—also official—*were essentially entangled in the Munich policy and had a certain responsibility for it.* The U.S. Ambassador in London, *Joseph Kennedy*, stood expressly and consistently behind Chamberlain's policy of appeasement. He supported it everywhere and unreservedly identified himself with it both during his stay in Great Britain in 1938 and 1939, after his return to the U.S. and during the presidential election campaign for Roosevelt's third term. Chamberlain more than once took advantage of Kennedy's attitude.

The American Ambassador in Berlin, *Hugh Wilson*, fully believed even in August, 1938, that a peaceful orientation of German policy was not impossible. When in August, 1938, events in Prague neared the culmination of the crisis, he came to Prague from Berlin to inform himself of our situation. He spoke with the American and British Ministers in Prague.

He had a long talk with Lord Runciman and finally, on August 6th, 1938, he also visited me. His naive belief in the peaceful intentions of the Berlin Government amazed me. He told me expressly that Göring did not want a war and that he was surely working for peace and for an agreement both with us and the others.

Hugh Wilson was sincere. He had a sympathetic feeling for us dating from the first World War and he did not want to harm us. But he was quite erroneously informed about Germany and its intentions and plans. Probably he also informed Washington on these lines. And as he himself stressed at a meeting of bankers and economists in Chicago in 1939, after he had been recalled from Berlin, the first and paramount interest of the United States at that time was to avoid a new war in Europe in which America would again have to intervene. It was from this standpoint that he looked at the policy of 'appeasement.'

The United States Ambassador in Paris, *William Bullitt*, did not at first express himself publicly in favour of 'appeasement' like J. Kennedy, but he worked for it incessantly. His attitude towards us during the crisis of September, 1938, was wholly negative. He did not hide this. Daladier clearly hinted on many occasions that his policy of 'appeasement' had the support of the American Ambassador and therefore also of the United States. Bullitt himself did all he could to prevent a new great war. He made it clear though with reservations (thus providing himself with an alibi) that in his view Prague was not behaving with sufficient circumspection towards the German minority and that President Beneš was a dyed-in-the-wool anti-German chauvinist whose policy was endangering European peace.

Bullitt's own policy at that time and later was mainly dictated by his dislike—his personal dislike—of the Soviet Union which he acquired while he was Ambassador in Moscow. His actions were directed principally against the Soviets and found expression again in a decisive manner later when together with Daladier and Bonnet he planned and secured the expulsion of the Soviet Union from the League of Nations for making war against Finland. He was said at that time to have sent a telegram to Washington in which he declared that he had at last got full satisfaction— that is to say, for what he had experienced in Moscow as Ambassador. He pursued this policy in Paris until the fall of France and later—it seems—in America also where, according to all reports, he supported to some extent the Pétain regime at Vichy against De Gaulle.

On the whole it was natural and comprehensible that the United States should view the possibility of an armed conflict in Europe with anxiety and that they should work deliberately and systematically against such an eventuality both in September, 1938, and later. A more than clear indication of the United States' attitude is given in the official publication of the State Department, *Peace and War*,[1] issued in January, 1943, and containing an official account of U.S. foreign policy from 1931–1941.

This document proves how the United States worked for the preservation of peace throughout this period; how on September 26th, 1938, President Roosevelt in his message to Germany, Czechoslovakia, France and Great Britain appealed to them not to stop negotiations for an agreement between Berlin and Prague; how, furthermore, on September 27th, 1938, Cordell Hull sent instructions to all U.S. representatives abroad to urge the Governments to which they were accredited to approach Berlin and Prague with similar appeals.[2] And it adds, that on the same day (September 27th, 1938), Roosevelt turned directly to Mussolini asking him to use his influence in Berlin so that the conflict between Prague and Berlin might be solved by peaceful negotiations and not by war. But the same document immediately proceeds to point out—and I stress this—that after the signature of the Munich Agreement, State Secretary Cordell Hull said quite clearly in a public address, *that the Munich Agreement neither assured peace nor did it rest on sound political and moral principles.*

These facts are the best indication of the general direction of U.S. foreign policy at the time of the crisis which led to Munich.

When I went to the United States in February, 1939, I saw at once that in North America as elsewhere the isolationists and appeasers were powerful enough. But the whole American public as well as official circles in Washington were aware of the fact that a great wrong had been done to Czechoslovakia. They said so openly. In all parts of the United States which Jan Masaryk or I visited on our lecturing tours in 1939, we found that public opinion, the press, most of the intelligentsia, important politicians and responsible people in general were agreed on this point. At that time this was a great moral support for us, It kept our hopes alive and encouraged us in our future activity.

I have already recounted how President Roosevelt and the Washington Government reacted to the occupation of Prague on March 15th, 1939, and to the attempts to destroy Czechoslovakia, and also how Minister Hurban saved our Legation which the American Government continued to recognise. In this way, the American Government showed clearly that from the point of international law and policy it did not regard the Czechoslovak chapter as closed. I have also mentioned my talk with President Roosevelt at Hyde Park on May 28th, 1939, and with State

Secretary Cordell Hull and Sumner Welles on June 29th and 30th, 1939. All these things meant that when the time came we would be able to start up our activities in the United States—with due regard to existing laws and the U.S. policy of neutrality—and link them with our liberation campaign as soon as war broke out in Europe.

Here three facts were of essential importance for our future:

(a) The United States—as a cardinal principle of policy which had already been publicly proclaimed by President Coolidge—did not recognise the occupation of any State by force.

(b) They were not, nor did they feel, bound by the unilateral decision of the four European Great Powers at Munich in which they themselves had taken no official part.

(c) They did not intend to change their attitude towards Czechoslovakia, the Legations and Consulates of which did not cease to function and continued to be officially recognised by the Government of the United States.

The U.S. Government, having taken this far-sighted legal and political attitude, which morally was the only right one, *maintained it consistently up to the final favourable legal solution of our whole problem in the United States in 1943.*

3. The United States and the Recognition of Our London Government

When we established the Czechoslovak National Committee in France and Great Britain after the outbreak of war in September, 1939, we desisted on the advice of Minister Hurban from trying to obtain recognition of the Committee by the United States. The position of our Legation was very strong and the U.S. Government had taken a firm legal stand in our affairs. Furthermore, the United States were neutral and it was therefore of greater advantage to await developments. But when on July 21st, 1940, the Provisional Czechoslovak Government in London was recognised by the British Government and then by a number of other Allied Governments, we asked confidentially in Washington whether the American Government was ready to extend the legal position which it had taken towards the Czechoslovak diplomatic and consular authorities, to cover in addition the newly-established Czechoslovak Government.

The most important point was that the Government of the United States had no objection to our representatives in America at once proclaiming their submission to the authority of our new Government nor to their accepting its leadership and instructions by becoming an integral part of our State organisation. It furthermore hinted to us that the logic of events might lead to the recognition of the Government having regard to the fact that the U.S. Government's policy towards Czechoslovakia remained unchanged—*the legal continuity of the Czechoslovak State had never lapsed so far as the U.S. Government was concerned*—and that the question of the recognition of the Czechoslovak Government was being examined carefully at Washington.⁴ This was the starting point from which Minister Hurban proceeded with his cautious and tactful moves and from which other people, too, helped us in Washington from the beginning of 1941— as, for example, our American friends in political and University circles, our National Council in Chicago and others.

Early in 1941 the American Ambassador J. G. Winant, arrived in Great Britain and I contacted him on March 28th, 1941. This was the beginning of regular political co-operation. I kept him systematically informed of our progress, of the development of our affairs and of our international position as well as of our negotiations for recognition by Great Britain. He showed a very positive attitude towards us from the outset and helped Czechoslovakia very effectively in Washington.

By June, 1941, Minister Hurban himself thought the situation was already ripe for the recognition of our Government by Washington. On July 24th, 1941, President Roosevelt himself received him personally to discuss this matter. Minister Hurban again outlined to the President the whole situation of the Nation at home as well as the political and legal position of our London Government. At the same time he delivered my personal letter to the President dated June 4th, 1941, in which I formulated our request for the recognition of our Government. In it I reminded Roosevelt of our conversation in Hyde Park in May, 1939, informed him of the state of our resistance movement at home and abroad and the position in regard to our recognition by other States. I acknowledged how much the United States had already done for us during this war and emphasized the importance for our people at home if the United States were now to show, by recognising the London Government, what was their final policy towards our country.⁵

On July 29th the State Department informed Minister Hurban that it had been decided to recognise the Czechoslovak Government in London, that I would receive a direct answer to my letter from President Roosevelt to this effect and that the American Ambassador, Mr. J. G. Winant, would at the same time be instructed to deliver an official Note to Minister Masaryk.

Some days later Ambassador Winant brought me this personal letter from President Roosevelt:

'White House, Washington *July 30th, 1941*
DEAR DOCTOR BENEŠ,

I read your letter of June 4th with great care. I remember with pleasure the conversation we had at Hyde Park two years ago. We discussed as you will remember the unhappy events which had befallen Czechoslovakia and your future plans for the fight to restore your country's freedom.

The cause of the Czechoslovak Nation has always been near to the heart of the American people. We have not forgotten its struggle for independence and we remember with pride how the Government and people of the United States in the preceding generation took part wholeheartedly in the efforts of that great statesman Thomas Masaryk and his collaborators, you among them, to establish a democratic republic in Central Europe in order to secure the liberty, and to permit the free political existence, of the Czechoslovak people.

Since that day there have been specially close relations between our two democracies. We have unlimited confidence in the vitality of your people as a nation and look forward eagerly to the day when democratic institutions shall again flourish in your beautiful country.

In order that the ties between our two nations should not be broken, we have not ceased to recognise the diplomatic and consular representatives of Czechoslovakia in the United States in the full exercise of their functions. We have also borne in mind the courage and ability of the armed forces and political leaders of Czechoslovakia who organised themselves abroad to continue the struggle for the re-establishment of liberty in their country. It is therefore with real pleasure that I can inform you—and I am sure that my feelings are shared by the whole American Nation—that the American Government has decided to accredit an Envoy Extraordinary and Minister Plenipotentiary to the Provisional Czechoslovak Government in London for closer contact in the common interests of the two countries until the institutions of free government are re-established in Czechoslovakia. We are at the same time sending instructions to the American Ambassador in London to inform the provisional Czechoslovak Government.

I take this opportunity to assure you of the firm hope of the people of the United States that the cause of Czechoslovak freedom will triumph.

Very sincerely yours,
FRANKLIN D. ROOSEVELT.'

On August 1st, Jan Masaryk received a Note from Ambassador Winant which defined the attitude of the Government of the United States as follows:

'*London, July 31st, 1941*

YOUR EXCELLENCY,

The Secretary of State has directed me to inform Your Excellency that the Government of the United States, mindful of the friendship and special interest which has existed between the peoples of the United States and Czechoslovakia since the foundation of the Czechoslovak Republic, has watched with admiration the efforts of the people of Czechoslovakia to maintain their national existence, notwithstanding the suppression of the institutions of free government in their country.

The American Government has not acknowledged that the temporary extinguishment of their liberties has taken from the people of Czechoslovakia their rights and privileges in international affairs, and it has continued to recognise the diplomatic and consular representatives of Czechoslovakia in the United States in the full exercise of their functions.

In furtherance of its support of the national aspirations of the people of Czechoslovakia, the Government of the United States is now prepared to enter into formal relations with the provisional government* established at London for the prosecution of the war and the restoration of the freedom of the Czechoslovak people, under the presidency of Dr. Beneš, and while continuing its relations with the Czechoslovak Legation at Washington would be pleased to accredit to the provisional Government an Envoy Extraordinary and Minister Plenipotentiary, to reside in London, for the conduct of relations pending the re-establishment of the Government in Czechoslovakia.

I shall later communicate with Your Excellency regarding the diplomatic representative whom my Government would like to designate.

Accept, Your Excellency, etc.

JOHN G. WINANT.'

We were informed at the same time that the Government of the United States had no obligations in respect of the question of definite frontiers.

These events brought near to a successful end our struggle for the restoration of their former international, political, diplomatic and legal position to our country and Nation. The decision of President Roosevelt was a final and decisive blow to the whole German action of that time against the re-establishment of Czechoslovakia and against the freedom of its people. It was also the *last* step needed for the re-establishment of the international legal, political and diplomatic pre-Munich position of

Czechoslovakia in the whole world. It is necessary to stress especially that this recognition was secured *when the United States were actually still neutral* and that our move for recognition by the United States had actually begun before our full and definite recognition by Great Britain and the Soviet Union.

Afterwards it was not even necessary to negotiate for a *definitive* and full recognition by the United States. The events themselves provided for this. After the British and Soviet recognition on July 18th, 1941, our international legal and political situation improved rapidly and it was gradually rounded off by recognitions from all the free countries of the world. From that time in the spheres of diplomacy and international law it was impossible to doubt what the political result of the war and of Allied war policy would be for our country.

The Czechoslovak Government headed by the second President of the Republic was again recognised as the fully legal Government of the former State by the following countries: China as the fourth Great Power waging war against the Axis countries on August 27th, 1941, Norway on October 12th, 1940, Poland on November 27th, 1940, Belgium on December 13th, 1940, Egypt on March 13th, 1941, the Netherlands on March 15th, 1941, Yugoslavia on May 19th, 1941. Diplomatic relations were established with Ireland on July 28th, 1941, with Luxemburg on February 27th, 1942, with Mexico on March 26th, 1942, with Iran on May 27th, 1942, with Bolivia on June 5th, 1942, with Uruguay on June 29th, 1942, with Cuba on July 4th, 1942, with Peru on July 6th, 1942, with the Dominican Republic on July 10th, 1942, with Greece on August 19th, 1942, with Brazil on September 16th, 1942, with Ecuador on January 13th, 1943, with Colombia and Venezuela on January 9th, 1943, with Chile on March 31st, 1943.

As is well known the United States entered the war only after the Japanese attack on Pearl Harbour on December 7th, 1941, by which spectacular act Japan joined the imperialist war launched by Germany and Italy. From that moment Washington changed from its semi-belligerent participation, during which it had not taken part in armed operations against Germany and had remained legally neutral in spite of its extensive help to the democratic Powers, to full and many-sided participation in the political, diplomatic and military activities of the democratic Powers against German, Italian and Japanese Nazism and Fascism.

With the Fighting France Committee, led by General De Gaulle, the Czechoslovak Government began official relations immediately after its first British recognition. It regarded 'Fighting France' from the beginning

N

as the real representative of the French people, and later, in the autumn of 1943, it transferred this co-operation automatically to the Committee for National Liberation at Algiers. In the League of Nations and the International Labour Office the representation of the Czechoslovak Republic had never ceased to exist. With some neutral countries our representatives were either recognised *de facto* or at least were tolerated in spite of the pressure and the difficulties which these States experienced from the Germans.

It was in such circumstances that the United States of America conceded to us, without new formal diplomatic negotiations or formalities in regard to international law, the same diplomatic status as the other Governments in exile. They accredited their envoy to us and finally *informed Minister Masaryk officially on October 26th, 1942, that the recognition by the United States was to be regarded legally as complete and definite.* A similar statement was made to me two days later, on our National Independence Day, by Minister Biddle who added that the United States were looking forward to my paying an official visit to Washington in due course as Head of the State in the same way as the Heads of State of the other exiled Governments in London had already done. The visit took place in May, 1943.

4. The United States Enter the War—My Official Visit to Washington

At Christmas, 1942, our Minister in Washington, Vladimír Hurban, came to London to acquaint himself with our position in Great Britain. He also brought me a message from President Roosevelt in which that eminent, leading Allied statesman asked me to pay an official visit to the United States and to discuss our own and allied war problems. Our London Government at once decided that I should go.

I therefore answered at once to that effect and decided that politically I would link my visit with my, already planned, journey to the Soviet Union. The whole war policy of the Allies was for me one unified whole because in World War II all world problems were more than ever intertwined and it was quite impossible to solve one independently of the others. I therefore mapped out a comprehensive plan for myself. In the spring I would go first to Washington and then soon after my return I would go from London to Moscow.

It was, of course, necessary to prepare for the journey politically by conversations with the British as well as, in particular, by discussions with Moscow. During March and April, 1943, I placed a number of questions before Envoy Bogomolov with a view to defining our relations with the

Soviet Union, ascertaining the attitude of Moscow to a number of European questions (especially concerning Germany) and finding out the general attitude of the Soviet Union to important individual questions of Allied war policy as a whole. In the course of these conversations all the articles of our future treaty of alliance with the Soviet Union which we wanted to conclude during my visit to Moscow were agreed upon in principle.

All these preparations and conversations were concluded during April and I started on my journey to the United States on May 6th, 1943. On a beautiful May day we flew from London—first to an airport in Scotland from which the Transatlantic planes normally started. On the same evening we flew to Iceland. This was our first stop. There we were taken over by the Americans who with true American lavishness had built a huge air and military basis for the American Army some 10 kilometres south of Rejkjavik. After sunset we started again and early on the second day completed the second lap of our journey when we landed on the South-Western coast of Greenland. From here we started for the third stage from Greenland to Canada where we again made a short stop. On the afternoon of the same day we arrived at the well-known La Guardia Air Port, New York.

The air journey of myself and my companions who included Minister Smutný and my Secretary Dr. Táborský was kept secret because we were officially due to arrive in New York some days later. In those days when flying was still a somewhat unusual way to cross the Atlantic, this was a most interesting experience and a politically valuable one in view of the interest it aroused.

On the following day I at once met Minister Hurban and Dr. Papánek. I discussed with them the situation in the United States and all the problems which would arise during my conversations with President Roosevelt and his collaborators. Then we officially announced our arrival to Washington.

During my stay in Washington in May and June, 1943, I had above all a number of personal political conversations with President Roosevelt, State Secretary Cordell Hull, the high officials of the State Department, Sumner Welles and Berle, Vice-President Henry Wallace, the Secretary for Finance, Morgenthau and Secretaries Stimson and Knox, as well as with a number of Senators, Congressmen and political, military, economic and financial personalities. I gave an official address on Czechoslavakia, its mission, its policy and its position in Europe to both houses of the American Congress and in the name of the Nation I reaffirmed my confidence in the strength and vitality of our future democracy.' Once again I could watch the people of the United States, their mood, their views and endeavours, their morale, their war effort—which at that time was already so enormous that it can hardly be expressed in words—and their plans for future victory and future peace.

On the invitation of the Canadian Prime Minister, Mr. Mackenzie King, I went on June 2nd to pay an official visit to Canada, too. There, from June 2nd to 5th, I had a similar experience and I was able to make precisely the same estimate of the views and war efforts of Canada. In conversations with Prime Minister Mackenzie King and a number of other members of the Canadian Government, I learned how strongly Canada felt about the injustice of Munich and how the sympathies of the people with Czechoslovakia had been maintained to their full extent. For the rest, my political talks in Canada dealt with the same problems as in the United States. The chief of them was the Soviet Union.

The political aspect of my journey and all my conversations in Washington were, above all, a public and, in a sense, almost a demonstrative confirmation and ratification of our official international position in the United States and the rest of the world. This stressed further that the United States did not recognise anything that had happened to us in the years 1938 and 1939, that the Republic still fully existed for them from the international standpoint, that the Munich frontiers and everything connected with them whether concerning Slovakia, Hungary, our Germans or anyone else*, had no international validity and that the Slovak question, the question of our Germans, the question of Sub-Carpathian Ruthenia were regarded as our internal questions.

All our official conversations were conducted in this spirit. Between us and the U.S. Government everything was quite straightforward: there were no misunderstandings or legal obscurities, neither were there at that time any differences of opinion concerning our basic problems. It stood to reason, of course, that the final solution of a number of important questions would be authoritatively discussed by us only at the moment of the armistice and peace—*especially details about frontiers*—but that was the same with all other countries.

The whole war against Germany, Italy and Japan with all their satellites was simply considered to be one common war. Here, too, I became convinced of the horrible danger into which Slovakia had been brought by the treason of Tiso, Tuka, Sidor, Mach, Čatlos and all the other traitors. And especially the fact that they were waging war not only against the

*The Poles had annexed Tešin (Tr.).

Soviet Union but also against Great Britain and the United States, prejudiced us greatly in the eyes of many Americans and very seriously endangered the interests of the Slovak people.

I was in America at the time of the gravest military failures of the Germans on the Eastern Front when German anti-Soviet propaganda ran amok in trying to evoke differences between the Soviet Union and the United States. This was one of the last attempts to save Germany. But during my sojourn in the United States I could myself see the results of this campaign. It not only brought about official talks between the United States and the Soviet Union but also great public discussions. I myself took part in these conversations and discussions both by personal contact with Roosevelt, Cordell Hull, Sumner Welles, Berle, Hopkins and others, and also in public meetings and in various pronouncements.

As is known, the result was that German and Hungarian propaganda gave me the title of a Bolshevik agent and agent of Stalin. But I was very satisfied at that time with the results of this great international discussion. It was more than ever before clear to everybody in America that the war could be won only by the close and loyal co-operation of the United States, Great Britain and the Soviet Union—and, of course, the other Allied Nations, too. This was already paving the way for the well-known Moscow Conference of the three Foreign Ministers (Molotov, Hull, Eden) which took place in October, 1943, and which in its decisions was of such great importance for the final victory of the Allies.

I came to Washington at rather a special moment. The United States were entering a period of the war which for them pointed to certain victory. For a foreigner that feeling of certainty about ultimate victory was quite overwhelming. The military consequences of the Anglo-American occupation of North Africa which had been carried out courageously and successfully at the end of the preceding year now began to show themselves. And as the Soviet Union was not taking part in the Italian campaign, the necessity of reaching greater harmony in the political and diplomatic and, of course, in the military direction of the war was also becoming apparent. There was continuous contact between Roosevelt and Churchill and just one day before my arrival in Washington, Winston Churchill himself had arrived in that city for new consultations.

The most serious items in my discussions at that time (after our relations with the United States and all the Czechoslovak political and diplomatic problems) were the question of France, the Pétain regime, the recognition of De Gaulle, the future of the campaign against Italy, the forthcoming negotiations about Poland and its relations with the Soviet Union and the final elucidation of the position of Great Britain and the United States towards the Soviet Union—all these were always on the daily programme. Finally there was already arising very urgently the question: What did each of the Allies intend to do with Germany at the end of the war.

After an official dinner in the White House on May 12th, 1943, at which most of the members of the U.S. Government, a number of Congressmen and Senators and some military advisers of President Roosevelt were present, we went with the President to his study and remained there until 2 a.m. in a lively and frank discussion of all the diplomatic and military questions mentioned above. Minister Vladimir Hurban and Minister Jaromir Smutný were present.

The discussions opened with the question of France. Roosevelt explained to me the reasons for his caution towards De Gaulle. He analysed conditions in France, Algiers and Morocco, as he had seen them during the Casablanca Conference with Winston Churchill, and expressed rather pessimistic views of the further development of the whole country and the French Empire. He reckoned with a very long duration of convalescence of France even in case of a full victory over Germany. His views of the matter gave me a clear sense that he felt a kind of personal disappointment about France in general. This was visible in his behaviour towards the Pétain regime as well as towards the De Gaulle movement.

I tried to defend France and to prove the necessity for all of us, without regard to his and Churchill's differences with De Gaulle, to help France find its feet quickly and to put that country into the ranks of the fighting European Great Powers. 'On the European Continent', I argued, 'it is necessary in the interest of Europe and the rest of the world, and having in view the future situation of Germany, that there should be again in addition to the Soviet Union one other strong democratic Great Power— France.' But the President criticised the French régime in the colonies as he had seen it during his recent sojourn in North Africa, and he doubted whether post-war France would be able to keep all its colonies. I think that, broadly speaking, he appreciated my arguments but for the time being his attitude continued to be reserved.

Then we turned to Poland and the Soviet Union. It was at the moment when the differences between them were reaching their climax and when the Allies—especially Great Britain and the United States—had to take a definite decision in this question. Millions of American Poles intervened strongly in this dispute and their influence on the forthcoming American presidential elections played a great rôle. From the attitude of Roosevelt as expressed in the discussion—and even more from the opinions of Harry

Hopkins, the personal adviser of Roosevelt, which Hopkins explained to me himself in another talk on the following day—I realised that the United States had already taken a definite attitude: that, essentially, they had accepted the view of the Soviet Union on the question of changing the former Eastern frontier of Poland and that in principle they agreed that there would have to be an agreement between Poland and the Soviet Union and some co-operation between them. Failing this, the United States were not inclined to support the action Poland was taking at this time. In particular, I came to the conclusion (this was *my* estimate of the outcome of the Washington talks) that the ideas of the London Poles— and, of course, of their Government, too—who believed that the Polish demands against the Soviet Union were supported by the United States were illusions or pious hopes and that it was a total mistake to think that the influence of the American Poles could work a fundamental change in this regard. State Secretary Sumner Welles formulated this attitude to me on the following day just as definitely.

In the course of the discussion, I raised the question of our relations with the Soviet Union. I shall tell in detail elsewhere how these relations developed. At present I shall only stress that when preparing in London for the journey to Washington, I sent word to Moscow through Ambassador Bogomolov that it would be well if, before my visit to America, I could know some of the fundamental views of the Soviet Union concerning Germany, France, Poland and ourselves, too, so that I could give the correct answer to questions on the subjects in Washington. As I explain elsewhere in this book*, I put a number of very precise questions to Bogomolov and I also got precise answers. Among those which were put and answered were the question of our formal treaty with the Soviet Union, the question of Soviet policy in regard to Germany, the Soviet attitude to the whole Polish problem, etc. Substantially I had already agreed with Bogomolov—and through him with Moscow—on the wording of our treaty of alliance and on the support of the Soviet Union in the ultimate solution of the problem of our relations with our Germans. I therefore went to Washington with, in the main, a clear idea of how our relations with the Soviet Union would very soon develop.

These then were the lines on which the conversations with Roosevelt developed concerning all these questions. I told him that I knew what course the Soviet Union intended to take and realised that this necessitated our accommodating ourselves to its policy. I told Roosevelt openly that we could not accept another Munich in future and that this already obliged

*See pp. 241 sqq. (Tr.).

us to consider a treaty with the Soviet Union. I told him further that it was clear to me that we would be neighbours of the Soviet Union and that this fact would exercise a certain influence on our internal policy in connection with our future social and economic development. Finally, I told him that after my return to England from America I intended to go immediately to Moscow and conclude a formal agreement with the Soviet Union. I added that I believed Poland, too, should follow a similar policy and should thus enable the three chief Powers to reach final accord in the Polish question.

After some further discussion of these matters Roosevelt expressed his full understanding of this policy. I have already mentioned that Harry Hopkins, the intimate political collaborator of Roosevelt, spoke to the same effect and so also did Sumner Welles. While I was still in Washington I received from London Bogomolov's report of the positive attitude of the Soviet Union in regard to the transfer of our Germans after the end of the war. I hinted to Roosevelt how we and the Soviet Union looked at this question. Roosevelt said plainly that Munich had been such a lesson for the whole world that the problem of our Germans would have to be examined in detail and *that it would have to receive a radical and courageous solution in accordance with the results of our detailed studies*. I therefore regarded it as a certainty (and rightly) that when the question of the transfer of the Germans became a concrete one, the United States would support us. And this actually happened.

I had two more opportunities of speaking to Roosevelt of all these questions—and some others—on the above lines.

From Washington I went for longer trips through the United States. I visited a number of industrial, military and other centres. I saw the enormous war efforts of the United States and I came again to the conclusion that the Allies would win a complete and decisive victory. In particular, I visited New York, Chicago, Detroit and other cities. Everywhere I gave public addresses in which I spoke openly of my attitude to current political and diplomatic problems. In Chicago I was received with full ceremony at the University of which I was still a professor. Everywhere—and on every occasion—I was asked about the future development of the Soviet Union, of its possible co-operation with the Western Powers, of its attitude to its future neighbours and to small countries in general, of its intentions to revolutionise and to communise the world, etc., etc. In general my answers were variants of the views I expressed later in the last chapter of my book *Democracy Today and Tomorrow*, and of what I said about Slav policy in my book *Essays on Slavism*.

I would also like to mention briefly our conference with Roosevelt and Winston Churchill on May 13th, the day after my arrival at Washington. Roosevelt asked me to this meeting so that I could tell them both my views about the question of the partition of Germany. I was cautious because I did not consider this matter to be ripe yet and because I did not know the precise attitude of the others—especially of the Soviet Union. But I expressed my firm conviction that it would be absolutely necessary to try the German war criminals, that it would be necessary to organise a profound and durable re-education of the German people and that without considerable decentralisation and substantial changes in the German social structure, post-war Germany would not develop into a really peaceful and democratic Germany.

I considered this visit and my talks with Roosevelt—which I have summarized here very briefly—to be another great milestone in our war policy. The visit was wholly successful and the results of the political talks which took place were for us decisive. Especially I want to stress *that in the course of the discussion of our problems with Roosevelt I twice examined with him in detail all the reasons and the procedure for the transfer of our Germans from Czechoslovakia to Germany. I found with the President the same full understanding which he had shown in all questions concerning Munich. And already on that occasion he gave me his full consent to the execution of the transfer of the greatest possible number of our Germans.*[8]

I left Washington confirmed in the conviction that it was necessary to round off my negotiations in London and Washington by means of a visit to Moscow and that I should make this visit immediately after my return to England from the United States.*

There are but few examples in history of a small State in times of storm and revolution securing such satisfaction for its policy and recognition of the correctness of its conduct as was afforded by this journey of mine. Already in the summer of 1943, I obtained a very strong impression of this fact—so important politically for my country and Nation—in the reception accorded to me when I visited the United States and Canada.

NOTES TO CHAPTER FIVE

[1]During my stay in the United States in 1938 the American broadcasting companies presented me with copies of all speeches, addresses, news items and commentaries issued by the American radio systems during the Munich crisis. These made a large and imposing pile which proved with what political earnestness the United States had watched the Munich crisis.

*Dr. Beneš's account of the visit to Moscow is given in the final chapter of this volume (Tr.).

²*Peace and War, United States Foreign Policy, 1931-41*, published by the American State Department in January, 1943.

³I had already realised in September, 1938, that the telegrams of all the South-American States firmly requesting me not to go to war with Germany in any circumstance and to save peace, were sent on the initiative of the United States of America. In September, 1938, such an appeal—contrary to the intentions of the United States and of President Roosevelt—served the interests of Hitler. At that time German propaganda exploited this telegram of Roosevelt's and the appeals of the South American States to our disadvantage, interpreting them as aimed against us and for Munich. Thus, against the intentions of their authors, these telegrams dealt us the final blow before Munich.

⁴State Secretary Cordell Hull replied in this sense to a question on May 14th, 1941, from Congressman J. Sabath and to one from Senator J. Lee on June 12th, 1941, concerning the attitude of the United States to the Czechoslovak Government in London. His letter to Senator Lee read as follows:

'DEAR SENATOR LEE,

I am acknowledging your letter of May 29th, 1941, with which you enclosed the communication from Mr. Petr Rabštejnek on the relations of the United States to Czechoslovakia. *The Government of the United States has never revoked the recognition of the Czechoslovak State and will continue to recognise the national integrity and the international status of Czechoslovakia.* It is continuing to recognise Mr. Vladimír Hurban as the Czechoslovak Minister to the United States and also the Consular officials under his direction. In this connection I wish to state that Mr. Hurban was nominated Minister in the United States in 1936 by Dr. Beneš before he resigned the Presidency of Czechoslovakia in October, 1938.

As you doubtless know, a Czechoslovak Committee was established in Paris and was later transferred to London. It is common knowledge that this Committee has been recognised by the British Government in the course of the war as the Provisional Government of Czechoslovakia under the Presidency of Dr. Beneš. Our Government has taken note of the situation thus created and the relative facts in this connection are constantly under consideration.

Truly yours,
CORDELL HULL.'

⁵This letter read as follows:

'London, June 4th, 1941.

MR. PRESIDENT,

I hesitated somewhat before deciding to address this personal letter to you. Many things have happened since the last conversation which I had the honour to have with you just two years ago (on May 28th, 1939) and in which, when discussing with you the approaching war and the events which have now actually taken place, I told you about our intended plans for the re-establishment of Czechoslovakia.

My plans have now been realised. In agreement with our country, we have established a new Czechoslovak Army on British soil and we have organised our flying corps which for a full year has already been fighting together with the British airmen against German attacks on Great Britain. We have united our political emigration and are in close co-operation with our country: with the political leaders of the Nation at home, with the intelligentsia and all classes of the Nation. We are marching in step with them and it is beyond doubt that the Nation is behind us. We have formed a Government and a whole governmental machine on British soil.

The British Government and all the British Dominions, after ascertaining these facts, have recognised us. At this moment we have agreed with Great Britain to raise our international status to one of full recognition *de jure*. We have also been recognised by a great number of other countries.

On May 28th, 1939, I had the honour of discussing with you the valuable aid which the Government of the United States gave to President T. G. Masaryk in his fight for the liberation of our Nation during the last war. Similar assistance given by the United States to my country in these hard times, after all that has happened to our Nation since Munich, its present sufferings and its really heroic resistance against the German invasion, would mean for us a quite inestimable service and encouragement, conferring upon the Nation at home an invincible moral and political strength.

By not recognising the occupation and destruction of Czechoslovakia in March, 1939, you, Mr. President, have performed a service to my country which our Nation will never be able to forget and which is a pillar of strength for us. But the fact that the U.S. Government has not yet thought it possible to recognise our Government resident in London is being misused by the Nazis in their efforts to suppress the resistance and the fight of our people for the restoration of freedom and democracy in our country, to weaken it morally and to destroy all its hopes for a better future. If on the other hand we were recognised by the United States, this would be a really far-reaching act in the struggle not only of Czechoslovakia but of all Central Europe against Nazi dictatorship. Our State and Nation were really democratic. Czechoslovakia was the only democracy which was able for fully twenty years to defend its happy and successful democratic freedom and but for the events of Munich our country would even now be one of the best European democracies. In the present war it is carrying on the same military and political fight, and it is in the same position, as present-day Poland, Norway and the Netherlands. I believe for these reasons that it deserves your confidence and that of your Government.

If the United States were to decide to do in our case the same as Great Britain has done, I believe their action would merely fulfil the spirit of your policy of aiding and saving freedom and the dignity of modern man, of saving democratic institutions in Europe and of removing from the political world that barbaric regime, today represented by Nazi dictatorship, which is destroying the small European Nations.

The Czechoslovak Minister in Washington, Mr. Vladimír Hurban, has already put our request before the State Department and he is continuing his negotiations. I myself have had the honour to contact your Ambassador in London, Mr. J. G. Winant, in this matter and I have given him all necessary information concerning it. But it seems that some difficulties still stand in the way of the recognition of our Government by the United States. I therefore beg you to forgive me, Mr. President, if, remembering again my visit with you in Hyde Park, your friendly reception and the sympathy which you then showed in the affairs of Czechoslovakia and its people, I again turn to you now after two years, when our cause has made such progress and our Nation at home has shown beyond doubt and uncompromisingly in which camp it stands, with a fresh request for your help.

If you are able to grant it, history will show that your help was not given to an unworthy recipient. Above all, you will be helping a Nation against which a great injustice has been committed and whose cause is just.

I wish all your undertakings real success. I thank you for all your sympathy and friendship to my country, and for every future enterprise in which your great and powerful country engages for the freedom of the oppressed European Nations and for democracy and world freedom.

Sincerely yours,

DR. EDUARD BENEŠ.'

*Negotiations for the recognition of the Czechoslovak Government by the U.S. Government were begun before full and definitive recognition *de jure* was granted by Great Britain and the U.S.S.R. The American answer was therefore addressed to the 'Provisional' Czechoslovak Government.

⁷The address read as follows:

'Mr. President, Members of the United States Senate, it is now a quarter of a century since Thomas G. Masaryk, the first President of the Czechoslovak Republic and my great predecessor, came, in the last year of the first World War, to Washington to inform American leaders how his Czechoslovak countrymen were fighting for their freedom and independence and to obtain the American support for their struggle. His Mission in the United States met with favour and encouragement everywhere. He found a great understanding of, and sympathy with, the national aspirations of the Czechoslovak people in the President of the United States, Woodrow Wilson, in his Government, and the people.

It was known that for centuries, beginning with the Middle Ages, this small Nation in the heart of Europe had been a glorious independent kingdom, the Kingdom of Bohemia—and a prosperous State—the State that first began the fight for religious freedom in Europe. In the fifteenth and sixteenth centuries, Prague, its capital, was a great centre of learning, contributed largely to European cultural, spiritual, and material development, and played an outstanding rôle in European history and particularly in the history of the Holy Roman Empire and the Austro-Hungarian monarchy. Perhaps your Government knew, too, the famous declaration made by the German Chancellor Bismarck after his victory over Austria in 1866:

'Whoever is master in Bohemia is master of Europe. Europe must, therefore, never allow any nation except the Czechs to rule it, since that nation does not lust for domination. The boundaries of Bohemia are the safeguard of European security, and he who moves them will plunge Europe into misery.'

In my estimation, there can be no better comment on the position of my country even today. The recognition of our cause here in this country in 1918 was also undoubtedly due to the unmistakable determination of our people to live as a free and independent nation. More than 150,000 Czechoslovak soldiers fought for their country's liberation in the first World War in Russia, France, and Italy. When the war was drawing to a close, the epic march of the Czechoslovak legionaries across the Siberian plains to Vladivostok fired the imagination of the American people.

When the collapse of the Central Powers was imminent, Masaryk made our Declaration of Independence in Washington on October 18th, 1918. It was promptly accepted and recognised by the American people and by their Government. That is why Czechoslovakia was considered and often called the god-child of the United States of America.

Czechoslovakia's 20 years' record as a free and independent democratic State is one of which we are justly proud. Surrounded on all sides by authoritarian countries and governments, she remained faithful to the democratic traditions which came to her very largely from the United States. Her social legislation and her educational system were progressive and advanced; her financial system was stable, her currency, one of the soundest in Europe; her general economic standard was very high, and her import and export trade greater than that of Italy. Until 1938 this Republic was one of the most prosperous and happy countries in Europe. Even the concentrated campaign of Nazi Germany, beginning in 1936, using corruption, lying propaganda, and threatening war and violence, failed to shake the inner harmony of the Czechoslovak Republic.

In her foreign policy Czechoslovakia resolutely and consistently followed the policy of peace, international arbitration and collective security. She fostered and encouraged friendship with her neighbours—Austria, Yugoslavia, Poland, and Rumania.* She was the most loyal member of the League of Nations. She supported the Locarno policy, was an original signatory of the Briand-Kellogg Pact, and was ready to play the part demanded of her in any generally accepted system of collective security. In Geneva she resolutely opposed the Japanese invasion of Manchuria and China; I was President of the Assembly of the League of Nations when we voted the sanctions against Italy upon her invasion of Abyssinia. Czechoslovakia was ready to oppose militarily the occupation of the Rhineland and Austria. Our Army and Air Force were ready and thoroughly efficient. Up to the year 1939 we did our duty completely, not only to our Nation, but to Europe and democracy as well.

Czechoslovakia was in mortal danger from the moment that Hitler and the Nazi leaders came to power.

When Hitler saw that the policy of sanctions against Italy was not strictly applied and when the German remilitarisation of the Rhineland was not opposed by force, he thought that the countless seeds of bitterness and mistrust sown by the dictators would permit him to reap a harvest of destruction in Europe and bring about the realisation of his pan-German plan. The success of the annexation of Austria in March led to the September crisis in 1938.

My own view then was that Hitler's demands and attacks against Czechoslovakia should have been rejected even at the cost of a war. We were ready, but the Western Powers were not. By the sacrifice of Czechoslovakia, Europe and the world gained a year's time in which to prepare for the defence against the coming onslaught. In my opinion, the second World War began with the criminal occupation of Prague. And from the very day of occupation, March 15th, 1939, all Czechoslovak citizens have been at war with Germany.

Since 1938 the Czechoslovaks at home have endured great hardships, sorrows, and suffering. They know that many of their soldiers and airmen, who escaped from their enslaved homeland, lost their lives while fighting for its liberation in Poland and in France. They know that after the Franco-German armistice, Czechoslovak soldiers and airmen reassembled in Great Britain and that in the decisive battle of Britain, Czechoslovak airmen played an honourable part. They know, too, that Czechoslovak soldiers are now fighting in Russia and in Africa and manning the defences of Great Britain.

*Note the omission of Hungary (Tr.).

On the other hand, they see their own country being converted into an arsenal for a war against the United Nations. Many are now working as forced labourers in Germany and elsewhere. Those who resist the oppressors are either executed in masses or tortured in prisons and concentration camps. Their country is pillaged and germanised, their national education completely destroyed. The undying memory of the martyred village of Lidice forbids us ever to relax in the world struggle now waged against the powers of evil and darkness. The all-out participation—after Pearl Harbour —of the United States in this fight for the freedom of the world has turned into certainty what until then had been the hope of the ultimate liberation for the Czechoslovak people and the other occupied nations.

Mr. President, permit me to say before this august body, in conclusion, with gratitude and appreciation:

It was here in this great democratic country that in October, 1918, the freedom and new independence of my Nation were solemnly proclaimed and its first free Government recognised. When on March 15th, 1939, Nazi Germany destroyed the new Czechoslovak liberty, and I personally, as member of the faculty of the University of Chicago, respectfully asked President Roosevelt to refuse to recognise this insulting and lawless act of violence, it was the Government of the United States which first among all Great Powers categorically repudiated this wanton aggression. It gave its full approval to the refusal of the Czechoslovak Minister in Washington to hand over his Legation to the Nazi authorities. The Government of the United States never recognised the German occupation of the Czechoslovak Republic. By this decisive act this great historic land of freedom defended the national liberty of my country at the most tragic moment of our modern history. Later your Government recognised our reconstituted Government and independent country and accepted our Republic as a free and equal member of the United Nations. Through all these acts the immortal spirit of the great American tradition, of Washington, Jefferson, and Lincoln, rose to defend the highest undying principles of human and national liberty at the time when a small, democratic, peace-and-freedom-loving Nation was assassinated by a vulgar authoritarian aggressor.

The entire Czechoslovak Nation expresses its warmest thanks and gratitude to the great American people, not only for all that they have done on behalf of Czechoslovakia but also for the enormous and outstanding contribution of your great country to the war effort of all the United Nations.

They do not doubt that this great struggle, in which the United States are playing so decisive a rôle, will end with one of the greatest victories in your and our national annals. They are greatly encouraged and proud that I have the privilege of addressing the Members of the Congress of the United States. I know that they will accept the promise I make to you, today, as theirs.

As President Masaryk in 1918, I, today, feel authorised to declare on behalf of my Nation, here in the Washington Capitol, that after the final victory in this great war is achieved, the Czechoslovak Nation will reconstruct its old home rapidly and successfully by its untiring efforts, remaining faithful—as it always was during the difficult period of its long, chequered, and glorious history—to the democratic way of life, to the principles of spiritual and religious freedom, to the ideals of peace and peaceful international collaboration, considering itself again the god-child of the great and glorious Republic of the United States.

⁸While I was in Washington, I sent to the Czechoslovak Government in London regular reports of the results of my visit. I quote here some of the reports which show how I saw things at that time. On May 13th, 19th and 30th and on June 7th, 1943, I cabled to our London Government some details of my discussions in Washington. They read as follows:

'For Minister Masaryk and the Government—Confidential.

I.

May 13th, 1943

I thank the Government cordially for their greetings. On the first day I had a discussion lasting five hours with Roosevelt in which we covered most of our political problems. The talks took place in a very cordial, friendly and frank atmosphere in the presence of Hurban and Smutný. My short résumé follows:

1. In regard to Russia the President's attitude is that it is necessary to trust Russia and also to continue to co-operate loyally and fully after the war. He wants to give practical expression to this by meeting Stalin soon and by discussing all questions with him quite frankly and realistically. For the time being please do not speak of this possibility.

2. Roosevelt also takes a realistic view of Polish-Soviet relations. At least he has succeeded in stopping any further polemics. But he is taking the right view of the difficulties on the Polish side and on the form of a solution of the Polish-Soviet frontier dispute.

3. He looks with sincere and friendly eyes at Czechoslovakia the full liberation and restoration of which as a State is to him self-evident.

4. He agrees that after the war the number of Germans in Czechoslovakia must be reduced by the transfer of as many as possible. He asked no questions about Slovakia.

5. I informed the President about my negotiations with the Soviets and of their and our point of view for the regulation of our mutual relations in the form of a treaty—also of their assurance that they do not intend to interfere in our internal affairs and of their readiness in principle to come to an agreement with democratic Poland also. The President took note of this with visible satisfaction and recognised that in our attitude to Russia we were proceeding on the right lines.

6. Roosevelt gladly accepted my memorandum for the Vatican (published in the Appendix) and will forward it with his recommendation.

7. In further conversations we discussed the question of post-war Germany, the question of general international control of the enemy countries and of the new international security organisation. The President's views on all these problems are very concrete. He tries to find a solution which will be as uncomplicated and at the same time as effective as possible, preserving the full liberty and independence of the component States. But he does not intend to go so far as the League of Nations did.

8. The whole of our talk about the organisation of security was within the framework of our discussions on this matter with Eden in London. The conversation though in general terms was nevertheless sufficiently concrete to make his whole conception clear to me. This was my first conversation with Roosevelt and it was successful from every point of view and favourable for our cause. Our reception and the whole proceedings were such as to give us every satisfaction.

BENEŠ.

II.

May 19th, 1943

(a) For the time being I have finished our discussions in Washington. Harry Hopkins visited me to confirm all the decisions reached in my conversations with Roosevelt and we discussed my future political contact with the President, who is especially interested in the regulation of the political and economic affairs in Europe at the moment of the fall of Germany, and everything that may directly or indirectly result therefrom.

(b) Though the visit to Cordell Hull at which Hurban was present, was a formal one (I thanked him for our reception in Washington), I discussed our problems again with him. Our main topic was Russia. Hull, like the others, is chiefly interested in getting guarantees that Russia will not interfere in their interior affairs and will not deliberately support communism and communistic programmes.

Hull, obviously on purpose, gave me a concrete example from his office of how after Munich he held up all decisions concerning matters arising from Munich, because, as he said, the Munich Agreement was actuated by the spirit of injustice, dishonour and dishonesty. For that reason, so far as the United States was concerned, all its effects on Czechoslovakia were null and void.

I thanked him for this statement and for the behaviour of the United States up to the present time and I declared that from our standpoint Munich did not exist and that legally we were, and would only stand for, the pre-Munich Republic, as had been expressly confirmed to us in our agreement with Russia.

The Washington talks surpassed all our expectations and we are satisfied with the understanding and really cordial reception which our cause received in all the circles with which I came in touch.

BENEŠ.

III.

May 30th, 1943

(a) Today I returned to Washington in accordance with an earlier arrangement and I had another long conversation with Sumner Welles in the presence of Hurban. Welles said that the President insisted that we should meet again—especially to discuss the Russian problems before my journey to Moscow. I am therefore leaving on Monday to attend a military review and see some factories and then I shall go straight to Canada. In consequence of Welles's request I shall then have to return once more to Washington for a last conversation with the President.

(b) The conversation with Welles was very important. We again discussed the question of general security and I learned how the organisation of a World Council will crystallize following the discussions here with Churchill and also the structure of the proposed regional councils and other forms of participation by the smaller Nations in the organisation of security. It seems that this is developing on the right lines.

(c) Welles confirmed to me how well the dissolution of the (Communist) International has been received here. He said it came just in time and that the reports of Davies from Moscow are quite favourable. It can be stated that the prospects of an agreement with Russia are certainly making good headway.

(d) We once more discussed the question of Germany and the arguments for and against partition. I stressed very strongly that if they should decide in favour of partition, the security system would really have to work because Czechoslovakia would be the first to be endangered—as in 1938 after the annexation of Austria. They are aware of this. He asserted that Great Britain and, it seemed, Soviet Russia, too, were for the time being in favour of partition, adding that a definite solution would especially have to be found for the problem of Prussia.

(e) He again confirmed the American attitude concerning Poland and Russia. I called his attention to the necessity of preparing a solution in time so that in the end it would not come to a *military* solution between Poland and Russia. He stressed also that the treaty we intended to conclude with Russia could be regarded as proof that the independence of Poland, Rumania and other neighbours would also be respected and that in this way we would be emphasising that our policy was European not binding us to an exclusively Eastern or an exclusively Western policy. But he understood that we do not want another Munich. He confirmed that they fully appreciated our policy and that they had no objections to it. I stressed that we were anxious to see complete unity between the Great Powers as well as *to promote our uniform line towards Russia, Great Britain and the United States!* I think that our whole attitude has been made clear, that it is now understood here in detail and that so far as America is concerned there will be no difficulties. On the contrary they understand that by a similar clarification of our policy in the case of Russia we shall be helping all the others. As to what points it will be necessary to stress in Russia about the situation here, this matter will be discussed in my final conversation with the President.

BENEŠ.

IV.

June 7th, 1943

Today I had my final farewell conversation with Roosevelt in the presence of Hurban. The conversation covered the whole ground of our former talks and again confirmed all the discussions and views exchanged earlier.

The following individual questions were discussed:

(a) Roosevelt requests that in my conversations with Stalin in Moscow I should present his views in the matter of the Baltic States. The United States are not able and do not intend to hinder their final annexation to the Soviet Union, but must respect world public opinion and therefore it is a question of finding the form and procedure which will calm public opinion. In the matter of Poland he considers Sikorski to be the best Prime Minister but he does not know what will happen among the Poles themselves. He knows that even Stalin would not personally reject Sikorski. He expects that the final solution will be the Curzon line somewhat modified in Poland's favour and the incorporation of East Prussia in Poland. He considers this a just and right compensation which the Poles could and should accept.

(b) He agrees to the transfer of the minority populations from Eastern Prussia, Transylvania and Czechoslovakia. *I asked again expressly whether the United States would agree to the transfer of our Germans. He declared plainly that they would.* I repeated that Great Britain and the Soviets had already given us *their views to the same effect.*

(c) As for Germany, he rather inclined to partition into five or six States. He was satisfied with the visit of Davies to the Soviet Union adding that a further rapprochement has been reached and that matters were developing on the right lines. About the dissolution of the Comintern he said that he accepted it in good faith. Now, he said, it depends on the Soviets.

o

(*d*) He is in favour of the establishment of free ports in the Northern Adriatic. He named Trieste, Fiume and Pola.

(*e*) He spoke very decidedly in favour of the system of as free international trade as possible as proposed in the Cordell Hull plan of reciprocal trade agreements.

(*f*) While speaking of Russia, I again stressed that we had agreed with Russia about our future relations and I repeated the essential parts of the agreement to him. He confirmed our former discussion and again took note of, and agreed with, my intention to conclude all the agreements on occasion of my next journey to Russia. I promised to inform him of the result. He also asked for reports about Poland.

(*g*) On the subject of the organisation of security, Roosevelt said that he was a realist differing in this respect from Wilson. He wants to secure peace for fifty years and leave the rest to posterity. Differing from Churchill, he does not want a *European* Council but a single central World Council with effective power.

(*h*) I thanked Roosevelt again very much for my reception in Washington, for our conversations, for the generally favourable attitude to Czechoslovakia and for the help the United States have given us in the past and during my present visit.

BENEŠ.'

CHAPTER VI

THE WESTERN POWERS ANNUL MUNICH

1. *Negotiations with Great Britain about the Revocation of Munich*

NEVER—not even when the situation looked its worst—did I believe that the Munich dictate would be a basis of lasting peace or of a lasting legal status for Central Europe. Invariably, my doubts concerned only the duration of that fearful and immoral political injustice. I was afraid only of what would happen to our Nation if the dictate should last even a few years in what purported to be peace.

I feared for the morale of the Nation if this should happen. Fascists and Nazis, political adventurers, cynics and immoral political schemers, so-called political realists and advocates of the immoral policy of having a number of irons in the fire, uneducated political opportunists—unscrupulous class egotists—all our political and spiritual reactionaries could have claimed to be in the right as opposed to the political conceptions and political morality of Masaryk and myself! And the Nation as a whole would have suffered an alarming retrogression politically, economically, socially and morally and its injuries would remain for decades, if not for centuries.

I repeat: I did not believe that this would actually happen. But that it should not do so necessitated, as always in politics, fighting against the possibility at once, with resolution and indefatigably. Equally, I never doubted that Munich *was not the end of a great crisis* but the *beginning*. Nazi Germany needed Munich to begin its expansion in earnest. The egotistic and (in all that concerned us) unscrupulous tendencies ruling in the Western democracies, either did not, or did not want to, understand this.

Feeling sure that I was right, I expected—as I always stress—war. Immediately after Munich therefore I started my preparations to attain our political objectives: to annul the Munich dictate, to restore the Republic, to obtain redress for the injustice done to us, *to secure political and moral satisfaction.* From September, 1938, sleeping and waking, I was continuously thinking of this objective—living for it, suffering on its account and working for it in every one of my political actions. In fact, it was already my only aim in life.

My determination was so much the stronger because before even six months had passed Germany itself destroyed Munich. Both the democratic guaranteeing Powers, on the most specious excuses, evaded—for a second time—the solemn obligations they had undertaken at Munich: namely, to defend the international existence of the truncated Czechoslovakia. This new act of German gangsterism culminated after another six months in the attack on Poland. Thus even the final and principal excuse for Munich—the preservation of world peace—which carried with it the fictitious justification for demanding sacrifices from Czechoslovakia (namely that it should give so-called liberty to its minorities) lost all validity or sense. The whole policy which led to Munich was brought to the height of absurdity, was demonstrated to be wholly impracticable and fundamentally wrong while all those who (whether they believed in it or not) initiated and sponsored it were shown to be altogether credulous, entirely frivolous and manifestly ridiculous.

Objectively, therefore, the conditions for the annulment of the Munich dictate and all its consequences had already existed for a long while.

Subjectively, however, this was not the case. All the western politicians who prepared and executed the Munich dictate were still in power when the war began and they remained in power for a long time afterwards—some even throughout the war. For three whole years the war took an adverse course for the Allies and the self-evident axiom of politics and diplomacy—not to assume obligations prematurely when one is not sure that it will be possible to honour them—was applicable to all these people, particularly in a case which would have meant disavowing their own actions and condemning both themselves and their former political achievements.

The fact that Munich was so intimately bound up with internal policy in France and Great Britain was another strong argument for postponing the reversal of that wrongful act. The obscurity of the relations of the Western Powers with the Soviet Union, against which the Munich dictate was as clear an offence as against Czechoslovakia, caused the ruling circles of the Western democratic Powers to proceed in this case, too, with caution and sometimes even negatively.

This was why the fight for the public and binding annulment of the Munich dictate was so extremely difficult even though revocation had been greatly facilitated both legally and politically by Germany's war policy and though the legality of Munich had indeed been destroyed, deliberately and cynically, by Berlin. For an incredibly long time the curse of the evil deed continued to operate in London, in Paris and elsewhere. Nevertheless, I began the fight as a private person immediately after my arrival in Great Britain and later in America. The occupation of Prague on

March 15th, 1939, gave me the first opportunity to take public action and to begin to advocate the principle of the legal continuity of the First Republic. The war waged by Germany against Poland, France and Great Britain enabled us to declare this to be the cardinal principie of our policy.

I made the first concrete attempt to secure a public declaration in this sense by Great Britain on the second anniversary of Munich in 1940. This was after our Provisional Government had already been recognised by Great Britain—at the moment when our Army which had arrived from France, was re-organising in England and when our airmen were already taking part over the Channel in the Battle of Britain. In recognising the Provisional Government, the British Government had informed us not that it was recognising *any of our frontiers, but simply that it had no obligations whatsoever in regard to frontiers in Central Europe.* This did not satisfy us and I asked for a clearer declaration, specifically in respect of Munich.

I discussed the matter with the representative of the British Government to the Provisional Czechoslovak Government, Bruce Lockhart. I urged that the British Government should take the opportunity offered by the second anniversary of the Munich dictate to make a solemn pronouncement to the Czechoslovak people, as to one of the Allies, declaring the Munich dictate to be invalid. The Foreign Office agreed to my request in principle and discussed with me the contents of the address which was to be made in the Czechoslovak broadcast from London either by the Foreign Secretary, Lord Halifax, or by the Prime Minister, Winston Churchill, himself.

I gave Lockhart my draft about Munich in which two essential facts were stated, namely that the Munich agreement was legally non-existent:

(*a*) because the Czechoslovak Government had been forced to accept it under special pressure and according to Czechoslovak law the Czechoslovak Constitution had been forcibly violated;

(*b*) because the agreement had been destroyed when Germany invaded Czechoslovakia by force on March 15th, 1939.

The Foreign Office only accepted the second point for inclusion in the official address refusing—in 1940—to admit publicly British participation in the pressure of the four Great Powers on Czechoslovakia in September, 1938, and publicly accepting a share in the guilt of Munich. As I have already mentioned the address was then delivered by Winston Churchill on September 30th.

In view of the fact that the address made no mention of our frontiers some of our people in the emigration and also in the Government sharply criticised it as insufficient and even held that it sounded as though Churchill had accepted the Munich dictate. The Foreign Office therefore confirmed to me by means of another official letter from Bruce Lockhart *that Churchill's address expressed the view that the Munich treaty had been cancelled, that in so far as frontier problems arose from this fact the British Government did not intend to bind itself in advance to recognise or support in the future any frontiers in Central Europe including, of course, the so-called Munich frontiers.*[1]

All these negotiations showed me very clearly how difficult it would be even at a later stage to get from the Foreign Office a categorical and clear repudiation of Munich involving a definite revocation of the whole Munich policy with all its consequences. Nevertheless, these negotiations were our first great success as they ended with the recognition of two great facts of essential importance for us:

(*a*) The British Government declared that it did not feel legally bound by the Munich Agreement.

(*b*) It did not recognise the Munich frontiers but regarded the question of *all* Central European frontiers as open.

Thus was stated what had ceased to exist. It was not yet stated what did or would exist.

I was therefore anxious that the next discussions should take us a step further and that there should be set out positively what actually existed or would take the place of the Munich dictate after victory had been won. I tried to obtain a positive declaration on this point in the summer of the following year when the change of the recognition of our Government into a full and definite one was being discussed and when, at the same time, we successfully asked and obtained that Czechoslovakia, in respect of international law, should be put on the same footing as all other Allied Governments residing at that time in London. I then asked that this equalisation should also *cover recognition of the legal continuity of the First Republic.* From this, would have implicitly followed *the recognition of the full 'status quo ante'* and therefore also the recognition of our pre-Munich frontiers.

Though the Foreign Office accepted the principle of the full international legal and political equality of Czechoslovakia with the other States, it requested that the question of legal continuity—and therewith all its consequences—should be postponed on the ground that this was too complicated a problem which would have to be studied further in detail in all its legal aspects and consequences.

As we did not want to postpone our definite recognition with the important political advantages arising from it, we accepted provisionally the Foreign Office's view but immediately started to prepare another move for the final liquidation of the Munich dictate. I began more intensive discussions on the manner and form of this liquidation in the autumn of 1941 after the full recognition of the Government of the Czechoslovak Republic by Great Britain, and after the arrival of Heydrich in Prague on September 27th, 1941, and the first wave of massacres in Bohemia and Moravia. I showed how the annulment of Munich would, so to speak, morally strengthen our people in their valiant resistance against Germany and what a blow this step would strike against Nazi power in our country.

In my letter of April 18th, 1941, which I sent to Foreign Secretary Anthony Eden through Lockhart (and to which I personally drew the attention of Prime Minister Winston Churchill when he visited the Czechoslovak Brigade in Leamington on April 19th, 1941), I summed up Czechoslovakia's legal attitude to the unworthy act concluded at Munich without our participation and to our great harm. My memorandum mentioned the principles of a declaration by which Munich would be definitely expunged as between Czechoslovakia and Great Britain.

From the beginning of 1942 I discussed this question with the British Minister Nichols who had been accredited with the Czechoslovak Government shortly before* and who helped in drafting a formula for the British revocation of Munich. The exchange of views was rather protracted. I imposed the greatest patience on myself and put forward proposals for the British text *which meant the legal status quo ante* and therefore did not infringe the British principle of not binding the Government in the matter of the frontiers of the different countries waging war before the war actually ended. The text was several times corrected or adapted by me to meet the objections of the Foreign Office. All my proposals contained these main principles:

(*a*) In view of the fact that the Munich Treaty of September 29th, 1938, was arbitrarily violated by the German Government on March 15th, 1939, by the occupation of Czechoslovak territory, it was thereby destroyed;

(*b*) In view of the fact that the Munich Treaty itself was forced on the Czechoslovak Government by pressure, it was therefore, from the Czechoslovak point of view, unconstitutional and illegal;

(*c*) The British Government to declare that they were not in any way bound by this treaty or by its consequences;

*Full legal recognition of the Czechoslovak Government involved an exchange of full-time accredited envoys. Sir Robert Bruce Lockhart as permanent Under-Secretary had other duties (Tr.).

(d) The British Government to regard the pre-Munich status of Czechoslovakia in international law as having been restored.

But all these 'integral' formulas about Munich—this is how my proposals were described in official British circles—always came up against insurmountable opposition in the Foreign Office.

My unvarying arguments that this alone would wash away the whole matter from the mind and memory of our people; that this alone would fully clear up the situation and really repair all the injustices done to us; that our sufferings gave us a right to such a declaration and that the whole course of the war had fully justified our pre-Munich policy and our behaviour during the Munich crisis—all this was not enough.

The chief reasons given officially by the Foreign Office against such an 'integral' condemnation of Munich were broadly speaking as follows:

(a) The formula proposed by Czechoslovakia means that we now make a definitive pronouncement in regard to the post-war frontiers of Czechoslovakia. We cannot do so, firstly, because all other States whose frontier problems are equally controversial (even though there is no Munich in their case) would ask for the same treatment; secondly, we are under an obligation to the United States not to make such a declaration before the end of the war and before joint negotiations have taken place at the peace conference. As a result of the war, *all* frontier problems of all States have substantially been reopened in one respect or another and therefore we cannot bind ourselves today unilaterally with respect to Czechoslovakia only;

(b) A declaration that the Munich Agreement has ceased to exist does not annul the historical and legal fact that such an Agreement was concluded and, according to British legal theory, such a historical and legal fact does not cease to exist as a result of a unilateral British declaration but only by a new international agreement or treaty in which those who concluded the original Munich treaty participate in some form or other. For this reason the invalidity of the Agreement as between Czechoslovakia and Great Britain must be proclaimed by a 'less integral' formula.

(c) However, our pressure to obtain recognition of the legal continuity of the First Republic induced the Foreign Office to concede that it respected our point of view as a strictly *Czechoslovak* point of view and had no objections to it. But it asked us for the time being not to urge the British Government to give international approval to our attitude.

We replied to the above arguments that we were ready to accept that the Peace Conference should occupy itself with our frontier problems to the same extent as with those of other States. I myself added that we ourselves would—perhaps—after a victorious war make new proposals and new frontier demands and might therefore ask for some small rectifications in our favour. We also rejected the second British argument on the ground that it involved a fact which for us was unacceptable: namely that the Churchill-Eden Government still advocated the preservation of part of Chamberlain's Munich.

These arguments did not change the point of view of the Foreign Office. The discussions were sometimes very lively and stubborn. But they were carried on with complete confidence and full loyalty on both sides. In particular, I refrained from putting the whole question before the British public, the press and Parliament thereby evoking an internal party-political British quarrel though some of our more uncompromising friends urged me to do so.

But I always had the impression that the real obstacle to the acceptance of my 'integral' formula and to striking at the roots of the matter by a complete disavowal of the whole British foreign policy since 1932 was the fact that there still remained in the Churchill Cabinet a number of persons who had pursued this policy and who had supported Munich in 1938 from conviction, that such a step would have been a great public rebuke for the prestige and reputation of the whole former foreign policy of Great Britain, and especially of the Foreign Office, and this could have its effect on the internal situation and give rise to quarrels, discussions in Parliament, etc., which in time of war would have very disagreeable consequences. Of a certain importance was also Churchill's very honourable, quite personal conception of the loyalty which he owed to his personal collaborators and former ministerial colleagues.

In short: After my discussions which went on for a number of months, first, very secretly between myself and Bruce Lockhart, Minister Nichols and Foreign Secretary Eden, and later from the spring of 1942 with the participation of Minister Masaryk and Minister Ripka, we reached the conclusion that the British Government (including the War Cabinet whose approval was needed for such an agreement between ourselves and the British Empire) would in no circumstances go beyond a certain point. At the same time we realised that the Foreign Office would do its utmost to postpone for as long as possible the solution of this question which for the Foreign Office was surely most delicate.

2. *Great Britain Revokes Munich*

At that stage the Soviet Union indirectly helped us to the final solution of Munich as between ourselves and the British Government. During the winter of 1942* the Soviet Union and Great Britain began to discuss a closer agreement and the conclusion of a new treaty of alliance which would remove mutual distrust and doubts concerning the future course of the war and future peace. We took part in this work—very intensively and so far as we were able—being anxious that this agreement should at all costs be reached. We were vitally interested and the signature of such an agreement would have provided a fresh confirmation of the policy for which we had striven so hard and so long before Munich. If it had existed then, there would have been no Munich and no second World War. Finally the matter matured, the agreement was ready and in May, 1942, Foreign Minister Molotov came to London to put the finishing touches to the treaty and to sign it.

I had a long talk with him in London on June 9th, 1942. We agreed on the lines of our common war policy and I obtained from him a declaration that the Soviet Union had recognised the Republic in its pre-Munich frontiers and that it never had recognised nor would it recognise what had happened at Munich and after Munich. *I also obtained Molotov's consent to my officially announcing this to our people at home and to the international public as a binding obligation.*

On June 4th, Foreign Secretary Eden invited me to the Foreign Office to inform me confidentially of the contents of the British-Soviet Pact. He thanked me on that occasion for our help in realising this policy. We discussed a number of other questions and finally we came to our unfinished discussion about the British liquidation of Munich. At the end I said to Eden quite frankly: 'It is time to liquidate Munich as between Great Britain and us. Our discussions are prolonging themselves indefinitely and they are beginning to have a bad influence on our mutual relations.'

Foreign Secretary Anthony Eden entirely agreed. He promised that he would look into the matter himself and that we would settle it as soon as possible. New discussions followed on June 25th and July 7th, 1942, the first in the presence of Minister Nichols, and on our side of Minister Ripka. At the second Minister Masaryk who had meanwhile returned from the United States was also present.

In the first conversation we discussed the British-Soviet Pact and its

*i.e. 1941–2 (Tr.).

consequences, my talk with Molotov and our negotiations with the Poles and Polish-Soviet relations. Eden especially wanted to know whether we and Molotov had concluded any detailed agreements about Munich, what had been decided about our future relations, about the Poles and our common frontier with the latter and whether we and the Russians had linked our London talks with our own discussions with the British Government about the liquidation of Munich. On the last point, I assured him that nothing of the kind had happened and that Czechoslovakia wanted to regulate its Munich problem loyally with the different States directly, separately and without pressure. We also intended to do this with France in due course.

In the discussion which followed, Eden brought forward British proposals for a compromise on the basis of which, he said, a final agreement for the liquidation of Munich could be reached and in which these basic principles would be recognised:

(a) The Munich Treaty does not exist because it has been violated by Germany itself.

(b) The British Government therefore recognise nothing concerning Czechoslovakia contained in the Munich Treaty nor do they recognise anything that has happened since 1938 in respect of the original Czechoslovak frontiers as a consequence of Munich.

(c) The British Government undertake that in future international discussions, and in particular during the peace negotiations, they will do nothing that may be influenced, in any way, by the events of 1938.

Elaborating this clause, all the British representatives participating in the talks confirmed to us officially and expressly that this meant the same as what my integral formula demanded because Great Britain wished Czechoslovakia to be as strong, as consolidated and as secure as possible. It was substantially a return to our former natural frontier. What we would have to talk about later, formally, during the general and final peace negotiations would be the detailed frontiers in connection with the wider regulation of our German and Hungarian questions.

(d) Further it is proposed to omit any reference to the question of the legal continuity of our State from the discussions about Munich. *The British fully respect our point of view as being the Czechoslovak point of view* to which the British Government have no objections.

(e) With regard to the discussions which had also been in progress since 1941 about the British reservation, made at the time of the recognition of our Provisional Government and our State organisation in 1940, namely that the legal competence of our authorities on British soil was not to extend to some categories of our citizens—those individual Germans and Hungarians from the occupied territories who did not join us—the British Government now proposed a new formula whereby we should nominate representatives of these categories of citizens to our State Council. The British Government would then drop this reservation.

(f) At the same time Minister Nichols informed us that the British Government had given careful consideration to our attitude *in the matter of the transfer from our Republic of minority populations which had conspired against us* and had reached the conclusion, in view of what had happened in 1938 and during the war, that at the time of the final solution of our minority problems after the victorious end of the war the British Government *did not intend to oppose the principle of transfer of the minority population from Czechoslovakia in an endeavour to make Czechoslovakia as homogeneous a country as possible from the standpoint of nationality.*

In this form the discussions about Munich received the character of a great and far-reaching political negotiation about the future. From the beginning of April, 1942, when I submitted my last draft formula, to the end of July, 1942, these discussions were uninterrupted, systematic, strenuous and sometimes very animated. But they were always friendly and conducted in a spirit of mutual understanding. Extreme patience and self-control were necessary on both sides, and especially also, I would say, political wisdom and foresight in view of the difficulties which again and again arose in and for Great Britain, internally and externally, and the bitter memories conjured up for us all by Munich—including myself.

After this decisive discussion with Eden, I considered the British proposals in detail and I also examined the question whether we should continue the discussions or bring them to an end by accepting these proposals. After consulting Prime Minister Jan Šrámek and Minister Ripka we finally decided to omit the question of legal continuity from our demands and to accept the British view which fully respected our own Czechoslovak view. But we rejected categorically the proposal to connect the question of our jurisdiction in Great Britain with the nomination of German members to the State Council and with the question of Munich. We then informed Foreign Secretary Eden that we were prepared to accept the British proposal in principle but that we would first like to see the precise wording of the whole formula and assess its real political content. Mr. Eden suggested that we should meet again on July 7th when he would hand us the draft of his final proposals on Munich, adding that he hoped that after all our previous discussions we would be able to accept it.

The formula put before us on July 7th contained the three points mentioned above, omitted the reference to legal continuity and retained the clause about recognition of our jurisdiction over all our citizens in Great Britain as soon as we accepted their representatives in the State Council.

We reserved our final answer until we had had another consultation among ourselves about the proposed British text. But we asked Mr. Eden at once and emphatically—Ministers Jan Masaryk and H. Ripka were present—to exclude the clause about the jurisdiction over our Germans and their membership in the State Council from this fundamental question and to omit it from the Note concerning Munich. During the two days which followed, we informed Minister Nichols that we accepted Eden's text in principle and we agreed on the next steps to be taken:

(a) The declaration would be delivered in the form of a diplomatic Note from Foreign Secretary Eden to Minister Masaryk.

(b) Minister Masaryk would acknowledge receipt of the British Note at the same time clearly stating that we had not changed our integral point of view and that in regard to Munich we were determined to persevere in the policy we had announced in our diplomatic Note sent to all Allied Governments on the occasion of our declarations of war against Japan, Hungary, Rumania and Finland after the Japanese attack on Pearl Harbour and after the United States of America had entered the second World War.[3]

(c) Foreign Secretary Eden would speak in Parliament about our whole discussions on the liquidation of Munich and would issue the text of both Notes to Parliament.

Thus ended these important and memorable negotiations.

In further discussions with Minister Nichols, the British Government's standpoint regarding our principle of the legal continuity of the Republic and of the attitude to the transfer of the German population was again confirmed. The decision of the British Cabinet, that it had no objection to the Czechoslovak principle of the transfer of our Germans, was shortly afterwards communicated to us by Minister Nichols.

On August 5th, 1942, Mr. Eden made the speech in the House of Commons on which we had agreed. The relevant parts of the speech read as follows:

'I am glad to have this opportunity to inform the House that I have today exchanged notes with the Czechoslovak Minister for Foreign Affairs in which I stated that His Majesty's Government's policy in regard to Czechoslovakia was guided by the formal act of recognition of the Czechoslovak Government by His Majesty's Government in July, 1941, and by the statement of the Prime Minister in September, 1940, that the Munich Agreement had been destroyed by the Germans. I added that as Germany had deliberately destroyed arrangements concerning Czechoslovakia reached in 1938, His Majesty's Government regarded themselves as free from any engagements in this respect and that, at the final settlement of Czechoslovak frontiers to be reached at the end of the war, His Majesty's Government would not be influenced by any changes effected in and since 1938.

'In his reply Monsieur Masaryk informed me that the Czechoslovak Government accepted my note as a practical solution of the questions and difficulties of vital importance to Czechoslovakia which emerged between our two countries as a consequence of Munich Agreement, while maintaining their political and juridical position with regard to that agreement and to the events which followed it.

'The text of this exchange of Notes is being laid as a White Paper.

'I should not like to let this occasion pass without paying tribute on behalf of His Majesty's Government to the tenacious and courageous stand which the Czechoslovak people are making against their ruthless German oppressors. Acts such as the destruction of Lidice have stirred the conscience of the civilised world and will not be forgotten when the time comes to settle accounts with their perpetrators.'

This was the last act of the Munich tragedy so far as the British Government and the British Parliament had participated in it.

In the whole struggle to annul Munich we proceeded without fuss. The British looked upon the matter with mixed feelings. Many of them did not hesitate to show me what they felt in a frank and manly way. The British Parliament dismissed the whole matter quickly either not having the desire or not taking the trouble to go into the question at length. Even in August, 1942, the Churchill Government still contained some members who had directly participated in the Munich policy and in Munich itself and the Parliament which now took note of the end of Munich was the same Parliament which had welcomed Chamberlain when he returned from Munich with his scrap of paper signed by Hitler and promised a lasting peace for both countries . . .

What reflections, what moral essays and ironical comments on political morality, on the march of events and on historic justice could be added! Perhaps it will be best if I simply quote instead extracts from what I said on August 8th, 1942, over the B.B.C. in my address to our people in Czechoslovakia about this final chapter of our struggle against Munich:

'Almost from the very moment when Butcher Heydrich stepped on to our Prague soil and began his bloody work; from the moment when for the first time the so-called Prague Government allowed itself to be driven into attacking us here and me personally as traitors and denouncing us solemnly; from the moment when the treacherous so-called Slovak Government declared war on the Soviet Union and later on Great Britain and the United States thus committing the outraged Slovak people completely to the bloody service of the Berlin Nazi Government—those same Slovaks who today are almost the only Slav race fighting against all its Slav brothers; at the moment when the Hungarian Government paid the Germans a second time for its booty in Slovakia and Subcarpathian Ruthenia by sending a military expedition into the Ukrainian plains and when the representatives of a large part of our Czechoslovak Germans, led by the infamous Frank, raged at their worst in Prague, Brno and other Czech towns, basely killing our patriots who remained true to the independence and indivisibility of our Republic—it was at this moment that we here prepared for the last diplomatic action which still had to be negotiated after the preceding successes of our liberation activity, *after the recognition of the Government and of the independence of the Republic: namely the erasure from recent history of the event which actually introduced this fearful war: the Munich Agreement and all its consequences.*

'We conducted these negotiations objectively and confidently, without fuss, without unnecessary excitement and propaganda and in the spirit of friendship and alliance, in the spirit of co-operation during and after the war—with Great Britain as well as with the Soviet Union. Even at this date these negotiations have not been without difficulties. These questions are so far-reaching not only for us but for everybody and they will be decisive for a number of Central European problems after the war. We do not hesitate to tell you about these difficulties ... The negotiations too were not without difficulty because Munich was an event which had such far-reaching consequences for Europe and the whole world. *As I have repeatedly emphasized it was with Munich that World War II began and since that time Czechoslovakia has been at war ...*

'I do not conceal from you, my friends, that the discussions with

Mr. Molotov as well as those with Minister Eden and everything I have just mentioned, have been a great satisfaction to us all and to me as President of the sorely tried Republic. I have been so closely connected personally with what happened before Munich, at Munich and afterwards, and I lived through it all so painfully, that my efforts together with those of my friends and helpers to annul Munich and its consequences have for the last four years perhaps constituted the only aim of my life. Munich and everything connected with it was a great affliction and humiliation for the Nation. Today we have as compensation the full appreciation of the world. And the raising of the British and Soviet Legations to the rank of Embassies at the moment when Munich has been annulled, at least symbolizes the *moral appreciation* which is coming to you—the Czechoslovak people—for your sufferings.

'Furthermore, I know today as an absolute certainty, that we shall win this war and that the gains registered in the negotiations we have just concluded with the Soviet Union and Great Britain will be realised. I therefore regard this diplomatic task which I had set to our whole liberation movement and to myself, as having been substantially fulfilled.'[4]

3. The Transfer of the Germans from Czechoslovakia

It was clear to me immediately after Munich that when the annulment of Munich and of its consequences came in question in the future *the problem of State minorities* and especially the problem of our Germans would also have to be solved radically and finally. Innumerable times and full of grief I considered the problem of our Germans and its meaning and importance for the existence of our State and Nation. Already at the time of my legal studies in Paris and Dijon in the years 1905–1908 my first literary effort was devoted to this problem.[5] During the struggles and discussions in the first World War I considered it afresh and I discussed it many times with T. G. Masaryk.

After our liberation in 1918, not a day passed without my discussing it with Masaryk, without my coming up against it and without my being brought into painful contact with it during Masaryk's and my fights against Dr. Kramář, the National Democrats and Agrarians. Especially as Minister for Foreign Affairs, I had for decades perhaps greater trouble with this problem than with the whole of our internal policy. How many explanations and admonitions had to be administered to our politicians and parties to try to get them to look at these problems from a broader international point of view! How many campaigns of propaganda and information had to be undertaken in friendly and hostile countries! How many extremely exhausting struggles there were at Geneva so that we might stand before the world as a mature Nation and State educated in matters of world policy! In the main, we succeeded!

When Germany entered the League of Nations in 1926 and shortly afterwards joined forces first with the Hungarians and then with the Italians for a comprehensive campaign to use national minorities as a weapon in the political fight against all its neighbours (ourselves of course included) I had to examine this whole problem in its wider aspects and I had to ask myself repeatedly: how long will we be able to hold out? *Our State was born with this problem and must either solve it at whatever cost or succumb!* In the thirties when there came first aggressive Fascism and then the even more aggressive Nazism and Hitlerism, this truth could be overlooked only by those who politically speaking were deaf and blind. There were enough of these in our midst!

This was why Masaryk as President of the Republic dedicated so much effort to these problems and why I as Minister and then as President never lost sight of them and shepherded them gradually to their solution. Often and intentionally I even put minority problems before the solution of social questions because I saw clearly that it was via these problems *that the first and foremost attack would be launched against our independence and existence and against our State as a whole.*

Our efforts in this direction are all known and I will not occupy myself with them here though I shall examine them again in detail in my book dealing with the Munich crisis. Munich posed the problem of the minorities especially of our Germans in so categorical a manner that nobody could be in any doubt about it. Munich also showed with complete clarity that what was in question was the fate of our State and of our very existence.

When I went abroad in October, 1938, I therefore put to myself once again that fateful question: When Munich is liquidated after a new dreadful crisis and a European war how can we solve our nationality problem once and for all and as far as possible justly? As always, I told myself that in solving such a difficult problem I must above all find the right method for tackling it: make myself acquainted with the procedure and political tactics to which I would have to adhere consistently and unchangeably from the very beginning of our struggle to its conclusion. *At the same time or even earlier I must decide what the fundamental solution of the problem was to be and this would have to remain our unchangeable aim both during the new war and after it.* But it would always be necessary to adapt oneself also to the

P

general political developments and the march of time including the course of the war itself.

Guided by these considerations, I decided above all in favour of the *continuity of pre-war policy*. I interpreted this as meaning that the solution of our nationality problem would have to start, as far as possible, from our historical and local conditions; that it would have to be governed by absolute goodwill and loyalty to all our partners and that it would have to be linked to our stand at the time of the fight at Munich when we went to the furthest limit of possibilities and compromises. At the same time, however, our political procedure must actually enable the solution which we had chosen and were supporting *to be applied generally, on a European scale, and that therefore it must be a solution which would be acceptable to all in the new post-war conditions in the European States all of which would assuredly undergo great and revolutionary social changes after this new catastrophe.* This meant that the solution of our nationality problem would have to be systematically tied to social and economic changes. *That is to say, the national revolution must be merged with the social-economic one.*

In other words: in the nationality problems there would also have to be *progress—real progress both from the human and evolutionary point of view.* This meant in practice that it would be necessary to convince the British, French, Americans and Russians—and, if possible, also the Germans themselves—that in order to preserve pre-Munich Czechoslovakia it would be necessary to adopt the principle of a very radical reduction in the number of its minorities. It would also be necessary to convince the Czechoslovaks that *they, too, would have to make some sacrifices in pursuit of this aim.*

This political objective to which I held consistently throughout the war was pursued as the progress of the war demanded—before and at the beginning of the war cautiously and with moderation, more decidedly and more fundamentally as the war proceeded. It was adapted to fit in with the social and economic changes which the war necessarily evoked in the structure of the newly-created post-war society. *But it was fundamentally influenced by the brutal behaviour of the Germans towards our Nation at home and it was proclaimed uncompromisingly to all parties concerned without making any differentiation between great and small. It was also resolutely and consistently applied to all of us at home and, naturally, our whole struggle for the liquidation of Munich was based on it. We were all convinced that the immediate fate of the Nation was intimately bound up with this question.*

Whenever international difficulties stood in the way of the acceptance of our thesis, I always resolutely and with a full sense of responsibility asked the question which always made everyone pause : *Do you want to prepare a new Munich.* Throughout the war the European consequences of Munich were really so fully understood everywhere that this question silenced everybody.

When I saw that we were likely to reach a satisfactory solution of the Munich problem with the British, I was even more convinced of the correctness of my considered and resolute attitude in the matter of nationalities. But I felt that absolute unanimity was essential in regard to those questions in our Czech and Slovak emigration abroad, between us and our people at home and between us and our Germans in so far as they were represented in the emigration: that is to say, the German Communists and Social Democrats first and eventually the others too. I decided not to hide anything from anybody—though these were very delicate diplomatic questions—but to put the whole matter openly to everyone especially our Germans and to try to reach complete agreement with them in advance. In this issue too, 'Fair play'* was my political principle.

It was thus that I began my discussions with the German Social Democrats—in practice, with Deputy Wenzel Jaksch and his associates. I discussed the matter frequently with the group of German Communists (Deputy Karel Kreibich)† as well and then with the Zinner-Lenk-Kirpalová group. Jaksch came to see me for the first time at Putney as early as August 3rd, 1939, soon after my return to London from the United States. He told me of his own grievous hardships, of the annoyances and difficulties which beset him when with British help he left Czechoslovakia and he described to me the situation in Germany, in Austria and, of course, also among the members of his party in Bohemia.

He estimated that among the German emigrants from Bohemia in Great Britain, 50 per cent were for Greater Germany and 50 per cent for the re-establishment of Czechoslovakia in the old pre-Munich frontiers. He said that the Social Democrats émigrés from the Reich and from Austria and their policies were exercising strong influence on our Germans. But among the Germans themselves, those from the Reich and from Austria, there was a similar controversy. Both camps were counting on war coming soon but one of them expected the speedy defeat of the Third Reich and at best the re-establishment of Weimar Germany while the other, especially the Austrian Social Democrats, foresaw a vast Greater German revolution and were planning the reorganisation of Europe accordingly—that is to say by applying all Greater German aims.

Jaksch said that in this hot-headed atmosphere our Germans were in a

*In English in the original (Tr.).
†Appointed Czechoslovak Ambassador in Moscow in 1950 and afterwards purged (Tr.).

difficult position. If their leaders could at least put before their émigrés some constructive Czech programme for the federalisation of Czecho-slovakia in which there was a special territory for the Sudeten Germans (not less than in the so-called Fourth Plan which I had offered to Henlein) then, perhaps, Jaksch and his comrades could support this solution and work in the emigration for the acceptance of this plan as a final agreement between Czechs and Germans. The latter could, of course, not again accept a dictate from our side because none of them would accept the sort of situation which had existed in the pre-Munich Republic.

I listened to Jaksch's views which were patently based on the plans of the other Germans, which shared their great hopes and counted on a quick tempo in the war and on a vast political revolution by all German workers. In regard to our purely Czech matters, Jaksch at that time was reserved. Therefore I maintained reserve too and did not tell him about my plans. I merely asked him to remain in contact with me so that we could exchange views as the situation developed especially as soon as war started. I simply rejected his proposals and pointed out that we would never again return to the old theories and ideas more especially not to bilingual districts or regions. We 'emigrants', of course, were all expecting war.

After the war had started and after my return from France, Jaksch visited me again (December 4th, 1939). He again complained how difficult it would be for his Party to decide the future fate of the Bohemian Germans. He asked me whether the leaders of our emigration could meet and discuss the whole situation with our Germans. Events, he said, would move fast and we could be taken by surprise by a premature peace. I myself thought a meeting with the Germans would be premature and I did not agree to it. But I suggested to him that they themselves should discuss the whole situation of Germany, Austria and themselves and formulate their future political programme accordingly—and that they should then submit it to us.

By that time I knew that Jaksch at the very beginning of the war had already elaborated an extensive programme of Greater Germany—that is to say, a programme covering Germany and the whole of Central Europe —that he had pushed it in British political circles, especially in the Labour Party, and that in it he had already envisaged not only the Bohemian Germans as an independent unit not connected with us, but also had put the whole of Czechoslovakia into a special Central European federation in which there would be a German preponderance.⁸ I therefore decided to wait realising that objective and reasonable discussions with our Germans would only be possible when the course of the war had brought home to them the position of the whole of Germany, how the world viewed this position and how our Germans were themselves inevitably involved in this situation.

Moreover, I had already received very detailed reports about how matters were developing at home in the 'Protectorate' including what had happened in Prague on October 28th*—and on November 17th in regard to our students and our universities†; also in the wider field: how our people were being treated, our politicians, our common people, our political parties, our clubs, our whole cultural life, how many of our people were already in concentration camps, etc., etc.

My expectations were fulfilled. Six more months of war taught us and our Germans much although this period was filled with great German victories against Poland and France. Jaksch came to see me again immediately after the recognition of our Provisional Government in London. This was on July 4th, 1940, when the question of our recognition was still secret and the whole political world was still occupied with the defeat of France and speculating about what would happen next.

But Jaksch surprised me by declaring, quite rightly, that for the time being a discussion of the fate of our Germans was impossible, that he was no longer occupying himself with such questions and that the paramount question was really to defeat Hitler. Therefore, for the time being, he did not ask me for a programme for the future or for any declaration about our Germans. He simply declared unconditionally his solidarity with our cause and said that he was ready to co-operate with us wherever co-operation was possible. I think that at the time this declaration was sincere.

I therefore decided to tell him more about our plans. I informed him that in a short while our Provisional Government would be set up and recognised by the British Government but that the situation was not yet sufficiently mature to enable us to agree with our Germans upon a positive or final solution of their problem. The Germans therefore would not immediately be in the Government but we were establishing at the same time a quasi-Parliament—the State Council—in which our whole emigration was to be represented and I intended to invite our Germans to enter it and then to start political discussions with them. After that, it was our desire to solve all their political problems in stages in accordance with the way the situation developed. *We were decidedly and in principle in favour of*

*Czechoslovak Independence Day, attempts to celebrate which had been ruthlessly suppressed.

†The Germans closed all the Czech Universities—a step which was followed by riots in which several Czech students were killed (Tr.).

co-operation with our anti-Fascist Germans. But, of course, we could not solve all these problems connected with this co-operation without the British. After all, we had in the first place to deal with *the liquidation of Munich,* a matter which closely concerned our Germans. Furthermore, it would be necessary to reach agreement with the Nation at home. 'We do not want to do all this without your participation and we therefore welcome what you have said today'—I concluded.

This statement made a very great impression on Jaksch. Intensive propaganda was being carried on at that time among our German émigrés and often very fantastic ideas and reports were circulating among them. Many of them were in principle against all compromise with us and continued to believe in the Greater Germany' programme. Others watched our actions attentively, especially in the military sphere, criticised it sharply and drew from the strong anti-German feeling among our soldiers very critical inferences about us and our movement in general. For a long time therefore there were no conversations between us on fundamental issues. Moreover, some of the British with whom Jaksch had been in contact had given him the impression that no important development could take place in our affairs without an agreement with our Germans.

On September 22nd, 1941, Jaksch came again. That was after the Soviet Union had entered the war against Germany and after our final recognition by Great Britain and the Soviet Union. I was therefore already able to speak more plainly and definitively.

I told him in particular what the attitude was at home towards our Germans and I did not hide from him the extremely uncompromising mood in our country under the impact of the brutal way the Germans had behaved to all the Czechs. I read out dispatches from home showing how our people were planning to solve the German problem. Nevertheless, I said, I regarded our really democratic Germans as equal partners and I asked for a clear declaration on their side—without reservations or conditions—proclaiming their loyalty to our Government-in-exile and to the Republic in its historic pre-Munich frontiers. I further told him that though I was in favour of the nomination of German representatives to the State Council, this would have to be postponed for the time being in view of the situation at home (and in accordance with the express wishes of our people in the homeland) and that meanwhile Jaksch's party and we should proceed on parallel lines. I said further that we should not force our German citizens in Great Britain to enter our Army and that the punishment of war criminals from the ranks of our Germans at home would be carried out within the framework of general retribution after this great war exactly the same principles as the punishment of Czech and Slovak war criminals. I added that I would soon have a further opportunity of discussing and clearing up all these questions with him and his friends and that I hoped we would reach agreement both about principles and about procedure.

I asked Jaksch and the other representatives of our Germans to come to tea on January 7th, 1942, for a general exchange of views about the war as a whole and our affairs in particular. I told them on that occasion that I expected the final defeat of Germany some time in 1943—at that time I, too, was somewhat over-optimistic about the progress of the war—and that it was necessary to make preparations accordingly. We should all be ready—not only ourselves but also the people at home. *We must of course expect great and revolutionary social changes* which would mean at the same time great changes in our nationality problems too.

I asked them to realise that immense and permanent changes had taken place in consequence of the behaviour of the Germans and of their regime: the plundering and looting (cultural as well as material) throughout the country, the widespread terror, etc. I said: '*Until now nothing similar has ever happened in the whole history of our country and the memory of it will never fade from our midst.* Such things cannot, and will not, be without grave consequences.' I called their attention to the fact that radical nationalism was growing daily at home because of the dreadful and unimaginable terror in the concentration camps where probably hundreds of thousands of our people were suffering and where tens of thousands of our people were dying.* The Protectorate as a whole is nothing more than one vast torture chamber the horrors of which could not be described. This had evoked in our people a dreadful longing for revenge. Their minimum demands included *not only a great and revolutionary act of retribution at the end of the war* in the course of which many people were prepared to rid our country by force of all our Germans in Bohemia and Moravia without distinctions or exceptions and to consummate *our final separation from the Germans, their transfer to the Reich. In a word: the end !*

I went on: 'I do not indeed believe that this bloody and extreme course will be adopted. I know our people and I know also that they are not so bloodthirsty as that. But the leaders of our German emigration must so

*The official Czechoslovak estimates of material losses due to the German occupation were Kčs 900,000,000,000 (£4,500,000,000 at Kčs 200=£1). The number of persons killed by the Germans was estimated at 38,000 while 200,000 (the majority being Jews) did not return from the German concentration camps. No information is available as to how these figures were computed (Tr.).

much the more take account of the fact *that the plans for the readjustment of our post-war internal relations which they submitted to me at the beginning of the war* and which they are still discussing in their publications *will not and cannot be realised either.* I have been considering all these matters very carefully, I have examined and compared the various plans for a solution of these problems and the least common multiple at which I have arrived is *that in the social revolution which will certainly come it will be necessary to rid our country of all the German bourgeoisie, the pan-German intelligentsia and those workers who have gone over to Fascism.* That would be a final solution and, so far as we were concerned, the only possible solution which we would be able to implement, *namely the coupling of our social revolution with the national one.'*

I added to Jaksch and his friends: 'We must have the courage to speak about this openly. And especially you Social Democrats must have the courage to do so. This plan even contains an element of marxism and marxist dialectics in the revolutionary process which must inevitably accompany the changes in the social structure of the Nation as an outcome of this great and world-wide catastrophe. After the first World War, I wrote a book about the nature of the Czechoslovak national revolution and in it I foretold that the German nationalist bourgeoisie in our country would sometime in the future attempt a counter-revolution and that there would be no peace between us until this bourgeoisie was forced to undergo a similar revolution to that the Czechs had to undergo in former centuries. Now, after the second World War, this revolution is inevitable. And the whole nationalities problem in our country will be radically solved at the same time'.

I invited my guests to give careful consideration to these ideas so that they should understand that they would be the apostles of this ideological transformation of the Germans, joining forces also for this purpose with the German Communists. I explained my whole plan to them quite frankly. I did not wish to, and did not, hide anything from them. If any of them entered the State Council, they would necessarily have to know what plans and discussions they would encounter there. Of course, I should have to conclude the negotiations with the British about Munich and our frontiers. I expected that they would be ended within a few months. I told them frankly about this, too—that I was also discussing this matter with the Allies and that I was sure of bringing the negotiations to a successful conclusion.

I invited Jaksch to luncheon the following day, January 8th, 1942, to finish our discussions. (Ernst) Paul, Jaksch's friend who had organised the

Social Democratic 'Rote Wehr' in our country during the struggle against the Henleinites was also present. He had come to London from Sweden. After lunch we went over the whole ground again. I saw that since the previous day Jaksch had considered my views and *that his reaction was clearly negative*. He did not say so expressly but his attitude was clear to me from his behaviour and that of his friend. Neither of them wanted to hear of such a combination of social and national revolution. They regarded the Germans in our country as a unit and did not consider themselves to be the representatives of the workers only but of the Germans as a whole. Perhaps at that time they did not clearly realise that by so doing they automatically took full responsibility for what the Germans were doing to us as a Nation in the war . . .

From that time we met less often. We had another, longer, conversation on May 29th, 1942, in which Jaksch expressly admitted the two principal mistakes he had made in exile: '*I expected the war would be short and I counted on a German revolution*', he told me. 'I did not expect either the first or the second,' I replied. 'In particular I did not believe that the German working class would stage a revolution against Hitlerism and for a victory of the Soviet Union over Germany. As in 1918 this will only happen at the moment Nazism collapses and the object will also be the same as in 1918: to try to save Germany with its whole Nazi bourgeoisie from the worst. In Germany this will mean dreadful chaos for a long while.'

Even at the beginning of 1943, Wenzel Jaksch was still waiting for some miracle which would prevent the complete collapse of Germany and thus save the Sudeten-Germans as well. I was not astonished nor did I reproach him as a German for his attitude. It was more than natural in existing conditions in Germany and in the German Nation as well as among the so-called Sudeten-Germans. *These, too, were political errors on Jaksch's part equally with his idea that he who was obviously a Social Democrat was not simply a representative of a section of the anti-Fascist German workers in our country but of all the Germans in general—that is to say also of the more than 80 per cent of our Germans who had gone over to Hitlerism and who, during the war, were always ready to do anything they could to help destroy our Czech people.*

My last personal talks with Jaksch (who was accompanied by his associates De Witte, Reitzner, Wiener and Katz) were on September 17th and 25th, October 2nd and December 1st, 1942, when the revocation of Munich had been publicly announced in the British Parliament in August, 1942, and when our point of view and our whole thesis had finally prevailed. Our conversations were more or less in the nature of reminiscences about all our former political problems. I stressed that Munich and the question of our Germans were to be regarded as finally solved; that it was now only a question of reducing to a minimum the number of Germans who were to remain in our country; but that in this question I was urging, and would continue to urge, an attitude of *compromise and humanity*, especially with regard to the real anti-Fascist Germans.

A short time before Jaksch had likewise received a statement on this subject from the Foreign Office. *Personally I never wished that decent Germans who had fought as brothers on our side for democracy and had remained true to democracy should be forced into a tragic situation.* But at the same time I frankly told Jaksch and his associates that I would like to see the words 'sudetendeutsch' and 'Sudetengebiet' (region) vanish from Czechoslovakia definitely and permanently and also that the political and wrongly-interpreted German concept of 'Selbstbestimmungsrecht' (self-determination) should disappear too. Politically speaking it had led our Germans astray and had completely prevented us from building our State after the first World War. Moreover, neither Masaryk nor I had accepted it in the sense in which the Germans were using it. We said this to Lansing, Wilson's Secretary of State, very firmly at the peace conference in 1919.

During the final conversation De Witte pathetically described the dreadful situation in which the Bohemian Germans now found themselves. In a phrase, it was: 'If Hitler wins the war, we Socialist Germans are lost and if the Czechs win it, we are lost too.'

I answered: 'Yes, I recognise your tragic situation and I am deeply grieved about it. But such things happen to Nations through the fault of their leaders and by the chain of historical events. That is why I am opposing and always will oppose the claims of some of our people for exaggerated rectifications of our pre-Munich frontiers in respect of a defeated Germany after the war. And that was why I made those super-human efforts during Munich for a real agreement with our Germans and with Germany as a whole.'

'But in what a situation have we been since 1938? Never forget what efforts I made for an agreement with you during the struggle over Munich! But what did Hitler prepare for us—and with him more than 80 per cent of your German co-nationals in Bohemia and Moravia, the representatives of whom you claim to be today? In what have we been guilty? Only consider what we have had to go through since 1938 and how we fought for democracy and peace! And our people at home are still suffering dreadfully. What are Hitler and the Germans doing in the Czech countries today and every day? The world will only come to learn about this when the war is over.

'From this, my dear friends, we can draw but one calm, but stern conclusion: *A just retribution for all direct and indirect, active and passive war criminals as a lesson for the future and—complete separation !* Otherwise after this dreadful war, *an unheard of massacre will ensue between our two races !* We can and must prevent this *by our complete separation !* Only in this way will we be able to meet again later—when the present sufferings are forgotten—as neighbours and live each in his new home without bitterness and in peace, separated, *side by side* with one another.

'In that connection I shall never forget that you, the true German Social Democrats from Bohemia and Moravia, have never sullied the German name during this great historical crisis and that you bear no guilt in the dreadful fate of the German Nation. Furthermore, the Germans will certainly not be destroyed as a Nation in this great struggle. They will live on—since 1938, it has not been so sure that we Czechs would do so ! We shall still learn more about that subject after the war. In any case perhaps your fate and that of the Germans as a whole *will contribute to the future moral and political democratic rebirth of Germany.*'

Our last meeting with Jaksch in exile was on December 1st, 1942. On that occasion, I gave him my written statement in answer to the declaration of the national conference of the Sudeten-German Social Democrat Party held in Great Britain in October, 1942. The Party was in regular operation in England with its whole organisation. It took decisions regularly and forwarded them to me if they concerned matters of principle. In some cases I answered them. In some ways, our correspondence was of importance, especially Jaksch's letter of January 3rd, 1941, the resolutions of the German Social Democrat Party of September 28th, 1941, and October 4th, 1942, and most of all the Party's resolution of June 7th, 1942, with Jaksch's letter of June 22nd, 1942, together with my reply which took the form of a declaration of principle in regard to the June resolution. I handed this to Jaksch in our Embassy in London on December 1st, 1942. Especially in this declaration and in my letter of January 10th, 1943, are summed up the fundamental principles of the problem of our former* Germans and of the minority question in general.[8]

In this chapter I have set forth the general conclusions I reached during the war about the question of our minorities and the solution of the problem of our Germans. They were natural conclusions valid for our Hungarians and Poles as well and I tried to apply them consistently to these minorities, too.

*This is the first occasion on which Dr. Beneš speaks of the Germans of Bohemia and Moravia as though they were no longer included in Czechoslovakia. (Tr.).

I also advocated this solution in all talks with the British, Americans, Russians and French. In their case, I started from the general principle accepted during the war by all Great Powers, namely, *that there would be no repetition of the attempt which was made after the first World War to apply the minority treaties with the help of the League of Nations because they had not stood the test of practical experience and had been most disappointing. In 1938 our country—how absurd it was—had been brought to Munich by means of these treaties!** So there was no other course open but to try to reduce the number of minorities in foreign States by transfers of population—to be carried out, as far as possible, universally, decently and humanely—and either to assimilate the remaining fractions of minority populations on a reasonable basis or to give them the free choice of emigrating voluntarily wherever they wished to go.

Though this would mean a grave and long drawn-out crisis for the persons actually involved, it would nevertheless provide *a better and more humane solution than fresh inhuman massacres in the post-war period through outbreaks of civil war and brutal vengeance causing the continuation of nationality struggles for centuries* thus frustrating again and again the social and economic progress of mankind. Moreover, the transfer could be closely controlled and co-ordinated and could be carried out under decent and humane conditions.*

Such a solution was also and especially suitable for our Hungarians and we mobilised all our efforts to win over all the Allies to this policy and to secure by this means *final reconciliation and post-war co-operation between Czechoslovakia and Hungary, too.* During our discussions in London with the Poles for a definite Polish-Czechoslovak settlement in the years 1940–1942 we made the same proposals.

After the negotiations with the British Government, I also discussed the question of the transfer of our minorities in detail with Moscow, through Ambassador Bogomolov, in the spring of 1943 before my visit to Washington, when I was also negotiating the text of our future treaty of alliance with the Soviet Union. Moscow gave its consent in principle to transfer by a declaration of Ambassador Bogomolov, which was handed to Dr. Ripka on June 5th, 1943. At the request of Bogomolov, Dr. Ripka cabled it to me in Washington on June 6th[10] and I then discussed it immediately with President Roosevelt.

*The minority treaties, in the drafting of which Dr. Beneš played a leading part, gave minorities a right to arraign the majority Government of the country in which they lived, before the League of Nations. They were thus an admirable weapon for would-be trouble-makers. Dr. Beneš's views on this subject are summarised in my book, *Beneš of Czechoslovakia*, p. 163 sqq. (Tr.).

Having therefore obtained the views of London and Moscow I submitted this question at once to President Roosevelt. He gave me his personal approval on the spot and added that *what had caused such a world catastrophe as Munich must be completely removed once and for all.* And when I arrived in Moscow at the end of 1943 I discussed the whole problem again, this time with Stalin and Molotov personally. I also gave them a written memorandum on this question. Both again confirmed the attitude which Moscow had already announced to me before. The practical aspects of the whole question of our Germans were afterwards dealt with at the Potsdam Conference of the Soviet Union, the United States and Great Britain in July, 1945, when the transfer of the Germans from our country was internationally approved. It was carried out by us to its conclusion in 1945 and 1946 under the leadership and full and permanent control of the United States of America.

A great and fateful chapter in our national history, one which had so often moulded our whole destiny—and which at least twice might have caused the destruction of our Nation—was thus finally closed.

An unexpected outcome, this, of the Munich policy !

Postcript to the story of the Transfer of the Czechoslovak Germans.

Speech by Deputy Hans Krebs* before he was sentenced to death by the People's Court on January 15th, 1947:

'Honourable Court! This is the last speech of a former German deputy addressed to the Czechoslovak public and this honourable People's Court.

'Today we stand before you as defendants and you are our judges. In this moment a full thousand years of a common, hard, but also great, historic period are closing. The Czech Nation will now, at the last, live alone in its national State, which not only in name, but also in fact is really becoming a national State.

'Three million Germans have been transferred. This is the greatest transfer since the migration of nations, perhaps even the greatest in the history of the world. Nearly one-third of the population of Bohemia, Moravia and Silesia have left or are leaving their old homes. They are leaving behind their homes, what they once called their property, their past and their dead. They are leaving the work of millions and the work of many centuries, never to return. It is hard for anybody who has not gone through it to measure the moral and spiritual burden we are bearing now. I believe that the Czech Nation will appreciate it, either

*A witness of Hitler's will (Tr.).

now or later, the Czech Nation whose magical song has often moved our hearts too—your "Kde domov muj" (Where is my country). I know that you will feel with us, you who are always singing with so much emotion ". . . and that is the beautiful country, the Czech country, my homeland."★

'I, too, have loved that country fervently and I am entitled to say that because I can prove that my family has been in this country since 1558. I think I may say: We fought for our Nation in good faith. We have been deceived but nobody can dispute our good faith. I always believed that the Czechs and Germans could establish a common State like Switzerland, each in his canton, in his autonomy. This did not happen. History decided otherwise. Before you, stand the rest of our parliamentary representatives, once more than seventy deputies and senators, today fifteen men, and you are to judge them. Think also when you do so of the greatness of the occasion.

'From this time, you will have no more nationality disputes in your country. I only wish that the great sacrifice we are making may not be without profit, but that from them there may at last be born a peaceful fellowship between us—which, alas, we did not succeed in establishing in one State—namely, the fellowship of the German State and the Czech State which will again be neighbours in the future.

'And so the question with which I ended the introduction to my book *Struggle in Bohemia*: "When will there be peace in this country?" has been answered—in a different way, of course. But I hope and pray it has been answered not only for the present but also for the future. Then even the personal sacrifices which we have to make will not have been in vain.

'Honourable Court! Convict me if you think that this is necessary in order that your laws may be observed and that it is necessary for peace and for the future. But convict me for faults that I really committed, not for what I never did and never wanted to do. The Public Prosecutor at the end of his comprehensive speech has declared: *Nothing may be forgotten and may never be forgotten!* But we cry out on parting: May the separation of Germans and Czechs finally bring peace to both! May the sufferings of our time end our sufferings for all time! Only so will all these immeasurable sacrifices have any meaning which we Sudeten Germans must now make and which the Czechs also have had to make in so great a measure. They will have served the highest ideal of mankind—a lasting and honourable peace.'

★From Smetana's Má vlast (My country) (Tr.).

I comment on this:

Alas! This profession of faith and confession are too late. Our whole struggle at the time of Munich proved more than clearly who was sincere and whose good faith cannot and must not be questioned. During the culminating and fatal struggle of the second World War in which the life of our Nation was literally at stake,* our Germans did not show good faith in any particular.[11] *Such will be the final judgment of world history on this subject.*

Prof. Reinhold Trautmann ! 'The Way of One Nation.'

From the *Leipziger Zeitung* of January 17th, 1947.

Professor Trautmann lived for a long time in Czechoslovakia before becoming Professor of Slavonic Studies at Leipzig University. (The Editor.)

I would first like to dispose of the easily-made objection: that I am inhumane.

Everybody who despite the terrors of war and post-war conditions has preserved his soundness of judgment knows that for the overwhelming majority of people the permanent loss of the home is a source of lasting, often unbearable suffering and hardships, be it as now the very roots of our existence in the country of our birth, or the accustomed professions which we have often inherited in the places where we spent our youth or our deep inner ties with our ancestors and relatives. All this I know very well. I would also like to point out that it is the sublime duty of other cultured Nations to prevent as far as they can, the sad and tragic transfers of peoples by making war impossible. I do not expect that those who are concerned personally will be able to consider their fate quietly and without passion. This would be superhuman. So much the more it is the task of others to examine the truth clearly and prosaically.

It is incontrovertible that for the future of the new Europe the transfer of the German population is something healing and a blessing. In particular looking back over the last 35 years (I went to the German University in Prague in October, 1911, and I worked there until 1921) I regard it as irrefutable that the real consolidation of Czechoslovakia was impossible while it was under the influence of the German element—at least of the overwhelming majority of the Sudeten Germans.

During the winter of 1918-1919 the Czechs re-established their State in exemplary order and on exemplary lines. If there were any mistakes they

*During the war, the German Government at one time seriously considered a project to uproot the whole Czech Nation and resettle it in the Ukraine (Tr.).

were not worth mentioning especially if we measure them with what happened under Hitler. German schools and universities remained. German civil servants were taken over without re-examination. But the Czechs had to pay heavily for their moderation and tolerance towards a quite unarmed Nation.

For twenty years, beginning with 1918, the Sudeten Germans were losing ground. They could not bear not being still the governing class. They did not want to admit—they even ignored conceitedly, short-sightedly and retrogressively the fact that the Czechs and Slovaks had already outgrown the Austrian—I would rather say: the German—cane, that they had matured culturally in the latter part of the long reign of Francis Joseph and that they had become independent. The value of the Slav share in the national economy and administration and in cultural life was not recognised. On the contrary, the majority rejected it in blind self-conceit: Such is the palpable, inexcusable, grave, perhaps even tragic, failure and guilt of the majority of the German population.

There were (and still are) exceptions. There were for instance the Prague Germans, sobered by Jews in high positions who rightly understood their part as mediators between two efficient Nations. There was the group of German farmers whose most striking representative, Franz Spina, in the end fully assimilated Czech culture. There were the members of the two Socialist Parties who stood side-by-side with the Czechs in the fight against Hitler . . . But over the majority there lay a thick veil of blindness and approaching disaster.

It was Hitler's lot to precipitate this catastrophe and bring it to a climax. It was at his instigation that there began the stormy development which no Czech could have anticipated not even in his wildest dreams and which was worth all sacrifices: the establishment of a purely Slav State.

It is not my object to write an obituary notice for the German Nation in Czechoslovakia. It would have to be very long, comprising seven centuries and there would be many famous pages in it.

That there is a positive side to the contribution of the Germans in Czechoslovakia no calmly thinking Czech would contest. But every Czech would have to point out, and rightly, that the positive traits became beneficent only when his own vitality and intelligence had permeated it and that he had to win both these qualities from the dragon's mouth. In reality, the struggle with the Czechs has already lasted many centuries and already about the year 1300 expressions of Czech national consciousness are on record. In the fourteenth century a very valuable Czech prose and verse literature originated in Prague. The prose reached European standards and importance with Jan Hus and Petr Chelčický. Under the Hussites, Czech national consciousness was embodied in a mighty movement which emanated not only from religious ideals but also from strong social and national impulses. But all that the Czechs won from the Germans during the fifteenth and sixteenth century in honest and hard fight, they lost again after the catastrophe of the White Mountain on November 8th, 1620. Germanisation and catholicisation worked so strongly that in the eighteenth century it was possible to doubt whether the Czech Nation existed because the 'nation' then meant only the nobility and bourgeoisie. Finally, about 1800, there began what is called the Czech renaissance, long unnoticed, uncomprehended and unrecognised by the Germans.

Now the Czechs and Slovaks have matured and by the verdict of history, against which there is no appeal to a higher court, their beautiful country has become their own property. Their diligence and industry, their meditative intelligence, ability and dexterity, their burning thirst for knowledge, for civilisation and all its gifts and, last but not least, their profound and strong national consciousness must open the way to an important future for them in Central Europe.

All this means for Europe that great obstacles which hid many dangers have been removed by a hard but necessary operation. We Germans recognise these developments as final and will enter into relations with this excellent and very gifted Slav Nation on a new spiritual and political basis.

Let the adversary and victor of yesterday contribute in the coming years to the healing of the scar. In a free, self-confident and really democratic Europe the opportunity will surely present itself.

4. *France also Revokes the Munich Outrage*

After settling the matter of Munich with the British Government, we considered how and when we should liquidate Munich *vis-à-vis* France. The problem of Munich hung round our necks like a millstone throughout the war and, let us confess it, this millstone hangs in our memories even today and will continue to lie there for a very long while. In the history of European politics the policy of appeasement which was practised by the Governments of the individual Great Powers with such calculating coldbloodedness in regard to the small States will always be a great and terrifying example of political egotism *which will for ever be a classical one*. That it was also a policy of incredible political levity, inexperience and criminal ignorance on the part of the Western Powers—and of criminal

Q

gangsterism on the part of the Germans, is simply another aspect of this sad period in European history. The Nuremberg Trials and all that transpired at them about German preparations to destroy the existence of Czechoslovakia are a more than eloquent testimony to the whole tenor of the Munich Agreement.

Czechoslovakia was the last and most characteristic victim of this policy —a victim in regard to whom it was no longer possible to bring forward excuses or arguments and justifications. The well-known British cartoonist, David Low, put it very well: his cartoon showed President Beneš on the operating table with Hitler and Mussolini hacking off his limbs while Chamberlain and Daladier held him so that he could not move. That was the policy of appeasement with an obvious commentary on the responsibility for its execution in Munich. The fact that France and Great Britain did feel guilty; the fact that nearly every Englishman with whom any of us talked about Munich during the war felt guilty and ashamed forced us to be tactful and decent in our procedure, to speak about the matter as little as possible, not to revert to it unnecessarily, not to make reproaches or incriminations. Above all, not to forget even in times which for us were bad, how both Powers, especially France, had really helped us to achieve our first liberation during the first World War! And this is the way we must go on behaving even in the future.

Now that we were allies and friends again, both countries—especially France—had to pay so heavily for Munich and, whether they wanted to or not, they also had to fight for the annulment of Munich and for our liberation whereas we—through their fault—could not participate in the fight as effectively as we would have liked so that we contributed comparatively smaller sacrifices during this period.

While the war lasted, our special position often brought us into difficult psychological situations. Naturally there was on all sides a tendency to push Munich to one side, to forget Munich, to act as though there never was a Munich. *But, of course, there was and is, and will be . . . It will stand for ever as a warning to future generations !*

This situation will persist for a long while. On one occasion, I spoke about it to some Frenchmen. They themselves started the conversation. They wanted to know my feelings about Munich, towards them, towards France. I told them that the first need was that both Governments, the British and the French, should liquidate Munich already during the war —also that this should be done as quickly as possible and without leaving any legal or political odds and ends. The second essential would be to help us regain our full liberation and to annul Munich also in this way. The crime of Munich must not, and would not be, misused by us against any-body, but *we had a right to full restitution*. And finally, somewhere in the future, the question would arise of a—perhaps formal—declaration, mani-festation or solemn pronouncement from one nation to another or between our Parliaments and peoples—I did not yet know if it would be conveni-ent. But it would be necessary that this event, which for us was so dreadful, should be forgotten and *pass from politics to the realm of history* so that it would no longer touch our sentiments and we could talk of it in the future calmly as of a single, bad, isolated moment of the past. In that way we would be able to think chiefly of what France had done for us in the war of 1914–1918.

Will this be possible? I hope and believe it will. Great Britain has already done so much in this direction during the second World War that it would be wrong not to recognise this fully. Of course we must never forget the lesson Munich teaches for our future national and State policy. And both France and Great Britain, too, cannot and must not forget it.

It was on this basis that I had worked for redress with Eden from the beginning of 1942. I now reflected what to do in the case of France. My view was that Munich should be annulled quickly, without unnecessary public acts but simply as a matter of course and without emphasising our satisfaction. In short: *in a dignified and manly way and without much fuss*. Such a method corresponded to the situation and to the whole character of this act as well as to the war situation as it existed at that time.

I therefore decided to liquidate the matter with France on these lines at once—at least in principle. Unlike other people I immediately saw in Charles de Gaulle after the fall of France the man who would play an important part in the military renovation of France and who would, at least for some time, be the mouthpiece of post-war France. After Pétain's treason and after the fall of the Third Republic he was the first to raise his voice and to continue the fight against Hitler. *He symbolised Fighting France*. Such a stand will never be forgotten. It is incorporated in the Nation's history.

De Gaulle visited me in my suburban London home soon after his first broadcast address to France on August 8th, 1940. He explained to me his attitude towards Vichy, and the Pétain Government, to the war and to France's future tasks. He at once told me plainly what he thought of the France of 1938 and of Munich. We agreed easily. We said that we would remain in contact, would support one another and would unostentatiously renew the former co-operation between our two countries, because we were both equally convinced of the final defeat of Hitler. Shortly afterwards I returned his visit and we once more confirmed our standpoints.

When he established his 'National Committee of Fighting France' and when he succeeded in bringing under its rule whole great territories in the French Colonies, I did not hesitate to tell him that we would regard this Committee as really representing France and as her Provisional Government without regard to what others would do. Afterwards, when he tried to obtain full recognition of his Committee as the Government of the French Republic and the admission of France as an equal into the ranks of the Allied countries and Governments fighting against Germany, he came into conflict with Great Britain and America. I considered the negative attitude of the Western Powers towards France to be a mistake and I showed them that I thought so tactfully but unmistakably. I regulated the policy of our movement accordingly.

I did not agree with those who thought that France had gone under for a long period, that it had perhaps already lost its former position for ever, and that it was already necessary now, during the war, to act on this assumption. I agreed that the collapse was a terrible one though not permanent. On the other hand, I did not exclude the possibility that though the process of regeneration in France would be difficult, perhaps even—as others thought—long, it would not take place in such a condition of weakness as some feared and others sometimes even hoped.

My policy towards defeated France was after all simple. It was in the interests of Czechoslovakia—and of Europe—that a new and strong France should be reconstructed again as soon as possible in the West of the European Continent. Otherwise the new peace and the post-war political order of Europe would again be built on the wrong lines. For this reason Czechoslovakia would work for the quick reconstruction of France and would contribute to it wherever possible. What France did to us in 1938 should stimulate us to repay evil with good, to ask nothing for doing so and to expect nothing, simply remembering gratefully what France did for us in the first World War. What conclusions France itself would draw was its affair and what the future relations between our two Nations would be concerned primarily the French people and ourselves. The attitude of our Nation towards France had always been, was and always would be quite clear and unambiguous.

It was in this spirit that our whole policy towards France was conducted during the second World War. In this spirit I also wanted to liquidate at once with de Gaulle the whole problem of the Munich policy. And in this spirit this was finally done . . .

On August 6th, 1942, after Eden's speech about Munich in the British

Parliament, I asked the Commissioner for Foreign Affairs in De Gaulle's National Committee, Maurice Dejean, to come to see me (Dejean afterwards became the first French Ambassador in liberated Prague). I again assured him that I considered the French National Committee to represent the real France and I declared that now the British Government had liquidated Munich the French should do the same.

At the time of Munich, Dejean had been an official of the French Embassy in Berlin where he had watched and experienced the complete penury of the French policy and diplomacy at that time. He had never agreed with Bonnet's policy. He had always remained loyal to our former common front and he had joined De Gaulle's revolt immediately after the capitulation in June, 1940. He was one of the few French diplomats who remained faithful to Fighting France. He fully agreed with me and he added his own reasons for embracing this policy and for carrying it out.

In answer to his question, I confirmed that he could officially tell De Gaulle—who at the moment was out of London—what I had told him.

On August 24th Dejean presented himself again and came to see me at Aston Abbots. He told me that De Gaulle agreed with my views and plans and had authorised Dejean to discuss all these problems with us. De Gaulle also approved of our deciding jointly as to whether the liquidation of Munich should be effected in the form of a treaty, a declaration or an exchange of letters as in the case of Great Britain.

I discussed the various possibilities with Dejean at once. I told him what I thought the liquidation documents should contain and finally asked him to discuss the technical details with Minister Masaryk and Minister Ripka. In the end it was agreed that the liquidation should be carried out by an exchange of letters which would be signed by De Gaulle and by Dejean as Commissioner for Foreign Affairs. On our side, the signatories would be the Premier, Dr. Šrámek, and the Minister for Foreign Affairs, Jan Masaryk.

In the following weeks, Masaryk, Ripka and Dejean discussed the wording of the two letters. Dejean brought a draft of the French text which Masaryk and Ripka regarded as incomplete and Dr. Ripka therefore made a new draft. To this new draft and to the amendments made by the French I added my own remarks. Ultimately, on September 23rd, Dejean and Ripka agreed in principle about the wording of the Notes which were solemnly signed and exchanged in the office of Premier Šrámek on the day of the fourth anniversary of the signing of the fateful Munich Agreement.

De Gaulle's letter read as follows:

'MR. PRIME MINISTER,

I have the honour to inform the Czechoslovak Government that the French National Committee,

Confident that it is expressing the feelings of the French Nation, the ally and friend of Czechoslovakia,

Convinced that the present world crisis can only deepen the friendship and alliance between the French and Czechoslovak Nations which, united by the same destiny, are now experiencing a period of common suffering and hope,

Faithful to the traditional policy of France,

Declares that in spite of regrettable events and misunderstandings in the past it is one of the fundamental aims of its policy that the Franco-Czechoslovak Alliance should rise from the dreadful trials of the present world crisis strengthened and secured for the future.

In this spirit, rejecting the agreements signed at Munich on September 29th, 1938, the French National Committee solemnly declares that it considers these agreements as null and void from their inception as well as all other acts committed during the execution, or as a consequence, of these agreements.

Recognising no territorial changes concerning Czechoslovakia which took place in 1938 or afterwards, it undertakes to do all in its power to ensure that the Czechoslovak Republic, in its frontiers of the period before September, 1938, shall obtain all effective guarantees for its military and economic security, its territorial integrity and its political unity.

Accept, Mr. Prime Minister, the assurance of my most profound respect.

GEN. CHARLES DE GAULLE,
President of the French National Committee.

Maurice Dejean,
National Commissioner for Foreign Affairs.
To Monseigneur Jan Šrámek,
Prime Minister of the Czechoslovak Republic.'

Our answer[12], signed by the Prime Minister and Minister Jan Masaryk, read as follows:

'GENERAL,

In your letter of September 29th you have been so good as to inform me that the French National Committee,

Confident that it is expressing the feelings of the French Nation, the ally and friend of Czechoslovakia,

Convinced that the present world crisis can only deepen the friendship and alliance between the French and Czechoslovak Nations which, united by the same destiny, are now experiencing a period of common suffering and hope,

Faithful to the traditional policy of France,

Declares that in spite of regrettable events and misunderstandings in the past it is one of the fundamental aims of its policy that the Franco-Czechoslovak Alliance should rise from the dreadful trials of the present world crisis strengthened and secured for the future.

You add that in this spirit, rejecting the agreements signed at Munich on September 29th, 1938, the French National Committee solemnly declares that it considers these agreements as null and void from their inception as well as all other acts committed during the execution, or as a consequence, of these agreements.

You state further that not recognising any territorial changes concerning Czechoslovakia which took place in 1938 or afterwards, the French National Committee undertakes to do all in its power to ensure that the Czechoslovak Republic, in its frontiers of the period before September, 1938, shall obtain all effective guarantees with regard to its military and economic security, its territorial integrity and its political unity.

I would like to thank you in the name of the Government of the Czechoslovak Republic for this declaration as well as for the obligations which the French National Committee has agreed to accept towards Czechoslovakia, the importance and range of which we value greatly.

The Czechoslovak Government which has never ceased to consider the French Nation an ally and friend of the Czechoslovak people is convinced that the present common trials will only strengthen this alliance and friendship to the greatest advantage of both our countries and of all peaceloving nations.

I have the honour to inform you that the Government of the Czechoslovak Republic for its part undertakes to do all in its power to ensure that France, renewed in its strength, its independence and the integrity of its metropolitan and overseas territories, shall receive all guarantees with regard to its military security and territorial integrity, and that it shall occupy in the world that place to which it is entitled by its great past and the worth of her people.

Accept, my General, the assurance of my most profound respect.'

I considered these two documents to be *the first step* to France's liquidation of Munich. It was symbolical and of political value that it should have happened thus at the earliest possible moment and that the gesture was made by a man whose personality and actions as a soldier and politician were a symbol of resistance to the policy of 1938 as well as to the capitulation of 1940. He was also an implacable adversary of the men of 1938 as well as of those who capitulated in 1940, even though politically the first group followed Daladier and the others his chief adversary, Pétain. Both groups have the same responsibility for France's misfortunes. The capitulation of June 21st, 1940, signed in the railway carriage at Compiégne by the Pétain Government was simply the direct, inexorable and dreadful consequence of the capitulation signed at Hitler's house in Munich on September 29th, 1938.

5. We and the French—Journey to Algiers

Some fifteen months elapsed and France's liquidation of Munich was emphasised by new political actions and declarations. Perhaps it will be best to mention them at this point.

In January, 1944, when I was on my way back from Moscow to London, General de Gaulle invited me to pay an official visit to Algiers. The French National Committee had already built up its whole administration here and after the liberation of North Africa—mainly as a result of the American and British invasion in November, 1942—it was already in full control of the former French colonies in Africa. Though the relations of De Gaulle's France to Great Britain and the United States were not yet fully settled, the National Committee at Algiers was in reality a Provisional French Government and it behaved as such.

I accepted De Gaulle's invitation and was welcomed by him and the Algerian National Committee on January 2nd, 1944, with all the ceremonies and honours due to the head of an Allied State on the soil of liberated France (Algeria was constitutionally part of Metropolitan France). It was a politically important demonstration. In the course of my visit, I had friendly conversations with General De Gaulle and the members of the National Committee as well as with leading French soldiers about Franco-Czechoslovak matters the political importance of which it is unnecessary to stress. I was agreeably surprised to see how comparatively quickly France was consolidating and recovering both from a political and military standpoint, how General de Gaulle and other leaders were well aware what the dreadful crisis in 1938 and 1939 and France's fall in 1940 had meant for their country, and how well they realised what France would have to do to regain her old and historically well-deserved position in Europe.

As I have already mentioned, in spite of all that had happened I had never ceased to believe in France and I still believe firmly in its new and great future. I saw many symptoms of French recovery during my stay in Algeria and I noted them especially in my conversations with men who had come from France.[1a] The relations of the National Committee to Great Britain and the United States were improving, with the Soviet Union they were good. French armies were already successfully taking part in heavy fighting in Italy and in the approaching invasion of Metropolitan France De Gaulle's movement was to play that political and military role which belonged to it by right in the new relationships which were arising among the Allied Nations. Though this France still had very many difficulties to face, it nevertheless seemed to me that from it might arise the new France which with its Government might again make an entrance on to the stage of allied Europe.

Thus the old problems were again on the order of the day and gradually also our French-Czechoslovak affairs. Once more I realised that true, patriotic Frenchmen had not substantially changed their attitude to Czechoslovakia and that they regarded everything that had happened during their country's years of fearful crisis from the correct angle of their national interests. This was brought out in two speeches, one by General De Gaulle and the other by me* during my official visit to French territory.

General De Gaulle said about Munich:

'When your Government and the French Committee of National Liberation concluded an agreement on September 29th, 1942, it replaced on a new basis our alliance which had been interrupted not long before by the hateful episode of Munich. After reaching a similar agreement with Great Britain, after renewing the foundations of the friendship between the Nation of which you are the head and the United States of America, you are now on your way back from Moscow where you and the Government of the Soviet Union have signed an unequivocal and firm treaty which from now onward determines, and makes secure for the future, the political co-operation of your two countries against the perpetual German danger. I can assure you, Mr. President, that no other Power is more delighted than France at the well-founded and brilliant

*Not printed (Tr.).

success of your policy—the policy of a great patriot and a great European.'

In May, 1944, when the British-American invasion of the European Continent was being prepared and when it had been decided that the invasion would be directed into France, General De Gaulle wanted to bring the dispute over the recognition of the National Committee as a Provisional Government to an end and thus decide in his favour the battle he had been waging (principally with the United States) for control of the civil administration in the liberated French territories. So he simply declared his Committee to be a Government and announced the fact through diplomatic channels to the Allied Governments. Faithful to our policy towards France, as described here, we at once decided to give official recognition to De Gaulle's National Committee as the Government of the new France. We and Belgium were among the first to do so.

M. Dejean who had meanwhile become French Minister with our Government in London proposed that we shall make a new declaration on the occasion of this act of recognition once more defining the relations between the two countries and reclarifying the question of Munich. He told me that General De Gaulle would come to London at the end of May and that we could then discuss this proposal with him. He was ready to prepare the text of the declaration.

I gave my consent and authorised Dr. Ripka to draft a declaration with Dejean. Shortly afterwards, when I had amended the proposed text in certain details and when the French Government in Algiers had similarly made its amendments, the new declaration was accepted by De Gaulle in principle on June 8th, 1944, when he visited me in London. The declaration was signed on August 22nd by De Gaulle and Dejean for France and by Monseigneur Šrámek and Jan Masaryk for us. It read:

'While again declaring that they consider the treaties of Munich with all their consequences null and void from their inception, the Government of the Czechoslovak Republic and the Provisional Government of the French Republic declare that the relations between the two States have been restored to the same state as before the signature of those treaties.

'In confirming that the traditional policy of friendship and alliance which unites them and their common attachment to the principles of liberty and independence have been strengthened by the struggle side-by-side against the common enemy, the Government of the Czechoslovak Republic and the Provisional Government of the French

Republic have agreed that at the appropriate time such modifications and amendments will be carried out in the existing agreements as shall be considered necessary in order that the collaboration between Czechoslovakia and France within the framework of the general security and reconstruction of Europe and the world is rendered closer and more effective.'

Thus, at this moment, France too had finally liquidated Munich during the very course of the dreadful war which Munich had started.

NOTES TO CHAPTER SIX

[1] See Appendix, page 302.

[2] This promise was implemented in July, 1945, at the Potsdam Conference.

[3] The text of this very important Note which contained our whole *legal standpoint* on the relations of Czechoslovakia to the second World War is contained in my book *Six Years of Exile and the Second World War*, pp. 446-72 (Czech edition).

[4] The complete address is printed in my book *Six Years of Exile and the Second World War*, pp. 168-75 (Czech edition).

[5] See Eduard Beneš: 'Le problème autrichien et la question tchéque. Etudes sur les luttes politiques des nationalités slaves en Autriche.' Paris, 1908.

[6] I also learned later that after the British revocation of Munich, Wenzel Jaksch in the name of his Party sent an emphatic protest against it to President Roosevelt. He never gave a copy of this protest to me personally.

[7] I shall describe all my efforts to reach agreement with our Germans in my book on Munich, now in course of preparation.

[8] See the Appendix. I also gave copies to the British Foreign Office with which Jaksch was also in regular contact.

[9] In general, the transfer of our Germans was really carried out in this manner in 1946, as can be proved by documents issued by the American authorities. I do not deny that our subordinate authorities committed some, very few, excesses which were unworthy of the country of Masaryk but I always opposed them very strenuously. I condemned them publicly and categorically several times and denounced them—for example in my speech at Mělník on October 14th, 1945. My vigorous protests were published in our country and afterwards even these excesses by subordinate organs definitely ceased.

[10] See Note, Chapter VII, p. 286.

[11] On this question there is still documentation to be published including Henlein's documents on the German plans for the Czechs and the Czech provinces. For example there is a very substantial document which provides the most convincing proof of the 'good will' our Germans bore to us: *Grundplanung O.A.* found in Henlein's archives. This document is no less revealing than all the so-called 'Nuremberg documents' of Germany's 'peaceful intentions'.

¹²I commented on this event in my broadcast to Czechoslovakia from London on September 30th, 1942, in this brief statement:

'Four years ago yesterday the agreement of the four Great Powers about Czechoslovakia was signed at Munich. One of the signatories was France in the person of its Premier, and one of the chief architects of that agreement was the French Minister for Foreign Affairs. Many foolish people in Europe thought at that time that peace had been saved by this agreement. But it was a declaration of war and the beginning of a whole series of catastrophes which were then disseminated so bountifully over the European continent by those two criminals who are still ruling over Germany and Italy and whose perjured hands signed at Munich that delusive and fateful pact of a dictated peace.

In London on the fourth anniversary of this pact the Chief of Fighting France, General Charles de Gaulle and his Commissioner for Foreign Affairs, M. Dejean, met the Czechoslovak Premier, Dr. Šrámek, and the Minister for Foreign Affairs, Jan Masaryk, with the object of solemnly effacing the signature of the French Premier on September 29th, 1938, from the history of our two countries. After the exchange of letters between the British and the Czechoslovak Ministers for Foreign Affairs on August 5th, 1942, which liquidated Munich between us and Great Britain, France has now solemnly done the same. General de Gaulle, who is doing this in France's name, has all the requisite moral qualifications. He revolted on June 19th, 1940, when the spirit of Munich which had paralysed the moral and military forces of France led the Government to capitulate to Hitler and then to shameful collaboration with Nazism. He raised the famous French tricolor. He gathered new military forces around it and great territories. He again conducted the French Nation after a short period of stunned delusion into resistance against the Germans. Today together with the whole movement of Fighting Frenchmen he is the real embodiment of future France, a resuscitated France, again great, fighting and revolutionary. If General de Gaulle rose against the capitulation of 1940 and if he today is liquidating the signature of Munich, he does this also because the French capitulation of 1940 had its real fatal beginning at Munich.

Whatever the internal organisation of France will be after the war, a new and liberated France is already speaking today in the signature of General de Gaulle. Together with the signatures of our Ministers, it means that France is returning to her old traditional friendship and is proclaiming solemnly that our two Nations together with Great Britain, the Soviet Union, the United States and the other Allies will re-establish European order and freedom and re-establish the fame, greatness and strength of France and Czechoslovakia.'

(The full speech was published in Dr. Beneš's book *Six Years of Exile and the Second World War*, pp. 176-84. Czech edition.)

¹³In particular, I had a very friendly talk with M. Vincent Auriol, afterwards President of the French Republic.

CHAPTER VII

EAST AND WEST—
CZECHOSLOVAKIA AT THE CROSSROADS?

1. *Before My Visit to Moscow*

AS I have already mentioned, when I decided to visit the United States I had already begun my preparations for my journey to the Soviet Union which was to be our last decisive political step of a military and diplomatic character during our liberation fight and before our joint victory was finally attained. It was intended as a diplomatic move which was to round off and complete the whole line of our war-time policy of liberation. In the future, I think it will also be possible to regard it as the logical culmination of the policy and journeys of our great predecessors in 1848, 1867, at the beginning of the present century and, of course, of the policy and journeys of Masaryk before and during the first World War.

My visit to Russia was closely connected with the negotiations for our treaty with the Soviet Union against a possible future recrudescence of German imperialism. From the moment the Soviet Union entered the second World War, I had planned to renew the treaty concluded with Moscow in 1935 by means of a new treaty of some kind concluded before the war was ended. Already in June, 1941, I had formulated the idea that we should resume our relations with the Soviet Union at the point at which they had been interrupted by Munich. Having always of course counted upon the participation of the Soviet Union in this war, on our side, I had therefore, from the beginning of the war, always conducted all our negotiations with other countries, especially with Poland, in such a way that they would never cause any differences to arise between ourselves and the Soviet Union. We had loyally kept the other allied countries, and especially the Poles, informed about our attitude towards the Soviet Union and of our intention never to get into conflict with it.

I always had this in mind in my written statements and when discussing agreements about Central European problems. In my speech to the State Council on November 12th, 1942—I was referring on that occasion to the joint Polish-Czechoslovak Declaration of November 11th, 1940—I emphasised this as follows:

'I regard the present war as *the decisive historic opportunity to bring to an end once and for all time the pan-German "Drang nach Osten". This same war has proved that in order to do so, real, friendly and loyal co-operation between Poland, Czechoslovakia and the Soviet Union is essential.* Our relations with both are those of allies and friends and they are to remain so permanently. We hope that when full agreement has been reached between Poland and the Soviet Union, this will be followed by a full agreement between the three of us *for the specific purpose of ending the imperialist and bloodthirsty Drang nach Osten.* If we succeed in bringing this about, the whole future of Poland and of Czechoslovakia will be guaranteed. This would benefit all Europe. If not, Germany will again evoke a new catastrophe in some other form. In this I am expressing only what is my real, profound political conviction.'[1]

When, on July 18th, 1941, Ambassador Ivan Maisky and Minister Masaryk signed our first treaty of alliance with the Soviet Union for the duration of the second World War only, I considered the possibility of some more permanent and substantial declaration on the lines of the policy we had inaugurated with the Soviet Union in 1935. But I saw that at that time this would be premature. The idea had not yet ripened either in Moscow, in London, or with the other allied countries.

But when I made my preparations for my visit to the United States in 1943, I decided to try to solve this question. I was always aware of the fact that Munich with all its catastrophic European consequences would not have occurred but for the hostility of Western Europe towards the Soviet Union and the differences between them. It was clear to me that—if we were to win this second World War—such differences must be removed. If they persisted even after the second World War, either another world catastrophe would follow at once or we would be subjected to some new form of Munich and there would be another world catastrophe afterwards. Hitler's attack on the Soviet Union started from the assumption that the differences between the world and the Soviet Union were of such a character that Germany would in any eventuality and at the right moment succeed in making peace with Western Europe *which then would give it a free hand against the Soviet Union.* It was clear to me that this, *the real world catastrophe,* could only be prevented by devoted work for a firm and *permanent* agreement between the Anglo-Saxons and the Soviet Union— that it was our chief task in this situation to work for such an agreement and that, within the frame of this agreement, our own special agreement with the Soviet Union during the war would be a self-evident and internationally feasible proposition.

Being anxious to use my visit to the United States as an opportunity to work for a closer rapprochement with the Soviet Union and thus secure a

CZECHOSLOVAKIA AT THE CROSSROADS ?

speedy victory over Hitler, I wanted to get a clear picture of the wartime and post-war policy of the Soviet Union towards the Great Powers as well as towards the smaller countries, both the Allies and the others—especially of its relations to all its neighbours, the question of non-interference in the internal affairs of the neighbour States, recognition of their full post-war sovereignty, its relations to Germany during and after the war and, *naturally, above all, its attitude towards us* and its views about our permanent relationship to the East and to the West.

It seemed to me that if full understanding were reached between ourselves and the Soviet Union in regard to all these questions, and if we trusted one another completely, it would also be possible—in the United States, too—to refer *to this actual example just as an example.* I believed that this would substantially draw all the Allies together, especially the bigger ones, that it would tend to allay wrong suspicions about the Soviet Union or even remove them and that it would help to pave the way for what happened later at the Allied conferences in Moscow and Teheran.

Early in 1943, therefore, before my visit to the United States, I started discussions in London on these lines with the Soviet Ambassador, Bogomolov. I explained the sense and the aim of my visit and ended my explanation with this conclusion: 'During my visit I shall have to explain our whole policy towards Germany, Poland and the Soviet Union. I would therefore like to ask Moscow in advance about some essential matters which are important for you as well as for us. The answers will show all our Allies what are the aims of the policy which we are following not only with regard to you but to all the others, especially Poland. This last question is the most burning one at the moment both here in London and in Washington.'

We had been trying to come to an agreement with the Poles since the beginning of 1940 in order to co-ordinate our policy with that of Poland and the Soviet Union and even in order to attempt closer Polish-Czechoslovak co-operation in future.* But these negotiations had been suspended at the end of 1942, partly because Polish-Soviet relations were in a state of crisis—a crisis which concerned the other Allies, too, including ourselves— and partly because the London Poles could not give us satisfactory guaran-

*A joint declaration providing for close political and economic association was signed on November 11th, 1940. Another document of a similar nature entitled 'Joint Polish-Czechoslovak Agreement' was signed on January 23rd, 1942—after the U.S.S.R. had been forced into the war. The closer association (which almost amounted to federation) was not, however, to come into force until ratified by the Parliaments of the two countries. Even in 1942, therefore, it was widely held that the agreement would never come into operation (Tr.).

tees about their policy in regard to all the points at issue between us arising
from territorial disputes and from Poland's attitude at the time of, and
before, Munich.

I therefore asked Ambassador Bogomolov to procure for me from
Moscow answers to the following questions before my departure for
Washington: Was Moscow ready to conclude with Czechoslovakia a
reaty similar to the Anglo-Soviet Pact and adapted to Czechoslovak
conditions? Would Moscow consider it possible to stress in the treaty the
mutual obligation of both partners not to interfere in the internal affairs of
the other partner? Could the Soviet Union tell us in principle what its
attitude towards Germany would be after the war and could it support our
view of the necessity to transfer Fascist Germans from Czechoslovakia?
Could Moscow accept in principle our proposal for an agreement to halt
any future German *Drang nach Osten* for all time? Could it accept this as a
basis for our future alliance and also consent to post-war Poland being
included in this treaty and in our system of co-operation by means of a
common agreement between our three countries?

These were the questions which I discussed from all angles in a number
of conversations with Ambassador Bogomolov in March, 1943, and which
I finally put to him in the form of a direct inquiry to the Soviet Government when he visited me in Aston Abbotts at the end of March.

The answer arrived on April 23rd. On the same day Bogomolov asked
if he could come to see me at Aston Abbotts. He arrived in a cheerful and
excited frame of mind. It seemed to me that he regarded the success of
these negotiations as his own. He brought a positive answer in essential
points and he stressed, rightly, how extremely important this was for the
future from the point of view of Moscow—as well as from our own. He
gave Moscow's answer as follows:

'If you were to put forward a comprehensive draft of the treaty we have
been discussing during the past weeks, the Soviet Government would not
in principle give a negative answer. The idea of non-interference in internal
affairs could be incorporated and the Soviet Government would have no
objection to post-war co-operation with Poland on the lines set out in the
Czechoslovak question. The Soviet Government therefore invites you to
prepare a draft of the treaty and submit it to the Soviet Government.'

With regard to Germany, the Soviet Government was not able to
formulate its views in detail at this stage. It was determined to prosecute
the war against Germany to the very end but its detailed views on post-
war Germany were greatly dependent on those of Great Britain and
America. Moscow would therefore only be able to tell me more on this

basic matter in the near future. Its views about the transfer of German Fascists from Czechoslovakia, although at present not negative, could only be formulated definitely at a later stage.

Not long afterwards—on June 5th, while I was in America—Bogomolov visited Minister Ripka and told him that he could confirm Moscow's above attitude towards Germany and further that Moscow was now definitely in favour of the transfer of the German Nazi population from Czechoslovakia. Ambassador Bogomolov then asked Dr. Ripka to pass this information on to me at once in Washington.[2]

I loyally informed the British Government after my return from America about these discussions in which Ministers Masaryk and Ripka also participated at various stages. I also told President Roosevelt and the representatives of the State Department (Cordell Hull and Sumner Welles) about them personally during my stay in Washington. My speeches in America and Canada in May and June, 1943, were naturally influenced by these discussions with Moscow.

I wanted to leave for Moscow already in the summer of 1943 immediately after my return to England from the United States. But discussions supervened between London, Washington and Moscow and ourselves about the proposed treaty and this postponed my departure until December, 1943.

In Washington I found full understanding for our policy vis-à-vis the Soviet Union in my very first conversations and Roosevelt as well as Cordell Hull and Sumner Welles agreed to it in principle. Our treaty was regarded by the American Government as typical of what the Soviet Union's other neighbours should do, in time, so as to secure their independence and non-interference in their internal affairs or in their social structure on the side of the Soviet Union.

In London the situation was somewhat different. Winston Churchill was, broadly speaking, rather favourable to our point of view. But in the Foreign Office two opinions existed among the officials. One section agreed with us; the other considered that we were leaning too far to the East to the special disadvantage of the Poles, who, they said, would thus be alone in their attitude towards the Soviet Union and the Soviet desire to solve its frontier problems with Poland in the spirit of the Curzon Line. The great majority of the London Poles, when they heard about our plans were very strongly opposed to our policy. They saw in it the end of their earlier plans to establish a Central European Federation led by Poland which was to be a barrier against Germany as well as against the Soviet Union.

R

Between June and November, 1943, after my return from Washington, I met Mr. Eden three times for long conferences, in which (in the presence of Jan Masaryk and Hubert Ripka on our side and Mr. Strang and Mr. Nichols on the other) we discussed all aspects of this policy. At the outset, Eden, without opposing either the treaty or my visiting Moscow, was inclined to think that in view of British public opinion, I might indeed go to Moscow at once and agree on the treaty but that I should only sign it later, preferably after the conclusion of the armistice with Germany, when the position with regard to the Soviet Union and Poland and the Soviet Union's post-war policy would be quite clear to all the Allies.

I did not agree with this postponement.* I argued that the precedent we established and our agreement with the Soviets might provide the best proof of what the real policy of the Soviet Union probably would be and could be after the war; that it was in our interest and that of all others to show the world by the example of our treaty with the Soviet Union what the Soviet Union wanted and what policy it intended to follow; that far from driving them apart it should and could draw the Soviet Union nearer to Great Britain as well as to the United States and that it could finally set the minds of all the other Allies at rest with regard to the aims of the Soviet Union. Moreover, above all, it would ultimately make for the normalisation of conditions and for the peaceful development of the Soviet Union itself in Europe and the world! In reply to all questions I repeated emphatically that I accepted at its face value what the Soviet Union was promising us and that in my experience I had hitherto had no reason at all to mistrust its word.'

At first there was a rather wide difference between us though—I emphasize this again—Great Britain *never opposed this treaty in principle*. On the contrary, Great Britain stressed that in principle it agreed to the conclusion of our treaty with Moscow. The only question was *when* to sign it. On the other side the Soviet Government—when we had decided to have a treaty and agreed about its contents—made it a condition and insisted on it firmly that if I went to Moscow the treaty would have to be signed on that occasion.

But the British Government—and Eden personally—drew the very important conclusion from these negotiations that considerable uncertainties and differences of opinion existed between London and Moscow, even possible conflicts in their mutual policy—during the war and still more

*There is every possibility that if Dr. Beneš had not gone to Moscow the Soviet Government would have set up a rival Czechoslovak Government as it did in the case of Poland (Tr.).

after the war—and that the background of our treaty negotiations showed these possible differences very clearly. They came to the conclusion that these differences should be looked into and that it would be advisable to reach substantial unity of views on the chief problems of war and peace between the three chief Allied Powers, Great Britain, the United States and the Soviet Union. This, in my view, gave birth to the idea of calling the Moscow Conference of the three Allied Foreign Ministers in October, 1943, which was followed by the Teheran Conference between Roosevelt, Churchill and Stalin in November and December of the same year.

I think, therefore, that I am not wrong in supposing that the Moscow Conference *was the direct result or was at least hastened by the negotiations for our treaty with Moscow.* At all events during our discussions in London in August and September, 1943, Mr. Eden finally urged that I should not go to Moscow until after the meeting of the three Ministers—Hull, Molotov and Eden—who, he said, would meet as soon as possible in *London* when it was expected that all questions concerning the general co-operation of the three Powers would be cleared up so that nothing would then stand in the way of the conclusion of our treaty. The conference actually met within a month, *but at the request of the Soviet Government its sessions were held in Moscow.*

I agreed with the procedure and declared that I would go to Moscow in any case after the meeting of the three Ministers and would agree to the signing of the treaty between us and the Soviet Union and also put it into operation. At the same time I urged in Moscow that the Commissar of Foreign Affairs, Molotov, should place the question of our treaty on the agenda of the conference and inform the representatives of the United States and Great Britain of the agreed text of the treaty. Molotov did so. Eden and Hull took note of our actions and expressed their satisfaction at the wording, the sense and the aim of the treaty.

I think that the whole result of our loyal attitude towards all our Allies and of our policy in general may be considered a real success for Czecho-slovakia. My visit and the signing of the treaty took place shortly after the Moscow Conference. To a certain degree it became one of the sensations of war policy and diplomacy in the year 1943, and without doubt it had a great importance not only for our future policy and that of the Soviet Union, but for the whole camp of the Allies and also of the Axis.

2. The Great Conferences : Casablanca and Washington— Moscow, Teheran and Cairo

Broadly speaking, the year 1943 was a turning-point not only in military sphere, but to a considerable degree also in the war ideology and the plans and ideas of co-operation between the Allies during the war and still more so in regard to peace and the post-war period. For a long while, uncertainty about the progress of the war events delayed the clarification of Allied views about war aims and peace. But when in the course of 1943 it became clear on the Eastern front that the Soviet Union was no longer suffering defeats but that the Western Powers could not achieve full victory over Germany and Japan without the Soviet Union, the political situation among the Allies crystallised to the extent that all saw and recognised that clearer formulations of peace and war aims had become quite indispensable.

Up to the end of 1942, the Allied war ideology was stated in quite general terms only, in the Atlantic Charter and the British-Soviet Treaty. But these were not sufficient for the concrete solution of all problems and a *practical*, successful and joint day-to-day war policy. Further discussions and agreements were necessary. These took place in the course of six conferences held during 1943, first between President Roosevelt and Prime Minister Churchill at Casablanca (January 14th–24th), at Washington (May 11th–24th) and at Quebec (August 11th–24th) and then between the three Great Powers at Moscow (October 19th–November 1st), at Cairo (November 22nd–26th) and at Teheran (November 28th–December 1st).

The course of the negotiations and the decisions at these conferences were naturally dependent upon and controlled above all by the Allied war successes. Gradually as military victories were won new *political* decisions became necessary. As the Allied Armies progressed, a new war ideology was formed and developed and the practical war policy of the Allies changed and was completed. The occupation of Morocco and Algeria and the victory of General Montgomery in the Eastern Mediterranean demanded preparations for a decision on the whole Mediterranean campaign, on the future fate of Italy and, especially, on the definite form of co-operation with France.

Thus came about the Conference at Casablanca in January, 1943. It discussed in detail the whole future of the Mediterranean campaign, *but its most important public act was the agreement between Roosevelt and Churchill* that there would be no armistice discussions with the Axis—that the Axis States would have to *surrender unconditionally*. This decision had the effect of a bomb. The Soviet Union subscribed to it fully. Also at the Casablanca Conference the problem of France was discussed and in spite of a number of difficulties the first foundations were laid for the agreement which followed in May, 1943, between the French themselves—General Giraud and General de Gaulle—for the transfer of the French Committee from London to Algiers and for the gradual but complete recognition of the new international legal position of the Fighting French representing France both militarily and politically as a great power.

The discussions about the Mediterranean which began at Casablanca were continued between Churchill and Roosevelt in Washington and Quebec in the summer of 1943. Preparations were made for the final attack on Italy, for an agreement between America and Great Britain on the concrete conditions for ending hostilities with Italy and for further discussions to clarify the situation of France. After moving from London to Algiers, the French National Committee created new conditions on its own national territory, consolidated its internal affairs militarily and politically, built up a democratic State organisation and thus became a real Provisional Government preparing the direct liberation of Metropolitan France in agreement with Great Britain and the United States. The Soviet Union effectively supported this evolution so that the camp of the Allies was consolidating very appreciably in the political sphere and political conditions in the Mediterranean were clearing up considerably, though not completely, with regard to the imminent fall of Italy.

But the sudden—and so pitiful—fall of Mussolini's Fascist Italy (on June 24th, 1943) which came unexpectedly soon after the attack on Sicily, showed how necessary it was to be prepared in time for the end of the war. The Anglo-Saxon Powers had no sufficiently clear ideas about what they would have to do in Italy's internal policy after the fall of Fascism. Similarly, the Soviet Union until then had not been sufficiently engaged in the Mediterranean campaign just as the other two Allies were not in the Eastern sector. The Soviet Union waged its own war on the Eastern front —though with the very abundant help of Great Britain and America on sea, in the air and in materials. But there was insufficient unity of ideas. The dispute about the so-called second front continued and was even increasing. Since the war on the Continent of Europe was being waged chiefly on the Eastern front there still remained an impression of two wars: an Anglo-American war and a Soviet one.

This fact was very effectively used by German propaganda. After their defeat at Stalingrad the Germans knew that they could only end the war without total disaster if they were able to split the Allies politically and diplomatically. From the spring of 1943, therefore, propaganda against the so-called danger of Bolshevism and for the so-called saving of civilisation from the Soviet Union was continually stepped up with increasing vigour.

The Germans depicted the dreadful future facing Europe and the world if Great Britain and America did not separate from the Soviet Union and let Germany defeat it or perhaps even help Germany to do so. In disorganised Europe—especially in the countries poisoned by Fascism and quasi-Fascism of various kinds—there were still millions of people in 1943 so blinded by the crisis of the past few years and psychologically so deadened by their class, national or personal egotism, that this propaganda trick had a certain success.

This was plainly Germany's last desperate attempt to save itself. It seems that it came at the right moment because it called forth the right reaction. In the end the Allies *had to try* politically, diplomatically and militarily to discuss all the war problems which till then had remained in doubt and to unify their policies at least in their main aspects. It was necessary to *demonstrate clearly that the war was one and indivisible, that its chief aims were common to all* and that this war comradeship must not and would not be destroyed by anybody. It was necessary to emphasize that this comradeship was of such a nature that the Allies were really not bargaining about the second front but that the question of the second front was a question of *joint* preparations, *joint* calculations, *joint military plans and at the end a joint and united victory.*

In addition, the three—or four—chief powers conducting the war (Great Britain, the Soviet Union, the United States and China) also had to formulate jointly a practical policy on their main post-war aims for Europe and the world—for example: what was to happen with Germany, how would practical effect be given to the political and economic co-operation of the Great Powers and how would the future security system of Europe and the world be prepared, what would happen to some small States and what about the so-called federation plans in Central Europe, how did the Soviet Union view its own post-war position, what was to be done about the Soviet-Polish quarrel and so on?

Only if these concrete questions were sufficiently cleared up could the fears of some countries be removed that the Soviet Union had some particular revolutionary plans in respect of the rest of Europe and only so could all the Allies be completely convinced that no so-called Bolshevisation or Sovietisation of Central, Southern and Western Europe was being prepared—as was assiduously spread by the German propaganda machine.

At that vitally important moment, two Allied conferences were held—in October, 1943, in Moscow and from November 28th to December 1st of the same year in Teheran. In addition there was the Anglo-American-Chinese conference in Cairo towards the end of November, 1943. These conferences brought a substantial elucidation of all these questions, and of others, and caused a far-reaching and favourable change in the atmosphere of the Allied camp.

The Moscow Conference was held from October 19th to November 1st and Ministers Molotov, Eden and Cordell Hull participated with their political and military advisers. Vyatcheslav Molotov, the Commissar for Foreign Affairs, presided. It discussed a number of vital military and political problems arising from the situation of the Allies at the beginning of the fifth year of war; it prepared a basis for real and loyal military and political co-operation at the start of the last phase of the war and for securing quick and final victory. The Conference also laid foundations for real agreement and friendship between the three participating Powers. It approved some resolutions of principle which, completed later by resolutions adopted at Teheran, laid a foundation for the joint policy of the three, or four, principal Powers for the prosecution of the war to final victory and for jointly preparing the construction of the subsequent peace.

The Conference then agreed on a joint policy towards Italy. Fascism and its whole heritage would be destroyed. Conditions would be laid down for Italy's return to a democratic régime and the Italian Nation itself would have to bring about this return. To draft the final conditions of peace for Italy a special Allied Committee was set up in which, in addition to Great Britain, the United States and the Soviet Union, three other countries, France, Yugoslavia and Greece were represented. The Conference adopted a definite decision on Austria's independence and on the punishment of all Axis criminals who had been guilty of military or other cruelties against the population of Allied Nations. This declaration was fundamental, resolute and categorical. It dealt with all German persecutions and cruelties in all the countries they and the Allies of the Axis had occupied. It thus guaranteed that our people too would get justice for their sufferings and that those guilty of crimes and terror in our country would be mercilessly punished.

Finally the Conference took these two important decisions:

It declared that it was in the national interest of the three Great Powers and of all the Allies that their existing close co-operation should continue both in war-time and *in peace-time after the war*, because only in this way would victory be won, an advantageous peace secured and made safe for generations. The Conference established in London an Advisory Committee of the three Great Powers for the permanent exchange of views on current political and military questions, to maintain this full and systematic political co-operation and to prepare the conditions for ending hostilities.

And it completed this basis of future co-operation by a far-reaching decision on *future post-war security*. The enemy States were to be completely disarmed after their capitulation, the whole system of their future disarmament would be insured, and the international regulation of post-war disarmament maintained, by joint agreement. The Allied States would establish a new security system to preserve peace which would be general, on a world scale, open to all countries, great and small, and after victory had been secured the Allies would remain in close co-operation to guard peace in such a way that—until the permanent and actual introduction of a joint security and international order—they themselves could at once undertake the necessary military steps to defend peace against any new violation.

Finally it was decided that after the end of the present military operations the Allies would only employ their military forces on the territories of other States for reasons of security and then only after joint agreement. This meant after the war ended *the military occupation of any part of the whole Continent of Europe would only be on a basis of full unity and the mutual agreement of all three Powers.*

The Moscow Conference was generally considered to have been very successful. And in my opinion it really was a great success at the time. It was the first general conference of the three Great Powers of such a kind and such a compass. And, if due consideration is given not only to the uncertainty, the vagueness and mutual distrust hitherto prevailing in the Allied camp, but also to all the decisions of the Moscow Conference together with all their consequences, one must draw the conclusion that the three Great Powers had achieved real unity in their *principal* war and peace aims.

This important agreement was then supplemented and rounded off at the Conference of the three leading Allied statesmen, President Roosevelt, Prime Minister Churchill and Premier Stalin with their advisers, held at Teheran from November 28th to December 1st. The purport of this second Conference was defined in the official declaration issued in Teheran, the contents of which are very explicit:

'We, the President of the United States of America, the Prime Minister of Great Britain and the Premier of the Soviet Union have met these four days past in this the capital of our ally, Iran, and have shaped and confirmed our common policy.

'We expressed our determination that our Nations shall work together in war and in the peace that will follow.

'As to war, our Military Staffs have joined in our Round Table discussions and we have concerted our plans for the destruction of the German forces. We have reached complete agreement as to the scope and timing of the operations which will be undertaken from the east, west, and south.

'The common understanding which we have here reached guarantees that victory will be ours.

'And as to peace, we are sure that our concord will make it an enduring peace. We recognize fully the supreme responsibility resting upon us and all the United Nations to make a peace which will command the goodwill of the overwhelming masses of the peoples of the world and banish the scourge and terror of war for many generations.

'With our diplomatic advisers we have surveyed the problems of the future. We shall seek the co-operation and the active participation of all nations large and small whose peoples in heart and mind are dedicated as are our own peoples to the elimination of tyranny and slavery, oppression and intolerance. We will welcome them as they may choose to come into a world family of Democratic Nations.

'No power on earth can prevent our destroying the German armies by land, their U-boats by sea and their war plants from the air. Our attacks will be relentless and increasing.

'From these friendly conferences we look with confidence to the day when all peoples of the world may live free lives untouched by tyranny and according to their varying desires and their own consciences.

'We came here with hope and determination. We leave here friends in fact, in spirit and in purpose.'

It can be said of the Teheran discussions that this was the first conference at which the leaders of the three world Powers spoke to one another with a frankness and sincerity which till then was unparalleled between them about all the steps which were necessary to clear up the military and political problems existing in the Allied camp. *They agreed on the military decisions* required for the establishment of the so-called *second front in Western Europe in the spring of 1944* and on the future direction of the Allied war which this involved and they exchanged views about the solution of all the chief problems of international post-war policy without shirking even the most difficult and most delicate questions.'

Both in its form and course the Conference at Teheran was something quite new. The discussions were not merely decisive negotiations between the three leading Allied Powers but also an agreement between the three most characteristic leading personalities of the Allied camp—personalities who differed very greatly the one from the other. The meetings took place in the form of free discussions at the Soviet Embassy in Teheran 'around the table'. They were friendly, without formal resolutions, and consisted of entirely frank expressions of the views and opinions of each partner so that each was able to know not only what the other was expressly asking for, but also, to a considerable degree, what he was thinking and how he viewed their common future. Besides Roosevelt, Churchill and Stalin there were also present: The American Ambassador Harriman and Harry Hopkins, Anthony Eden and Ambassador Kerr for the British, Molotov and Voroshilov for the Soviet Union.

All parties were generally agreed that the results of the talks were satisfactory as I was personally able to ascertain from my discussions with most of the participants in this Conference. There were no wide divergencies about the main problems of Germany. All agreed on the necessity for a hard peace and they did not exclude strong action against it even in the matter of frontiers. Stalin received detailed information about the second front: about the state of British and American preparations and when, at the latest, they intended to invade the European Continent (May-June, 1944). The Soviet participants accepted and agreed to this. The joint policy of the three States towards France and China and some colonial problems were also discussed.

Stalin quite plainly and frankly outlined the policy of the Soviet Government in regard to the Western frontiers of the Soviet Union and reiterated that he wanted an independent and strong Poland adding that they could not give up the amended Curzon Line (according to which Vilno and Lwow would also remain in the Soviet Union) but that they supposed Poland would be compensated at the expense of Germany—especially by receiving Eastern Prussia, part of which, however, including the town of Königsberg, would be incorporated in the Soviet Union. Great Britain and the United States took note of this point of view. This conference also showed the first signs of the intention to fix military—and therewith also political—spheres of influence for the Eastern front as well as for the Western front. It was clear to both East and West that they would have to invade Germany. Where these spheres should or would meet was not definitely fixed. But it can be supposed that the Soviet Union was already hinting that it was counting on its sphere including in any case North-Eastern Germany, the whole of Poland, Czechoslovakia, Rumania and Hungary. Probably there were no objections from the side of the British or the Americans seeing that the invasion of France was only to come about in the spring of the following year. *As I have already mentioned, we were not told anything of these plans at the time either by the Soviets or by the Western Powers.* The extent of these arrangements only became clear to us at the time of the Slovak revolt, when for this reason we sensed that certain difficulties existed on the side of the British and Americans in giving aid to the revolt.

As to the future system of security, it was clearly indicated

(*a*) that it was sure to be established,

(*b*) that it was to be a general system, not for Europe only (Roosevelt and Stalin stated plainly that their countries could not participate unless this was the case),

(*c*) that it would be based on the military strength of the leading Allied Powers,

(*d*) that though the Great Powers would play the leading rôle, all smaller Allied countries would participate on a fair basis.

Thus it can be seen that the most far-reaching problems of the future peace was discussed at Teheran. So far as our country was concerned, the decisions on the whole coincided with our long-pursued policy of securing first victory in the war and then a victorious peace—victorious for us as well as the others. I therefore regarded the Teheran Conference as a great success and I moulded all my further discussions in Moscow as well as my later ones in London and our negotiations with the Americans to fit the results of Teheran. This also covered the advance of the Soviet Army into Central Europe and on to our territory which I regarded as a certainty—especially after Teheran—though I did not exclude the possibility that the Western Allies would also try to reach it.

When Roosevelt, Churchill and Stalin parted after the Conference of Teheran, they had also drawn closer together personally and had strengthened the feelings of co-operation and friendship between their States and Nations. I am convinced that at this Conference these three leading men together with all their advisers did great service to their countries, to all Allied Nations and to their war effort, and above all to promote the final victory. The Conference at Teheran therefore has a really important place in the history of the second World War though some of its decisions caused differences to arise later but not till 1945 and the years which followed.

To recapitulate: considered together with the Moscow Conference, the Conference at Teheran meant that the three Great Powers were agreed in matters of principle as regards the war, victory and peace. Furthermore, it was now certain that while the war lasted nothing could destroy the agreement of the three States and enable Nazism to escape destruction by exploiting their differences. Finally, in spite of difficult discussions and divergencies of views which began to be apparent later in a number of questions and which caused considerable difficulties for all three countries, in spite of the differences between the regimes and governmental systems of the Anglo-American Powers and the Soviet State, the three countries, after the Conference at Teheran, were so strongly aware of the substantial identity of all their vital interests in the war, that they subsequently did their utmost *to enable us to fight one single war and prepare one single peace, together.*

Between November 22nd and November 26th, 1943, there was a military and political conference at Cairo between President Roosevelt, Prime Minister Churchill and the Chinese Generalissimo Chiang Kai-shek in which their military and political staffs and advisers took part. The political and military situation of the whole war against Japan was discussed, plans for further military operations against Japan were agreed upon and a far-reaching decision was made which, if realised, would mean the complete transformation of conditions in the Far East. Japan was to be forced to capitulate and would be made to hand back not only all the territories of which it had taken possession by force and betrayal during the present war, but also those which it had conquered since 1914 and at China's expense since 1894–1895. In particular, independence was also to be restored to Korea. This would mean a real revolution in existing conditions in the Far East and in the whole Pacific.

The decisions of the Allied Conferences of 1943 were thus of the utmost importance—indeed they were decisive in regard to many problems. They brought the certainty of a joint and united prosecution of the war to a victorious conclusion. They also gave at least a *hope* of agreement in principle about mutual co-operation *even after the war* and the preservation of mutual confidence even when the interests of the Powers concerned should conflict in the future. They gave *promise* that world peace would be safe—perhaps for some generations. *And they promised, in the spirit of international democracy*, that the other Allies as well, *especially the small States*, would acquire a legal place in the new world organisation.

3. *Signature of the Soviet-Czechoslovak Treaty*

After his return from the Moscow Conference, Foreign Secretary Anthony Eden informed me that the question of our treaty had been fully clarified during the negotiations in Moscow and that therefore nothing stood in the way of my going to Moscow nor the signing of the Soviet-Czechoslovak Treaty.

My draft of the treaty which I had submitted to Ambassador Bogomolov on August 22nd, 1943, had already been discussed between us and
the Soviet Government during August, September and October, 1943,
and was therefore fully agreed before my visit. Later it was changed in
some details by Envoy Fierlinger and the Soviet Foreign Office in Moscow.[5]
On December 12th, 1943, the day after my arrival the treaty was solemnly
signed by Molotov on behalf of the Soviet Union and Ambassador
Zdeněk Fierlinger on behalf of the Czechoslovak Republic in the presence
of Kalinin and myself, of Stalin, Voroshilov and a number of Czechoslovak and Soviet politicians and soldiers. And the Treaty was ratified
immediately afterwards.[6]

The text of the 'Treaty of friendship, mutual aid and post-war co-
operation between the Czechoslovak Republic and the Union of Soviet
Socialist Republics,' signed at Moscow on December 12th, 1934, is as
follows:

'The President of the Czechoslovak Republic and the Presidium of
the Supreme Soviet of the Union of Soviet Socialist Republics,
wishing to amend and to supplement the existing treaty of mutual aid
between the Czechoslovak Republic and the Union of Soviet Socialist
Republics, signed at Prague on May 16th, 1935,' and to prolong the
Agreement between the Government of the Czechoslovak Republic
and the Government of the Union of Soviet Socialist Republics on their
joint prosecution of the war against Germany signed in London on July
18th, 1941; wishing to co-operate after the war for the maintenance of
peace and the prevention of a new attack by Germany and to secure
their lasting friendship and mutual peaceful co-operation after the war,
have decided to conclude to this effect a Treaty and have nominated as
their representatives:

The President of the Czechoslovak Republic—Mr. Zdeněk Fierlinger,
Ambassador of the Czechoslovak Republic to the Soviet Union.

The Presidium of the Supreme Soviet of the Union of Soviet Socialist
Republics—M. Vyatcheslav Mikhailovitch Molotov, People's Commissar for Foreign Affairs,

who, after exchanging their full powers and finding them in good and
due form, have agreed upon the following provisions:

Article 1

The High Contracting Parties, after mutually agreeing to unite in a
policy of permanent friendship and friendly post-war co-operation as
well as of mutual aid, undertake to give one another military and other

aid and support in the present war against Germany and against all the States allied with it in acts of aggression in Europe.

Article 2

The High Contracting Parties bind themselves not to enter during the present war into any negotiations with the Hitler Government or any other Government in Germany which does not clearly renounce all aggressive intentions, and not to negotiate or to conclude without mutual agreement any armistice or peace treaty with Germany or any other State allied with it in acts of aggression in Europe.

Article 3

Confirming their pre-war policy of peace and mutual aid expressed in their Treaty signed at Prague on May 16th, 1935, the High Contracting Parties undertake that if either of them shall in the post-war period be drawn into military action against Germany on account of a renewal of its policy of *Drang nach Osten*★ or with any other State which allies itself with Germany in such a war directly or in any other way, the other High Contracting Party will immediately give to the Contracting Party which has been drawn into military actions in this manner all military and other support and aid at its disposal.

Article 4

The High Contracting Parties having regard to the interests of their mutual security, have agreed to maintain close and friendly co-operation after the re-establishment of peace and to regulate their actions according to the principles of mutual respect of their independence and sovereignty and non-interference in the internal affairs of the other signatory. They have agreed to develop their economic relations on the broadest possible scale and to grant one another all possible economic aid after the war.

Article 5

Each High Contracting Party undertakes not to conclude any alliance and not to participate in any coalition directed against the other High Contracting Party.

Article 6

This Treaty becomes valid immediately upon signature and is to be ratified in the shortest possible time. The instruments of ratification shall be exchanged at Moscow as soon as possible.

★It is noteworthy that the treaty is only operative in the case of a German attack *eastwards* (Tr.).

This Treaty remains valid for twenty years from the time of signature. If one of the High Contracting Parties does not give notice of its intention to denounce the Treaty not less than twelve months before the expiration of this twenty years' period, the validity of the Treaty shall be prolonged for another five years and shall so continue until one of the High Contracting Parties shall not less than twelve months before the expiration of the current five years' period declare in writing that it intends to end the validity of the Treaty.

In witness hereof the representatives have signed the Treaty and have attached thereto their seals.

Executed in two copies, each in the Czechoslovak and Russian languages.

Both copies have the same validity.

Moscow, December 12th, 1943.

On the authority of the Presidium of the Supreme Soviet of the U.S.S.R.:

(signed) V. MOLOTOV.

On the authority of the President of the Czechoslovak Republic:

(signed) ZD. FIERLINGER.'

At the same time we and the Soviet Government signed a special *'Protocol to the Treaty of friendship, mutual aid and post-war co-operation between the Czechoslovak Republic and the Union of Soviet Socialist Republics concluded on December 12th, 1943,'* which contained the so-called 'Polish clause' and met our wish for future agreement with Poland.[8] It read as follows:

'In concluding the Treaty of friendship, mutual aid and post-war co-operation between the Czechoslovak Republic and the Union of Soviet Socialist Republics, the Contracting Parties agree that if any third country having common frontiers with the Czechoslovak Republic or the Union of Soviet Socialist Republics and having in this war been an object of German aggression, expresses the wish to adhere to this Treaty, it will be given the opportunity to do so after mutual agreement between the Governments of the Czechoslovak Republic and the Union of the U.S.S.R. and this Treaty by such adhesion shall acquire the character of a trilateral treaty.

This Protocol has been signed in two copies each in the Czechoslovak and Russian languages.

Both copies have the same validity.

Moscow, December 12th, 1943.

On the authority of the Presidium of the Supreme Soviet of the U.S.S.R.:

(Signed): V. Molotov.
On the authority of the President of the Czechoslovak Republic:
(Signed): Zd. Fierlinger.

On December 21st, before returning to London, I spoke on the Moscow radio about the sense and significance of this treaty for ourselves, for the Soviet Union and the rest of Europe.[9] I think that everything I said on that occasion has afterwards been confirmed by events. I considered my visit and all that was done during it for Czechoslovakia a great success of our policy. The international public which had watched this visit with close attention, evaluated these events in the same manner. When I returned to London, I made a report about the treaty to the State Council in which I added the following to what I had said from Moscow to Prague and to Slovakia:[10]

(a) We regard this treaty as one of the links in the post-war system of security. Another specially important link, in our opinion, is and will be the British-Soviet treaty of May 26th, 1942, which with our treaty fits into the general security system of the world in which the United States, France and the other Allied States are also taking part.

For us this treaty, by its whole character, its twenty years' term and its automatic renewal, means a *permanent* defence against the recrudescence of pan-Germanism, against the *Drang nach Osten* and against another bandit acquisition of German 'Lebensraum'. It is a guarantee of our frontiers and a guarantee that Munich shall never be repeated. In short, it provides a high degree of security for our independence and our Republic, such as we never had before.

(b) Our joint proposal and desire to concert this policy of defence against German imperialism with an independent, democratic Poland, friendly to us both, *is sincere, real and lasting*. In this way could be brought about the final settlement of all disputes between the three of us and the preparation of a secure future for these three Slav Nations and States as well as the final establishment of peace in Eastern and Central Europe and therewith perhaps in Europe as a whole. No future Germany could ever dare to provoke a new World War against the alliance and harmonious co-operation of these three Slav States for the defence of peace in this part of the globe. Such an agreement could therefore be of the greatest importance for the future peace of all Europe.

We agreed in Moscow that we will not cease to work for such an agreement. It would involve agreement between Czechoslovaks, Poles, Ukrainians, White Russians and Russians. Such an agreement has never yet existed between these Slav Nations. This is no attempt to construct some new special form of pan-Slavism. It is an attempt to bring a definite end to historic German banditism and pan-German imperialism by the harmonious co-operation of three free, independent democratic Slav States.

That is our project and our object.[11] Its success depends upon us all. The Germans will do all they can to ensure its failure. Fascism and Nazism will regard it as their deathblow. This fact should serve as a challenge for us all, in spite of momentary difficulties and disputes, to take advantage of this war and these immense historical events to bring about our rapprochement and the liquidation of all differences still existing between us. Hardly will there be in history another moment so propitious. If we are able to fulfil these tasks we will have done great service not to ourselves only but also to the other peace-loving Nations of Europe and the whole world.

4. My Political Discussions with Stalin and Molotov in Moscow

My political discussions with Moscow actually began during my journey from London to the Soviet Union when I was met at Habaniyah Airfield, near Bagdad, by Alexander Korneytchuk (Molotov's Deputy in the Commissariat for Foreign Affairs) who came to meet me.

We[11] left England by plane during the night of November 23rd and travelled via Gibraltar, Tripoli and Egypt. In and around Cairo I refreshed all my memories of old Egyptian culture and civilisation. I inspected the relics and excavations, visited the places of interest and thus quickly absorbed the ancient past. From Egypt we flew via Palestine, the Dead Sea, Transjordan and Iraq to Bagdad; then across Iran to Teheran. It was a beautiful trip during which I went over in my mind all that these countries had meant for the history of mankind.

In Teheran we were received with all ceremony by the young Shah of Iran. Both he and those around him (people, intelligentsia, university authorities, Army and Parliament) were anxious to repay the service I had had occasion to render to Iran at Geneva many years before in Iran's oil dispute with Great Britain.* The Shah also expressed his full satisfaction about his meeting with Stalin during the Teheran Conference. Teheran University conferred on me in the course of a special Iranian ceremony the honorary degree of Doctor.*

*In 1932. This service had evidently been forgotten when Iran nationalised its oilfields in 1951 (Tr.).

S

From Teheran we went by air to Baku and from Baku by train for nearly four days through Caucasian regions to Moscow. Our route was almost entirely through regions which the Germans had already devastated in their barbarian manner. It was a long tiring journey filled with vivid impressions and reflections and, of course, also with anticipations and preparations for the discussions in Moscow.

Alexander Korneytchuk and Ambassador Fierlinger were waiting for me at the airfield in the desert near Bagdad. We spent a whole week there because of bad winter weather over the Caucasus and Southern Russia. While waiting to continue our journey we discussed all the questions I wanted to raise in Moscow: questions about the war, peace, Germany, Hungary, especially Poland and the future Slav policy of the Soviet Union, our relations to the Russians and Ukrainians and our future joint policy with the Soviet Union. From what I was told by Korneytchuk, our good friend, a talented writer and a great Ukrainian and Soviet patriot, I judged that we would agree well together in Moscow on every point. Korneytchuk himself prepared notes about our talks for Stalin and Molotov so that when our discussions began in Moscow, both Molotov and Stalin were informed about my views on the chief problems.

My stay in Moscow began with an official visit to Kalinin and a ceremonial dinner given by Kalinin in my honour. Molotov and Stalin were present as well as the whole official political and military world together with the heads of the Politburo. On our side Ambassador Fierlinger and General Pika,* Deputy Klement Gottwald, Professor Zdeněk Nejedlý and Dr. Vrbenský, and my suite from London took part in the official receptions. It was during this dinner that I had my first conversations with Stalin[13] and Molotov. We went cursorily but objectively through all the chief problems of the war and the future peace. I saw at once that we really would agree—our views were fundamentally identical. On this occasion I also met all the important political personalities of the Soviet Union, a number of the chief soldiers and leading officials. I saw on what terms they were with one another, the main lines on which they worked together and how Soviet home and foreign affairs were conducted. This told me much about the Soviet Union itself.

In the political discussions which followed I first had two talks about all our problems with Foreign Commissar V. Molotov. With him were Korneytchuk and Lebedev[14] and with me, Ambassador Fierlinger and Smutný. Then I had two long talks with Stalin at which Molotov and

*Afterwards executed by the Communist Government of Czechoslovakia on a charge of having spied for the West while in the U.S.S.R., see p. 146 (Tr.).

Fierlinger were present. We discussed every point which needed elucidation and exchanged and co-ordinated our views in full and friendly agreement about our joint problems and our future joint policy in Czechoslovak and other European questions.

I paid many visits to factories, to military installations and institutions, to cultural and scientific institutes, libraries, theatres and cinemas. I spoke to a number of people from simple workers to technicians and managers, from simple soldiers to officers and generals, to politicians, diplomats, artists, professors, writers. Everywhere I carefully watched the life, the work, the people: men, women, children. All was focused on war, the front, victory, post-war reconstruction, and—in connection with us on our mutual co-operation and the future Slav partnership. Czechoslovakia was everywhere received with joy, with sincerity, with cordiality.

I brought back unforgettable impressions. Of all the political journeys I have undertaken in the course of my political life, I consider this one, which took place in circumstances so exceptional both for the Soviet Union and my own country, to be one of the most important for our post-war future. I think also that once more I obtained a good picture of life in the Soviet Union and was able to deepen my understanding of the nations of the Soviet Union.

Instead of going into detail about my conversations with the Moscow leaders, I shall put on documentary record here a part of the cabled report which I sent from Moscow to London to Foreign Minister Jan Masaryk and the Government about the Moscow negotiations as a whole as soon as I had finished my principal conversations:

1. The political discussions and negotiations have taken place up to this point in the utmost harmony, friendship and cordiality. The discussions were carried on chiefly with Kalinin, Stalin, Molotov and Voroshilov. Of special importance were two conversations with Stalin, two evenings in succession in the presence of Kalinin and Molotov, and two meetings with Molotov which were devoted to political negotiations about questions on our standing programme.

2. With Molotov we discussed in detail and systematically all problems of our joint policy, the post-war situation of Germany and Hungary, the question of the transfer of our German Nazis, our frontiers and our military and economic co-operation with the Soviet Union; then France, Yugoslavia, Rumania, Poland, Austria, the punishment of war criminals—especially, too, how we envisaged the end of hostilities. We spoke in detail about future Slav policy and the conferences at Moscow and Teheran. All these questions were again discussed with Stalin, especially

the problems of future Germany and Hungary, the transfer of our Germans, the Polish question, our frontiers and a number of other things. There is complete unity of views. On Saturday will be the final and conclusive conversation with Stalin.

3. I consider all our negotiations as wholly successful. It can be stated that personally I did not expect that the problems would be posed so clearly, so definitely and with such a prospect of cordial and harmonious co-operation for the future.

4. Progress here in the development of ideas since 1935 and especially since the war is great, real and definite. To imagine that the present outlook towards the Internationale, religion, *co-operation with the West*, Slav policy, etc. is merely tactical would be a fundamental error. The growth of a new Soviet Empire, a decentralised one, with a firm place for the other Soviet Nations in the spirit of a new popular democracy, is undeniably and definitely on the march. A new Soviet Union will come out of the war. Economically and socially it will retain the Soviet system in its entirety but will be quite new politically. It will stand at the head of the Slavs and will exact for itself and therewith for them, too, an entirely new position in the world. The consciousness of victory here is universal. And there is an unalterable determination to be merciless in settling accounts with Germany. For us there is general sympathy. Observers here say that our reception was first-rate and our political position is firm. The treaty is regarded here as the beginning of a new and politically very important phase in our mutual relations—eventually even as a prototype for all Slavs.

5. I handed to the Soviet Government our memoranda on the (minority) transfers, on economic co-operation, on military co-operation and on our questions regarding the cease-fire. These matters will be further discussed here by our Ambassador and our soldiers. In general it can be said that our proposals and our demands will be supported as by an ally. Our frontier problems are understood and it can be expected that Moscow will fully support us in this respect as our ally.

6. I think it can be regarded as certain that all treaties and agreements not only with us but also with the British and with America will be kept. Fulfilment of the promises made to the Anglo-Saxons in Moscow and Teheran will be regarded here as a matter about which there can be no doubt. Furthermore, the Soviet Union already feels itself to be an equal in the world, is proud of its rôle and position and will not want to lose it again.

7. Throughout our discussions there was not a single occasion on which our partners did not stress that whatever question might arise they are not

concerned with our internal affairs and that they would not interfere in them.

8. I have had long discussions with our Communist deputies and after a detailed exchange of views on the past, present and future of the Republic, *there is general agreement between us about what should be done in the immediate future, at the time of transition at home after the fall of Germany and about the procedure for establishing a single national front at home immediately after the revolution.* Discussions about these questions are still continuing.

Especially important were the talks with Marshal Stalin and officials of the Commissariat for War about our Army on Soviet territory, its future, its extension and its reorganisation, and also about supplying us when Germany fell with arms and equipment for the speedy formation of our new Army at home and about the future military co-operation between our two States after the war ended. All the measures agreed upon at that time, especially about our Army on Soviet territory, were afterwards gradually carried out while the war was in progress.

We also discussed quite frankly—with Stalin at the Kremlin in the presence of Molotov—the eventuality of the Red Army entering our territory. I expressed the wish that we should agree clearly on these matters in good time. I expected—though the Soviet armies were at that time only in Rostov and in front of Kiev—that they would soon enter Polish territory, that they would advance westwards and also enter our own country. I therefore asked that, when this happened, our own military units should always enter our territory with the Red Army; *that the occupation of our territory should always be left to us provided our numbers were sufficient, that our internal order should be respected and that our territory should be progressively handed over to our own civil administration.*

Marshal Stalin unhesitatingly accepted this view and confirmed it to me. He declared that the Soviet Union had no intention of proceeding otherwise in our regard, that the measures concerning our military units would be prepared and that at the proper time all military and political preparations and steps to put them into operation could be arranged with our Government and with our Military Mission in Moscow. As I shall show, this more detailed agreement was in fact concluded later. It was signed in London on May 8th, 1944, at our request and on our proposition as an amendment to our treaty with Moscow.

The question of Poland was discussed several times in Moscow following the full discussions I had already had on this subject with Korneytchuk during our journey to Moscow.

The most detailed discussion took place during our joint official visit to the 'Great Theatre' in the presence of Stalin, Kalinin, Molotov, Voroshilov, Korneytchuk, Fierlinger and Smutný. There was a lovely performance of *Snegurotchka* and in the long intervals and after the end of the performance, deep into the night we discussed the Polish problems in a salon behind the Government box. The Soviet politicians wanted to know my opinion about the state of the London Poles, about the British and American attitude, on whether any agreement with the London Poles was possible, etc.

I told them sincerely what I knew and what I believed. But I stressed two points, firstly that we Czechoslovaks sincerely hoped that an agreement between Moscow and Warsaw would in any case be brought about. It was we in Czechoslovakia who were the first to suffer from any quarrels between them—this had been the case for the whole twenty years after the first World War and it had contributed to Munich—which was why I insisted upon the 'Polish clause' in our treaty. Secondly, that I would always believe agreement was possible with the present Polish Government in London—at least with some of its leading representatives even if with others this seemed quite hopeless. Those who were followers of Pilsudski —and among the London Poles they had a decisive majority—would never come to an agreement with Moscow. But Prime Minister Mikolajczyk and some others were in my opinion sincere democrats and were perhaps convinced that agreement and co-operation with Moscow after the war were necessary for Poland. I therefore urged that Moscow should try once more.

And I again repeated to them, as I had already done to Korneytchuk during our journey to Moscow, my last talk with Mikolajczyk at Aston Abbotts before I left for Moscow. Mikolajczyk knew that I was going to Moscow and had himself asked to see me to explain his attitude as Polish Premier in regard to the Polish-Soviet dispute. He no longer advocated the views which General Sikorski had advocated. He recognised that the Poles would have to come to an agreement with the Soviet Union and that they would have to make great concessions in the matter of frontiers. He was only interested in keeping Lwow and a part of Eastern Galicia and in the non-interference of the Soviet Union in Polish internal affairs. He wanted to do all he could to renew relations with the Soviet Union and he was ready to go again to Moscow. He authorised me to inform official circles in Moscow accordingly.

I and my two collaborators who were present—Fierlinger and Smutný —were favourably impressed about this conversation with our hosts at the Great Theatre. In general the views of the Soviets were to the point, calm and sincere. As Stalin expressed it, they really wanted an independent and strong Poland. But they did not forget the twenty years of Polish policy after the first World War and they did not want this repeated. It seemed to me that my exposé had interested and, perhaps, influenced them. I advocated that Moscow should agree to the eventual renewal of diplomatic relations with the Polish Government in London which had been interrupted after the Katyn incident*; that Moscow should explain clearly its whole policy towards Poland, Germany and ourselves; that Moscow should give the Poles the same assurances as it had to us—that it would not interfere in Polish internal affairs and that it should make another sincere attempt to reach an agreement.

Before we left the theatre, Stalin summed up the specific points in our conversation and clearly formulated the Soviet attitude to me in regard to Poland. When I asked whether I could pass this information to Mikolajczyk as the official view of Moscow, he agreed.

Perhaps it will be best if I end my account of my Moscow conversations about Poland with a brief postcript. When I was on my way back from Moscow, I received at Cairo, and again at Algiers, an invitation from Churchill to visit Marrakesh where the British Prime Minister was staying to recuperate after his recent rather grave illness. He wanted to know the results of my visit to Moscow and he was especially interested in the Polish question, telling me that agreement had to be reached at the earliest possible moment if Allied policy as a whole was not to suffer and if above all the Poles themselves were to avoid the worst consequences. He also wanted to discuss with me the question of Yugoslavia where the crisis had reached its climax.† My visit to Churchill at Marrakesh took place on January 4th and 5th, 1944.

I told him about my negotiations and impressions and about my views on Polish-Soviet relations. His reaction was very strong and decided. He felt that the Poles should accept what I was bringing Mikolajczyk from Moscow; that when I reached London I should first tell Eden and then

*This concerned the discovery, while the Germans occupied the area, of the mass graves of a number of Polish soldiers. According to the Polish Government in London, the dead soldiers had been missing since the Soviet Government took over this part of Poland after the country had been partitioned between Germany and the U.S.S.R. in October, 1939. According to the Soviet Government, the men had been murdered by the Germans and it broke off diplomatic relations with the Polish Government in London when the latter refused to accept this explanation. A proposal that the Red Cross should investigate the matter was rejected by the Soviet Government (Tr.).

†As between Marshal Tito and the supporters of the exiled Government in London under King Peter (Tr.).

Mikolajczyk, and that then in conjunction with Eden I should urge the Poles as their friend to decide at once to negotiate with Moscow and to accept Stalin's offer.

I arrived in London on January 6th, 1944. On January 8th in the presence of Jan Masaryk I discussed the whole matter with Eden who was of the same opinion as Churchill and I invited Mikolajczyk to come to Aston Abbotts on January 10th. There I summarised my impressions and information from Moscow and the Soviet attitude to Polish matters as formulated to me by Stalin as follows:

(a) Moscow did not exclude negotiations with the new Polish Government in London and would be ready to establish diplomatic relations with it at once. But the present Polish Government would have to be reconstructed and old points at issue (Katyn, systematic hostile propaganda against the Soviet Union, etc.) would have to be dropped. Moscow was willing to negotiate with Mikolajczyk if he cared to form a new Government, from which unsuitable elements were excluded, and if he would negotiate with Moscow in this spirit.

(b) Moscow could not give way about the Curzon Line but was ready to consent to territorial compensations for Poland at the expense of Germany in full agreement with Poland, Great Britain and America— Moscow would accept any western line upon which they agreed even if it were the Oder line.

(c) The Eastern frontier of Poland could be moved from the line on which the Soviet Union had agreed with Germany in 1939, to a 'corrected' Curzon Line—that is to say Lomza, Bialystok and Przemysl would evidently fall to Poland.

(d) The Soviet-Czechoslovak Treaty was the basis for both countries of their eventual agreement with Poland and also of any future joint guarantee for Poland against Germany. Both countries would loyally work for the conclusion of a tripartite treaty.

(e) The Soviet Union had no thought either of procuring a revolution in Germany or of siding with Germany against the other Allies. In this matter, it would go forward jointly with Great Britain and America, and, of course, also with Czechoslovakia and Poland, and was ready to accept the policy of the territorial weakening of Germany.

(f) The Soviet Union would not interfere in Polish internal affairs and there would be no Bolshevisation and no Sovietisation.

I felt at the time that my remarks had made a strong impression on Mikolajczyk. It seemed to me that till then no one had been so outspoken to the Poles about these matters. On the same occasion I told Mikolajczyk what had been said about our affairs in Moscow and to what extent I considered Soviet policy towards us to have definitely crystallised:

(*a*) Our pre-Munich frontiers—corrected perhaps in some small details —were considered a matter of course in Moscow.*

(*b*) Czechoslovakia would be a neighbour of the Soviet Union.

(*c*) We would pursue a uniform or similar policy towards Germany.

(*d*) The proposal to transfer our Germans had been accepted by Moscow.

(*e*) We would also pursue a uniform or similar line of policy towards Hungary.

(*f*) The Soviet Government had promised me help in the occupation of our territory and the equipment of our Army.

This conversation with Mikolajczyk was very friendly and frank. Mikolajczyk answered quite openly that he feared he would not be able to persuade the Poles to accept the new Polish-Soviet Eastern frontier. If Lwow at least could be saved for Poland! He said he knew the Poles. Even if they made matters still worse for Poland, nobody perhaps could get them to yield voluntarily about the Curzon Line. If only it were possible to shift the Polish-Soviet frontier line further to the East and to combine this with an exchange of populations!

He said that nevertheless he would consider all I had told him and would discuss it with his friends. He personally had a fairly strong position politically. Four parties were wholly with him, in England and at home. *Everything I had told him would be regarded as satisfactory and as an acceptable basis for agreement except the question of the Eastern frontier—as I had put it to him. This difficulty could probably not be overcome.* The growth of a desire among the Poles for agreement with the Soviet Union was already quite considerable, there was also at present more confidence in the Soviet Union and it was especially recognised *that in the interest of Poland itself an agreement should be concluded as soon as possible.* He himself was decidedly in favour of an agreement.

I told him that I had seen Churchill at Marrakesh, that he had urged me to speak to Mikolajczyk and tell him that Churchill thought this was the last chance for an agreement. I had therefore delivered this message and added that Churchill thought the Poles should accept the offer I had brought them. He had asked that Mikolajczyk should perhaps visit Churchill as soon as possible so that they could agree on the next step.

*This involved Poland's giving up Tešin and other places which it occupied at the time of Munich (Tr.).

Finally, Mikolajczyk asked me whether I considered the Soviet Union to be full of vigour or exhausted and whether I thought that it would keep up its offensive. I assured him that the offensive would continue and that to count on the exhaustion of the Soviet Union would be a most unwarrantable assumption. He told me that he thought so too. He rejected the whole well-known ideology of some Polish officers concerning the present-day Soviet Union and Poland and he was working to ensure that Polish feudalism should fall utterly. He added that in Poland itself feudalism had in reality fallen already and social and economic radicalism were much more advanced in Poland than in the emigration. The new Poland would also be quite different, completely changed in fact from the Poland of Pilsudski and Beck.

I emphasised again that I did not want to interfere in Polish affairs and that I had simply delivered my report as I had promised him I would do before I left for Moscow. I was not intervening between them and the Soviet Union—they would have to find a solution themselves. I was only giving information about what I had seen and heard and I was only trying to contribute to a rapprochement. *But I was not acting as a mediator* and I repeated that I did not want to interfere in their affairs and any agreement would have to be their own work and only theirs.[15]

I had the impression that Mikolajczyk was convinced of the necessity for immediate negotiations. But it was clear to me that he did not believe he would be able to overcome the objections of the London emigrants and force them to negotiate.

5. *Discussions in Moscow with our Political Emigrants about the Revolution at Home*

The account of my visit to Moscow in December, 1943, must include a report of my negotiations with our Communists who were living at Moscow.

I was in Moscow for two weeks and the second week was dedicated to conversations and discussions with the Czechoslovak political elements there. Chief among them were: Klement Gottwald, Jan Šverma, Václav Kopecký, Professor Zdeněk Nejedlý, Rudolf Slánský, Dr. Bedřich Vrbenský and some others. We met four times in the house which had been placed by the Soviet Government at my disposal for the period of my stay in Moscow. The Moscow group was represented at these talks, which were very friendly, by Deputies Gottwald, Rudolf Slánský, Jan Šverma and Václav Kopecký.

My plan for the discussions with our Moscow emigrants involved describing to them with complete frankness our conditions in the West, telling them what political, diplomatic and military difficulties and successes we had had there, to what extent we had been in contact with the people at home during the war and what our plans were for the future. Similarly I wanted to know in detail what were the views and plans of those in the East.

All our conversations took place on these lines.

(*a*) In particular, I informed our Moscow politicians in detail about the state of our activity, about the political attitude of our western emigrants and of course about the whole situation of our Government;

(*b*) I was ready to answer all their questions arising out of this statement, to clear up any misunderstandings there might have been between London and Moscow and to invite the Moscow emigrants to take a direct share in our work by sending two delegates to our London Government;

(*c*) I wanted to discuss thoroughly what would happen at home, what questions would arise there in the moment of the revolution and to settle a uniform procedure for the final anti-German revolution at home and for our internal policy during the first phase after our Republic had been liberated.

In my accounts of the situation of our Government and of the emigration in the West, I stressed all the circumstances and difficulties with which we had to contend in Paris, London and in America immediately after Munich. I explained the steps we had taken during the negotiations for the recognition of the Government, our difficulties in organising the Army, our contact with our people at home, with Dr. Hácha and the Protectorate Government and our view of conditions at home in general both in the Czech provinces and Slovakia. Finally I explained how the competent authorities in Great Britain and America saw the future course of military and political events—here I mentioned my visit to the United States—and what conclusions I drew for *our* policy and what the full result of the allied war effort would be *from our standpoint.*

In the second part of my explanation I referred to certain differences in procedure as between London and Moscow, our more moderate line in London and the great radicalism of the Moscow group in estimating conditions at home as well as general differences in tactics as between London and Moscow—especially differences in the radio propaganda to our people at home. I did not consider these differences as a grave deficiency or mistake. I simply regarded them as natural—an inevitable result of the differences of environment in West and East. I also explained the way our various groups and political parties co-operated in London and I stressed the fundamental accord and general harmony between Communists and non-Communists in the work of our Western emigration.

I ended with a request that those in Moscow should co-operate directly with us in the London Government and should instruct their London comrades accordingly. Before I left London I had secured the approval of the Government and the Czechoslovak emigration for this step—and also the approval of the British Government which I had informed of my intention. And I suggested that all conceivable difficulties had already been disposed of so that there were now no obstacles from the London end.

Those living in Moscow had a number of questions to put regarding my exposé. This served to clear the ground and to remove obscurities and some misunderstandings. The most important discussion arose about the third point : future developments at home, how the revolution was to be carried out especially against the Germans and what our internal policy was to be after liberation. Klement Gottwald thereupon opened the discussion with a long discourse depicting in detail the standpoint of our people in Moscow.*

He emphasised that they held that this war could not end in the same way as the war of 1914-1918. We would have to fight, we would have to carry out a real revolution together with all our people against the Germans as well as against our war criminals at home. I replied that in general we did not greatly disagree with this conception of the end of the war. It was a matter of course that, after what had happened in our country, this war could only end in such a way. And we in London were already making our preparations in this sense. In all our contacts with our country we had this object in view. In addition I had been speaking on these lines publicly for a long time already in my broadcasts from London and I had been sending confidential reports to our country about this subject for many years. So we all were agreed on this main point.

Gottwald then explained his idea of the procedure to be followed in preparing for this revolution. He stressed the necessity of forming national committees which would have to be used not only for the organisation of revolutionary cells for the insurrection itself but also as the basis for the whole revolutionary civil administration. I did not oppose this conception. I explained that it was essential to think it well over and to formulate it on correct lines, that a similar peace-time administration had existed in Great

*i.e. Of the Soviet Government. (Tr.).

Britain since long before the war,* that a democratic administrative organisation of this type had already been discussed in our country in 1848 and again in 1918. The introduction of these ideas after the last war, however, had been prevented chiefly by the existence of the minorities: the Germans and Magyars.

We finished these discussions in agreement that if the question of National Committees were well considered and put before the public in the right way, there would be no rooted objections in our country. My final comment was that the most important consideration would be *to prevent legal and administrative chaos and to replace the previous legal order quickly by a new post-revolutionary legal order.*

Deputy Gottwald next asked what the party structure in our country would be after the revolution. He took it for granted that there would be a great revolutionary shift to the Left, a clear Socialist majority and an overwhelming defeat of our former pre-war Right-wing bloc (Agrarians, National Democrats and Traders). Our Moscow Communists also appeared to regard co-operation of the three Socialist parties with the Šrámek Party as acceptable. In December, 1943, our Communists did not commit themselves definitely on the future existence of the Agrarian Party. All of us without exception regarded the ruthless liquidation of all Fascism as a matter of course.

I put the question of the possibility of merging all Socialist workers' parties; but this matter was left in the air. When I asked whether the Communists would aim at a merger of all the Socialist Parties and would eventually renounce the independence of their own Party, they replied that at that date—December, 1943—they could not yet answer such a question. I drew the conclusion that the Communists would certainly not renounce their independence and I therefore inferred that the Social

*The National Committees (Národní Výbory) as originally conceived and actually introduced into Czechoslovakia after the war were elected in every commune, town and Province on a system of proportional representation. After the Communist coup d'état in February, 1948, they were remodelled and given wide judicial and administrative powers to enable them to enforce Communist economic, social and political regulations entrusted to them by the Government. The members, though 'elected' were first nominated by the Communist Party and no opposition candidates were allowed to stand. During the war, of course, the National Committees were also nominated and though other political parties were represented, the Communists, through their better organisation, often secured an undue proportion of the executive posts. In the borderland, this state of affairs tended to persist after the war, but elsewhere the other parties were able to establish a proper balance and to keep it until the *coup d'état.* (Tr.).

Democratic Party would also remain.* During this discussion the question of the *National Front* was mentioned for the first time. It was declared to be necessary that the Government Parties should form a united national front after liberation, that they should jointly prepare a single post-revolution programme and that they should jointly undertake to fulfil it. I also agreed to the plan for the National Front on this occasion.

Then came the question of elections. I advocated the view that they should be prepared and held within six months after the end of the war. To this there were no objections. Then it was asked how the first Government would be formed—in practice, this meant *who* would be Prime Minister. Klement Gottwald demanded that the first Prime Minister should be from the Left as it could be taken for granted that after the revolution there would be a shift to the Left. After the elections this question would solve itself: it would be the representative of that Party of the Left which emerged strongest from the elections who would become Prime Minister. To this I had no objections. Besides these questions, we touched a number of others, most of them only tentatively: the question of the further development of gymnastic organisations,† the question of punishing war criminals and subversive elements acting against the patriotic anti-German home front, various financial questions, etc.

Finally we arrived at matters in regard to which unity of views between us was not so easy or complete. Above all our Moscow friends doubted whether we in London—and I personally—had not gone farther than we should have done in our contacts with the home country, with Dr. Hácha and the Protectorate Government. As I at once realised, they were asking themselves, and cross-examining me, about whether we had not thus assumed some obligations for the future. I tried to convince them that our behaviour had been correct, that we retained our full liberty of action, that we had no secret obligations to anyone—in accordance with the general principle upon which I had acted in every question throughout the war. *But I was not quite sure whether I had fully succeeded.* It seemed to me that doubts and suspicion remained.‡

---

*A few months later, the Communists absorbed the much larger Social Democratic Party of Slovakia, thus clearly showing that a 'merger' was only acceptable from the Communist standpoint if it left their own independence unimpaired. (Tr.).

†In Czechoslovakia, gymnastic organisations were patriotic and political bodies too (Tr.).

‡The Communists in exile boasted later of the underground organisation they themselves had built up in Czechoslovakia during the war and it was evident that they wanted as far as possible to have the field clear for themselves. (Tr.).

Various questions and objections arose over my request that the Communists should now enter the London Government. They did not put themselves on record as opposing the London Government and gave general approval to what their Communist friends were doing in the London State Council but they hinted that if they were to become members of the London Government at once, this Government would have to undergo *total* reconstruction. They therefore put the direct question: was the situation in London such that I desired or could proceed with a reconstruction of this kind? They clearly did not believe that it was. I confirmed their doubts. We then agreed that in these circumstances they would not enter the Government, that their Communist friends in London would continue to co-operate in the State Council and would also support the Government politically as before but that the question of their direct participation in the Government itself would be left over for future consideration.

Lastly, came the questions about which there was a direct conflict of views which still remained even after our discussions. The men in Moscow objected to what I had done in 1938 in two respects: firstly, they said I should not have resigned the Presidency, and secondly, that we should not have 'capitulated' but should have gone to war in any circumstances.

I explained in detail all the reasons for my actions at that time: the situation into which we had been brought by Great Britain and France, the line the Soviet Union had chosen to take, the open hostile behaviour of Poland in agreement with the Hungarians, the direct threat to Czechoslovakia, confirmed in writing, from Great Britain and France concerning their attitude if we went to war in spite of their warning. I also explained what our internal position had been at that time and the attitude of the parties comprising the Government coalition: the preparations for open treason by some elements in the homeland and my serious doubts about the attitude of some of our Agrarians, our Ludáks* and our Germans as a whole—finally some of our military weaknesses such as lack of fortifications on our Austrian frontier, infiltration or penetration by not entirely reliable Germans into the rank and file and Staff of our Army, etc., etc.

Above all: the inevitable and forseeable international complications for the Soviet Union[16] as well as ourselves if we had gone to war against the express wish of Great Britain and France!

I ended by declaring that I had done my utmost that we should be able to fight: we had mobilised twice, we had put nearly the whole Nation on

*Members of the Ludová Strana (People's Party)—an extreme Right-Wing Separatist Party in Slovakia formed by Father Hlinka. (Tr.).

a war footing and in September, 1938, we were ready up to the last moment to plunge into war . . . Could more have been done on our side ?
. . . 'In the conditions which ultimately developed I finally came to the conclusion, according to my conscience and my common sense, that there was no other solution or way out than the solution for which I decided. Of all possible evils, it was the least bad and only by adopting this course did we have the possibility to prepare morally and materially for the event (i.e. the war) with which I had to reckon already in 1938 as a possibility.'

After thus concluding my reasons for acting as I did, I added:

'Besides, what is happening today has fully justified my point of view. You will see that our Nation will hold out better compared with other nations, that it will continue its anti-German resistance and that it will survive the war better than anybody could have imagined—and with comparatively speaking smaller losses.'

Our Moscow politicians disputed my views very hotly and stressed especially that no such conclusions could be drawn before the end of the war. Only when Germany collapsed would we see what havoc the Germans had caused our people in property as well as in lives ! 'And then'— added Gottwald—'only consider what evil *moral* consequences Munich has had for our people. It made even March 15th possible ! And what else might have happened to Czechoslovakia ! It is only by accident that all these catastrophes have not yet fallen on us. That they have not done so, *is no thanks to us !* But above all: we must still wait to see what the final outcome will be ! We will have to wait and see !'

I agreed with Deputy Gottwald that in 1943, when the war was raging in all its fury, one could not assume that its end would be advantageous to us. It was therefore necessary to weigh the events to see whether from the end of 1943 they turned out as advantageously for us in comparison with others as I expected and as they had proved till then. Nor did I underestimate in the slightest the moral influence of what had happened in September, 1938, and in March, 1939, and I admitted also that I took the effect of this on the spirit of the Nation into my calculations.

With regard to his second point—what might have happened in our country and his assertion that we could not claim credit for its not having happened—*I retorted by asking the much more justifiable question : what would have happened if in 1938 in our dreadful plight and isolated from nearly all the world we had gone to war !* And I added that indeed *I claimed the merit of having foreseen in 1938 that certain things would happen and that other things would not*—as can be clearly seen from some of my speeches as well as from some of my actions at that period. Because to *pursue the correct policy means also to forecast events correctly—gouverner c'est prévoir !*   And that is what had happened in our case !

In December, 1943, *each of us held firmly to his own opinion* in these disputed questions. We left the decision *partly to the march of events, partly to the judgment of history* in so far as this was, will and can be a matter of impartial history.

In general, even in these discussions of domestic affairs we also did a great piece of work—good and successful work. On the whole, I was satisfied. I realised at once that in spite of some very important differences it would be possible for our national camp to reach agreement at critical moments about the fundamental problems of our post-war policy. And above all, I did not rule out *the possibility of avoiding civil war at home.*

When I left Moscow, Ambassador Fierlinger accompanied me to Teheran. He told me that our Moscow politicians had agreed that our conferences had taken a satisfactory course and that results had been reached which they themselves had not expected.

So I was full of hope that what happened a year later to the Poles and Yugoslavs would not happen to our movement.

6. *The Soviet Revolution and the Second World War*

I have already mentioned that at the end of 1943 my journey and our treaty were a political event of importance in the framework of the second World War and in a certain sense even a sensation. Though the Soviet Union had already been winning immense military victories for nearly a year, the current opinion among the Allies about the Soviet Union was still reserved. Indeed with many of its opponents its great and unexpected victories over Germany even renewed and strengthened their former apprehensions which were used by German propaganda in an unprecedented—*and successful*—manner.

Our treaty—the first of this kind during the war—made at least a partial breach in this wall between the Soviet Union and the Western world which regarded our action as a kind of experiment—a 'test case' which would show what the Soviet Union intended to do with its smaller neighbours after the war. At first there were rather vehement polemics. Conservative circles in England and America and to some extent elsewhere, Catholics all over the world, the Poles and, of course, the Germans and Hungarians too pounced upon us. Our policy passed through a somewhat difficult phase and it was necessary to explain, react, make statements and to counter-attack on all sides. It was not easy but in the end we convinced all people of goodwill, especially when it was proved, very

T

soon, that the reverse policy adopted by the Poles led first to great complications among the Allies themselves and soon afterwards to the great
discomfiture of the Poles ending with the collapse of the whole Polish war
emigration movement in the West.

The problem was always one and the same. The Soviet revolution was
a great turning point in Liberal society, which in its main characteristics
still continued in the rest of the world though in far more advanced forms
than in old Russia. The prejudices against the new revolutionary regime in
the Soviet Union and, from a purely Western point of view, the understandable objections to the Soviet system were not removed by the second
World War. The fear of social revolution after a new war which had led
the Western world to 'appeasement' in 1937–1938 was in some places
actually strengthened by the events of the war and by the Soviet victories.
And German propaganda knew very well how to use this fear even if
'à la longue' its extremely unintelligent procedure in this regard made it
appear ridiculous in the eyes of all sensible people. There remained, of
course, the fundamental question: *what would be the relationship between
West and East when the war ended ? And what influence would this have on us ?*
Naturally, for us, what happened to Germany would always be decisive in
this matter because we are not merely between the West and the East.
Above all we must remain neighbours of the Soviet Union and Germany.

In our policy towards the Soviet Union—though the larger public of
the Allies only took notice of it a whole year after the signing of the Anglo-
Soviet Pact—we were still the only pioneers of *systematic and definite co-
operation between Western* and Eastern Europe and we had to bear all the
unpleasant consequences of this fact. It was not always easy. And so after
my return from Moscow our whole policy, our propaganda, our Minister
for Foreign Affairs, Masaryk, and Minister Ripka, who were in charge of
our information service, were for a number of months occupied in Great
Britain and America chiefly with efforts to neutralise and overcome these
difficulties. It must be confessed that a certain mutual distrust never completely vanished. It was also clear *to us* that post-war co-operation would
depend on the reasonableness of *both* sides. In this too we had no illusions.

I also devoted myself to this task as I emphasised what I had seen in the
Soviet Union and I spoke about the development of the Soviet Union in
and after the war to people in Great Britain and in the United States. I
stressed that many things which were being described as Soviet achievements at the end of 1943, I had already seen on my journey to Moscow in
1935. This was why I had marched with the Soviet Union against Nazism
until 1938 and why I had believed in the Soviet Union in the second

World War and had never doubted its strength. Even if I had expected the war to take a different course in some details, especially in the West, and had accordingly decided in favour of a different political plan, I was convinced that the Soviet Union would ultimately be on the winning side. On this particular point I had never hesitated and had guided our liberation struggle in the second World War from this standpoint. My second journey to Moscow had confirmed the facts and the truth to me to an extent which in some directions had perhaps even exceeded my expectations.

The development of the Soviet Union and the effects of this development since 1935 made that country quickly accommodate itself to the new conditions of internal and international life which under the influence of the war and of wartime requirements proceeded at a much quicker pace than could have been expected. After my return from Moscow I described the situation of the Soviet Union in the following summary written in 1943 :

(a) The Soviet revolution can be called a victorious revolution. The Soviet regime is solid and even if it continues to develop as every regime does, it is a regime which has definitely won its fight against Old Russia and is now establishing itself. It has won in the domestic sphere because it did not collapse even in the most cruel war which has ever been waged by any State against any country. It has won internationally because it has definitely established its new international position by its great prowess and successes. It has become the recognised and militarily powerful ally of the greatest empires of the world after defeating attempts to isolate it and it is preparing to play its great rôle in the world together with its Allies and other countries.

(b) It is conscious and proud of its victory in the war and proud of the part it has played and will continue to play till the end of the war in the struggle for the freedom of Europe and for the saving of democracy from Nazism. It regards itself as an equal of the other Great World Powers, claims recognition of this equality from the others and wants to maintain this equality, this mutual esteem and co-operation with the others in the future.

In organising its war effort it has equalled the ablest and has surpassed them in some respects. The Red Army was the first to defeat the German army machine on the land.* It has overcome all the difficulties of the notorious communications problem of the Soviet Union which hitherto have nearly always been insurmountable in time of war. It has overcome

*Dr. Beneš has overlooked Alamein which preceded the Soviet Union's first victory—at Stalingrad (Tr.).

all the dangerous difficulties in supplies of all kinds and is already out of all danger in this field. The Soviet war industry has worked almost faultlessly and with full success.

(c) Some changes in the Soviet Union which astonished the world recently were the natural outcome partly of the war, partly of developments already accomplished, partly of the changes in its whole position in the world. The dissolution of the Communist International, the new attitude to the Orthodox Church and to religion in general, the incredibly alive and deep cultural, artistic and literary life at Moscow and in other centres of the Soviet Union even during the war (in spite of its being State-directed), its profound Soviet patriotism and new national feeling, its favourable consideration of the so-called Slav policy—that is to say the understanding that German imperialism, directed in the first instance against the Slavonic nations, must be destroyed now, at once and for all time and that the Slavonic nations must be liberated and defended in future against a new German imperialist expansionism[18]—*all this was not a mere game, not mere tactics and not merely the opportunist use of tactics which might perhaps be discarded again after the war.*

Such was the new internal and international situation of a State which had emerged from isolation, fought its way through to the recognition of the new position in the world which belonged to it and was conscious not only of its new strength and power but also of its new international responsibility for Europe and the world and their peace. This was the natural and logical evolution of a great world State the international position of which had entirely changed through the final victory of its revolution which had once been so frowned upon. It had thereby acquired new tasks, new duties and new aims, no longer revolutionary and Soviet ones only. It simply began to use new ways, new methods and new political means which secured for it this new position in the world. *I do not think that this development has already wholly ended today.**

Some people saw in this new policy merely a return to the way other States normally acted. Others declared that the change was in those who had formerly opposed the Soviet Union. They therefore regarded the new attitude of the Soviet Union to this question or that as quite natural. I myself saw it as the natural attitude and development of victorious revolution progressing simply according to its laws—a development which was sociologically quite comprehensible. I had been convinced of this before and I believed it to be implicit in the very substance of Soviet doctrine. Therefore, from 1922 onwards, and really from the end of the first world

*1947 (Tr.).

war, I had tried to bring about a rapprochement and gradual settlement between Europe and the Soviet Union. Today I still think, perhaps more strongly than formerly, that if this had been understood in time on both sides there might not have been a second World War. *Moreover, the Soviet Union itself had substantially changed from the time when it first came into being* and it would be forced to go on changing in future because the main question for the Soviet Union, too, would be: how to keep its new world position permanently? It naturally demands understanding and tolerance from those who criticise its régime and methods. *But it is equally natural that in its own criticisms of the other regimes and their methods it must show the same understanding and tolerance. Full and definite recognition and respect for the principle that every independent State may go the way which suits it best are the necessary pre-requisites for all peaceful co-operation in the world. Otherwise the whole course of events will lead to another war and to a much more dreadful war than its predecessor.* Do we want this or not?

(*d*) The Soviet Union and the Soviet people were great not only because of the historically important results they had been able to achieve for themselves and the rest of the world in the course of their great national Patriotic War and in their national revolution as a whole, but above all on account of what they suffered in this dreadful war.* There is perhaps no Nation which could have borne its sufferings as the Soviet Union did. Its losses in men and property have been without doubt the greatest among the warring Nations.

On my journey I passed a great number of ruins of Soviet towns and villages, destroyed houses, demolished hamlets, railway lines and stations, bridges and roads. I passed endless dumps of destroyed German tanks, motor-cars, planes, railway-wagons and of weapons of all kinds. One beautiful bright night I went through Stalingrad and saw the incredible destruction wrought by the Germans: demolished houses of which only the four main walls were left pointing to heaven like dreadful and warning fingers and appearing even more sinister at night than such ruins do by day. The chairman of the town soviet told me in detail how, not far away near the Volga River, he had buried in one single grave thousands of Germans who had been killed and deservedly punished by the Red Army in a pitiful condition of incredible demoralisation. He had had them carried there on lorries like shot deer to be deposited like logs by thousands and tens of thousands in huge, deep pits.

*Dr. Beneš here uses the words 'národní revoluce' instead of 'Sovětská revoluce' and I therefore assume that he was referring to the great war-time upheaval in the U.S.S.R. and not to the Revolution of 1917 (Tr.).

Young heroes of Stalingrad told me incredible details of the defence of their town, of the sufferings of the whole population without distinction, of the unprecedented bestialities which the German soldiers committed against women and children before their merited fate overtook them for ever, of the desperate runnings to and fro and the cries for help of hundreds and thousands of children and old people in the burning streets during the hellish bombardment by German planes up to the moment when the Red Army broke and annihilated the attackers and when in that very town it smashed for ever the wretched and frantic dreams of German Nazism and of the Berchtesgaden Corporal.

And in Moscow I saw proofs in realistic films of the devastations in the Ukraine, on the Dnieper, at Kharkov, at Kiev: everywhere those unheard-of bestialities, masses of killed civilians, old men, women and children, in nearly every liberated town cultural memorials and buildings smashed insanely, uselessly and without military necessity, churches and monasteries destroyed, libraries, universities, hospitals, simple but remembered houses, without respect, without object, without necessity. I almost ceased to believe that the German Army was still composed of human beings. All these things could not be forgotten and for all of them there had to be a reckoning!

These sufferings brought the Soviet Union to its later, and present, realistic concept of post-war policy—to its decision to end all such things, to come to a sincere agreement with the Anglo-Saxons and with everybody who really wanted an agreement and to construct together with us all a new, more just Europe, a new world and a new peace.

I left Moscow with my collaborators on December 23rd, 1943, with feelings of extreme respect and gratitude to the whole Soviet people, to their Army and their leaders. Grateful as I was to the British and Americans for all they had done for us in this war, I was not less grateful to the Soviet Union both for its deeds of prowess in the war and the really friendly and cordial reception given us in Moscow and all over the country; for the favours and recognition which the Soviet Union bestowed with so much sincerity on our soldiers who fought on its front.* And I wished that what I saw and went through at that time—a time which was decisive for the whole future course of the war—might be viewed in the same spirit by our other Allies and friends and that they should orientate their future policy on this basis—for real post-war and peace-time co-operation between the West and the East. *It was, of course, clear to me that even after the war the Soviet Union must continue permanently in the lines of policy on which it had*

*Dr. Beneš was not allowed to visit the front himself (Tr.).

embarked so decidedly during the war and with so much statesmanship and which it was prosecuting so unreservedly. At this point, during my journey back to London, my thoughts continually came back to the question: Are we on the right path or not? Will what I pondered so deeply during all my years in London and what I wrote about in detail in my book *Democracy Today and Tomorrow* really come to pass, namely, a settlement between West and East—a settlement, moreover, which in the future and, above all, in our* own interest, remains *our great political task* for the future?

After my return from Moscow the Western world was intently watching how our relations would develop. Many predicted '*grave disappointments*' in our experience of the part played by the Soviet Union. Many declared in asides and also publicly, that 'Beneš had been in too much of a hurry'. German propaganda, of course, pelted us with fire and brimstone, explained to our people at home that I had sold the country to Stalin and that I had betrayed the Nation again. They founded an anti-Bolshevist league and rounded up the masses of our people with whips and revolvers to take part in demonstrations against Bolshevism into the hands of which I had allegedly sold myself.

But the reports we ourselves received in London were to the effect *that though the majority of our people were not Communists they fully understood and approved our attitude, my journey and the treaty. In short, that they understood the problems which would confront European policy after the war.* They understood that our Government abroad was taking the right course in view of what had happened in 1938 and 1939 and the fact that we would be neighbours of Russia after the war and the Nation at home fully approved the policy of timely agreement with Russia.

7. Czechoslovakia at the Crossroads between West and East .

These reflections of mine about what would happen after the war and my questions whether the policy I had hitherto defended and advocated so vigorously throughout the war would be fulfilled, namely, the necessity of making the war a joint one and of course also making joint preparations for peace and for a joint peace policy after the war, became the whole basis of all my deliberations and political activity after my return from Moscow.

The question has been put to us and is again being *put today :* Is our national culture Eastern or Western? And what inferences can be drawn from this? Indeed, our conduct during the war sometimes gave the West the impression that we were preparing to change over from our former Western cultural orientation to a so-called Eastern one. I thought and still

*i.e. The interest of Czechoslovakia (Tr.).

think that this question was and is *quite incorrectly formulated. It was not and is not a question of changing our cultural orientation.* The cultural development of a nation is not a value which can be put off and on like a coat, particularly not from one day to the other, one year to the other, or according to some momentary change of political regime. The cultural development of a nation consists of centuries-old values which build themselves up in the course of ages and are imperishable, which are continually developing and which adapt themselves to new cultural facts and values only by slow degrees. Such is the sociological development of every national culture. In that sense it is simply ignorant and unreasonable to speak of a change in our national cultural orientation. Furthermore, in our cultural development one great fact has never ceased to be valid. It still is valid. *We have always taken deliberately a general and universal line.* That is to say a line which includes not only the development and progress of the West, but also the progress and development of the East. Perhaps therefore we will in this or that direction deepen our cultural contact with the East after the war to a somewhat greater extent than in the past, especially during the twenty years preceding the war.

The best proof of this is our constantly recurring relationship to *German* culture: We have always reacted to it—even if this reaction has often been inspired by a purely national sentiment—by deliberately leaning towards French and Anglo-Saxon and also the Russian culture. In this way we have instinctively expressed our age-old effort to avoid simply and slavishly imitating cultural and other values of a particular nation and to cultivate instead a general human, an explicitly *universal* culture and progress while clinging passionately and obstinately to our *national* forms. All our great national leaders are clear examples of this tendency.

And so our answer to the question: West or East? is to say deliberately and plainly: *West and East.* In this sense—*and in this sense only*—did I sign and approve the treaty with the Soviet Union of December, 1943, *intentionally and consciously linking it with the Anglo-Soviet treaty of May 26th, 1942.* At the time I firmly believed that this treaty would continue in operation after the war ended. Was I right or wrong?

Today it is not, of course, a question of changing cultures and national orientations. The present revolution is a fundamental and deliberate change of *political and social-economic* regimes. Naturally this deep change will also have certain influences on national and cultural orientations and will affect them in many ways. But in essence the change will be of the kind which I described in my book *Democracy Today and Tomorrow* (pp. 247 *et sqq*). It can be summed up in the question: *Is a transformation of post-*

war democracy actually possible and is it possible for it to coexist and co-operate with the system of Soviet Socialism ?

I said that after this dreadful second World War the system of political democracy and the system of Soviet Socialism would both remain—first as allies, *later as rivals*. Could they and would they live side-by-side with one another? Would they co-operate or at least tolerate one another? Or would there be further conflicts between them until one or the other fell (perhaps after an interval which both would need in order to recuperate from their war exhaustions) and would they ultimately come to grips once more in a new and mighty struggle?

Consistent Marxism must of course *theoretically* believe in the final liquidation of the system of bourgeois capitalism. Communism therefore was devoting its efforts *theoretically* to the triumph of classless Socialist society and would continue to do so. Would it also do this *in practice*—after the war, as before it—despite the gigantic changes which the war had brought about? *And would Communism continue to be supported internationally by the Soviet State in this struggle regardless of what had happened in the present war? On the answers to these questions would, naturally, depend the actual post-war relations between the Western European democracies and the American democracies on the one side and the Soviet Union on the other.* The signature of the Anglo-Soviet treaty of May 26th, 1942, on co-operation during the war and on post-war co-operation in reconstruction and the maintenance of peace suggested and *held out the promise* that at that time there *really was an intention* and determination to secure friendly and allied co-operation between the two systems for at least twenty years after the conclusion of the peace.[19]

Or was the Anglo-Soviet treaty merely a means of securing mutual aid during the war with the intention of renewing the international social struggle ruthlessly between the systems after victory? There is no doubt that neither party showed this intention—rather that both showed the contrary—before signing the treaty. So are we to return to the pre-war system of murderous struggle between Western Europe and America and the Soviet Union, to mutual boycott and isolation which would culminate in some new catastrophe?

In my book, written in 1944, I continued: 'I myself answer all these questions about our present international situation *in general quite unambiguously. I believe that peaceful co-operation between the two systems is possible and that it is right and necessary. I believe that today, too, and not only in their war effort both systems should co-operate and that they should tolerate one another loyally even after the war. This would result first in their further temporary* rapprochement and finally perhaps even in a permanent evolutionary equilibrium through adaptation. I base this view partly on *theoretical considerations*, partly on *practical needs.*'

The process of socialisation of society is today* on the march all over the world, in all modern democracies in their present forms! (See for instance what is being done at present in Great Britain!) Not long ago, Great Britain was only limiting various kinds of private ownership and private-capitalist profits. Today it is already putting into operation downright nationalisation and socialisation of all forms of ownership according to Socialist doctrines. Today socialisation formulæ are even incorporated in various forms in new State constitutions. Scientific economic planning is already generally accepted. All this is a great step to the socialisation of modern democratic society and at the same time expressly a great step also towards a compromise with the ideas advocated by Soviet Socialism. Of course, these steps are not an acceptance of the theory of Communism. But the benefit from such a compromise might go in the first instance to world Socialism itself.

'Moreover the principle of State enterprise,† nationalisation and public control of the means of production, of distribution and of private profit, is in some democracies only in its first stages. In others it has progressed far. In some places it is still fighting for general recognition on principle. In others, there is no longer a fight over principles, but only for the degree of practical realisation in this or that direction.

'And here I again put the paramount question: Can the Soviet Socialist system live side by side with the new and transformed democracy which has in essence accepted the principles of nationalisation of the means of production and private profit and which seeks to apply them courageously, reasonably and step-by-step in addition to other so-called Socialistic measures? Yes or no? Again I answer: *Yes!* Here the road is really open. The realisation of this aim depends partly on gradual development, on new political methods and on the degree of maturity of the Society and State concerned.[10] Partly, too, it is a question of experience, of standing the test and of the comparative advantages of a smaller or greater degree and scale of socialisation in modern society.

'It is therefore a question of suitability of the choice of means: what actual position to assume and by what road to travel. It can be the road of violent revolution put through in one blow. It can be by a hurried and more or less violent process which most people would consider exaggerated,

*i.e. in 1947 when Dr. Beneš was writing his Memoirs. (Tr.).

†Dr. Beneš is again quoting from his book (Tr.).

rash, psychologically unsuitable for winning over the majority of the population and likely to raise a counter-revolutionary reaction. But it is also possible to move gradually, on an evolutionary path, empirically and by scientific economic planning, without catastrophes and without violence, by agreement and co-operation.'

I am in favour of this third method, categorically and unconditionally. I am in favour of it also because I am *a real democrat.* I know that in the development of Nations and States there are periods *when violent revolutions are necessary.* But I also know that at certain moments of national history, *attempts to stage a violent revolution may actually amount to a thoroughly bad attempt on the part of reaction.* And as a real democrat I want to exhaust all peaceful ways, all possibilities of agreement and all ways of democratic co-operation. The Communists, too, having already come so far on the way to real power, must understand that they must impose some restraint on themselves, that while they need not retreat anywhere they must have the patience to choose the correct moment for continuing in a reasonable way along the evolutionary road.

I do not want to stage a sectarian debate as to what is and what is not 'revolution'. Slow progress may be sometimes more revolutionary than unreasonable pressure and violence. A. S. Pushkin puts it admirably: 'Remember, young world, that the best and most permanent changes are those which have their origin in a moral improvement without any violent commotion at all.' For me, that is what matters. I am anxious that our State and Nation should build up the best and most lasting social structure. As a practical politician and not as a party-man or sectarian I want to do what is necessary, fitting, advantageous and, above all, what is possible and what is right under existing conditions of society and the country. *I want to do it by the path of evolution, without violence.*

I also believe that in these circumstances new post-war democracy and Soviet Socialism could live one beside the other in an atmosphere of real peace, without rivalry and hostility, in co-operation and mutual agreement. But already in 1944 I added very significantly—anticipating what is manifesting itself on both sides today: 'How this process will develop and end in regard to both these social-political systems, nobody can yet say.' Did I at that time see and foresee the present developments in the East and West correctly or not?

And will events continue to march to a final violent culmination or will both parties cease to boast about their revolutionary strength or their atomic bombs? Will they stop dwelling on the real or alleged weaknesses of their antagonist? Will they return to the statesmanlike policy which they followed during critical war days and turn the present untoward course of events into a channel which is vital, as well as favourable, for both? If not, then woe, woe betide us all, whoever we are!

On the answer to this fundamental question depends once again the peace and destiny of the whole world—its rational, or violent and unhappy, future.

NOTES TO CHAPTER SEVEN

[1]The full text of the speech is printed in my book *Six Years of Exile and the Second World War*, pp. 312–41 (Czech edition).

[2]Minister Dr. Ripka informed me of the negotiations and of their result in the following dispatches:

Dispatched May 29th, 1943.   Number 186/43
Bogomolov on talks in the U.S.A.
Telegram from Dr. Ripka to President Beneš:

(a) After Masaryk had done so, I have also informed Bogomolov today of your conversations in America. Bogomolov received this information with the utmost satisfaction and was visibly delighted at all the references to Russia. He said that he had already been informed about them by the Soviet Embassy in Washington.

(b) With regard to the fact that, following the British, the American Government is now also in favour of transfer of the Czechoslovak Germans, I explained to him that we expect the Soviet Government to take the same view and that it was not enough for us to be told that this was our internal concern. Bogomolov told me frankly that, if the Soviet Government had so far hesitated to express itself clearly, this was certainly because the Government had not yet decided what policy it would follow towards Germany. In his opinion this was now maturing . . . and he thought that there would be no difficulties . . . He promised he would make inquiries at once so that the whole matter should be arranged before your arrival in Moscow . . .

                                                                                RIPKA

Dispatched June 6th, 1943.   Number 202/43
Consent of the Soviet Government to the transfer.
For Beneš only:

On Saturday evening, Bogomolov telephoned to me in the country that he had just received a telegram stating that the Soviet Government agreed to the proposal to transfer the Germans. Bogomolov asked me expressly to inform you of this by cable at once.

                                                                                RIPKA

[3]Was I mistaken in either my opinion or my expectation or was I not? Only the future can answer. Come what may, I was to the fullest possible extent sincere and honest in my belief.

[4]The division of the war zones in Germany and Central Europe was decided between the West and East at this time. Poland and Czechoslovakia, Rumania, Hungary and Yugoslavia were placed in the Soviet Zone. Nobody told us at the time either officially

or unofficially. We only learned about it indirectly, much later, at the time of the Slovak Revolt.*

⁵In my draft, for instance, it was provided that the treaty should be ratified by our Parliament at home in Prague after the end of the war. I had also proposed the treaty should last for five years with the possibility of renewal. These provisions were changed in Moscow already before I arrived. As I did not want to prolong the discussions, I accepted the Moscow draft.†

⁶On the occasion of the signing of the treaty there were speeches by M. Kalinin, President of the Supreme Soviet and myself on behalf of Czechoslovakia.

Kalinin's speech ran as follows:
'MR. PRESIDENT,
'In the name of the Nations of the Soviet Union I welcome you in our capital, Moscow.

'The Treaty of friendship, mutual aid and post-war co-operation concluded today between the Union of Soviet Socialist Republics and the Czechoslovak Republic, is an important contribution to our common fight against German Fascism and against any new aggression on the part of Germany.

'The traditional friendship of our Nations, expressed already in the Treaty of mutual aid concluded in Prague on May 16th, 1935, and in the agreement of our two Governments on the joint prosecution of the war against Germany, concluded in London on July 18th, 1941, has now been confirmed by a new treaty which will constitute a very important historic stage in the development of this friendship.

'The strengthening of wartime co-operation between our Nations and all the freedom-loving Nations of the world is a guarantee of success in the struggle to destroy German Fascism and all who are associated with its sanguinary crimes in Europe.

'The hour of revenge approaches for the humiliations, the sufferings, the blood and tears of the Czechoslovak people whose tortures and hardships are near and comprehensible to our people who have felt the full weight of Hitler's invasion. The Russian Nation has organised a powerful resistance to the enemy aad wages war for the complete expulsion of the hated occupants from the whole of Soviet territory.

'It is important to emphasise that the principles of the Treaty for mutual aid in the war against Hitler's Germany are already being carried out. This co-operation has been sealed with the blood of the sons of our Nations who are fighting shoulder to shoulder for our common victory, for the common victory of the cause of the Allies. The Treaty establishes a firm foundation for post-war co-operation between our Nations and for the prevention of any attempts by Germany to return to its old gangster policy of conquests in the East—the *Drang nach Osten*. German imperialism's policy of conquest must be opposed by the Nations of our two countries with all their might.

*Before this revolt began, the British and American military authorities in Italy had accumulated considerable quantities of arms which they were preparing to take to Slovakia by air. The plan, which had been worked out in collaboration with the Czechs, had to be dropped because of objections raised by the U.S.S.R. (See p. 253). (Tr.).

†The Czechoslovak electorate was thus deprived of any opportunity of expressing its views about the Treaty—a fitting commentary on the Soviet interpretation of the word 'democracy' (Tr.).

'Allow me, Mr. President, to congratulate you and your collaborators on the conclusion of this Treaty which for long years is to serve the great future of our Nations.

'I thank you for your efforts which have been so happily crowned by the signing of this Treaty.'

I answered in this short address:

'MR. PRESIDENT, GENTLEMEN,

'I would like to express my feeling of deep satisfaction that we could today sign this Treaty which I consider an act of immense importance in our national history and in the history of the mutual relations between the Soviet Union and Czechoslovakia. This Treaty has crowned the efforts made by Czechoslovakia during the past twenty years to give security to our Nation and our State against German imperialism. Our Treaty is a natural milestone in the course of this war against inhuman and rapacious German chauvinism which has been striving above all to destroy the neighbouring Slav States: Czechoslovakia, Poland, Yugoslavia and the Soviet Union. This Treaty will be a link in the future organisation,* beneficent alike for us and for all the Allies and it will help to strengthen peace in Europe.

'Allow me, Mr. President, to thank you and all the Soviet political and military elements which have taken part in the realisation of this Treaty. The Treaty, as I have already said yesterday, will be a firm guarantee for Czechoslovakia of a happier future and close political, military, economic and cultural co-operation with the brotherly Nations of the Soviet Union.'

'I proposed this wording to show that the Treaty was a continuation of our former policy and the renewal of a treaty which our whole Nation, in a time of freedom, had approved through its constitutional institutions in 1935.

*The 'Polish Clause' was drafted as signed by the Soviet Foreign Commissariat.

*From this speech, addressed to our country, I quote:

'Above all we will, together with the Soviet Union, wage war against Germany and all its allies until final victory. And if—as the treaty expressly lays down—Germany again renews in the future its present criminal policy of the *Drang nach Osten* and of the so-called German Lebensraum we will again concert together our full and joint defence by war against Germany and its helpers. This German policy of violence must be destroyed once and for all and completely by this war. The Treaty is a clear formulation of the principle that the Soviet Union will never again in the future permit the German *Drang nach Osten*. This has been clearly and firmly stated for the first time and I am convinced that all Europe and the whole world will now realise that this bandit, imperialist, vile, typically Prussian policy of the former German armies of crusaders and knights as well as of the present German Junkers, aristocrats, bureaucrats, generals, capitalist land-grabbers and pan-German Nazis which has lasted for long years—and in a certain sense for whole centuries—that this policy *must end once and for all*.

*I assume this to mean the World Organisation to which Dr. Beneš has already referred several times. It is pertinent to add here that after the war when Czechoslovakia (of which Dr. Beneš was at that time still President) wished to renew its pre-war treaty of alliance with France, the Soviet Union prevented it from doing so. (Tr.).

'Secondly, this Treaty puts on record the joint and permanent friendship which will exist between our Nations in the future, a friendship which immediately after the war will begin by extensive economic co-operation. We here and you at home should already prepare for this co-operation and should make our plans and take practical measures to ensure it.

'This will mean considerable changes in our pre-war trade and industrial orientation. But it will also mean for us a great economic security, a new economic independence especially from Germany and from its future influence. It will be necessary to prepare the reconstruction of our railway, waterway and air communications. This does not mean that we should abandon our connections and economic interests in Western and Southern Europe and in the rest of the world. But it will complete them in an important direction, give us new security and be an expression of the fact that geographically we are in the very heart of Europe and in the immediate proximity and neighbourhood of the Soviet Union which until now has been so neglected by us economically and which itself is and will be so deeply interested in our economy in future.

'Thirdly, the Treaty expressly refers to our future co-operation in every direction as that of *two completely free and independent States*. It fully respects our sovereignty and provides for mutual non-interference in one another's internal affairs. By this, we both wanted to prove as plainly as possible to the whole world that the propaganda of the Germans and our treacherous Czech and Slovak Quislings is both stupid and extremely mendacious. It has already been emphasised during the Moscow Conference of the three Great Powers that these Powers in general and the Soviet Union in particular fully respect the independence of the smaller Nations and States, that they want a strong Czechoslovakia, a strong Poland, a strong Yugoslavia and, of course, also an independent Austria, Rumania, Bulgaria, Hungary and Finland.

'You at home, in Prague, in the Czech provinces and in Slovakia should not heed therefore the slanderous Nazi propaganda which so foolishly proclaims that the Soviet Union wants to devour us. Do not heed this propaganda from the standpoint of internal politics either. Immediately after the war our State will freely establish its political regime with a very limited number of political parties—I, personally, would wish only three. It will be a democratic State—a real People's State. Immediately after the fall of Germany it will have its new Government which will also represent our whole national home front. Only Fascists, Nazis and all treacherous evil-doers of the war period will be excluded from it and from its benefits. These of course must be swallowed up in the abyss of their catastrophe. They will have to atone for all their guilt, their crimes and their treason—just as in all the other liberated countries of Europe.

'Our State will also carry out a number of social and economic changes. It will accept in its policy and in its economy the *system of planning* for which already some of our economists worked before the war. I myself expect and will endeavour to secure that the whole political, economic, and social—and especially also the ethnical—post-war reconstruction of our new State shall be carried out at great speed, chiefly on the basis of the programme of our well-considered and scientifically-prepared *first Five-Year-Plan*.

'I do not want to continue the enumeration of these problems of internal policy—we will tell you about the matter in due course from London and also from Moscow. After my return to London our Government will make all the necessary preparations the definite execution of which will naturally be decided by our liberated people at home as a free and sovereign Nation.

'And fourthly: this treaty and all that comes out of the war in the way of the co-operation of the Soviet Union with Western Europe, *will once and for all prevent a repetition of Munich*, a repetition of the treason of our Fascists, a repetition of the treason of the Slovak Fascists and of their treacherous separation of Slovakia from the Republic in the interests of barbarian German violence, and it will mean that German Fascism and treacherous and base Henleinism will entirely vanish from our country. *This is one of the chief tasks and aims of the treaty*—I say this plainly and frankly. In other words: what we are now doing here, *is to frame one of the chief safeguards for the whole future existence of a united national Czechoslovak State, a State of the Czechs, Slovaks and Sub-carpathian peoples.**

'As long ago as August, 1942, after the visit which the Commissar of Foreign Affairs, Vyatcheslav Molotov paid to London, I informed you in the course of my announce-ment that the British Government had revoked Munich in a letter to Minister Masaryk dated August 5th, 1942, that Commissar Molotov had assured me that the Soviet Union had never had anything in common with Munich, that it had never recognised any of the consequences of Munich and that therefore—by entering on July 18th, 1941, into the Treaty of alliance with us in the war against Germany—he had recognised, and signed the treaty with, the pre-Munich Republic.

'The same is true today for both our States *and in particular it is true for our new Treaty*. In addition, the Soviet Union sincerely wishes the Czechoslovak Republic to be strong, consolidated, nationally as homogeneous as possible, to be a really good and strong friend and collaborator of the Soviet Nations in the future defence of permanent European peace. It has the same wishes with regard to the future Poland and does not merely desire good and friendly relations with it *but also full Polish-Czechoslovak friendship and co-operation*. This can be seen from the protocol appended to our treaty fore-shadowing and desiring that the Treaty should become in the near future a trilateral treaty of the Soviet Union, Poland and Czechoslovakia.'

The full (Czech) text of this speech was printed in my book *Six Years of Exile and the Second World War*, pp. 223–230 (Czech edition).

[10]The full text of my London speech was printed (in Czech) in my book *Six Years of Exile and the Second World War*, pp. 341–407 (Czech edition).

[11]We were asked a number of times in London whether we were not afraid that we had gone too far and that we had made our independence too dependent upon the Soviet Union. I answered that it was a question of securing ourselves against some future repetition of Munich *and that I firmly hoped we could trust the Soviet Union*. We, at any rate, were really sincere in this expression of our hope and confidence that we could do so was really sincere.

[12]Envoy J. Smutný, General Nižborský (Hasal), Envoy (Jaroslav) Kraus and Dr. Táborský were with me.

[13]My discussion with Stalin was interesting, very frank and sincere. It covered Munich, the Slavs, Communism and the Communists in our country and other questions.

*Towards the end of the war, the Soviet Government insisted on Sub-Carpathian Ukraine becoming a part of the Soviet Union. (Tr.).

[14]The Soviet Ambassador to our Government in London.

[15]In the afternoon of the same day Minister Stanczyk* visited me and we went over the same ground again. Stanczyk insisted even more strongly that there must be an agreement and as soon as possible. It was, he said, high time.

To his direct question as to whether there was no hope of saving Lwow, I told him that according to what I had heard in Moscow, I thought the Soviet Government could not and would not make any concession *with regard to the Ukraine*. It would also want a definite solution with us of the question of Subcarpathian Ruthenia.

[16]At that time I did not go into this question in so much detail and so precisely as I did later in my book *Essays on Slavism*, published in London in 1944,† in which I explained my opinion of our procedure and that of the other nations during the Munich crisis. See this book, p. 243 *et sqq.* and also the note on pp. 248–249 (Czech edition).

[17]I shall give a detailed account of all these problems in the volume of my Memoirs dealing with Munich.

[18]Compare these remarks with what I said in my book *Essays on Slavism*, Czech edition, Prague, 1947.†

[19]See my essay in *Democracy Today and Tomorrow*, p. 250 (Czech edition).

[20]See also my remarks when on accepting the honorary title of Doctor of Law of Charles University in Prague on December 15th, 1945.

*Minister for Foreign Affairs in the Polish Government in London (Tr.).

†The first edition was published in London in 1944 and the second in Prague in 1947.
(Tr.).

U

President Beneš's Farewell Broadcast to the Czechoslovak Nation on October 5th, 1938, on resigning after Munich.

Dear fellow-citizens,

I have just sent to the Prime Minister a letter in which I resign my presidential office. And I am addressing myself to you to say farewell to you as President, to say farewell to my political colleagues, to our splendid soldiers, to the Legionaries and to all those with whom as President I came into contact and used to work.

I reached my decision of my own free will and in accordance with my personal conviction after consultations with political and constitutional circles and with a number of other leading persons. I intended to take this step immediately after Munich. I postponed it in order to secure first a stronger and more lasting Government. I believe that in present circumstances my decision was right.

I do not intend to analyse the whole political situation which has led me to this step. I want only to emphasise that the whole system of the balance of power in Europe built up after the war has for some years been steadily growing weaker and during the last three years has substantially changed to our disadvantage and the disadvantage of our friends. In agreement with its friends, the Czechoslovak Republic has honestly tried through long years to support this system and to change it gradually by a process of evolution because this was the way its interests lay. At the same time it has always searched frankly and honestly for a possibility of adapting its policy to new developments and of reaching agreement with its neighbours.

During the last three years events have succeeded one another with unexpected speed. We in our country have done our utmost when these events took the form of racial strife. At the same time we have also sincerely tried to reach agreement with the other races. We went to the utmost limit of possible concessions. But influences from abroad and the whole course of European development intensified these matters into a grave international conflict in which it behoved us to look to the defence of our frontiers by military action.

All of us united to do this with energy, devotion and unparalleled self-confidence and our attitude is respected by our enemies as well as friends. But it became evident that a European and world catastrophe would develop. You know that in these circumstances four Great Powers met and agreed among themselves about the sacrifices which they asked from us in the name of world peace. You know that we were forced to accept these sacrifices.

Today I do not want to discuss these matters in detail nor to criticise them. And you need not expect me to utter a single word of recrimination against anyone. All will be judged in due course by history and history will give a just verdict. I will say only what we all feel most painfully: the sacrifices which we were asked to accept and which were then forced upon us are out of all proportion and are unjust. The Nation will never forget that fact though it is bearing its burden with dignity, calm and confidence which evoke general admiration. In this attitude can be seen the strength of the Nation and the moral greatness of its sons and daughters.

During this period, I have, as my duty demanded, defended with all the devotion of which I was capable the interests of our State and Nation and our present position in Europe. They are mistaken who did not rightly estimate the hundreds of attempts we made to preserve peace, to build up peaceful co-operation, to build up good neighbourly relations—who did not appreciate our real desire to come to an understanding with all around us. But the forces on the other side were stronger. In these circumstances I think it is advisable that the new developments and the new European collaboration should not be disturbed from our side through the fact that the personal position of its leading representative apparently constitutes an obstacle to this development. I was elected to my present position at a time substantially different from the present and I must consider whether I can remain at my post under the changed conditions now obtaining. I am by conviction a democrat. I believe I am acting rightly in leaving so that our State and Nation can develop quietly and undisturbed in the new atmosphere and adapt itself to the new conditions. This means that it should not renounce old friends and should gather new friends around it in a spirit of calm, of realism and of loyalty to all as I have always longed that it should.

Our State has had a special structure from the nationality standpoint. Now conditions will change greatly. Many of the causes of dispute with our neighbours will disappear. We shall have a national State as in one sense the development of the principle of nationality indicates. Herein will lie the great strength of our State and Nation. This will provide the State with a great and new source of activity and a strong moral basis which it has not possessed hitherto. Our national culture will deepen and grow stronger. We are still strong enough, numerous enough. Let us therefore look hopefully towards our national future. The Czechs and Slovaks by their origin, by their whole education for many generations, may be everything else but they are not a Nation of defeatists. We are a typically sober Nation and, as we did not grow proud in the hour of good fortune, so let us not lose our heads in our misfortune. Heroism of work and of self-denial for which we must now be prepared, are not less grand or less worthy than heroism on the battlefield.

The stem of the tree of our homeland has had some branches lopped from it but the roots of the Nation are still firm in the earth. Let us go back to our roots. Let us concentrate all the old strength of our race in them as we have done so often in our history, and after a while the stem will again put forth new shoots. Let us remember that what remains to us after all these sacrifices is the core of our country, a heritage which we must preserve for future generations, and which still constitutes a possession of eternal value. Remember that even now we remain a State which is not one of the smallest but a Nation with a culture equalling the culture of greater nations and excelling that of many. We have an obligation therefore to safeguard this our great inheritance with a firm and calm hand.

Dear fellow-citizens, friends!

In conclusion I appeal to you all with an earnest, sincere request which comes from my heart: The home of the Czechs and Slovaks is in real danger. It would be in still greater danger if at this moment we did not stand together in unity, concord and in the full moral strength of people who are devoted to one another. It is necessary above all to come to an agreement with the Slovaks. They, too, are in danger. Today it is not this or that concession which is of importance. Give way to one another wherever necessary.

Next, I address myself to all other elements in the population: to farmers, workers, the middle classes and intelligentsia. I say to you: preserve your calmness and concord, your unity, devotion and mutual love to one another, because—as Masaryk used to say—the country, the State and the Nation, are just all of you standing together in your homeland. Drop for the time all your quarrels and your daily petty interests and direct all your efforts to one aim only: united work for your country and State.

Especially warmly I thank our spendid Army. As President, I dedicated all my activities to its well-being. I am with it and I will never forget it. I believe in its successful development and in its future.

I end with the expression of my honest conviction, the expression of my profound belief, in the eternal strength and firmness of our Nation, in its energy, constancy, perseverance and, especially, in its belief in the ideals of humanity, in the ideals of liberty, right and justice, for which it has fought so often, for which it has suffered so often and with which it has always in the end been victorious. I, too, have fought for these things. And I shall remain true to them. Nor am I leaving the ship because there is a gale. On the contrary, I believe that at this moment my sacrifice is politically necessary. But this does not mean that I shall forget my duty to continue working as a citizen and patriot.

My wish for you all, for the Republic and the Nation, is that it shall soon see better days, that it shall live, grow and flourish again as a beautiful branch of the human race and as one of the noble, comely nations of Europe.

Fare you all well!

Note of the Commissariat of Foreign Affairs of the Union of Soviet Socialist Republics, delivered to the German Ambassador, Graf v. Schulenburg, a copy of which was sent by the Commissariat to Envoy Fierlinger :

Moscow, March 18th, 1939

MR. AMBASSADOR,

I have the honour to confirm the receipt of your Note of the 16th inst. as well as of your Note of the 17th inst., in which you announce to the Soviet Government the incorporation of Bohemia and Moravia into the German Reich and the establishment of a German protectorate over them.

Not considering it possible to pass over in silence the Notes mentioned above and thereby giving the false impression that it is not interested in the events in Czechoslovakia, the Soviet Government deems it necessary, in reply to the Notes in question, to express its real attitude to the events with which the Notes are concerned.

1. The political-historic concepts mentioned in the introductory part of the German Decree with the object of justifying and defending it, especially the reference to the Czechoslovak State as a source of permanent unrest and danger for European peace, to the lack of vitality of the Czechoslovak State and to the resultant permanent uneasiness arising for Germany, cannot be accepted nor do they correspond to the facts which are known to the whole world. In reality, of all the European States after the world war the Czechoslovak Republic was one of the few in which internal peace and a peace-loving foreign policy had been really secured.

2. The Soviet Government does not know of any State Constitution that would authorise the head of the State to destroy the existence of the State without the consent of the Nation concerned. It can hardly be admitted that any Nation would voluntarily consent to the abolition of its independence and to its incorporation into another State, much less so a Nation which for centuries has fought for its independence and which for twenty years has maintained its independence. The Czechoslovak President Hácha, when signing the Berlin document of the 15th inst., was not authorised to do so by his Nation and acted in clear contradiction of Articles 64 and 65 of the Czechoslovak Constitution and against the will of the Nation. Therefore the document in question cannot be regarded as valid.

3. The principle of self-determination to which the German Government often refers, presumes a free expression of the will of the Nation which cannot be replaced by the signature of one or two persons even if they should fill the highest offices in the State. In the present case there was

no decision by the Czech Nation, not even in the form of plebiscites such as were carried out for example when determining the fate of Upper Silesia and the Saar.

4. Having regard to the fact that there has been no expression of the will of the Czech Nation, the occupation of Bohemia by the German Army and all other actions of the German Government must be characterised as arbitrary, violent and aggressive.

5. All the above remarks apply also to the change of the legal position of Slovakia in the direction of subordination to the German Reich which was not legalised by any decision of the Slovak Nation.

6. The action of the German Government has brought about a violent invasion by the Hungarian Army into Subcarpathian Ruthenia and the suppression of the natural rights of the population.

7. Having regard to these facts, the Soviet Government cannot recognise the incorporation of Bohemia or, in some form or another, of Slovakia into the German Reich as valid or according to the generally recognised principles of international law and justice or to the principle of self-determination of nations.

8. In the opinion of the Soviet Government, the actions of the German Government not only do not avert the danger threatening general peace, but have on the contrary created and increased that danger, violated the political stability of Central Europe, strengthened the elements of insecurity which have already been created in Europe and brought about another weakening of the sense of security among the nations.

I beg you to inform your Government, Mr. Ambassador, and to accept the assurance of my respect.

(Signed) LITVINOV

To the Ambassador of the German Reich,
Graf von Schulenburg

President Doctor Eduard Beneš takes over the Leadership of the United Liberation Movement of Czechoslovakia all over the World.

From *New-Yorské Listy*
(a newspaper published in New York in Czech)
April 21st, 1939

On April 18th, 1939, Dr. Eduard Beneš received twenty delegates of the Czech National Association, the National Union of Czech Catholics and of important Slovak organisations at the Windermere Hotel, Chicago. Dr. Beneš thanked the delegates for their greetings and asked them to express his thanks to all the organisations concerned for their invitation to accept the leadership of the new movement for the liberation of the Czechoslovak Republic. Dr. Beneš stressed that he had been invited to do so by many organisations, clubs and associations of Czechoslovaks all over the world. He then gave a very detailed report of the international situation and reviewed the immediate prospects of the Czechoslovak Nation being liberated from the German yoke. Furthermore he also outlined what were the duties of Czechs, Slovaks and Carpatho-Ruthenians in this connection.

A discussion of the situation and of the duties of Czechs, Slovaks and Subcarpathian Ruthenians followed after which Dr. Beneš read a report on the conclusions reached at the meeting and made a personal declaration in which he stated *that he was accepting the request of all Czechoslovak organisations throughout the world to assume the leadership of the new Czechoslovak political movement. Dr. Beneš's report and his personal declaration were enthusiastically received and unanimously approved.* The general discussion of the difficulties with which the Czechoslovak Nation was faced took place in a spirit of the conscious unity of Czechs, Slovaks and Sub-Carpathian Ruthenians at the opening stage of the struggle for the independence of the Czechoslovak Republic. After the meeting the following statement was issued:

'On April 18th, 19th and 20th, 1939, the representatives of American citizens of Czech and Slovak origin met at Chicago. All the principal groups and important Czech and Slovak organisations were represented. They have agreed to concentrate and complete their existing central organisation under the name of the Czechoslovak National Council to which all Czechs and Slovaks in Canada, the South-American States and other countries will also adhere. The task of the Council is to consolidate in a great united movement all American citizens of Czech and Slovak origin—within the framework of American laws and American political traditions and as American citizens and patriots—to liberate Czechoslovakia, the land of their fathers and mothers, from the unjust, temporary occupation by a military dictatorship.

Today, Tuesday, April 18th, these organisations sent a deputation to Dr. Eduard Beneš to inform him of their decision and to ask him to assume the leadership of the Czechoslovak liberation movement and to consolidate all free Czechs and Slovaks in Europe, America and elsewhere under one leadership and a common political programme. It is essential that the world should hear the voice of those who also have a right to speak in the name of the suppressed Nation at home which today cannot defend itself.

Dr. Eduard Beneš received the delegation and answered as follows: 'I thank you sincerely for your confidence. I agree with you that it is necessary today to establish a movement and an organ which after the occupation of our country and the suppression of all its liberties, will speak in its name and will defend its right to freedom and independence before the world. I thank you also for the offer of your help within the framework of your duties as American citizens, and I repeat today, as I have done since I came into your free and beautiful country, that you should be, above all, its faithful, devoted and loyal citizens. That is your first duty— a duty with which your help to us will not conflict because we ourselves, as guests of this country, will never ask anything of you that is not in conformity with these duties.

'To your invitation to head the liberation movement, I reply: I have not ceased to work for my country from the moment when I left it last October after Munich. But I maintained an attitude of reserve and loyalty to our Government as well as to the Governments of the other interested States and waited for further developments. Now, when a new, great injustice has been done to us by the occupation of our ancient land, I am free again. As you know I have appealed to the leading men of the United States of America, the British Empire, France, Soviet Russia and to the League of Nations to refuse to recognise the injustice done to us. At the same time I began to negotiate with various Czechoslovak politicians who are now outside our country in preparation for what you are now proposing: the organisation of a new world-wide liberation movement for the re-establishment of our temporarily violated freedom.

'In this sense, in contact with the diplomatic Missions of our Republic which continue to function and after agreement with the leading representatives of these Missions, especially Envoy Masaryk in London, Envoy Osuský in Paris, Envoy Hurban in Washington, Envoy Fierlinger in

Moscow and Envoy and ex-Minister of the Interior of Czechoslovakia, Dr. Slávik, who has just arrived in America from Warsaw, as well as with other political personalities, I intend to form a Czechoslovak political directorate which will represent and head our movement as a whole. In these countries we have more than a hundred thousand Czechoslovak citizens, not only Czechs and Slovaks, but also democratic Germans and Ruthenes. They all are at one with us and large numbers from all over the world are already reporting to me with a view to co-operation. In these same countries we have more than two million friends of Czechoslovak origin who are now citizens of these friendly States. But we have also behind us all faithful democratic citizens in our oppressed country and they number more than ten million people. We have right on our side and the non-recognition of German violence by the Great Powers and by a great part of the rest of the world. These are enormous assets.

'*I reply therefore that I am glad to accept your invitation.* And in agreement with the colleagues in London, Paris, Moscow and Washington whom I have already mentioned we will shortly publish a proclamation to all our people as the starting point of our new political activities. This simply means that, in the name of the Czechoslovak Republic which today cannot speak itself, we will step into the ranks of those European States which are forming a new European front against dictatorial aggression. And, in the name of the Nation which cannot speak itself, we will also associate ourselves with the latest message of President Roosevelt.

'I therefore ask all of you to stand in full unity, harmony and co-operation without regard to party, religion, social or other differences, firmly and in unity behind the ideals of American democracy. Thus you will stand also behind the ideals of Czechoslovak democracy and freedom.'

Mr. Churchill's Statement* on Recognition of Czechoslovak Government.

The Prime Minister: Communications have recently passed between my Nóble Friend† on the one side and Dr. Beneš on behalf of the Czechoslovak National Committee on the other, concerning the recognition of the Czechoslovak National Committee as a Provisional Czechoslovak Government. As the result of these communications, Dr. Beneš informed my Noble Friend of the composition of the Provisional Czechoslovak Government, in which several new members joined the previous members of the Czechoslovak National Committee, and requested the recognition by His Majesty's Government of the newly-constituted Provisional Czechoslovak Government. This recognition was granted on 21st July in a letter from my Noble Friend to Dr. Beneš in the following terms:

'In the light of exchanges of view which have taken place between us, I have the honour to inform you that, in response to the request of the Czechoslovak National Committee, His Majesty's Government in the United Kingdom are happy to recognise and enter into relations with the Provisional Czechoslovak Government established by the Czechoslovak National Committee to function in this country. His Majesty's Government will be glad to discuss with the representatives of the Provisional Government certain questions arising out of this recognition which require settlement.'

*Hansard, House of Commons, 23rd July, 1940, Vol. 363, Col. 614. (Tr.).
†Lord Halifax. (Tr.).

Letter from R. H. Bruce Lockhart, British Representative with the Czecho-slovak Provisional Government, to Dr. Eduard Beneš, President of the Republic, concerning Churchill's Speech of September 30th, 1940.

'Office of the British Representative with the
Czechoslovak Provisional Government
November 11th, 1940

DEAR MR. PRESIDENT,

With reference to Your Excellency's letter of October 10, regarding certain comments in Czechoslovak circles upon the Prime Minister's broadcast message to the Czechoslovak people on September 30, I am now in a position to give you the following answer for Your Excellency's private information:

The Prime Minister's statement of September 30th should be read as a whole and not misinterpreted by taking certain passages out of their context. In speaking of the Munich Agreement, Mr. Churchill simply stated that this Agreement had been destroyed, and any further elucidation or interpretation of this remark would be profitless. In this connection I venture to refer Your Excellency to Lord Halifax's letter to yourself of July 18, 1940. In that letter His Lordship said:

'I wish to make it clear that by proceeding to this act of recognition His Majesty's Government would not commit themselves to recognise or to support the establishment in the future of any particular frontiers in Central Europe.'

I am authorised to inform you officially that this statement was intended to refer to all and any frontiers including, of course, the so-called Munich line.

I trust that this explanation will enable Your Excellency to rebut criticism which seems out of place at a moment when both our Nations are fighting for their existence.

I have the honour to be, with the greatest respect, Your Excellency's most obedient servant.

(*Signed*) R. H. BRUCE LOCKHART.'

Resolution of the Executive Committee of the Sudeten-German Social Democrat Party, June 7th, 1942 :

The Executive Committee of the Sudeten-German Social Democratic Party with the addition of members of our Trade Union and co-operative organisations in England, takes note of the report of the party leaders concerning relations with the departments of the Provisional Czechoslovak State organisation.

The Executive Committee wishes to emphasise that two invitations to the Sudeten-German Social Democratic Party to co-operate in the Czecho-Slovak State Council have been answered affirmatively. In this connection it calls attention to the relevant passages in the addresses of State President Dr. Beneš to the State Council on December 11th, 1940, and November 25th, 1941. The position was clearly described in the message of the President on November 25th, 1941, when he declared: 'As I have already stated last year, I have discussed matters also with some political representatives of our democratic Germans. By mutual agreement their co-operation on the floor of the State Council has for the time being been postponed in view of events at home.'

This declaration fully coincides with the declaration of the Party Conference of Sudeten-German Social Democrats in England of September 28th, 1941, intimating its readiness 'to inaugurate already abroad that measure of co-operation with the Czechoslovak State organisation which is rendered possible by psychological conditions at home.'

We abstain from all criticisms of the fact that meanwhile a representative of the Sudeten Communists* has been admitted to the State Council without any previous consultation as to whether this decision was in harmony with the agreement mentioned by the President on November 25th, 1941.

The Executive Committee of the Party does not ignore the tragic background from which the difficulties for closer co-operation between Czechs and democratic Sudeten-Germans arise at this stage. It is convinced that the formal question of participation or non-participation in the State Council is of lesser importance and that the final result of our policy of agreement will depend on the measure of goodwill on both sides. It always remains our aim to work for close co-operation between the democratic and socialist masses of the Czechs and Sudeten-Germans both in a revolt against Hitler's tyranny and after this revolt. But we do not

*Karl Kreibich who was appointed Czechoslovak Ambassador to the U.S.S.R. in 1950 (Tr.).

want to leave our Czech friends in any doubt that in the pursuit of this policy we can sacrifice our unity with the heroes and martyrs of the anti-Hitler struggle at home. Nor can we renounce our responsibility which history has imposed on us as the strongest democratic element in the Sudeten population. The undefeated ranks of our movement at home feel strong enough to settle their accounts with the Nazi criminals in the hour of the inevitable European revolution and to take into their hands the work of re-democratisation and of economic and social renaissance. They have fought against Fascism under most difficult conditions with perseverance and with no smaller sacrifices than the democratic elements among the Slovaks. Therefore we must already at this moment reject any inequality of treatment between democratic Germans and Slovaks in the new State organisation. We are especially opposed to the fact that the Sudeten-Germans are threatened with a transfer of population whereas for Slovakia the basis of policy is simply the principle of political and legal reckoning with the instruments of Hitler.

The Executive Committee of the Party is authorised to continue its efforts to work in the spirit of the Atlantic Charter and in accordance with the traditional policy of agreement of our movement for a solution of the Czech-Sudeten-German problem by negotiation.

The Executive Committee of the Party instructs the party leaders to make it clear to our Czech partners with equal friendship and urgency that a unilateral solution of the Czech-German question after this war by force could not be permanent and would not be in the interest either of the Czech Nation or of European peace.

Letter of Wenzel Jaksch to President Eduard Beneš of June 22nd, 1942 :

London, June 22nd, 1942

MR. PRESIDENT,

I have waited till today before delivering our resolution of June 7th for reasons which I need not explain. Allow me to assure you that the latest fearful events at home* have deeply concerned us too. Nothing has changed in our friendship to the Czech Nation and we mourn its victims as our own brothers.

After this introduction, dear Mr. President, allow me to ask you to take note of the enclosed copy of our protest. It has been broadcast and can surely be regarded as representing the views of our best fighters who since October 1st, 1938, have been exposed to the most severe persecutions. But important considerations force me when sending you this letter, to try to obtain an elucidation of political issues which can no longer be postponed. In our political resolution we have simply described the entirely negative result of all discussions up to this moment. I think I can claim some merit in the fact that this alibi of our goodwill is clothed in very moderate language. It does not express the deep exasperation felt by our responsible representatives at the way in which our movement has been treated since Munich. The astonishment can be hardly described, Mr. President, which was evoked in our ranks by the present propaganda for a mass transfer of the Sudeten population. Such measures would naturally be directed against the population of whole regions and would also affect those districts which before and after Munich stood the test with real heroism in the fight against Nazi Fascism. Our people who are schooled in fighting and inured to suffering have not overlooked the difference between the British thesis of the punishment of the culprits and the design of Czech policy not simply to reach a reckoning with the Nazi criminals but also to endeavour to secure an unnecessary increase in their own national influence. Remembering how deeply our working people are rooted in their homeland, it is clear that their evacuation from the whole territory could be carried out only by brute force against the unanimous resistance of all political forces (groups) still remaining after the fall of the Nazi Government.

Dear Mr. President, it is with a heavy heart that I must put before you all our fears. Let it be said clearly, and rather today than tomorrow, that the programme of the transfer of population would be a dangerous slogan and would unchain civil war along the language frontiers in Bohemia and

*The terror which followed the shooting of Reichsprotektor Heydrich on May 27th, 1942 (Tr.).

Moravia. There are other ways of punishing the Nazi criminals. In the Sudeten territory, too, a terrible reckoning will come. Our dead and many thousands of our best men are a guarantee of this. But reckoning with the Nazis does not justify the transfer of the population of the whole border-land region, a transfer which would necessarily have to be unselective. The transfer of population would be revenge without differentiation and that means, dear Mr. President—I wish to say it quite frankly—*to destroy every basis of democratic co-operation for a generation.*

In face of this danger we cannot simply renounce the moral heritage of a long period of national co-operation. Today perhaps much has been forgotten. But in the book of history it is written that in the fatal years of 1935–1938 one million Germans stood at the side of the Czech Nation. That the Catholics and the Farmers' Union capitulated after the fall of Austria must be judged more moderately when we consider how de-moralising was the influence of the great Czech parties on the German population. The heroism of our workers has compensated for much of the weakness which manifested itself in other sectors of the activist camp. The members of our movement will stand before the Czech Nation with the clearest conscience of the world. Their sacrifices and the active co-opera-tion which they are developing in spite of the continuing persecutions are positive items which cannot be overlooked in the final balance-sheet of the fight against Hitlerism.

Allow me, Mr. President, to sum up all these opinions in a single phrase: *we believe it is to our credit that Czechoslovak democracy fell heroically.*

Dr. Hodža has admitted in his last book that he had already offered Henlein general municipal elections in the autumn of 1937 which would have meant the extinction of the whole free administration in our border territories. If our party had not gone into the election campaign in spite of accusations of inner-political treason (and practically alone) then the battle of international propaganda for the fate of Czechoslovakia would have already been lost in the spring of 1938. In that case the Runciman Mission would not have been required, nor the Munich decision. Even the heroic gesture of the September mobilisation would have been denied to the country. Every objective examination of these tragic events will confirm that our organisations held the Sudeten territory politically even at the time when this region had already been practically abandoned by the State administration.

These are the reasons, Mr. President, why my best comrades are filled with profound resentment at the fact that the openly declared goodwill or their legal representatives abroad has met with so little response. Conscious that they have fulfilled their duty to 100 per cent, they are not prepared to accept discrimination against themselves in favour of the Slovak representatives in the Government or the State Council seeing that the claims of the latter are certainly not stronger than ours.

At this point, dear Mr. President, I refer to the exchange of Notes on the occasion of our party conference in London on September 27th and 28th, 1941, to prove how our honest readiness has remained unrequited and how the fund of personal confidence in the hearts of faithful people is being destroyed. Perhaps not without justification I may add that I am filled with deep despair at the path Czech policy is taking in the way of trying to dictate against old allies who stood at the Czech Nation's side when it was abandoned by all its friends.

I would therefore like to conclude this explanation of our last resolution with the following statement:

The absolutely negative attitude of the departments of the Provisional Czechoslovak State Organisation towards an agreement on political and economic transitional solutions deprives our policy of conciliation of all foundation.

The policy of transfer of population lies outside the scope of the principle of the legal continuity of the State in the name of which the Czechoslovak Government has until now demanded the loyalty of democratic Sudeten-Germans abroad.

Our resolution is an invitation to all responsible elements of the Czechoslovak State Government not to think only in terms of a violent solution and not to drive the democratic Sudeten Germans who feel attached to their homeland into a conflict which might have fatal consequences for both parties.

I am fully aware, my very dear Mr. President, of the implications of this statement.

Accept, Mr. President, the expression of my special respect.

Yours sincerely,
(Signed) W. JAKSCH

v

*Basic principles of the attitude of the President of the Republic, Dr. Eduard Beneš, to the Resolution of June 7th, 1942, from the Executive Committee of the Sudeten German Social Democratic Party handed to Wenzel Jaksch by the President of the Republic on December 1st, 1942 :**

On June 22nd, 1942, Mr. Jaksch sent to President Dr. Beneš the attached resolution of the Sudeten German Social Democratic Party agreed upon at the meeting of its Executive Committee in London in June, 1942. Though this resolution does not express the policy of the party in exile to the fullest extent, it gives the principles of the Party's attitude to some essential problems of Czechoslovak policy as conceived by the Government of the Republic at present in exile in London and already advocated by President Dr. Beneš since Munich.

We therefore think it necessary to clarify our attitude to this resolution in the following notes:

1. The resolution has every right to refer to President Dr. Beneš's declarations of December 11th, 1940, and November 25th, 1941, and the declaration of the Party's conference of September 28th, 1941. These declarations express the policy of the two sides at the times in question. President Beneš has not changed his standpoint and still stands by these declarations.

2. The nomination of Karl Kreibich to the State Council does not in any way change the President's declaration of December 11th, 1940, and of November, 1941. Both declarations, especially that of November 25th, 1941, were the result of discussions between Dr. Beneš and Wenzel Jaksch to whom their contents were announced before the declarations were made in the State Council. On December 11th, 1940, President Dr. Beneš said: 'I stress that as occasion arises I will accept as a matter of course the participation of some politicians and groups not yet among us today. I have discussed this with some politicians from among our German fellow-citizens. I have offered them participation and I have obtained an affirmative answer (these words refer to politicians of the party of German Social Democrats). I therefore suppose their representatives will join the State Council in near future. I have discussed the same question also with some of our Communists. The negotiations are not yet finished but I hope that an agreement will be reached in their case too. There are still some other elements, as for instance the Jewish Party, about whose co-operation in the

*This memorandum contains internal evidence that the views expressed were those of the Czechoslovak Provisional Government as a whole. See also President Beneš's letter to Mr. Jaksch of June 10th, 1943 (Tr.).

State Council a decision will be made—in some cases, soon, and in others when the State Council has been augmented in the manner mentioned above.'

From this declaration it is clear that those still not represented belonged to three independent groups with which negotiations were conducted separately. In 1940, before the opening of the first State Council no agreement had been reached with any of these groups. At that time the German Social Democrats made political demands which were unacceptable for President Beneš (the group of German progressives did the same); the Jewish groups could not reach agreement among themselves and the Communists were uncertain and not united in their policy towards our Liberation Movement.

This situation lasted until the autumn of 1941. Before the opening of the second State Council and after discussions between Dr. Beneš and W. Jaksch it was frankly agreed by both parties that political conditions at home and in the emigration and in the army were such (killing and persecutions at home and the strengthening of radical Czech nationalism) that the nomination of members from the German Social Democrats could not be carried out at that moment. It must be mentioned that though Wenzel Jaksch held at that time to his original general policy towards the Czechoslovak liberation movement, he was—if his attitude was correctly understood—ready to accept membership in the Czechoslovak State Council unconditionally in 1941 having regard to the definitive recognition of the Czechoslovak Government by the British Government and the Soviet Union's participation in the war.

But at that time the political situation had already developed sufficiently (after Germany's attack on the Soviet Union and the recognition of the Czechoslovak Government by the Soviet Government) to envisage an immediate participation of elements from the ranks of the Communists. They were again offered this by President Beneš—negotiations had already been started in 1940 after the provisional recognition of the Government and before the German attack on the Soviet Union—and the offer was accepted unconditionally. It was only asked that not only Czechs, but also Slovaks, Germans, Hungarians and Ruthenes might be nominated for membership. This was promised on the express condition that all nominations would be, *not as members of this or that nationality*, but as individuals close to Communist ideas and tendencies (as the State Council was not composed of *representatives of parties or nationalities, but of individuals* who expressed the various political tendencies in the Republic). The President then asked for a list of ten to twelve possible candidates from which he nominated four under these conditions. None were nominated to represent a particular nationality because in addition the Communists themselves do not have national groups in their party.

Full agreement was also reached with the Jewish group after discussions lasting a year and the nomination was therefore carried out.

With the Zinner group (German Social Democrats in Czechoslovakia) there were no differences either in the matter of the State Council or concerning their participation in the struggle for the re-establishment of the Republic and the group made no prior conditions so that there was no need for fresh negotiations. Nevertheless there were no nominations from their ranks for the same reasons as in the case of the Sudeten German Social Democrats, namely to avoid giving the impression that by nominating somebody from the Zinner group the Czechs were interfering in the quarrels of the two groups of German Social Democrats. And there were also no nominations from the other German groups for the reasons mentioned above (persecutions at home and radical nationalism in the emigration and at home).

These are the reasons for nominating a German Communist as member of the State Council to which the resolution of June, 1942, referred. There were no obligations to follow any other procedure and no obligations not corresponding to the situation just described would have been accepted if they had been suggested.

3. Nevertheless we agree with the point of view of the resolution of June, 1942, that participation or non-participation in the State Council is of minor importance in the matter of German co-operation in the Czechoslovak liberation movement. The essential point is whether it is possible to reach, abroad and at once, sincere co-operation between the democratic, anti-Hitler masses of Czechs and Germans in full goodwill on both sides and on the *basis of principles which both accept and recognise for their common fight against Hitlerism and for the re-establishment of the Republic as well as for settling accounts with all war criminals* and those guilty of all persecutions and crimes committed in our country against whomsoever it may be and *to settle accounts with the last remnants of Fascism and Nazism in the Republic.*

4. As to the question—the settlement of accounts with Fascism, Nazism and all the guilty men among Bohemian Germans—the resolution of the Executive Committee of the Sudeten German Social Democratic Party of June, 1942, says that the party wishes to carry this out itself and to take the work of re-democratisation of the Germans into its own hands.

To this the following observations must be made: It cannot be accepted for one moment that a party—any party—could be granted either the right or the power to re-educate by itself any particular part of the population of the Republic unless the party in question had got all authority and a political dictatorship into its hands. Such a thesis is to us unthinkable. The task is a great and extremely difficult one and can be carried out successfully only after the war as a result of a popular revolution of all inhabitants of the Republic and therefore by the State and the State administration as a whole, an administration which springs from a common victory and a common anti-Fascist revolution and which puts itself at the service of that revolution. *We hold this to be true for Czechs and Slovaks as well as for the Germans in the Republic.*

For this reason, President Beneš has formulated his attitude to the question of settling accounts with Nazism and with all guilty persons in the Republic in general terms and in a manner acceptable to all in his speech in the State Council on November 25th, 1941. Before addressing the Council he showed the draft of his speech to Wenzel Jaksch who agreed to it at once only asking for the addition of one point (which was accepted) The text of this declaration was as follows:

'As I have already announced last year, I have also had negotiations with some political elements among our democratic Germans who fought by our side in 1938 for the integrity of our Republic. By mutual agreement their co-operation on the floor of the State Council has been postponed for the time being in view of events at home.

'Some doubts and discussions have started in our ranks about these matters. I will repeat what I said last year so that it may be clear to all. Everyone who is sincerely fighting against present Germany is our ally. Every Czechoslovak citizen who sincerely stands against all that is Nazi and all that Nazis stand for, what they have done and are doing, can join our ranks and co-operate with us. The State Council is an organism which has as its first and most important mission to unite all political elements of all former political lines of thought and of all nationalities in the Republic owing allegiance to the State and the Republic, on the basis of their consistent opposition to Nazism and recognition of the present organisation of our Republic on British soil and on the basis of the oath taken by them in this spirit.

'We all know that the discussions to which I referred were concerned with what should happen to the Germans in our Republic after the defeat of Nazi Germany. I think it is essential to say a few words on this subject now. As far as I know the views of politically-minded people at home, they are in general identical with what is already being discussed between the Allied Governments and with what will probably, as Prime Minister

Winston Churchill himself has hinted, become one of the articles of the armistice and peace negotiations, namely, that it will be necessary to punish war criminals everywhere, without exception and without mercy. It will especially be necessary to punish all those who, directly or indirectly, have participated in acts of treason and bestialities perpetrated by the Henlein-ites, the Nazis and the Gestapo, who have helped to persecute our people, to humiliate them morally, humanly and racially, who have destroyed, robbed, plundered the occupied countries and their populations and who have betrayed, stolen and murdered.'

This justice which will not discriminate between Germans and Slovaks —or Czechs—will be meted out by the whole Czechoslovak democratic people without distinction of class or nationality, and *especially by the State itself as part of its whole post-war policy.*

5. The resolution of the Sudeten German Social Democratic Party of June, 1942, alleges that in the reconstruction of the State the Germans are to be treated less favourably than the Slovaks and that the Germans are threatened with a general transfer of population whereas the Slovaks are to receive individual political and legal punishment.

To this it must be remarked:

(*a*) From the very outset of the movement for the liberation of our Republic, President Beneš has formulated all his political concepts on the basis of the absolute equality of all our citizens. When resistance started in 1939 he asked for the political and military co-operation of all citizens and of all leading politicians irrespective of party or nationality with the excep-tion of the Fascists and he offered participation in the liberation movement *to all equally.* If in 1939 and in 1940 all had spontaneously accepted this offer, our campaign for the recognition of the Government and the formation of the provisional State organisation would have proceeded much more quickly to the moral and political advantage of all. Unfortunately not everyone took part in the struggle for the recognition of the Government and Republic. At that time only a few people had a clear understanding of the situation. Ideologically, many had rather chaotic ideas of the way the war was developing and of the political prospects of this or that Nation and State. Some expected a too great, too fast and too far-reaching revolu-tion and changes which would be to the advantage of themselves and their tendencies and ideas. Others did not realise the unexpected possibilities and the great consequences of this world revolution and anti-German war in unforeseen directions. The Poles, the Germans, the Slovaks and of course also some Czechs made a number of unrealistic and unreal calculations. For these reasons conditions were laid before Dr. Benes from the outset which he and those Czechs with whom the decision rested, considered then and consider so much the more now, to be unacceptable. Dr. Beneš rejected them in principle from whatever side they came : from Slovaks, Czechs or Germans. He acted, and is still acting, on the principle *that in the question of allegiance to the State and the fulfilment of civic duties during such a struggle as the one started by Nazism for Nazi pan-Germanism, for Munich and for the present war, no conditions are any more admissible now than they were in 1938. Our State has never ceased to have a legal existence and none of its citizens were relieved of their responsibilities towards it.* From this it follows that occasional concrete political demands can be addressed to the leading men and to the Government at this time and objections can be lodged against the composition or activity of the Government and the authorities, but the question cannot and must not *be raised as to whether or not or on what conditions this or that individual shall be a citizen of the State.* Neither should there have been raised the question whether this or that citizen was or was not to fulfil his military duty towards the State and towards the fight for its resurrection and continued existence.

The theory and practice of the Sudeten German Social Democratic group since 1939 has been different and precisely for that reason it was necessary to repeat the President's point of view which he had never ceased to expound. The fact that at the outset Great Britain and France may have shown some hesitation, which today no longer exists, does not excuse anti-Hitlerite, democratic Czechoslovak citizens of the Republic for having shared this hesitation or for having drawn grave political conclusions therefrom, seeing that all of them uncompromisingly opposed everything that happened at Munich and afterwards.

When war was impending and when it had actually begun, conditions of the kind mentioned above were put to Dr. Beneš by some Slovak and German politicians. Some withdrew them after Dr. Beneš had categorically rejected them. Those Slovaks who posed no conditions have co-operated with the liberation movement throughout. Those who withdrew their conditions on the ground that they had not realised the implications from the Czech standpoint were gradually admitted to co-operation. Those who made or are still making conditions of this nature, are not being admitted to co-operation. President Beneš advocated and advocates the view that the conditions made to him concern problems which only the whole Czechoslovak Nation is authorised to decide. He has never departed from this view in one single instance. This is a democratic stand-point and politically the only correct one.

The President takes this attitude towards all nationalities, parties and politicians of the Republic and he is applying it in practice to all with consistency and justice—to the Ruthenians, for example, as well as to others. Nor does he consider it justifiable for the Germans to regard the Slovak-Czech nationality question as being on a par with the German-Czech relationship. It is well known that among Czechs as well as among Slovaks the question of a special Slovak nationality is a matter of dispute and that a great percentage of the Slovaks and the immense majority of the Czechs do not recognise any national differentiation between Czechs and Slovaks. Although he has always respected and still respects the view of those who have felt or feel that they are only Slovaks, President Beneš since boyhood has considered himself to be not a Czech, but a Czecho-slovak (in the times of the Austro-Hungarian Monarchy the word used was 'Cechoslovan'—Czechoslav). In this matter, a large proportion of Czech as well as Slovak politicians are in agreement with him.

(b) As has been stated above, in the matter of liquidating Nazism and Fascism and of punishing the criminals, President Beneš takes a strict view which is applicable to all nationalities in the Republic equally whether Czechs, Slovaks, Germans, Hungarians, Ruthenians. If this punishment involves no transfer of larger groups of any population of the Republic, so much the better. But we must realise that it will be really a question of punishing *many thousands of Nazis and Fascists of all nationalities*. It is for all of us to consider together how this can be done in such a way as to avoid a repetition of what happened in connection with pan-Germanism, Nazism and Fascism in our country throughout almost the whole twenty years of the Republic and, what is even more important, to avoid a repetition of what happened at the time of Munich and after. The President and the Czechoslovak Government do not intend to pardon any guilty person to whatever group he may belong. The questions are: Should they all be slaughtered or should huge prisons or life-long concentration camps be established for them, or is it better that they should leave the country for ever?

This raises the question of the so-called transfer of populations. It must be stated that the Czechoslovak Government has so far reached no decision on this problem: that views on transfer are views which so far have only been formulated by individual political groups; that these ideas are not advocated or propagated only among our people but also among other allied Nations and even among politicians (as for instance ex-President Hoover) who are very strongly opposed to a post-war policy of revenge and reprisals against Germany. It must also be put on record that some of our people are also opposed to transfer.

The question of transfer therefore is not and cannot be an exclusively *Czechoslovak* question. *It is a question of general European importance, a question which concerns not only Czechoslovakia, but also many other countries and it may therefore be included among the international problems which must be solved at the final settlement of European post-war relations.* Only at that moment will the Czechoslovak Government and our whole liberation movement be able to take a definitive attitude to this question. It will do so *only on the basis of the situation at the end of the war in accordance with developments at home and the attitude of the other victorious Powers towards the armistice and peace terms.* Until then the official Czechoslovak position will certainly not be defined.

6. Concerning the Atlantic Charter it must be stated that President Beneš has already told Mr. Jaksch that when giving its adhesion to the principles agreed upon between President Roosevelt and Winston Churchill on August 14th, 1941, the Czechoslovak Government formulated reservations which it does not intend to withdraw.* What happened at Munich will remain a grave warning to all Czechoslovaks without exception not to be misled by imprecise general principles into political agitation which can never solve the vital problems of all the people in the Czechoslovak Republic. The races in the Czechoslovak Nation cannot and never will accept the principle of self-determination for three millions of

*Reservations to Atlantic Charter (from letter of 29th August, 1941):
... (1) that the final interpretation and application of these principles will be in accordance with the circumstances and needs of the different parts of Europe and the world;
(2) that the vital interests and sovereign rights of the Czechoslovak Republic as internationally acknowledged by the whole civilised world and temporarily disturbed by Germany's acts of aggression beginning in September, 1938, will be reinstated and safeguarded;
(3) that the application of points 2, 3 and 8 will result in securing such frontiers, such international, political, legal, military and economic guarantees for all peace-loving peoples, but especially for the neighbours of Germany, as to enable them to defend peace for themselves and for the world against any future attempts at aggression either by Germany or anyone else;
(4) that in the future economic structure of the world, small nations like Czechoslovakia, by access to a fair share of raw materials and other necessary help, will be given an opportunity as equal among equals in close co-operation with their neighbours, to reconstruct quickly and permanently their economic life, which has been so cruelly devastated by Germany and other aggressors, thus securing improved labour standards, economic advancement and social security for all.
'The Czechoslovak Government wishes me to place the above observations on record for His Majesty's Government and it does not intend to publish them.
(Signed) JAN MASARYK.' (Tr.).

Germans if formulated, interpreted and advocated in such a manner as was done previously at the last peace conference and throughout the following twenty years. Neither President Masaryk nor President Beneš ever concealed this because such a concept of self-determination *is a priori a denial of the right of self-determination of ten million Czechoslovaks and precludes the very existence of an independent Czechoslovak State.* It may certainly be expected *that after this war the principle of self-determination will be given a fresh formulation by international law and that its application will be on entirely new lines.* The unparalleled misuse by Nazism and Fascism of this principle as formerly conceived and its incredible and shameful pollution by Nazi gangsterism in our country and in all occupied countries immediately afterwards will surely have this result. The former concept of this principle has completely failed during the last twenty years. It is no longer operative and the war will certainly result in the establishment of other new concepts.

7. With regard to the so-called 'Vertragslösung des tschechisch-sudetendeutschen Problems' (solution of the Czech-Sudeten German problem by treaty) it must be stressed that such a formula will certainly give rise to misunderstandings between us. President Beneš rejected it when it was submitted by the Slovaks. And we mutually agreed to replace it by the formula of a *democratic* solution of all political, administrative and other disputes in the Republic. Such a formula will serve for the solution of all problems, the Czech-German problem in the Czech Lands included.

On this occasion it is perhaps right to give notice that at a suitable moment President Beneš and the Government intend to invite all our German citizens spontaneously and definitively to desist from describing themselves as 'sudetendeutsch'. The reasons are:

(*a*) Scientifically, geographically and historically the word 'Sudeten' has an entirely different meaning from the one at present attributed to it.

(*b*) The word has come to express the political fraud into which Henlein and German Fascism have turned the German question in Czechoslovakia. Henlein wanted to bring new political facts into being by the use of a special terminology. It was, and is, a fraud for which he is responsible. It is perhaps comprehensible that other parties in our country which wanted to fight Henlein's fraudulent political agitation should have used the same term for tactical reasons. Politically, this was an error. Difficulties are never solved by accepting the errors or the demagogy of one's opponent. If we want to emancipate ourselves completely from Henleinism and Nazism, let us do so consistently and not by succumbing to their methods! Let us return to our good traditions!

(*c*) The words 'Sudeten', 'Sudetenland', 'Sudetendeutscher' will always be connected in the Czech provinces with Nazi bestialities perpetrated on Czechs and democratic Germans too in the fatal crisis before and after 1938. We must seek a new agreement by freeing ourselves from these sad, politically fatal and (so far as we are concerned) unacceptable instruments of Nazi policy.

(*d*) The Czechs will not accept the word 'Sudeten' after the war. They will ban it. It is therefore in our interests to agree before it is too late that the word shall vanish from our political vocabulary on both sides. Political common sense requires that this should not be done by laws and decrees. It would be ridiculous if Czechoslovak anti-Henleinites and anti-Nazi democrats quarrelled among themselves over words after the war and if they created political problems out of the Henlein heritage and terminology. We believe that our German citizens will give this matter due consideration and will make all necessary preparations.

No one can doubt that President Beneš personally is and will consistently remain opposed to the so-called 'einseitige Machtlösungen der tschechisch-deutschen Frage' (unilateral solutions of the Czech-German problem by force). But we would not be realistic politicians if we did not tell ourselves plainly *that if the German Nation and State is defeated, they will have to bear the consequences of their defeat just as every defeated State and Nation have to bear them in every war.* Everyone who has in any way participated in the war or declared his solidarity with or helped the German cause in any way will be concerned in this defeat.

The great majority of Germans in the Czechoslovak provinces have adhered to the German State, have declared their solidarity with it and are still helping it effectively. They will therefore be concerned. How, is a question which none of us can answer correctly today. It will be decided in accordance with the circumstances in which the war ends. But it is also in the interest of Czechs and Slovaks that the settlement should be reasonable and just and not simply an act of revenge. The greater the number of those who unconditionally help the Czechs in the Republic and abroad to destroy Nazism the easier the settlement and the better and quicker will be the re-establishment of co-operation on the basis of equality and justice.

The President earnestly wishes this to come about and he will co-operate to that end justly and devotedly in the same spirit in which he acted until 1938 as Minister and still more as President. It is manifest to everyone that some Germans will and must live in the new Republic. We hope that they will be loyal citizens in equality with all others and that there will be no repetition whatsoever of their behaviour since 1934 under the influence of

German Nazism. It will be agreed that this would neither be in the interests of the Czech people nor in those of European peace.

But it would be a fatal error if it again began to be said that the realisation of this aim depends only on the Czechs and on what the Republic does in regard to the German question. There are 80 million Germans and *the small Czechoslovak Nation cannot live with a German revolver permanently against its breast.* So long as the Bohemian Germans fail to understand that the Czechoslovak Nation cannot possibly live politically under the permanent threat of having their State destroyed at any given moment, thus depriving them of the essential condition for their national existence, there will be no agreement but only strife and attempts to bring about 'einseitige Machtlösungen'. Appeals to the so-called 'Selbstbestimmungsrecht' (right of self-determination) regardless of the Czechs *in the area which is indispensable to the existence of our State and Nation*—such as have been made in the last twenty years under the Republic by nearly all our Germans with the support of the other Germans and of their great Reich—*constituted and always will constitute an 'einseitige Machtlösung'.* Hitler simply put into operation this 'einseitige Machtlösung' in the face of world opinion when, ideologically speaking, the situation was sufficiently prepared for him. *If this doctrine which from the standpoint of our country is wholly inadmissible is revived, then Hitlerism will be also, though perhaps in a new form, and this will lead to a new world war.*

The doctrine was called 'The right of the Germans to national unity'. But the effect—*whether intended or not*—*was a political pan-Germanism which is the real father of Nazism.* We conclude therefore that the inhabitants of our Borderland *have no right to a collective and territorial 'Selbstbestimmungsrecht' without the consent of the Czechs* who, if the right were exercised, would always be literally in the grip of the adjacent Reich and would be deprived of their own right of self-determination, that is to say, of their freedom.

Every German of course has and must have a right to *individual and personal* 'Selbstbestimmung' and can freely leave the State and the environment in which political conditions are not to his liking. The German Nation, as well as other Nations, has a right to its German State but not the right that all Germans wherever they live must be within the boundaries of this State. Other Nations—France for example—does not have this right. Whether all members of the same Nation shall or shall not be in one State is a question of political opportunity, of practical possibility, of geography, of economic viability and desirability, of historic development as well as, among other things, of the interests of other Nations. But it is never a question of principle.

The principle of territorial and collective 'Selbstbestimmungsrecht' for national minorities or fractions of nations which already have their own national States, is political dynamite calculated to destroy the life of all Central European States and nations and the existence of world peace. On this point as long ago as the last Peace Conference President Beneš agreed with Lansing against Wilson.

From this it follows that minorities are in danger of being outvoted. But they have the right to defend themselves against this possibility and to demand the highest possible degree of democracy. But so long as their defence consists in appeals to territorial and collective 'Selbstbestimmungsrecht' and in constant threats to disrupt the State, no majority will be ready to make any concessions. In its political struggle, a minority may appeal to all possible rights and use all methods with one exception: territorial and collective 'Selbstbestimmungsrecht' coupled with threats and programmes to secede from the State. Otherwise there will never be agreement between the minority and the majority.

In our opinion, this is *the psychological law on which is based all loyal internal and foreign policy.* If Czechs and Germans do not agree on this absolutely fundamental question concerning the future of the Republic, neither will they agree on solid, loyal and real co-operation in the Republic after the war. Once more, there will only be 'einseitige Machtlösungen'— as there have been between Czechs and Germans for the past five or six centuries. *There will again be pan-Germanism, a new Nazism, a new Hitler and a new and dreadful catastrophe.* Nobody who understands the present events and the laws of political strife and development in Europe, can doubt this for a moment. President Beneš and the Czechoslovak Government do not want this to happen and they trust *that all these questions may be solved between us sincerely, thoroughly, realistically and, therefore, permanently.* They consider this to be possible only on the lines on which they have started at the very outset of our fight for the Republic after Munich.

Letter from Dr. Eduard Beneš, President of the Republic, to Wenzel Jaksch, dated January 10th, 1943 :

London, January 10th, 1943

DEAR COLLEAGUE JAKSCH,

On June 22nd, 1942, you sent me, with a personal letter from yourself, the resolution of the Sudeten-German Social Democratic Party of June 7th, 1942. I expressed my own unofficial opinion of this resolution and the views of a number of members of our Government in a special memorandum which I have already given you.* That communication also contained answers to many matters mentioned in your *personal* letter to me and I will therefore not refer to them again in this *personal* letter to you. I will confine myself to essential points only. But as some of the views expressed in your letter are formulated as reproaches addressed to me personally, I am obliged to answer them.

1. I will pass over the reproaches in your letter concerning the period before Munich, whether they concern the 'Behandlung unserer Bewegung' (treatment of our movement) or the behaviour of some of the big Czech political parties in 1935–38, or the announcement of elections or the attitude of Dr. Hodža and the State machine towards the German Social Democrats in the Republic. This would be too long a chapter. As everywhere else, there was also a struggle between political parties in our Republic. As everywhere else, there was a struggle between Left and Right. As everywhere in Europe, there was a crisis in our country too and a struggle between Democracy, Fascism and Communism. And with us it had the same accompanying symptoms as elsewhere. But in our country the Left always kept the upper hand and its followers held their positions till the time of Munich. Among you Germans the difficulties were greater because in our country too the great majority of Germans succumbed to Fascism. To explain this as due to conditions in the Republic, to a wrong procedure *vis-à-vis* the German Social Democrats and others would certainly be wholly incorrect. You yourself admit in your letter that in the years 1935–1938 only one million Germans (that is to say about 30 per cent of the German inhabitants) stood at the side of the Czech people—in other words, at the side of the Czechoslovak State. And surely neither of us today will argue that Fascism and Nazism are phenomena which originated in a Czech milieu or from Czech faults or that the war which has broken out between Nazism and the whole world is a war which originated in Czechoslovak conditions.

If therefore there was a crisis of democracy in our country it originated

*See the preceding document. (Tr.).

in the same causes as in the rest of the world. And it is a fact that the Czech people and with them the Czechoslovak State put up a better resistance than the German people and the other continental States. I am proud to claim that much of this was my doing. But alas, on this Nation which is mainly Czechoslovak and on this democratic State there was put an unheard of and unjust pressure from outside, *which was visibly of a reactionary character* and which had—if not for its aim, certainly as its consequence—the downfall of Czech democracy. What happened in 1938 in our internal policy was not merely an attack against German democracy in our country. It was first and foremost an attack against the whole State and particularly against *Czech democracy*. That is why I, personally, was the first to fall after Munich. Therefore to address these reproaches to the Czechs and to me is not justified. A world war was in preparation and the Czechoslovak State and Nation were the object of an attack which aimed at the destruction and death of State and Nation. The Czechs *had to* prove to the world that they were not guilty and that they wished to do all in their power to avert war. They had to make national and political sacrifices and to make an attempt, under pressure from foreign reaction, to come to an agreement with the Fascist Germans. I was anxious that the war should break out in circumstances which from the standpoint of morality would put the whole democratic world on our side. In pursuit of this, we went to the very brink. *We ourselves made the greatest sacrifices in that dreadful crisis* and the German people as a whole could not but profit therefrom. And it is to the honour of the Czechoslovak people that, when I signed the decree of mobilisation, the Nation was united from the Left to the Right. It is my greatest satisfaction that as President I maintained this unity and that in the decisive moment our people would have gone firmly behind me into a life and death struggle without regard to left or right political tendencies. I gladly admit the merit of the German Social Democrats, that they held out with us valiantly to the very end even though *under influences from abroad and under the pressure of events* there were attempts to exclude them from the Government majority.

The simple fact is that after all that has already happened in this war I do not consider your interpretations to be correct from a historical point of view. Certainly, it has been a matter of concern to you as a party; but internationally, politically and morally our behaviour was correct. My heart bled when I saw the blows dealt to democracy and when I myself had to participate in them. Nevertheless I did not fear to take those various steps in the spheres of internal and international policy which were to save peace and our country. Today that is my, and our, great strength.

But I do not consider it at all right to hark back now to all these so much less important disputes or reproaches about the past. We all have before us the *war with Hitler* and Nazism in which one side or the other must be defeated once and for all. I have refused to discuss with our Czech people whether we ourselves should have declared and waged war with Germany. I have refused to quarrel with the Slovaks about which of us committed mistakes or the greater mistakes. Similarly in the matter of our Germans I do not wish to return now to such discussions of less importance. In the eyes of the international public, we would win this dispute today even more decisively than Hitler won it against us in 1938. But after the war we can come back to these matters. In fact, we will have to do so.

2. In the matter of the transfer of population my attitude is fully expressed in the enclosed notes on your Party's resolution of June 7th, 1942.

3. They also express my point of view towards the respective positions of the Slovaks and Germans in the resistance movement. I only want to add that beyond doubt the great majority of Slovaks (at least 80 per cent) have never changed their attitude to the Czechs and to the united Czechoslovak State either in the crisis of 1938 or in the present war and that today they are firmer in this respect than ever. Moreover, the great majority of Slovaks abroad, after the first mistaken steps of some of their leaders, have put themselves *unconditionally and unreservedly* at the service of the movement for the re-establishment of the united State though they have their own ideas about its internal structure. And though today there are personal quarrels—with, for instance, Osuský or Hodža—*there is, and was, no substantial political divergence concerning principles as between Czechs and Slovaks.*

On the German side this is neither the situation at home nor has it been from the beginning here abroad.

4. I have therefore only to answer the conclusion of your letter in which you allege in substance:

(a) After the exchange of notes between myself and your Party on September 27th and 28th, 1941, in which you expressed your readiness for co-operation, you were not answered by deeds: you were not invited to co-operate in the Provisional State Organisation nor even in provisional economic and political matters and that this destroyed the confidence of your people (if I understand correctly, their confidence also in me). You conclude from this that Czech policy has started on the road of trying to dictate to an old ally which had not deserted the Czechs at a time when all other people had done so.

(b) You stress that the programme of the transfer of population lies outside the principle of the legal continuity of the Republic.

(c) You stress that your Party's resolution of June 7th, 1942, is a request to all responsible Czechoslovak elements not to think in terms of violent solutions of the German problem which would drive you into a situation which would be fatal for both parties.

And in the beginning of the letter you take credit for the fact that in your Party's resolution of June 7th the 'alibi' disclaiming responsibility for our present mutual relations was formulated with such moderation.

As most of the discussions were between us two and several times your whole delegation has been to see me, this means that the responsibility for this state of affairs is on my shoulders. It is therefore necessary that I should also express my views of the matter.

5. I therefore state these facts:

From our first conversations in 1939 I have upheld to you, as well as to all Czechs and Slovaks, the continuity of the Republic, the necessity for a common front of all of us without distinction of party or nationality, common action for the annulment of Munich and the necessity of declaring ourselves unconditionally and unreservedly for the Republic. Already from the beginning I explained my programme to you of establishing a Government at the proper moment and I wished to organise our whole liberation movement with the participation of the German democrats in exile. I told you expressly that if Masaryk or I were in your place we would align ourselves with this policy without reserve, without hesitation and without conditions.

During the whole of the year 1939–1940 you answered that you could not do this, that your party-membership would not agree because they wanted me to give an undertaking concerning the future organisation of the Republic and the position of the Germans in it. I explained to you that I could not give such an undertaking, that I was not authorised to do so, that also I did not admit that anyone was authorised to put such a request to me whether he was a German, a Slovak or Subcarpathian Ruthenian because neither I nor he had received an authorisation on this subject. I refused to give way to Hodža and Osuský as I did not accept their claim to represent the *whole* of Slovakia. I also told you that I accepted you as entitled to speak for a *certain part* of the German Social Democrats of the Republic, but that you could not speak in the name of three million Germans, that you had no more right to agree to or take any decision affecting future policy than I had a similar right to do anything which might prejudice the future of the State in the name of ten million Czechoslovaks. From a democratic standpoint such decisions could only be made by all our people jointly.

w

I know that you put forward your demand because you thought that our liberation movement would have no success without an agreement of this nature. I thought otherwise. I also know that you were working on the assumption that the situation would evolve in a different way from that which actually occurred. In our last conversation, when I stressed that I considered your whole approach had been wrong, you said that you had been mistaken in two points: you had expected a revolution in Germany and you had expected the war would be a short one.

I, on the contrary, as you know from our conversations and from my public speeches—expected what actually happened. Broadly speaking I made no mistake in any of my principal war hypotheses: the course of events in Germany and in regard to the Soviet Union, America, the occupied Nations and finally the radical stand the whole world took against Hitler—all these things happened as I expected they would happen. It was on this basis that I wanted to organise our whole joint activities with you all before it was too late. I did not fully succeed with the Slovaks (Hodža) or with you.

I had therefore to start working for recognition *without Hodža and without you*. For your part, you mistakenly counted on help from the British. Mistakenly, because finally the British too—in spite of their former Munich errors, or perhaps just because they had committed them—now understand that Czechoslovakia must be re-established substantially in its original form and as strong as possible, thus receiving real justice. They understand that the natural frontiers of the Republic must be restored—Munish itself proved that this is necessary. That is why I obtained the first —'provisional'—recognition. Before this took place, I loyally invited you and kept you informed—as I did everyone who was not yet co-operating fully. And I told you that this was only the beginning and that we were sure to win further successes, that we were sure to reach agreement with the British and with the others. I told you also that I was counting on the participation of America in the war and on receiving American recognition as well as on the participation of the Soviet Union in the war and on Soviet help for our cause.

Nevertheless you did not give up your point of view until the summer of 1941. At that time I often emphasised to you how important it was that as many of our German citizens as possible should join our army spontaneously, voluntarily. I promised you that we should not try to impose compulsory military service on those who did not report voluntarily. Now, as from August 5th, we have agreed to a bill proposed by the British Government making it possible for the citizens of all the Allied Nations to enter the British Army. We did so because the British Government 'annulled' Munich. But I considered it was a cardinal mistake on your part that you issued calls to your followers to enter the British Army. This was equivalent to saying that *you did not pronounce yourselves unconditionally and unreservedly for the Republic.* I have always deeply deplored this fact, regarding it as a great political mistake which at home, in the Republic, will always be considered politically in the light of the action of those who entered our Army without hesitation.

Such was the state of affairs up to the autumn of 1941. The Soviet Union's entry into the war and the new recognition of the Republic and Government—now absolutely and finally—by Great Britain, the Soviet Union, China (in addition to the American recognition) had had the effect that in our next conversations (especially at the time of your visit to Aston Abbotts in the summer of 1941 and again later) you agreed to enter the State Council without conditions or reservations *though at the same time you kept your former fundamental view of the relations of our Germans to the Republic.*

But by that time at home, and here, too, Czech hatred against the Germans in our country and everything connected with Nazism and Germany in general had alarmingly increased. We were not the only ones to undergo this revulsion of feeling. It manifested itself daily on a gradually rising scale among all Nations and on all sides, including Great Britain. I told you about this very loyally in all our conversations. At Aston Abbotts I even showed you my confidential reports from home. At the time you appreciated this.

After September 28th, following the appointment of Heydrich and its sequel, you all recognised that your participation in the State Council would have to be temporarily postponed. As the result of a series of talks we agreed on the formula: The nomination of German Social Democrats to the State Council is at present impossible but we are agreed that both groups are proceeding on parallel lines along the same path of struggle for the liberation of the Republic without doing anything which could be considered disloyal to this common aim.

Neither from you, nor from others, nor from myself did I conceal my conviction that if you had taken a different line in 1940 and had given up in time your conditions and your reservations (concerning correlations for the future organisation of the Republic and the unconditional enlistment of our German citizens in the Czechoslovak Army), your people would probably have already been in the State Council in December, 1940, together with all the others and the problem of your co-operation would have been solved long before the arrival of Heydrich and the new wave of new nationalism at home. At that time the British would have regarded this as our great joint success.

Your own disputes about these matters did not, of course, go unnoticed by our people who considered them to be a lack of loyalty towards the Republic and the State on your part, as opportunism and a precaution against what might happen to Germany and in Germany when the war ended. This was used as an argument against your participation and the participation of any Germans at all in our liberation movement. You know what troubles I had about this in the Army.

I would like to end this analysis by stating:

(a) It was not right, and in my opinion it was a cardinal political error, that from 1939 to 1941 you made conditions and reservations about your co-operation and about making a definite declaration of your support for the Republic as well as of your participation in the common military struggle on its behalf.

(b) In consequence all acts of recognition for our Government at that time had to be reached without your participation (after the first such act, articles and pamphlets were even issued by your Party deprecating this recognition). I regretted then and I still regret that the Party which had so faithfully stood by the Republic in 1938 had got into such a position.

(c) When in the autumn of 1941 you changed your attitude (on one point, namely, conditions concerning the future organisation of the Republic—on the question of military service you still maintain the same attitude), the situation was already such that your nomination to the State Council could not be put into effect. This nomination had been intended as a public proof of full agreement and common action.

Such was the course of our discussions and this is how the question of an 'alibi' really stands. But I want to stress that I never concealed from you how the situation was developing, that I was never disloyal to you, that I always loyally kept you informed of my intentions and plans (and of my views about the punishment of war criminals and the transfer of population). Nor did I conceal from you that my aim was definite and full recognition and revocation of Munich and I always told you that we would quite certainly attain our object. I also want to remind you that I intentionally employed officials of German nationality in the Provisional State Organisation—in so far as there were any—and that I also intentionally and deliberately nominated a German member to the Legal Council to show how I wished the situation to develop in this direction too.

I must therefore reject the reproach of having been in any way guilty of 'non-co-operation' with you, by whomsoever it is made *against me and against our movement.*

6. I am unhappy about having to refer to the last point in this connection: *The Revocation of Munich.* I never concealed from you that I was working for it and I never concealed from you that it would be attained. *But you never disclosed to me your views about this question.* I know that you have been in contact with certain British circles from which you derived expectations which I held to be unjustified. I knew about your activities and your negotiations. I did not consider and I still do not consider that you acted correctly towards us, neither you nor the British circles in question, if and to the extent that your activities were to be used as a weapon against our united resistance movement, and to force us to adopt some other policy. *I took this line towards Hodža and others, I do so also towards you.* I also told the British elements concerned what my views were and I repeat it to you. Furthermore, I considered your broadcasts to Germany from London to be a cardinal error in view of your relations with us. And what is more, the procedure adopted to obtain permission for these broadcasts to be made was not altogether regular. I spoke to you several times about the matter. But when I found that you yourself did not feel you had no right to try to create an international problem out of our joint internal affairs I did not pursue the subject since we could not but feel that you were working *against us.* I did not want to pick a quarrel with you on this matter.* But I have to say this today in answer to your complaints. Did we not see eye-to-eye before Munich *that the Henleinites had not the right to solicit foreign intervention in these very issues?* We should have taken the opposite line in our work with the British—especially during the war—and should have co-operated, leaving our internal affairs to be solved between our own selves!

I have ascertained that after the exchange of notes of August 5th you have expressed a *negative* view on this issue which for us is so important and far-reaching! You are said to have expressed yourself in this sense to the British and your Party is said to have prepared a memorandum for President Roosevelt. I did not want to believe it. And I regret that your Party did not publicly and positively express its views about the triumph of justice for our State† for which it fought so devotedly in 1938.

7. I cannot close this letter without giving you proofs of the great, material and tactical political mistakes which you and your political friends must be held to have committed: the number of your publications and

*Recognition of the Provisional Government (Tr.).

†Revocation of Munich (Tr.).

statements which, from the Czech side, have evoked opposition and in my opinion much-justified criticism.

I will give here only the following examples: Wenzel Jaksch 'Was kommt nach Hitler' (What comes after Hitler), p. 16:

'Later the Versailles order (which denied the right of self-determination to the Germans) also broke down. We are therefore resolutely opposed to the dualist principle which would join the Austrian and even the Bavarian Germans to the Danubian combination, merely in order to disrupt once again the power-political factor of Great Germany by the one-sided application of the right of self-determination . . .

'. . . For the Sudeten Germans we demand also the right to decide freely whether they want to live as an autonomous sector of the historical provinces of Bohemia and Moravia, that is to say, in a closer State-union with the Czechs, *or whether they want to be attached as a province to a federal Reich.*'

De Witte: Commentary on W. Jaksch's essay: 'Was kommt nach Hitler':

". . . The union of Austria with Germany has been recognised by all States which matter, and the fusion (Anschluss) of the German Sudeten territory with Germany was expressly approved by Great Britain and France at Munich in 1938. What the Germans of the Reich, the Austrians and also we Sudeten Germans worked for in vain in 1918–19, is an accomplished fact of which the whole world has taken note . . .

'The Sudeten Germans want also to know whether they could expect no more from tomorrow's German democracy in the old Reich than from that of yesterday. And the echo from Vienna interests them at least as much as the echo from Prague. Germany from Memel to Bregenz and from Flensburg to Klagenfurt is just now a fact and this is the time for the democrats of this great Reich to speak up . . .

'The Central European federation as Jaksch imagines it is in reality the resurrection of Austria-Hungary on a different scale and under special conditions . . .'

'Sudeten-Freiheit' (Sudeten Freedom), No. 3, September, 1939, from the article 'Vor 20 Jahren' (Twenty years ago).

'. . . The Sudeten Germans should not be, as in 1919 and in 1938, a pawn in the policy of others. The Sudeten Germans should themselves decide their State citizenship and its form. Their own welfare as well as that of the Czech Nation and the safeguarding of peace make this necessary . . .'

From a circular, dated October 9th, 1939, by Wenzel Jaksch :

'As long as the constitutional future of the Sudeten territory has not been cleared up in a way that we could in due course advocate successfully to the working masses at home, the leaders of the "Treugemeinschaft" are not able to issue a general invitation to enter the Czechoslovak Army ... Most of our men who are able to perform military service *will in present circumstances prefer voluntary enlistment in the British Army.*'

Ditto, page 4, paragraph 7:

'For the rest, we expect from Czech policy, that it will put forward a new concept which could serve as a suitable basis for a free decision by the Sudeten territory ...

'The experience of twenty years teaches that a solution satisfactory to both parties is possible only on the basis of Sudeten German autonomy with a separate territorial Government. In any case, the promise of such autonomy would make it easier to *secure a Sudeten German majority for the idea that the Sudeten territory together with the Czechs should form a smaller or greater federal State.*'

De Witte and Katz: 'Einige Grundprinzipien in Sache ČSR und Sudetenland', October 18th, 1938 (some fundamental principles concerning Czechoslovakia and the Sudeten territory):

'... The decision *whether, and if so*, on what conditions and guarantees, the Sudeten Germans should form a joint State with the Czechs, *or whether they should join another State* must be reserved to this people themselves. It is necessary to ascertain their views by plebiscite under international control as was done in the case of the voting in the Saar Territory.

'All sympathy for the Czech liberation struggle cannot and must not change the fact that we are not a part of the Czech Nation and that the latter's aim *to re-establish the Czech State—simply cannot be our aim too. We cannot admit that our people should blindly or regardless of the cost enter the Czech legions* and that perhaps they should even fight against our German comrades at home for the re-establishment of the Czech State. Who among us goes to war must know that he is fighting for *his* Nation, for *its* freedom and *its* better future ...

'... We must not further Czech aspirations, or simply copy the Czechs of the years 1914–1918. We must not—remembering the Pittsburgh Agreement and the experience of the Slovaks in this regard—*be satisfied with agreements with the Czechs concerning mere intentions to grant autonomy or federation.*'

Wenzel Jaksch: Foreign Policy Aims of Sudeten German Social Democracy, October, 1939:

'Twice in twenty years it has been decided unilaterally to which State the Sudeten territory should belong. By the dictate of Saint-Germain Czechoslovakia has been burdened for twenty years with unsolved nationality problems . . . We demand the right of self-determination for the Sudeten Germans . . .

'We do not deny that the Munich frontiers have in many cases violated the principle of nationality and that inside those frontiers a re-established State of the Czechs and Slovaks would not be capable of living. But as a part of the Sudeten German Nation we must above all defend the interests of this Nation. After twenty years' experience, therefore, we must refuse to join the Sudeten German Nation to a preponderantly Czech State under the same or similar conditions to those which existed up to the time of the Munich Agreement. It is our profound conviction that such a solution would contain the seeds of new conflicts.

'Three million Sudeten Germans need an administrative centre in the form of an autonomous territorial Government . . . Any lasting democratic settlement of the relations between Czechs and Sudeten Germans must be based *on the recognition of a compact German linguistic territory in Bohemia and Moravia.*'

From a circular by Wenzel Jaksch, dated November 24th, 1939:
'There has been no deterioration in the situation of the refugees in spite of war conditions. But we are under no illusions that if the war goes on the present standard of care for the refugees can be maintained. *We have therefore decided to recommend in the enclosed directions that the able-bodied men should voluntarily enter the British Army.*'

From a circular by W. Jaksch, dated January 17th, 1940:
'Without the clearing up of certain preliminary questions concerning the legal position of the Sudeten territory, *we could not recommend unconditional enlistment in the Czech Army abroad. We have chosen rather to recommend our able-bodied friends to enlist voluntarily in the British Army. From the standpoint of international law the question of the Sudeten territory belonging to the Czechs is open and a fresh decision will not be taken without our participation . . .*'

From a letter of W. Jaksch published in *The New Statesman and Nation* of February 24th, 1940, under the title of 'Future of Czechoslovakia', p. 242:

'In the interest entirely of democracy in the Sudeten territory we must remain independent in our relations with the (Czechoslovak) National Committee while completely sympathising with it . . . While these questions are still unsettled *we must give Sudeten Germans abroad the choice of volunteering either for the British or the Czech Army*.'

From a speech by W. Jaksch at the meeting of the Executive Committee of the German Social Democratic Party on March 9th, 1940, at the Holmhurst Hotel, Loughton, Essex:

'In our deliberations we must not stand where we used to stand. *The reason is that this State (Czechoslovakia) no longer exists.* At that time we were in an abnormal position. *We were obliged to oppose autonomy for the Sudeten territory so that we should not be delivered wholly into the hands of the Henleinites* . . . Our declaration must be based on the following principles : (1) *A solution by treaty ;* (2) *equal rights for nations, not only for individuals.* As to the question of a Provisional Government : This is not only a question of a provincial form of Government but also of a provisional parliament of the Sudeten Germans. The theory of the legal personality of the Nation is in practice the Provincial Parliament and provincial sovereignty in regard to taxation . . .'

From the declaration of the Sudeten German Social Democratic Party 'Uber die künftige Stellung des Sudetengebietes im Rahmen einer demokratischföderalistischen Neuordnung Europas' (On the future position of the Sudeten territory in a democratic-federalistic reorganisation of Europe), March 10th, 1940, p. 8.

'We claim a peace of agreement also for the population of the Sudeten territory. Twice in twenty years it has been decided unilaterally to which State they should belong. By the dictate of Saint-Germain, Czechoslovakia was burdened for twenty years with unsolved nationality problems . . .

'*We demand the right of self-determination for three million Sudeten Germans.*'

From an article 'So sprechen unsere Canadier' (So speak our Canadians), published in *Freundschaft* (Friendship), No. 3, March, 1941:

'*It can hardly be expected that the majority of our comrades will recognise without compulsion the authority of the Czechoslovak Government abroad* so long as our competent representatives have not received assurances *which will make it impossible for the last twenty years of the Czechoslovak Republic to be repeated.* Voluntary recognition could only be realised if the present

Czechoslovak Government abroad were ready to accept the principles expressed in Point IV of our Party's declaration of March 10th, 1940.'

From a circular by W. Jaksch dated March 10th, 1941:
'. . . In permanent contact with our Executive Committee I therefore proposed: *We will support the pre-Munich frontiers but we demand* from the Government a declaration that the new Constitution will be drafted after mutual agreement and not be dictated to us . . .'

From the circular by W. Jaksch dated January 23rd, 1942:
'. . . The aim of Czech policy *is invariably a maximum increase of national power after the war.* It would be convenient for our partners if this development took place with our formal consent . . .'

From the circular by W. Jaksch dated March 23rd, 1942:
'. . . *That* a certain number of *our comrades belong to British units has a deeper meaning. In the days of decision, what happens will depend only on our strength.* Many, if not all of you, *will,* so far as human foresight can judge *be more easily transferred to the service of our cause* if you remain in some British unit till that time.'

From the circular by W. Jaksch dated June, 1942:
'Nevertheless, if there were readiness on the Czech side to solve these problems according to recognised democratic principles, we would not hesitate to issue the appropriate uniform directions to our comrades. *But if an attempt should be made* to exercise any *pressure* against our people and to call them individually to military service, *then such an attempt to dictate* to men who have had experience of fighting *will justify the political and moral decision of every comrade to join the British Army. The Executive Committee of the Party is fully aware of its responsibility in this question also.'*

8. I want to stress that the political memorandum you wrote and distributed *in the summer of 1939,* especially part IV, contains *an express demand that the Czechoslovak Germans should be able to choose freely between either Czechoslovakia or becoming a province in a great all-German Reich.* Moreover, that memorandum is founded on the quite incorrect views that the smaller Central European Nations—after the period of Nazism and after all that Germany has done to them—would be morally, psychologically and politically ready to enter a political union with a Germany whose future after the war and for thirty years to come is unpredictable.

After what has happened in Germany, the *German people* will have first to make amends for the past and then for a certain period follow such a policy that the European Nations may regain at least some measure of confidence in her. That means that a really final *peaceful* solution of European problems can only be expected after some considerable time, perhaps even several decades.

9. I hereby declare that in general all your Party's decisions which are also repeated in your resolution of October 4th, 1942, follow the political line contained in all the above quotations. In essence, their content and sense is the following:

(*a*) We do not accept and do not advocate the legal continuity of the Republic.

(*b*) Each of our declarations about the Czechoslovak State is conditional and leaves a way open for an alternative solution.

(*c*) It has never been clear whether your profession of Czechoslovak citizenship is *a matter of principle* or whether it relates only to the temporary fact that, formally, you hold Czechoslovak passports and that the British and other authorities consider you to be Czechoslovaks.

(*d*) Your people do not and did not feel themselves bound to fulfil their duty as citizens of the Czechoslovak Republic not only before the legal integrity of the Republic was fully recognised internationally but also not even when recognition was accorded. And they still maintain this attitude today (e.g. your resolution about military service).

(*e*) In our last conversation I told you privately that not even your last resolution was satisfactory. I will give you my reasons: Not only did you not use the occasion of the annulment of Munich to express a correct attitude towards the true international reality but you also repeated once more all the obscurities mentioned above, all the indecisions and your deliberately chosen policy of conditionality. *On the contrary, you say in the resolution that the annulment of Munich leaves your aims unchanged.*

I gladly admit that at the end of your resolution you say that you recognise the necessity of postponing all constitutional questions. This will facilitate your agreement with the Czechoslovak Government. But even now you have not said clearly and unambiguously whether you are Czechoslovaks or not, whether you have still any reservations with regard to your unconditional and clear allegiance to the State, whether you stand fully and unconditionally behind our State or whether you do not. Are these tactics? Or indecision? *Or is this a resolution intended to hold a back-door open for various alternatives?*

10. This is the present situation. Do you think it possible that any Czechoslovak—and not only a Czechoslovak but any Allied politician— would understand if there were nominated to the State Council or among the Czechoslovak civil servants someone who until now has never publicly declared himself to be a Czechoslovak citizen, who refuses to fulfil his civic duties and who still *makes conditions* about his belonging to the State and still leaves a door open so that he can advocate a different view later on ?

I do not think that this impossible situation can continue any longer.

With cordial greetings,
Yours,
(Signed) DR. ED. BENEŠ

Aston Abbotts, January 10th, 1943.
To Deputy W. Jaksch, London.

Memorandum from President Dr. Eduard Beneš to the Holy See, delivered to President F. D. Roosevelt on May 12th, 1943 :

I. On January 7th, 1941, President Dr. E. Beneš delivered to the Apostolic representative in Great Britain, His Excellency Monseigneur William Godfrey, a letter stressing the following:

Immediately after the armistice in 1918, as Minister for Foreign Affairs of the Czechoslovak Republic, I began diplomatic negotiations with the Holy See and started to discuss the delimitation of the dioceses, church property, etc. There were many difficulties in 1924 and again in 1927 when new and grave misunderstandings arose. But in 1927 I succeeded in definitely solving all these problems by creating a definitive legal basis for our future relations. The so-called *modus vivendi* between the Holy See and the Czechoslovak Republic was accepted and normal and friendly relations were definitely established. Since that time their mutual relations have been good and co-operation has developed without difficulties. In particular, I cannot forget the extremely sympathetic attitude of His Holiness Pope Pius XI towards Czechoslovakia during the September crisis of 1938 and the message sent to me in the most critical moment of the history of my Nation.

For these reasons I have come to the conclusion that the time has arrived when some kind of unofficial contact should be established between the new Czechoslovak Government, residing now in London, and the Holy See. All previous agreements on church problems between the Vatican and the Republic have been destroyed by the Nazi Government. Conditions in Slovakia are very bad and the subjection of the present Tiso Government will have a very profound influence on the position of the Catholic Church in Slovakia after this war. The persecution of Czech Catholics by the Nazis in the Czech 'Protectorate' will also be of great importance for the post-war policy of the Czech Nation.

Poles, Belgians and others continue to maintain such relations and they are enabled to discuss matters of common interest and their post-war policy with the Holy See. Since March, 1939, up to the present day, Czechoslovaks have not been offered such an opportunity. The Slovak delegate with the Holy See is the representative of a State which is wholly in the hands of the Nazi Government. I think that in these conditions it is extremely desirable to make timely preparations for the future.

I ask your pardon for explaining my view to you so frankly. But in this dreadful war in which the whole of Christian civilisation is at stake and in which the Holy See—as can be seen from the Christmas message of His

Holiness Pope Pius XII—has taken an unambiguous attitude by adopting the policy of a just peace for all small Nations, I deem it to be the duty of all responsible persons not to miss the smallest opportunity to do what they consider necessary in the interests of their people who have so much at stake.

II. On May 19th, 1941, His Grace Monseigneur William Godfrey delivered to President Dr. E. Beneš the answer of the Holy See in which it is stated:

'His Eminence declares that he has read with great interest of your participation in the negotiations which, in spite of considerable difficulties, ended in the *modus vivendi* of 1927. His Eminence is especially pleased with your courteous remark about the Church and the sublime Pope Pius XII whose chief concern is a just and lasting peace, secured not by hatred and revenge but by the sublime majesty of justice. His Holiness has already expressed this wish on June 2nd, 1940, and again not long ago in his Christmas message to the world.

'The Pope and the Holy See feel for every Nation in its sufferings and are always seeking faithfully to fulfil their pastoral mission entrusted by God to the Church and to help the suffering in every way.

'It is therefore quite natural that the Czechoslovak people have a special place in the motherly heart of the Church. With regard to the step taken by Your Excellency directed to the establishment of unofficial relations between the Czechoslovak Government, formed in London not long ago, and the Holy See, His Eminence is convinced that your Excellency will understand how delicate the present situation is and how difficult it would be at the present time to afford to the Czechoslovak people the advantages of such relations. His Eminence thinks that the proper moment for such a development has not yet come.'

III. More than two years have elapsed since then and the military and political situation of the world has undergone a fundamental change. Particularly in the military sphere there have entered the war on the side of the Allied Nations the Soviet Union in June, 1941, and the United States of America in December, 1941. By this the potential balance of power has shifted to the side of the Allied Nations. Since November, 1942, this has been shown on the battlefields and today it is quite clear, even in the Axis States, that they can no longer win the war. The Czechoslovak Government considers it to be certain, especially since the Casablanca Conference, that the chief military and political aims of the Allied Nations will undoubtedly be realised. One of these aims is the re-establishment of the Czechoslovak Republic. The fact that supporting this aim there stand

—in addition to all the other members—the four leading Powers of the Allied Nations, Great Britain, the United States of America, the Soviet Union and China, is a guarantee to the Czechoslovak Government, that Czechoslovakia will be liberated and re-established together with all other countries occupied by the Axis States.

IV. In the sphere of international policy so much has already been done in this respect that diplomatically and in international law we have no doubts today about the outcome of the war. Above all, in our view, the Czechoslovak Republic has never ceased to exist in international law. This is the view of a number of other States. Great Britain and the United States of America, for instance, have never recognised the events of March, 1939, *de jure* as is proved by the continuing recognition of the Czechoslovak Legations in London and Washington. The development of the war made it possible for the representatives of the Czechoslovak people in the allied countries to establish an organised military and political movement on the basis of the irreconcilable resistance of all classes of the Czechoslovak people at home against the Germans. This movement, which formed its Czechoslovak National Army and Government, was recognised politically and in international law in July, 1940, as the Government and Army of an allied Nation and State waging war against Nazi Germany and as the legal political representative of the Czechoslovak people at home and of the Czechoslovak State.

It must therefore be remembered that since July, 1940, the Czechoslovak State and its internationally recognised Government have resumed all their former rights and in respect of international law have once more become vested with the same competence and with the same political, diplomatic, military and international position as Poland, Norway, the Netherlands, Belgium, Yugoslavia and Greece today. The Czechoslovak Government, led by its former President, has again been recognised as the legal Government of the former State by nearly all those Governments and States which, before the outbreak of the second World War, maintained strict neutrality or have later entered the war against Germany, and have not recognised either what happened at Munich in September, 1938, or what Nazi Germany has done in March, 1939, against Czechoslovakia by violence and in disregard of all obligations.

In this sense Czechoslovakia has been fully recognised diplomatically and internationally by Great Britain (and most of the Dominions) and the Soviet Union on July 18th, 1941, by the United States on July 31st, 1941, and by China on August 27th, 1941. Diplomatic relations and mutual recognition was effected with Norway on October 12th, 1940, with

Poland on November 27th, 1940, with Belgium on December 13th, 1940, with Egypt on March 13th, 1941, with the Netherlands on March 15th, 1941, with Yugoslavia on May 19th, 1941, with Eire on July 28th, 1941, with Luxembourg on February 27th, 1942, with Mexico on March 26th, 1942, with Iran on May 27th, 1942, and with Greece on August 19th, 1942. In addition, the new Government of the Czechoslovak Republic was recognised by Bolivia on June 5th, 1942, by Uruguay on June 29th, 1942, by Cuba on July 4th, 1942, by Peru on July 6th, 1942, by the Dominican Republic on July 10th, 1942, by Brazil on September 16th, 1942, by Colombia, Venezuela and Ecuador on January 9th, 1943, and by Chile on March 31st, 1943. The representation of the Czechoslovak Republic at the League of Nations and the International Labour Office never ceased to exist and with some neutral countries, *de facto* representation and contact continues.

I emphasise this position in international law which best shows the present situation of the Czechoslovak Republic and the Czechoslovak Nation and its Government in London in international policy and which already today expresses the situation as it will be after the war.

The Government of the Czechoslovak Republic remarks that all these Governments have recognised a united Czechoslovakia (the Czech provinces and Slovakia) and also, that the Munich Agreement of September 29th, 1938, has been violated by Germany herself. In consequence of this, His Majesty's Government declared in their Note to the Czechoslovak Government of August 5th, 1942, that they consider themselves freed from all obligations concerning agreements about Czechoslovakia made at Munich in 1938. The French National Committee presided over by General De Gaulle has done the same. The Soviet Government has expressly recognised the Czechoslovak Republic in its frontiers of the time before September, 1938. The other States and Nations had no part in the Munich Agreement. The violent occupation of Subcarpathian Ruthenia by Hungary in 1939 has not been recognised *de jure* by any of the countries mentioned.

V. The Czechoslovak people, and later the newly recognised Government of the Czechoslovak Republic, have watched with special attention the actions of the Holy See in Czechoslovak affairs during the present dreadful international crisis. They have gratefully welcomed the action of the Holy See in the matter of filling the Archiepiscopal See of Prague after the death of His Eminence Cardinal Kašpar. They understood the difficulties arising for the Holy See from the behaviour of the German and Hungarian Governments in the Czech 'Lands' as well as in Slovakia and

Subcarpathian Ruthenia. They would have preferred that—as these were still unfinished war events—all countries and Powers with which the Czechoslovak Republic was in diplomatic relations until September, 1938, should have observed at least an attitude of neutrality in the same spirit as the United States of America or Great Britain, which never—neither before nor after the outbreak of the war in 1939—interrupted their diplomatic relations with the Czechoslovak Legations in Washington and London. The Czechoslovak Government realised that the Holy See was unable to take a similar attitude but this could of course give rise to certain complications between the Czechoslovak Republic and the Holy See at the end of this war.

The Czechoslovak Government, taking into consideration the present attitude of the Holy See and especially the presence of a representative of Slovakia at the Vatican, is already deliberating how these difficulties might be avoided. It takes this opportunity to state the following about the present internal situation in the Czechoslovak countries:

All Czechoslovaks, except an insignificant number of individuals, are against present-day Germany. They never did and never will recognise what has been done to our country by Germany since September, 1938, and they stand unreservedly behind the present Czechoslovak Government which has its seat in London.

Today, the great majority of Slovaks take the same attitude. In Slovakia political, social, economic and moral conditions are extremely deplorable. The majority of Slovaks consider the present Government in Bratislava responsible for this situation and consider it to be a traitor to the Slovak people and to the Czechoslovak Republic. The former Slovak Government parties of the days before March 15th, 1939 (the Agrarians, Liberals, Socialists) stand almost unanimously behind the Czechoslovak Government and against the present regime in Slovakia. According to our reports nearly 60 per cent of the former Catholic Popular Party which in 1939 accepted the management of Slovak affairs from the Germans are today opposed to the present regime. They reproach it for entering into alliance with pagan German Nazism, with agreeing to declare war against Poland, Great Britain, the United States, the Soviet Union and Yugoslavia as well as against the Czechoslovak Government and with having brought about the present politically untenable position in Slovakia. The Holy See may have received different information about the situation in Slovakia. But I consider it my duty to put before the Holy See objectively the information based on reports which have arrived regularly from our country during the past two years.

In these circumstances grave disturbances could take place in Slovakia at the end of the war, the consequences of which, if the situation is not taken in hand in time, could be very far-reaching. The fact that this Slovak régime, which will certainly fare very badly when the war ends, is recognised by the Holy See and that the Holy See has accepted its representative, is a cause of great uneasiness for all faithful Czechoslovaks and especially for the Czechoslovak Catholics.

VI. The object of this memorandum is to describe the whole international and internal situation of the Czechoslovak people and the Czechoslovak State in connection with Czechoslovak church problems. Without doubt Slovakia will again be part of the Czechoslovak Republic. The Czechoslovak Government in London considers that after the war the Czech and Slovak people will regulate their mutual relations themselves freely and democratically by a new revision of the former Constitution. It would therefore like to prepare the situation so that the post-war problems of religion and of the church should not be unnecessarily complicated and especially that the relations of the Czechoslovak Republic and the Holy See should be neither complicated nor again the object of any special and long negotiations or disputes in consequence of what happened during the war.

Since 1919 I have personally conducted all discussions for the Czechoslovak Republic with the Holy See and I remember how difficult they have often been. I would not like this to happen again. After long and difficult discussions not only did I reach full agreement with the Holy See, but the people and Parliament of Czechoslovakia ratified the agreement of December 17th, 1927, the so-called *modus vivendi* which was joyfully accepted by all Czech and Slovak Catholics. I have consistently advocated that these agreements should be kept and so between 1927 and 1938 the individual clauses of the *modus vivendi* have been carried out. I think the simplest solution would be if, before the end of the war, we could return to the former *status quo* without any further complications, explanations and discussion by simply renewing the former normal diplomatic relations between the Holy See and the Czechoslovak Republic and if we could solve the concrete problems arising from this dreadful war in the spirit of the *modus vivendi*, at the time of the fall of Germany. The Czechoslovak Government would welcome this. Without doubt this course would avoid many difficulties which otherwise will certainly arise in view of the chaos which will certainly supervene in Central Europe after the defeat of the Axis countries.

VII. If the Holy See does not consider this course to be possible or proper, or if the Holy See considers that such a procedure could be only applied to a limited extent in view of the circumstances of the war, the Czechoslovak Government would be grateful for an expression of the views of the Holy See on these delicate matters. In this connection the Czechoslovak Government wishes to emphasise that it considers it its duty to provide for the consolidation of post-war conditions already at this moment. The Czechoslovak Catholics will be a consolidating factor. We wish to secure their co-operation in the post-war Government. For their co-operation it will certainly be essential that the relations between the Czechoslovak Republic and the Holy See are regularised in time. I believe that Czechoslovakia will be one of the first Central European countries to consolidate after the present war. The Czechoslovak Government there-fore wishes to make all preparations in sufficient time to ensure continuity in its policy from the moment when the relations between the Holy See and our country have been consolidated and become normal and friendly.

At the present moment when—this of course is my personal conviction —it has become clear to me in broad outline what the course of events will be this year and how the present dreadful war will end, I consider it my duty to approach the Holy See with this memorandum. After the war I wish to render account to the Czechoslovak people of the activities of our Government in its church policy, among others, and to show that we have not neglected any angle of our international relations. I would be happy if we could take a real step forward and thus secure the future successful development of relations between the Holy See and the Czechoslovak Republic. After the tribulations, severe persecutions and immense suffer-ings inflicted by the Nazi Germans on the Czech countries, as well as on Slovakia under its present regime, this would be a well-deserved benefit for our Czechoslovak people.

Moreover, the post-war difficulties which might supervene in church and religious matters as a consequence of the war would be avoided or at the least limited to a minimum. This would be to the advantage of both interested parties: the Holy See and the Czechoslovak Republic.*

DR. EDUARD BENEŠ.

London, May, 1943.

*This memorandum was also sent to the Vatican on July 15th, 1943, through the British Government. (Tr.).

INDEX

THE END